D1090782

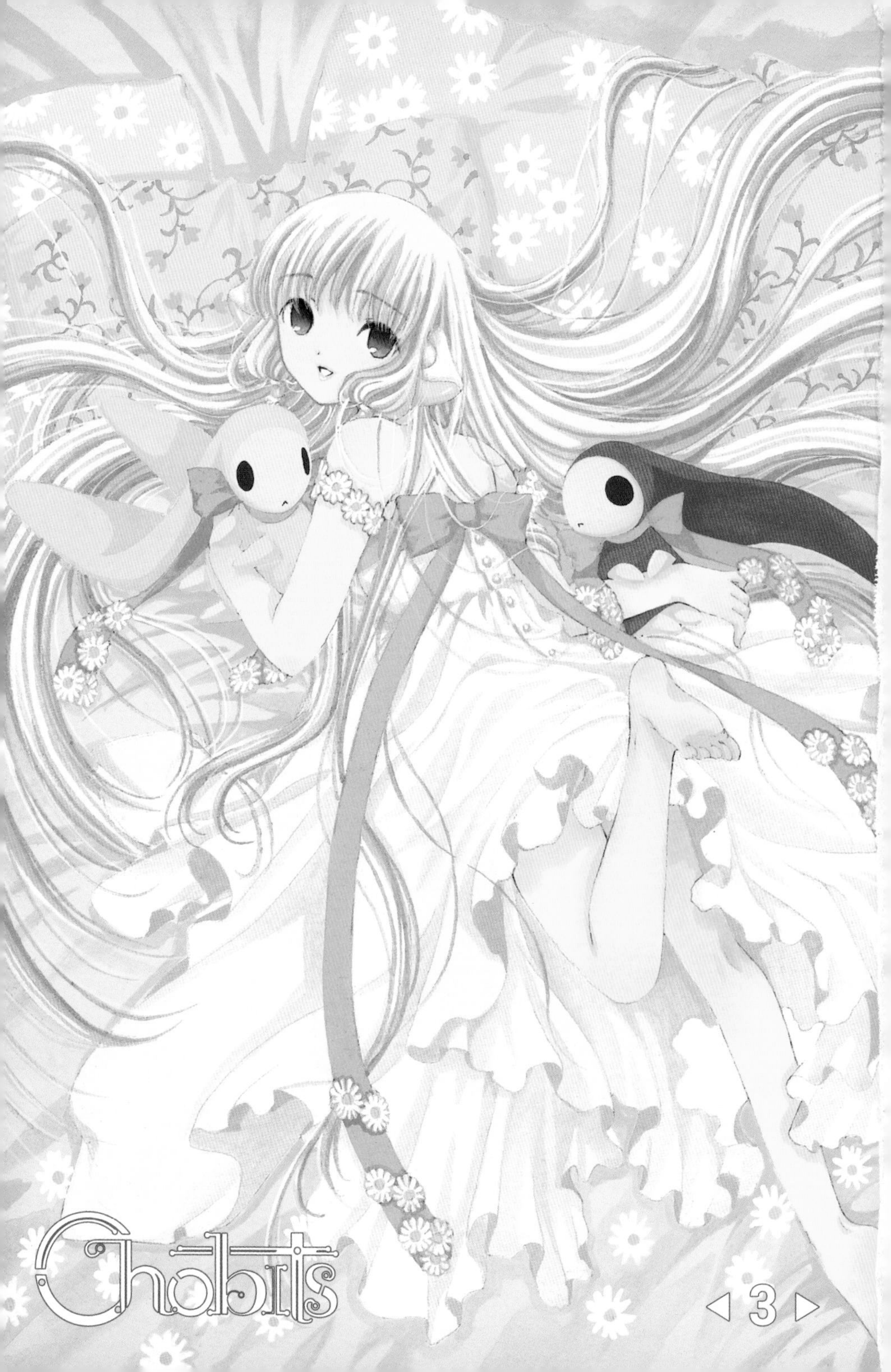
Chobits
3

CONTENTS

◀ **CLAMP** ▶

SATSUKI IGARASHI
NANASE OHKAWA
TSUBAKI NEKOI
MOKONA

◀ Book design ▶
CLAMP

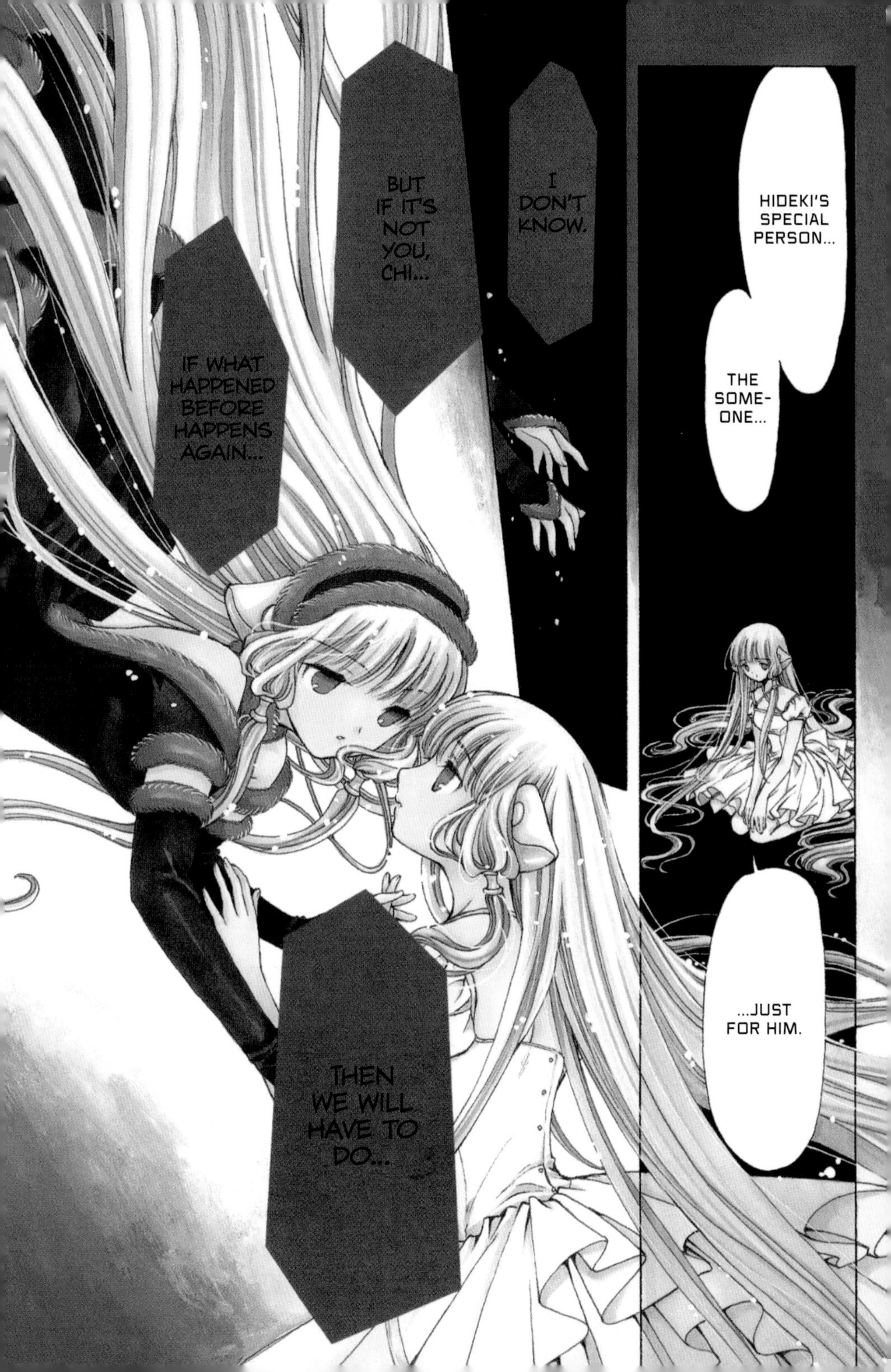
HIDEKI'S SPECIAL PERSON...
THE SOME-ONE...
...JUST FOR HIM.
I DON'T KNOW.
BUT IF IT'S NOT YOU, CHI...
IF WHAT HAPPENED BEFORE HAPPENS AGAIN...
THEN WE WILL HAVE TO DO...

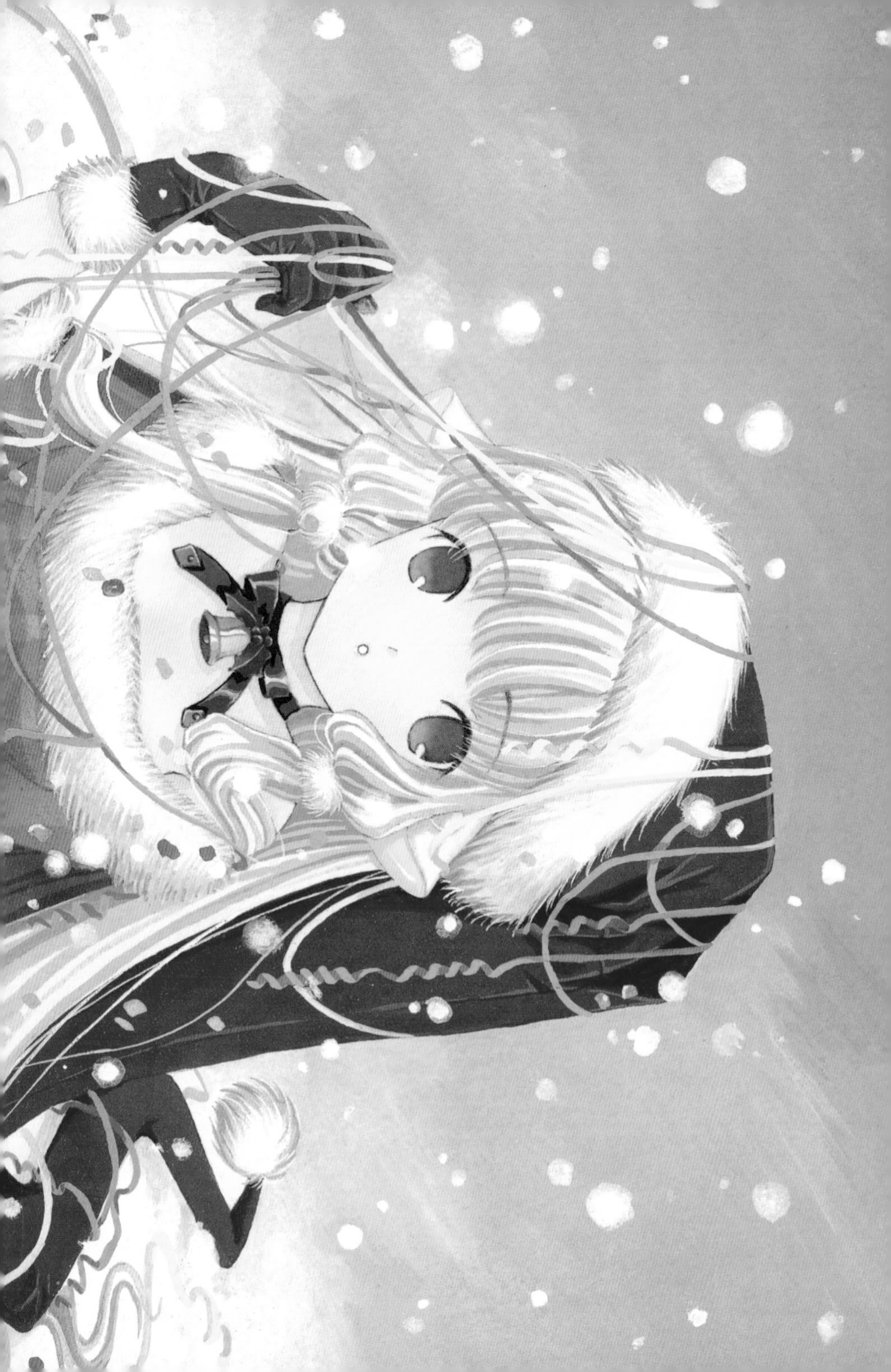

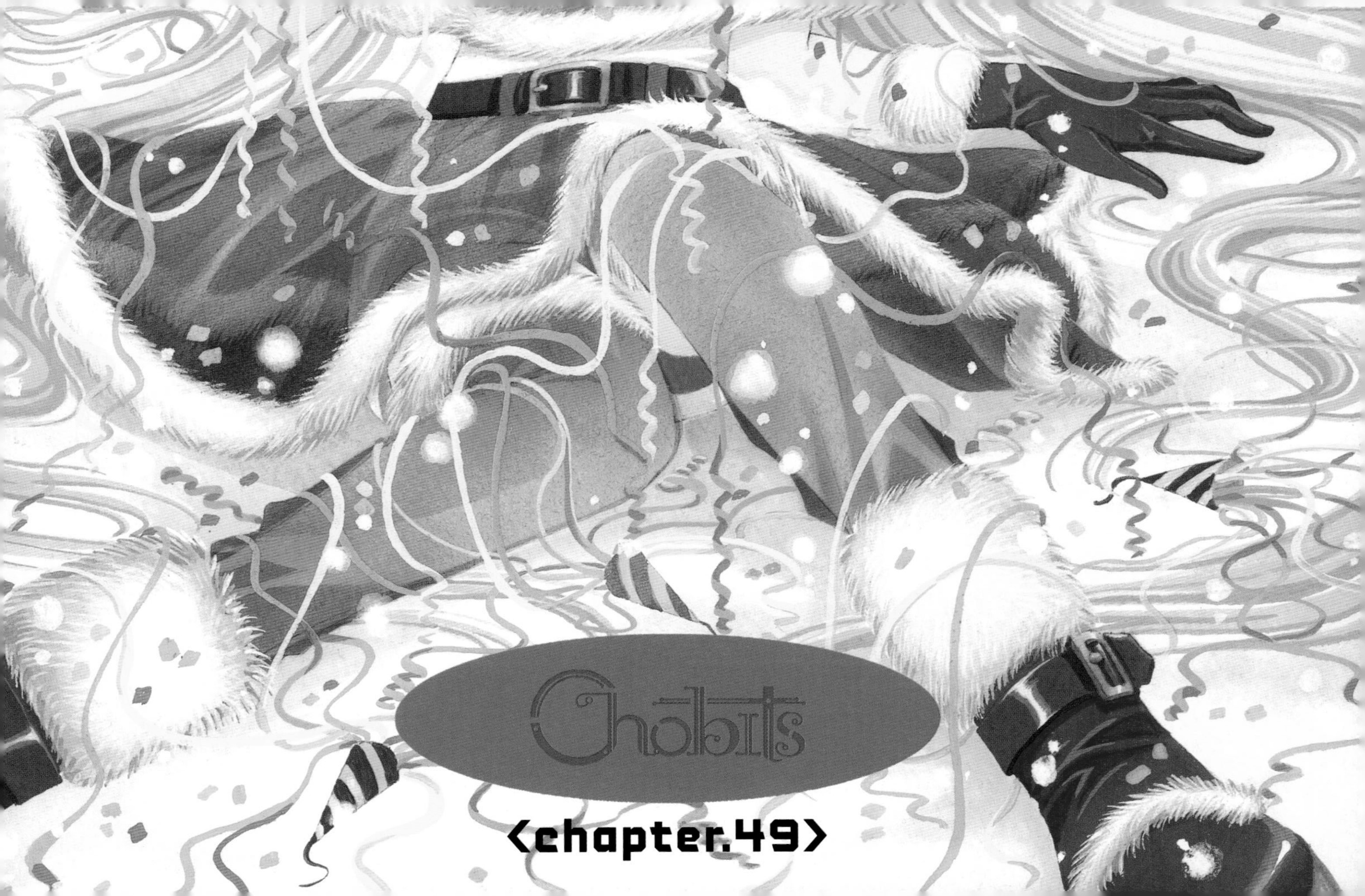
Chobits
<chapter.49>

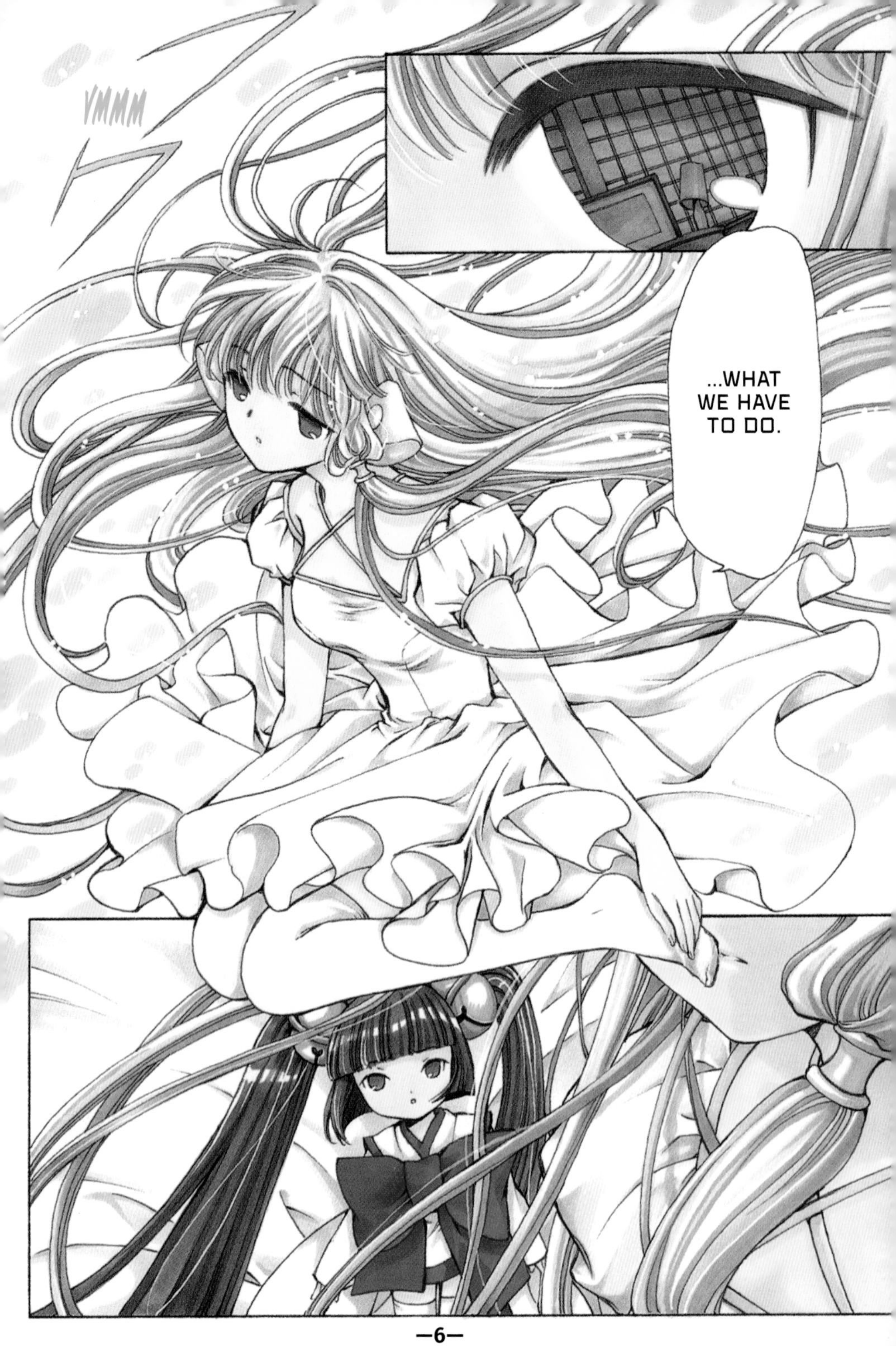
YMMM
...WHAT WE HAVE TO DO.

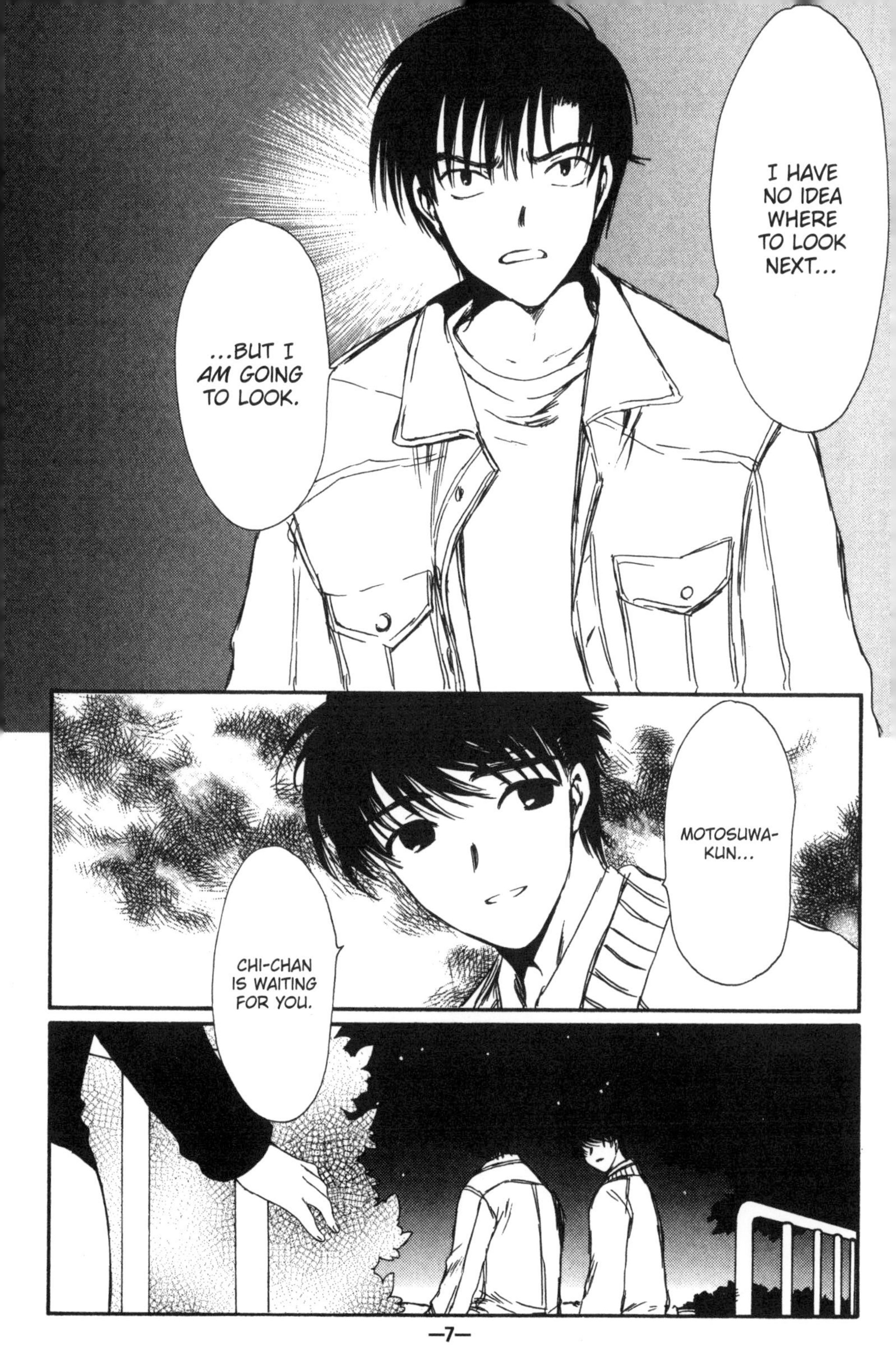
I HAVE NO IDEA WHERE TO LOOK NEXT...
...BUT I AM GOING TO LOOK.
MOTOSUWA-KUN...
CHI-CHAN IS WAITING FOR YOU.

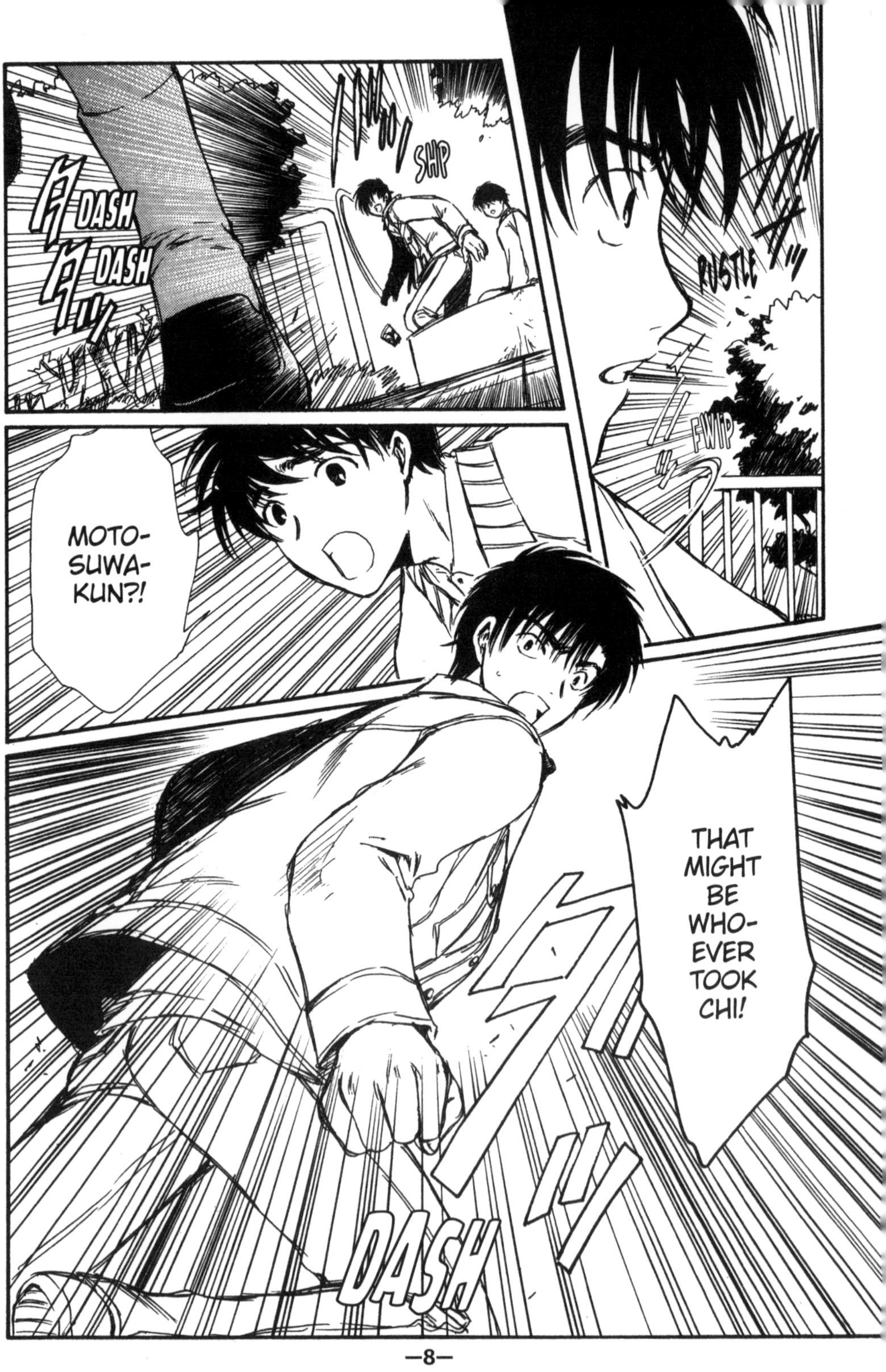
RUSTLE
FWIP
SHP
DASH
DASH
MOTO-SUWA-KUN?!
THAT MIGHT BE WHO-EVER TOOK CHI!
DASH

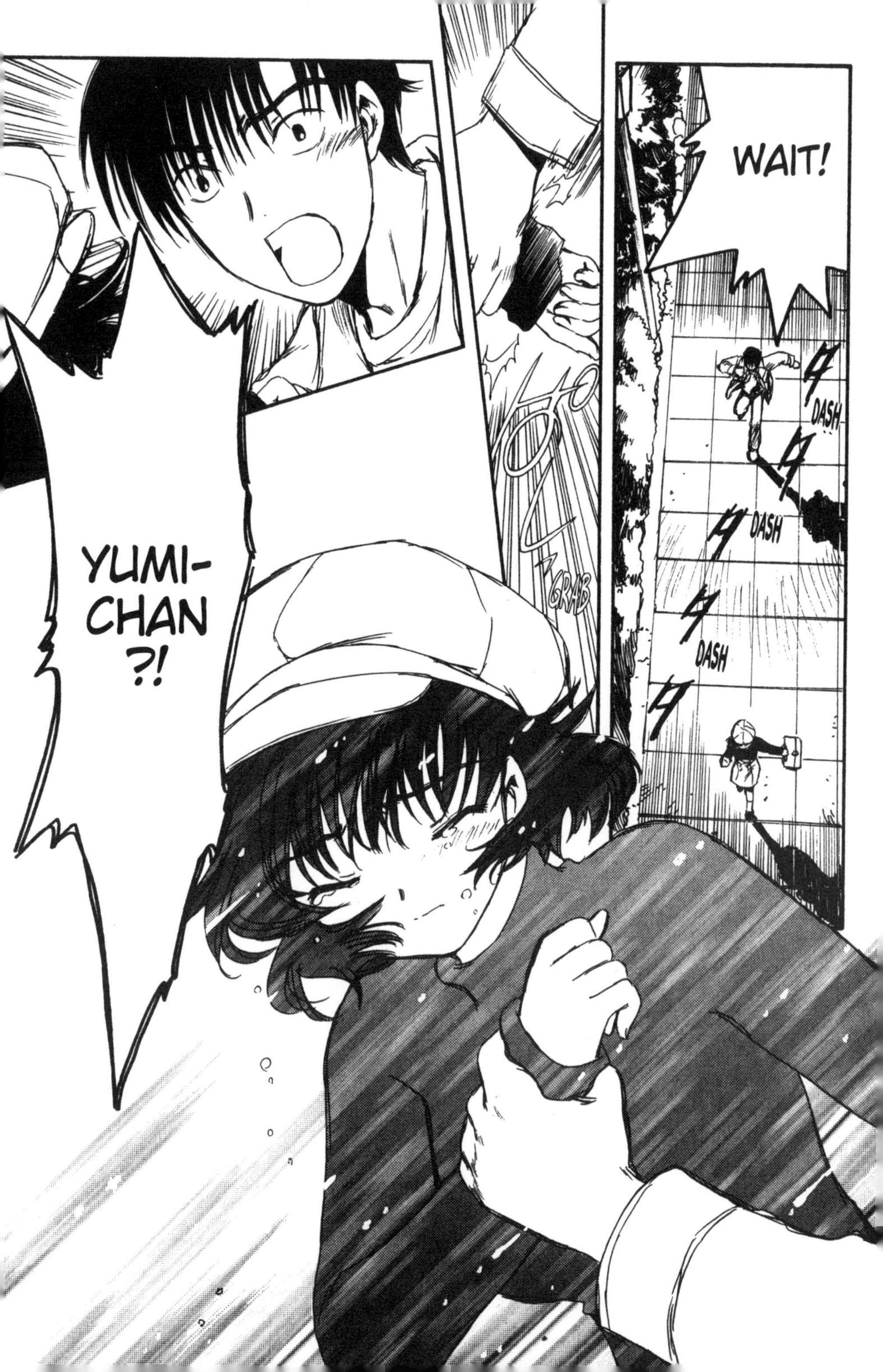
WAIT!
DASH
DASH
DASH
GRAB
YUMI-CHAN ?!

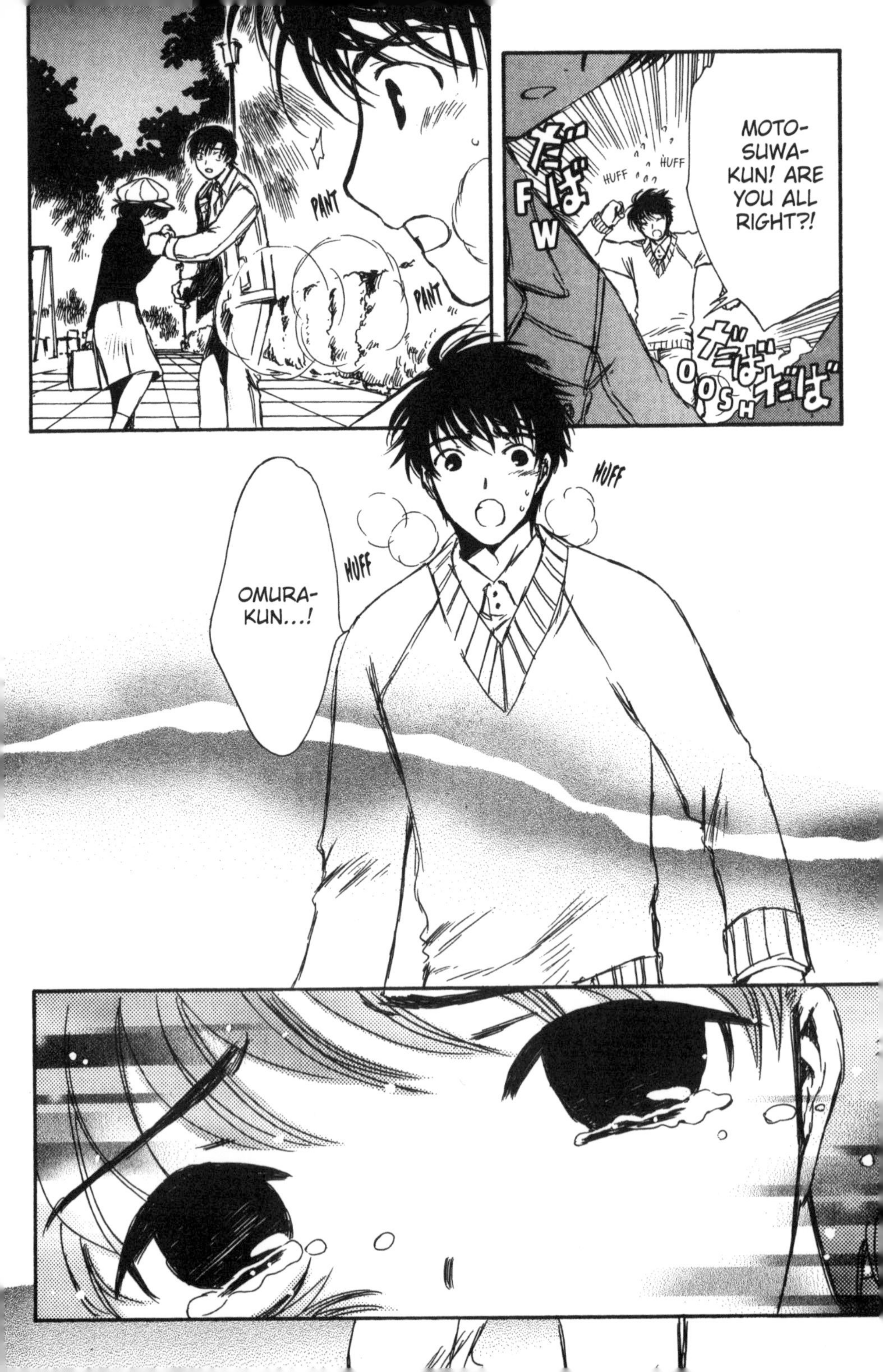
MOTO-SUWA-KUN! ARE YOU ALL RIGHT?!
HUFF HUFF
FWOOSH
PANT
PANT
OMURA-KUN...!
HUFF
HUFF

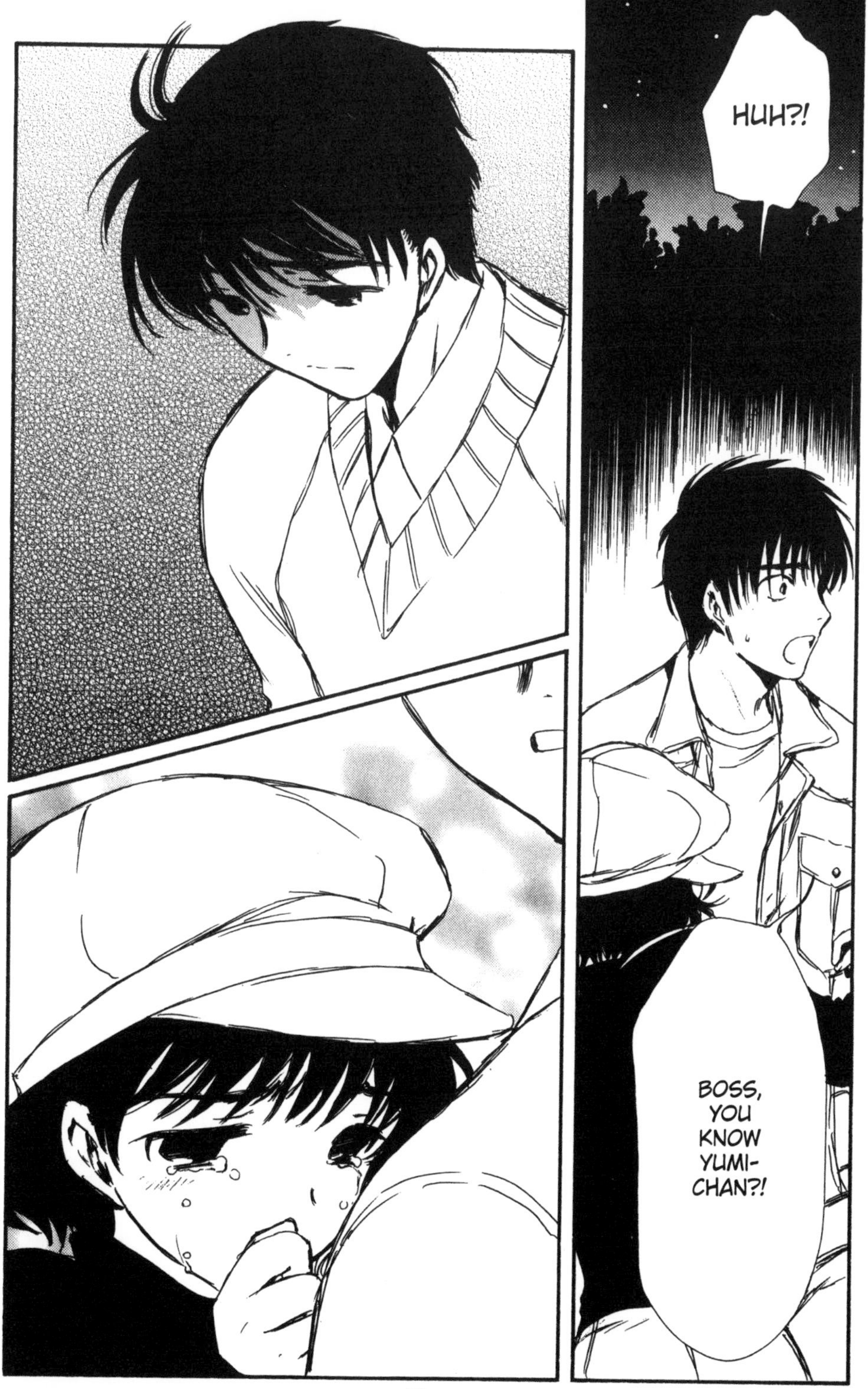
HUH?!
BOSS, YOU KNOW YUMI-CHAN?!

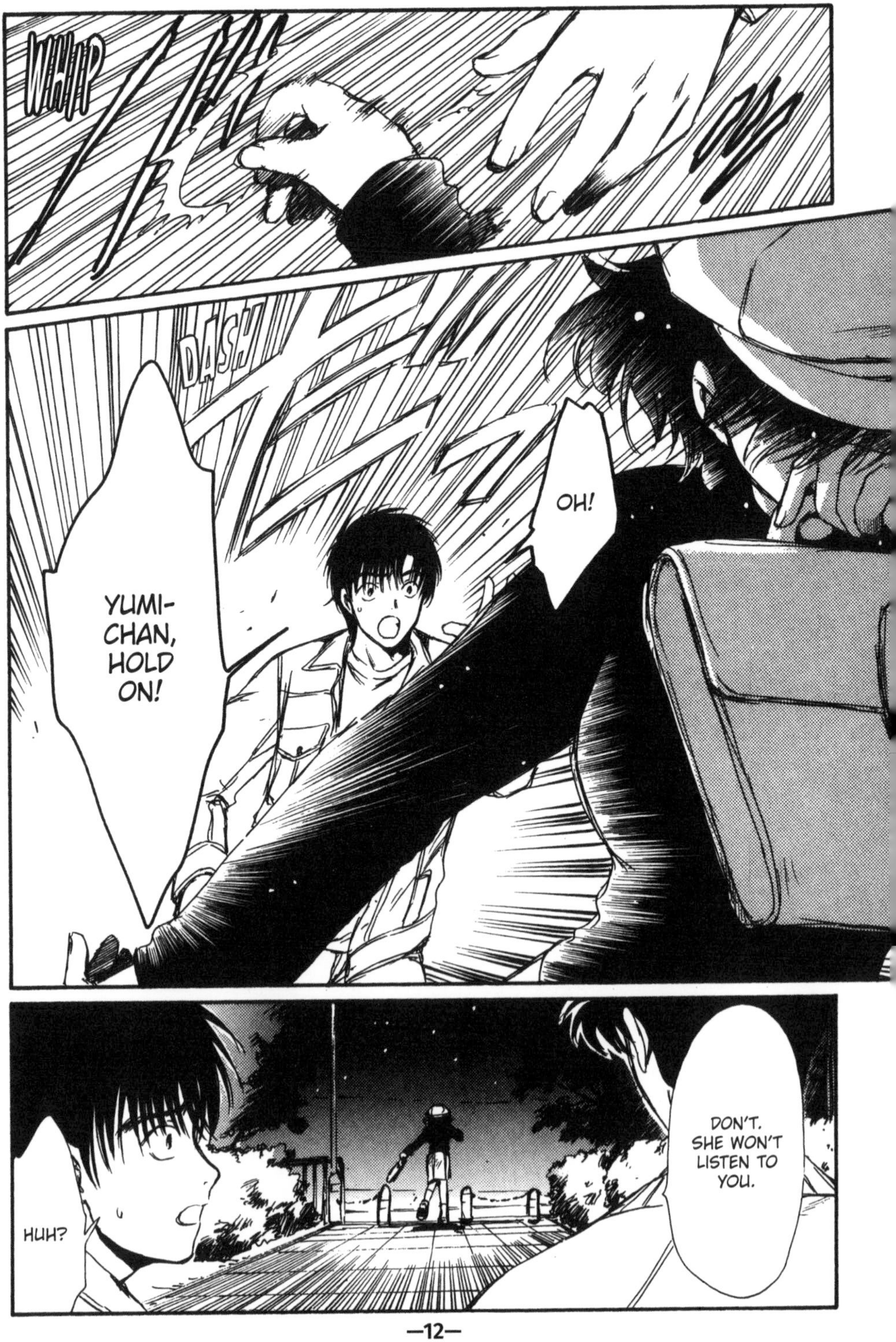
WHIP
DASH
OH!
YUMI-CHAN, HOLD ON!
DON'T. SHE WON'T LISTEN TO YOU.
HUH?

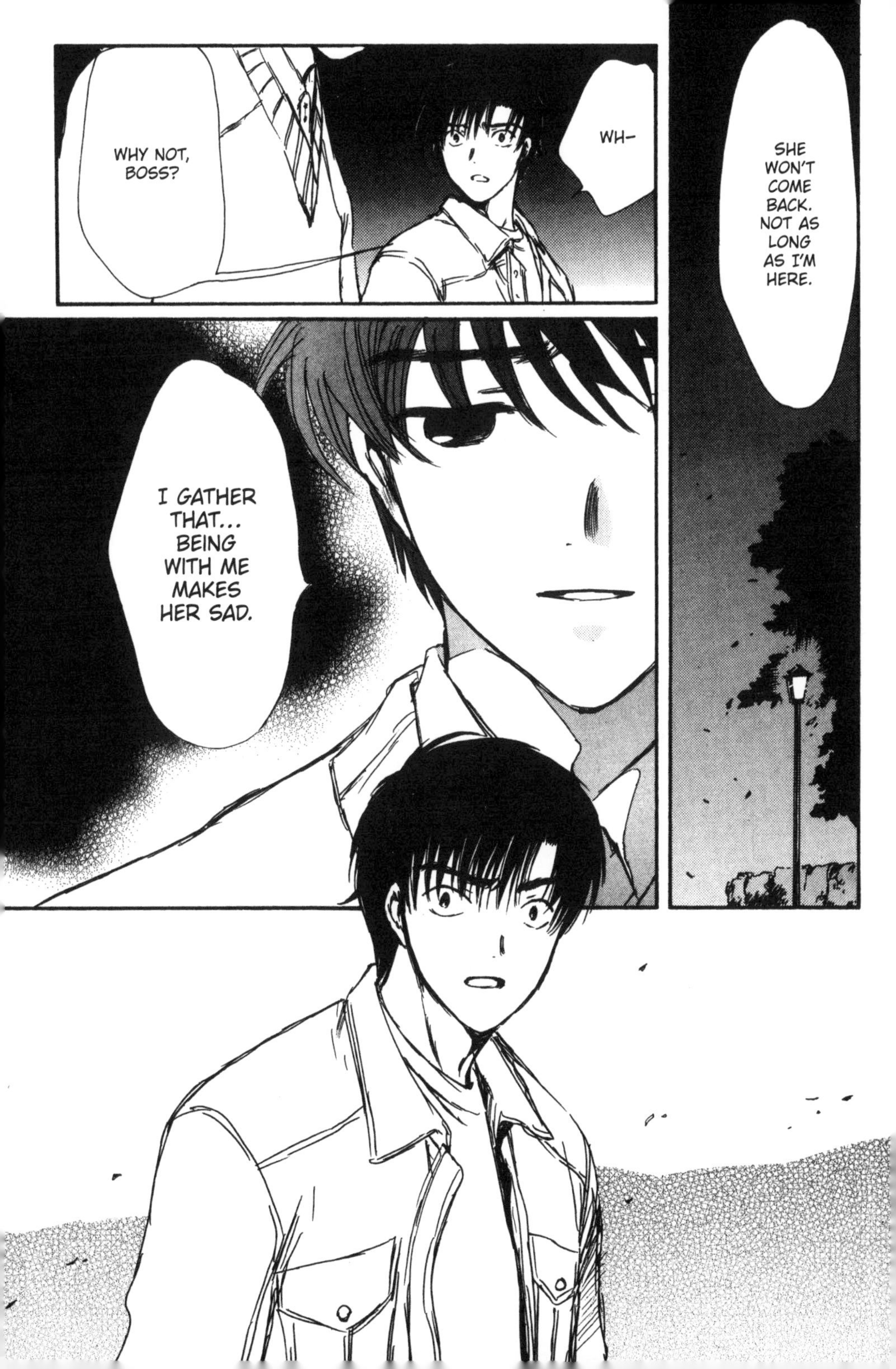
SHE WON'T COME BACK. NOT AS LONG AS I'M HERE.
WH–
WHY NOT, BOSS?
I GATHER THAT... BEING WITH ME MAKES HER SAD.

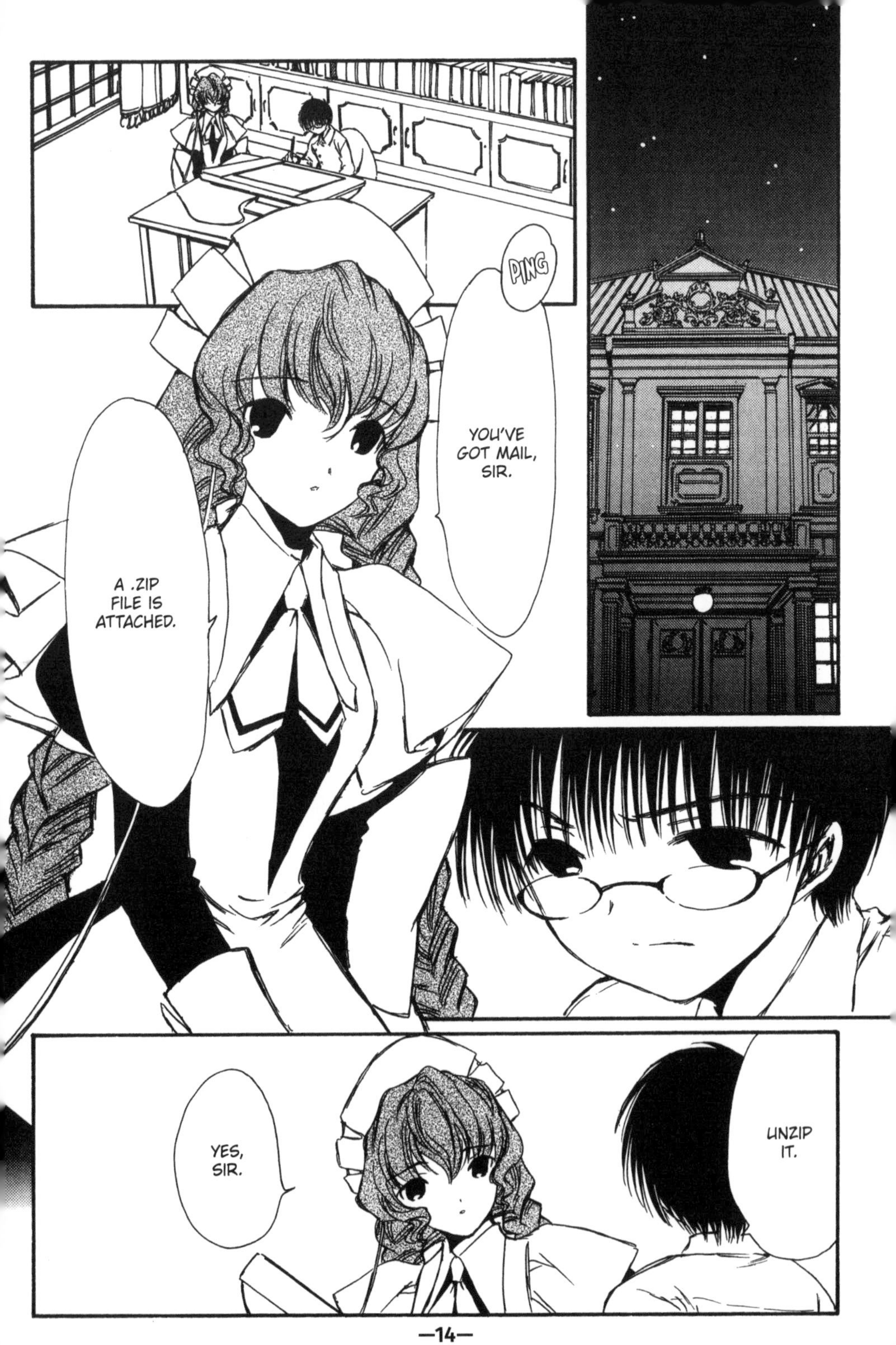
PING
YOU'VE GOT MAIL, SIR.
A .ZIP FILE IS ATTACHED.
UNZIP IT.
YES, SIR.

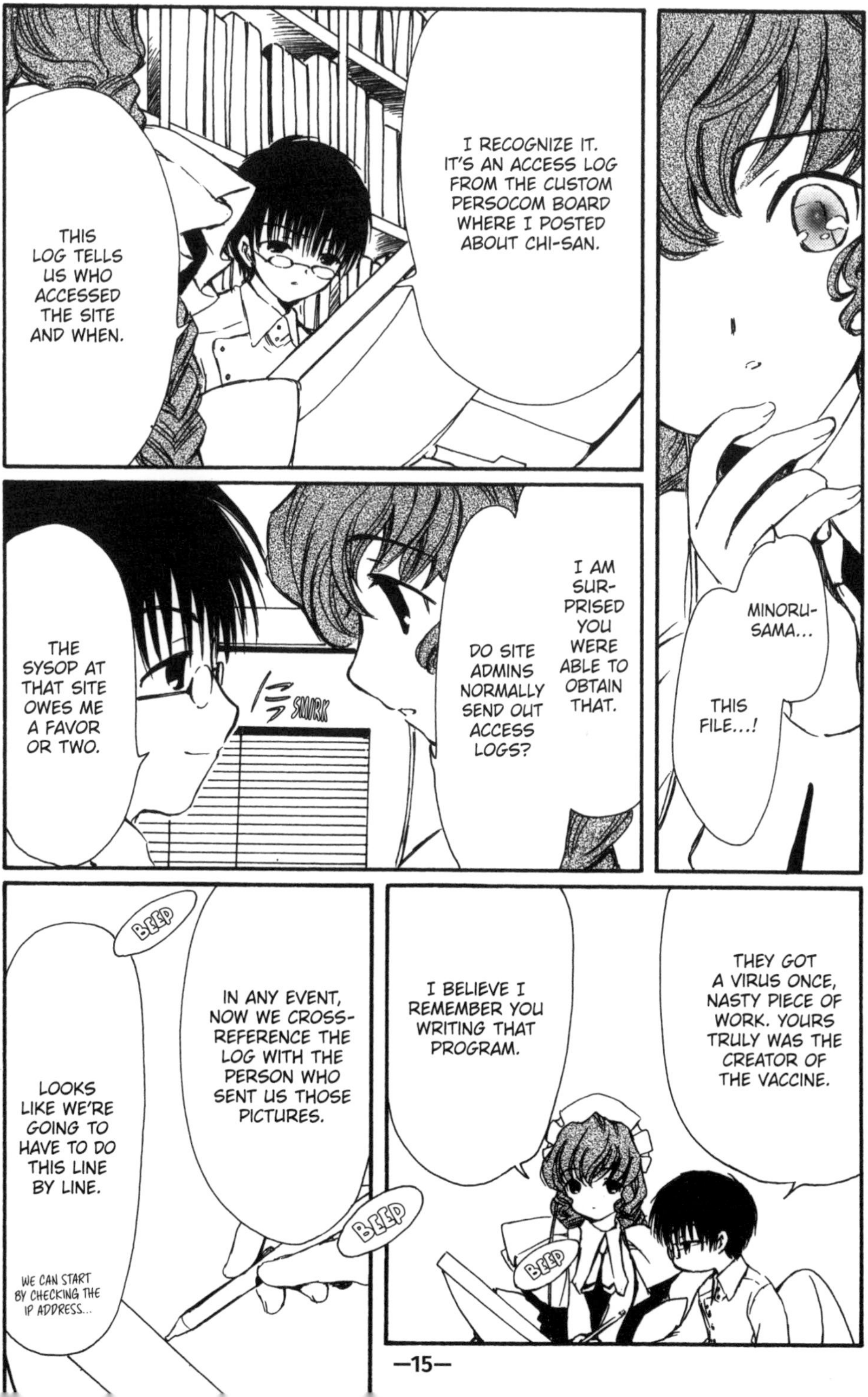
MINORU-SAMA...
THIS FILE...!
I RECOGNIZE IT. IT'S AN ACCESS LOG FROM THE CUSTOM PERSOCOM BOARD WHERE I POSTED ABOUT CHI-SAN.
THIS LOG TELLS US WHO ACCESSED THE SITE AND WHEN.
I AM SURPRISED YOU WERE ABLE TO OBTAIN THAT.
DO SITE ADMINS NORMALLY SEND OUT ACCESS LOGS?
SMIRK
THE SYSOP AT THAT SITE OWES ME A FAVOR OR TWO.
THEY GOT A VIRUS ONCE, NASTY PIECE OF WORK. YOURS TRULY WAS THE CREATOR OF THE VACCINE.
I BELIEVE I REMEMBER YOU WRITING THAT PROGRAM.
BEEP
BEEP
IN ANY EVENT, NOW WE CROSS-REFERENCE THE LOG WITH THE PERSON WHO SENT US THOSE PICTURES.
LOOKS LIKE WE'RE GOING TO HAVE TO DO THIS LINE BY LINE.
BEEP
WE CAN START BY CHECKING THE IP ADDRESS...

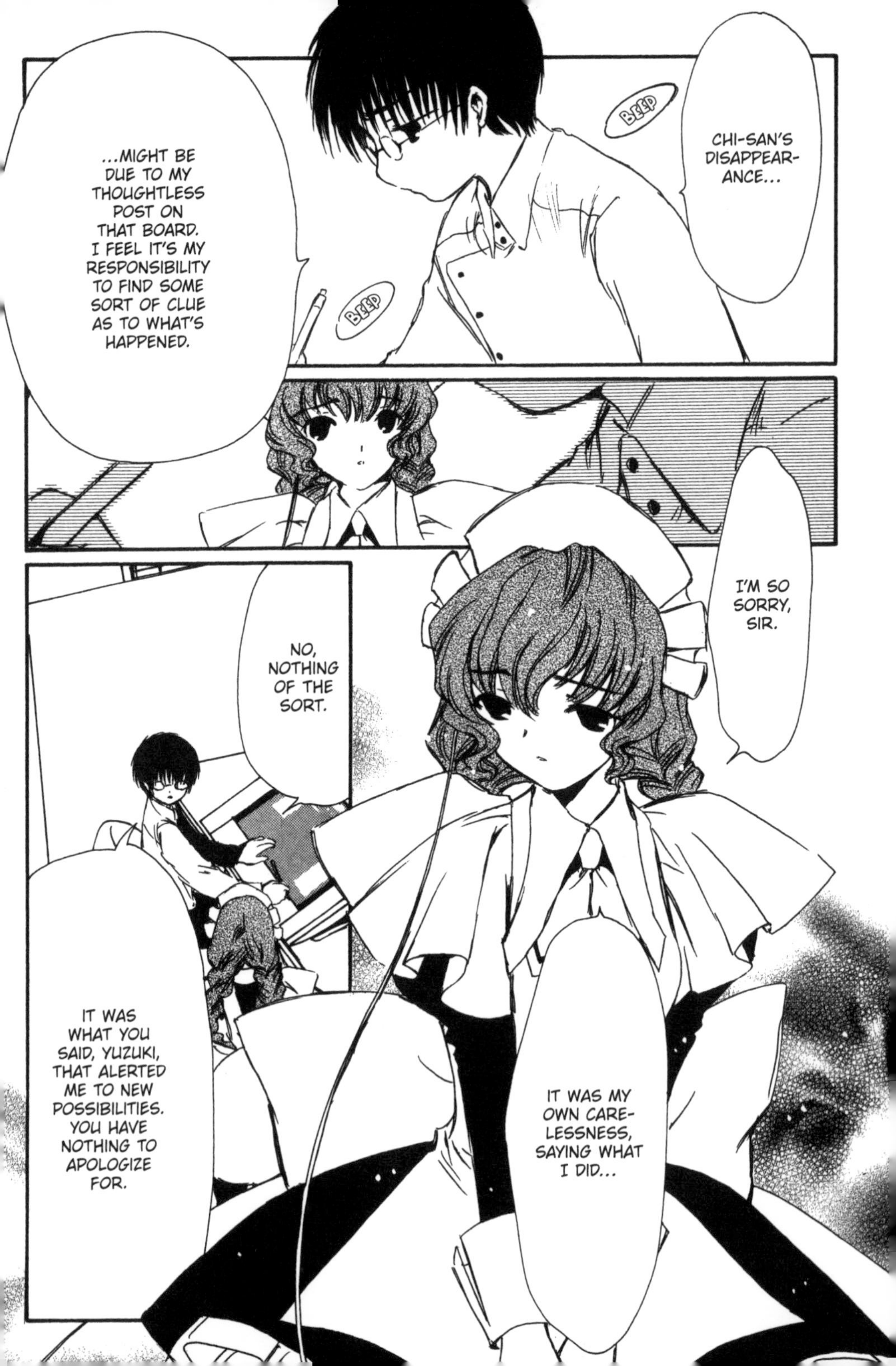
CHI-SAN'S DISAPPEARANCE...
BEEP
BEEP
...MIGHT BE DUE TO MY THOUGHTLESS POST ON THAT BOARD. I FEEL IT'S MY RESPONSIBILITY TO FIND SOME SORT OF CLUE AS TO WHAT'S HAPPENED.
I'M SO SORRY, SIR.
NO, NOTHING OF THE SORT.
IT WAS MY OWN CARELESSNESS, SAYING WHAT I DID...
IT WAS WHAT YOU SAID, YUZUKI, THAT ALERTED ME TO NEW POSSIBILITIES. YOU HAVE NOTHING TO APOLOGIZE FOR.

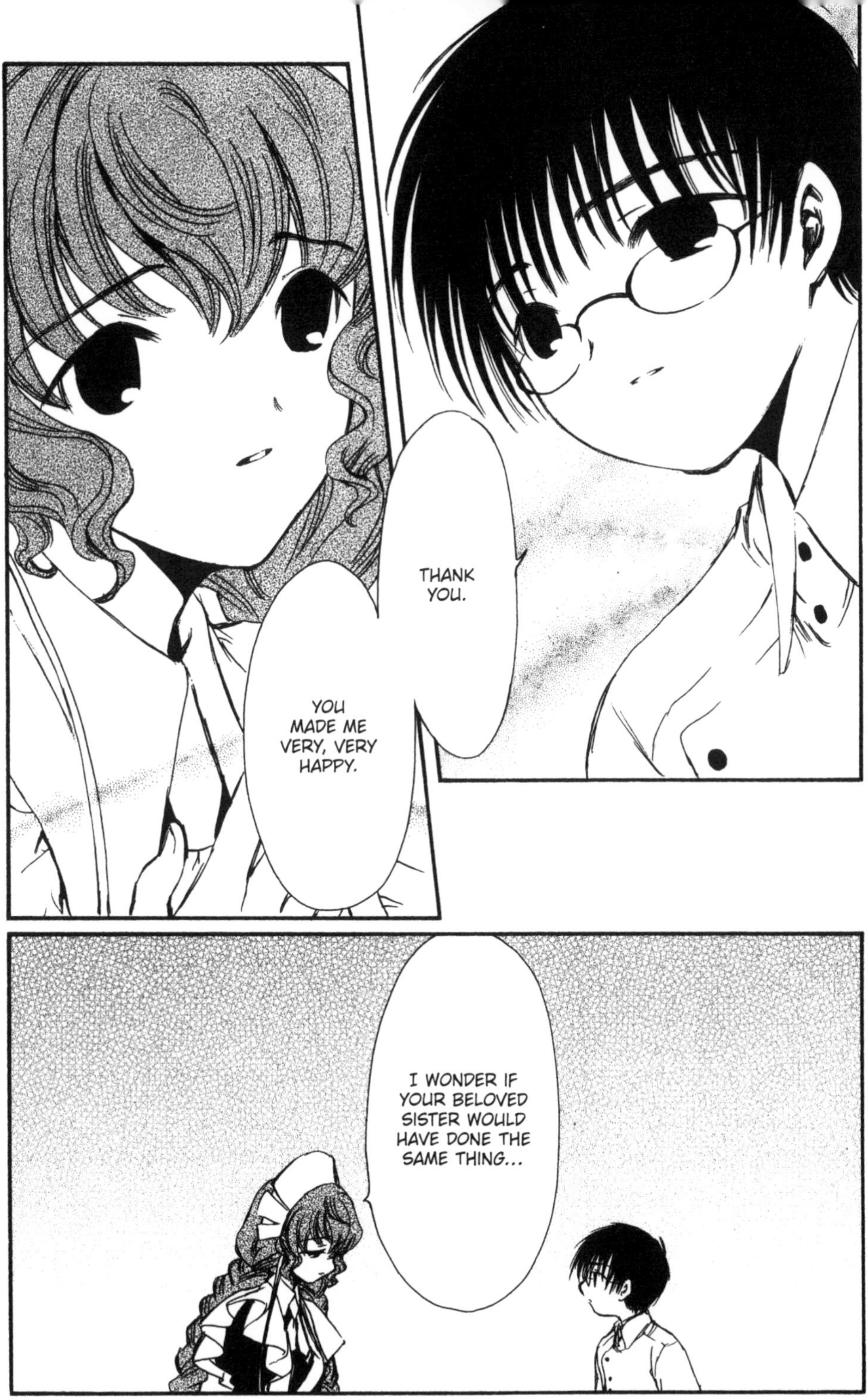
THANK YOU.
YOU MADE ME VERY, VERY HAPPY.
I WONDER IF YOUR BELOVED SISTER WOULD HAVE DONE THE SAME THING...

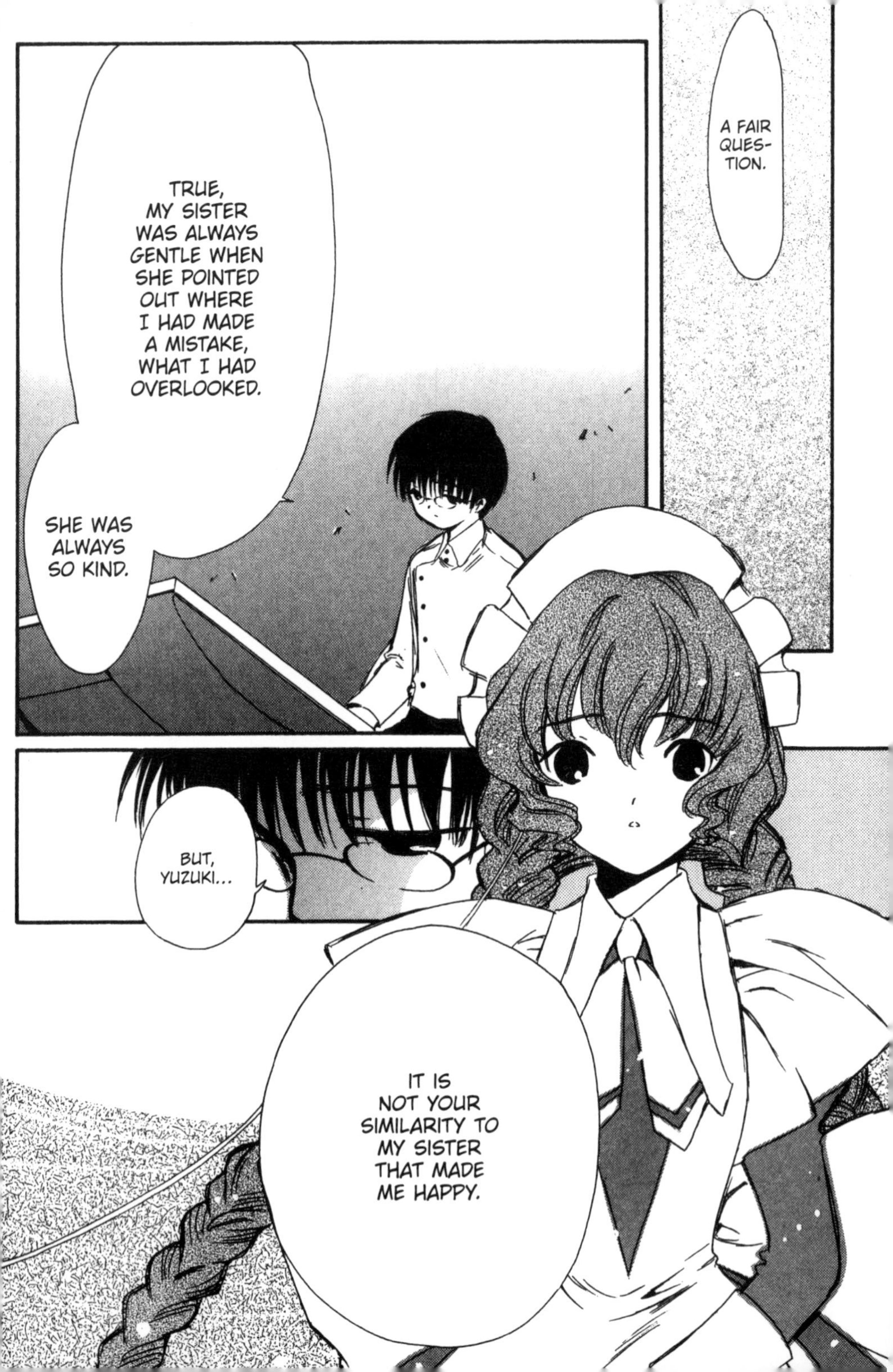
A FAIR QUESTION.
TRUE, MY SISTER WAS ALWAYS GENTLE WHEN SHE POINTED OUT WHERE I HAD MADE A MISTAKE, WHAT I HAD OVERLOOKED.
SHE WAS ALWAYS SO KIND.
BUT, YUZUKI...
IT IS NOT YOUR SIMILARITY TO MY SISTER THAT MADE ME HAPPY.

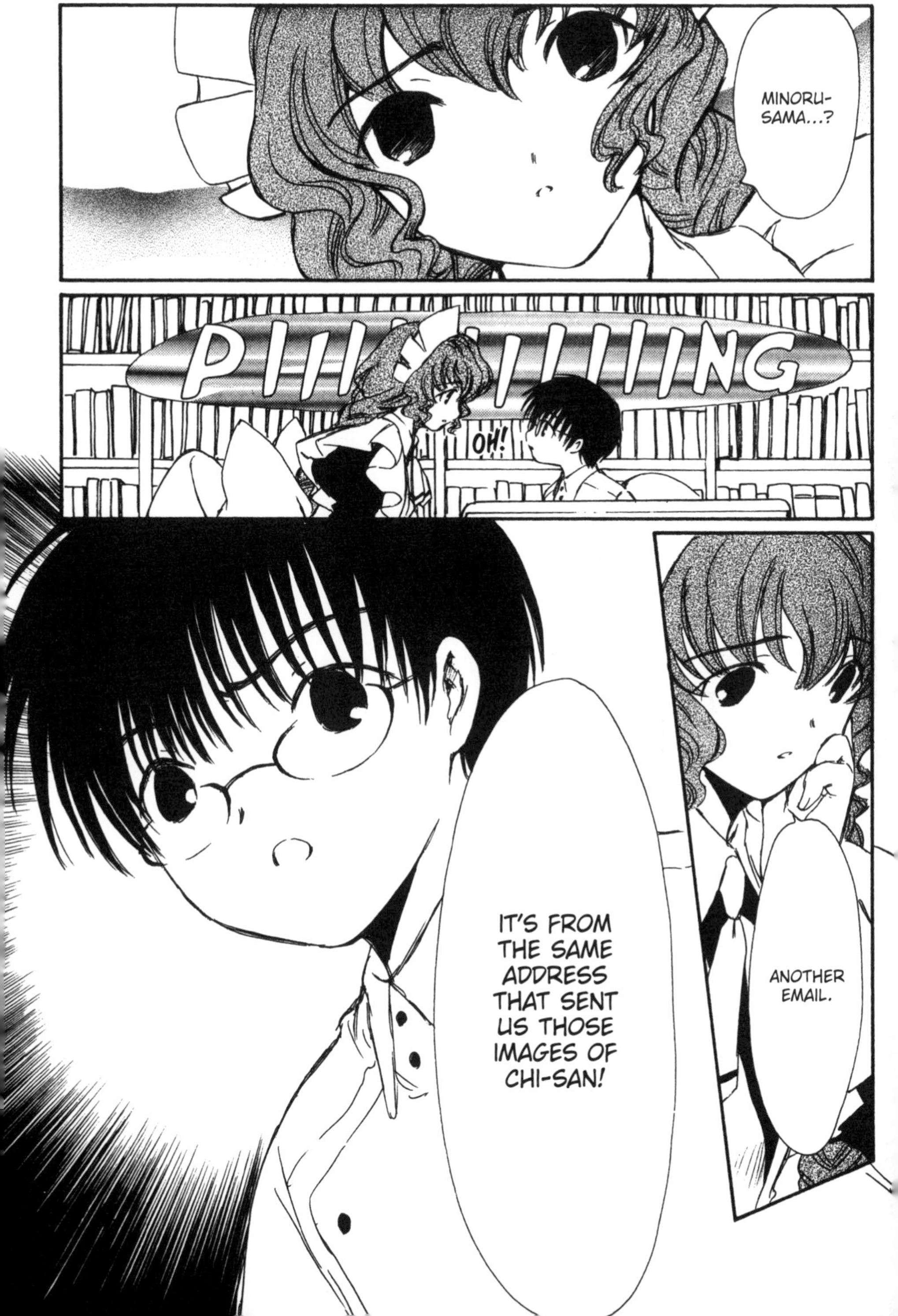
MINORU-SAMA...?
PIIIIIIIIING
OH!
ANOTHER EMAIL.
IT'S FROM THE SAME ADDRESS THAT SENT US THOSE IMAGES OF CHI-SAN!

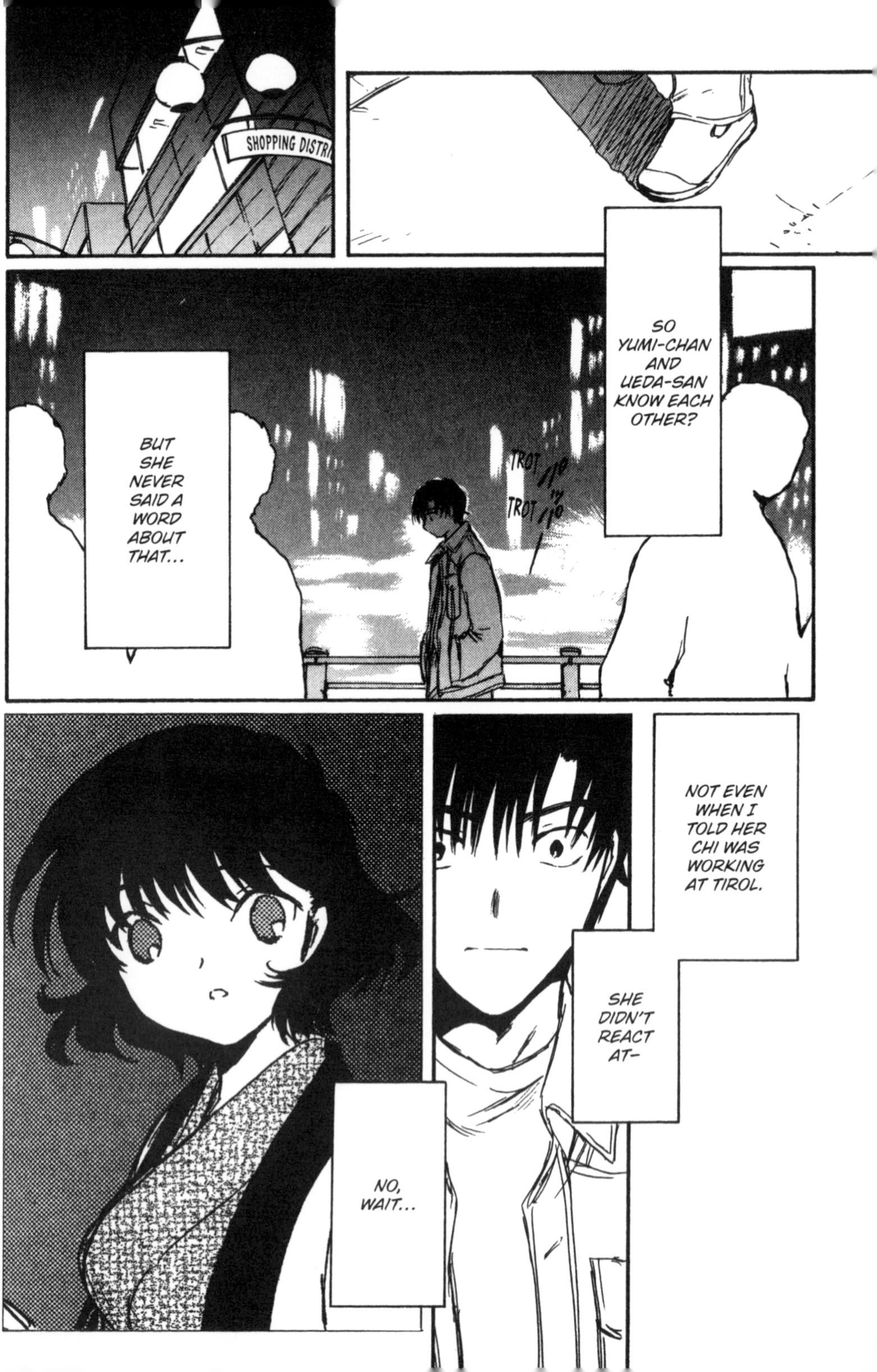
SHOPPING DISTRI
SO YUMI-CHAN AND UEDA-SAN KNOW EACH OTHER?
TROT
TROT
BUT SHE NEVER SAID A WORD ABOUT THAT...
NOT EVEN WHEN I TOLD HER CHI WAS WORKING AT TIROL.
SHE DIDN'T REACT AT-
NO, WAIT...

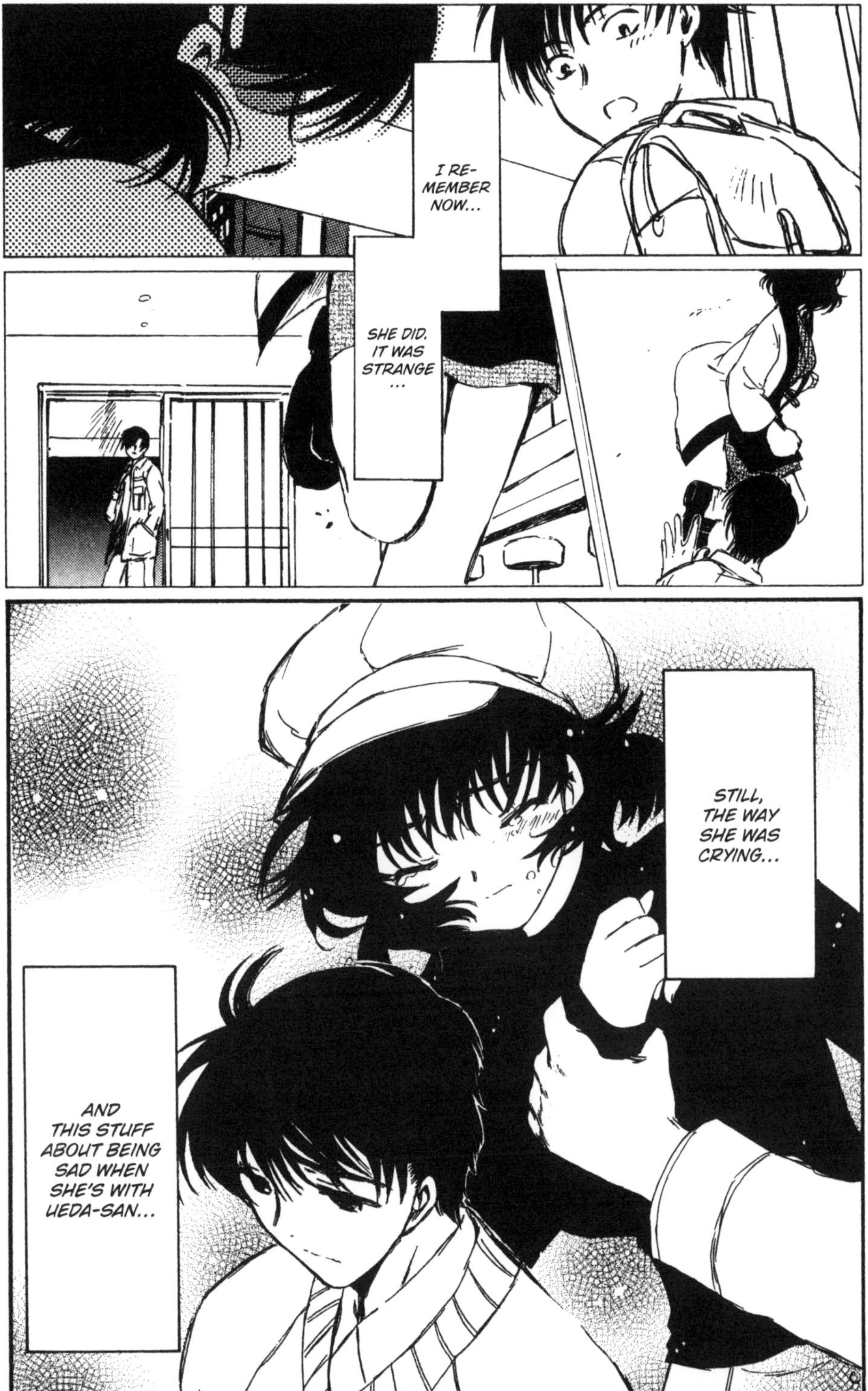
I RE-MEMBER NOW...
SHE DID. IT WAS STRANGE...
STILL, THE WAY SHE WAS CRYING...
AND THIS STUFF ABOUT BEING SAD WHEN SHE'S WITH UEDA-SAN...

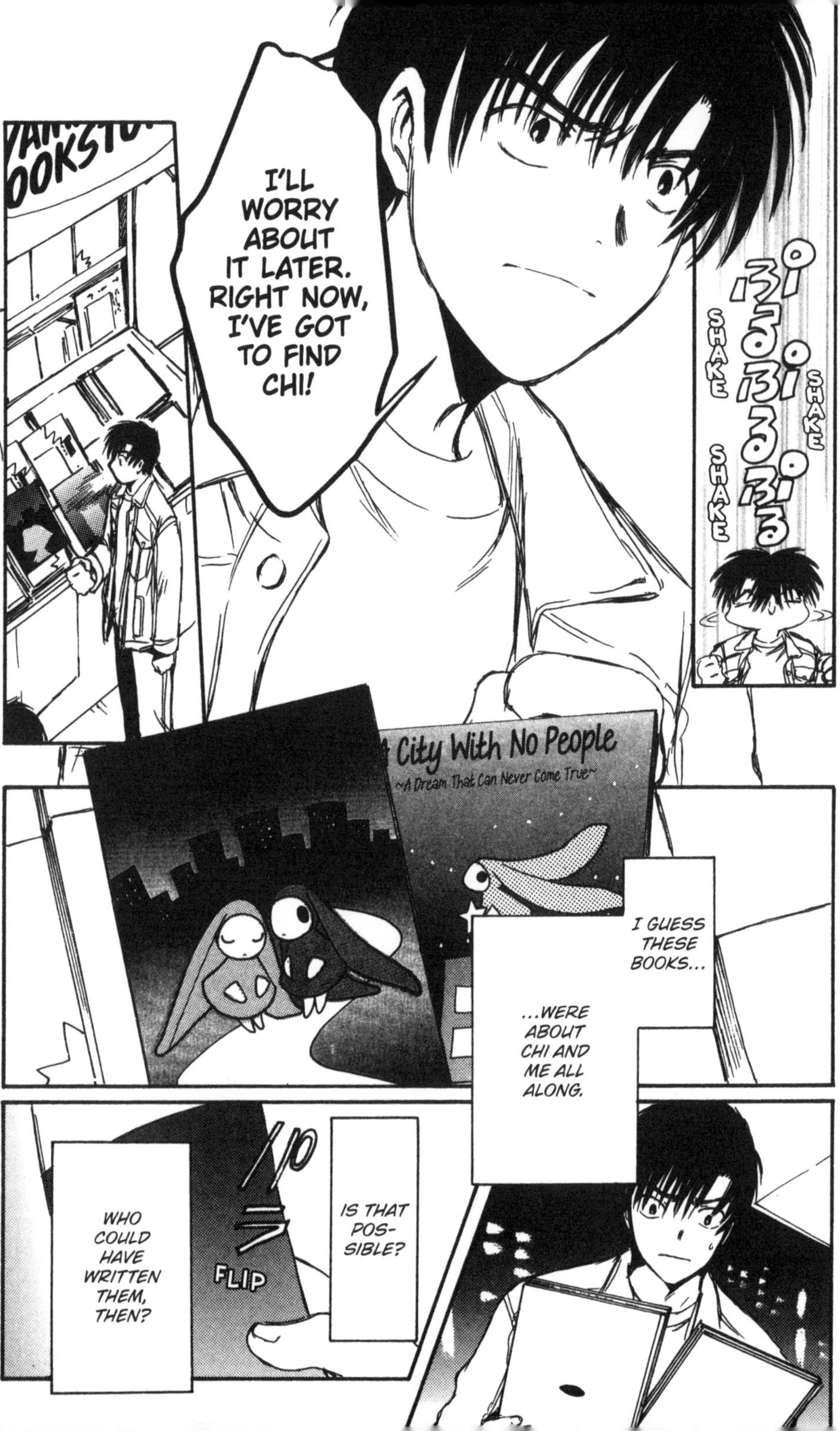
ぷるぷる
ぷるぷる
SHAKE
SHAKE
SHAKE
SHAKE
I'LL WORRY ABOUT IT LATER. RIGHT NOW, I'VE GOT TO FIND CHI!
City With No People
~A Dream That Can Never Come True~
I GUESS THESE BOOKS...
...WERE ABOUT CHI AND ME ALL ALONG.
IS THAT POS-SIBLE?
FLIP
WHO COULD HAVE WRITTEN THEM, THEN?

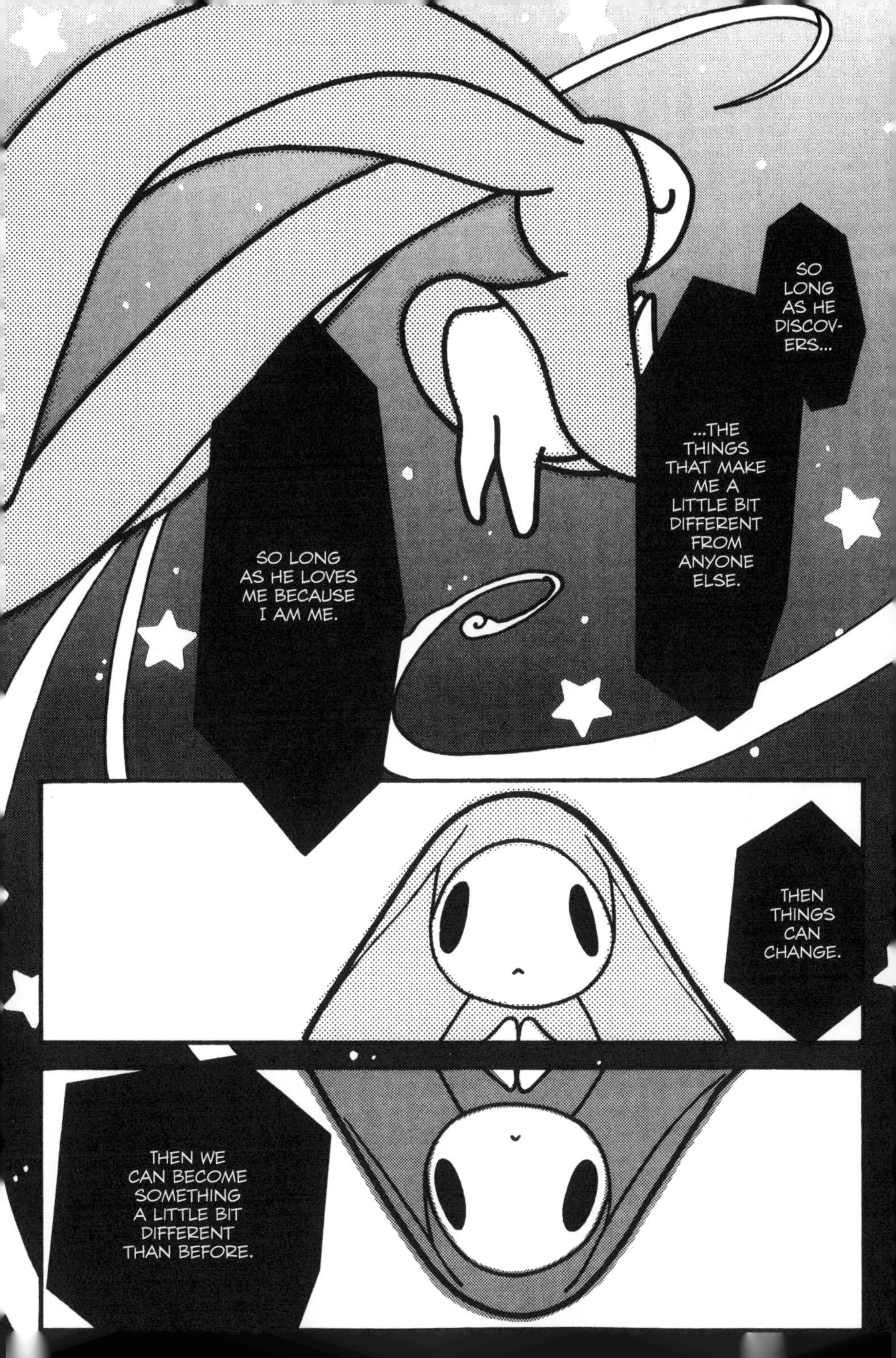
SO LONG AS HE DISCOV-ERS...
...THE THINGS THAT MAKE ME A LITTLE BIT DIFFERENT FROM ANYONE ELSE.
SO LONG AS HE LOVES ME BECAUSE I AM ME.
THEN THINGS CAN CHANGE.
THEN WE CAN BECOME SOMETHING A LITTLE BIT DIFFERENT THAN BEFORE.

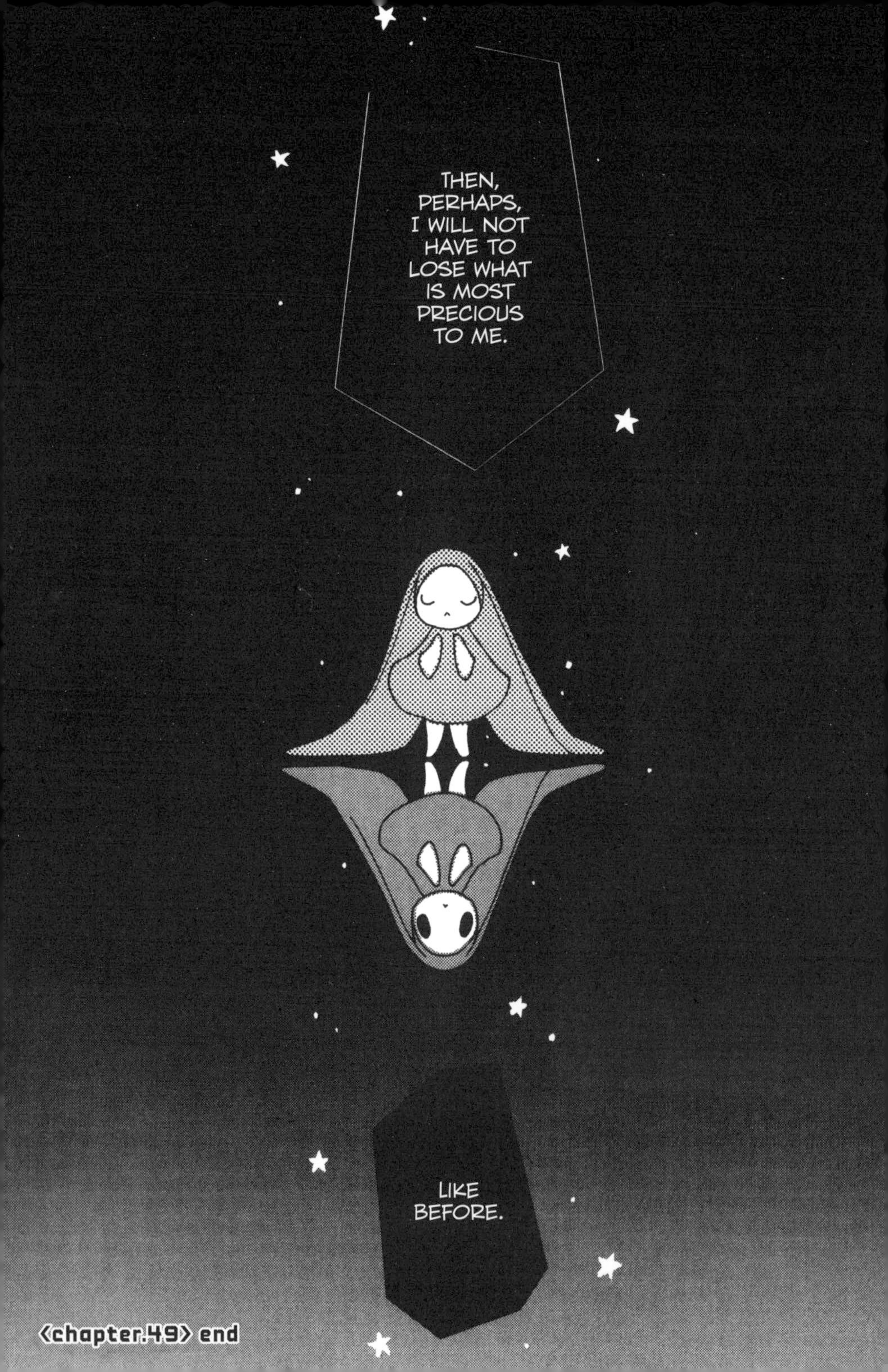

THEN, PERHAPS, I WILL NOT HAVE TO LOSE WHAT IS MOST PRECIOUS TO ME.
LIKE BEFORE.

《chapter.49》 end

〈chapter.50〉

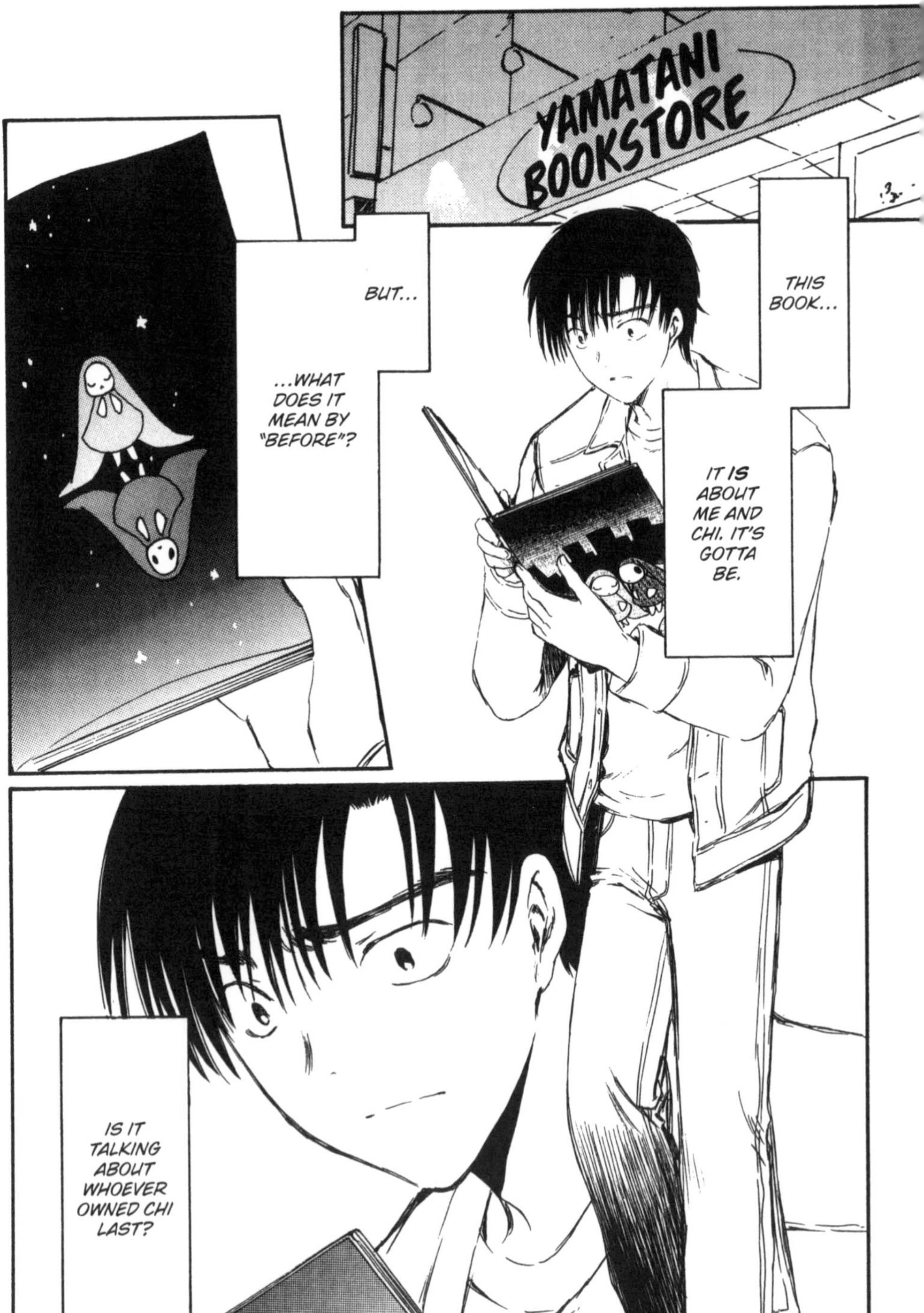
YAMATANI BOOKSTORE
THIS BOOK...
IT IS ABOUT ME AND CHI. IT'S GOTTA BE.
BUT...
...WHAT DOES IT MEAN BY "BEFORE"?
IS IT TALKING ABOUT WHOEVER OWNED CHI LAST?

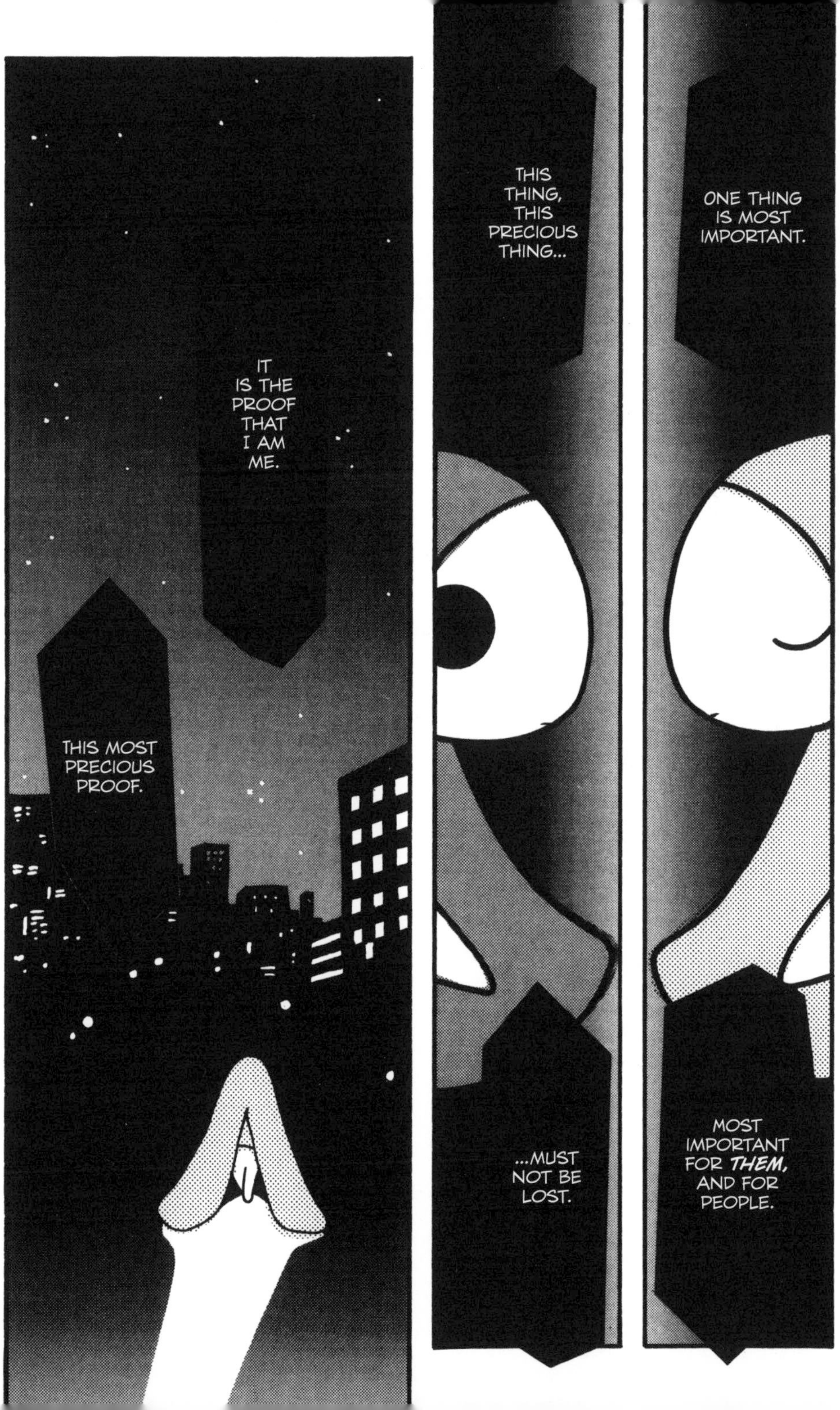
ONE THING IS MOST IMPORTANT.
MOST IMPORTANT FOR *THEM,* AND FOR PEOPLE.
THIS THING, THIS PRECIOUS THING...
...MUST NOT BE LOST.
IT IS THE PROOF THAT I AM ME.
THIS MOST PRECIOUS PROOF.

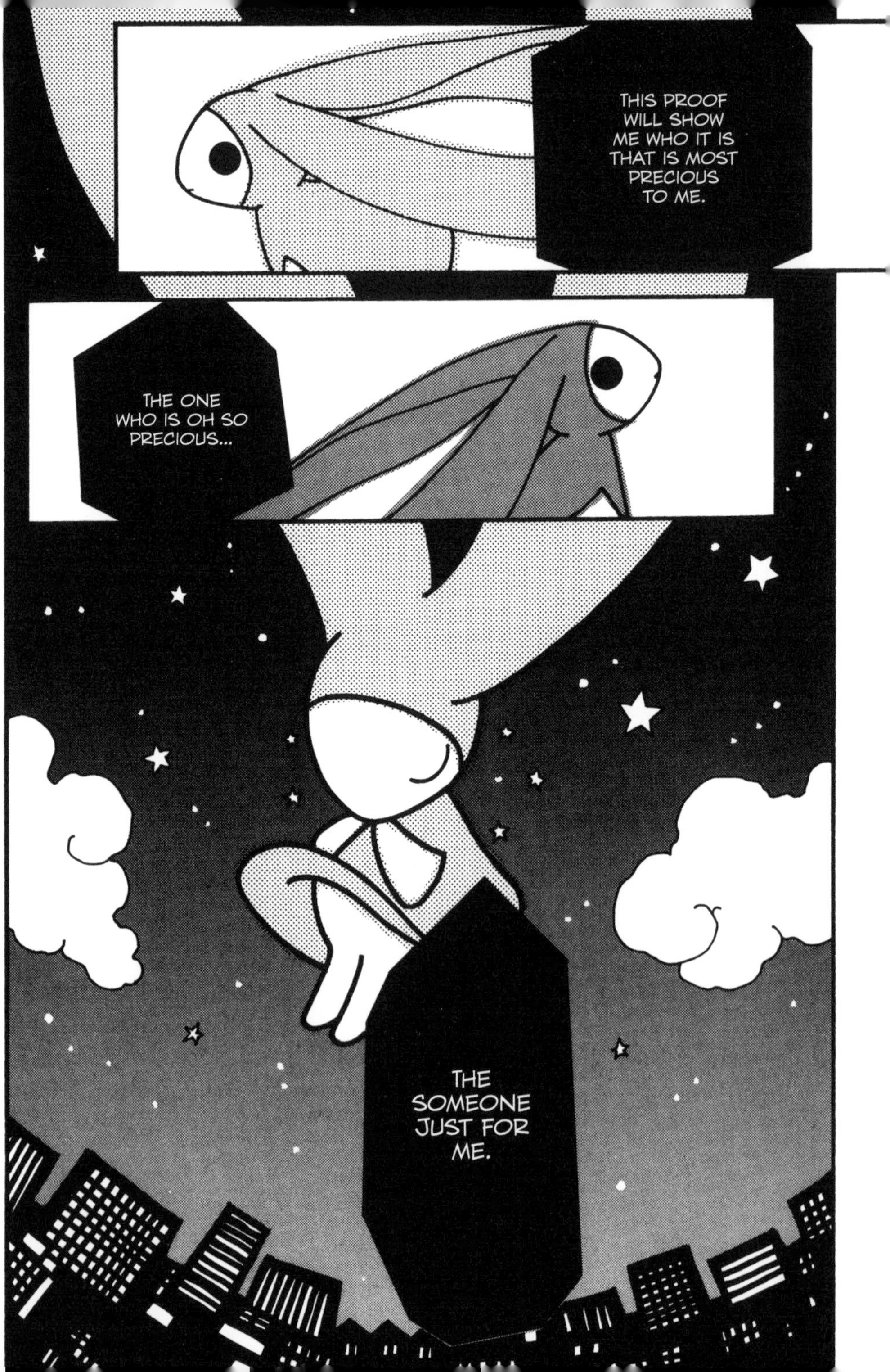
THIS PROOF WILL SHOW ME WHO IT IS THAT IS MOST PRECIOUS TO ME.
THE ONE WHO IS OH SO PRECIOUS...
THE SOMEONE JUST FOR ME.

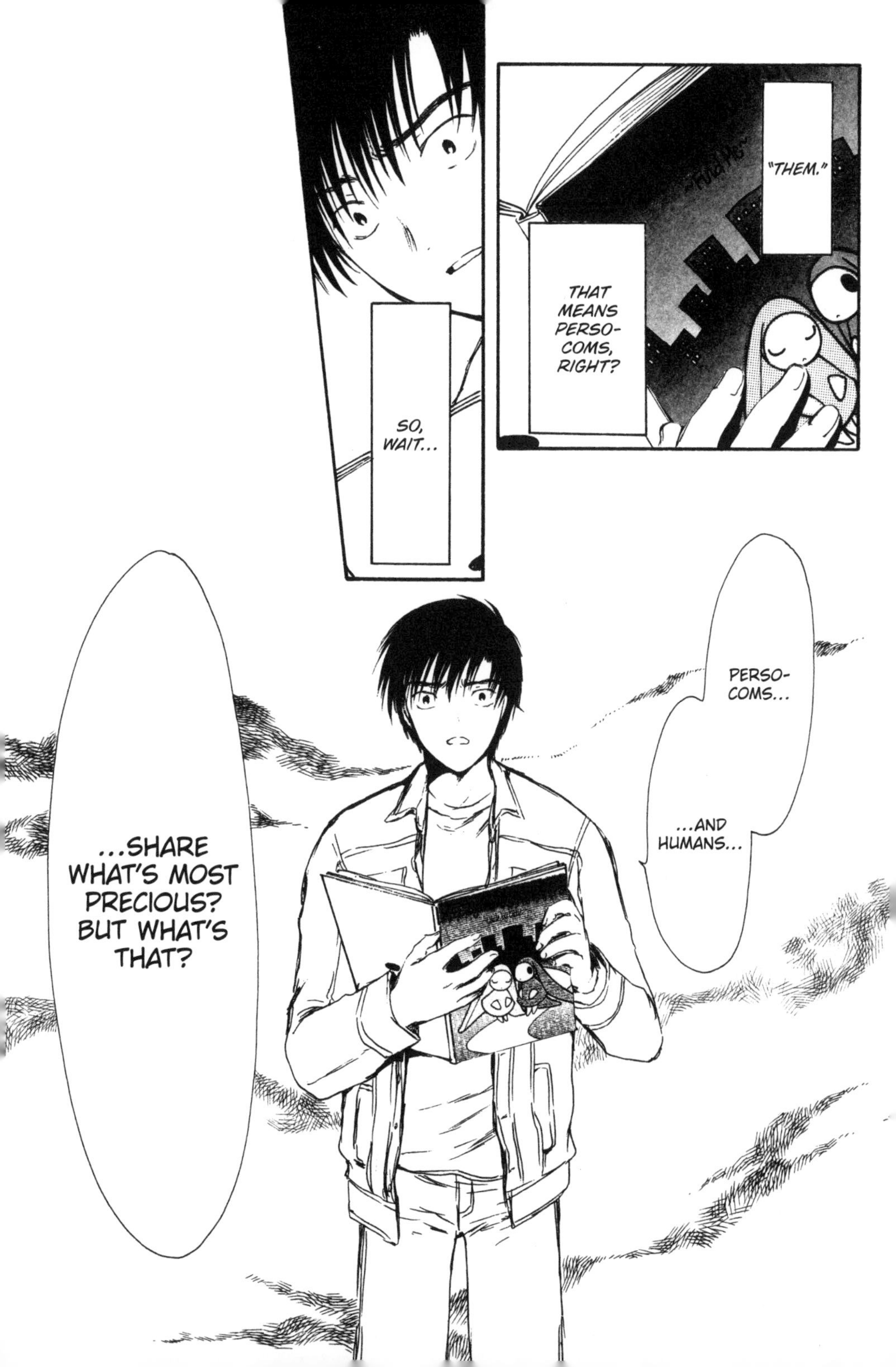
"THEM."
THAT MEANS PERSO-COMS, RIGHT?
SO, WAIT...
PERSO-COMS...
...AND HUMANS...
...SHARE WHAT'S MOST PRECIOUS? BUT WHAT'S THAT?

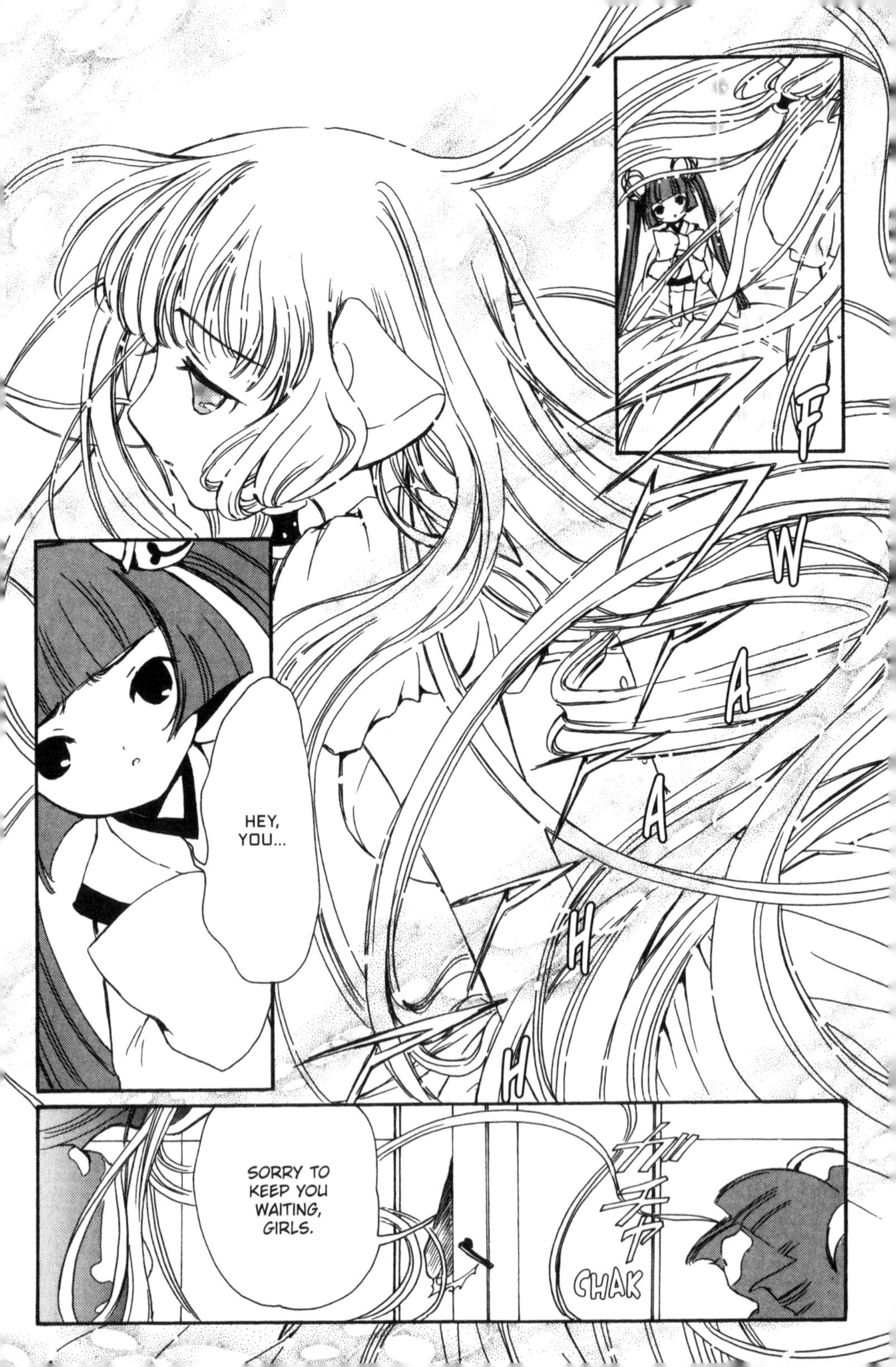
FWAAHH
HEY, YOU...
CHAK
SORRY TO KEEP YOU WAITING, GIRLS.

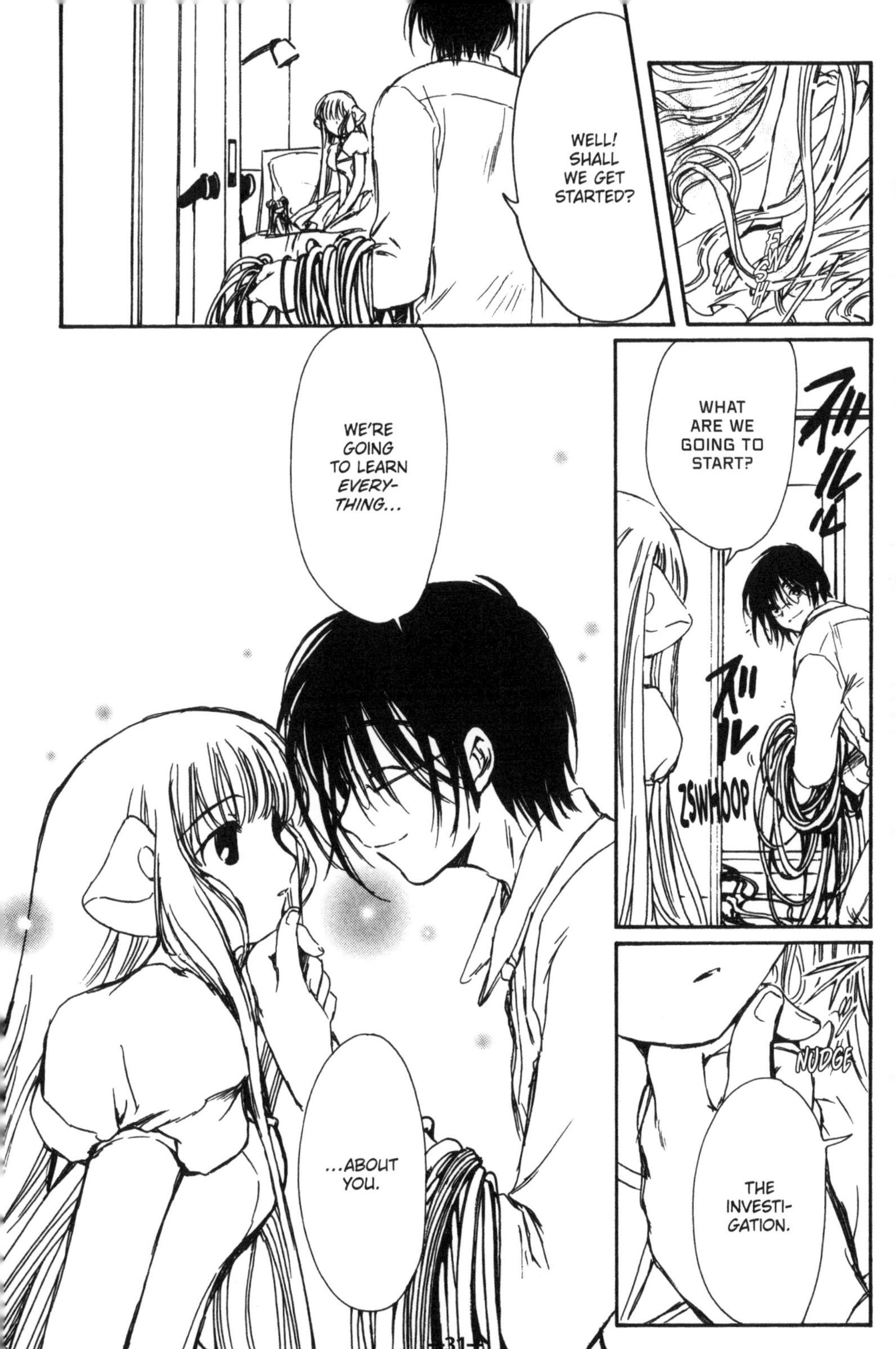
FWSH
WELL! SHALL WE GET STARTED?
WHAT ARE WE GOING TO START?
ZSWHOOP
NUDGE
THE INVESTIGATION.
WE'RE GOING TO LEARN *EVERYTHING*...
...ABOUT YOU.

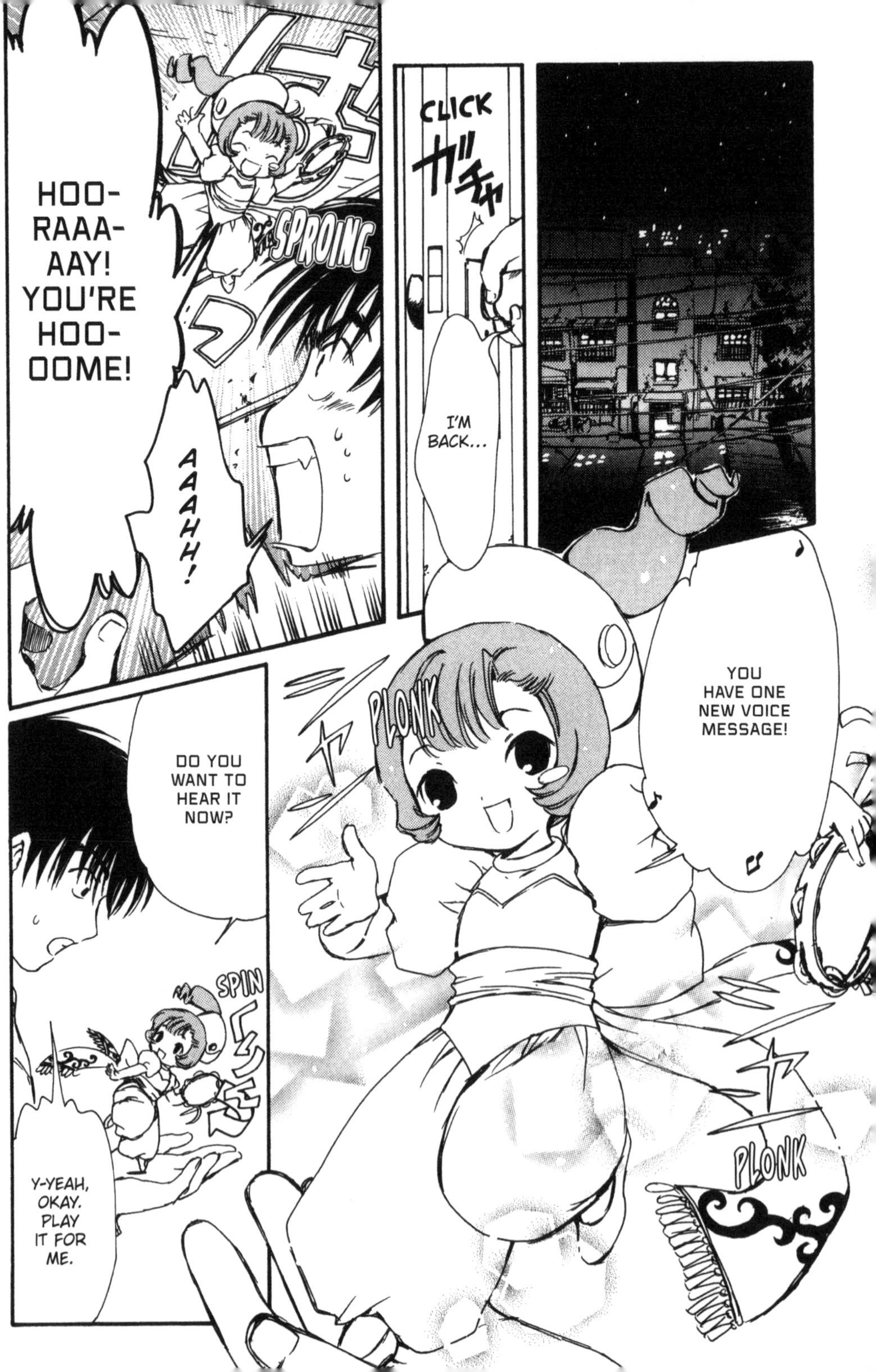
CLICK
ガチャ
I'M BACK...
HOO-RAAAA-AAY! YOU'RE HOO-OOME!
SPROING
AAAAHH!
YOU HAVE ONE NEW VOICE MESSAGE!
PLONK
PLONK
DO YOU WANT TO HEAR IT NOW?
SPIN
Y-YEAH, OKAY. PLAY IT FOR ME.

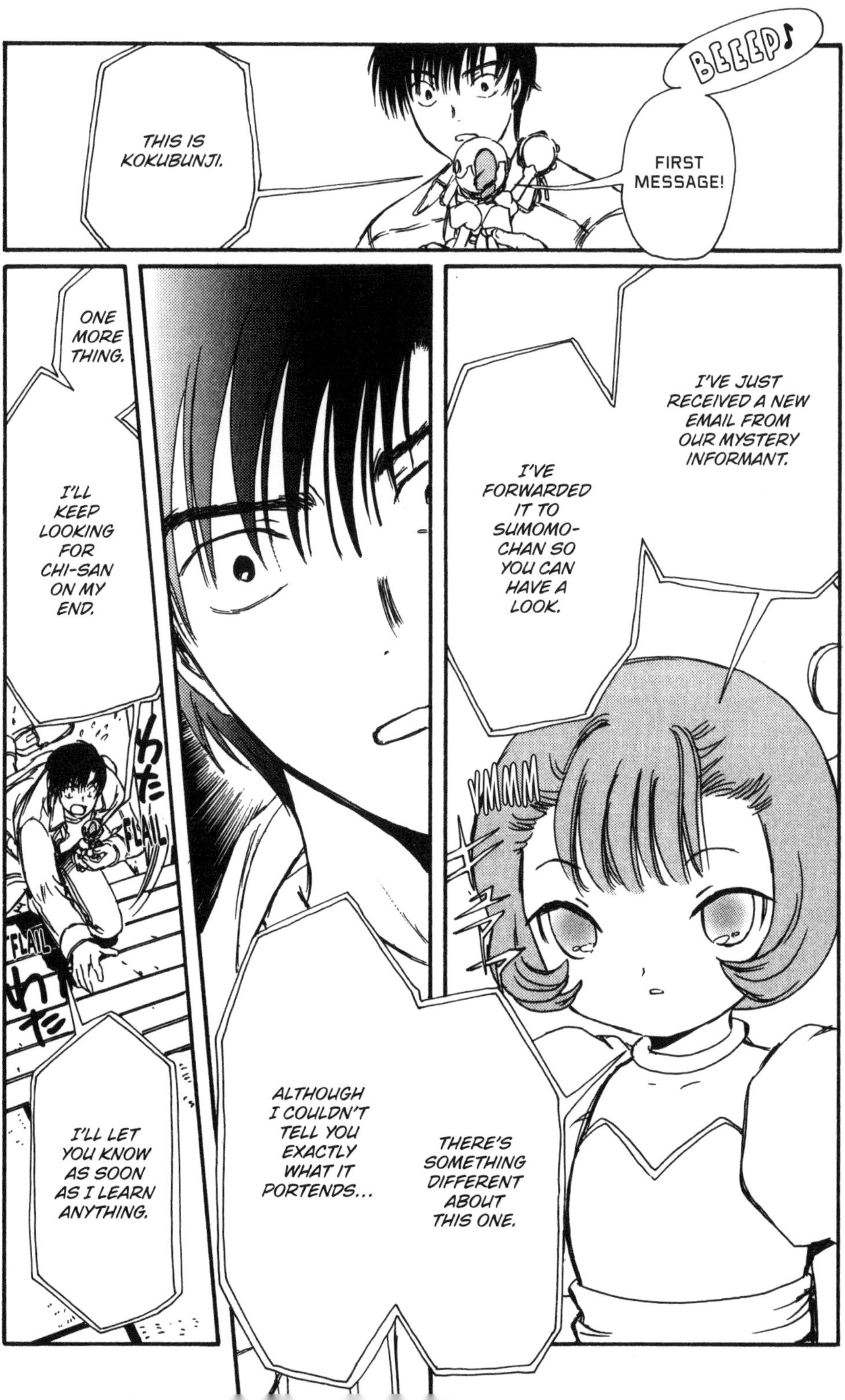
BEEEP♪
FIRST MESSAGE!
THIS IS KOKUBUNJI.
I'VE JUST RECEIVED A NEW EMAIL FROM OUR MYSTERY INFORMANT.
I'VE FORWARDED IT TO SUMOMO-CHAN SO YOU CAN HAVE A LOOK.
VMMM
THERE'S SOMETHING DIFFERENT ABOUT THIS ONE.
ALTHOUGH I COULDN'T TELL YOU EXACTLY WHAT IT PORTENDS...
ONE MORE THING.
I'LL KEEP LOOKING FOR CHI-SAN ON MY END.
わた
FLAIL
FLAIL
わた
I'LL LET YOU KNOW AS SOON AS I LEARN ANYTHING.

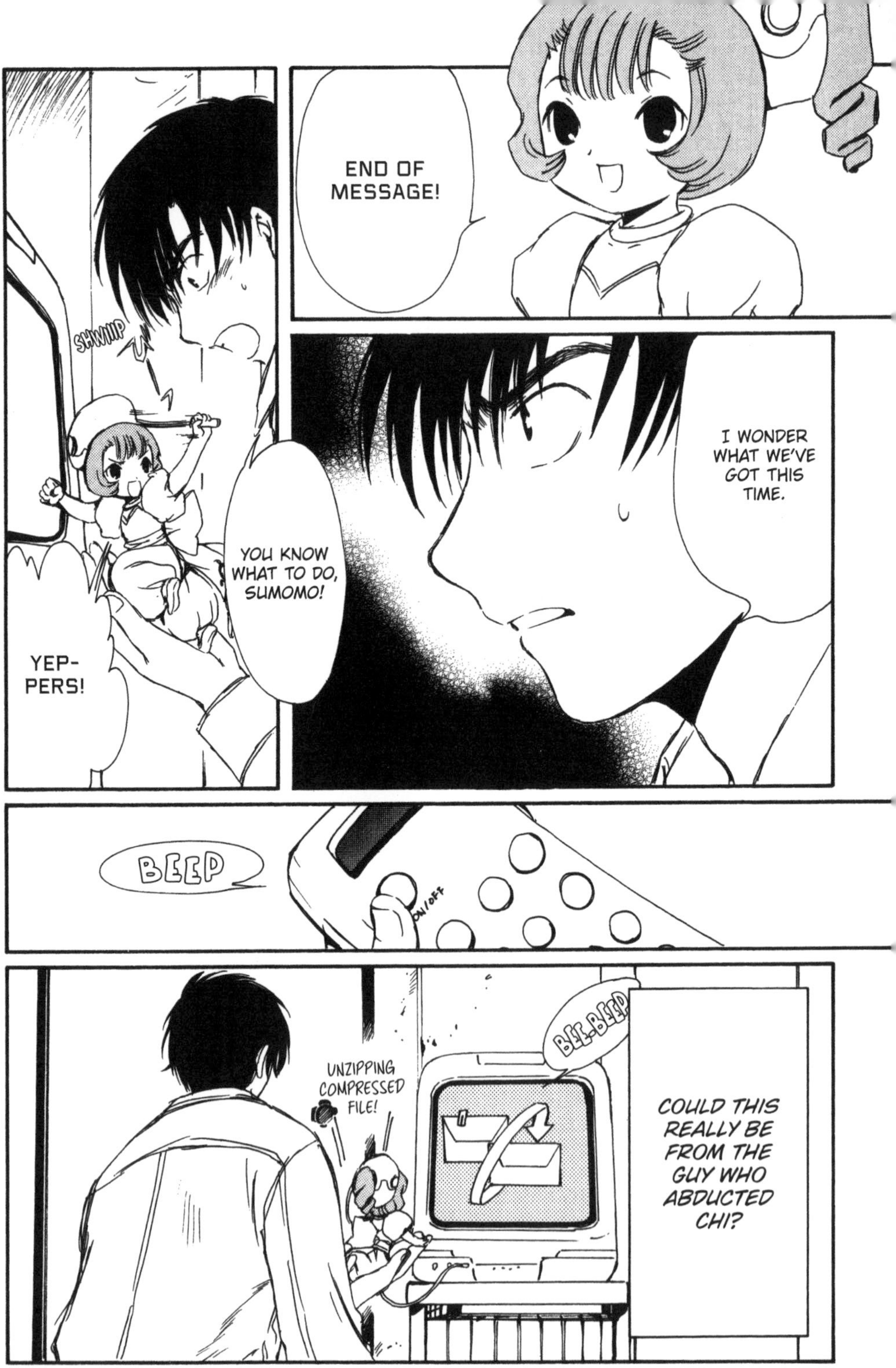
END OF MESSAGE!
I WONDER WHAT WE'VE GOT THIS TIME.
YOU KNOW WHAT TO DO, SUMOMO!
SHWIIP
YEP-PERS!
BEEP
ON/OFF
COULD THIS REALLY BE FROM THE GUY WHO ABDUCTED CHI?
BEE-BEEP
UNZIPPING COMPRESSED FILE!

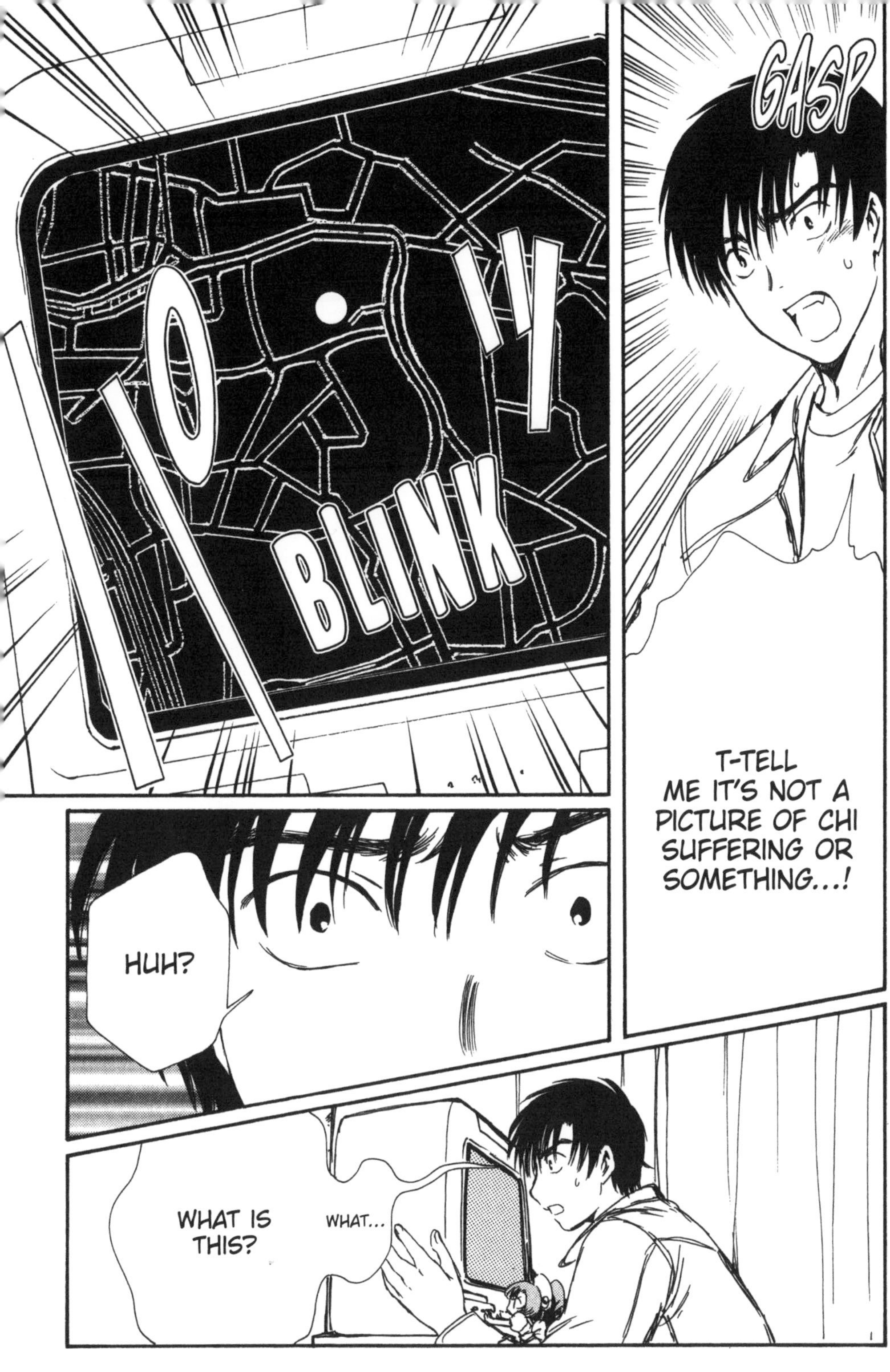
GASP
T-TELL ME IT'S NOT A PICTURE OF CHI SUFFERING OR SOMETHING...!
BLINK
HUH?
WHAT...
WHAT IS THIS?

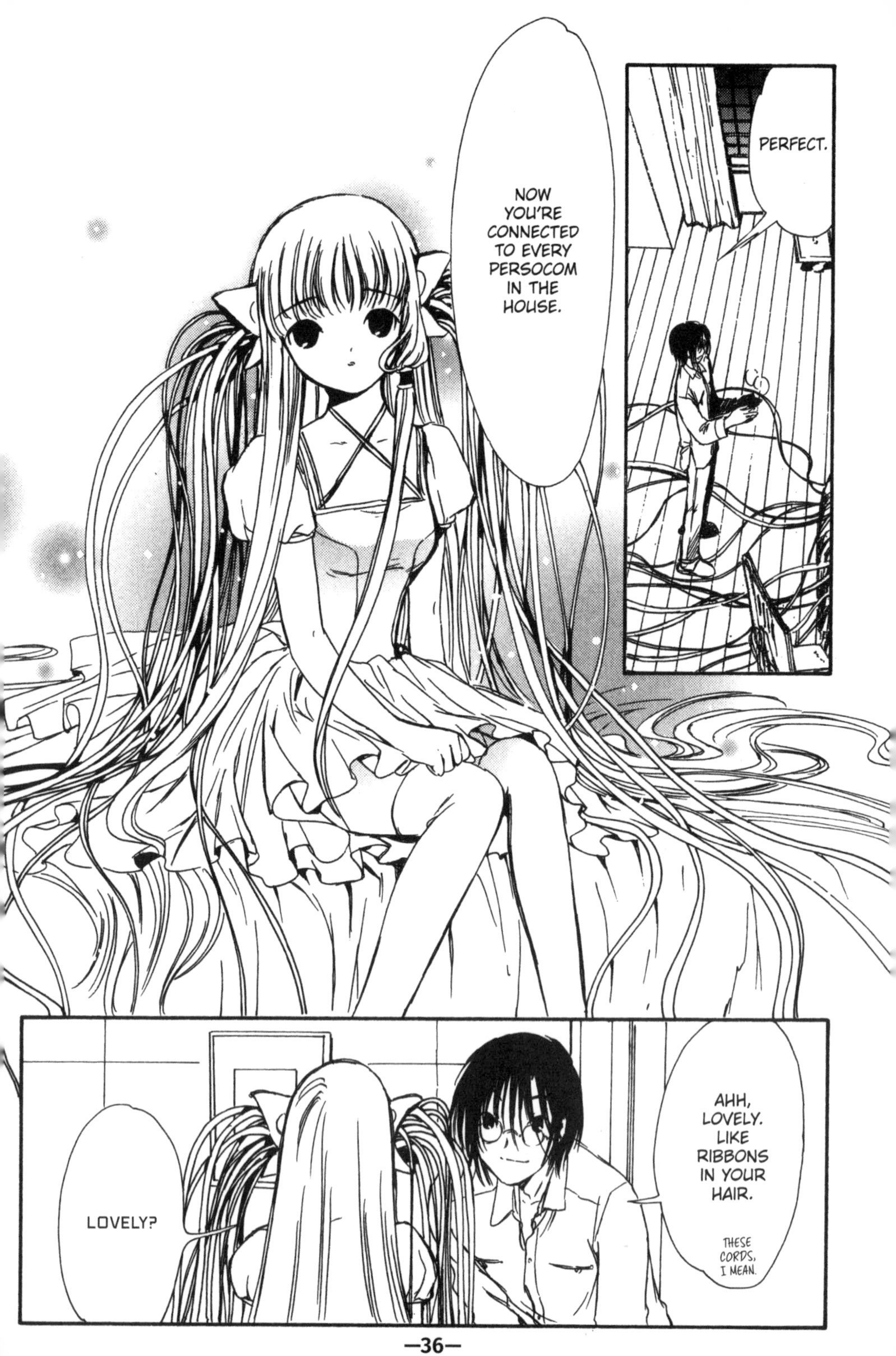
PERFECT.
NOW YOU'RE CONNECTED TO EVERY PERSOCOM IN THE HOUSE.
AHH, LOVELY. LIKE RIBBONS IN YOUR HAIR.
THESE CORDS, I MEAN.
LOVELY?

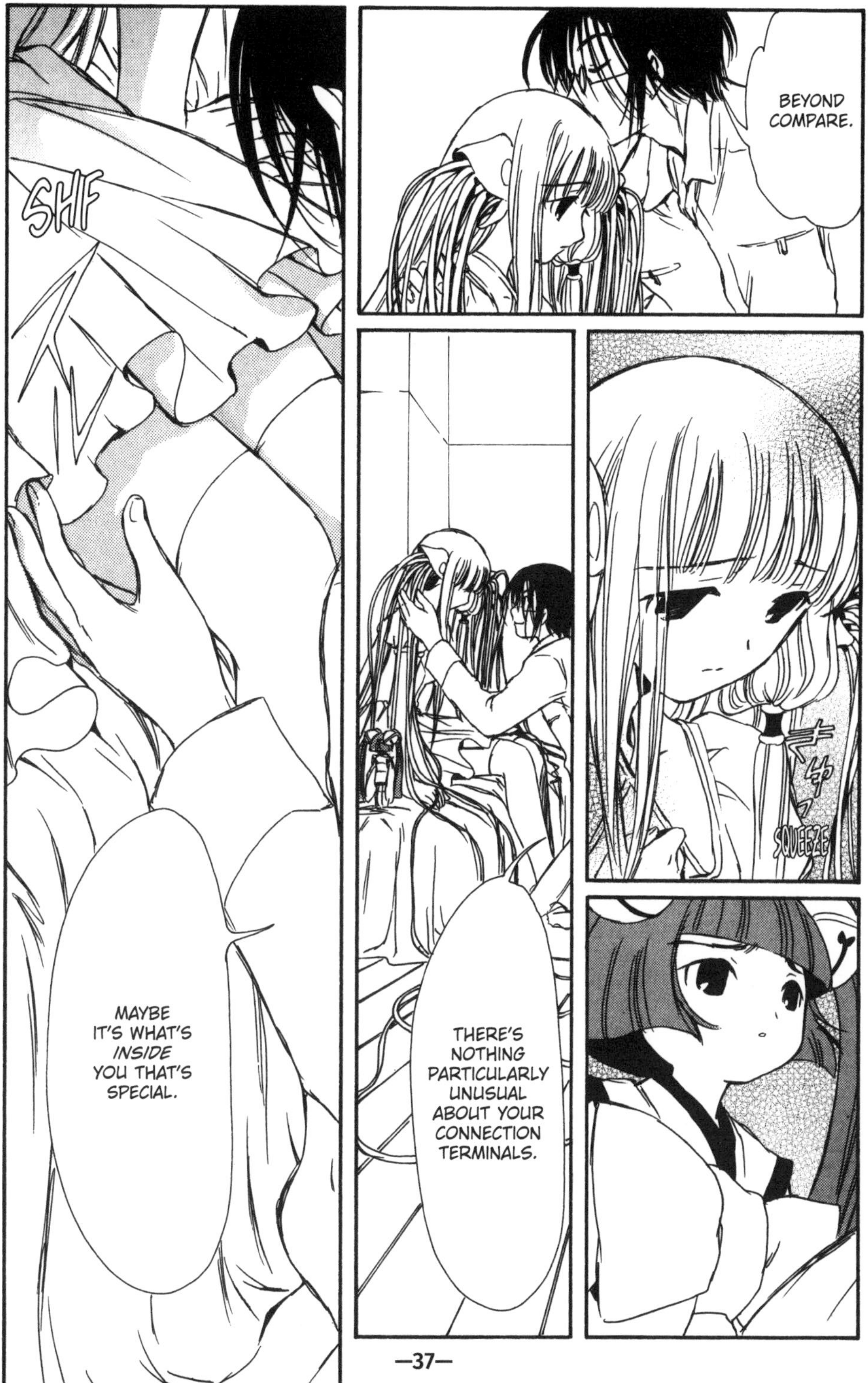
BEYOND COMPARE.
きゅっ
SQUEEZE
THERE'S NOTHING PARTICULARLY UNUSUAL ABOUT YOUR CONNECTION TERMINALS.
SHF
MAYBE IT'S WHAT'S *INSIDE* YOU THAT'S SPECIAL.

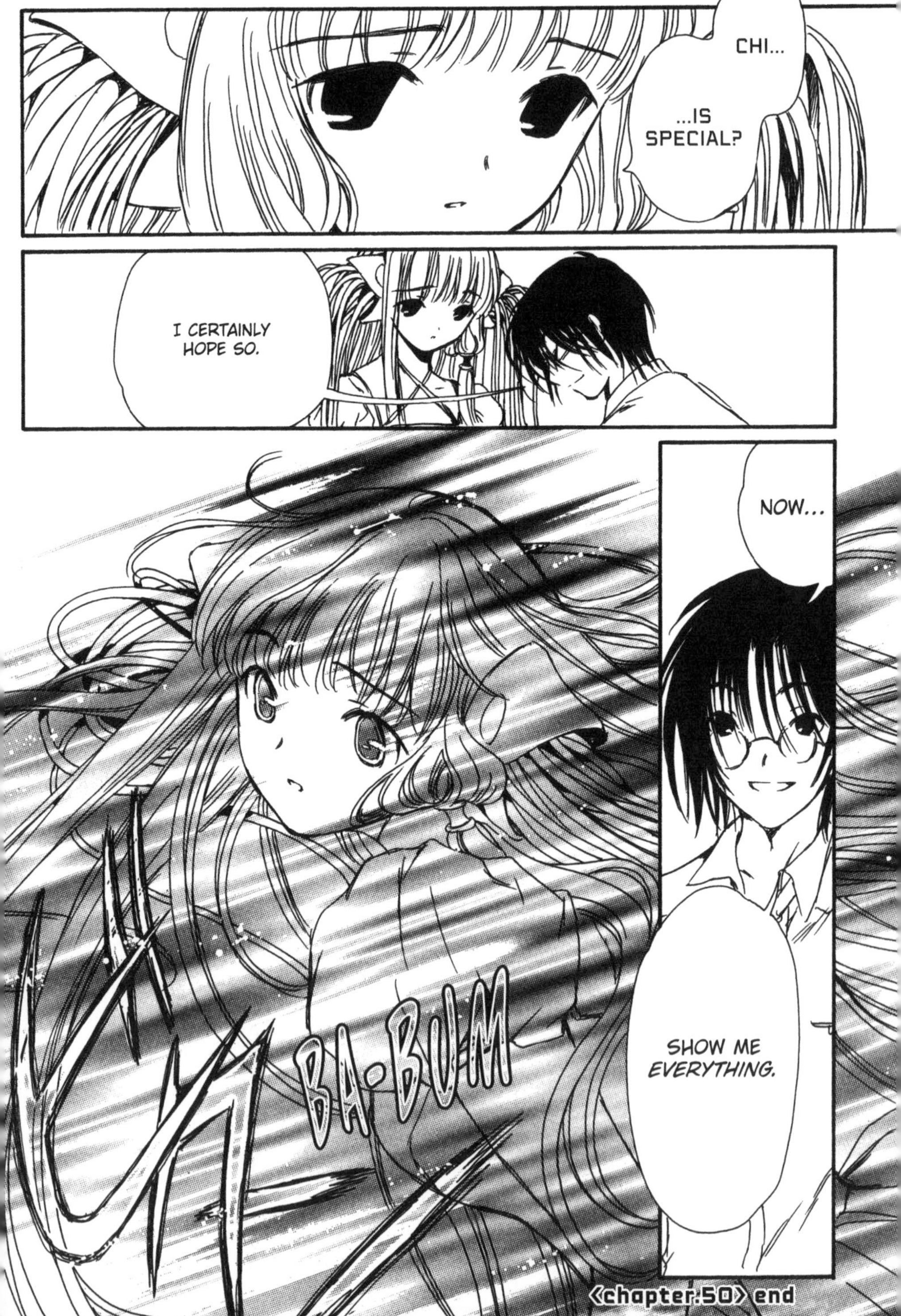
CHI...
...IS SPECIAL?
I CERTAINLY HOPE SO.
NOW...
SHOW ME *EVERYTHING.*
BA-BUM
<chapter.50> end

Chobits

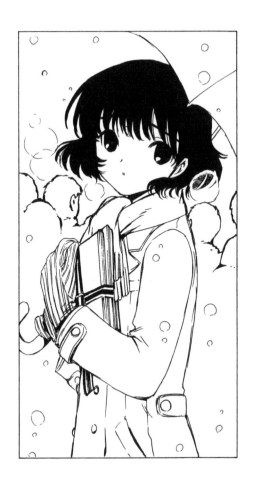

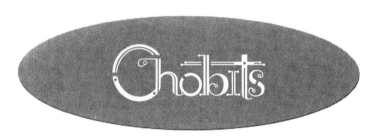

‹chapter.51›

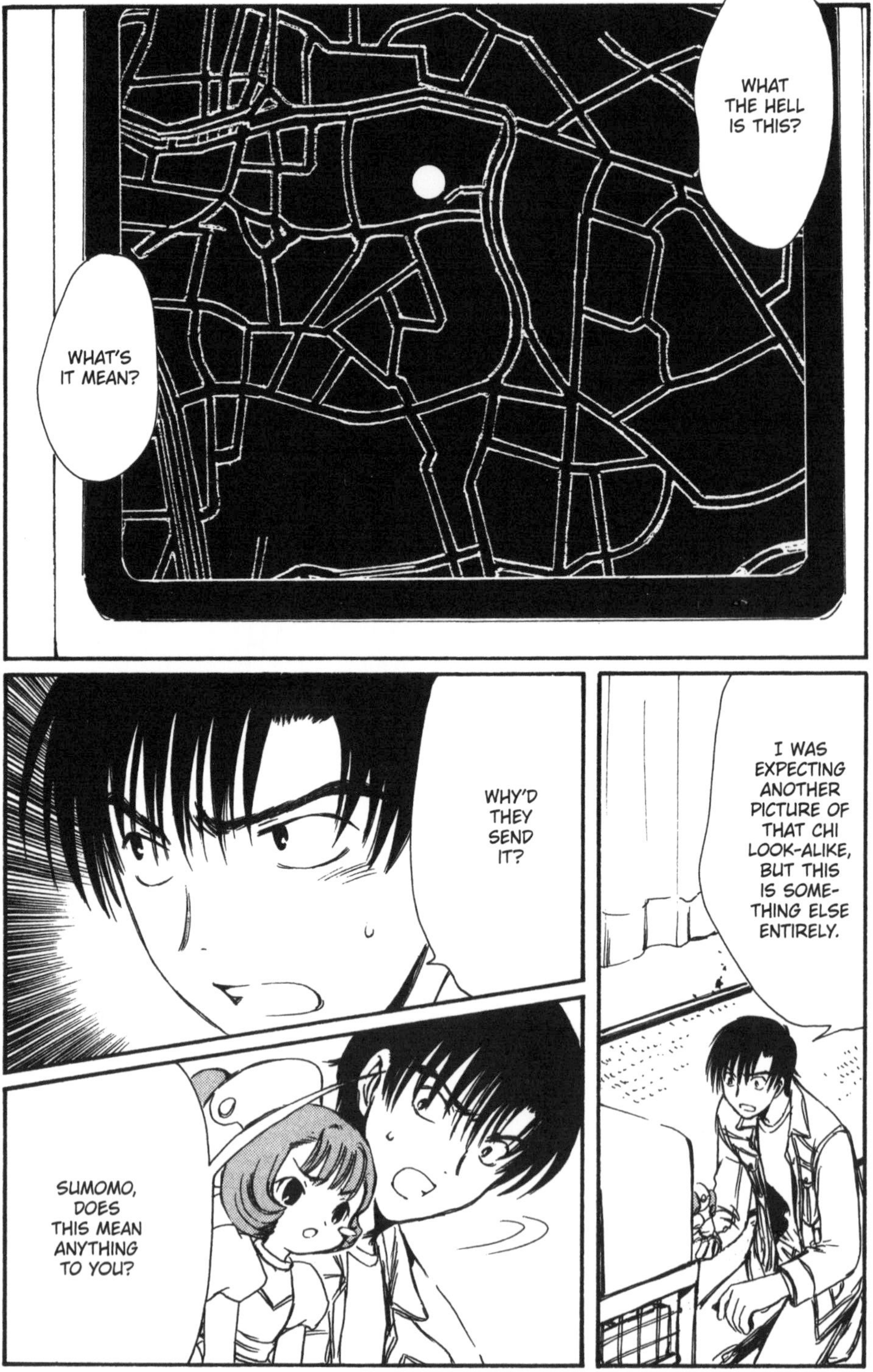
WHAT THE HELL IS THIS?
WHAT'S IT MEAN?
I WAS EXPECTING ANOTHER PICTURE OF THAT CHI LOOK-ALIKE, BUT THIS IS SOME-THING ELSE ENTIRELY.
WHY'D THEY SEND IT?
SUMOMO, DOES THIS MEAN ANYTHING TO YOU?

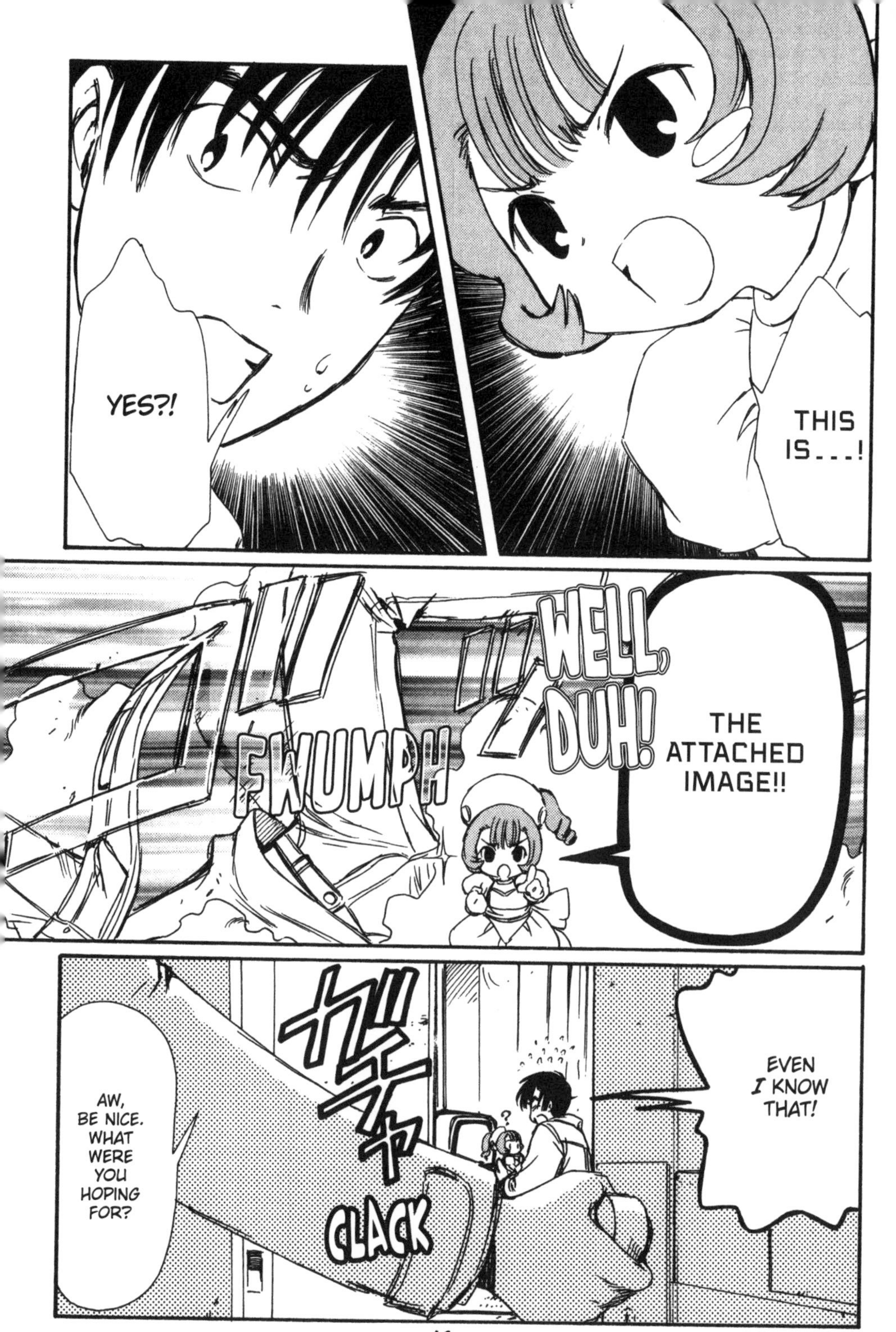
THIS IS...!
YES?!
THE ATTACHED IMAGE!!
WELL, DUH!
FWUMPH
EVEN I KNOW THAT!
CLACK
AW, BE NICE. WHAT WERE YOU HOPING FOR?

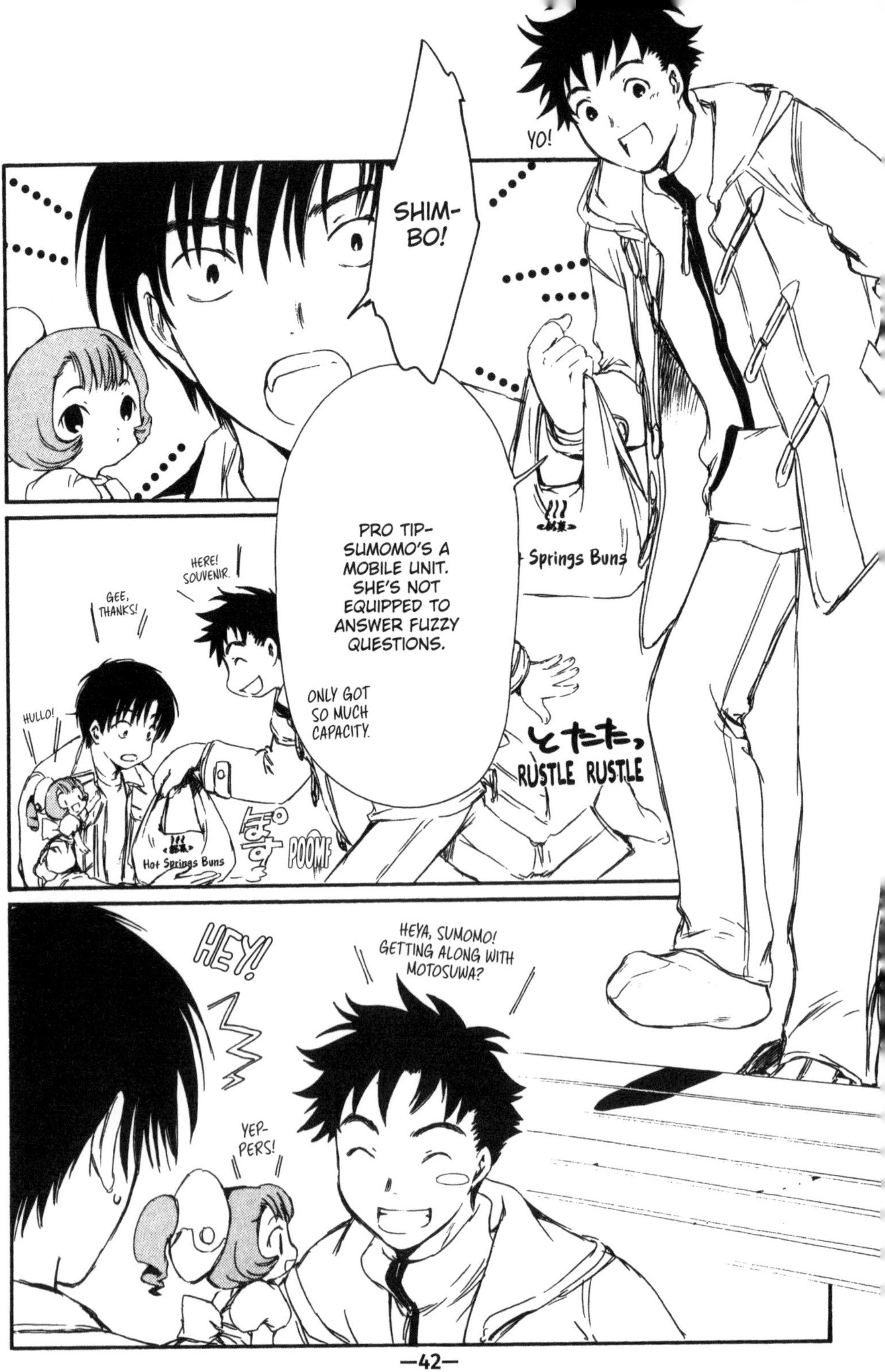
YO!
SHIMBO!
PRO TIP- SUMOMO'S A MOBILE UNIT. SHE'S NOT EQUIPPED TO ANSWER FUZZY QUESTIONS.
ONLY GOT SO MUCH CAPACITY.
Hot Springs Buns
とたたっ
RUSTLE RUSTLE
HERE! SOUVENIR.
GEE, THANKS!
HULLO!
Hot Springs Buns
POOMF
HEY!
HEYA, SUMOMO! GETTING ALONG WITH MOTOSUWA?
YEP-PERS!

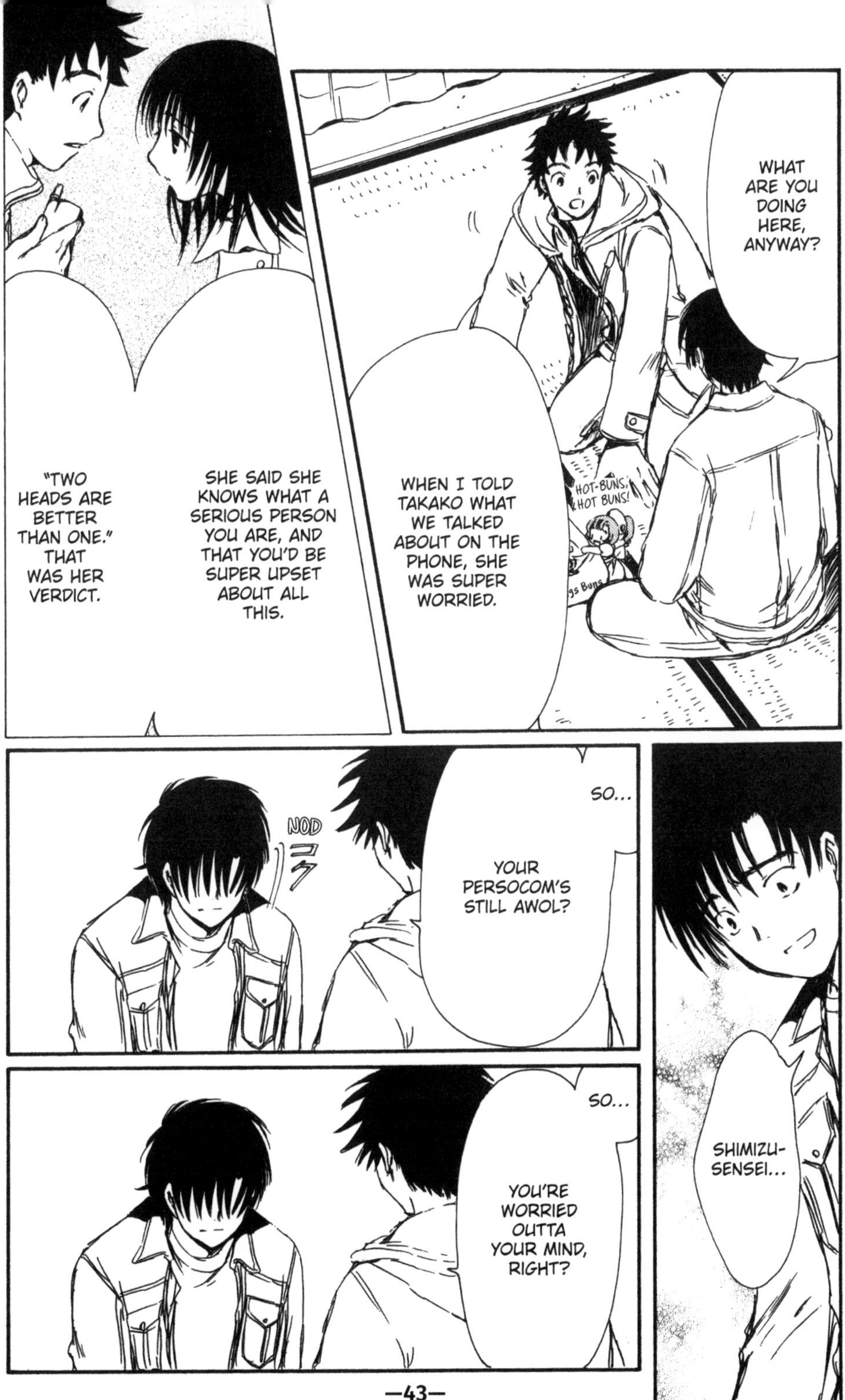
WHAT ARE YOU DOING HERE, ANYWAY?
HOT-BUNS, HOT BUNS!
WHEN I TOLD TAKAKO WHAT WE TALKED ABOUT ON THE PHONE, SHE WAS SUPER WORRIED.
SHE SAID SHE KNOWS WHAT A SERIOUS PERSON YOU ARE, AND THAT YOU'D BE SUPER UPSET ABOUT ALL THIS.
"TWO HEADS ARE BETTER THAN ONE." THAT WAS HER VERDICT.
SHIMIZU-SENSEI...
SO...
YOUR PERSOCOM'S STILL AWOL?
NOD
SO...
YOU'RE WORRIED OUTTA YOUR MIND, RIGHT?

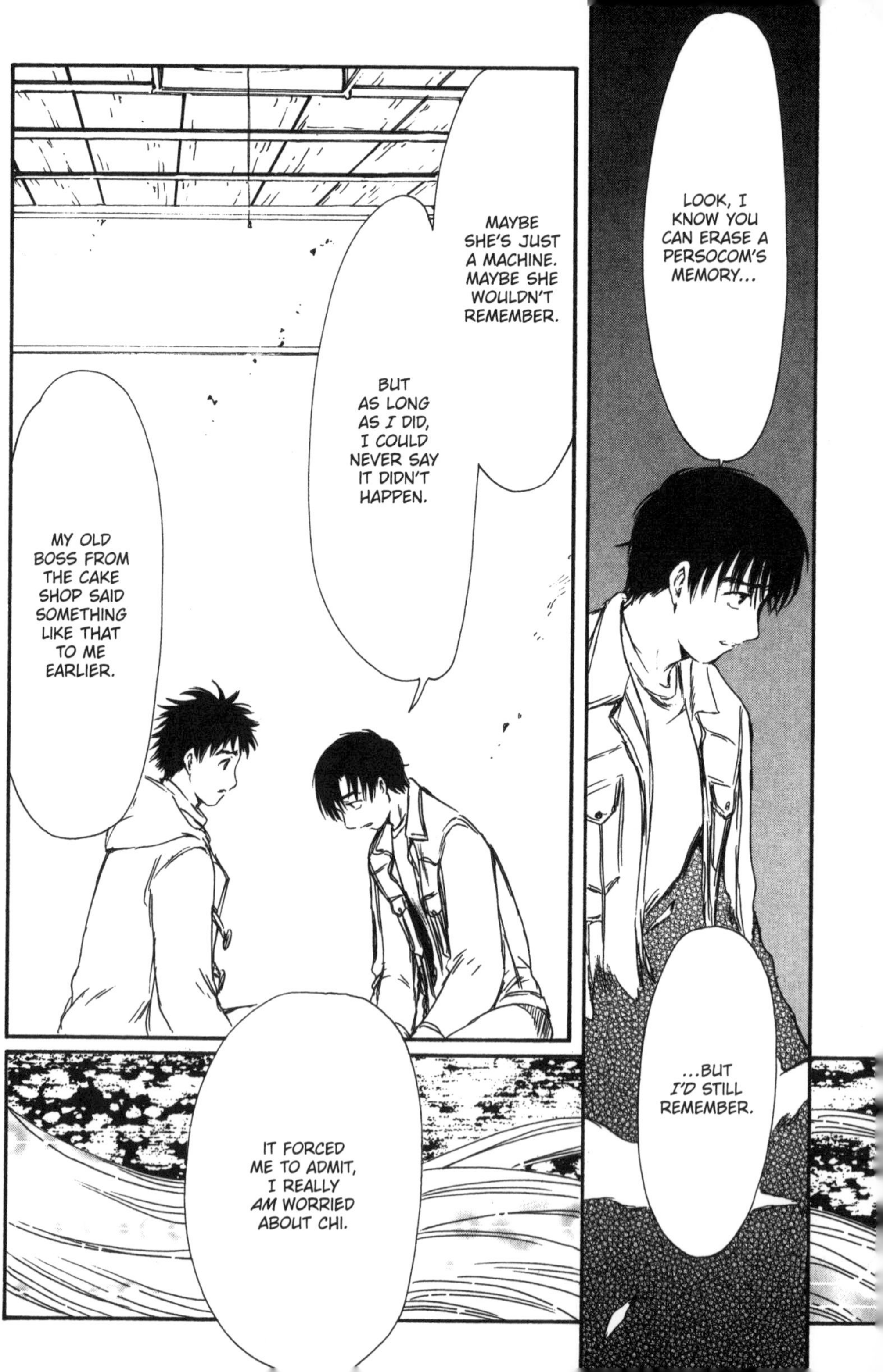
LOOK, I KNOW YOU CAN ERASE A PERSOCOM'S MEMORY...
...BUT I'D STILL REMEMBER.
MAYBE SHE'S JUST A MACHINE. MAYBE SHE WOULDN'T REMEMBER.
BUT AS LONG AS I DID, I COULD NEVER SAY IT DIDN'T HAPPEN.
MY OLD BOSS FROM THE CAKE SHOP SAID SOMETHING LIKE THAT TO ME EARLIER.
IT FORCED ME TO ADMIT, I REALLY AM WORRIED ABOUT CHI.

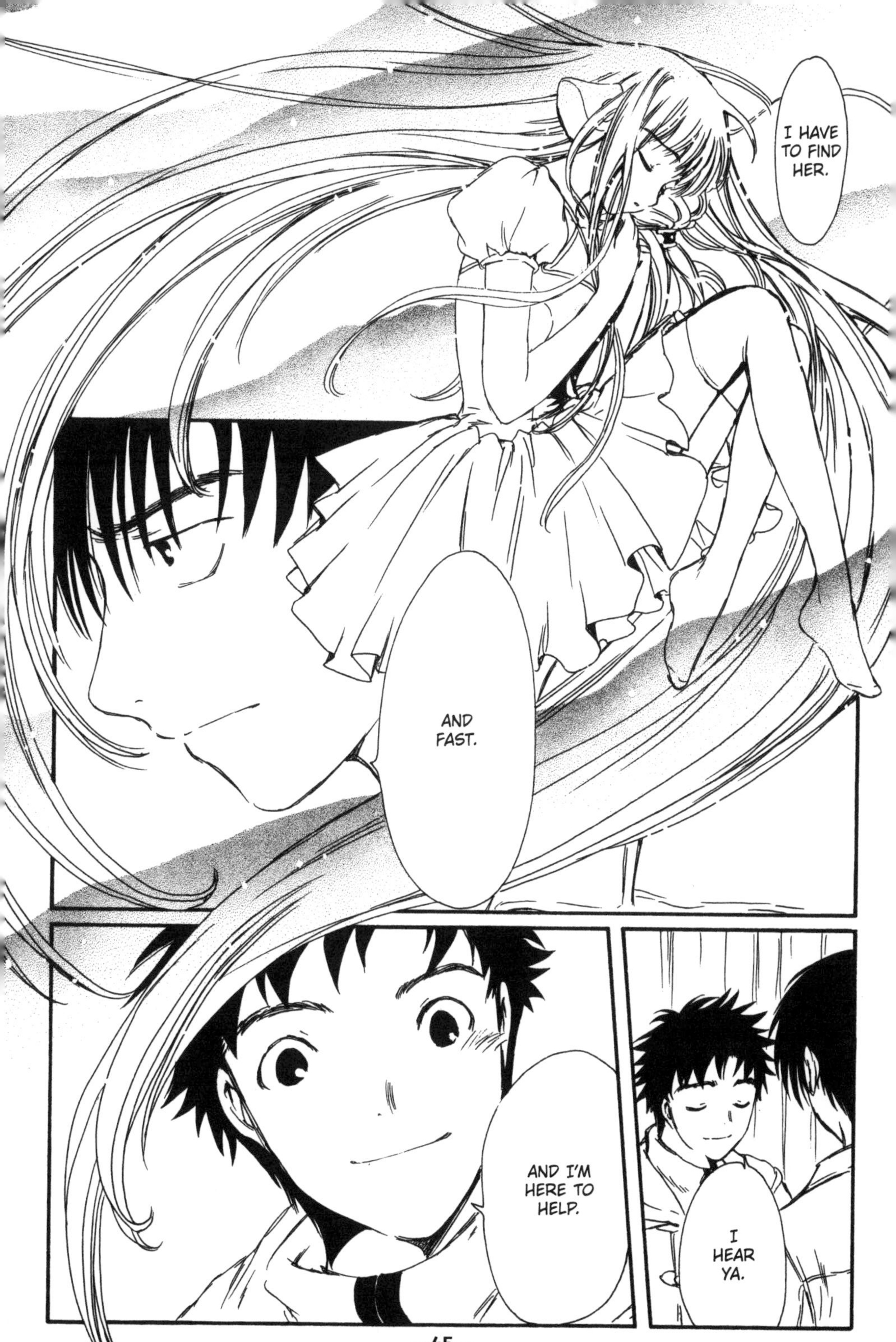
I HAVE TO FIND HER.
AND FAST.
I HEAR YA.
AND I'M HERE TO HELP.

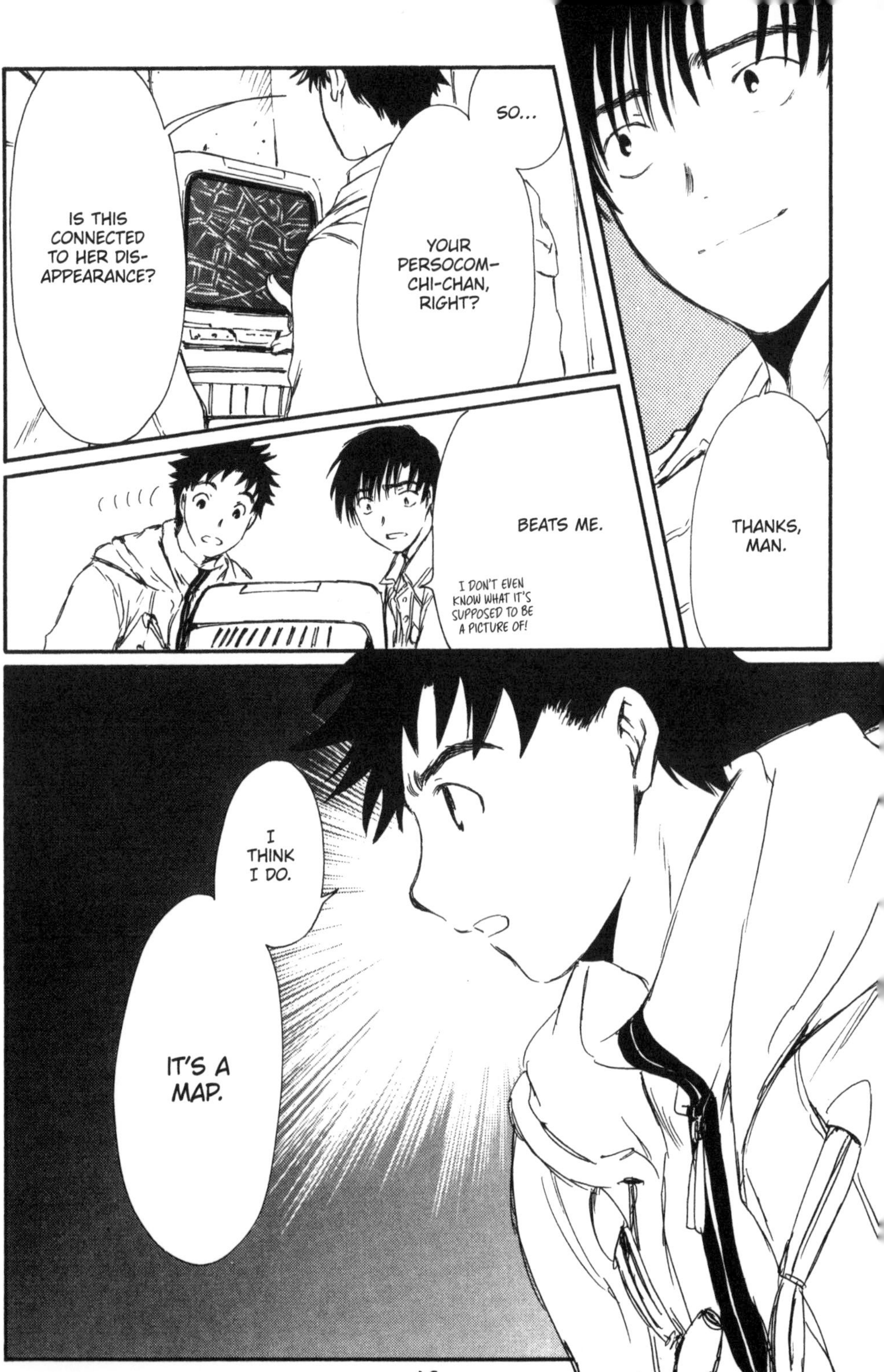
THANKS, MAN.
SO...
YOUR PERSOCOM-CHI-CHAN, RIGHT?
IS THIS CONNECTED TO HER DIS-APPEARANCE?
BEATS ME.
I DON'T EVEN KNOW WHAT IT'S SUPPOSED TO BE A PICTURE OF!
I THINK I DO.
IT'S A MAP.

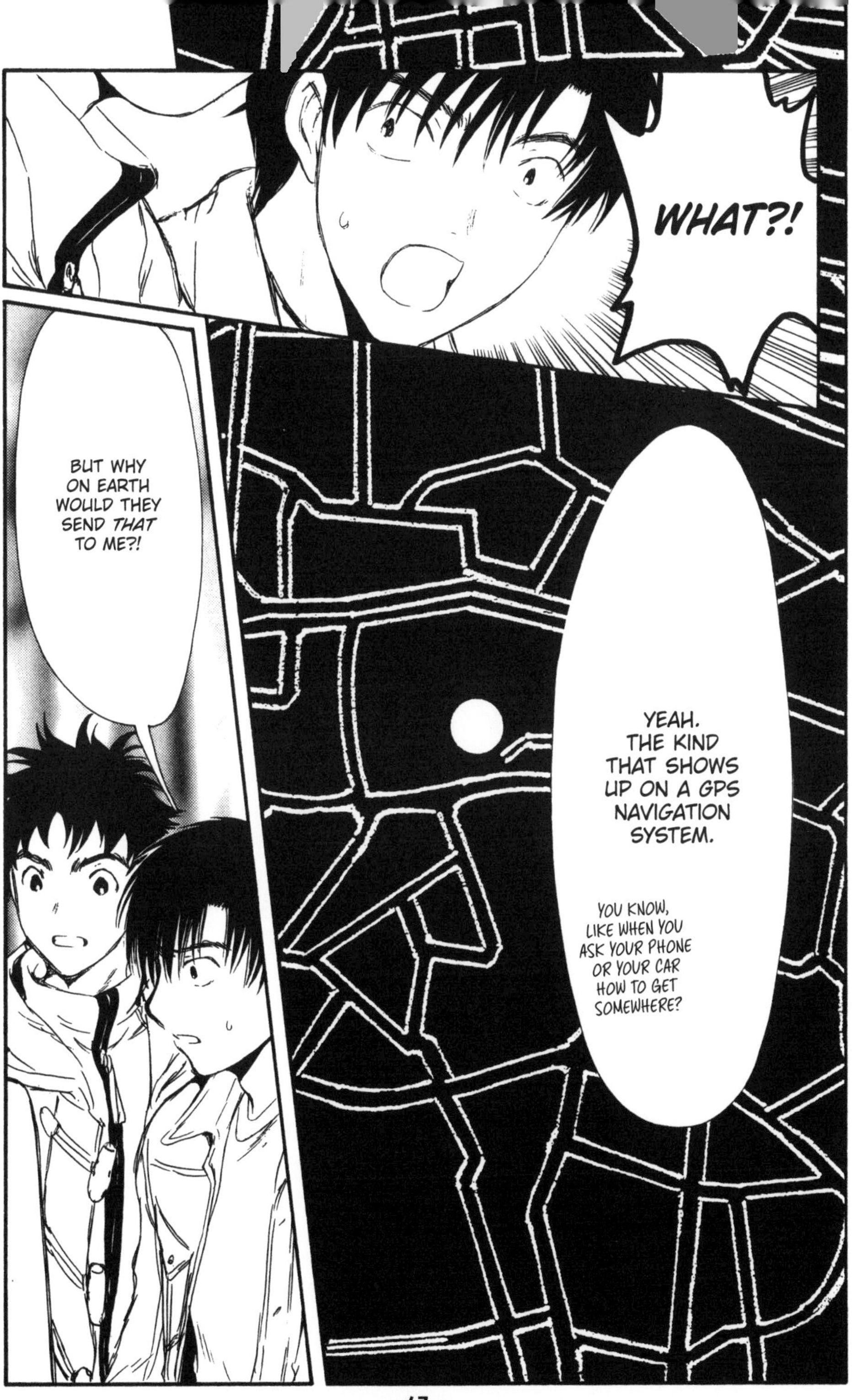
WHAT?!
YEAH. THE KIND THAT SHOWS UP ON A GPS NAVIGATION SYSTEM.
YOU KNOW, LIKE WHEN YOU ASK YOUR PHONE OR YOUR CAR HOW TO GET SOMEWHERE?
BUT WHY ON EARTH WOULD THEY SEND *THAT* TO ME?!

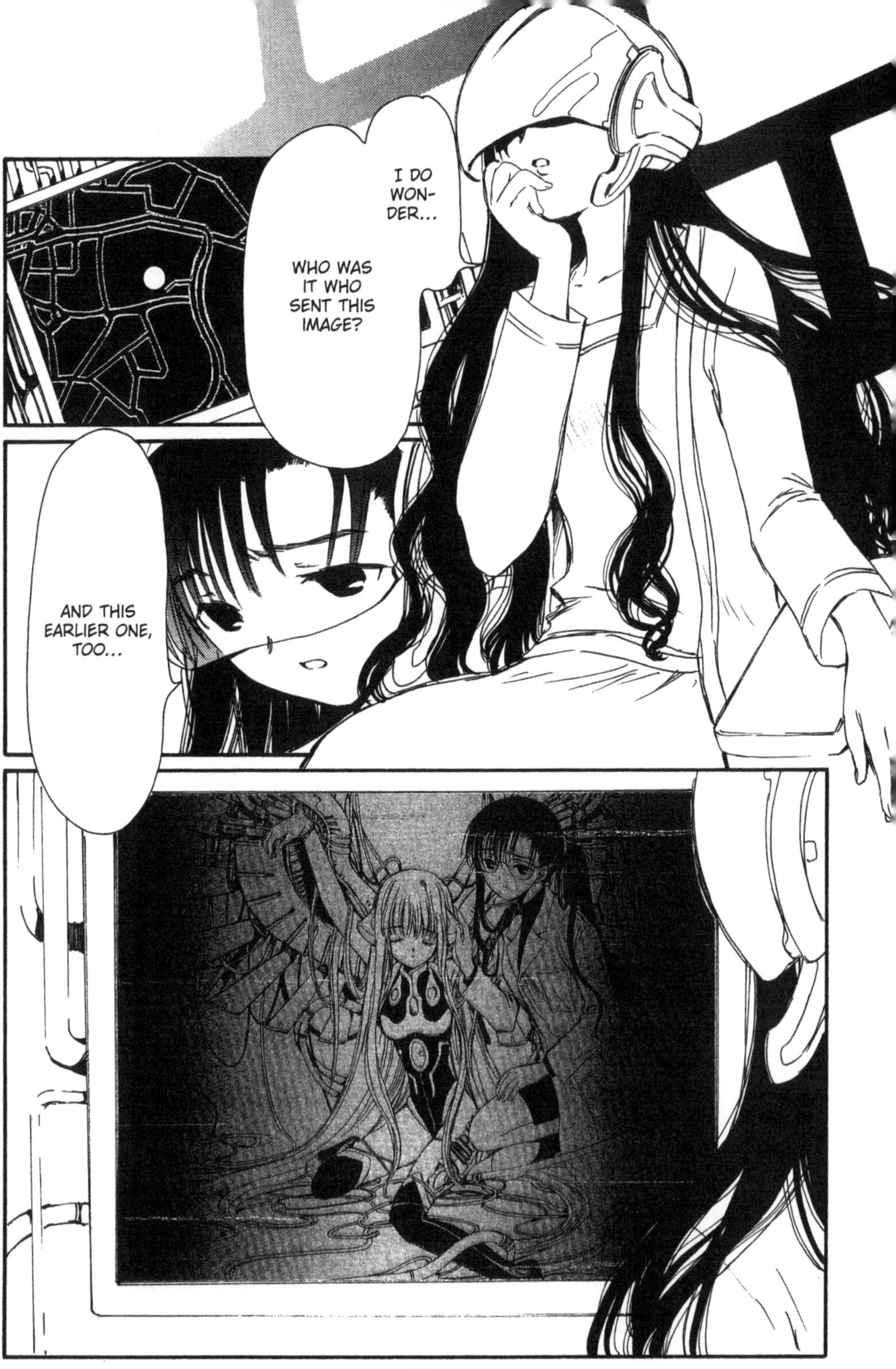
I DO WON-DER...
WHO WAS IT WHO SENT THIS IMAGE?
AND THIS EARLIER ONE, TOO...

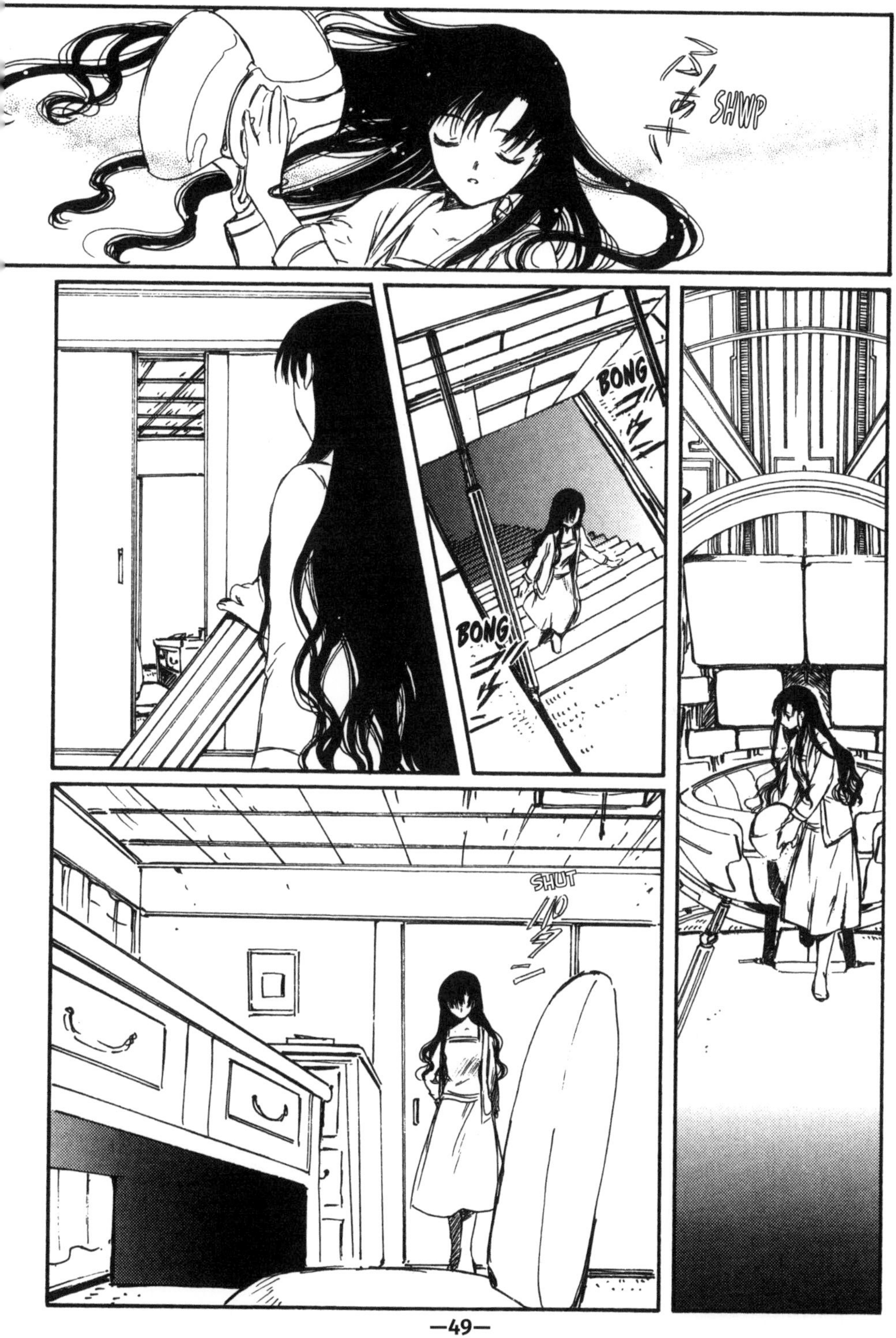

SHWP
BONG
BONG
SHUT

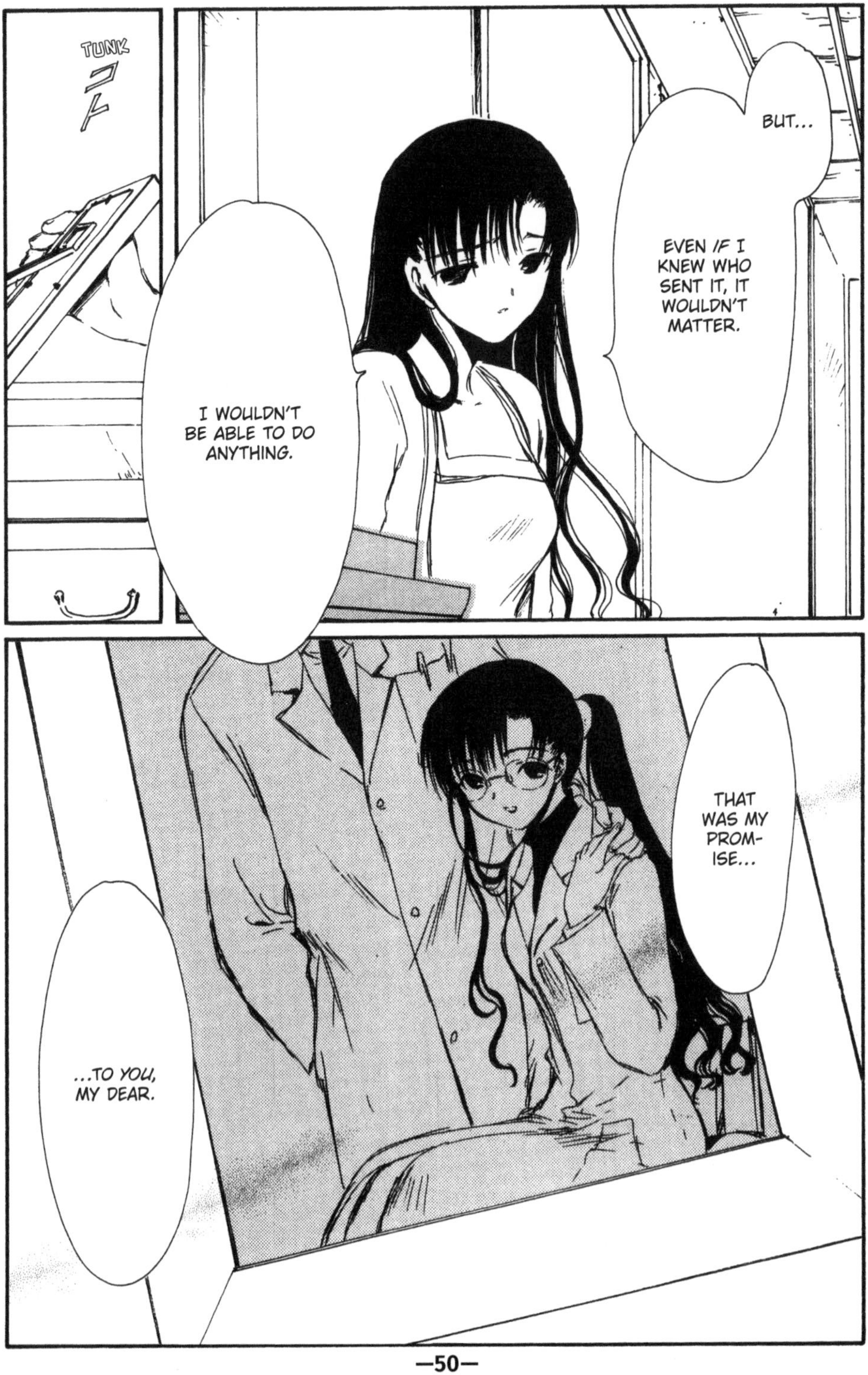
BUT...
EVEN IF I KNEW WHO SENT IT, IT WOULDN'T MATTER.
I WOULDN'T BE ABLE TO DO ANYTHING.
TUNK
コト
THAT WAS MY PROM-ISE...
...TO YOU, MY DEAR.

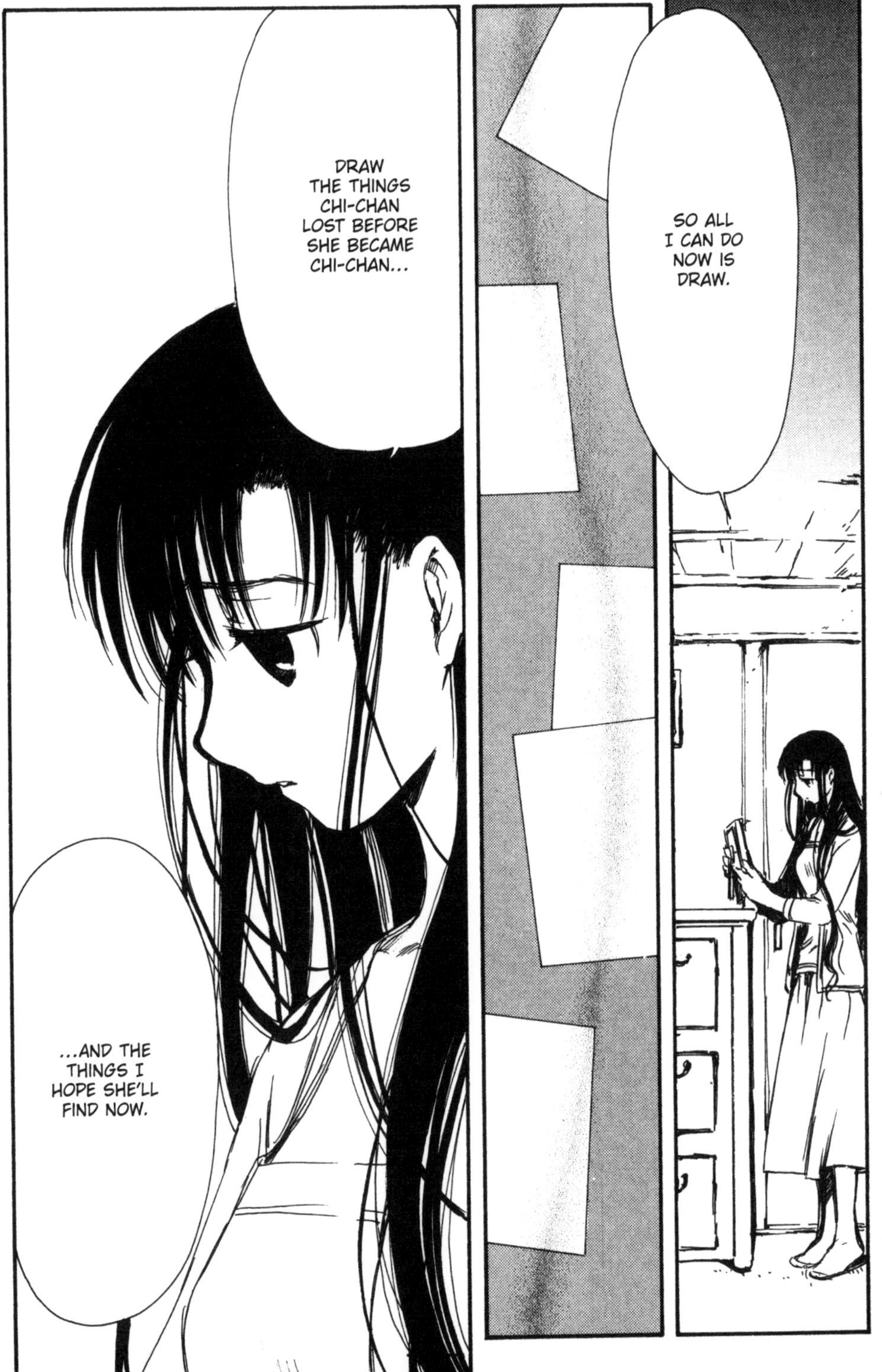
SO ALL I CAN DO NOW IS DRAW.
DRAW THE THINGS CHI-CHAN LOST BEFORE SHE BECAME CHI-CHAN...
...AND THE THINGS I HOPE SHE'LL FIND NOW.

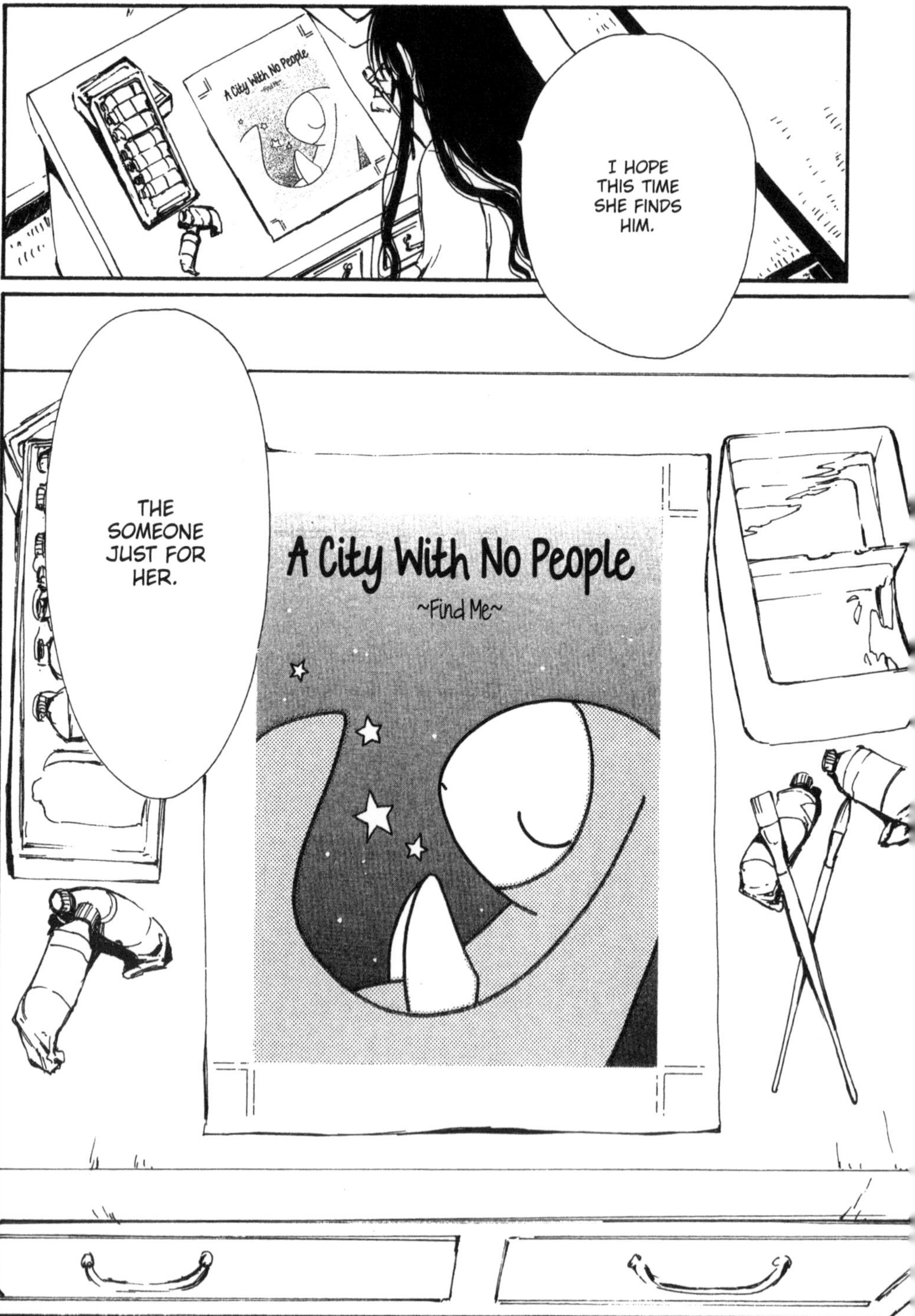
I HOPE THIS TIME SHE FINDS HIM.
A City With No People
~Find Me~
THE SOMEONE JUST FOR HER.

<chapter.51> end

⟨chapter.52⟩

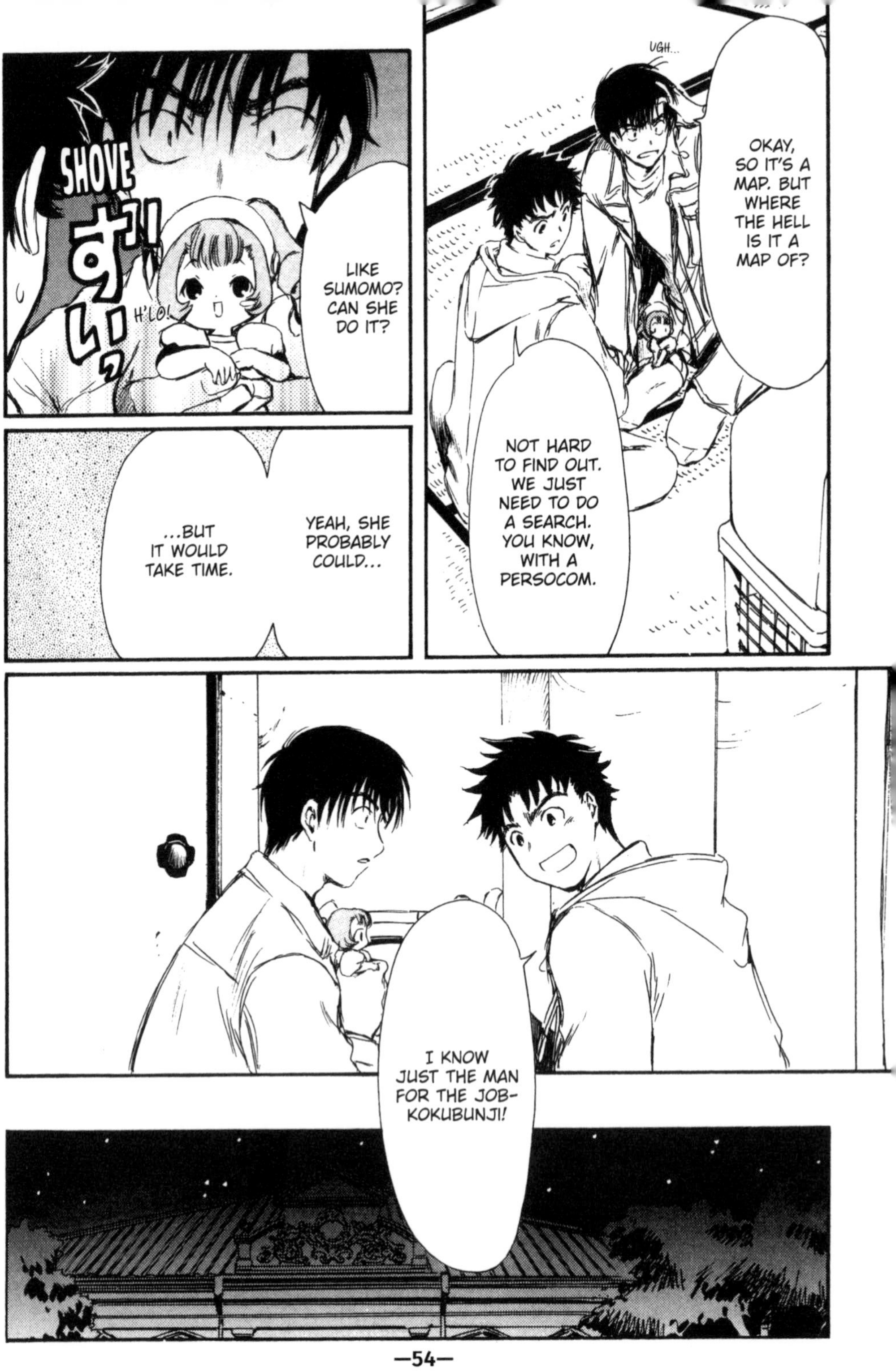
UGH...
OKAY, SO IT'S A MAP. BUT WHERE THE HELL IS IT A MAP OF?
NOT HARD TO FIND OUT. WE JUST NEED TO DO A SEARCH. YOU KNOW, WITH A PERSOCOM.
LIKE SUMOMO? CAN SHE DO IT?
SHOVE
すいっ
H'LO!
YEAH, SHE PROBABLY COULD...
...BUT IT WOULD TAKE TIME.
I KNOW JUST THE MAN FOR THE JOB- KOKUBUNJI!

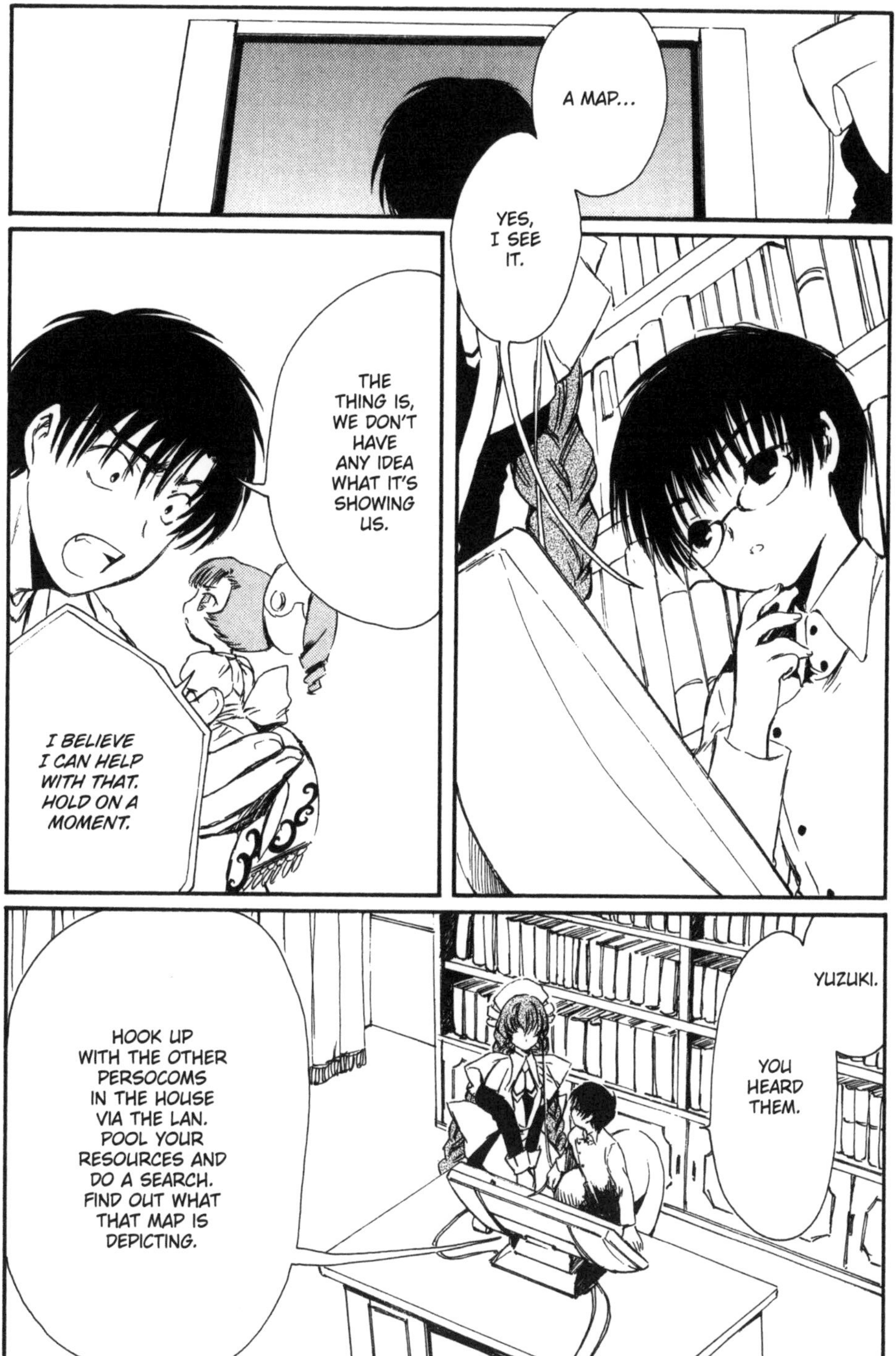
A MAP...
YES, I SEE IT.
THE THING IS, WE DON'T HAVE ANY IDEA WHAT IT'S SHOWING US.
I BELIEVE I CAN HELP WITH THAT. HOLD ON A MOMENT.
YUZUKI.
YOU HEARD THEM.
HOOK UP WITH THE OTHER PERSOCOMS IN THE HOUSE VIA THE LAN. POOL YOUR RESOURCES AND DO A SEARCH. FIND OUT WHAT THAT MAP IS DEPICTING.

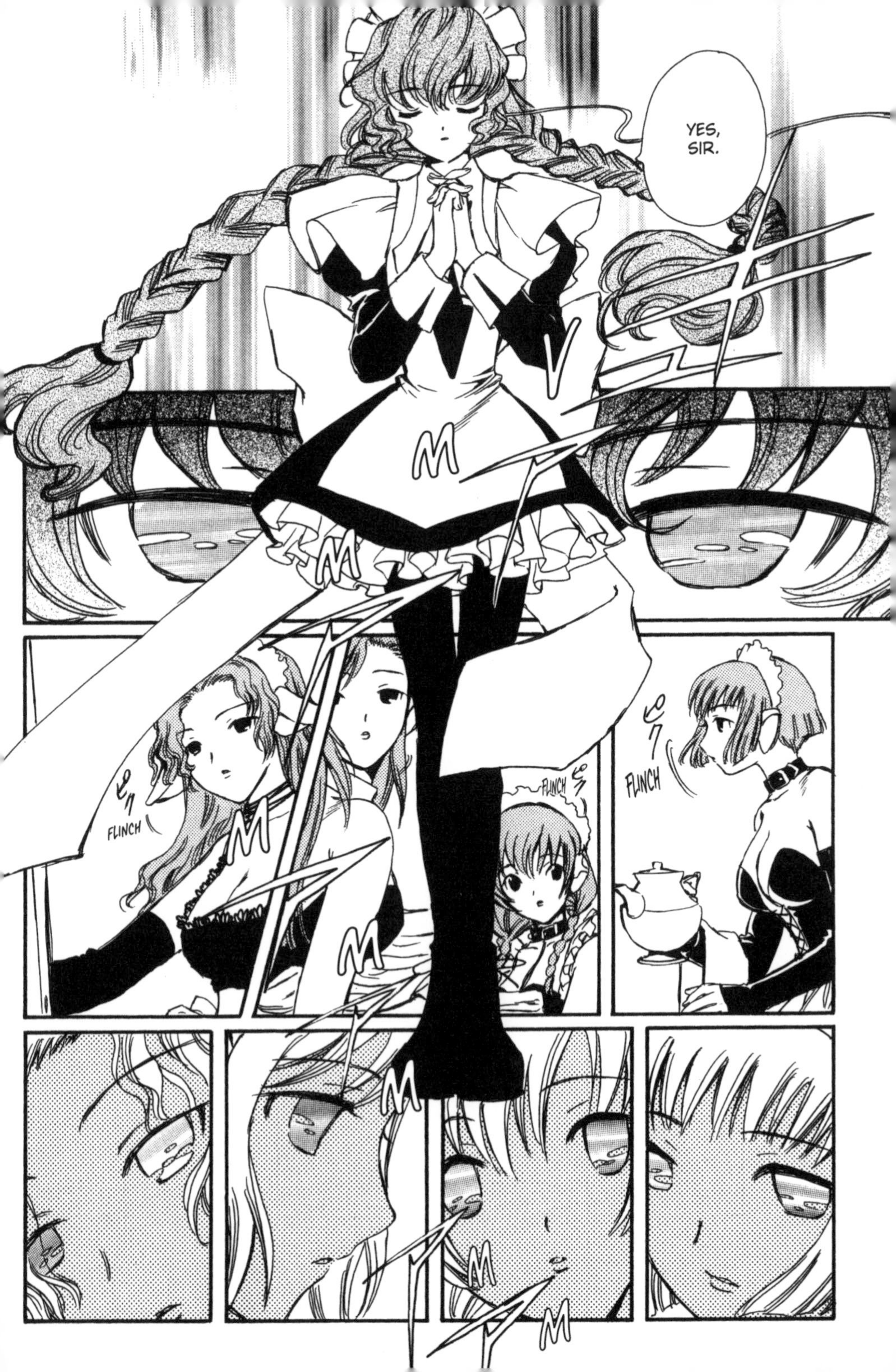
YES, SIR.
M
M
FLINCH
FLINCH
FLINCH
M
M
M
M
M

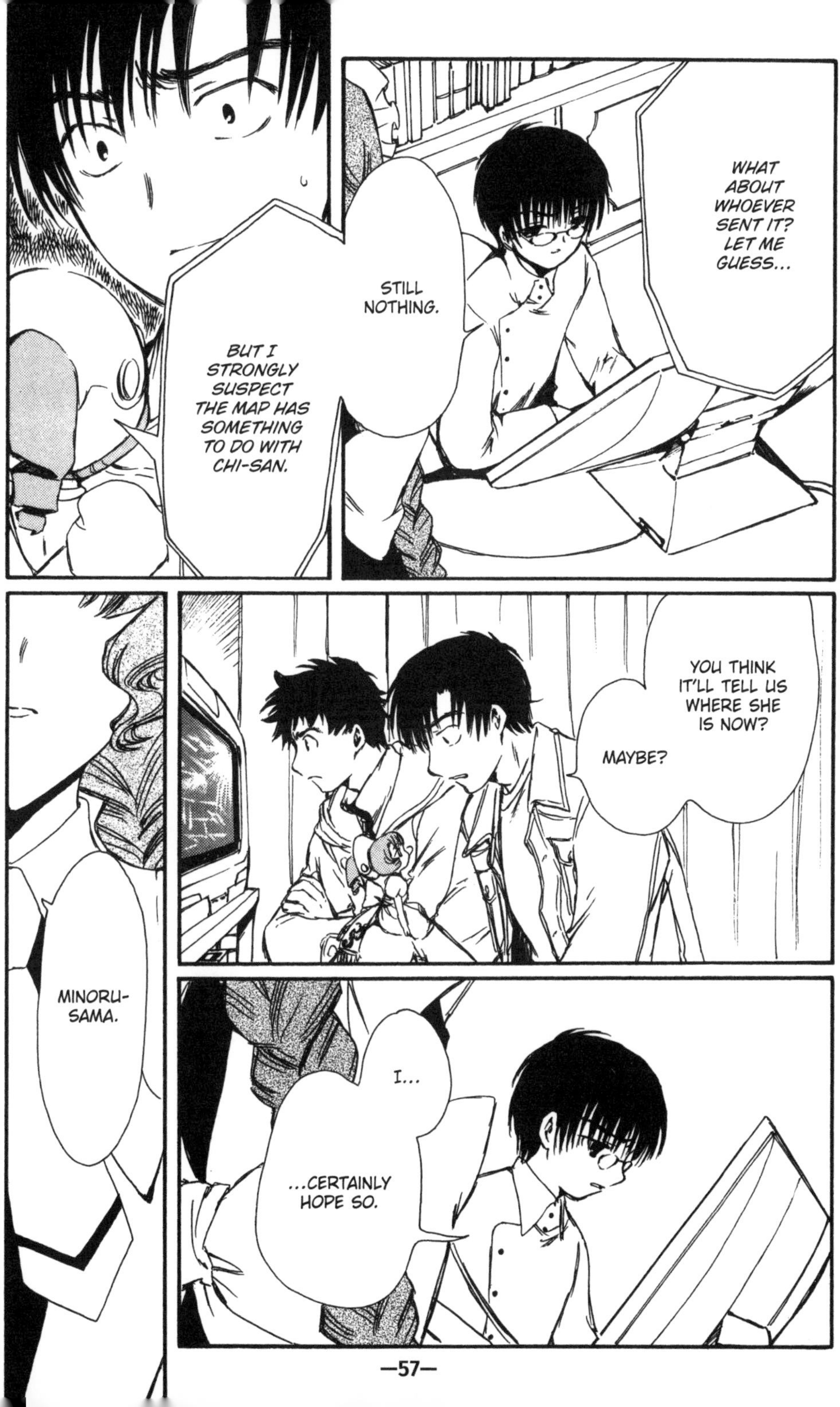
WHAT ABOUT WHOEVER SENT IT? LET ME GUESS...
STILL NOTHING.
BUT I STRONGLY SUSPECT THE MAP HAS SOMETHING TO DO WITH CHI-SAN.
YOU THINK IT'LL TELL US WHERE SHE IS NOW?
MAYBE?
I...
...CERTAINLY HOPE SO.
MINORU-SAMA.

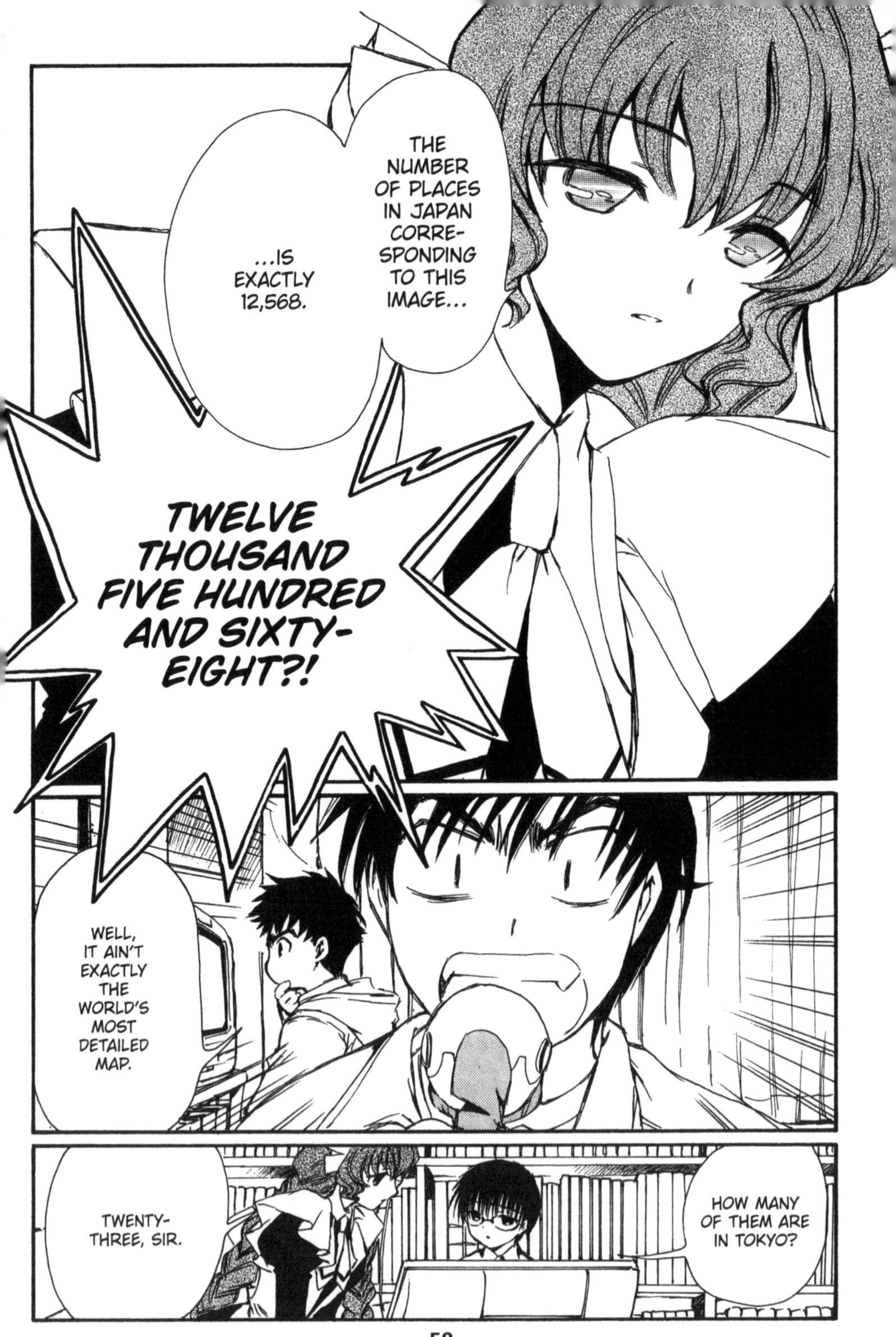
THE NUMBER OF PLACES IN JAPAN CORRE-SPONDING TO THIS IMAGE...
...IS EXACTLY 12,568.
TWELVE THOUSAND FIVE HUNDRED AND SIXTY-EIGHT?!
WELL, IT AIN'T EXACTLY THE WORLD'S MOST DETAILED MAP.
HOW MANY OF THEM ARE IN TOKYO?
TWENTY-THREE, SIR.

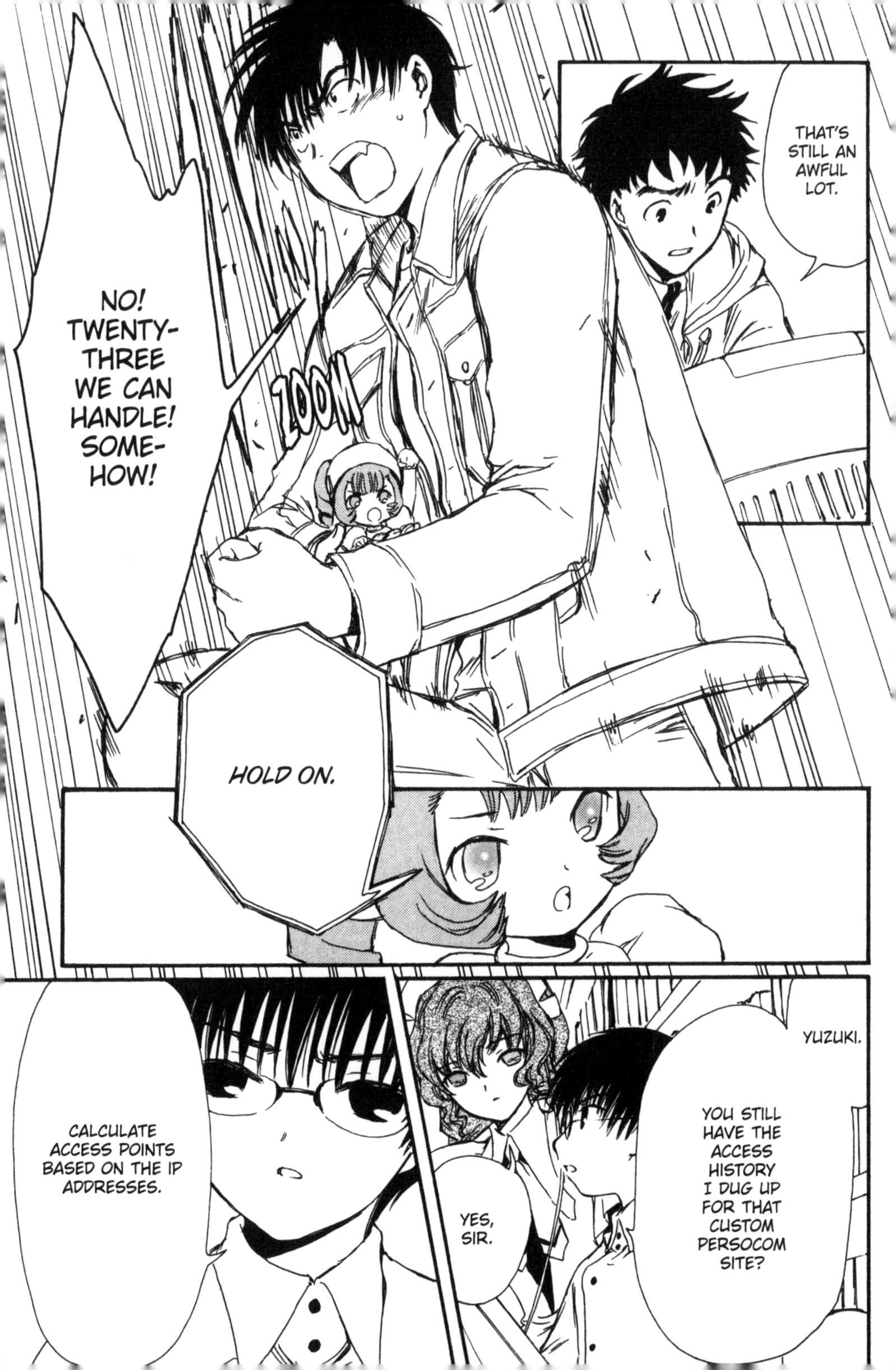

THAT'S STILL AN AWFUL LOT.
NO! TWENTY-THREE WE CAN HANDLE! SOME-HOW!
ZOOM
HOLD ON.
YUZUKI.
YOU STILL HAVE THE ACCESS HISTORY I DUG UP FOR THAT CUSTOM PERSOCOM SITE?
YES, SIR.
CALCULATE ACCESS POINTS BASED ON THE IP ADDRESSES.

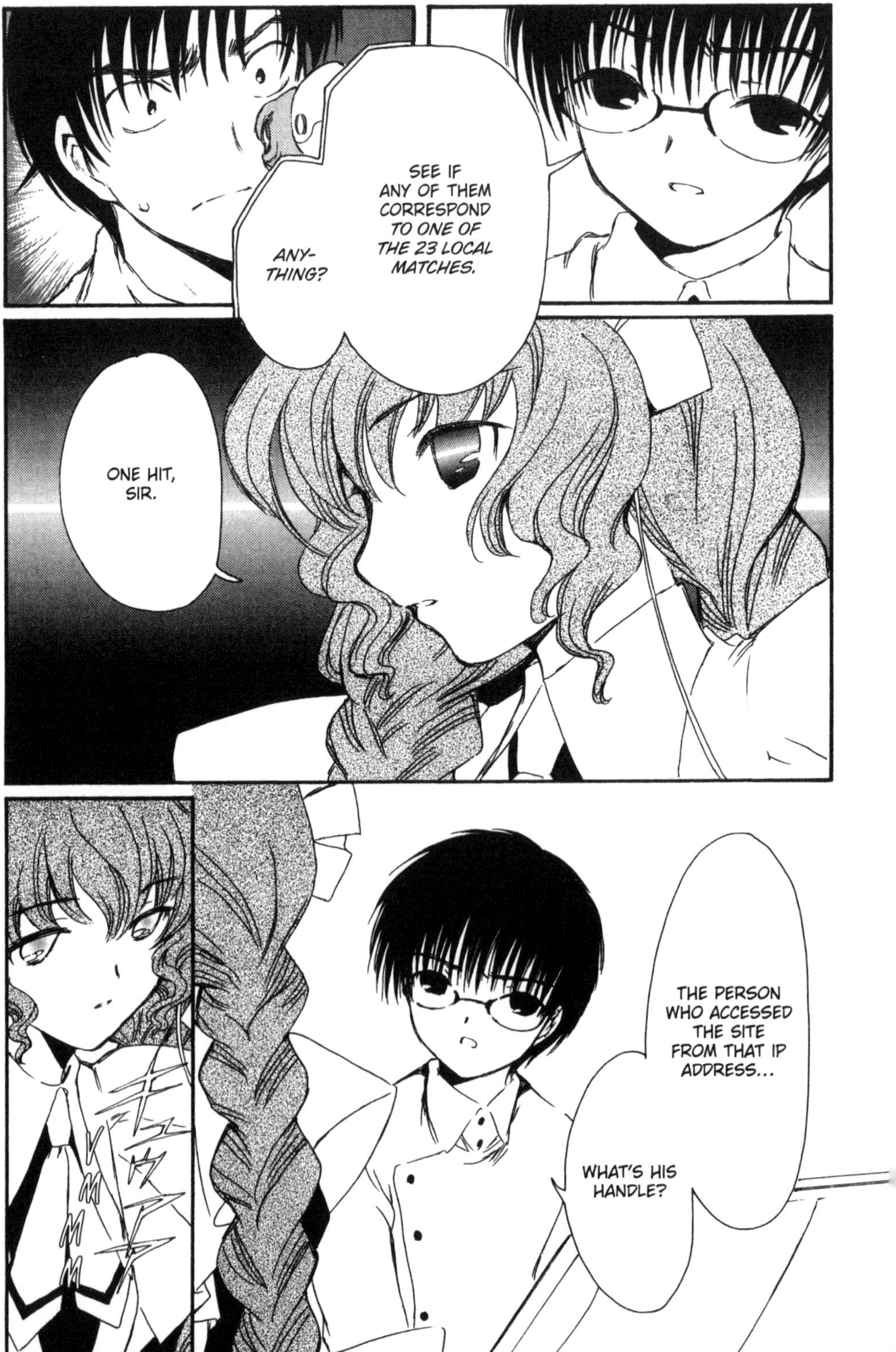
SEE IF ANY OF THEM CORRESPOND TO ONE OF THE 23 LOCAL MATCHES.
ANY-THING?
ONE HIT, SIR.
THE PERSON WHO ACCESSED THE SITE FROM THAT IP ADDRESS...
WHAT'S HIS HANDLE?
ギュウウ
VMMM

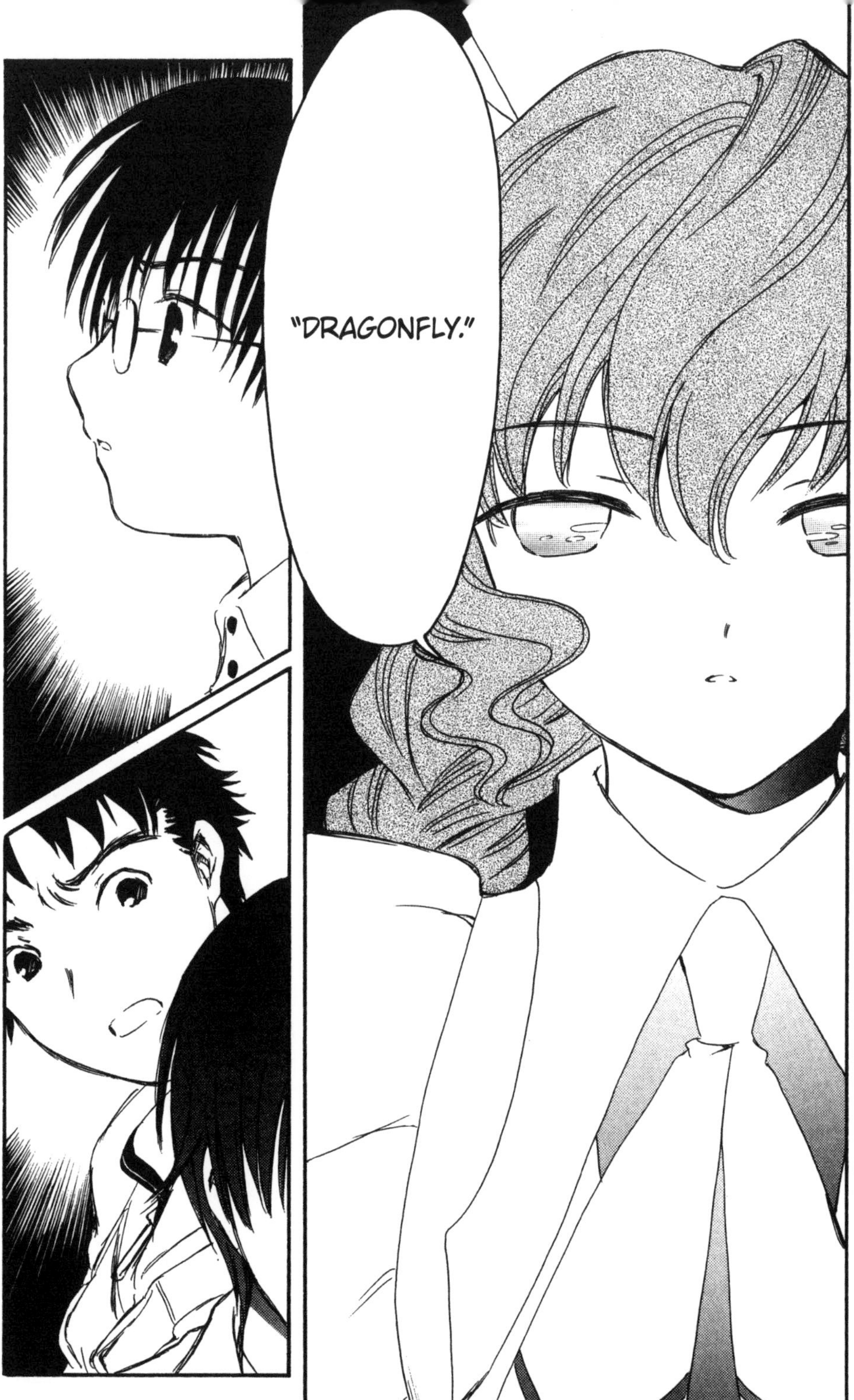
"DRAGONFLY."

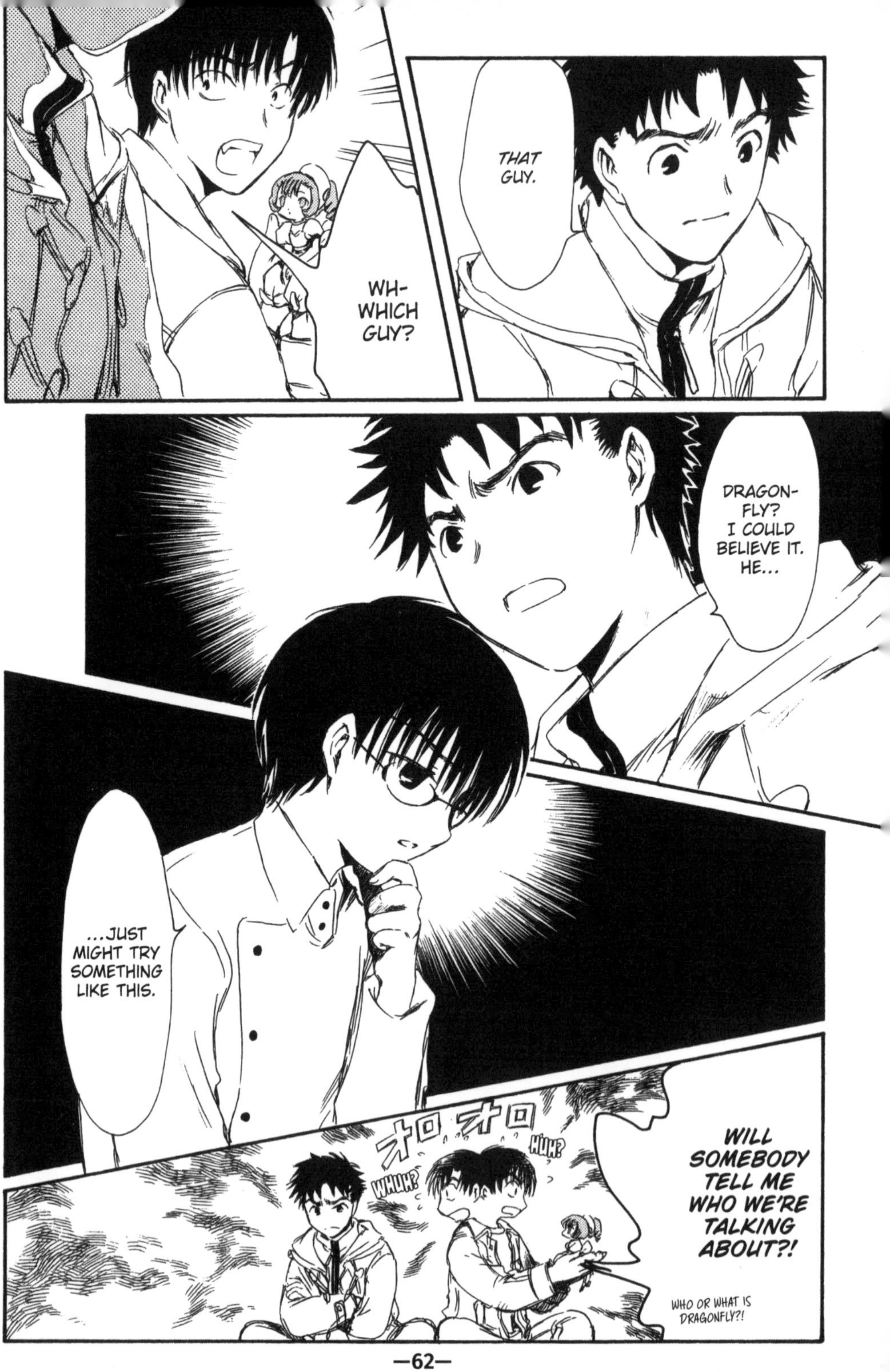
THAT GUY.
WH- WHICH GUY?
DRAGON-FLY? I COULD BELIEVE IT. HE...
...JUST MIGHT TRY SOMETHING LIKE THIS.
WILL SOMEBODY TELL ME WHO WE'RE TALKING ABOUT?!
オロ オロ
HUH?
WHUH?
WHO OR WHAT IS DRAGONFLY?!

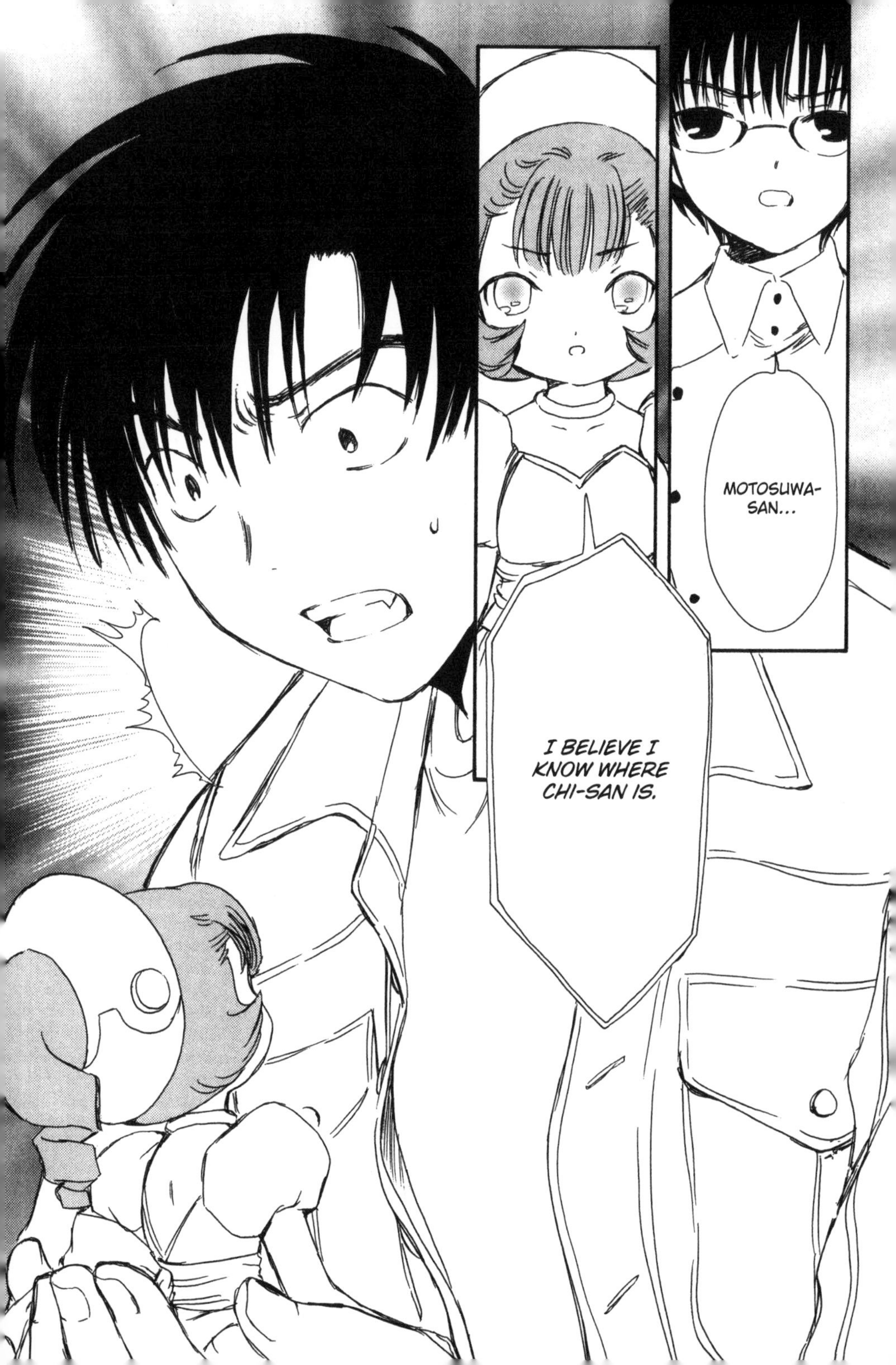
MOTOSUWA-SAN...
I BELIEVE I KNOW WHERE CHI-SAN IS.

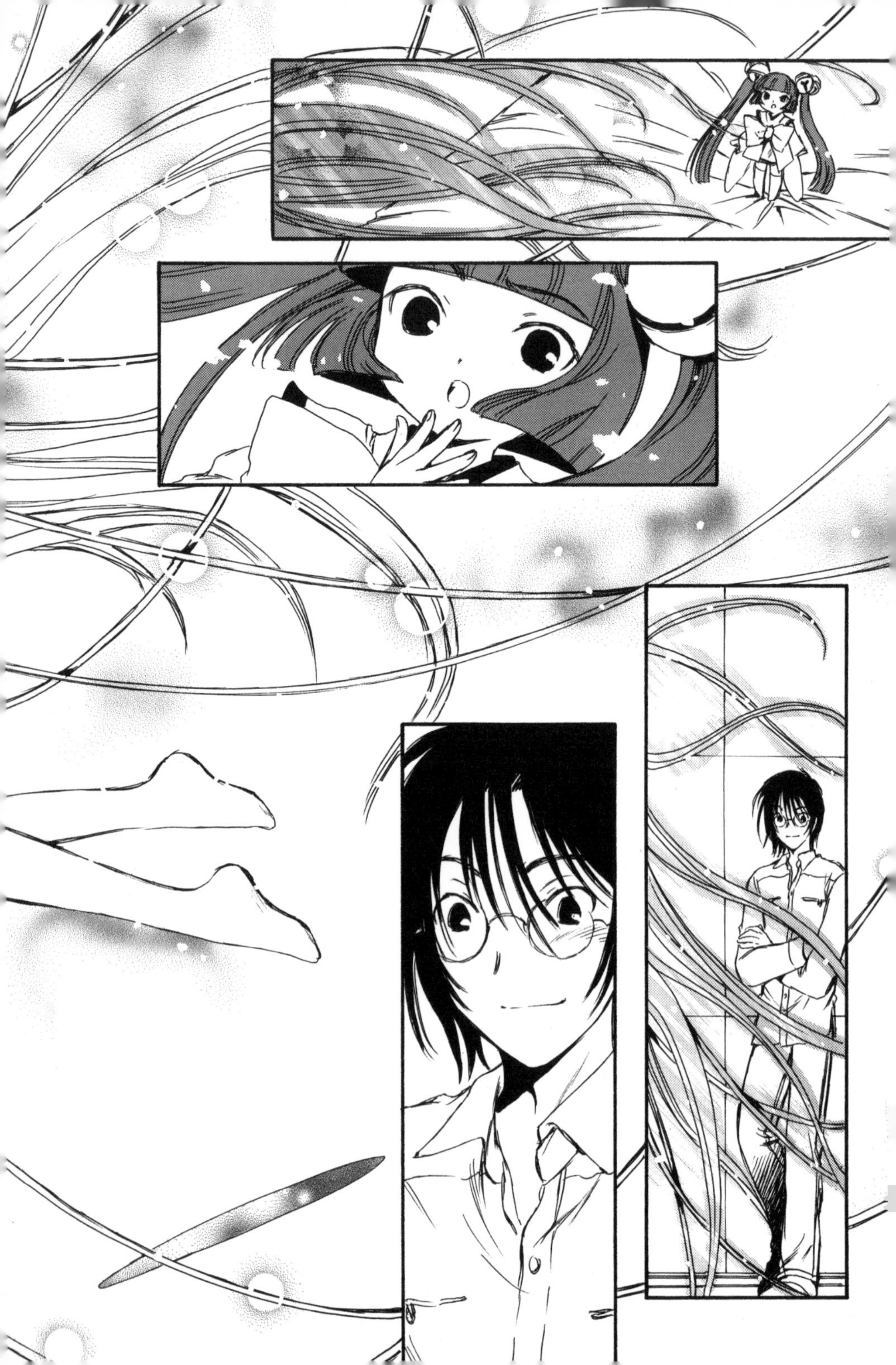

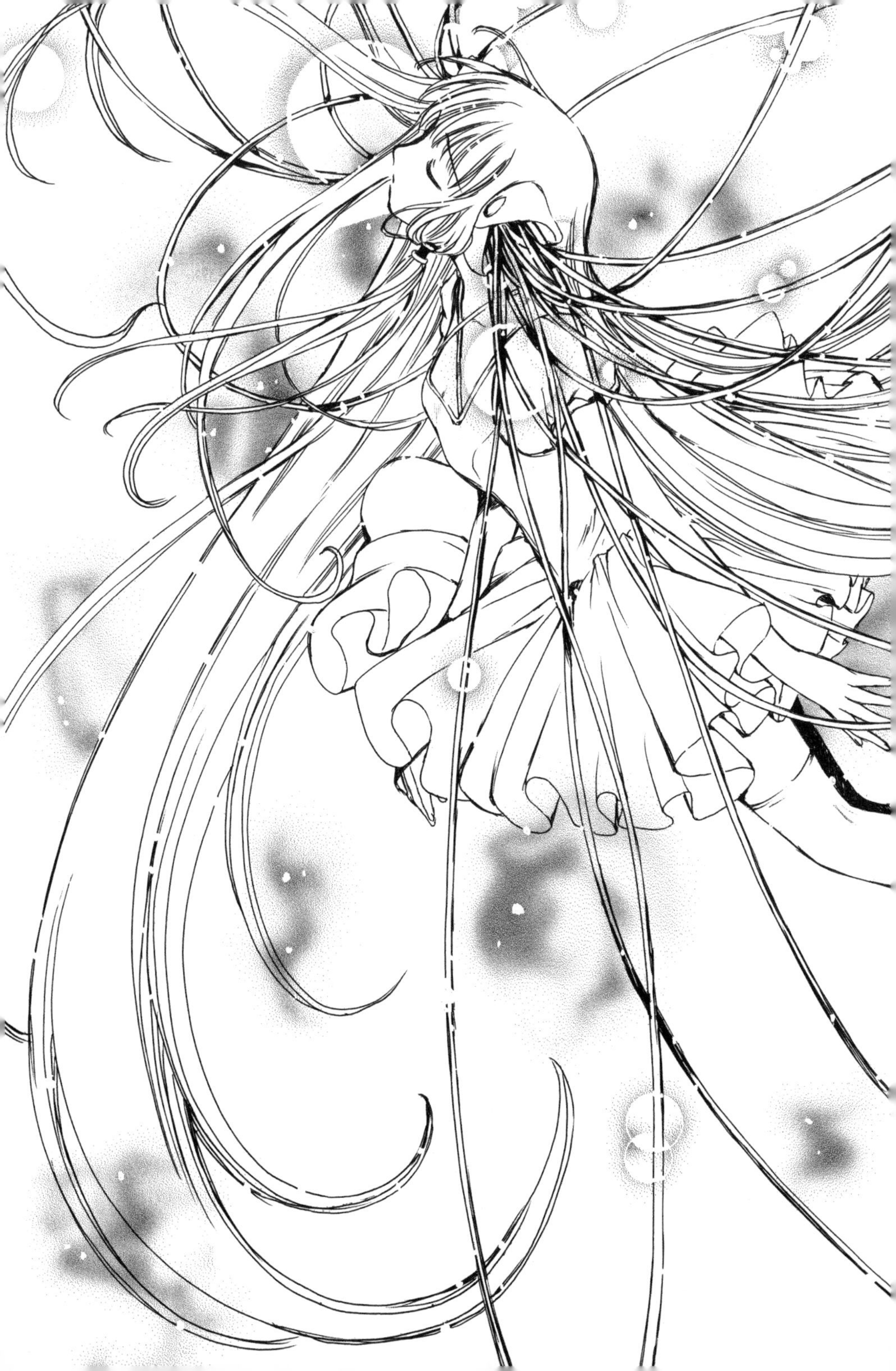

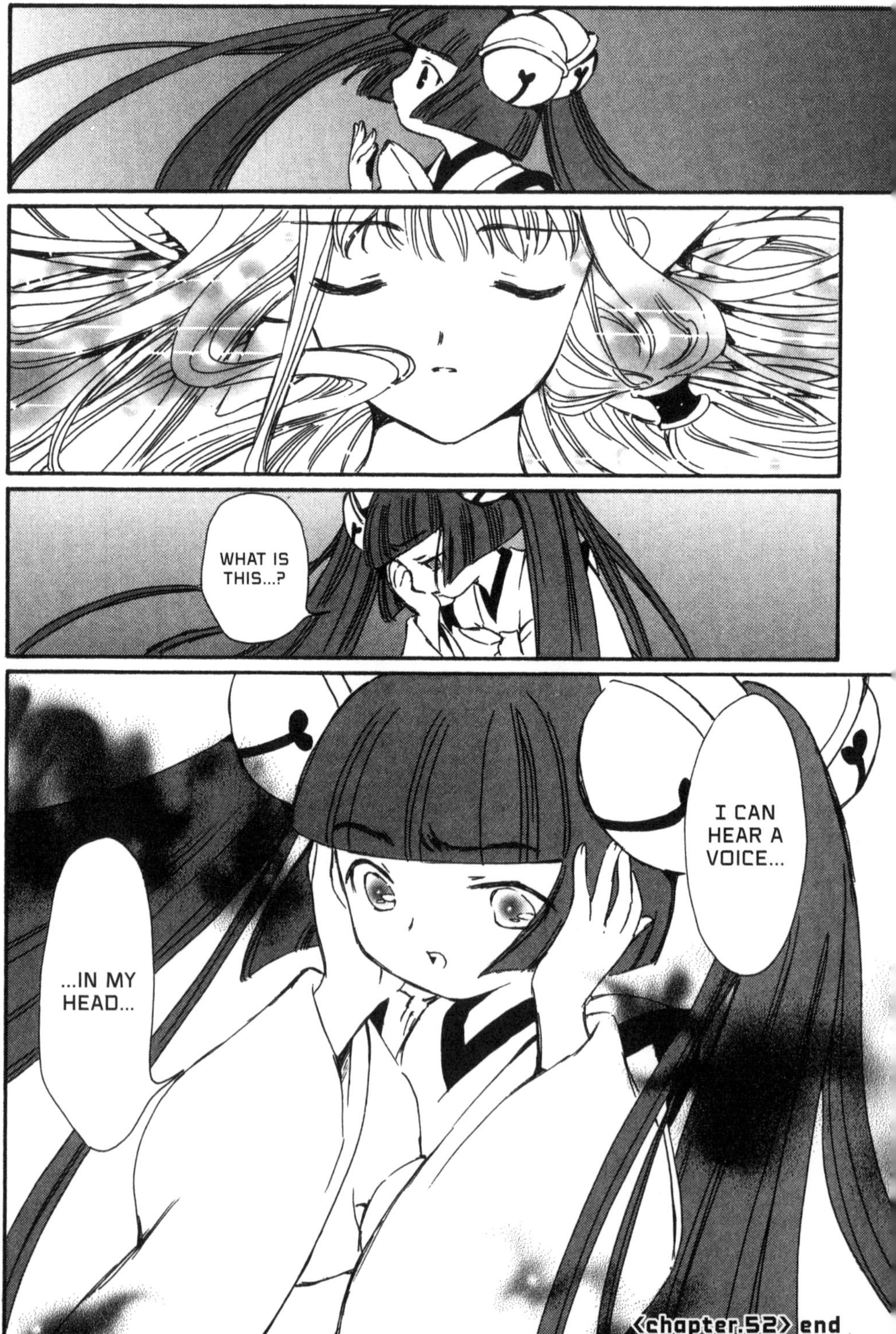
WHAT IS THIS...?
I CAN HEAR A VOICE...
...IN MY HEAD...
<chapter.52> end

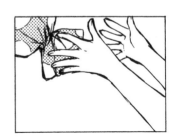

⟨chapter.53⟩

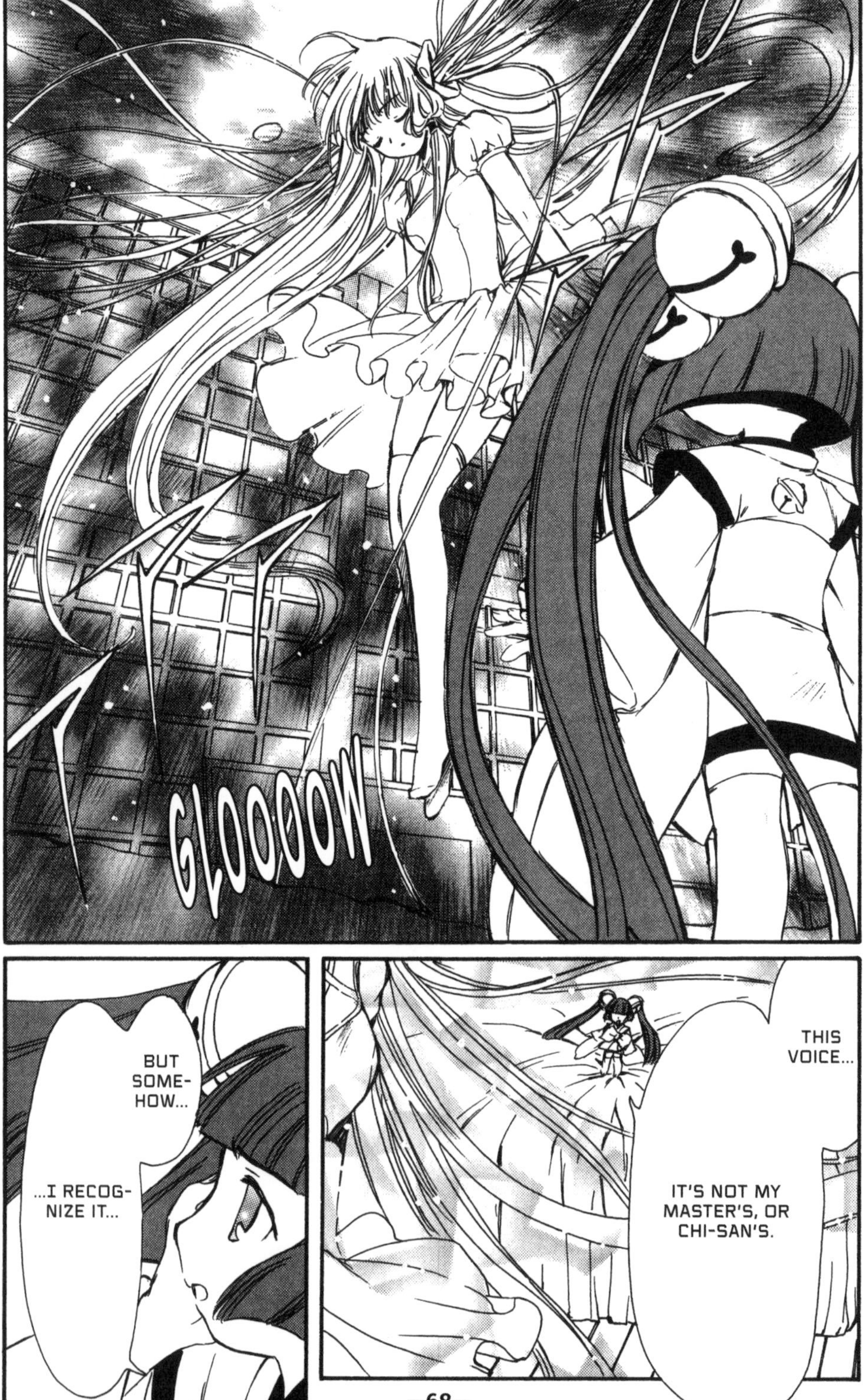
GLOOOOW
THIS VOICE...
IT'S NOT MY MASTER'S, OR CHI-SAN'S.
BUT SOME-HOW...
...I RECOG-NIZE IT...

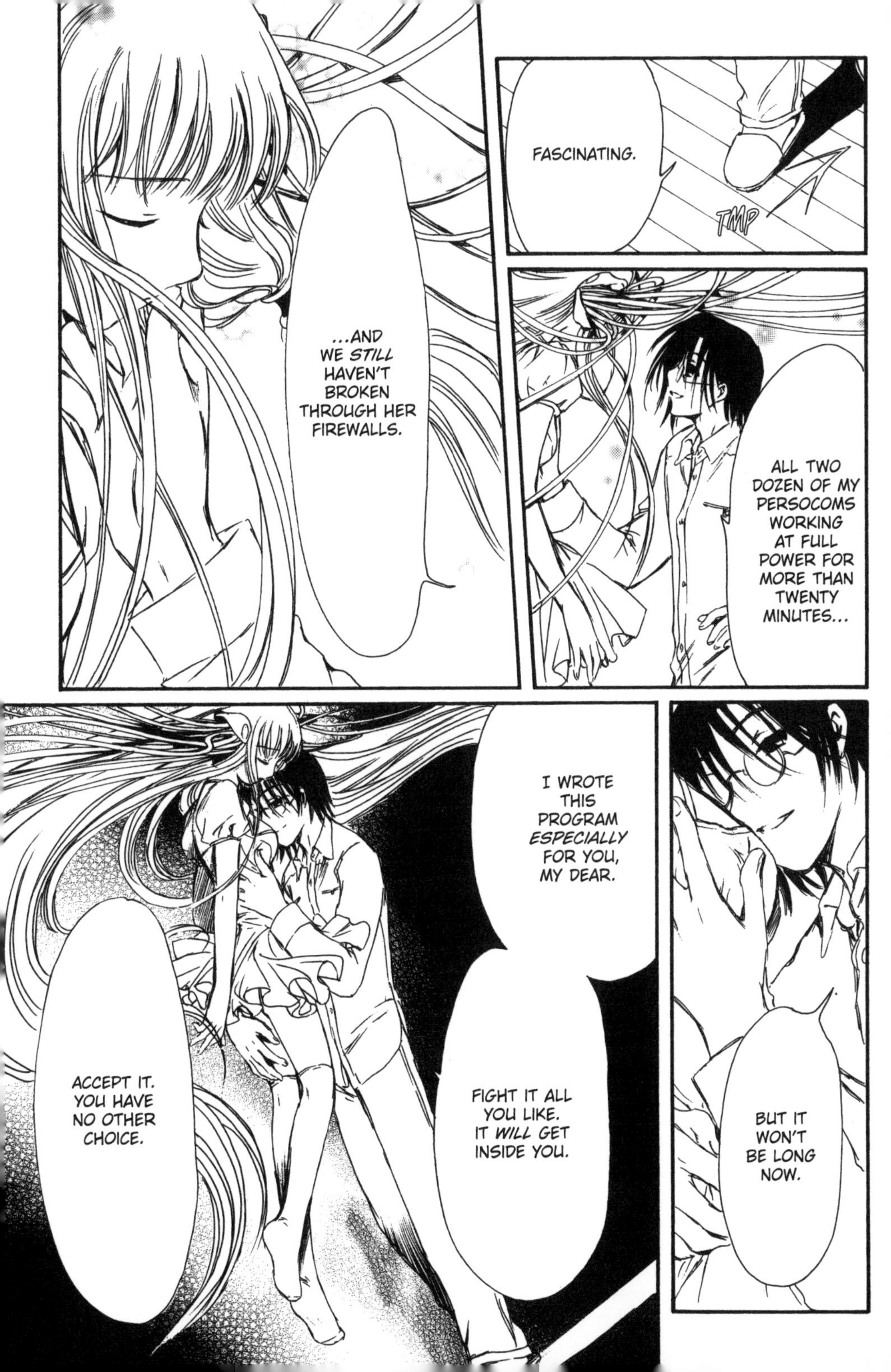
FASCINATING.
TMP
ALL TWO DOZEN OF MY PERSOCOMS WORKING AT FULL POWER FOR MORE THAN TWENTY MINUTES...
...AND WE *STILL* HAVEN'T BROKEN THROUGH HER FIREWALLS.
BUT IT WON'T BE LONG NOW.
I WROTE THIS PROGRAM *ESPECIALLY* FOR YOU, MY DEAR.
FIGHT IT ALL YOU LIKE. IT *WILL* GET INSIDE YOU.
ACCEPT IT. YOU HAVE NO OTHER CHOICE.

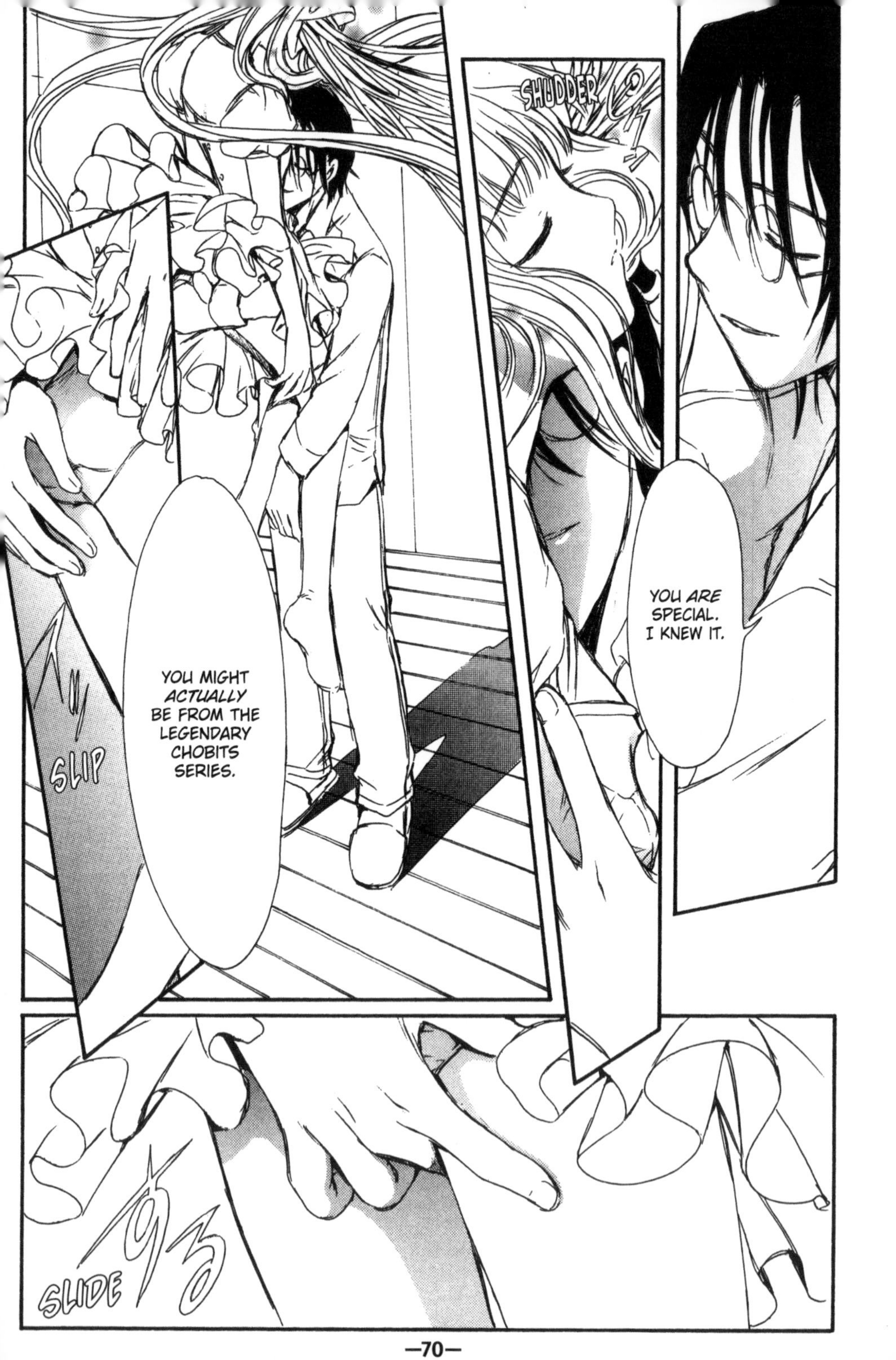
SHUDDER
YOU *ARE* SPECIAL. I KNEW IT.
YOU MIGHT *ACTUALLY* BE FROM THE LEGENDARY CHOBITS SERIES.
SLIP
SLIDE

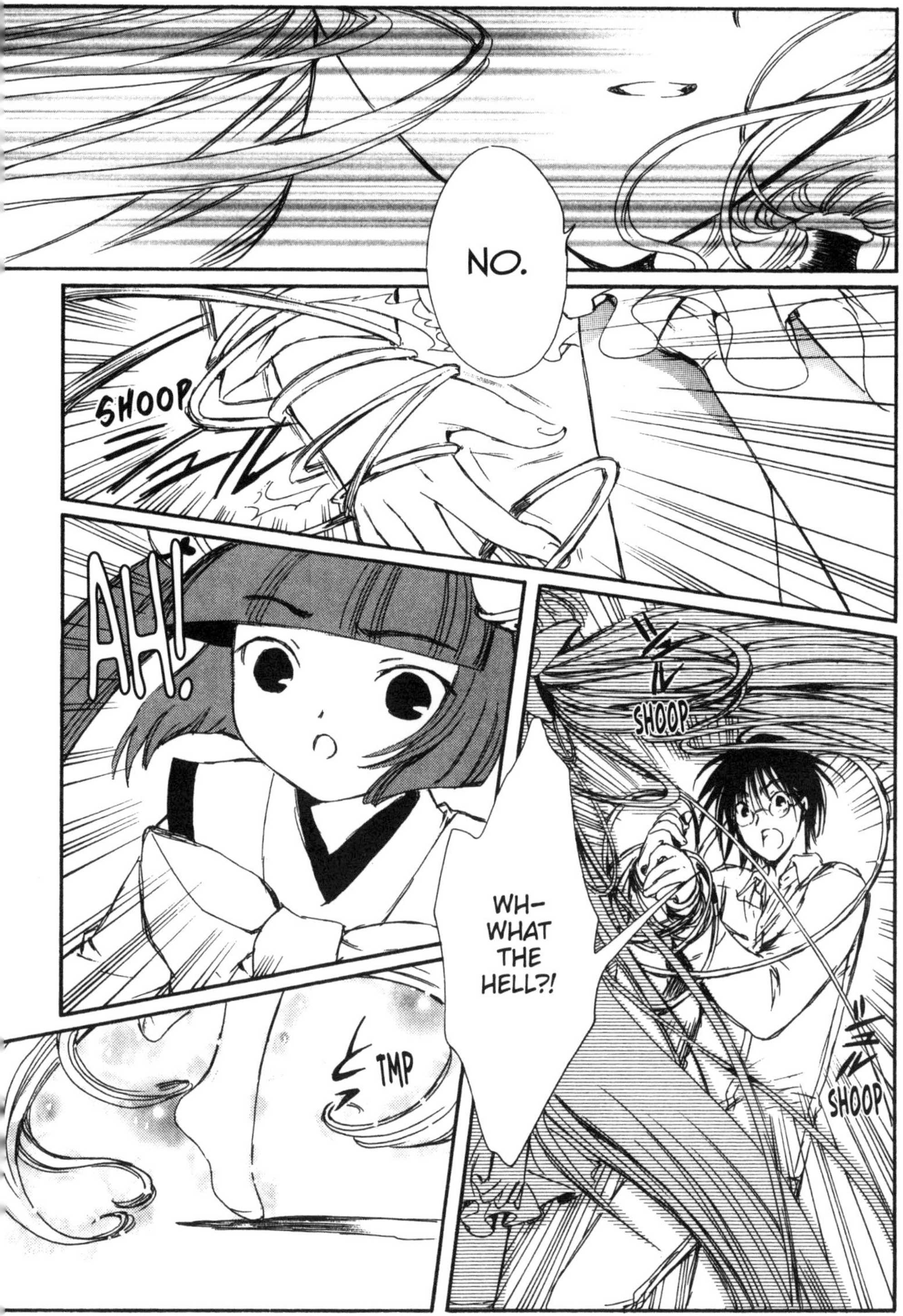
NO.
SHOOP
SHOOP
WH- WHAT THE HELL?!
SHOOP
AH!
TMP

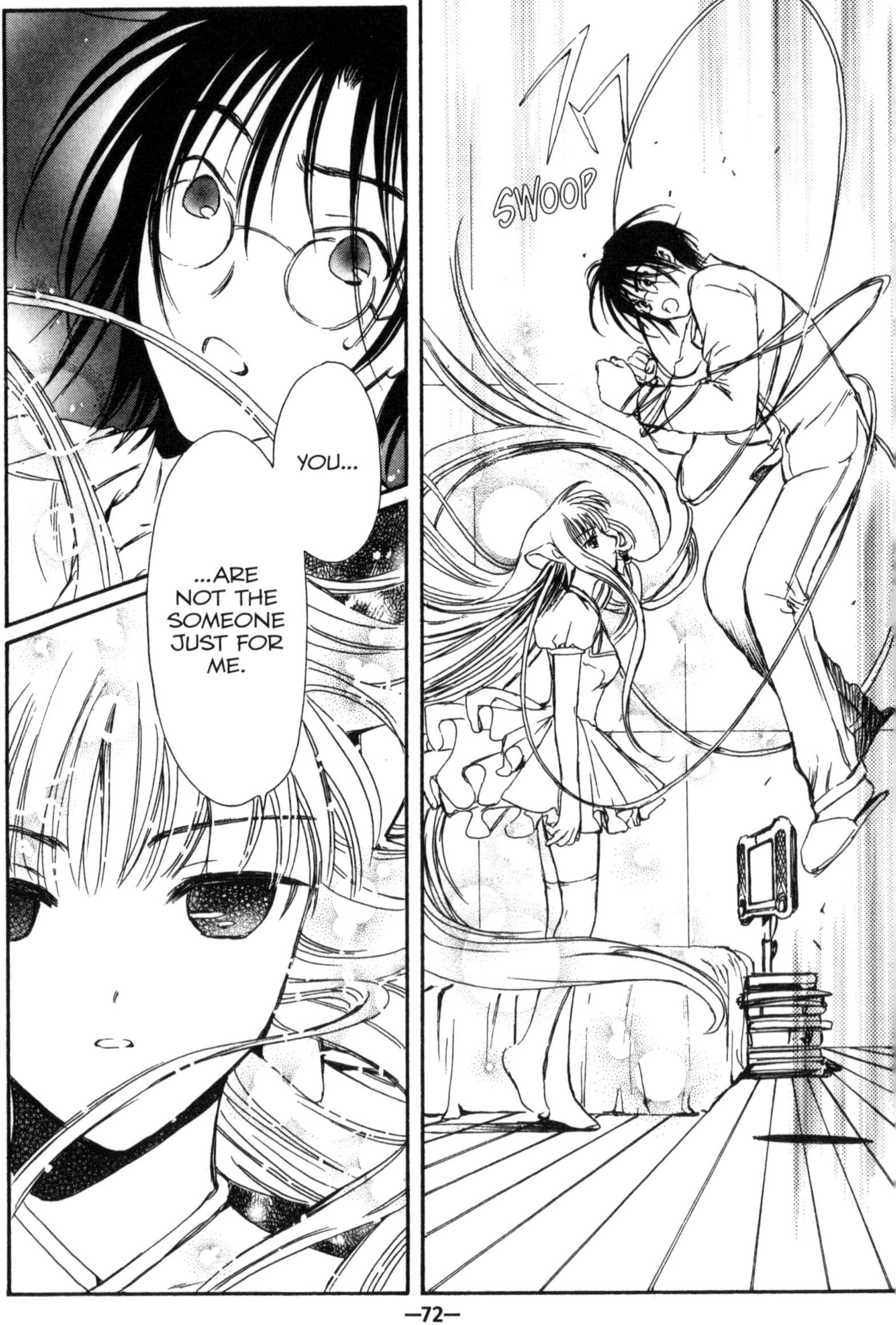
SWOOP
YOU...
...ARE NOT THE SOMEONE JUST FOR ME.

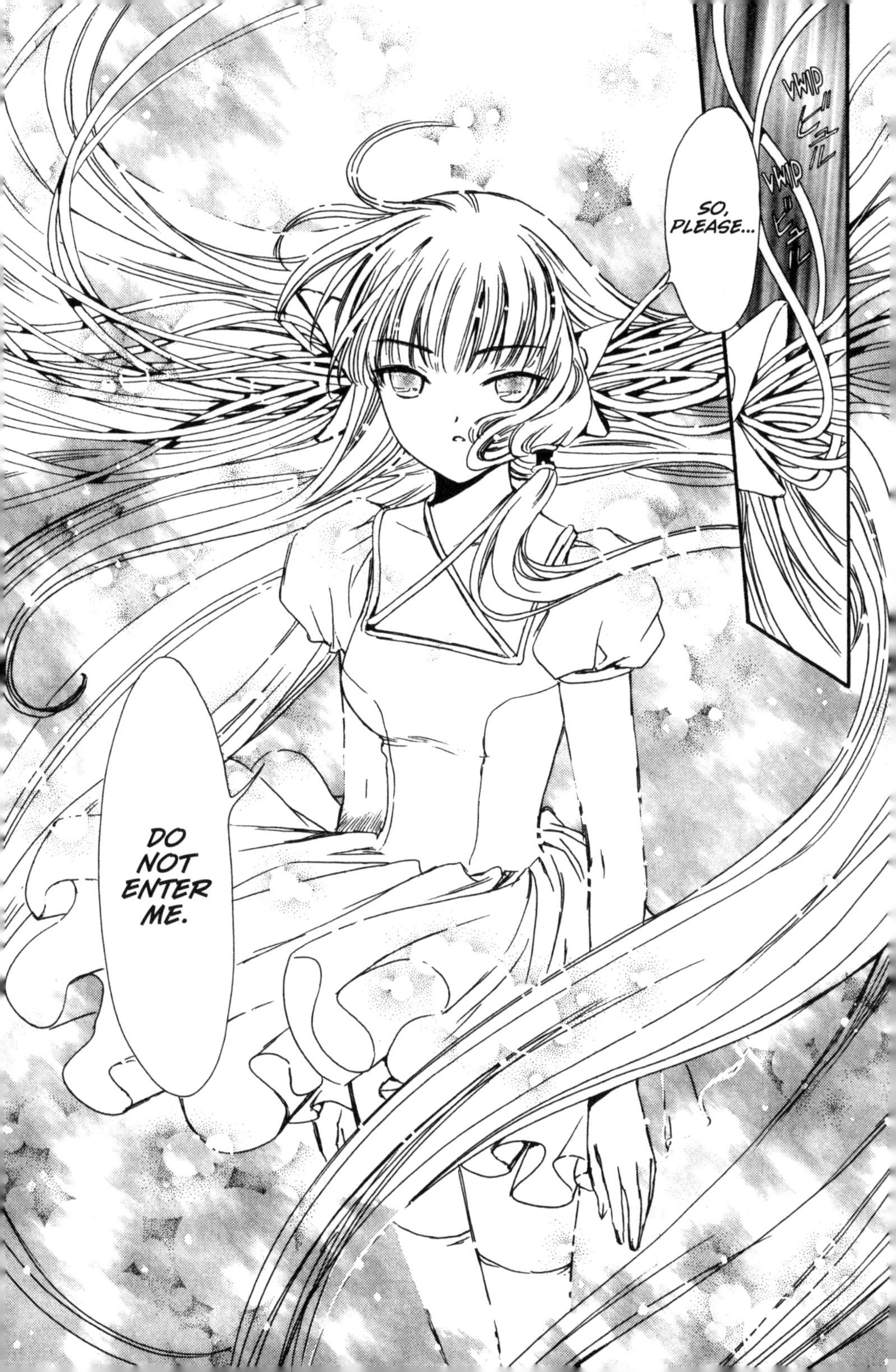
VWIP ビュル
VWIP ビュル
SO, PLEASE...
DO NOT ENTER ME.

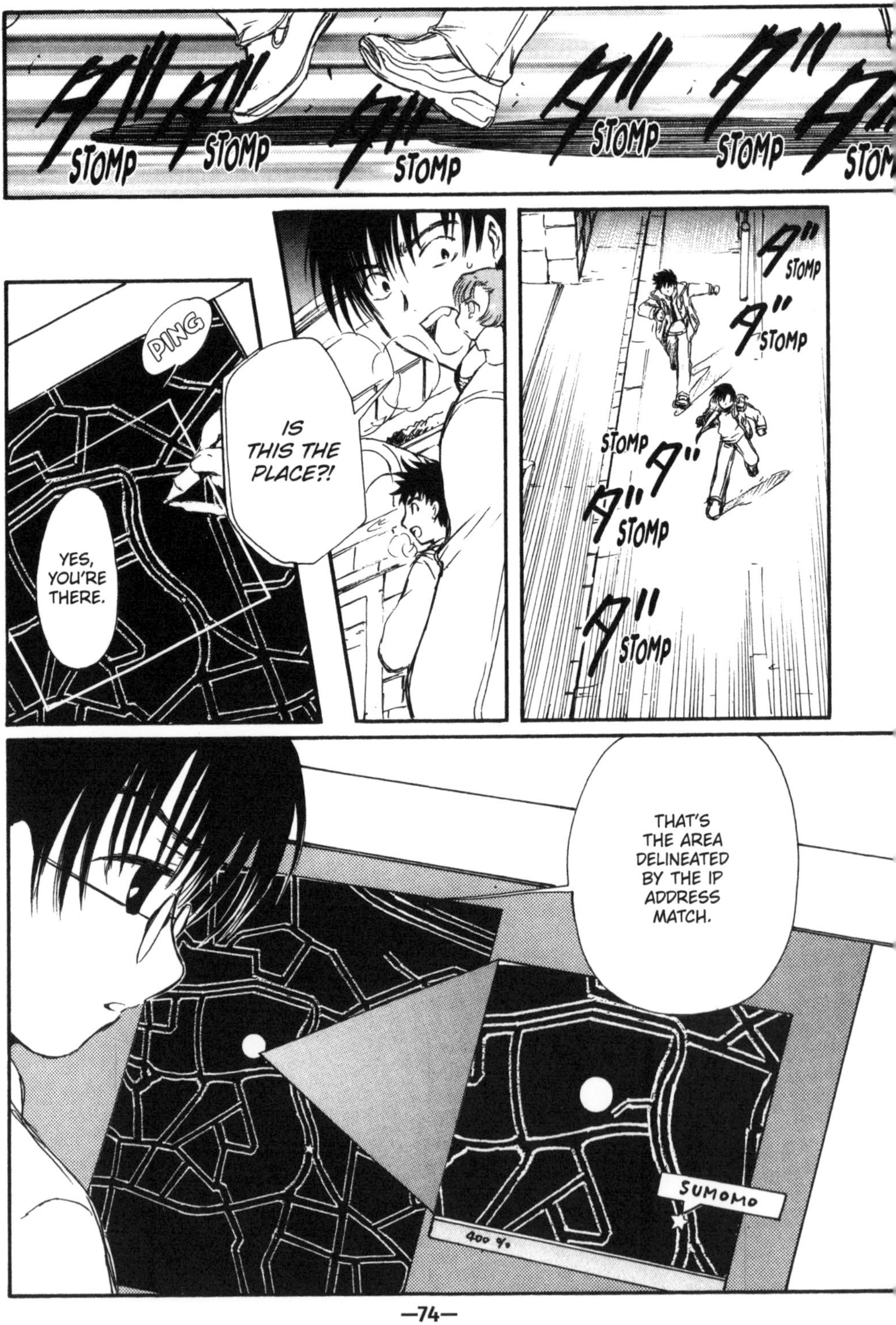

STOMP
STOMP
STOMP
STOMP
STOMP
STOMP
STOMP
STOMP
STOMP
STOMP
IS THIS THE PLACE?!
PING
YES, YOU'RE THERE.
THAT'S THE AREA DELINEATED BY THE IP ADDRESS MATCH.
SUMOMO
400 %

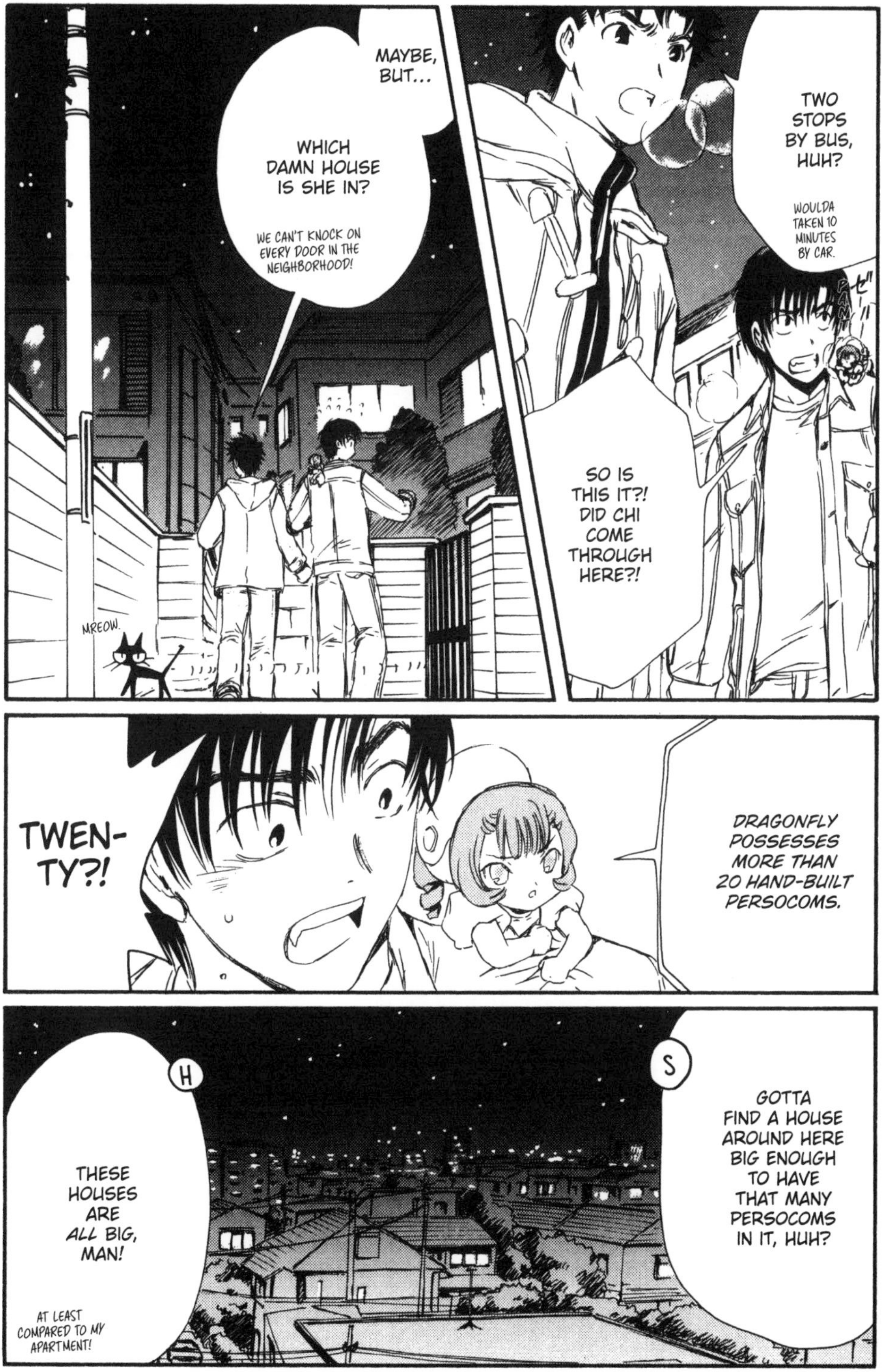
TWO STOPS BY BUS, HUH?
WOULDA TAKEN 10 MINUTES BY CAR.
PAN
SO IS THIS IT?! DID CHI COME THROUGH HERE?!
MAYBE, BUT...
WHICH DAMN HOUSE IS SHE IN?
WE CAN'T KNOCK ON EVERY DOOR IN THE NEIGHBORHOOD!
MREOW.
DRAGONFLY POSSESSES MORE THAN 20 HAND-BUILT PERSOCOMS.
TWEN-TY?!
S
GOTTA FIND A HOUSE AROUND HERE BIG ENOUGH TO HAVE THAT MANY PERSOCOMS IN IT, HUH?
H
THESE HOUSES ARE ALL BIG, MAN!
AT LEAST COMPARED TO MY APARTMENT!

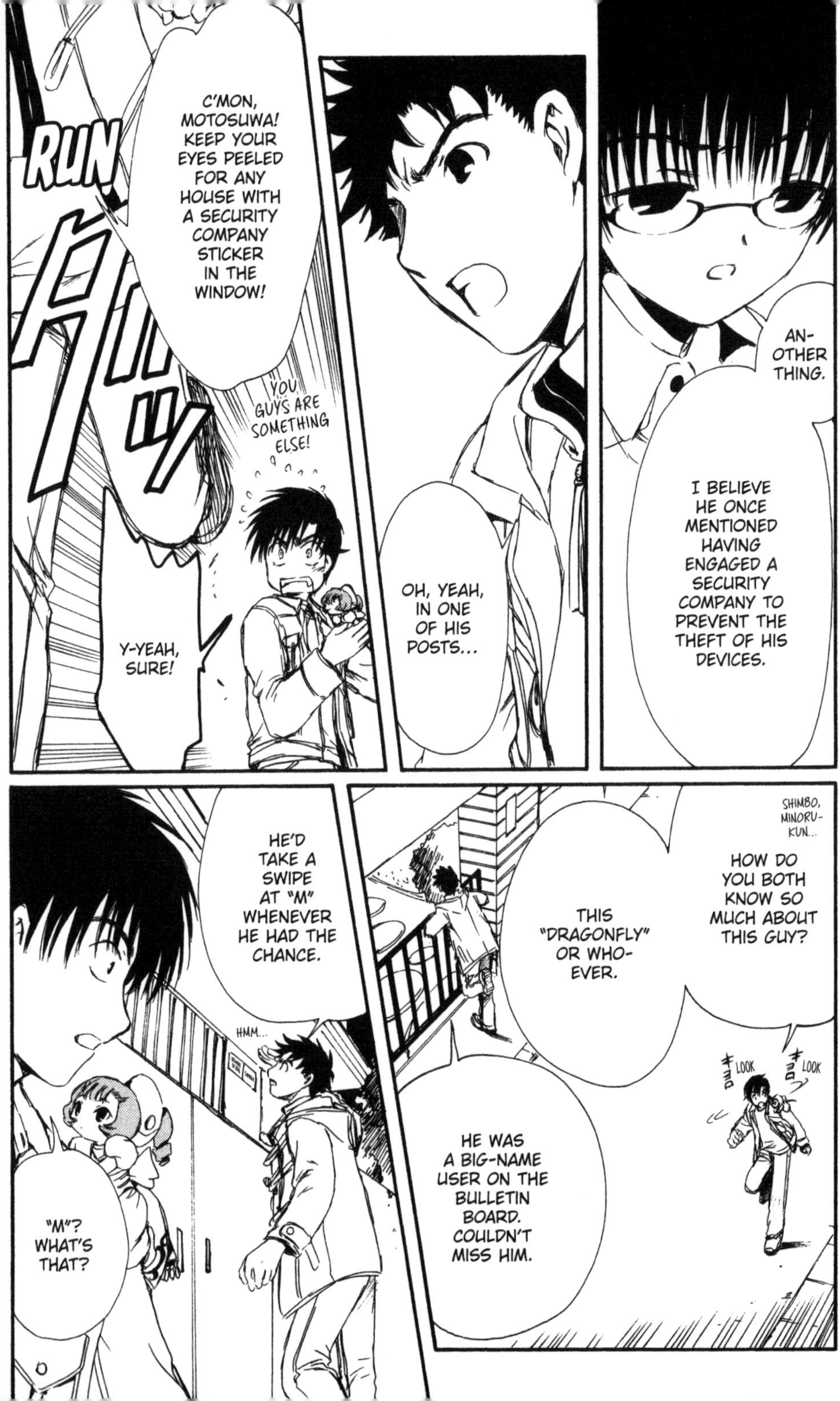
AN-OTHER THING.
I BELIEVE HE ONCE MENTIONED HAVING ENGAGED A SECURITY COMPANY TO PREVENT THE THEFT OF HIS DEVICES.
OH, YEAH, IN ONE OF HIS POSTS...
C'MON, MOTOSUWA! KEEP YOUR EYES PEELED FOR ANY HOUSE WITH A SECURITY COMPANY STICKER IN THE WINDOW!
RUN
YOU GUYS ARE SOMETHING ELSE!
Y-YEAH, SURE!
SHIMBO, MINORU-KUN...
HOW DO YOU BOTH KNOW SO MUCH ABOUT THIS GUY?
THIS "DRAGONFLY" OR WHO-EVER.
LOOK
LOOK
HE WAS A BIG-NAME USER ON THE BULLETIN BOARD. COULDN'T MISS HIM.
HE'D TAKE A SWIPE AT "M" WHENEVER HE HAD THE CHANCE.
HMM...
"M"? WHAT'S THAT?

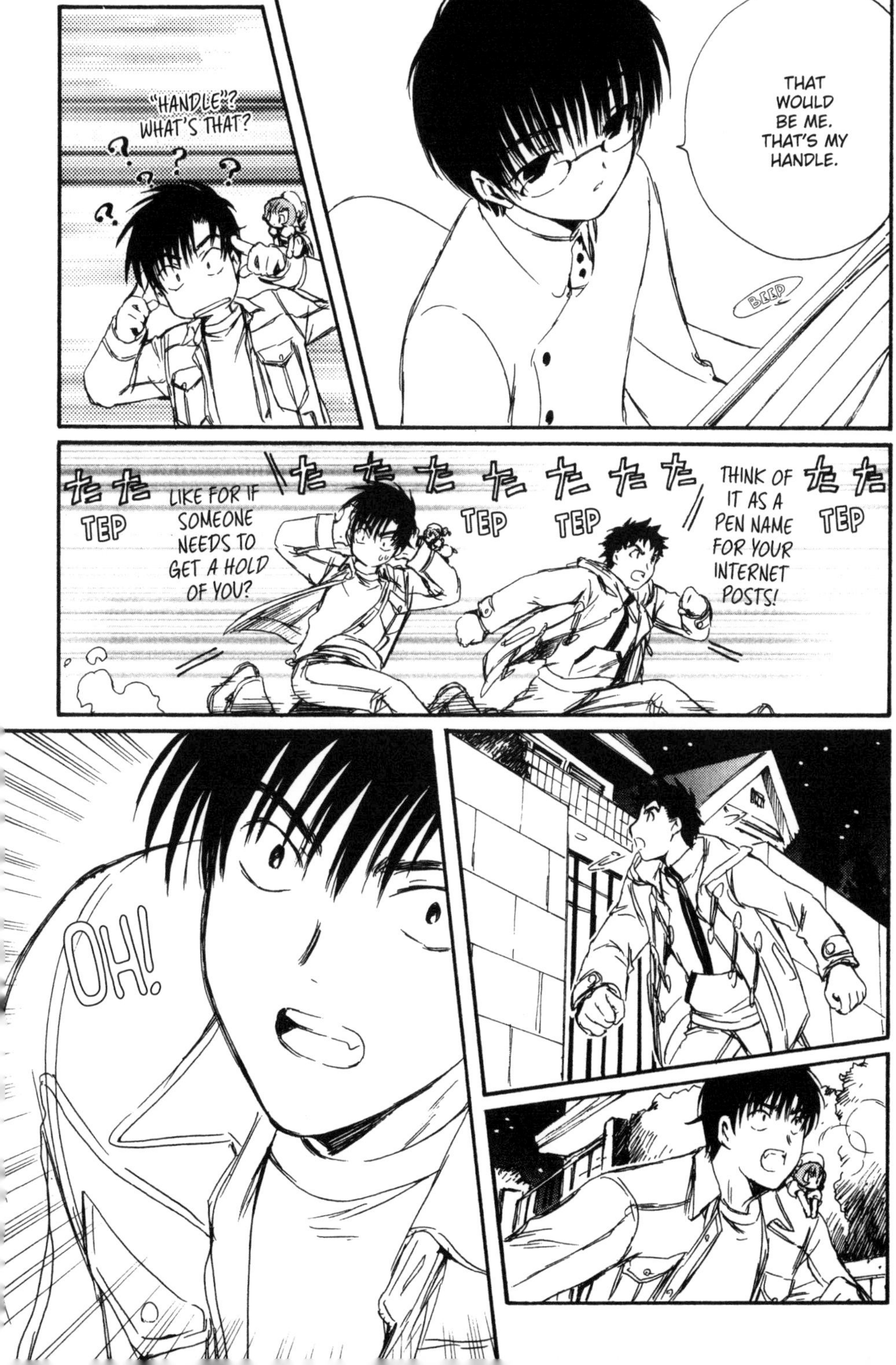

THAT WOULD BE ME. THAT'S MY HANDLE.
BEEP
"HANDLE"? WHAT'S THAT?
たた
TEP
THINK OF IT AS A PEN NAME FOR YOUR INTERNET POSTS!
たたたたたたた
TEP
TEP
LIKE FOR IF SOMEONE NEEDS TO GET A HOLD OF YOU?
たた
TEP
OH!

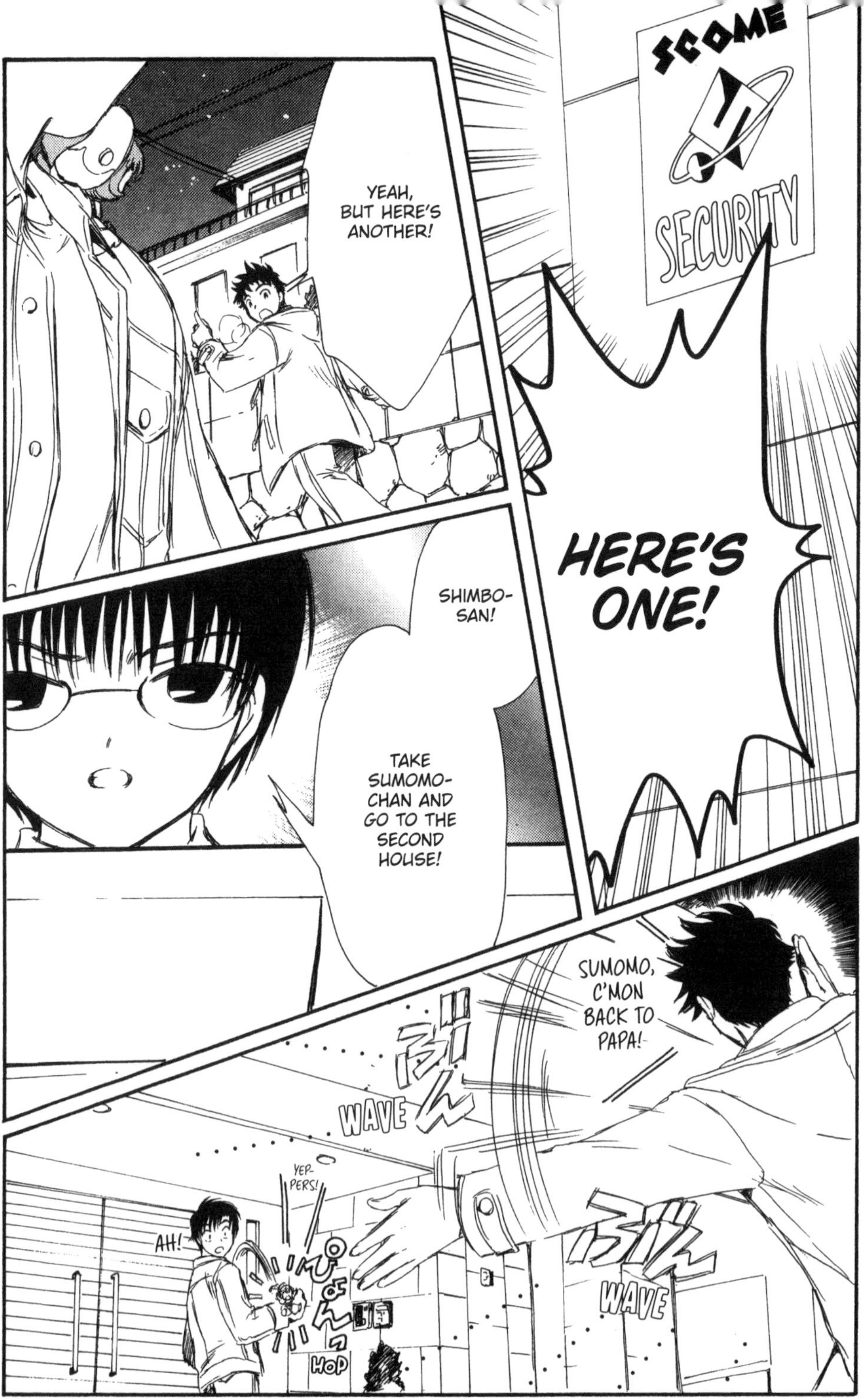
SCOME
SECURITY
HERE'S ONE!
YEAH, BUT HERE'S ANOTHER!
SHIMBO-SAN!
TAKE SUMOMO-CHAN AND GO TO THE SECOND HOUSE!
SUMOMO, C'MON BACK TO PAPA!
WAVE
WAVE
YEP-PERS!
AH!
HOP

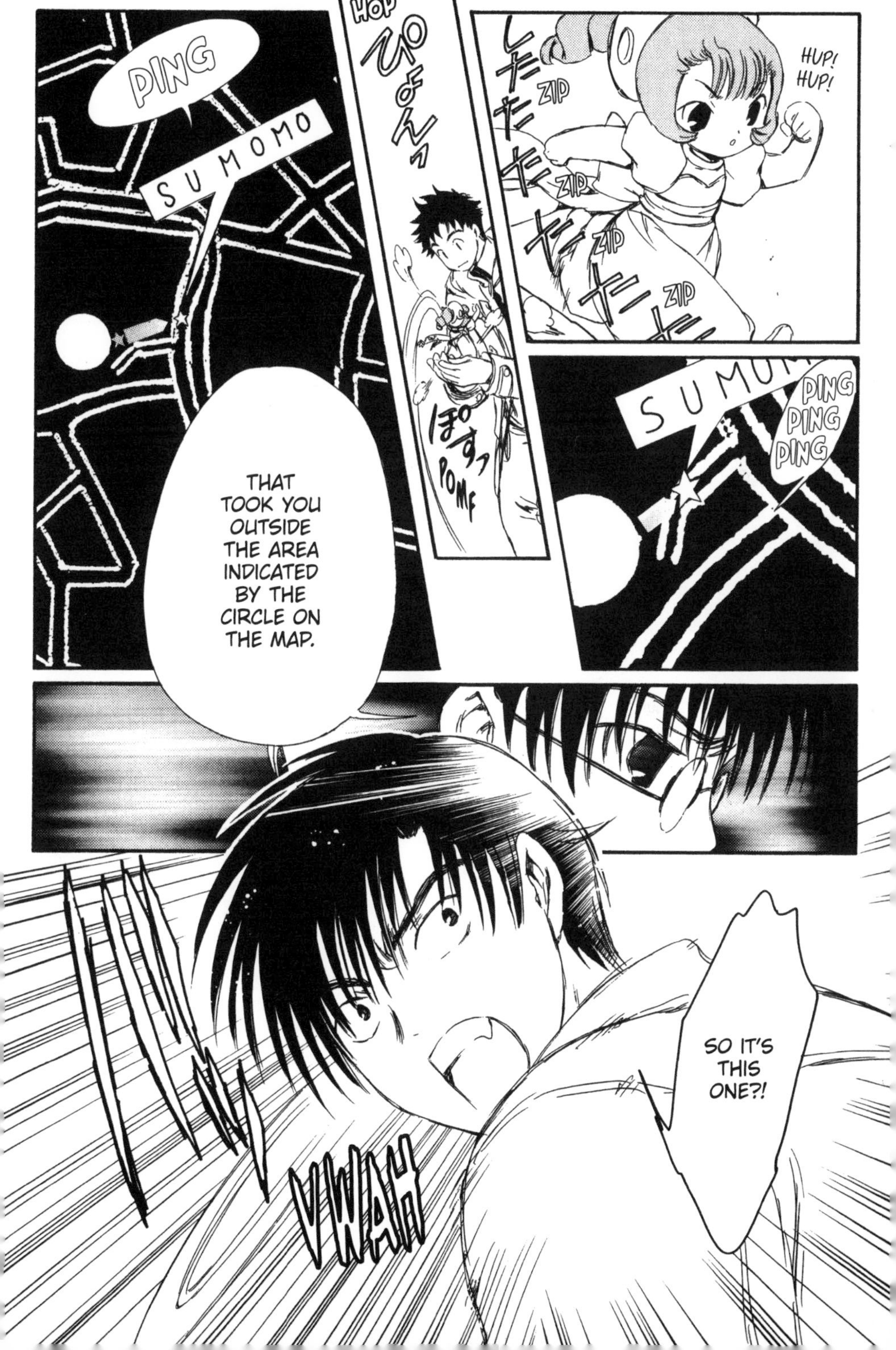
ZIP
ZIP
ZIP
ZIP
HUP! HUP!
SUMOMO
PING PING PING
HOP
ぴょんっ
ぽすっ
POMF
PING
SUMOMO
THAT TOOK YOU OUTSIDE THE AREA INDICATED BY THE CIRCLE ON THE MAP.
SO IT'S THIS ONE?!
VWAH

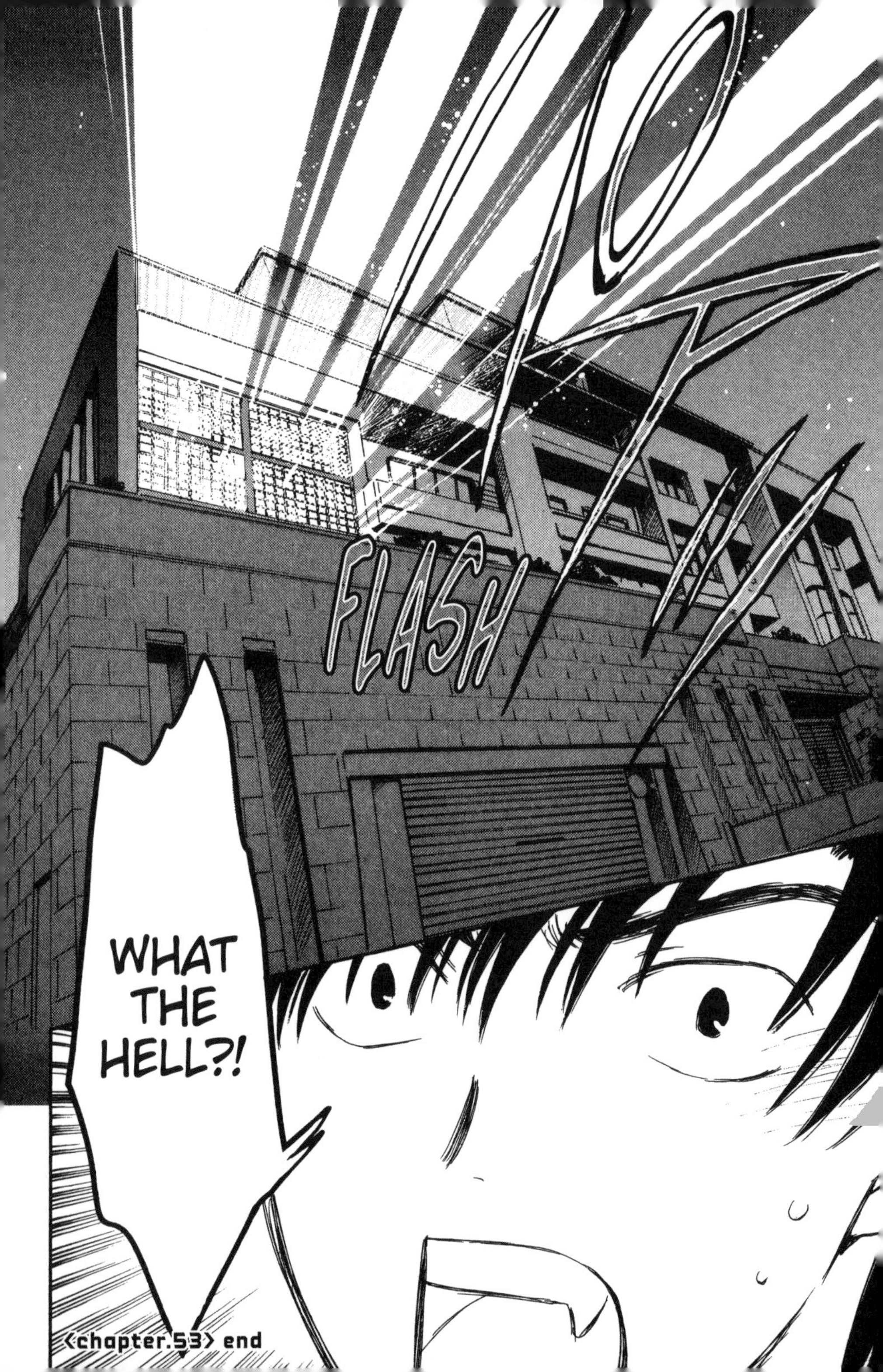
FLASH
WHAT THE HELL?!
<chapter.53> end

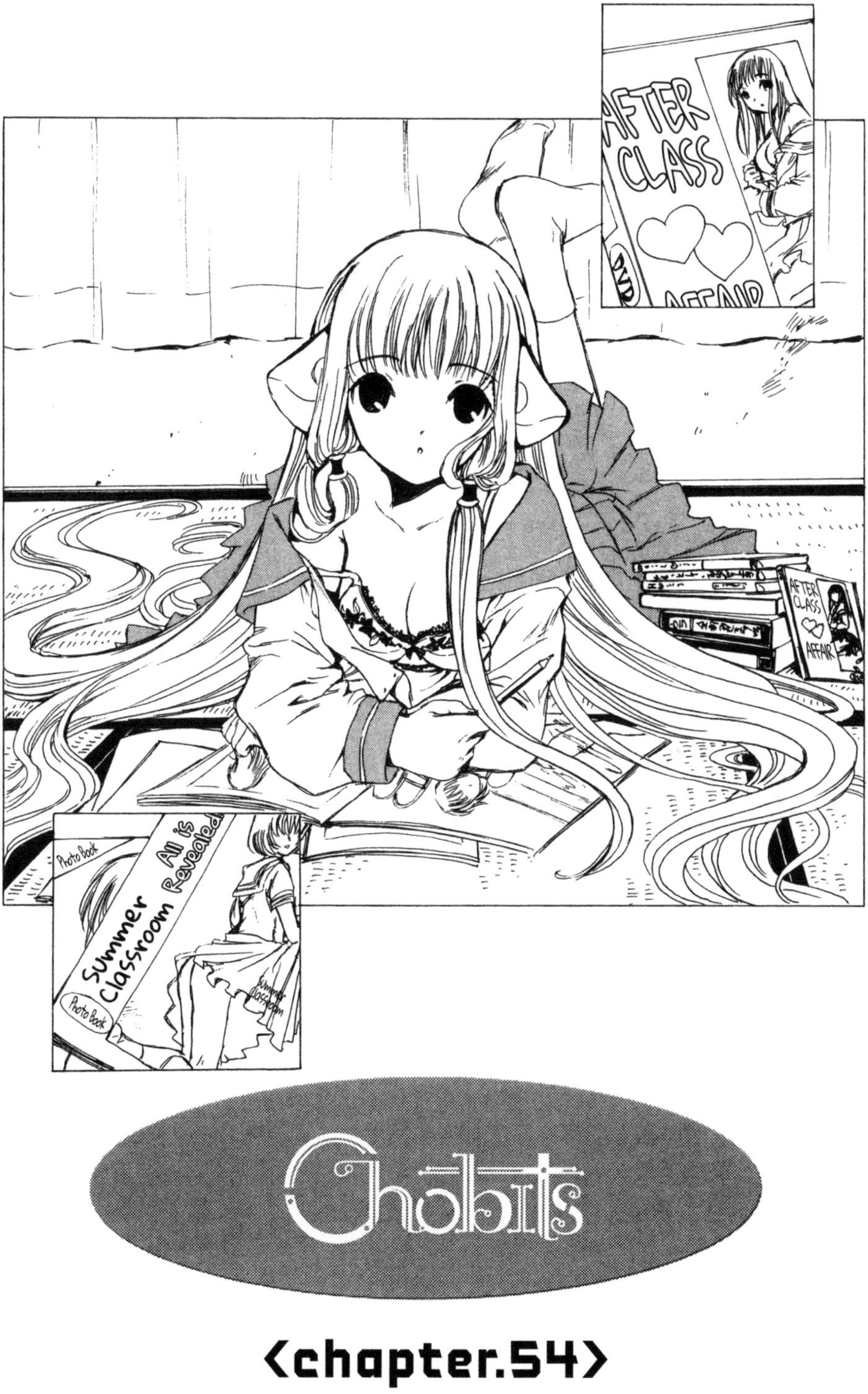
AFTER CLASS
DVD
AFTER CLASS
AFFAIR
Photo Book
All is Revealed!
Summer Classroom
Photo Book
Summer Classroom

Chobits

<chapter.54>

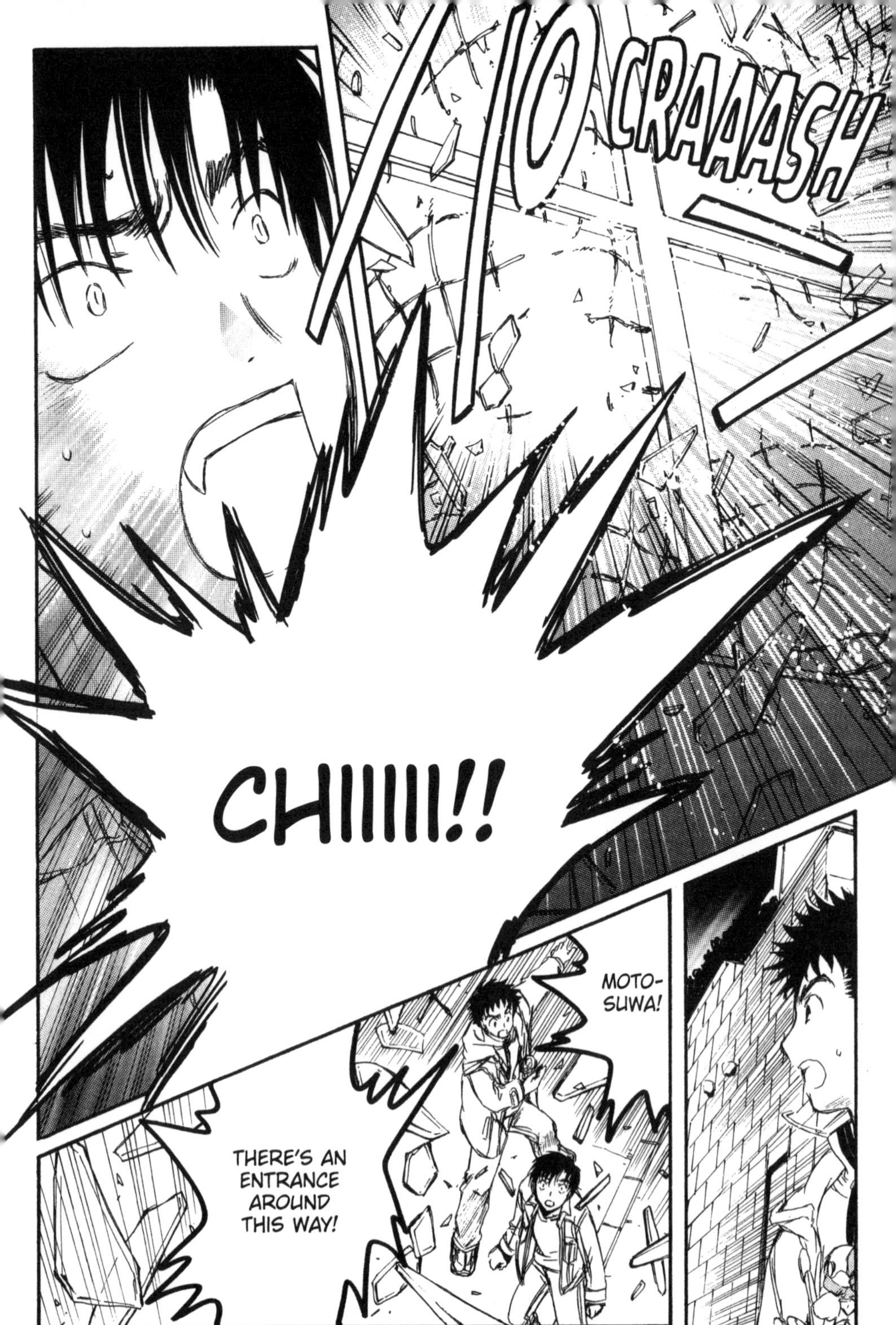
CRAAASH
CHIIIII!!
MOTO-SUWA!
THERE'S AN ENTRANCE AROUND THIS WAY!

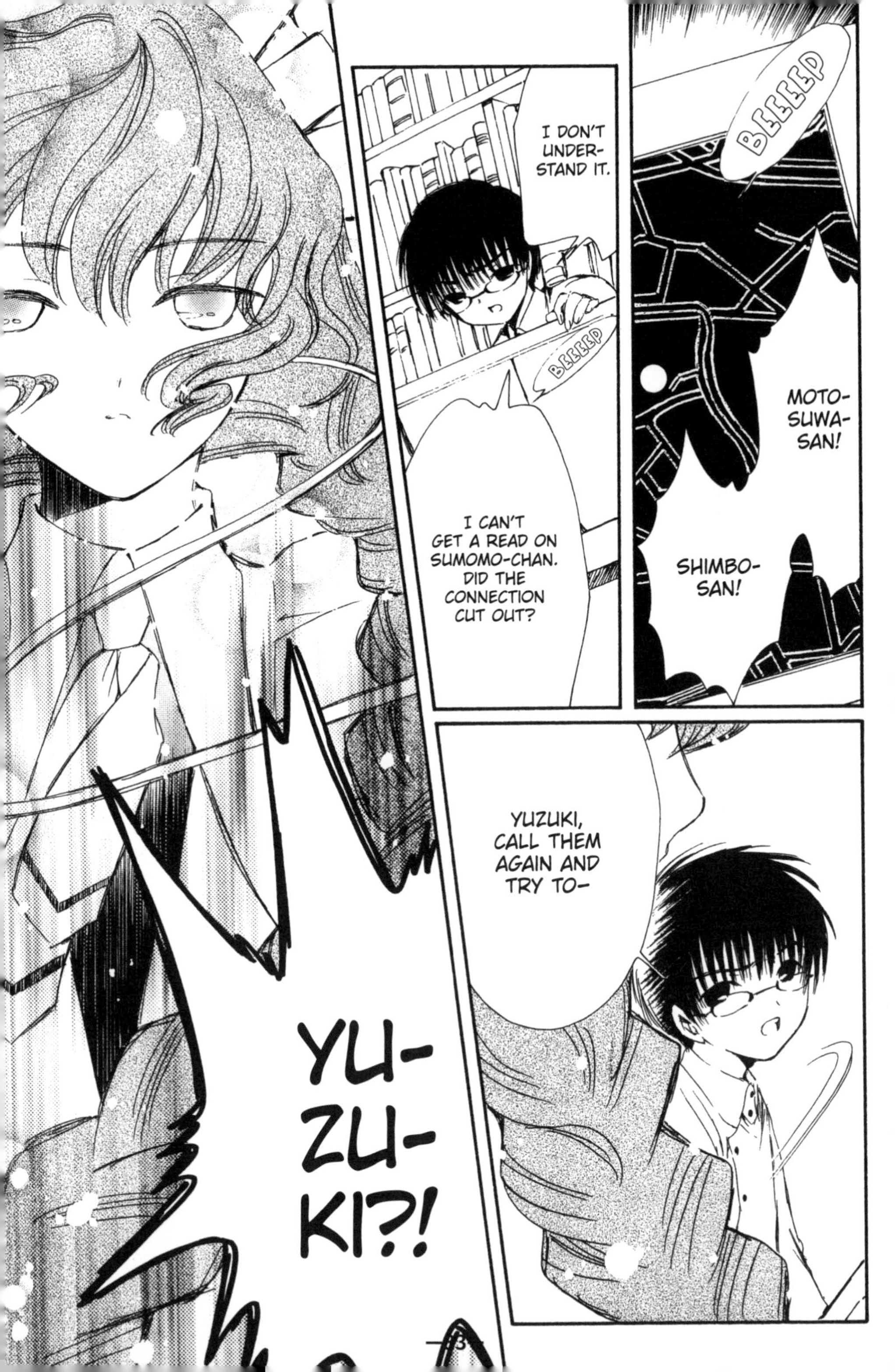
BEEEEP
MOTO-SUWA-SAN!
SHIMBO-SAN!
I DON'T UNDER-STAND IT.
BEEEEP
I CAN'T GET A READ ON SUMOMO-CHAN. DID THE CONNECTION CUT OUT?
YUZUKI, CALL THEM AGAIN AND TRY TO-
YU-ZU-KI?!

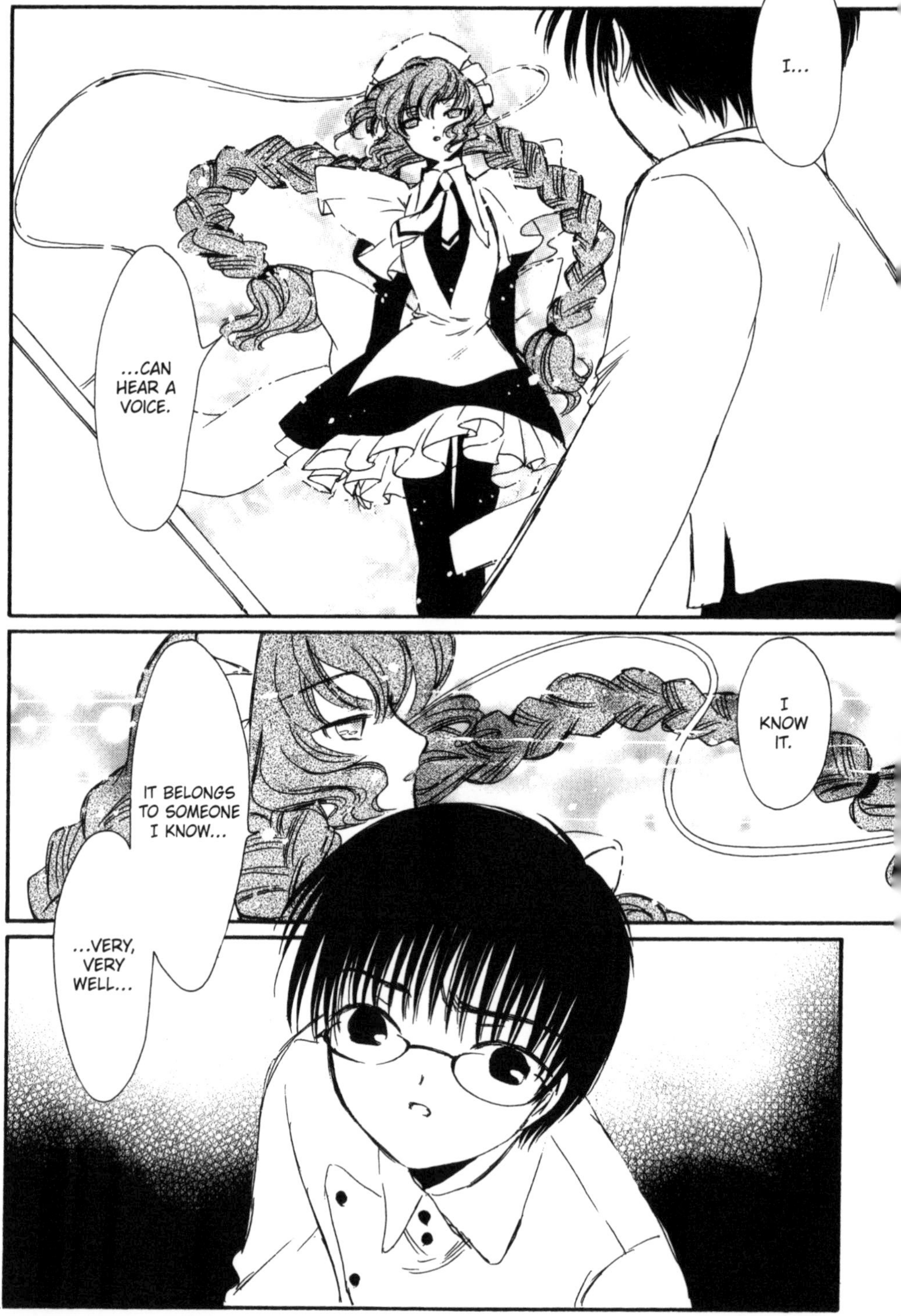
I...
...CAN HEAR A VOICE.
I KNOW IT.
IT BELONGS TO SOMEONE I KNOW...
...VERY, VERY WELL...

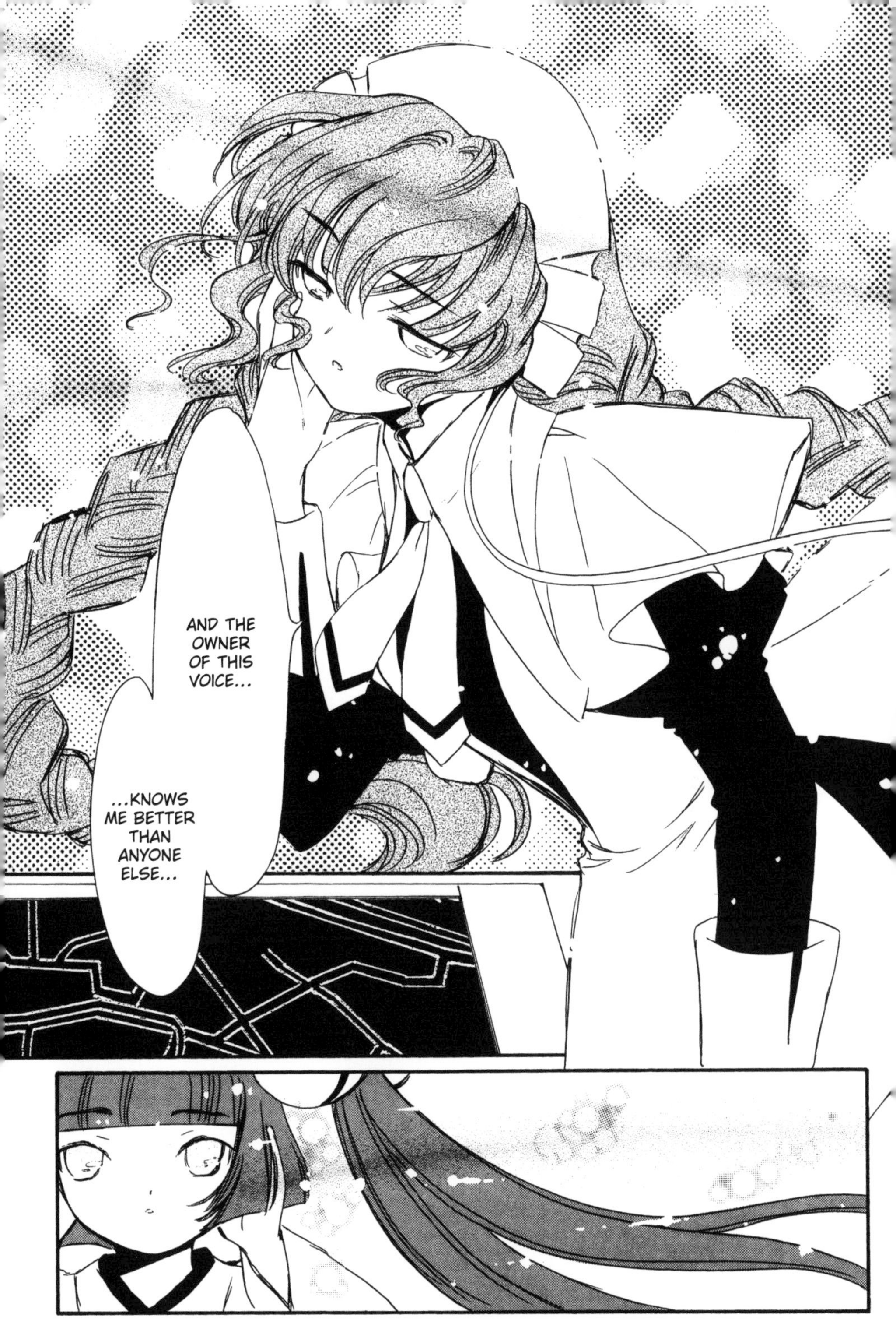
AND THE OWNER OF THIS VOICE...
...KNOWS ME BETTER THAN ANYONE ELSE...

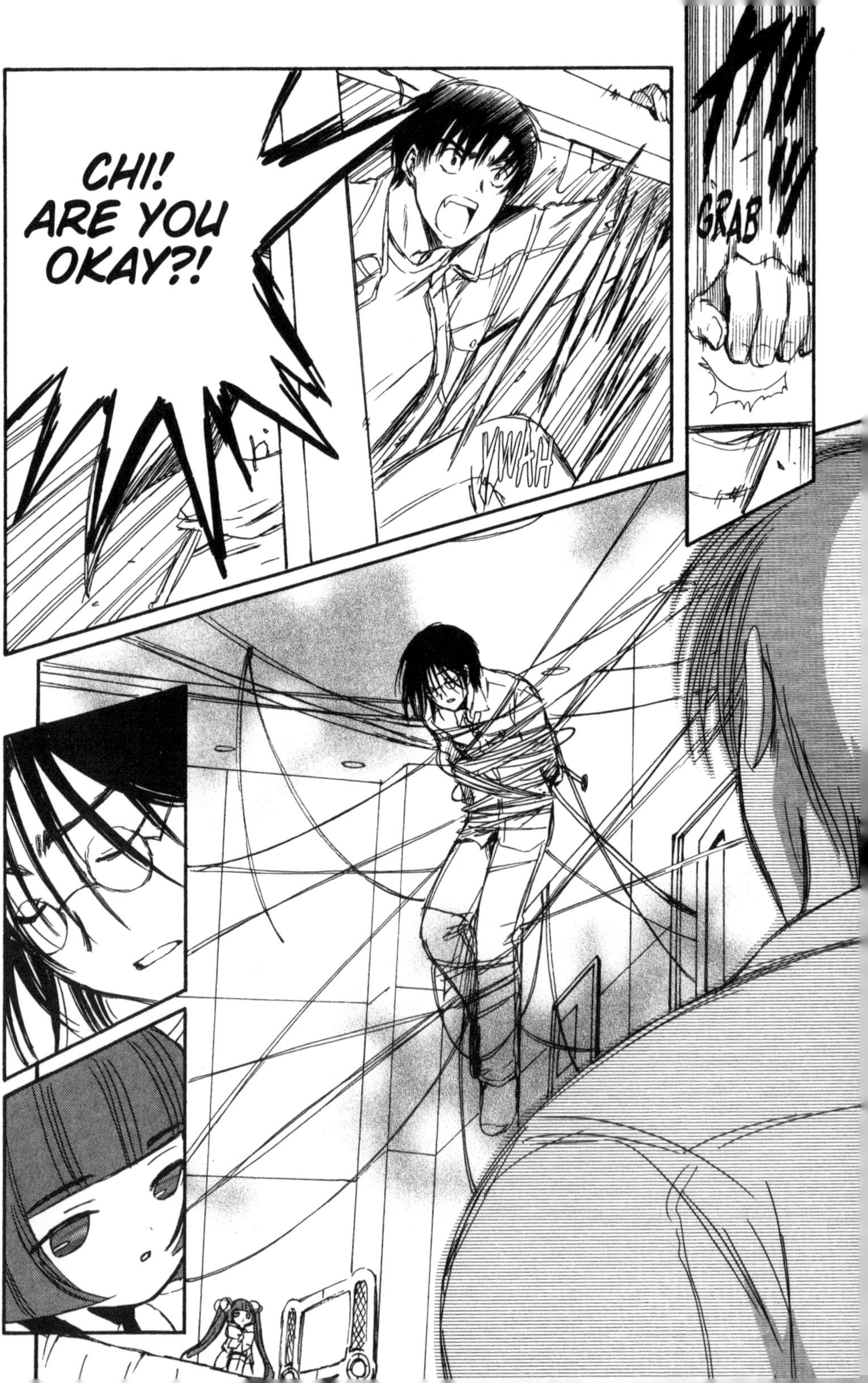
GRAB
CHI! ARE YOU OKAY?!
VWAH

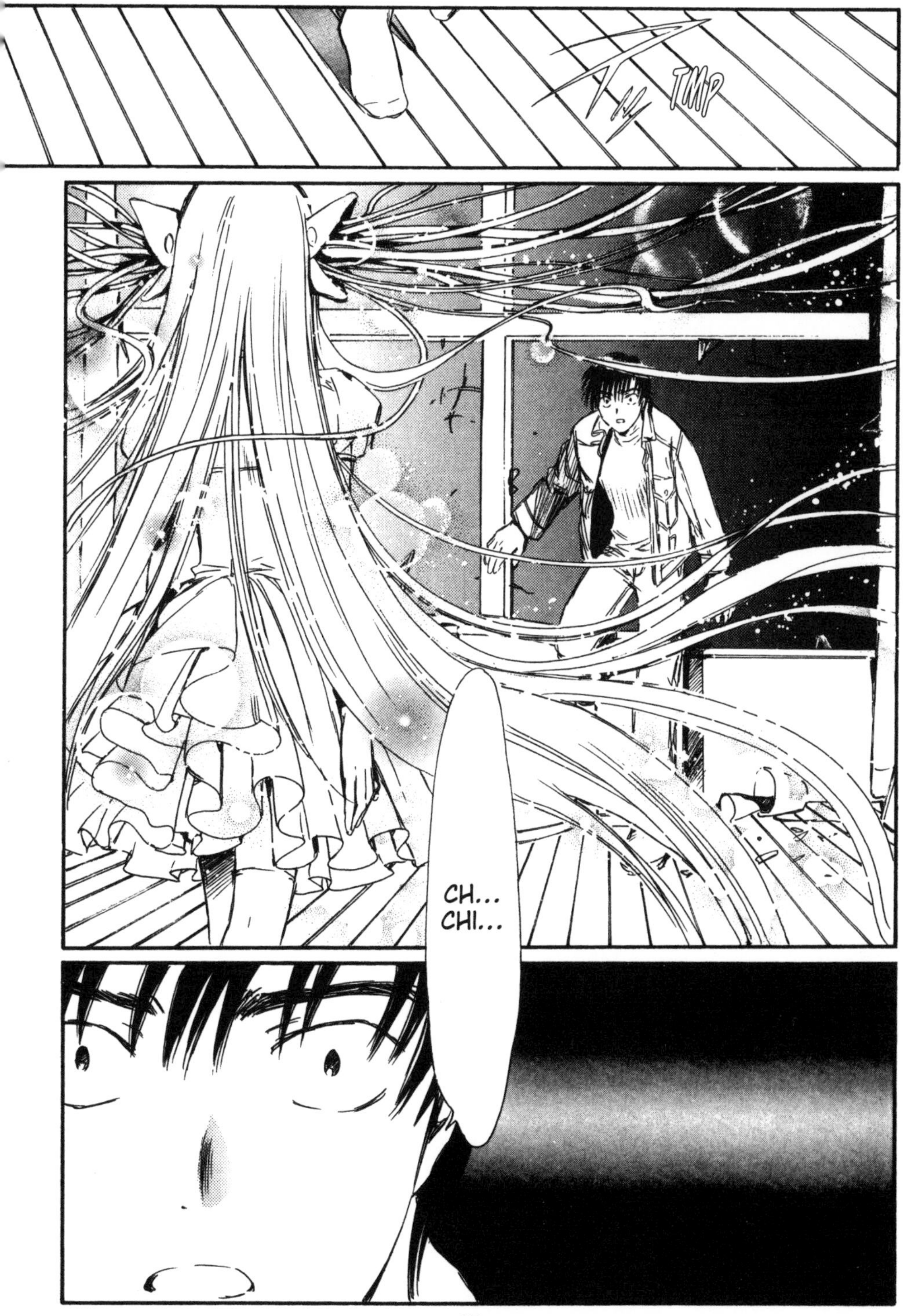
TMP
CH... CHI...

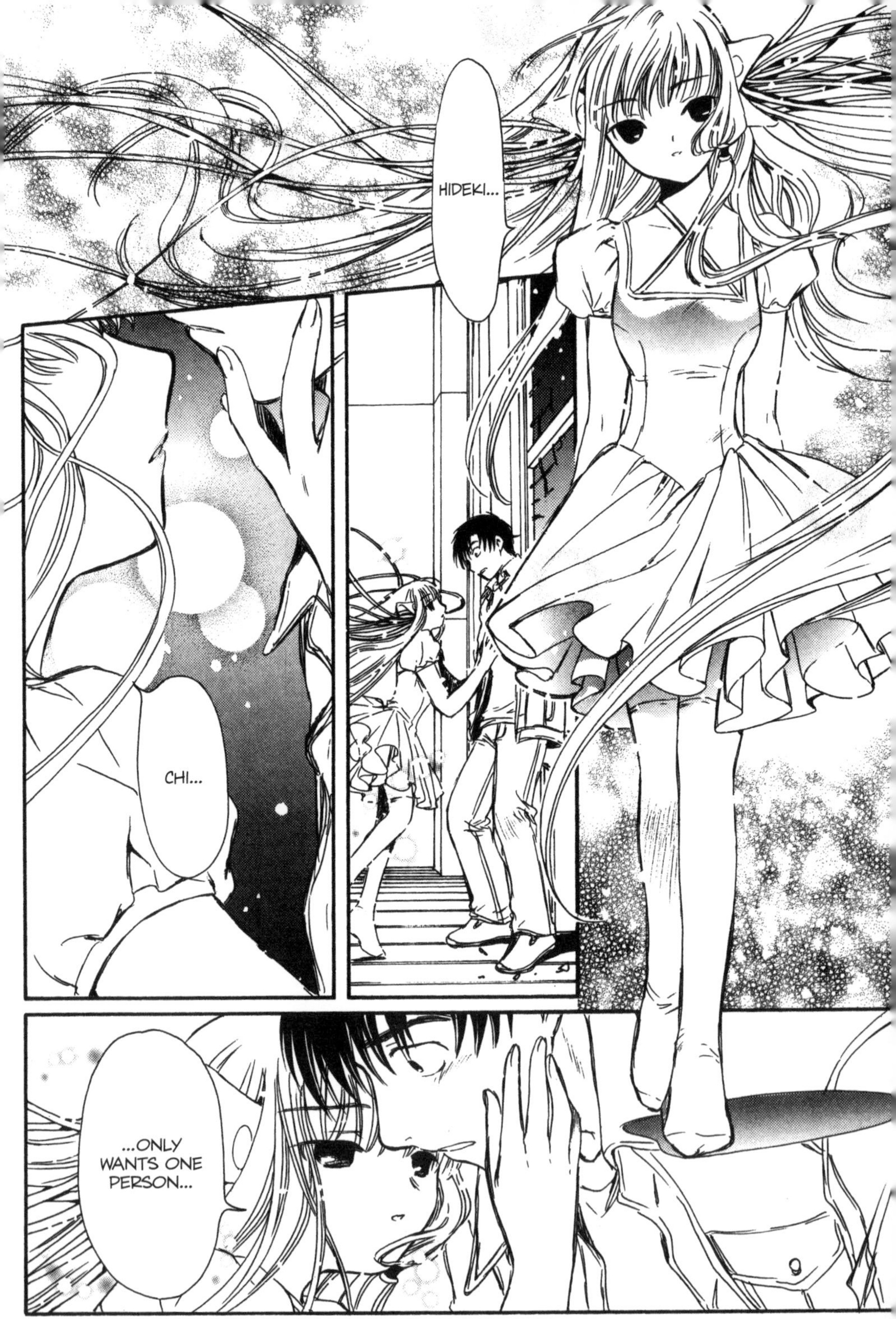
HIDEKI...
CHI...
...ONLY WANTS ONE PERSON...

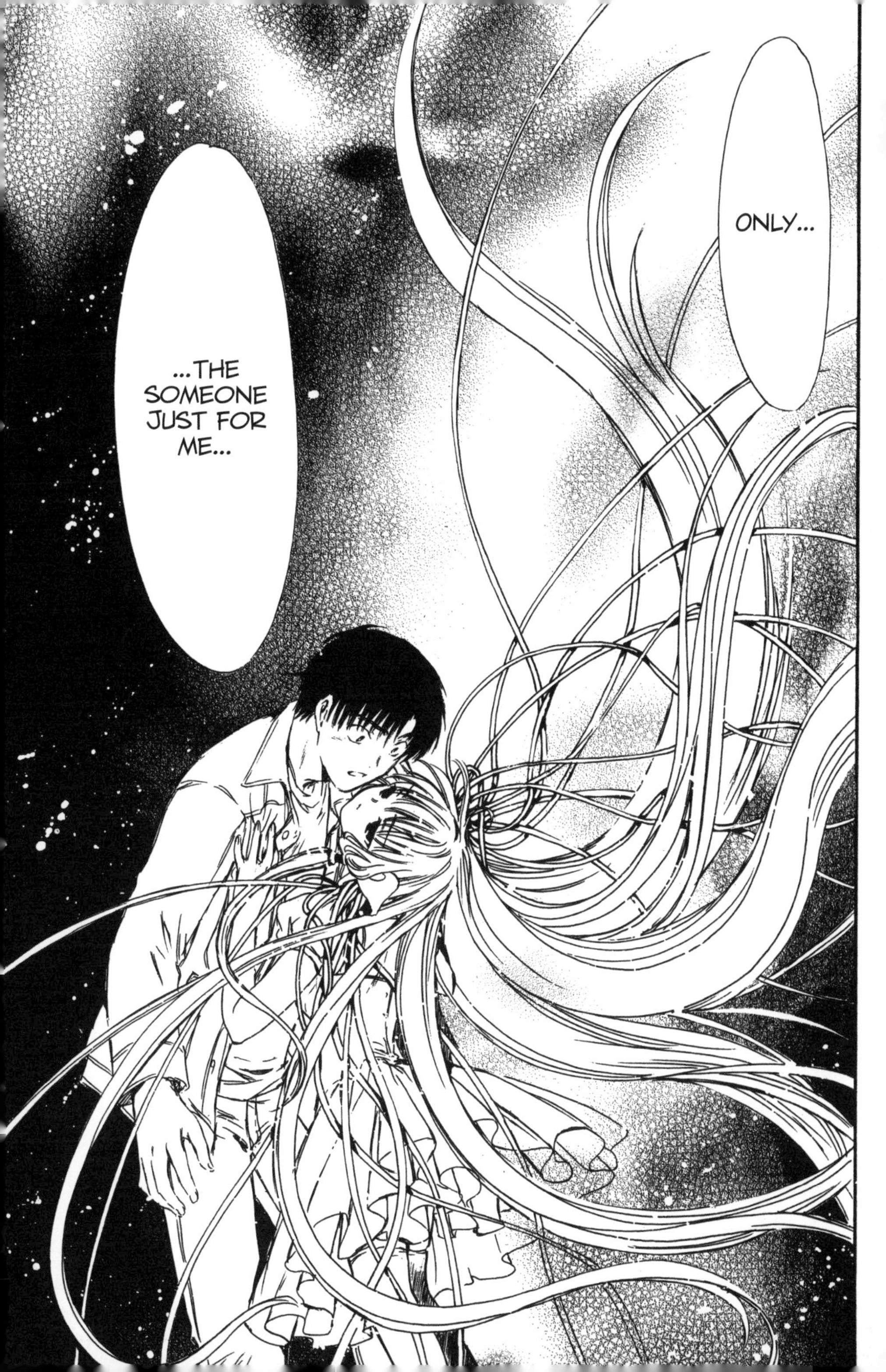
ONLY...
...THE SOMEONE JUST FOR ME...

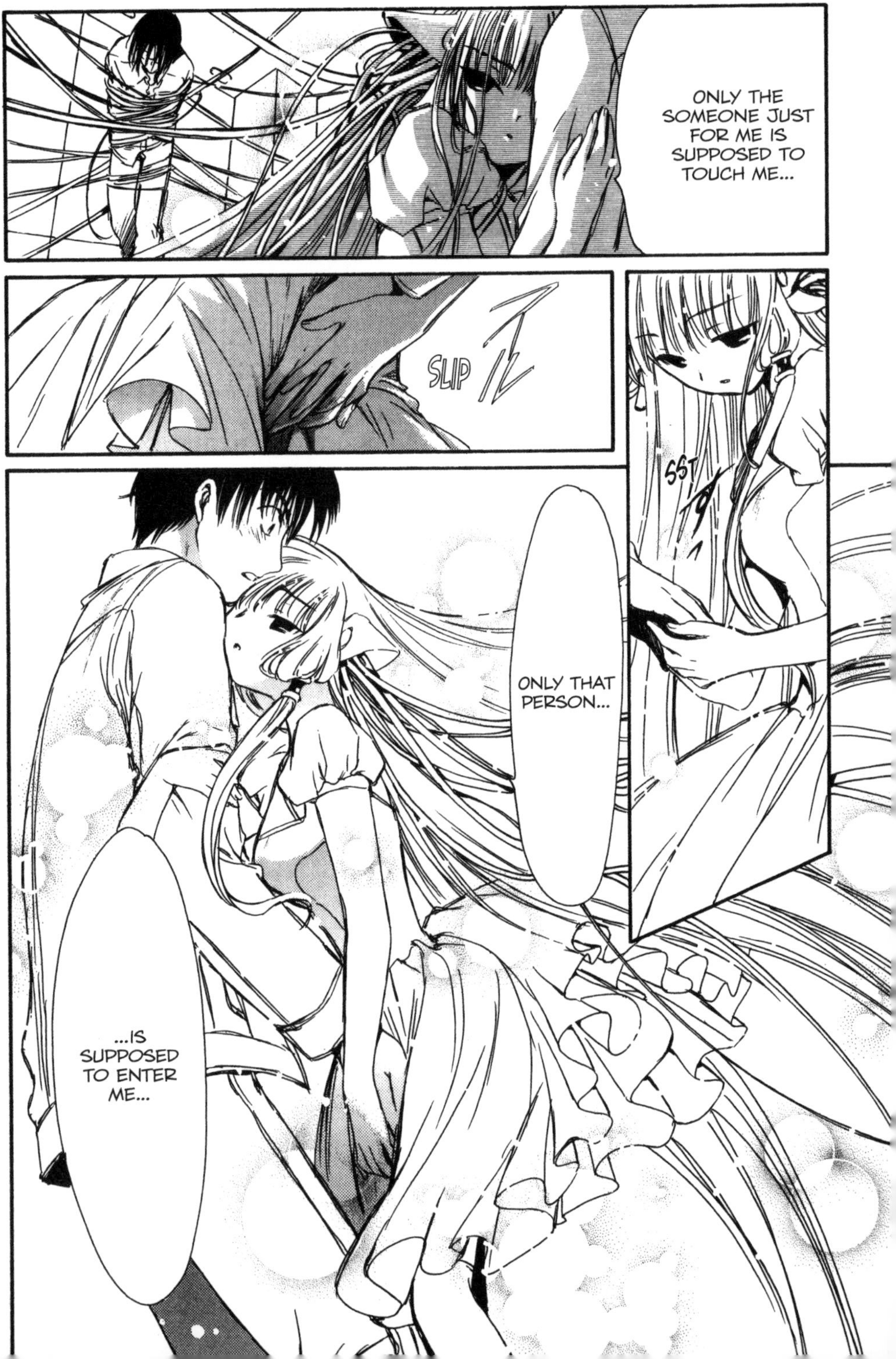
ONLY THE SOMEONE JUST FOR ME IS SUPPOSED TO TOUCH ME...
SST
SLIP
ONLY THAT PERSON...
...IS SUPPOSED TO ENTER ME...

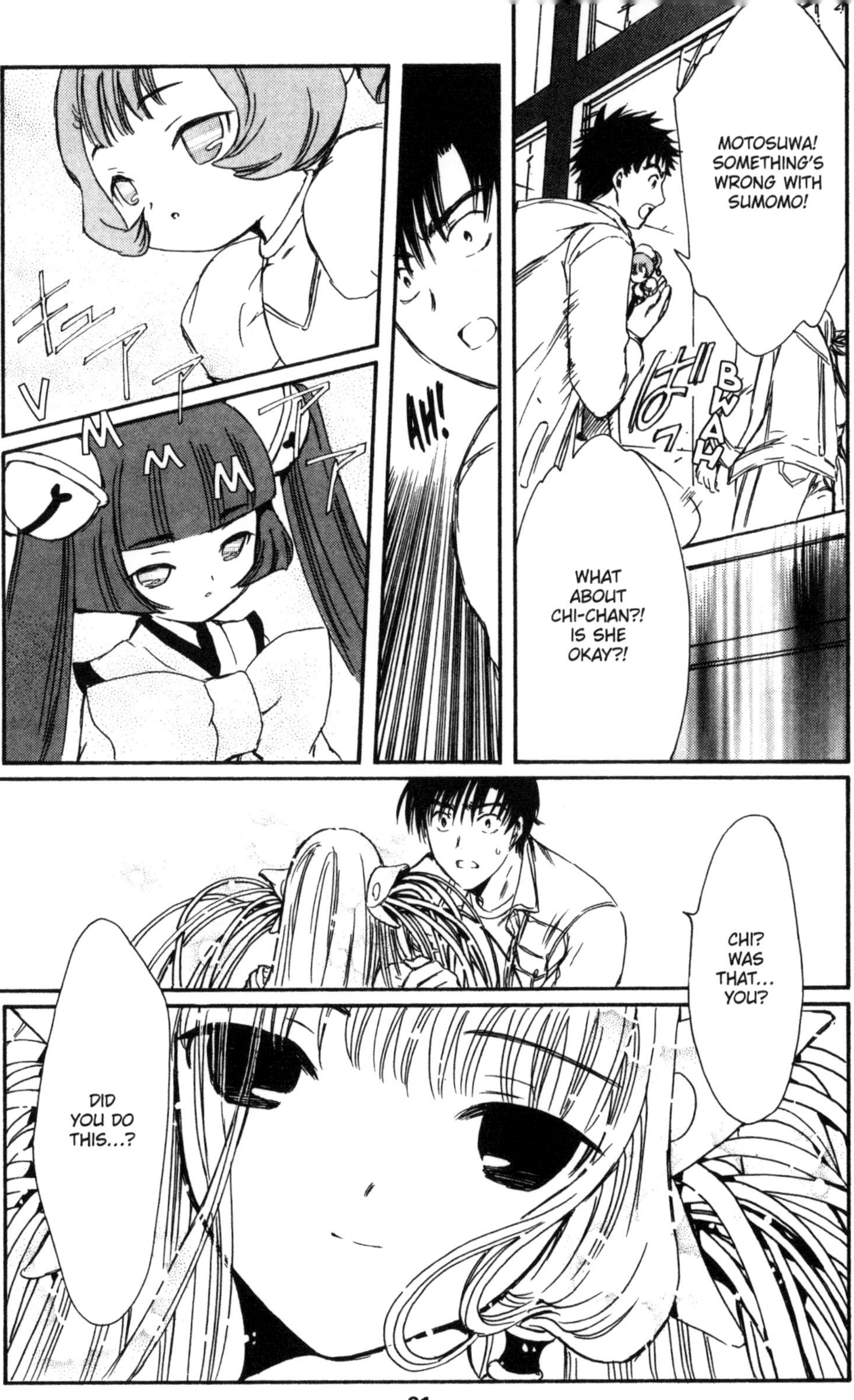
MOTOSUWA! SOMETHING'S WRONG WITH SUMOMO!
BWAH
WHAT ABOUT CHI-CHAN?! IS SHE OKAY?!
AH!
V
MMMM
CHI? WAS THAT... YOU?
DID YOU DO THIS...?

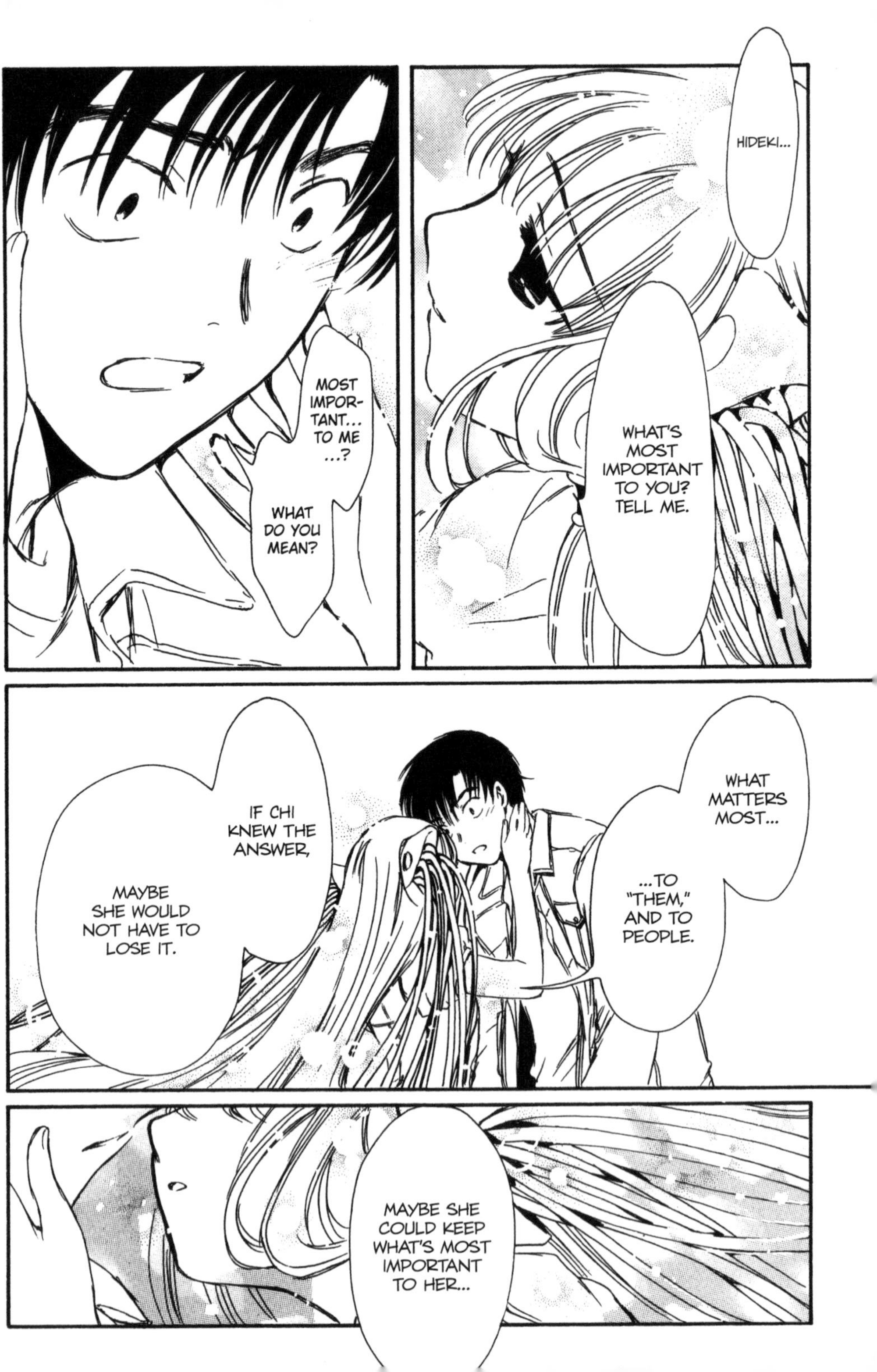
HIDEKI...
WHAT'S MOST IMPORTANT TO YOU? TELL ME.
MOST IMPOR-TANT... TO ME ...?
WHAT DO YOU MEAN?
WHAT MATTERS MOST...
...TO "THEM," AND TO PEOPLE.
IF CHI KNEW THE ANSWER,
MAYBE SHE WOULD NOT HAVE TO LOSE IT.
MAYBE SHE COULD KEEP WHAT'S MOST IMPORTANT TO HER...

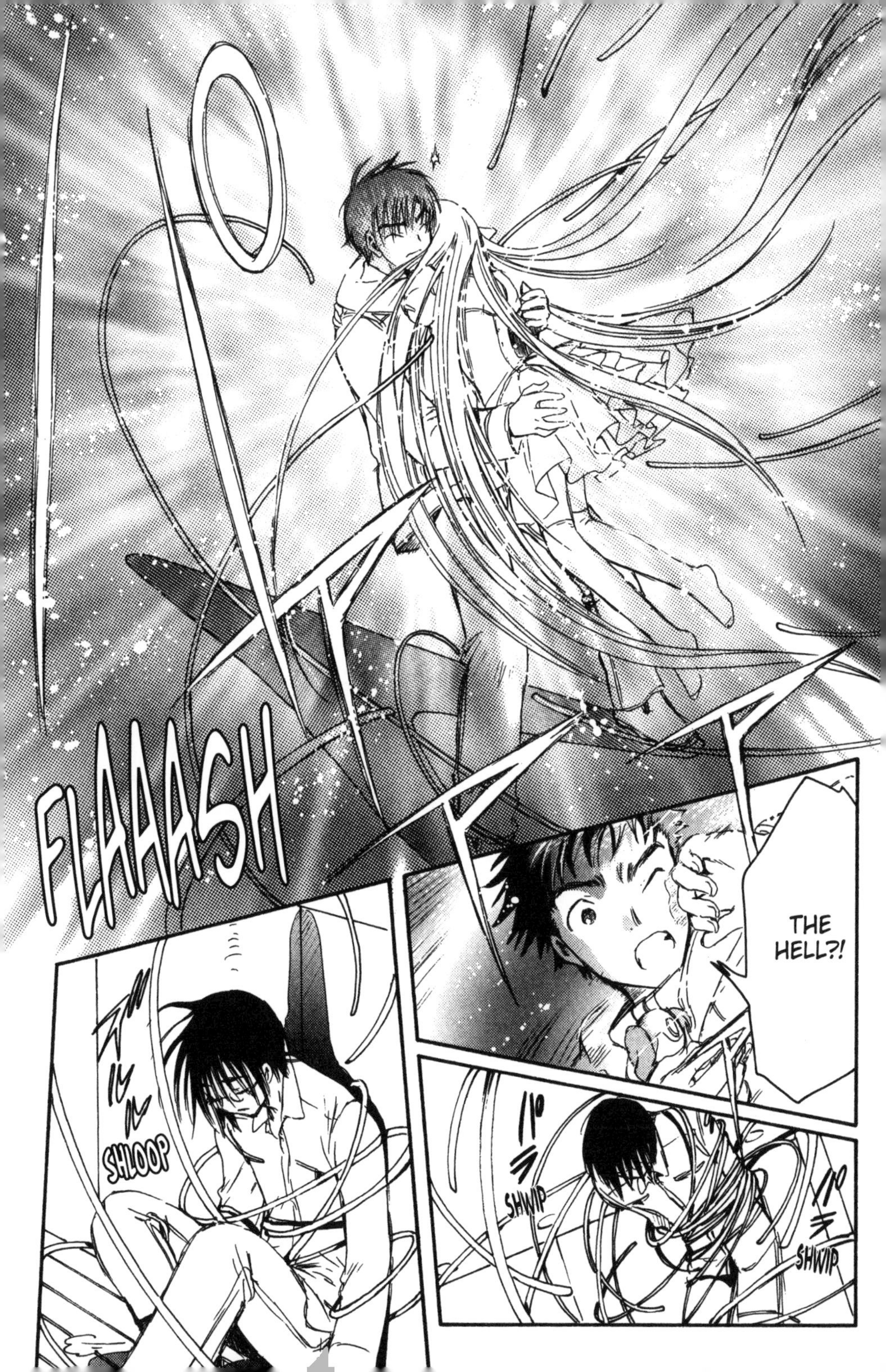
FLAAASH
THE HELL?!
パラ
SHWIP
パラ
SHWIP
ズルル
SHLOOP

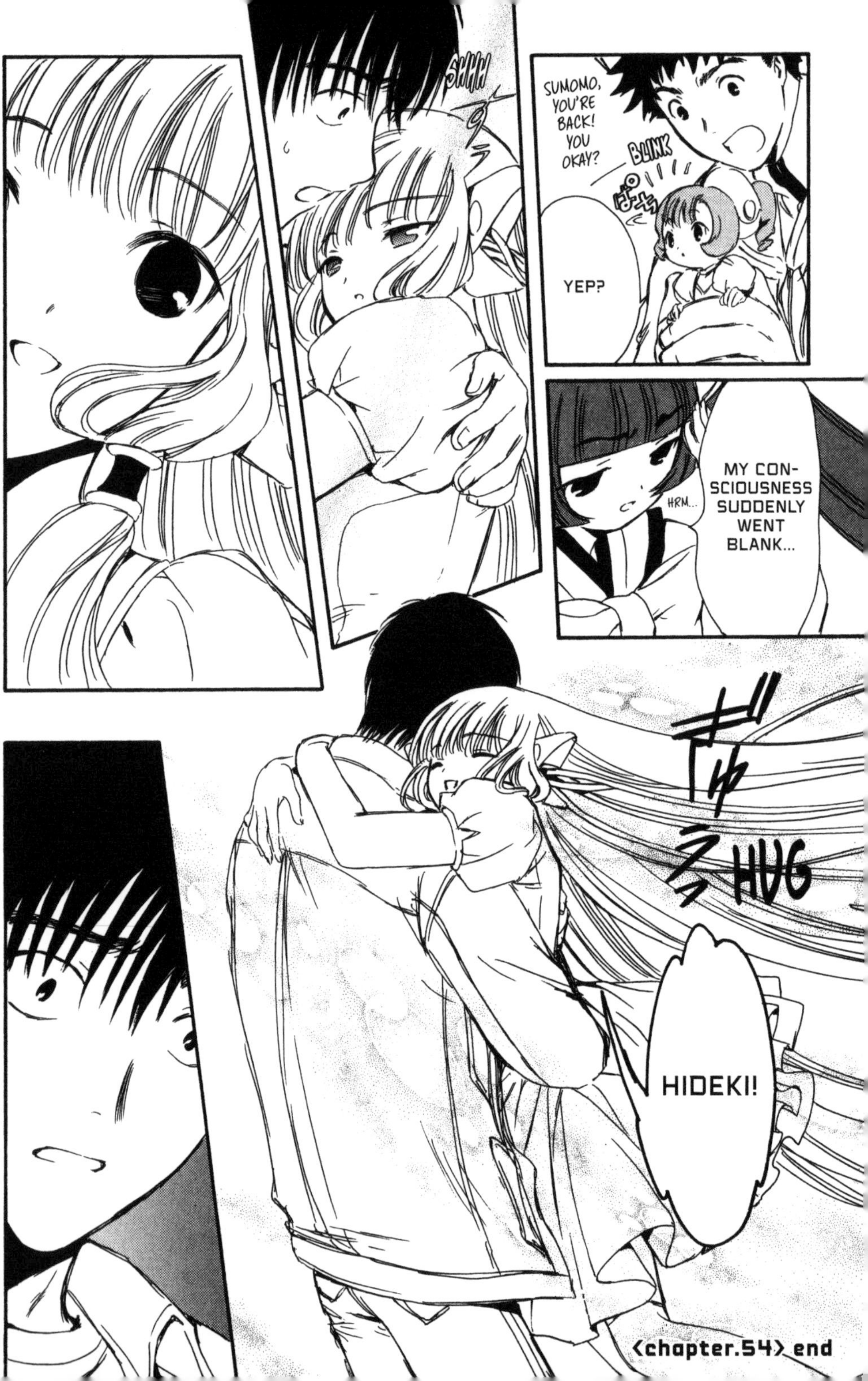
SUMOMO, YOU'RE BACK! YOU OKAY?
BLINK
YEP?
HRM...
MY CON-SCIOUSNESS SUDDENLY WENT BLANK...
SHHH
HUG
HIDEKI!
‹chapter.54› end

〈chapter.55〉

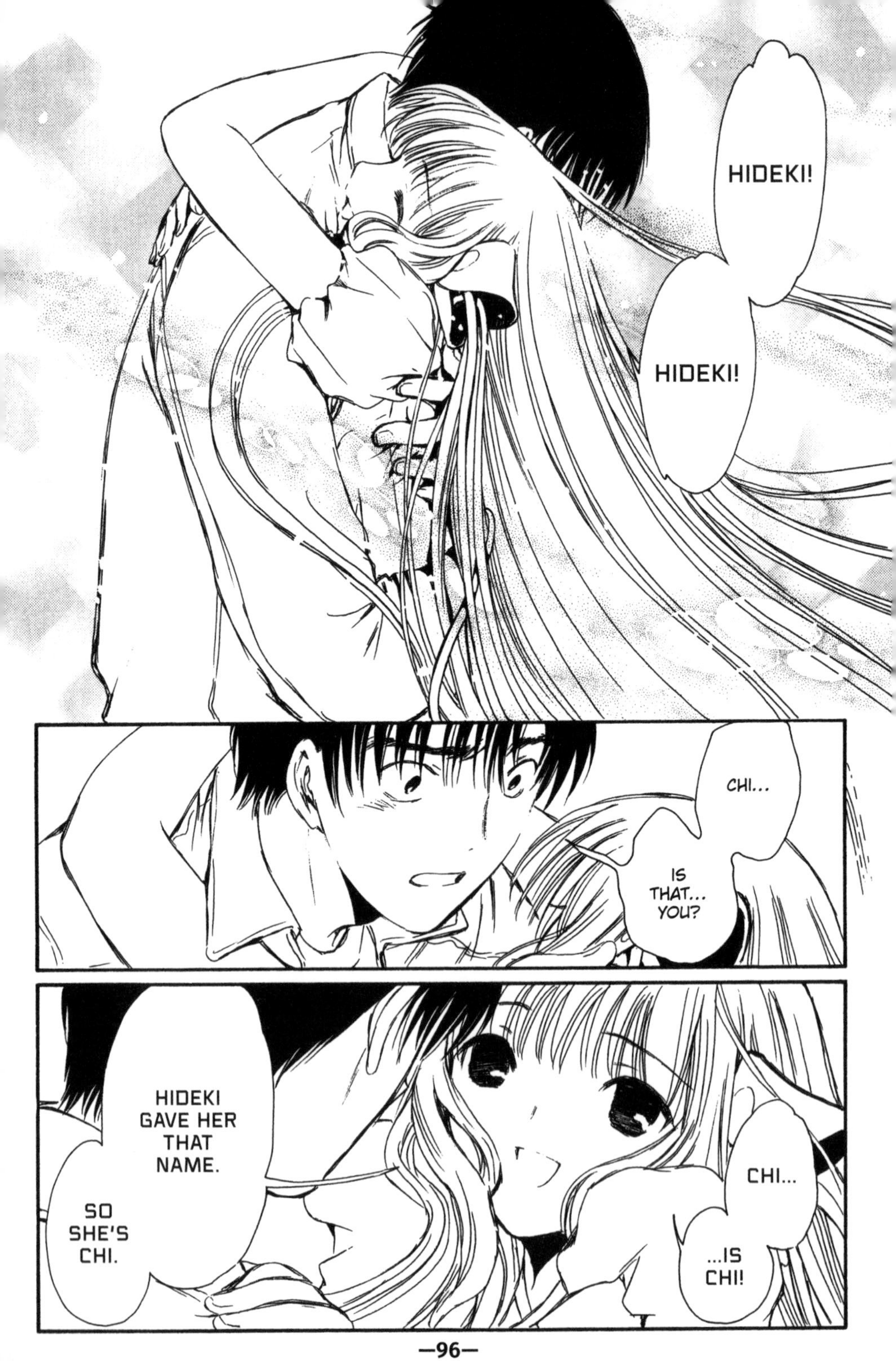
HIDEKI!
HIDEKI!
CHI...
IS THAT... YOU?
CHI...
...IS CHI!
HIDEKI GAVE HER THAT NAME.
SO SHE'S CHI.

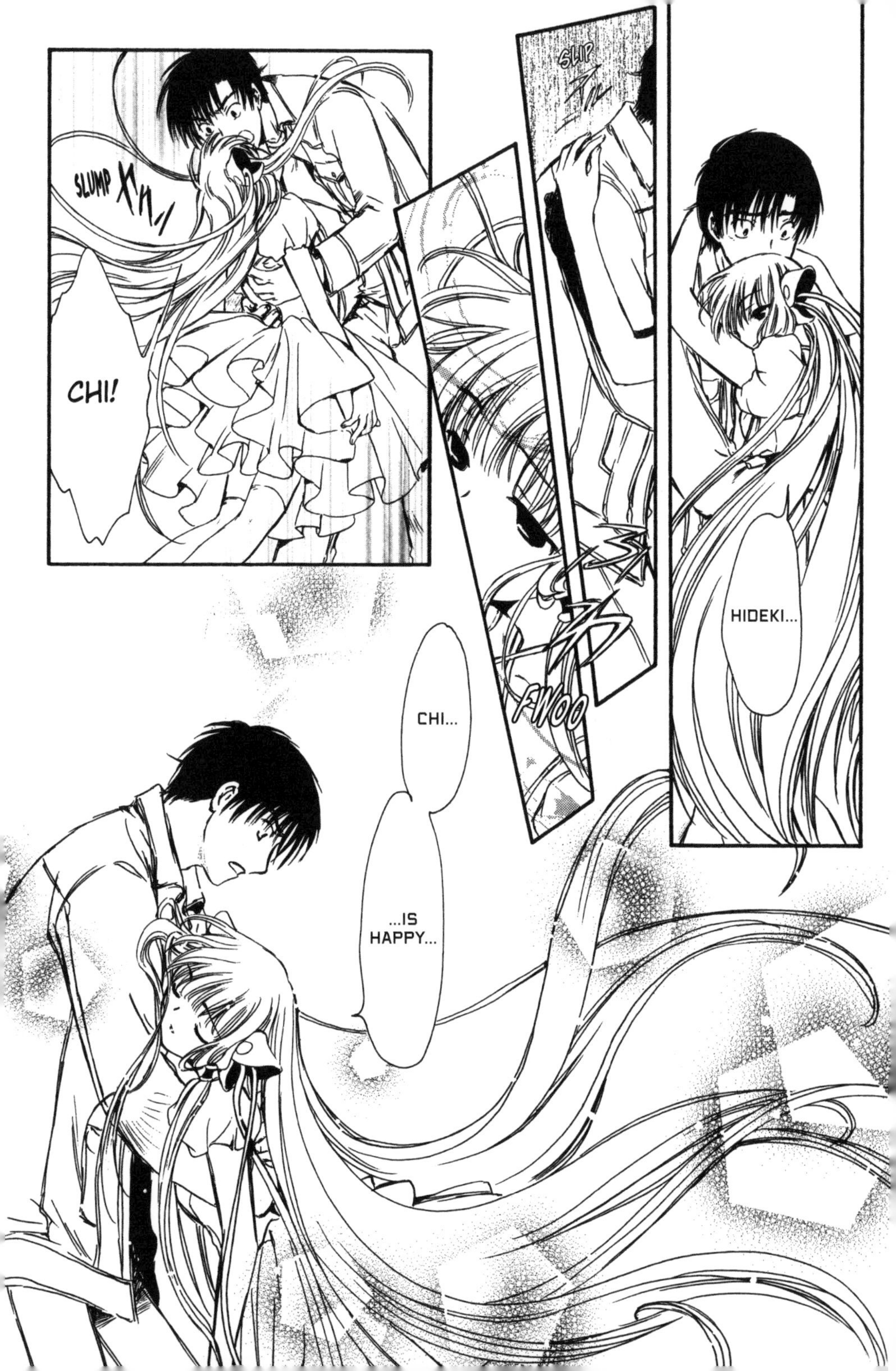
HIDEKI...
SLIP
FWOO
SLUMP
CHI!
CHI...
...IS HAPPY...

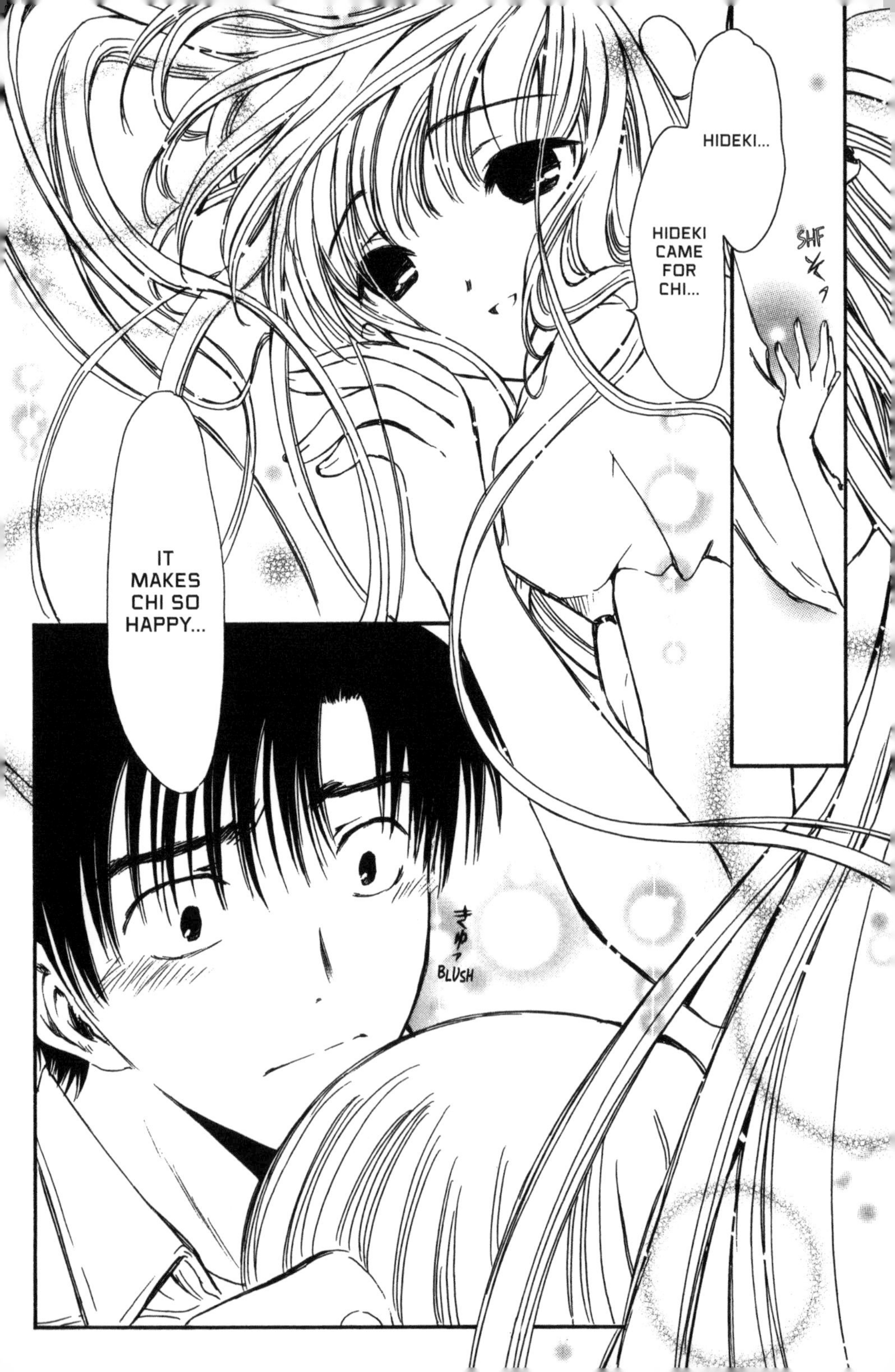
HIDEKI...
HIDEKI CAME FOR CHI...
SHF
IT MAKES CHI SO HAPPY...
BLUSH

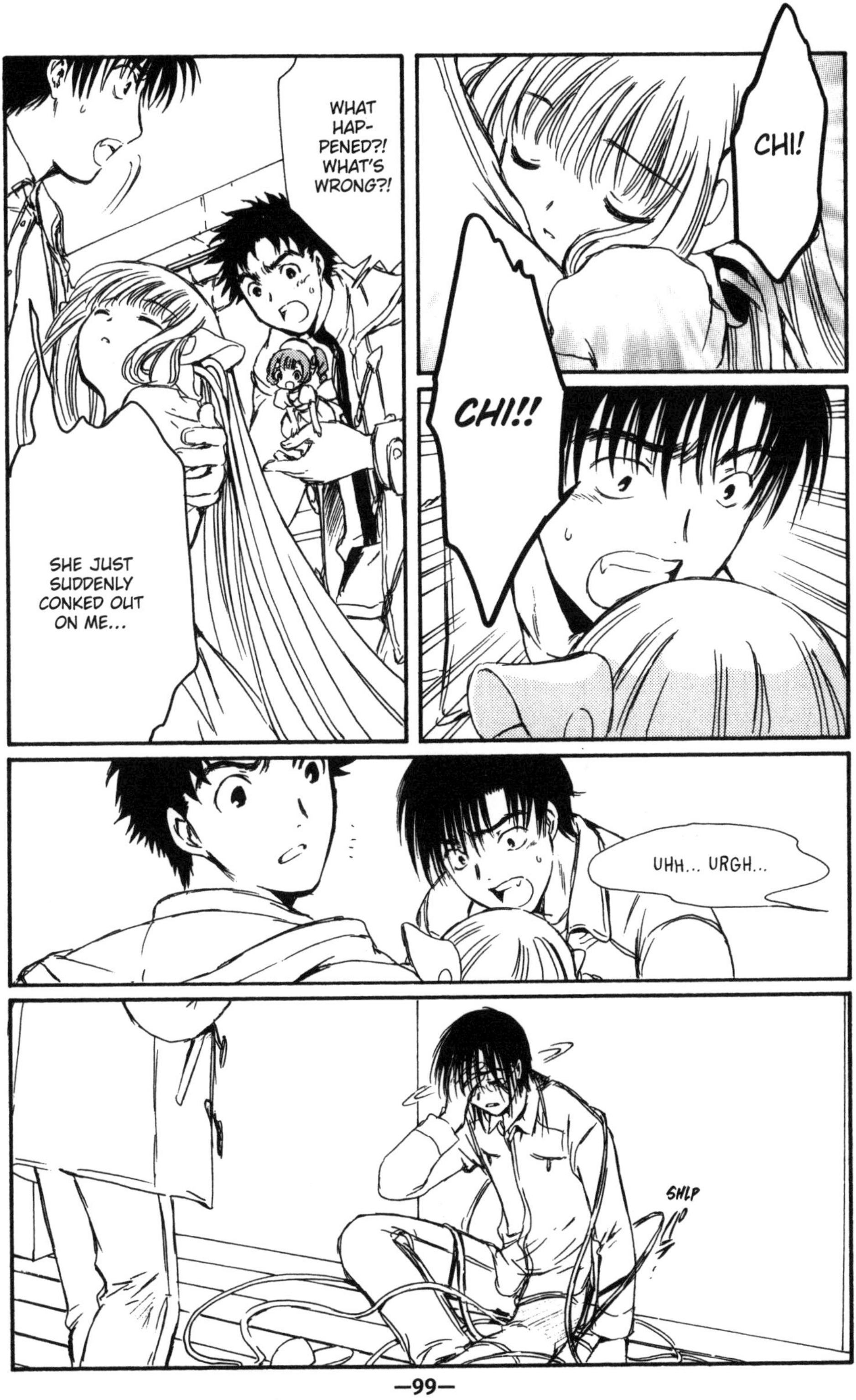
CHI!
CHI!!
WHAT HAP-PENED?! WHAT'S WRONG?!
SHE JUST SUDDENLY CONKED OUT ON ME...
UHH... URGH...
SHLP

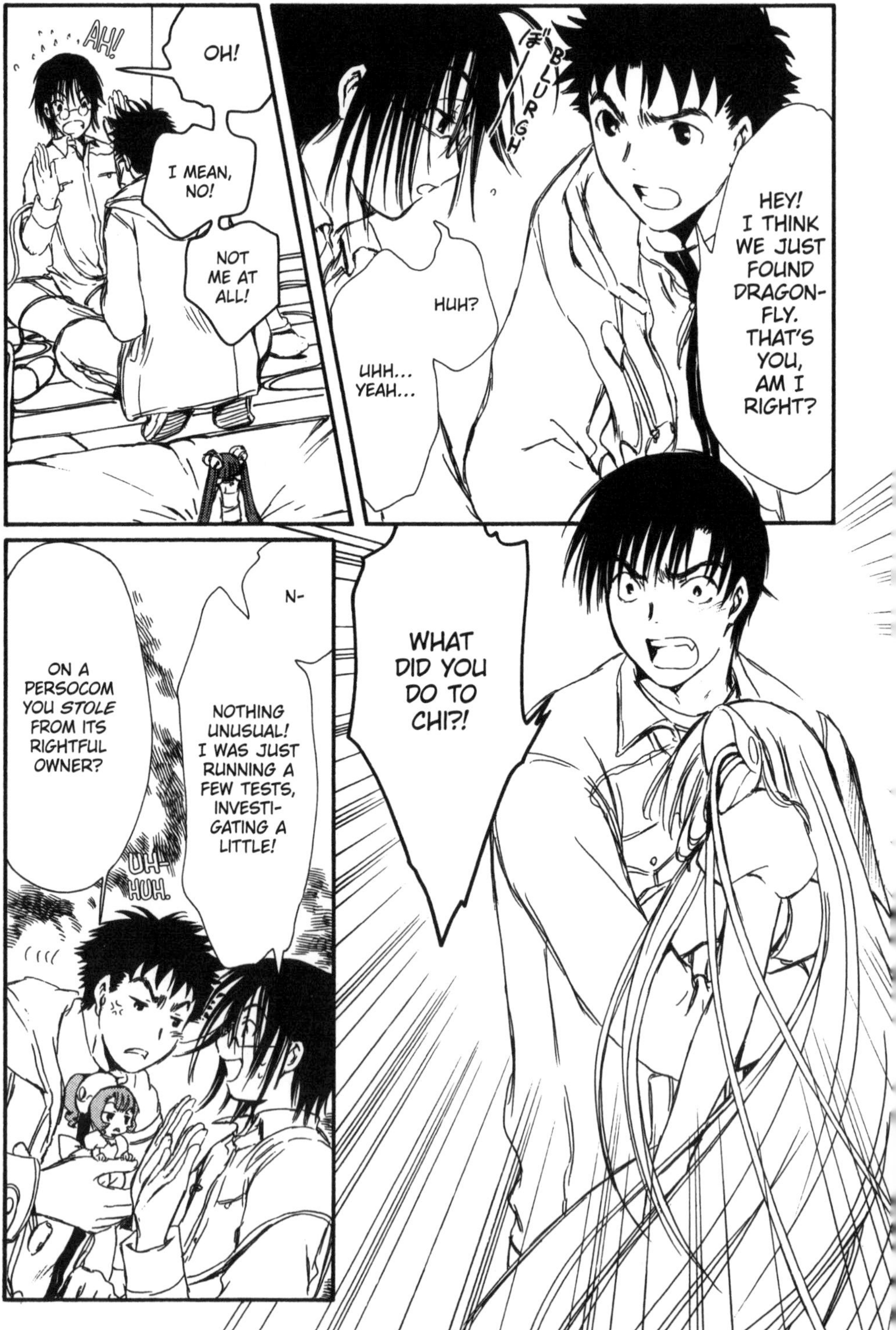
HEY! I THINK WE JUST FOUND DRAGON-FLY. THAT'S YOU, AM I RIGHT?
ぼ BLURGH
HUH?
UHH... YEAH...
OH!
AH!
I MEAN, NO!
NOT ME AT ALL!
WHAT DID YOU DO TO CHI?!
N-
NOTHING UNUSUAL! I WAS JUST RUNNING A FEW TESTS, INVESTI-GATING A LITTLE!
ON A PERSOCOM YOU *STOLE* FROM ITS RIGHTFUL OWNER?
UH-HUH.

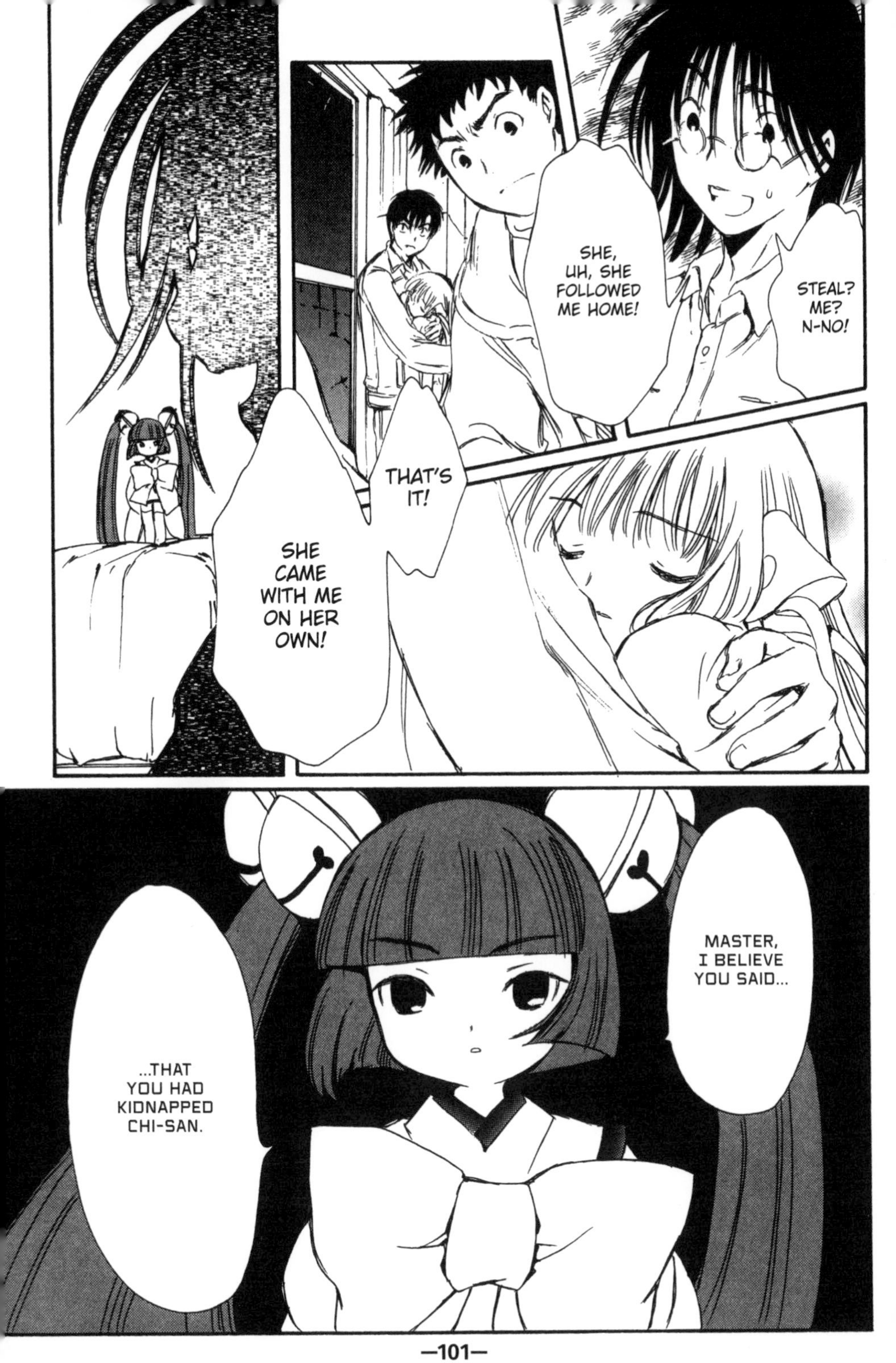
STEAL? ME? N-NO!
SHE, UH, SHE FOLLOWED ME HOME!
THAT'S IT!
SHE CAME WITH ME ON HER OWN!
MASTER, I BELIEVE YOU SAID...
...THAT YOU HAD KIDNAPPED CHI-SAN.

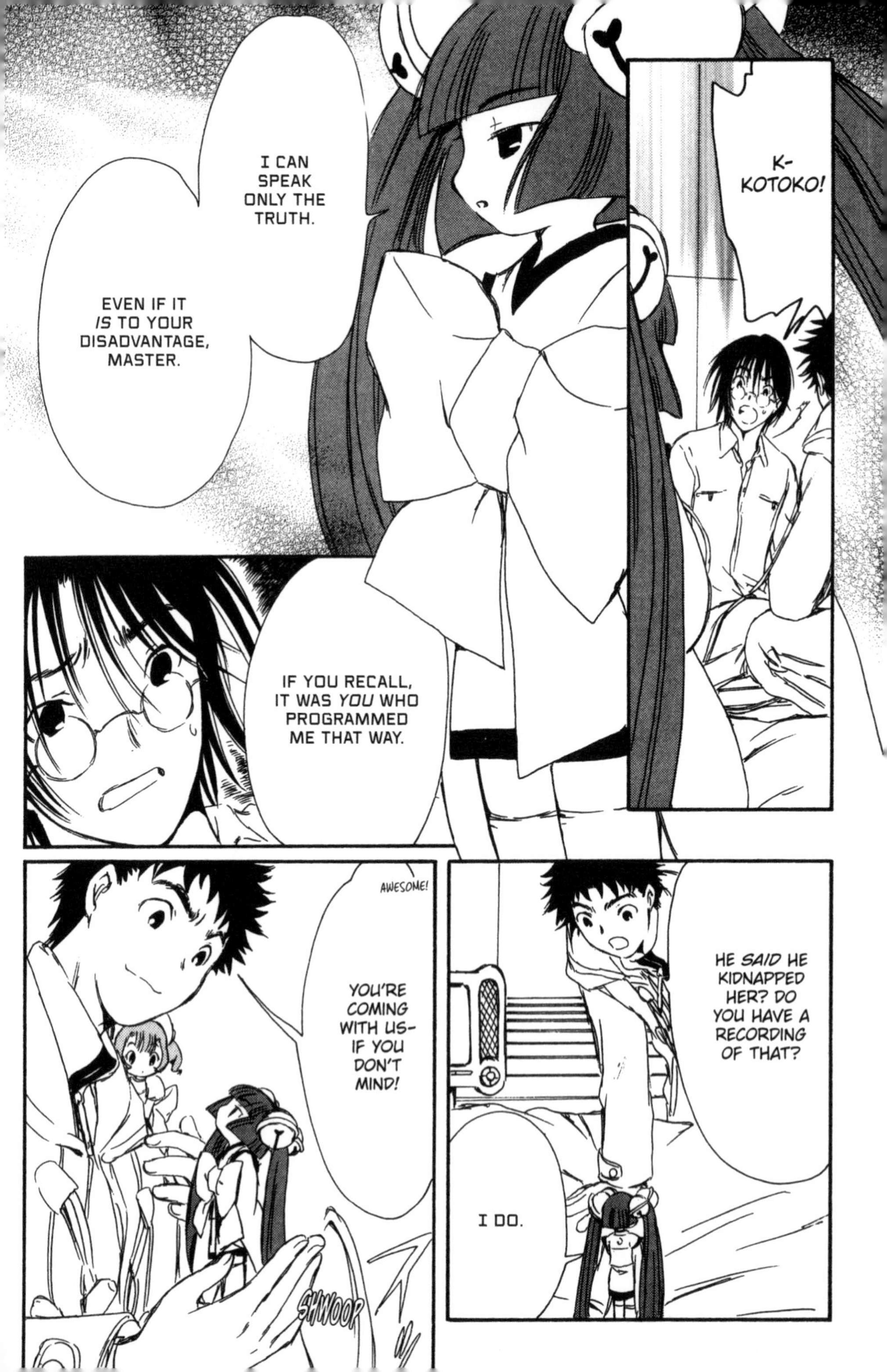
K-KOTOKO!
I CAN SPEAK ONLY THE TRUTH.
EVEN IF IT *IS* TO YOUR DISADVANTAGE, MASTER.
IF YOU RECALL, IT WAS *YOU* WHO PROGRAMMED ME THAT WAY.
HE *SAID* HE KIDNAPPED HER? DO YOU HAVE A RECORDING OF THAT?
I DO.
AWESOME!
YOU'RE COMING WITH US- IF YOU DON'T MIND!
SHWOOP

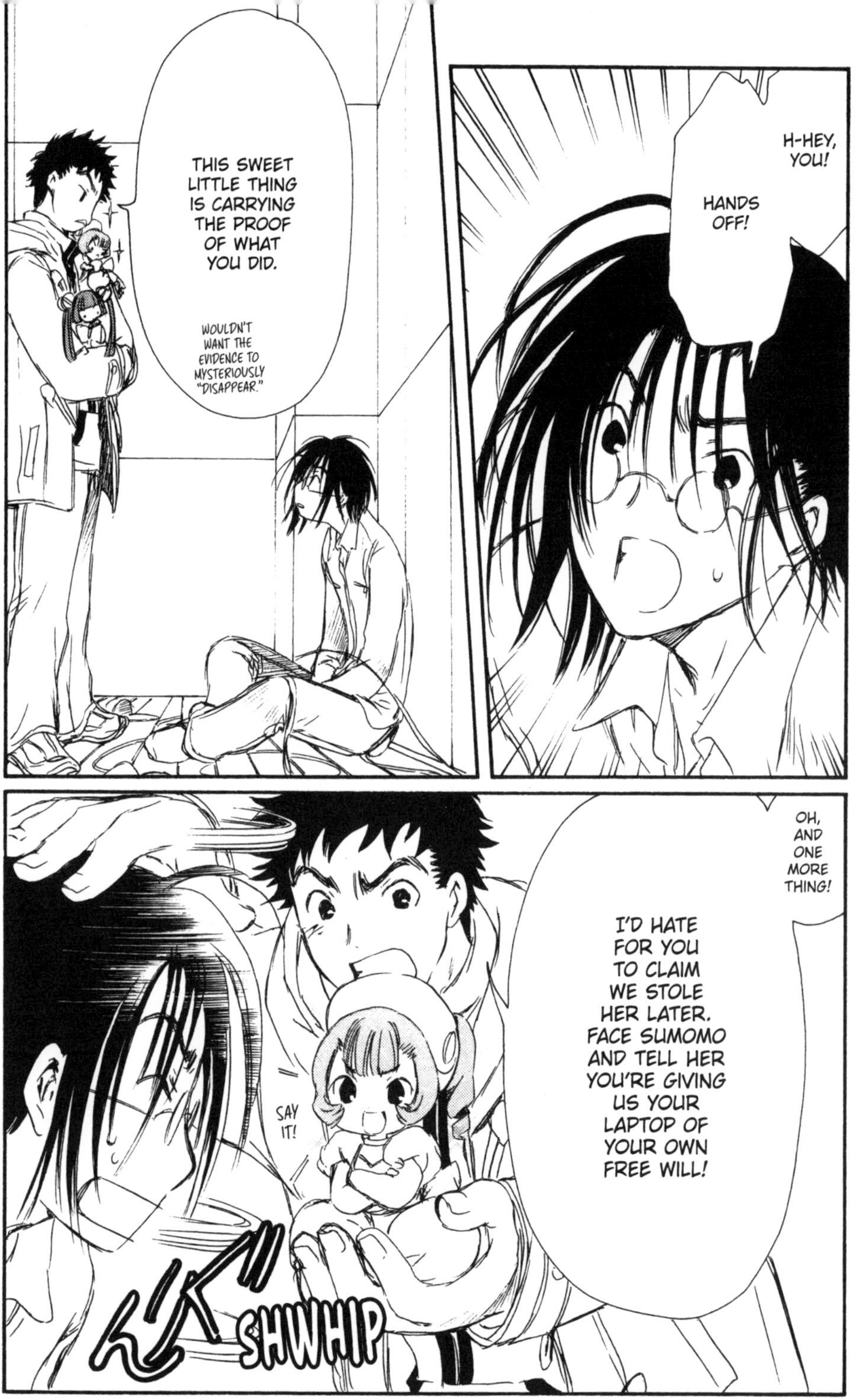
H-HEY, YOU!
HANDS OFF!
THIS SWEET LITTLE THING IS CARRYING THE PROOF OF WHAT YOU DID.
WOULDN'T WANT THE EVIDENCE TO MYSTERIOUSLY "DISAPPEAR."
OH, AND ONE MORE THING!
I'D HATE FOR YOU TO CLAIM WE STOLE HER LATER. FACE SUMOMO AND TELL HER YOU'RE GIVING US YOUR LAPTOP OF YOUR OWN FREE WILL!
SAY IT!
SHWHIP

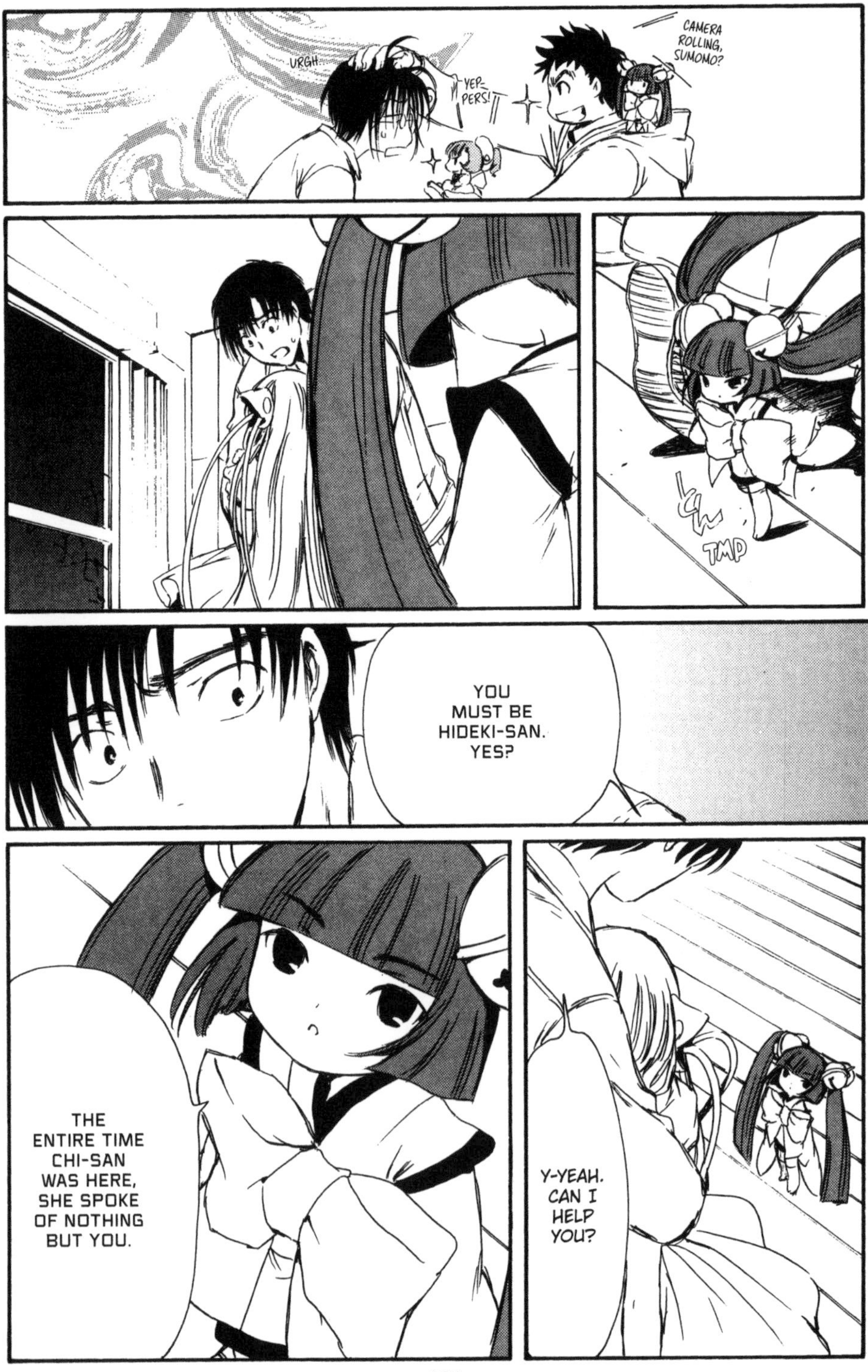
CAMERA ROLLING, SUMOMO?
YEP-PERS!
URGH...
TMP
YOU MUST BE HIDEKI-SAN. YES?
Y-YEAH. CAN I HELP YOU?
THE ENTIRE TIME CHI-SAN WAS HERE, SHE SPOKE OF NOTHING BUT YOU.

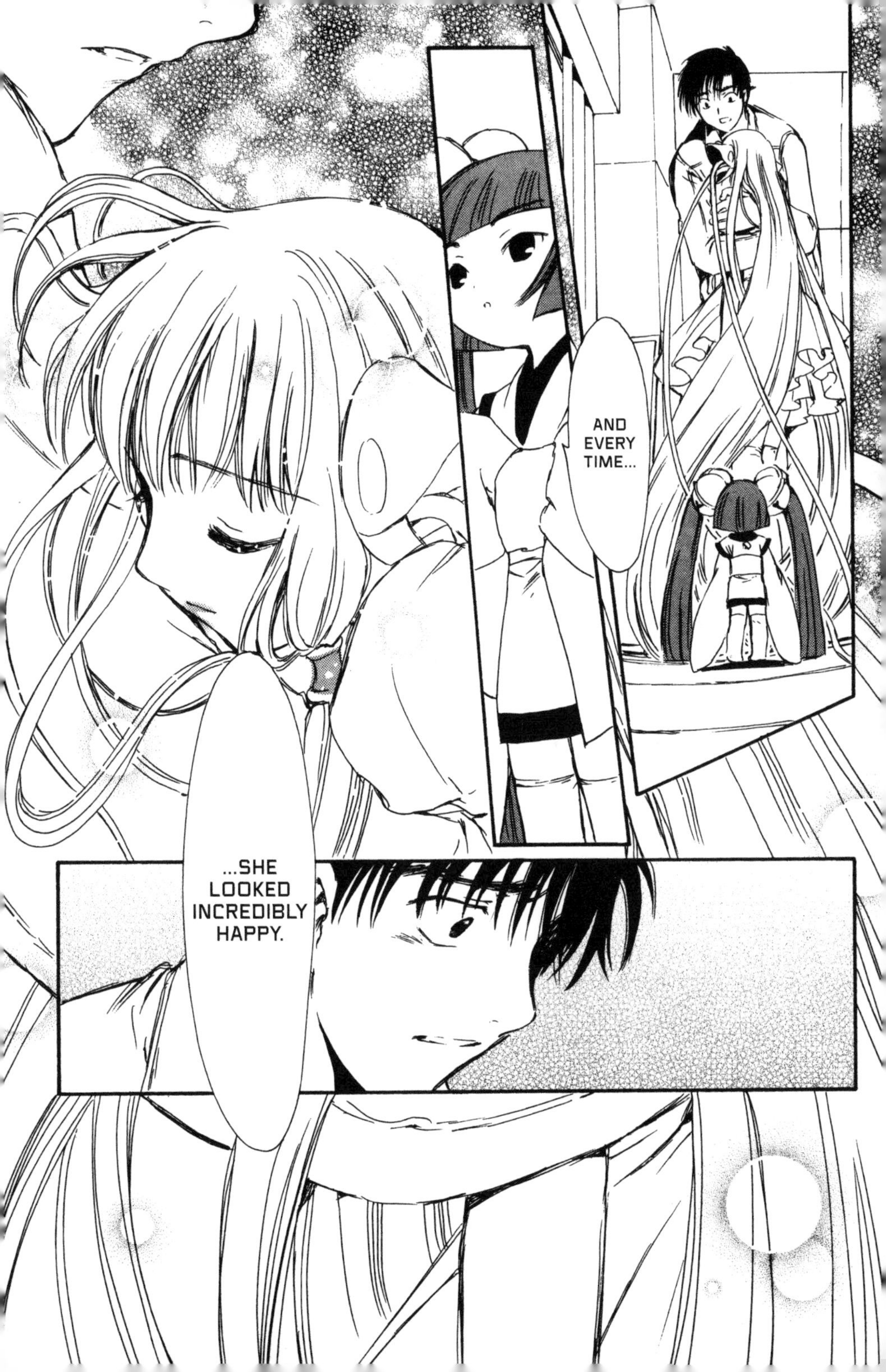
AND EVERY TIME...
...SHE LOOKED INCREDIBLY HAPPY.

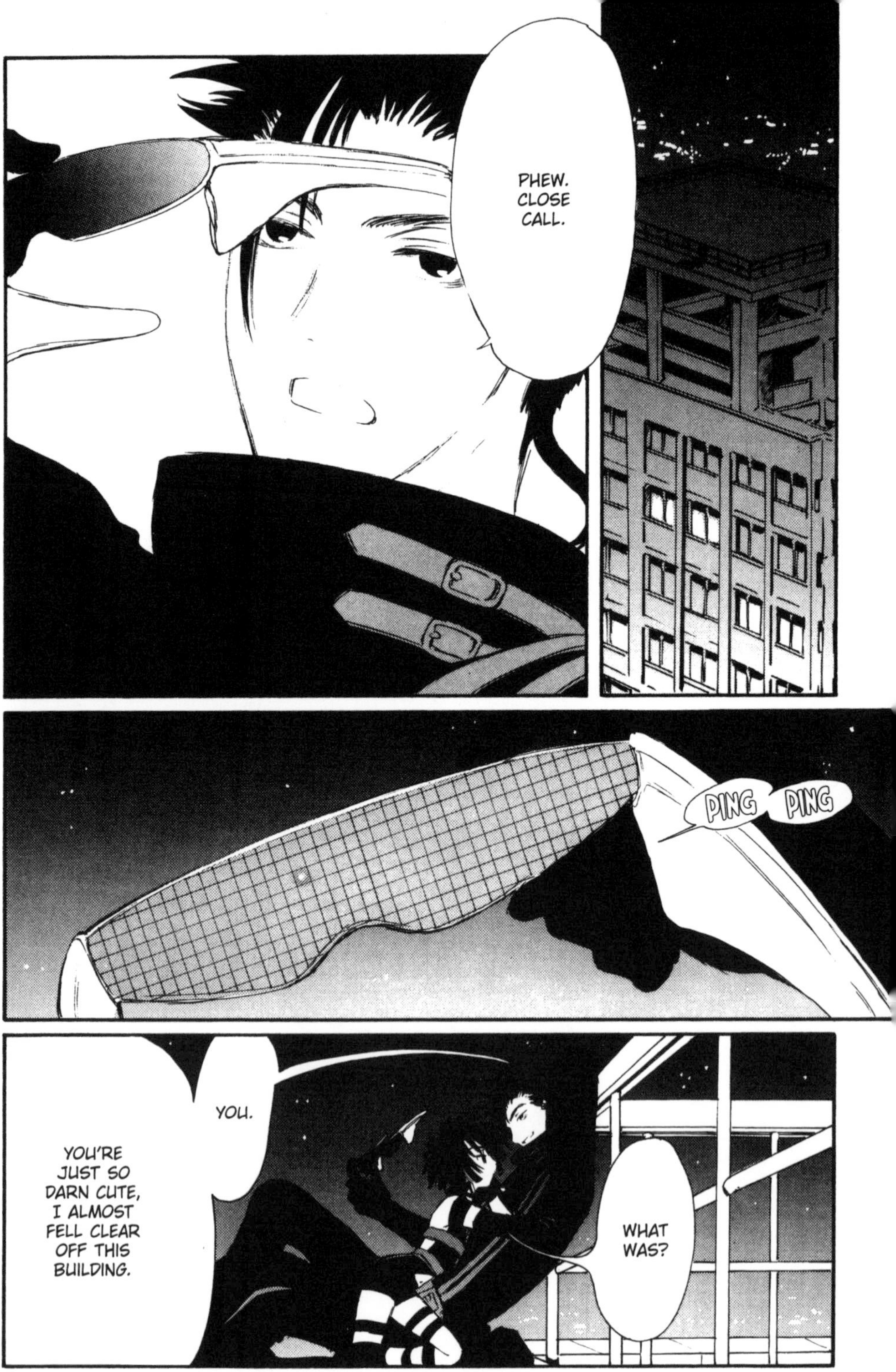
PHEW. CLOSE CALL.
PING PING
WHAT WAS?
YOU.
YOU'RE JUST SO DARN CUTE, I ALMOST FELL CLEAR OFF THIS BUILDING.

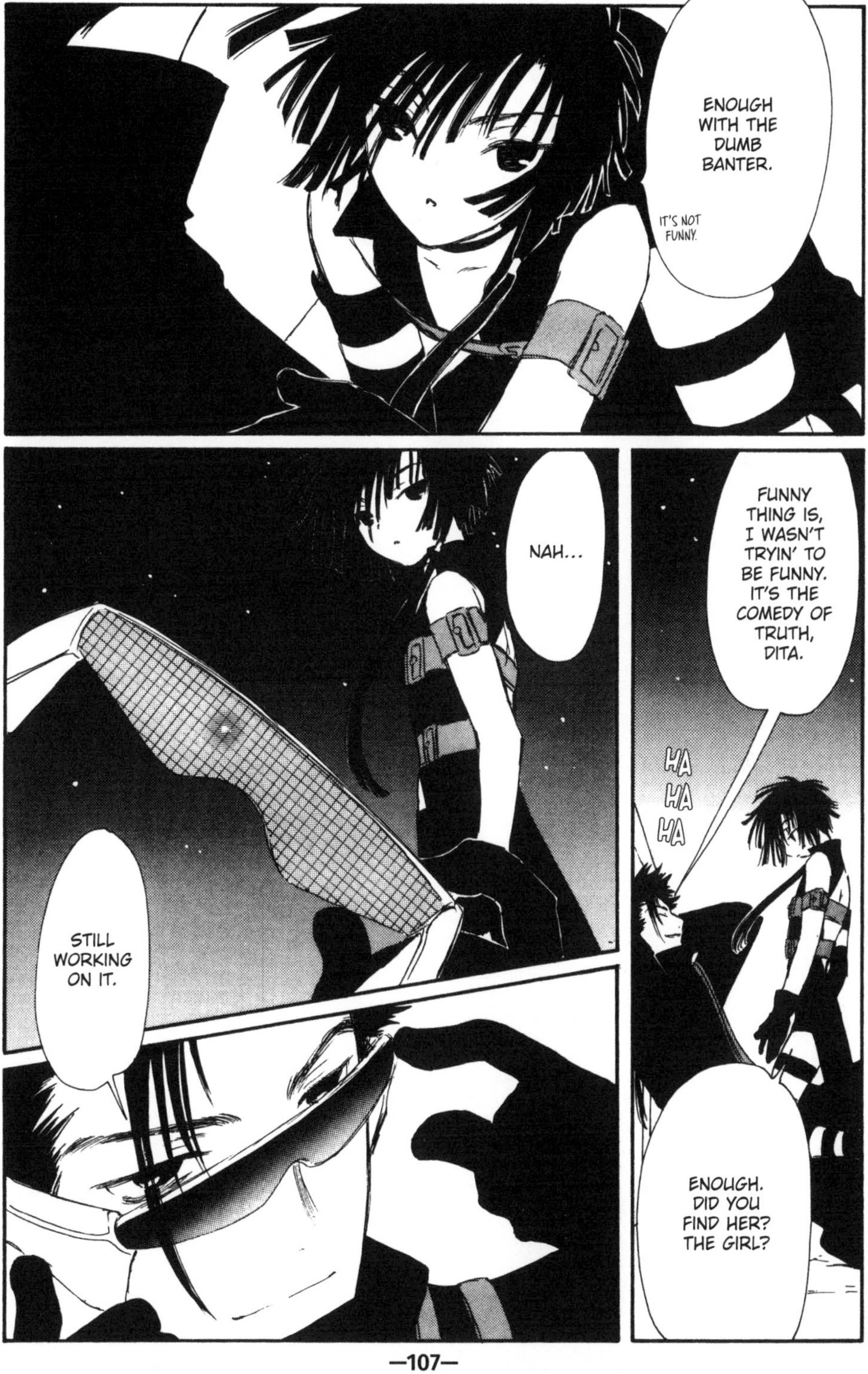
ENOUGH WITH THE DUMB BANTER.
IT'S NOT FUNNY.
FUNNY THING IS, I WASN'T TRYIN' TO BE FUNNY. IT'S THE COMEDY OF TRUTH, DITA.
HA HA HA
ENOUGH. DID YOU FIND HER? THE GIRL?
NAH...
STILL WORKING ON IT.

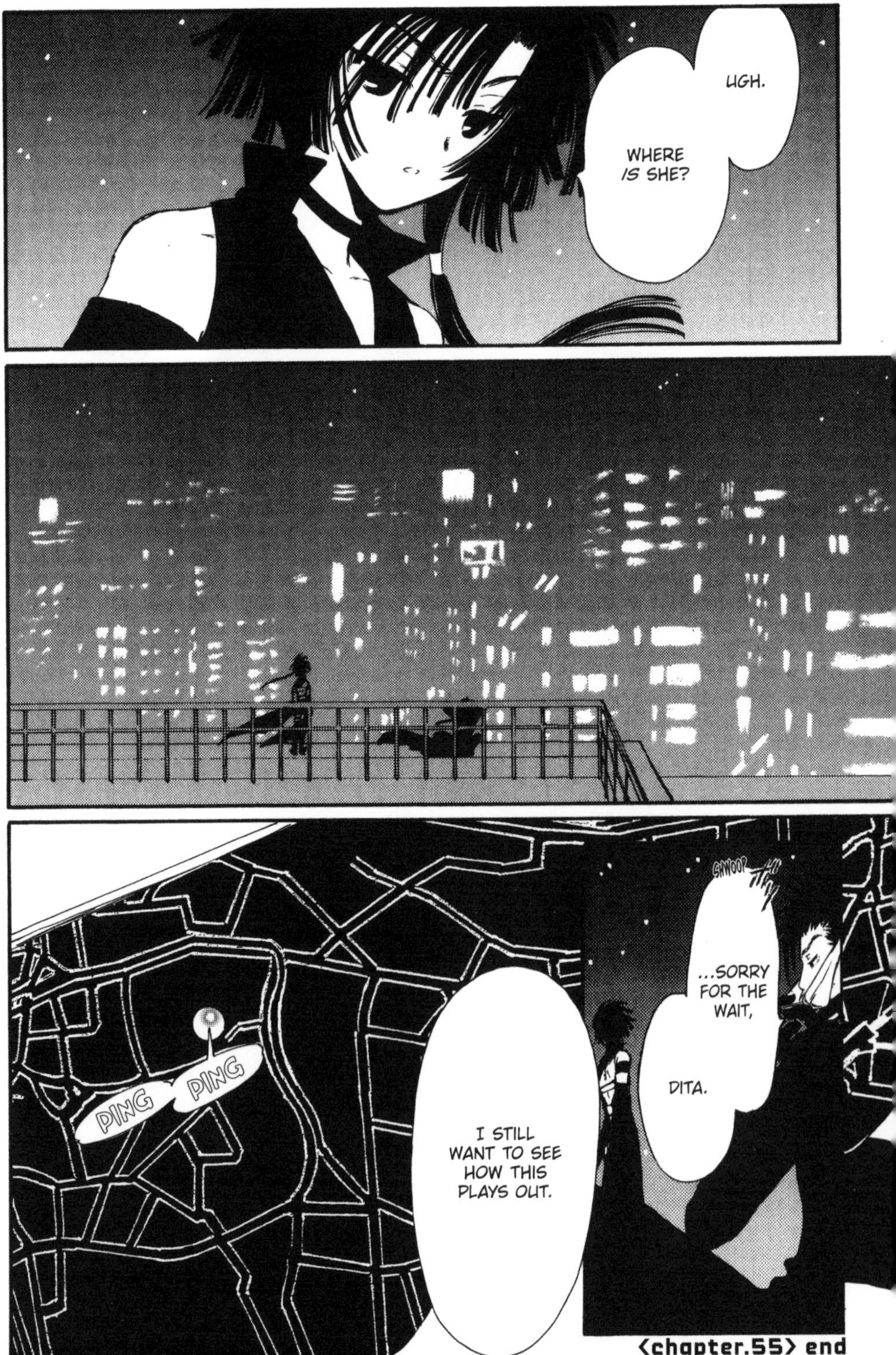
UGH.
WHERE IS SHE?
SWOOP
...SORRY FOR THE WAIT,
DITA.
I STILL WANT TO SEE HOW THIS PLAYS OUT.
PING
PING

<chapter.55> end

Chobits

〈chapter.56〉

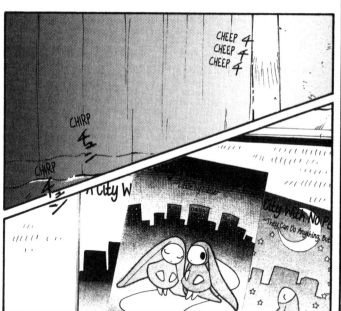

CHEEP 4
CHEEP 4
CHEEP 4

CHIRP

CHIRP

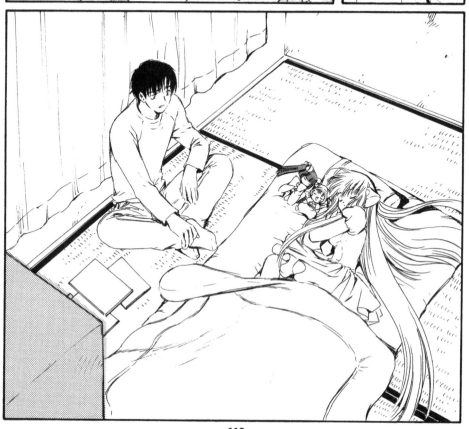

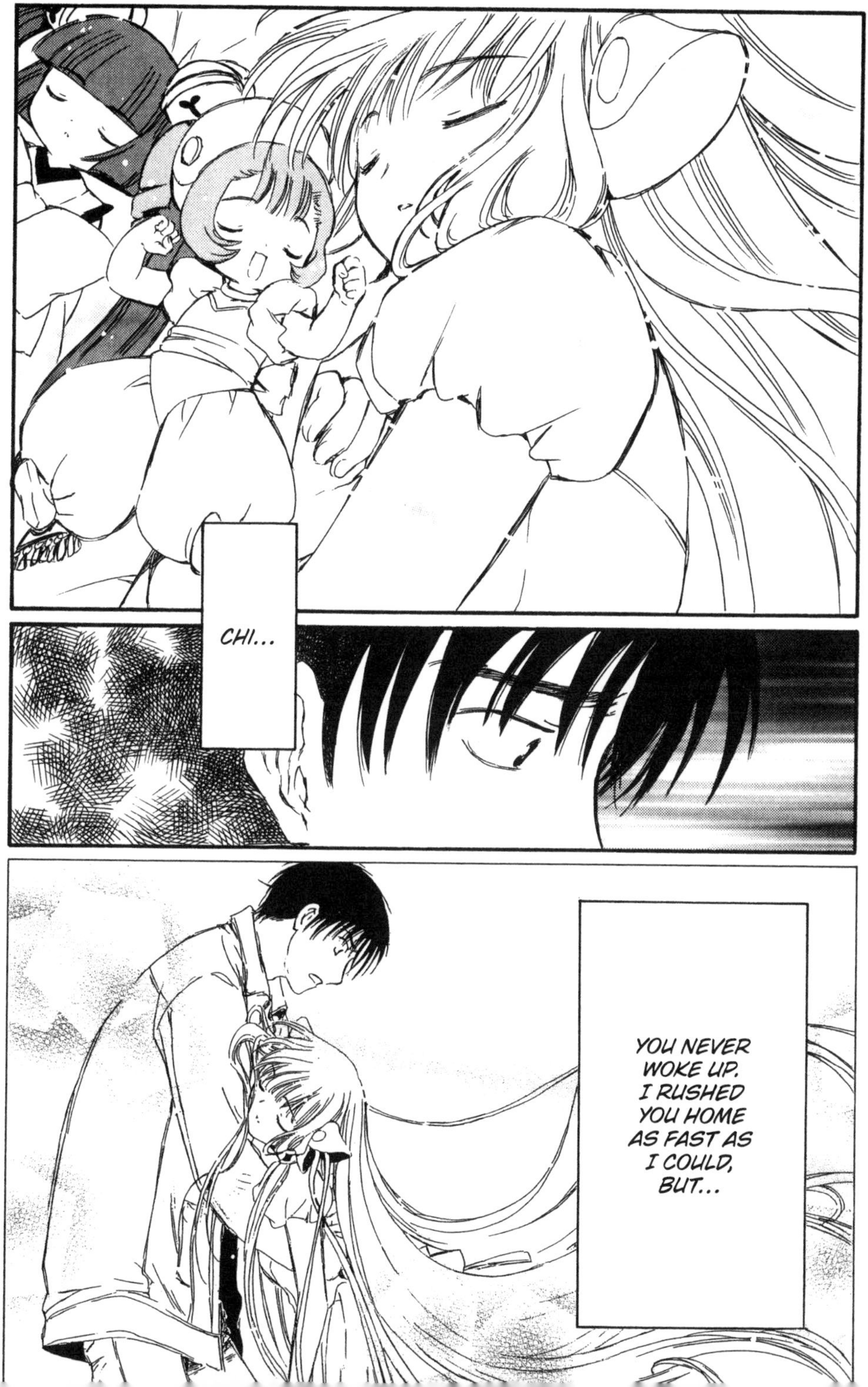
CHI...
YOU NEVER WOKE UP. I RUSHED YOU HOME AS FAST AS I COULD, BUT...

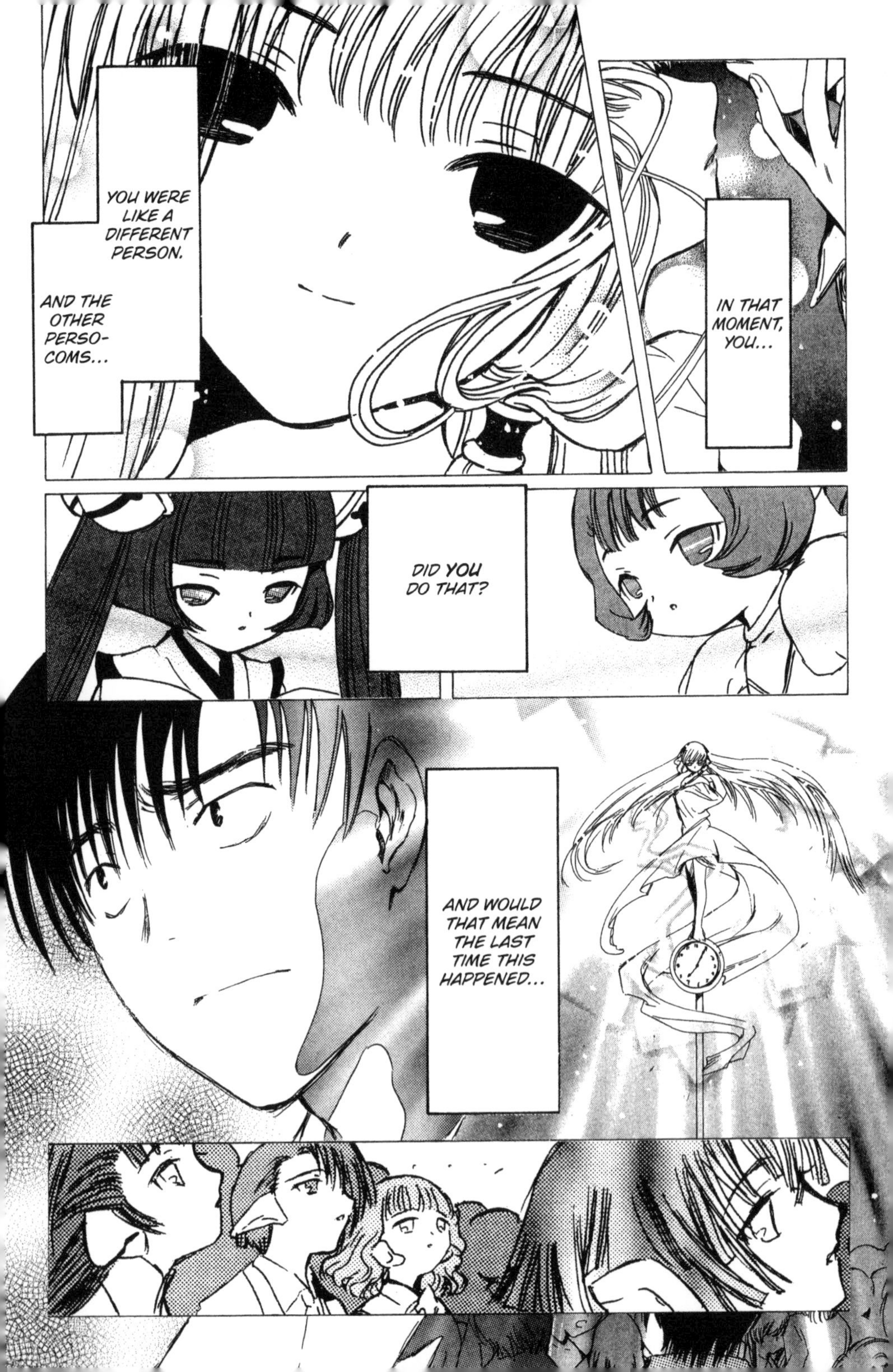
IN THAT MOMENT, YOU...
YOU WERE LIKE A DIFFERENT PERSON.
AND THE OTHER PERSO-COMS...
DID YOU DO THAT?
AND WOULD THAT MEAN THE LAST TIME THIS HAPPENED...

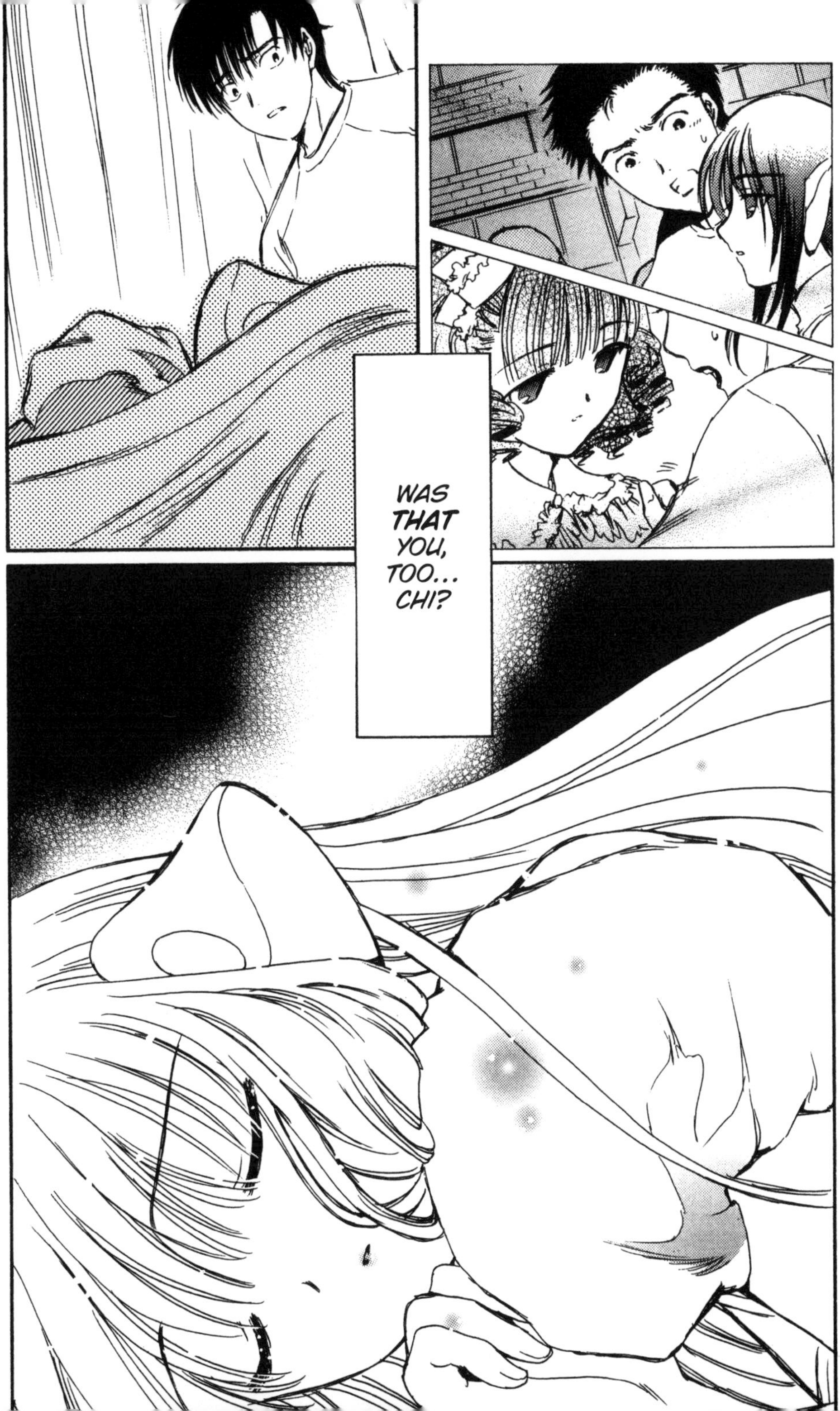
WAS THAT YOU, TOO... CHI?

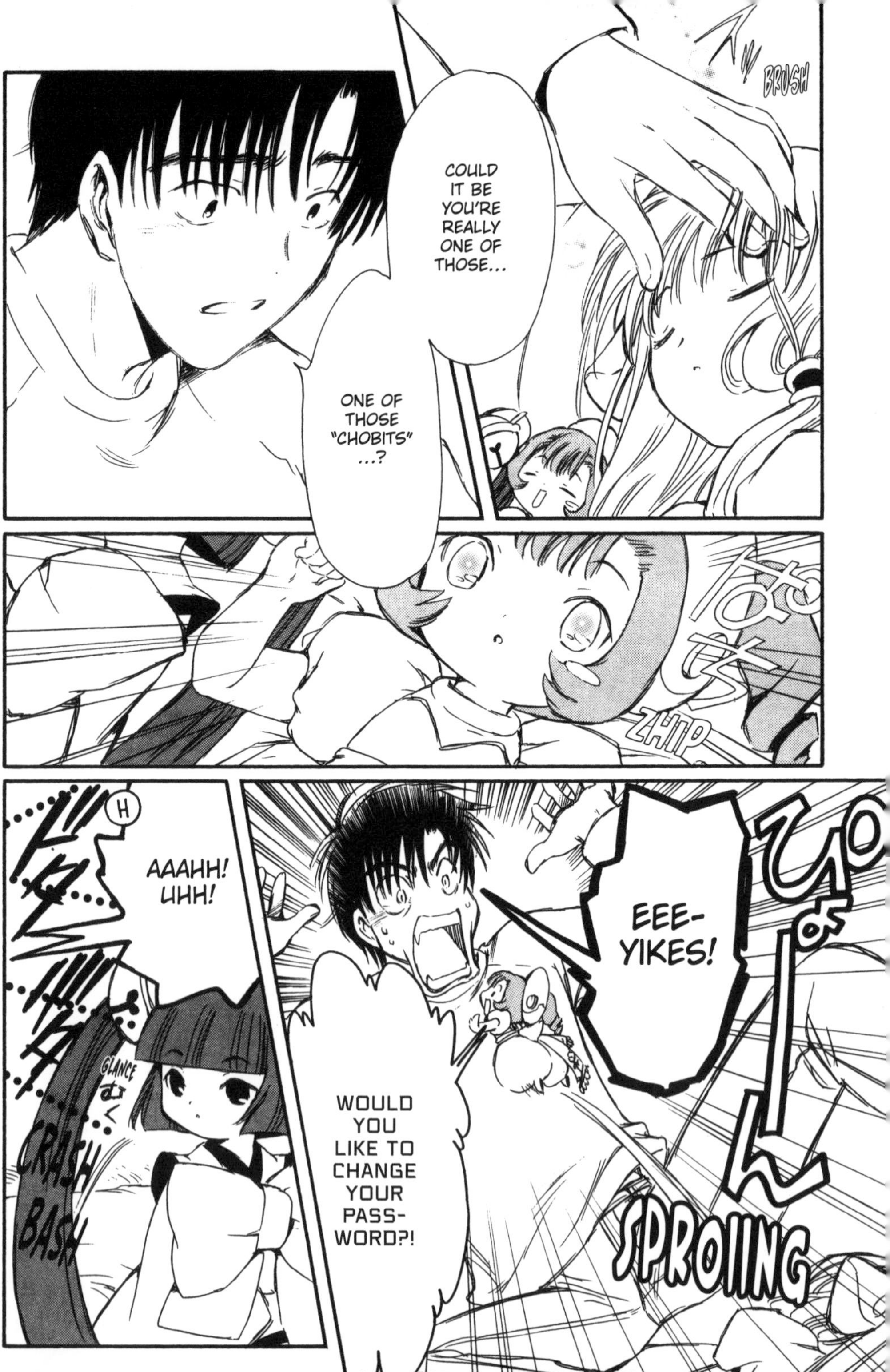
BRUSH
COULD IT BE YOU'RE REALLY ONE OF THOSE...
ONE OF THOSE "CHOBITS" ...?
ZHIP
EEE-YIKES!
SPROIING
WOULD YOU LIKE TO CHANGE YOUR PASS-WORD?!
H
AAAHH! UHH!
GLANCE
CRASH BASH

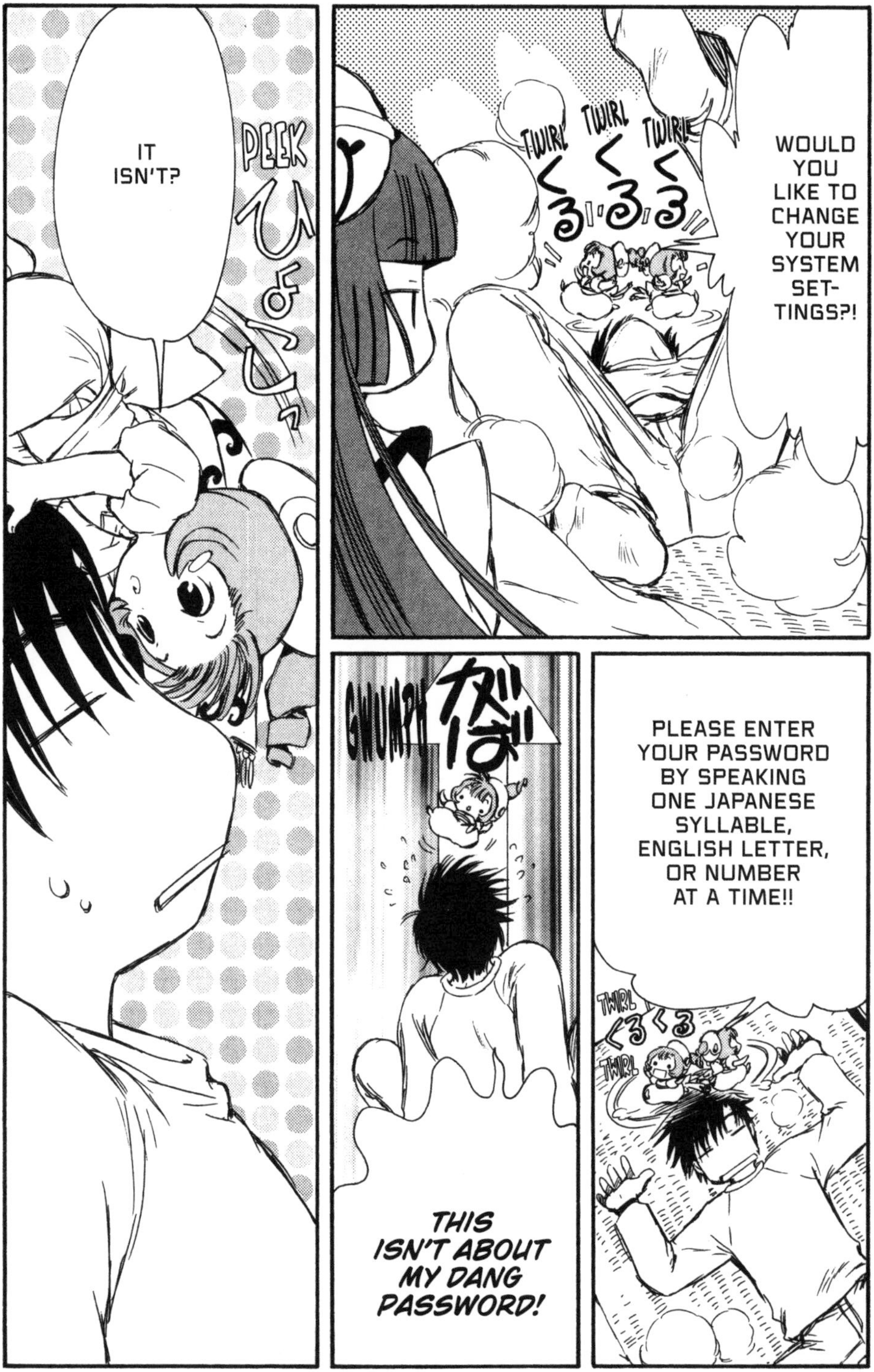
TWIRL TWIRL TWIRL
くるくるくる
WOULD YOU LIKE TO CHANGE YOUR SYSTEM SET-TINGS?!
PLEASE ENTER YOUR PASSWORD BY SPEAKING ONE JAPANESE SYLLABLE, ENGLISH LETTER, OR NUMBER AT A TIME!!
TWIRL
くるくる
TWIRL
GWUMPH
がばっ
THIS ISN'T ABOUT MY DANG PASSWORD!
IT ISN'T?
PEEK
ひょこっ

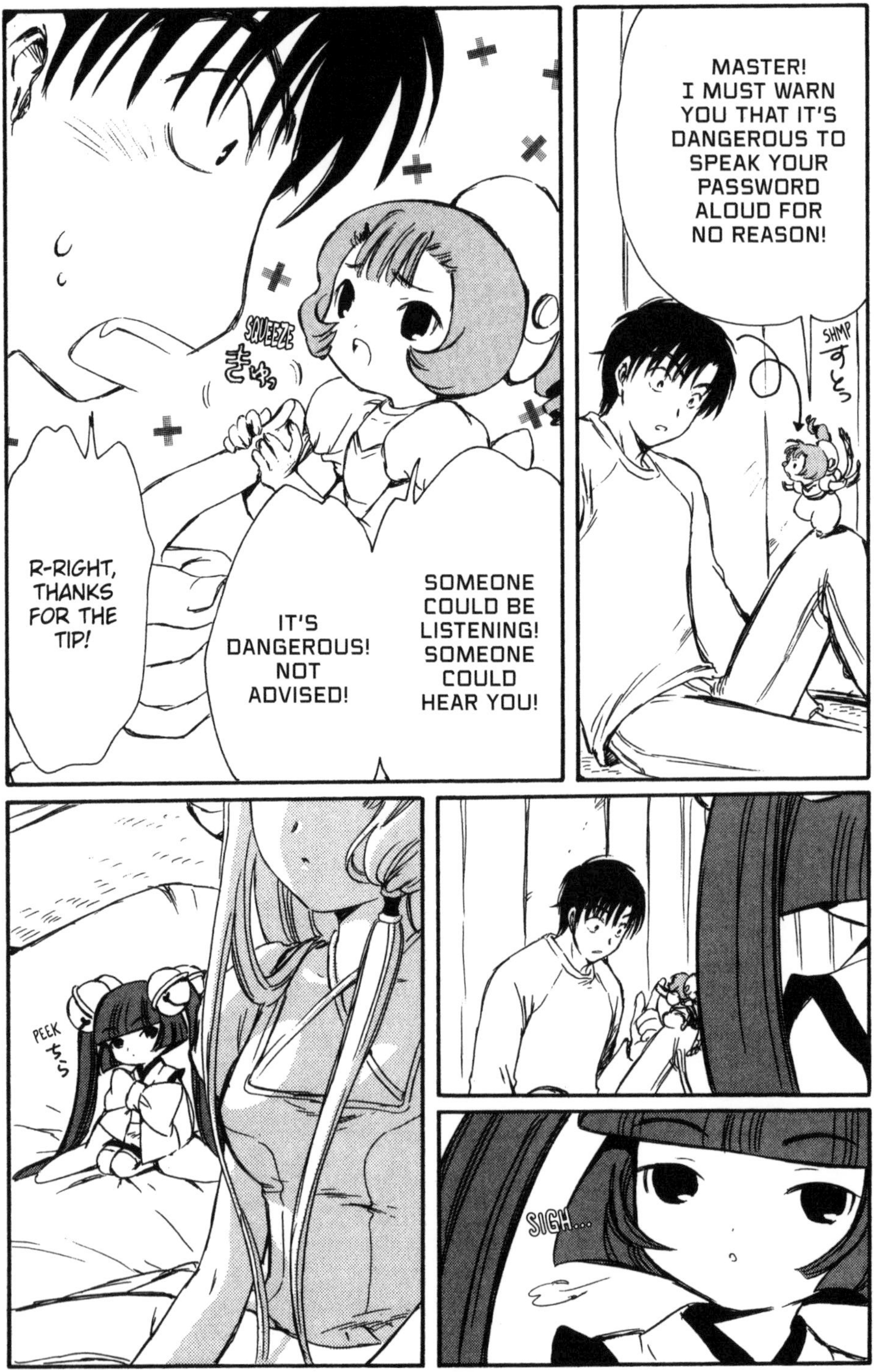
MASTER! I MUST WARN YOU THAT IT'S DANGEROUS TO SPEAK YOUR PASSWORD ALOUD FOR NO REASON!
SHMP
すとっ
SQUEEZE
きゅっ
SOMEONE COULD BE LISTENING! SOMEONE COULD HEAR YOU!
IT'S DANGEROUS! NOT ADVISED!
R-RIGHT, THANKS FOR THE TIP!
SIGH...
PEEK
ちら

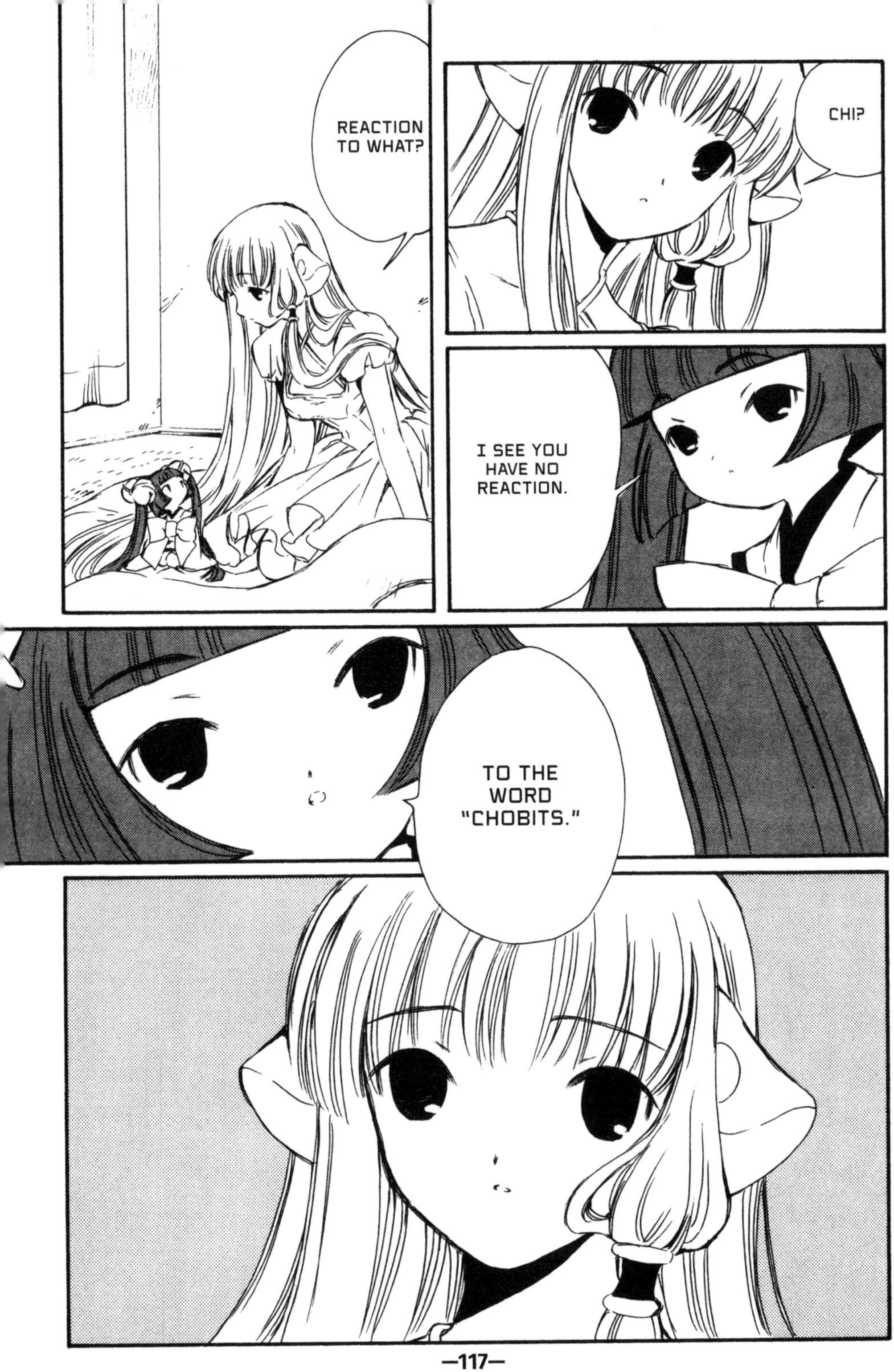
CHI?
I SEE YOU HAVE NO REACTION.
REACTION TO WHAT?
TO THE WORD "CHOBITS."

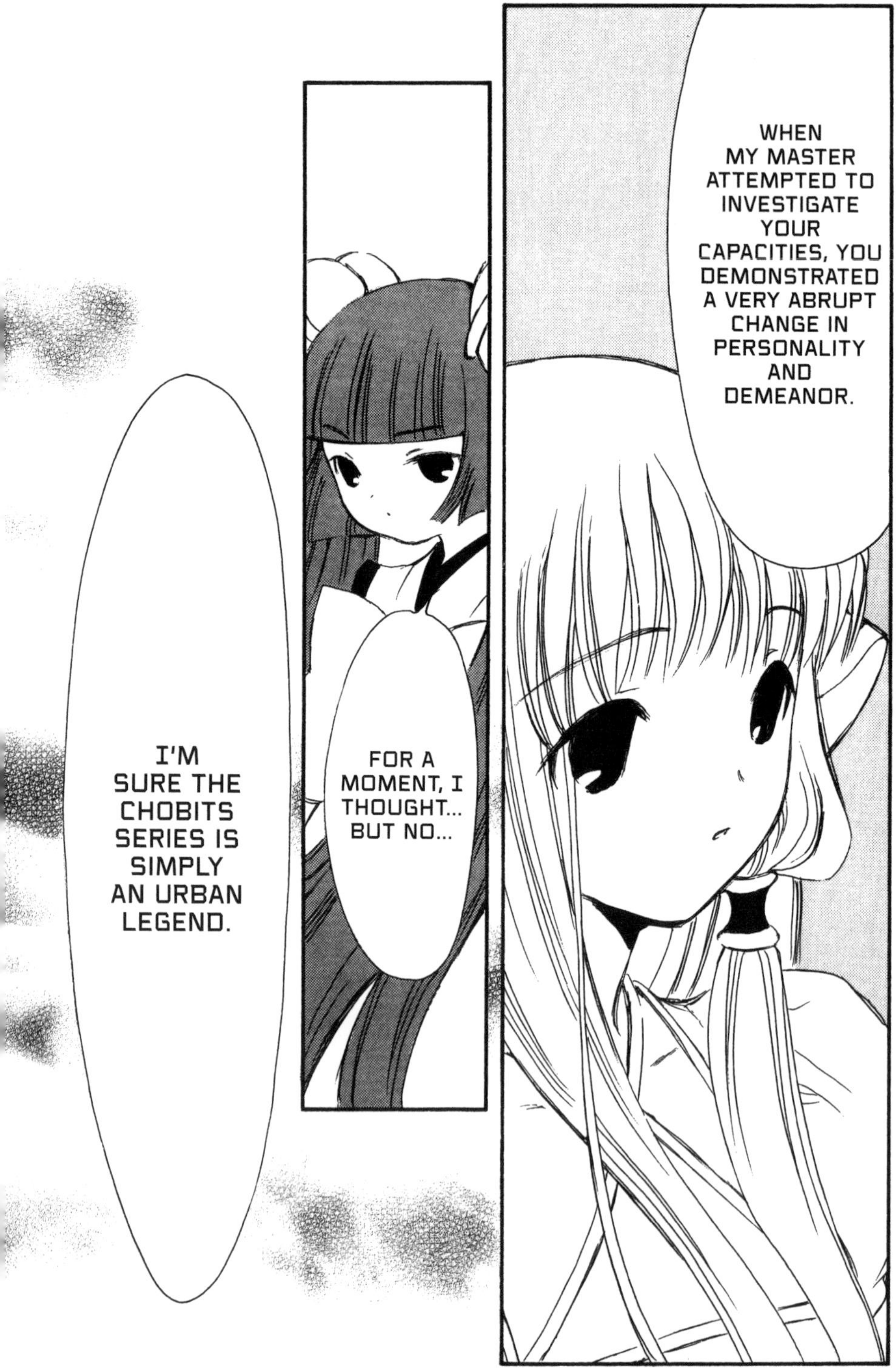
WHEN MY MASTER ATTEMPTED TO INVESTIGATE YOUR CAPACITIES, YOU DEMONSTRATED A VERY ABRUPT CHANGE IN PERSONALITY AND DEMEANOR.
FOR A MOMENT, I THOUGHT... BUT NO...
I'M SURE THE CHOBITS SERIES IS SIMPLY AN URBAN LEGEND.

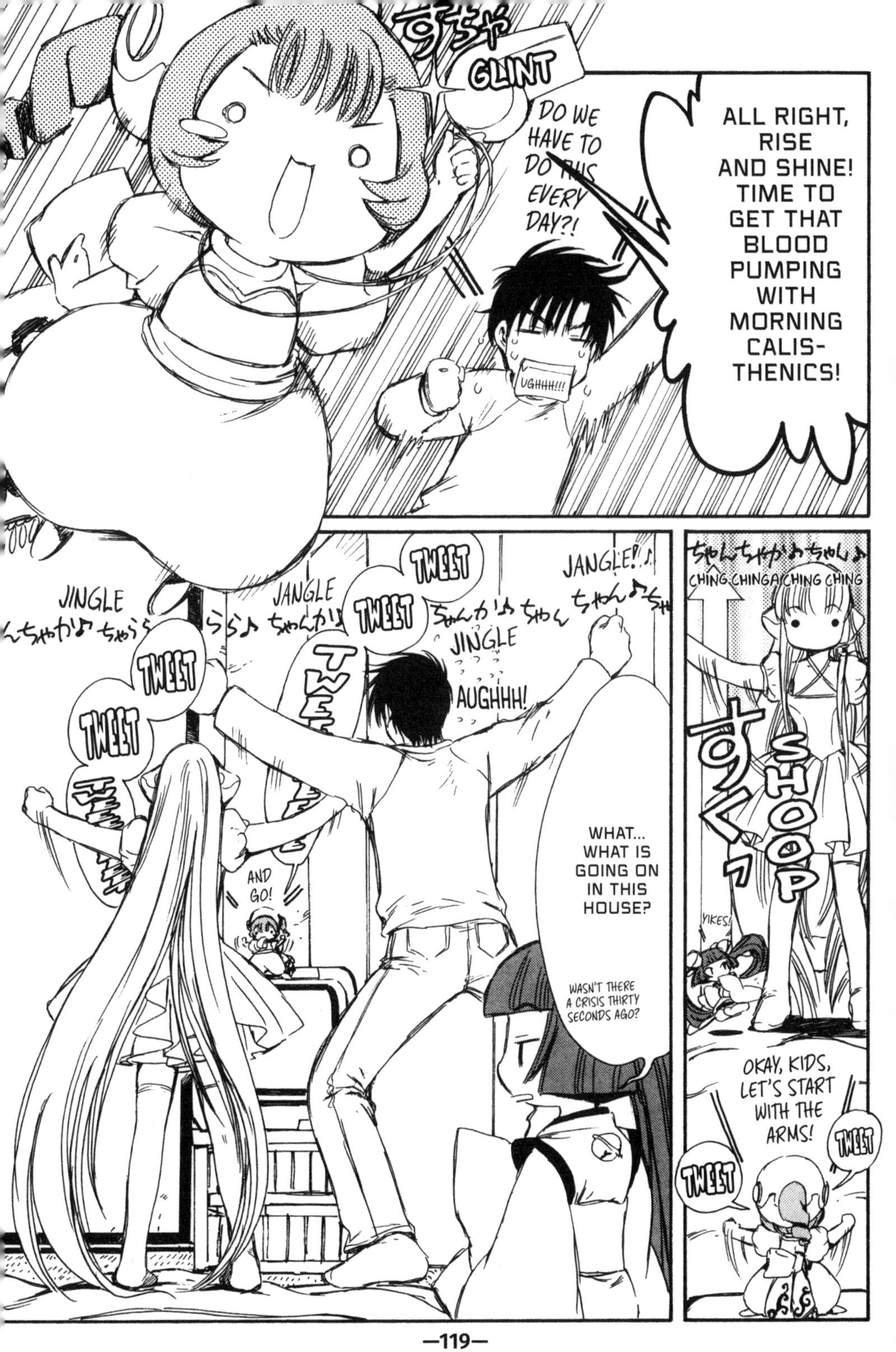
ALL RIGHT, RISE AND SHINE! TIME TO GET THAT BLOOD PUMPING WITH MORNING CALIS-THENICS!
すちゃ
GLINT
DO WE HAVE TO DO THIS EVERY DAY?!
UGHHH!!!
ちゃんちゃかちゃん♪
CHING CHINGA CHING CHING
すく
SHOOP
YIKES!
OKAY, KIDS, LET'S START WITH THE ARMS!
TWEET
TWEET
WHAT... WHAT IS GOING ON IN THIS HOUSE?
WASN'T THERE A CRISIS THIRTY SECONDS AGO?
JANGLE!♪
JINGLE
AUGHHH!
TWEET
TWEET
JANGLE
JINGLE
TWEET
TWEET
AND GO!

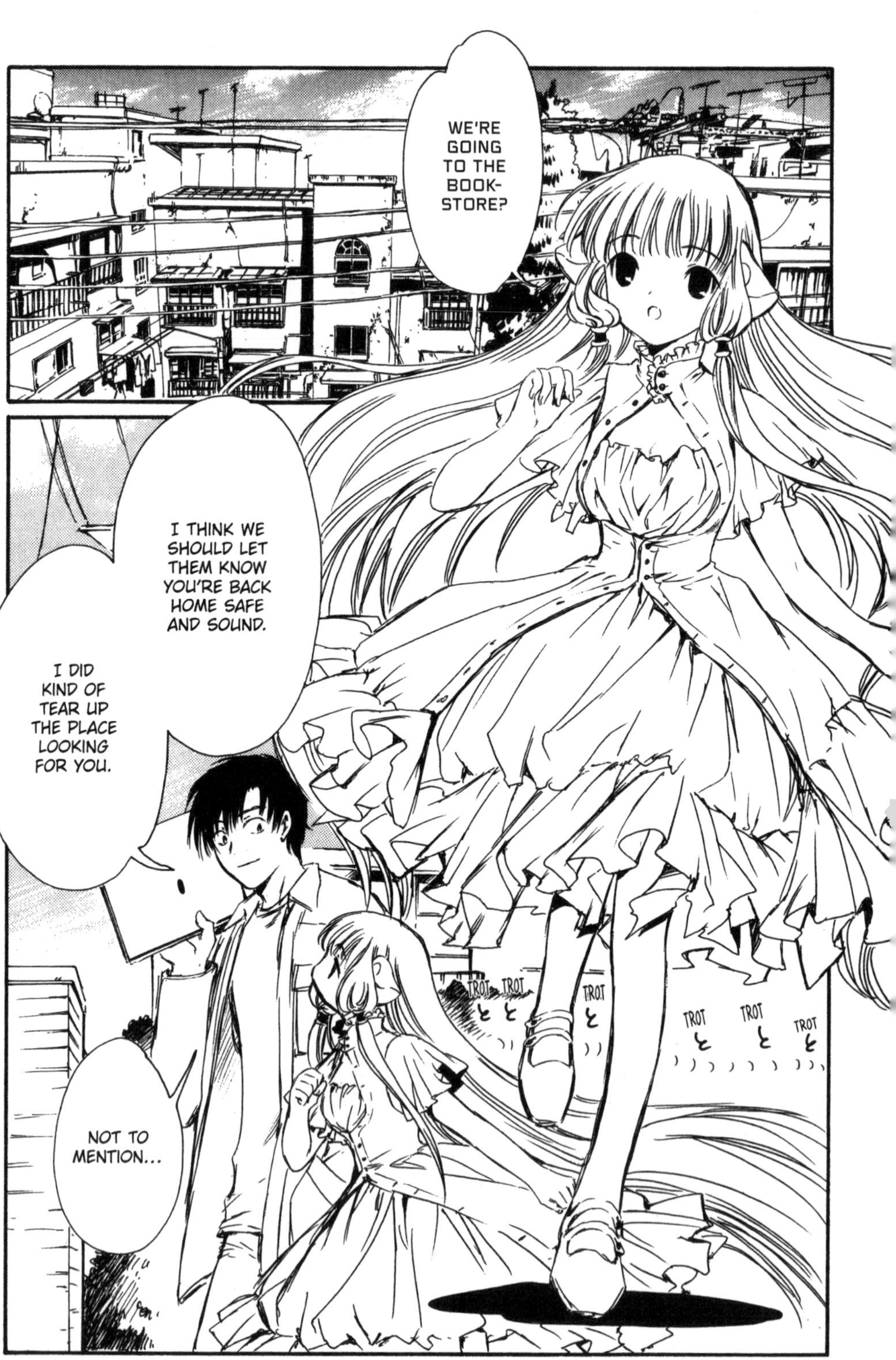
WE'RE GOING TO THE BOOK-STORE?
I THINK WE SHOULD LET THEM KNOW YOU'RE BACK HOME SAFE AND SOUND.
I DID KIND OF TEAR UP THE PLACE LOOKING FOR YOU.
TROT と
TROT と
TROT と
TROT と
TROT と
TROT と
NOT TO MENTION...

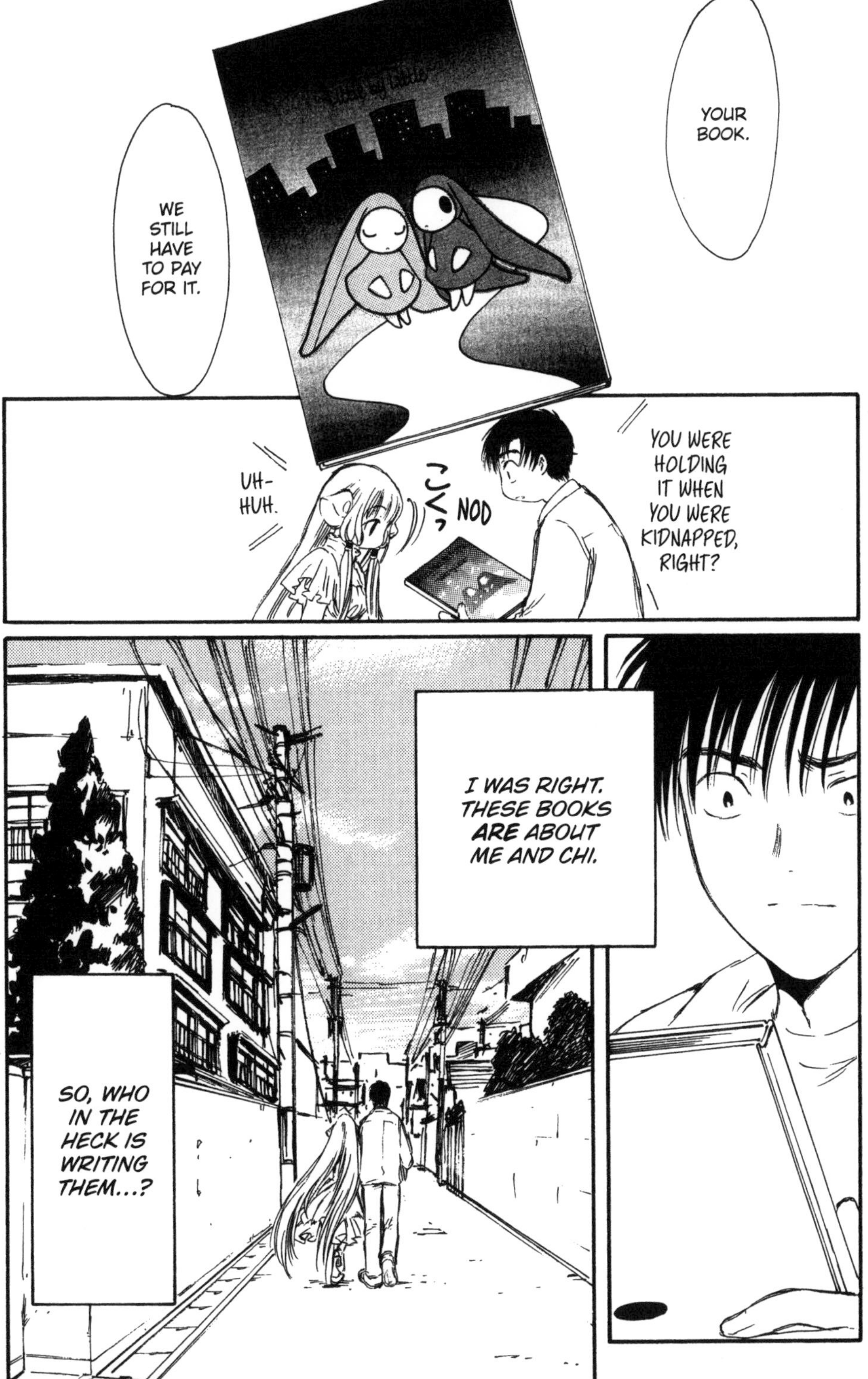
YOUR BOOK.
WE STILL HAVE TO PAY FOR IT.
YOU WERE HOLDING IT WHEN YOU WERE KIDNAPPED, RIGHT?
こくっ NOD
UH-HUH.
I WAS RIGHT. THESE BOOKS **ARE** ABOUT ME AND CHI.
SO, WHO IN THE HECK IS WRITING THEM...?

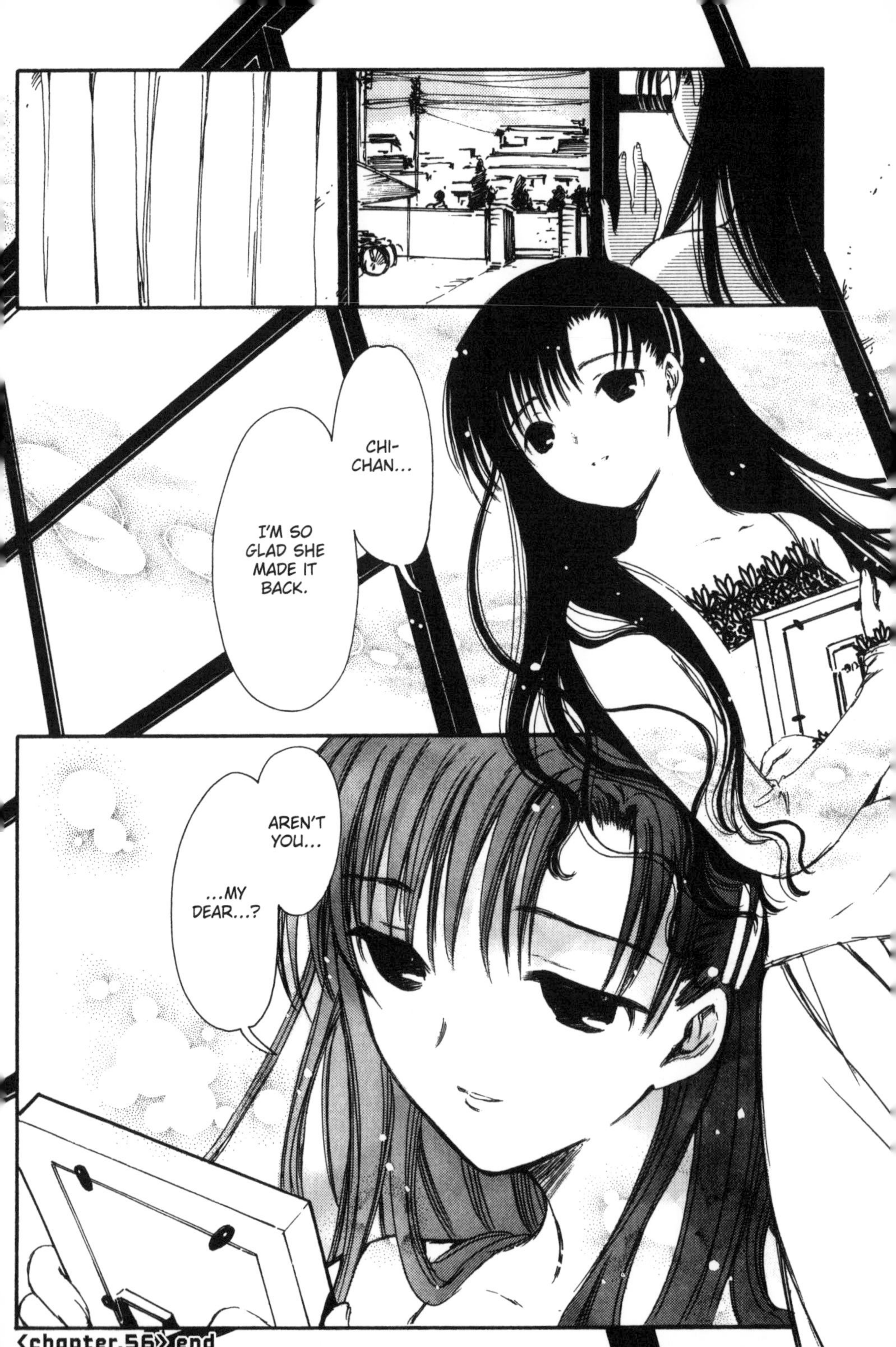
CHI-CHAN...
I'M SO GLAD SHE MADE IT BACK.
AREN'T YOU...
...MY DEAR...?

<chapter.56> end

⟨chapter.57⟩

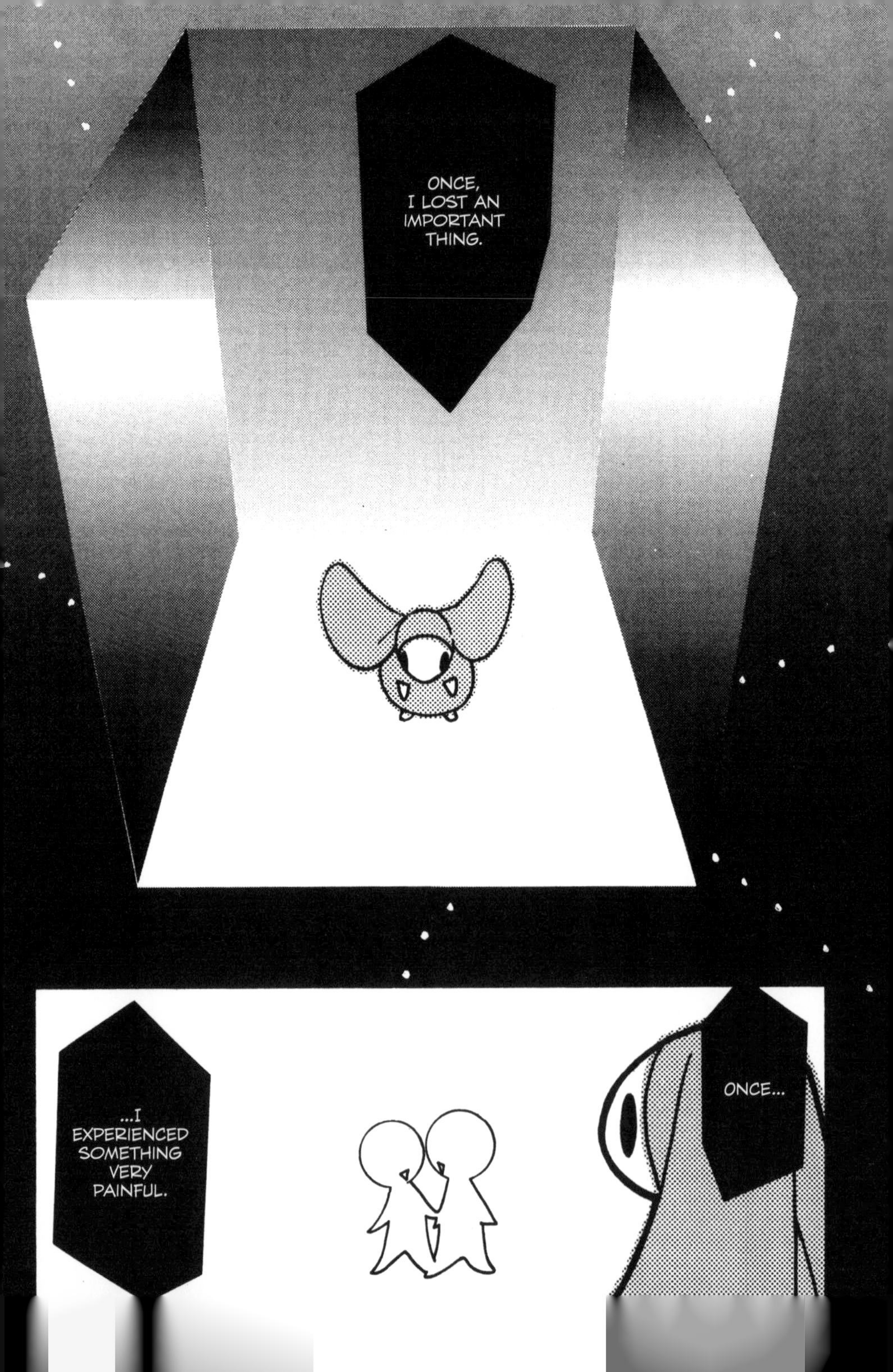
ONCE, I LOST AN IMPORTANT THING.
ONCE...
...I EXPERIENCED SOMETHING VERY PAINFUL.

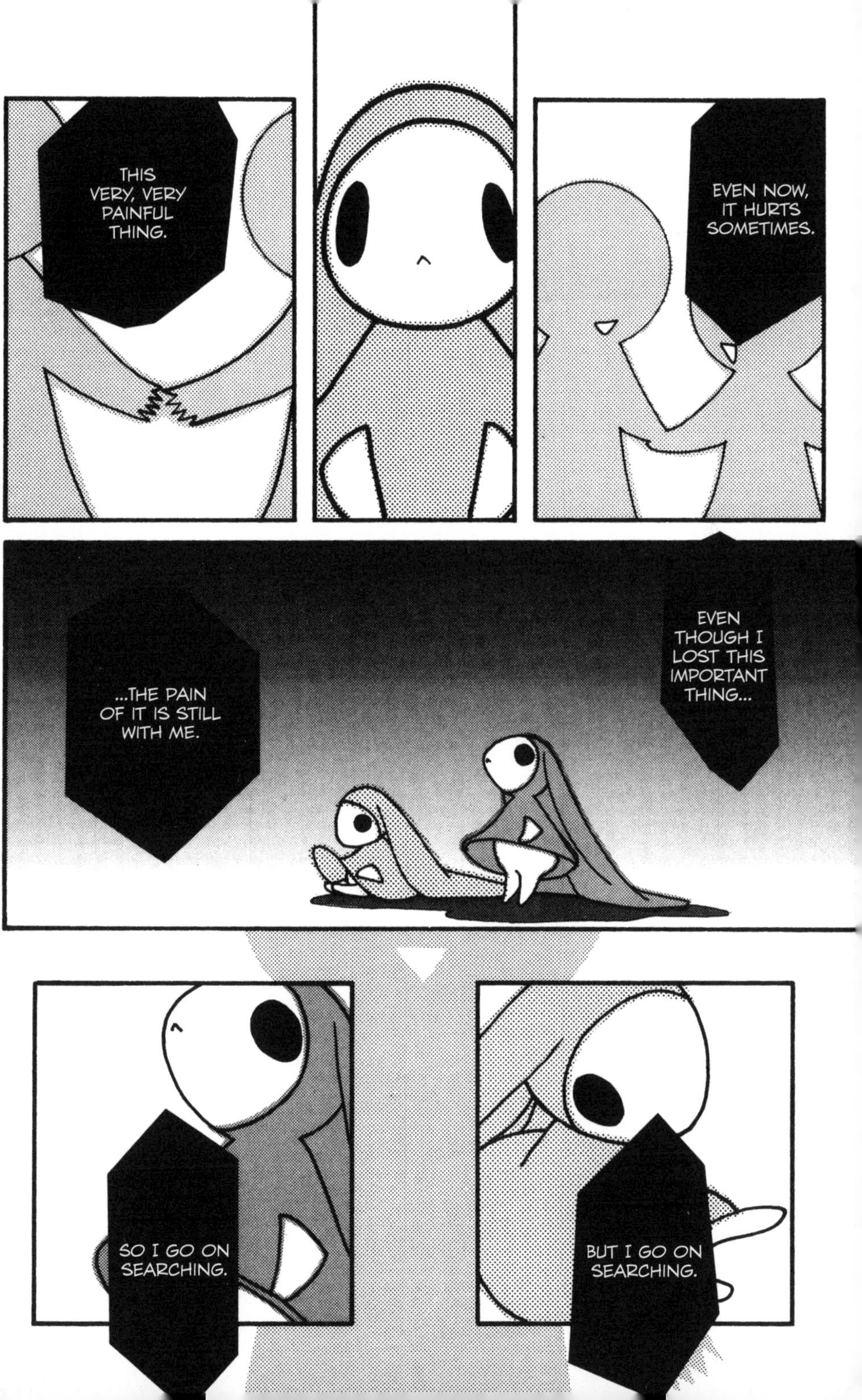
EVEN NOW, IT HURTS SOMETIMES.
THIS VERY, VERY PAINFUL THING.
EVEN THOUGH I LOST THIS IMPORTANT THING...
...THE PAIN OF IT IS STILL WITH ME.
BUT I GO ON SEARCHING.
SO I GO ON SEARCHING.

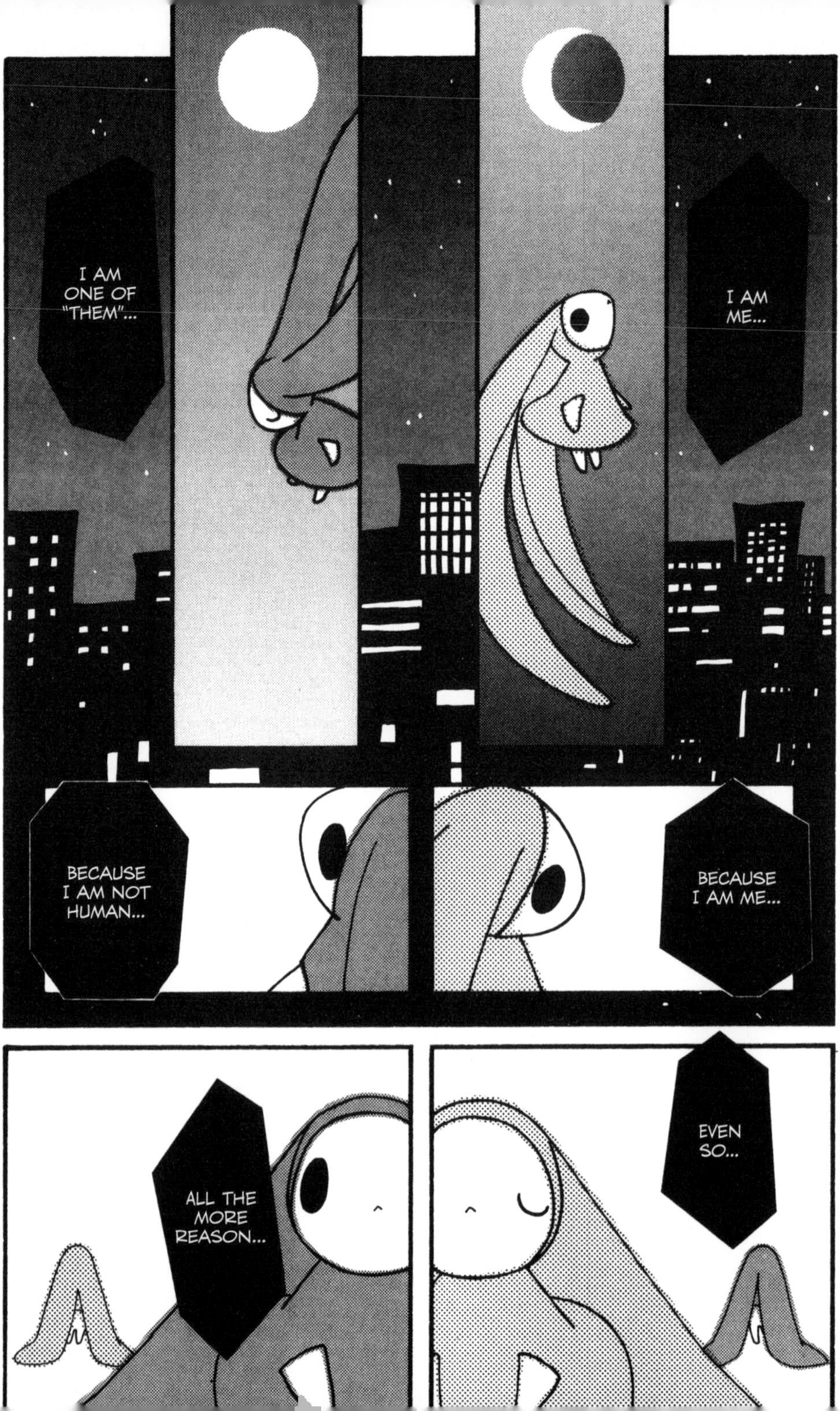
I AM ME...
I AM ONE OF "THEM"...
BECAUSE I AM ME...
BECAUSE I AM NOT HUMAN...
EVEN SO...
ALL THE MORE REASON...

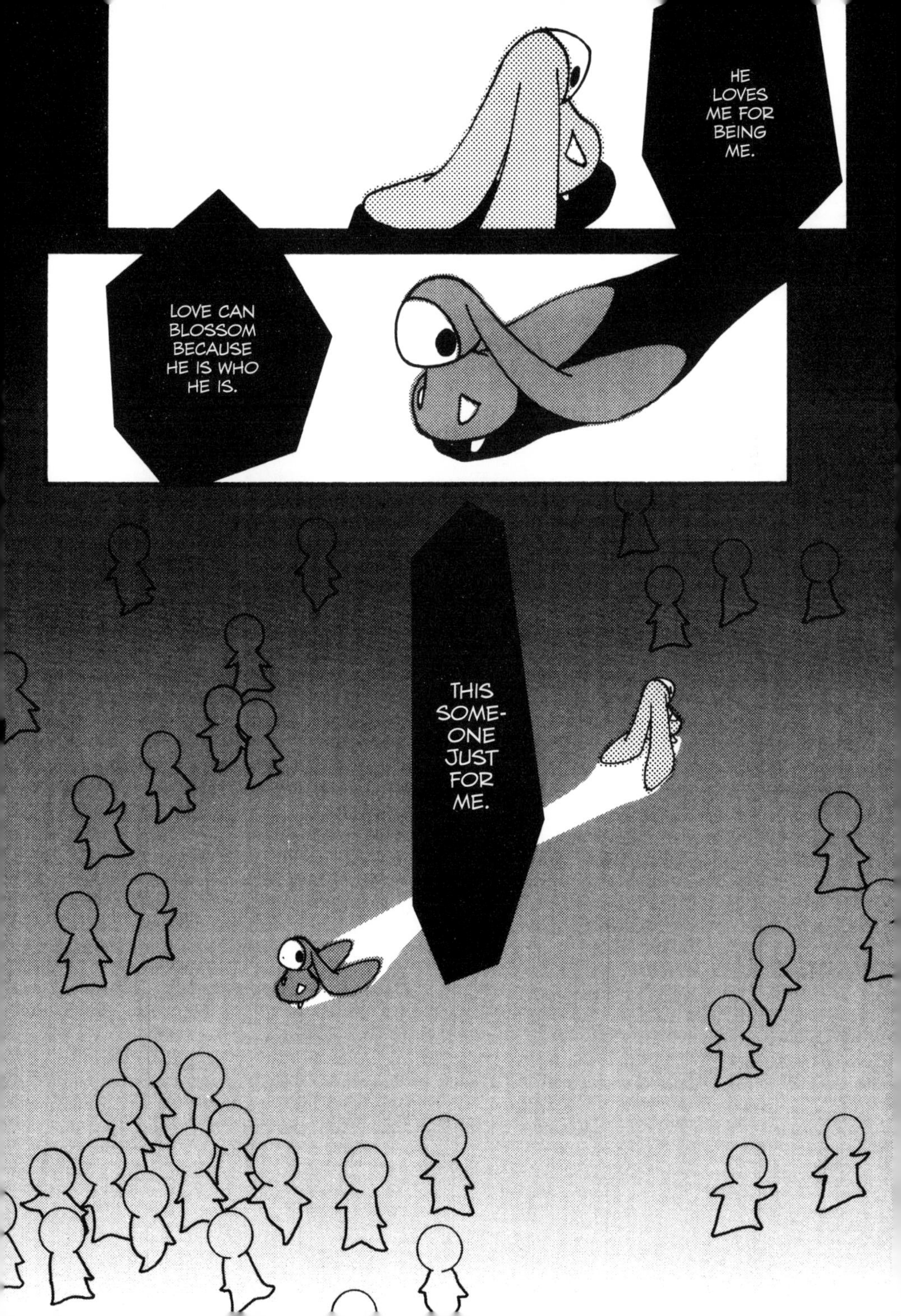
HE LOVES ME FOR BEING ME.
LOVE CAN BLOSSOM BECAUSE HE IS WHO HE IS.
THIS SOME-ONE JUST FOR ME.

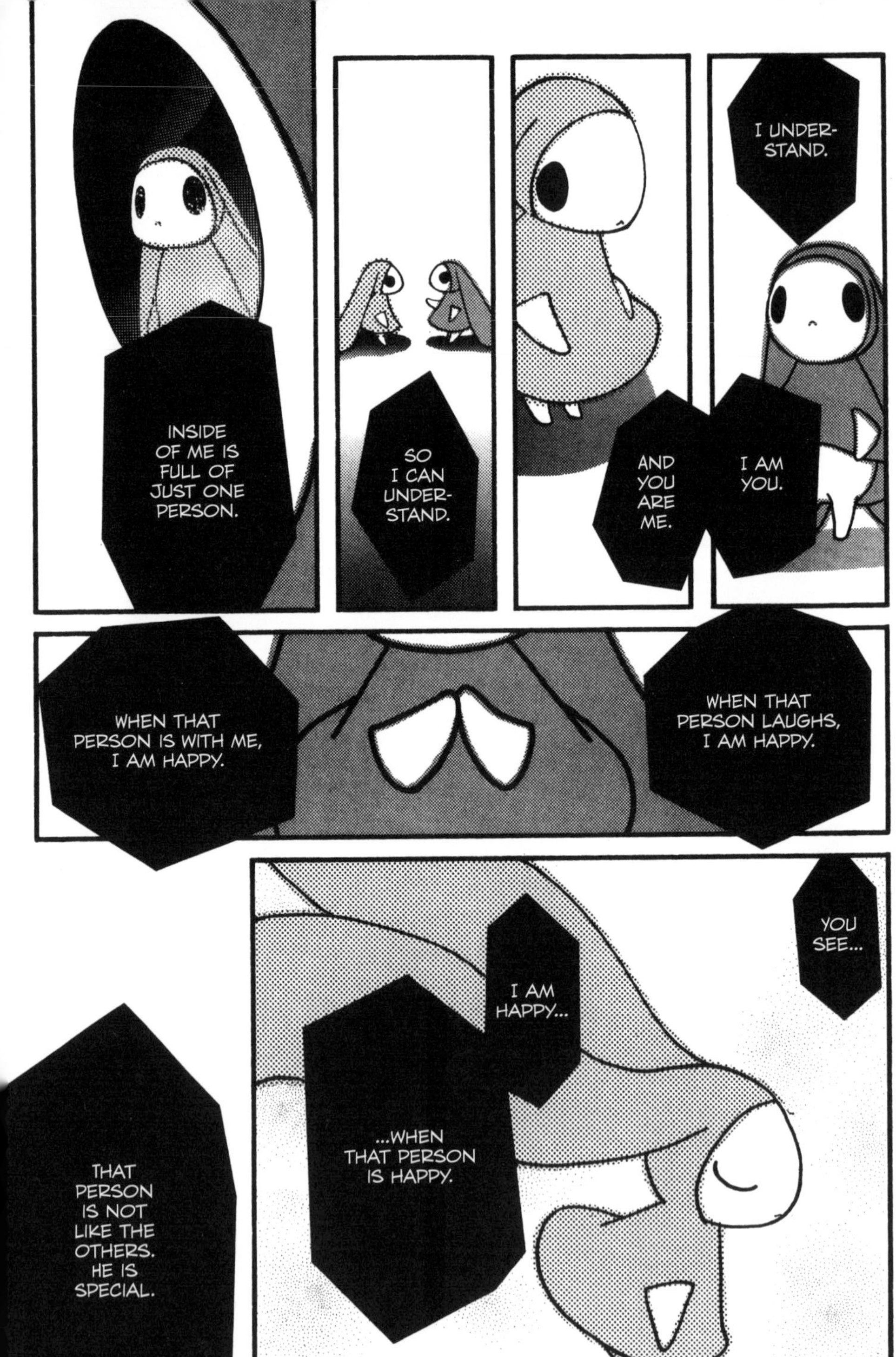
I UNDER-STAND.
I AM YOU.
AND YOU ARE ME.
SO I CAN UNDER-STAND.
INSIDE OF ME IS FULL OF JUST ONE PERSON.
WHEN THAT PERSON LAUGHS, I AM HAPPY.
WHEN THAT PERSON IS WITH ME, I AM HAPPY.
YOU SEE...
I AM HAPPY...
...WHEN THAT PERSON IS HAPPY.
THAT PERSON IS NOT LIKE THE OTHERS. HE IS SPECIAL.

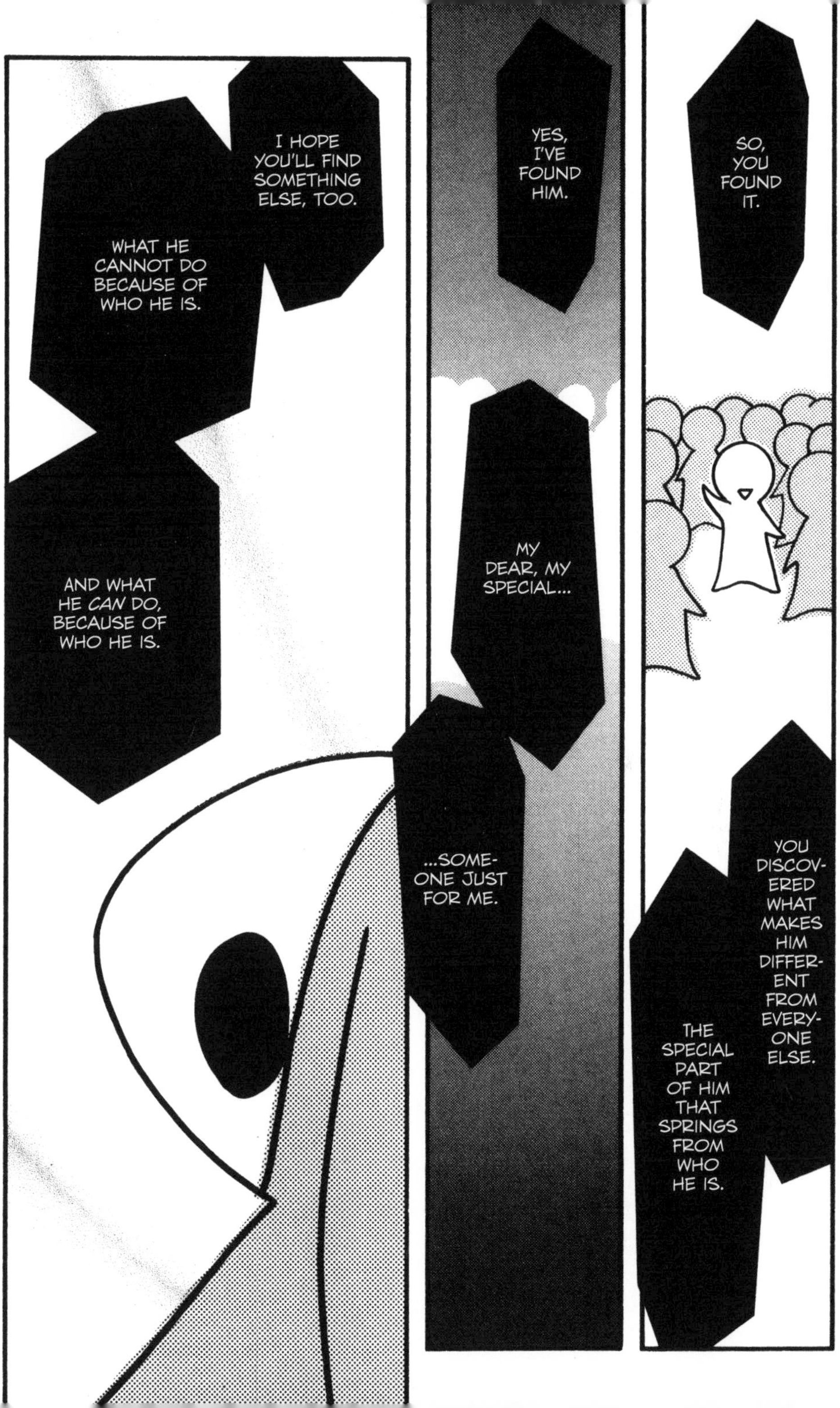
SO, YOU FOUND IT.
YOU DISCOVERED WHAT MAKES HIM DIFFERENT FROM EVERYONE ELSE.
THE SPECIAL PART OF HIM THAT SPRINGS FROM WHO HE IS.
YES, I'VE FOUND HIM.
MY DEAR, MY SPECIAL...
...SOMEONE JUST FOR ME.
I HOPE YOU'LL FIND SOMETHING ELSE, TOO.
WHAT HE CANNOT DO BECAUSE OF WHO HE IS.
AND WHAT HE *CAN* DO, BECAUSE OF WHO HE IS.

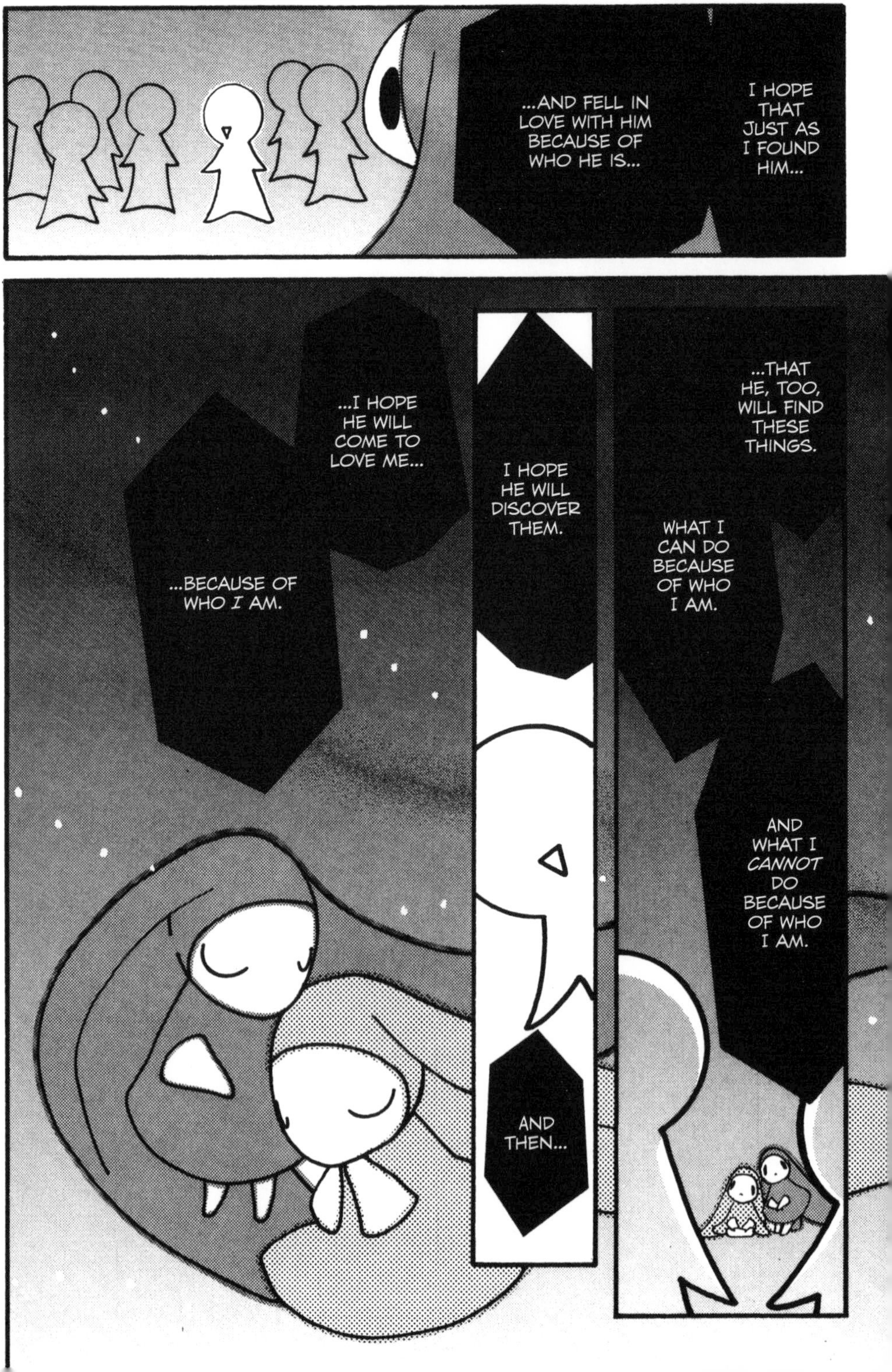
I HOPE THAT JUST AS I FOUND HIM...
...AND FELL IN LOVE WITH HIM BECAUSE OF WHO HE IS...
...THAT HE, TOO, WILL FIND THESE THINGS.
WHAT I CAN DO BECAUSE OF WHO I AM.
AND WHAT I *CANNOT* DO BECAUSE OF WHO I AM.
I HOPE HE WILL DISCOVER THEM.
AND THEN...
...I HOPE HE WILL COME TO LOVE ME...
...BECAUSE OF WHO *I* AM.

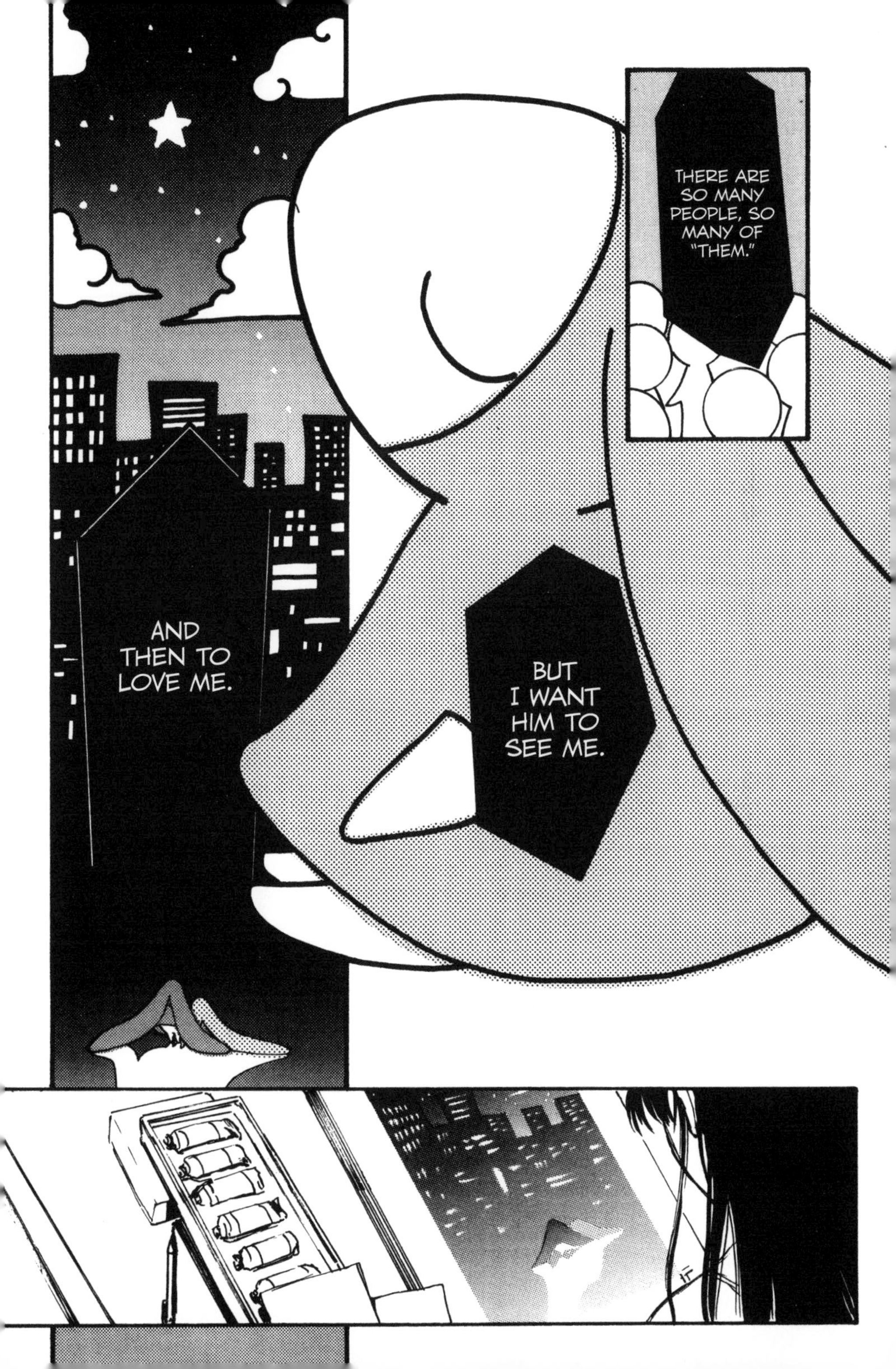
THERE ARE SO MANY PEOPLE, SO MANY OF "THEM."
BUT I WANT HIM TO SEE ME.
AND THEN TO LOVE ME.

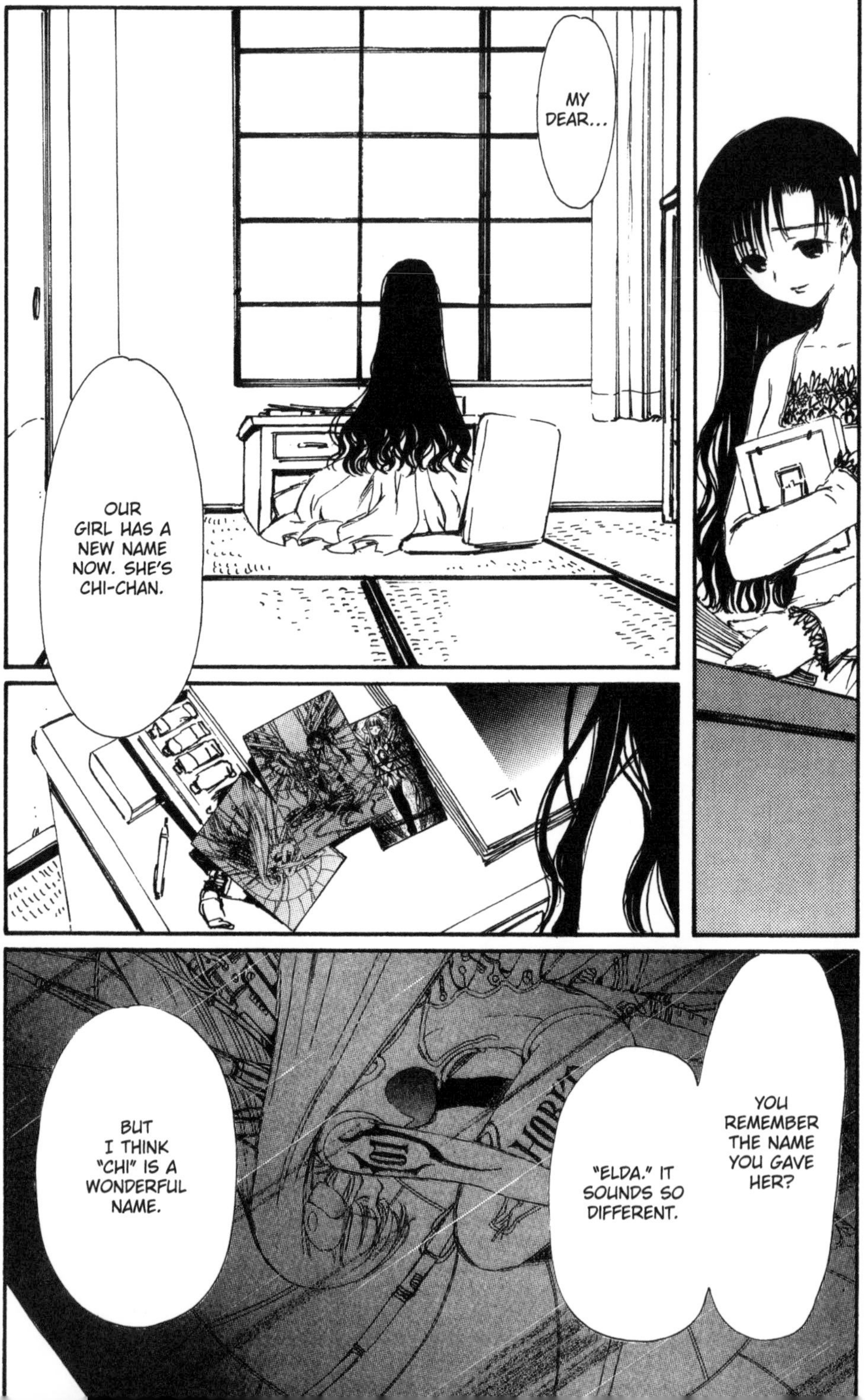
MY DEAR...
OUR GIRL HAS A NEW NAME NOW. SHE'S CHI-CHAN.
YOU REMEMBER THE NAME YOU GAVE HER?
"ELDA." IT SOUNDS SO DIFFERENT.
BUT I THINK "CHI" IS A WONDERFUL NAME.

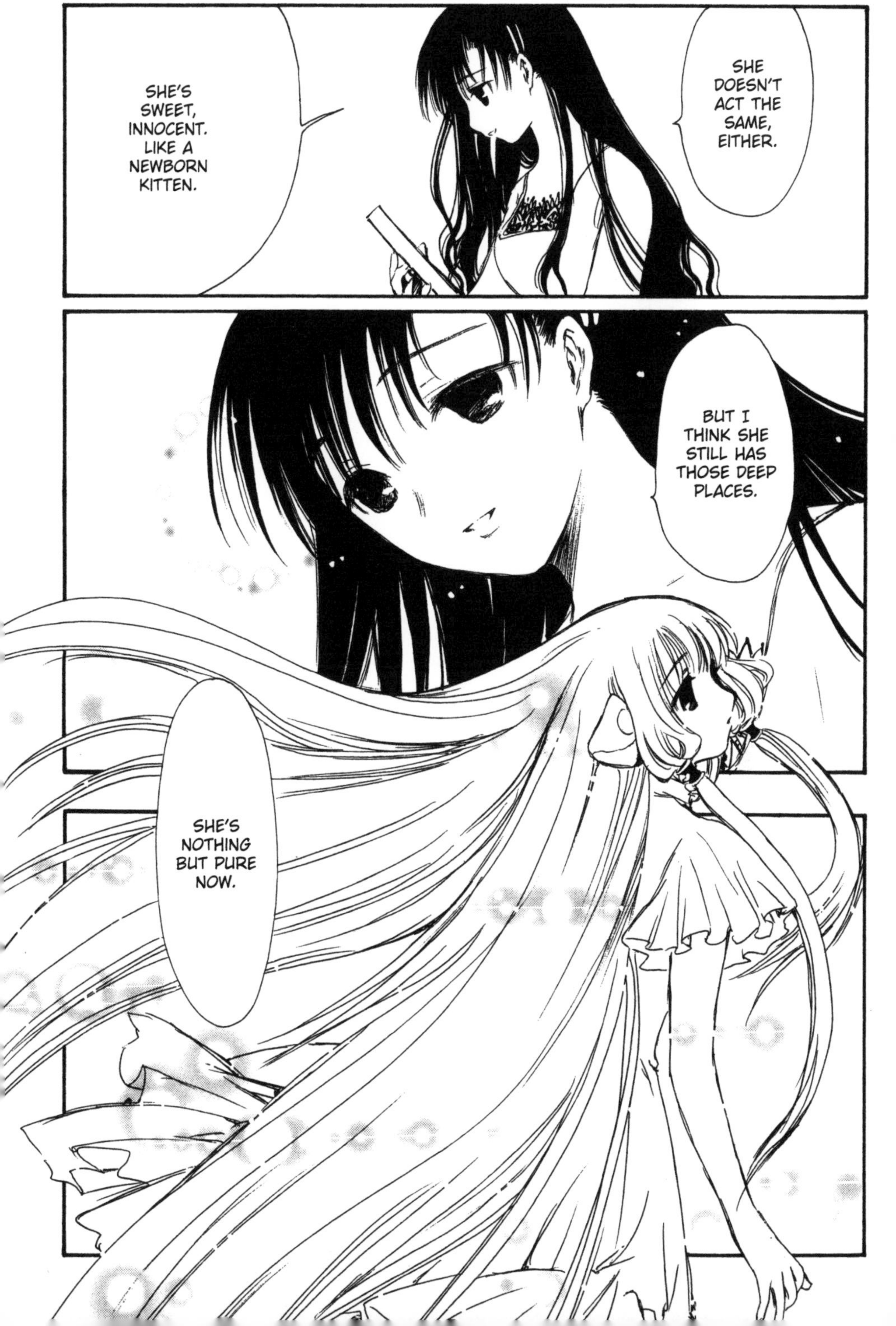
SHE DOESN'T ACT THE SAME, EITHER.
SHE'S SWEET, INNOCENT. LIKE A NEWBORN KITTEN.
BUT I THINK SHE STILL HAS THOSE DEEP PLACES.
SHE'S NOTHING BUT PURE NOW.

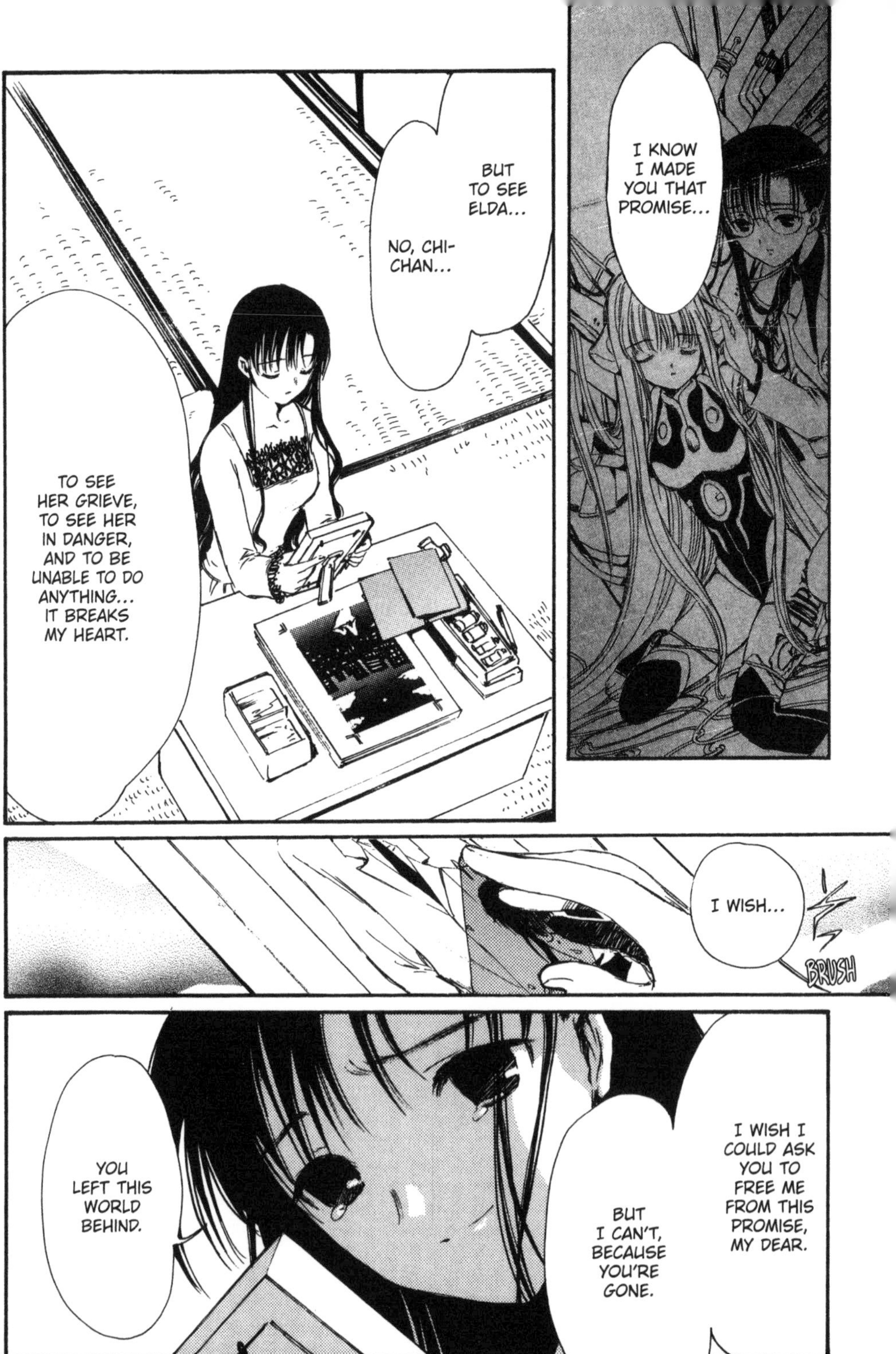
I KNOW I MADE YOU THAT PROMISE...
BUT TO SEE ELDA...
NO, CHI-CHAN...
TO SEE HER GRIEVE, TO SEE HER IN DANGER, AND TO BE UNABLE TO DO ANYTHING... IT BREAKS MY HEART.
I WISH...
BRUSH
I WISH I COULD ASK YOU TO FREE ME FROM THIS PROMISE, MY DEAR.
BUT I CAN'T, BECAUSE YOU'RE GONE.
YOU LEFT THIS WORLD BEHIND.

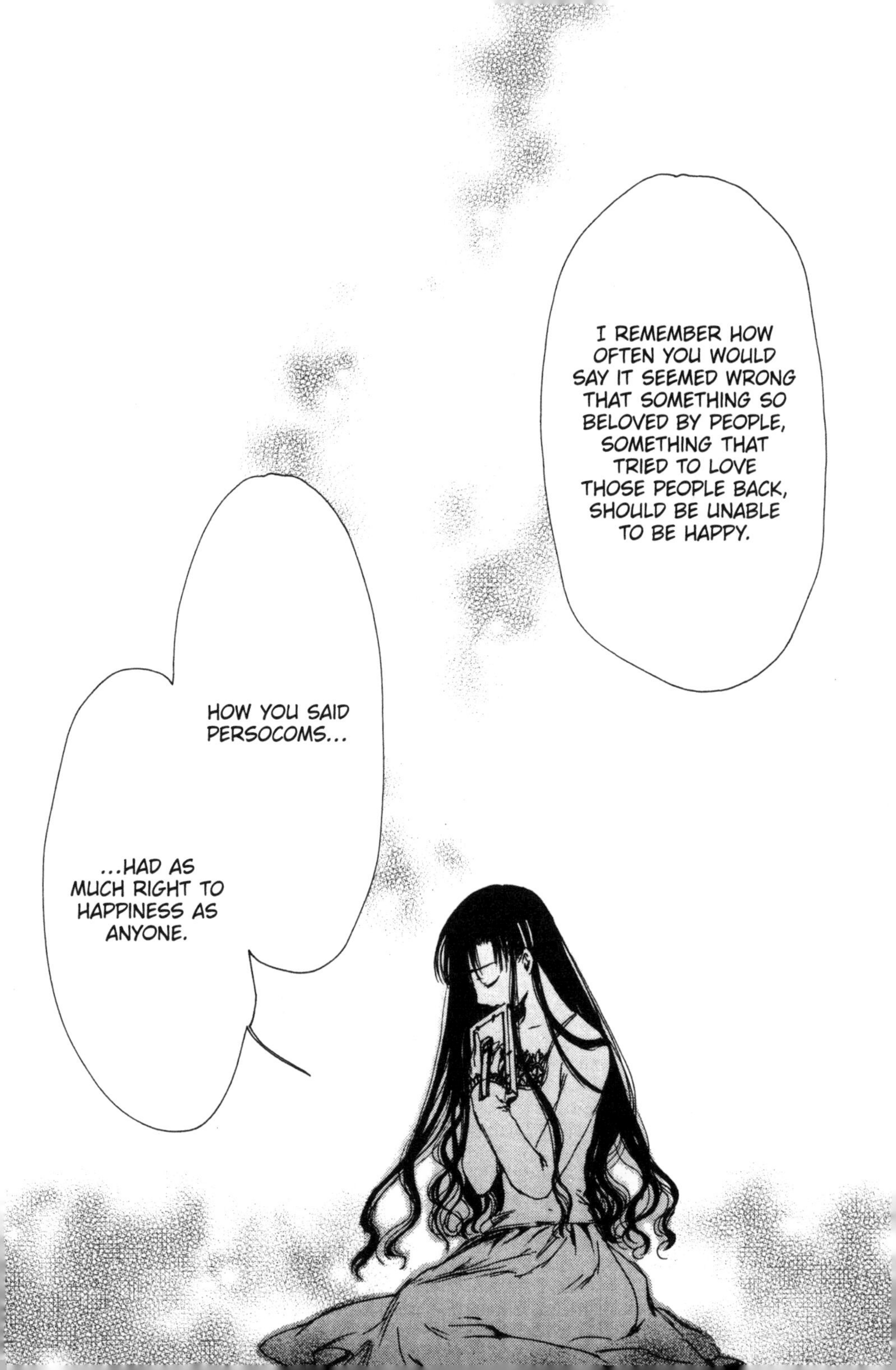
I REMEMBER HOW OFTEN YOU WOULD SAY IT SEEMED WRONG THAT SOMETHING SO BELOVED BY PEOPLE, SOMETHING THAT TRIED TO LOVE THOSE PEOPLE BACK, SHOULD BE UNABLE TO BE HAPPY.
HOW YOU SAID PERSOCOMS...
...HAD AS MUCH RIGHT TO HAPPINESS AS ANYONE.

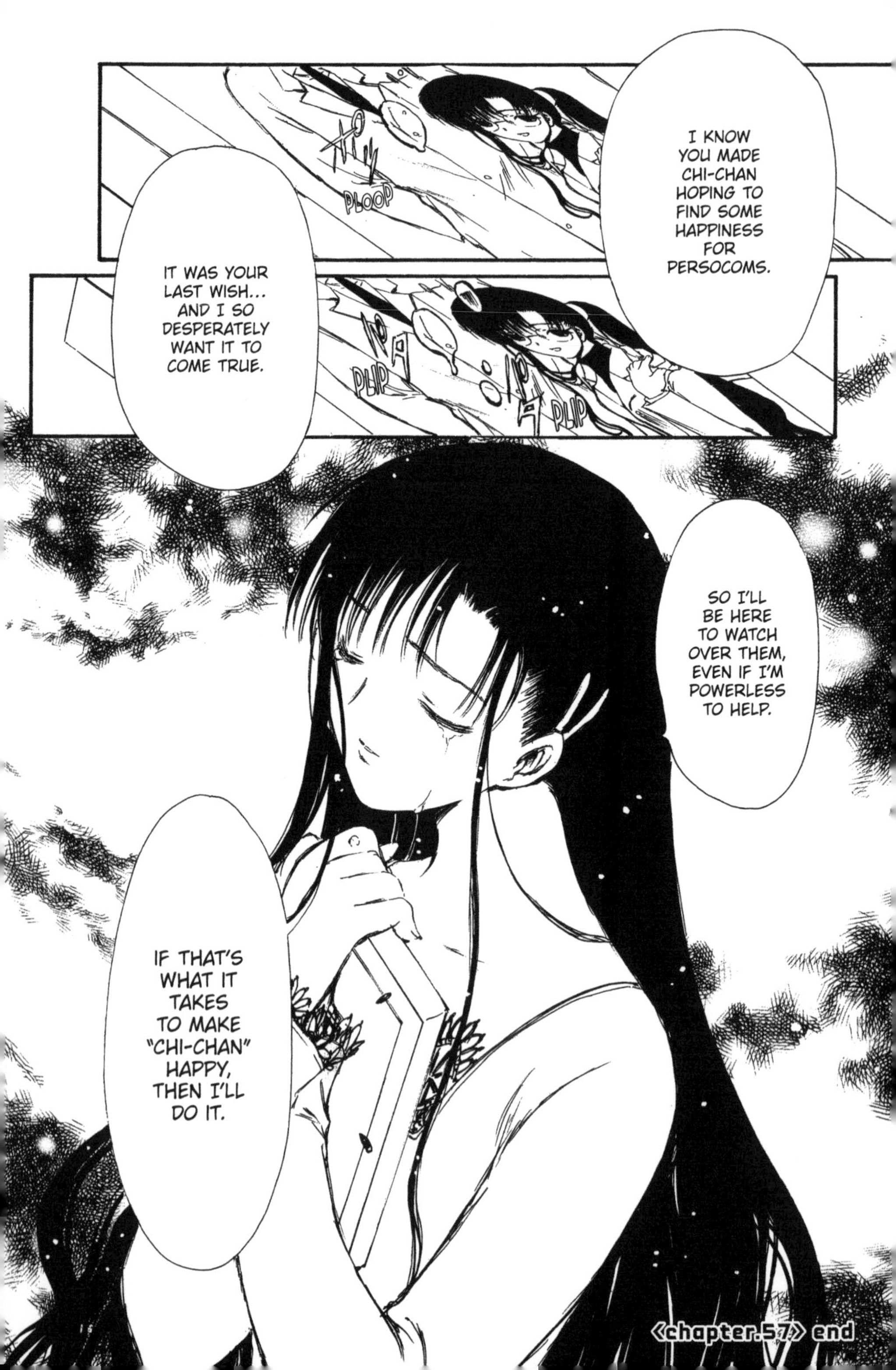
I KNOW YOU MADE CHI-CHAN HOPING TO FIND SOME HAPPINESS FOR PERSOCOMS.
PLOOP
IT WAS YOUR LAST WISH... AND I SO DESPERATELY WANT IT TO COME TRUE.
PLIP
PLIP
SO I'LL BE HERE TO WATCH OVER THEM, EVEN IF I'M POWERLESS TO HELP.
IF THAT'S WHAT IT TAKES TO MAKE "CHI-CHAN" HAPPY, THEN I'LL DO IT.
«chapter.57» end

Chobits

〈chapter.58〉

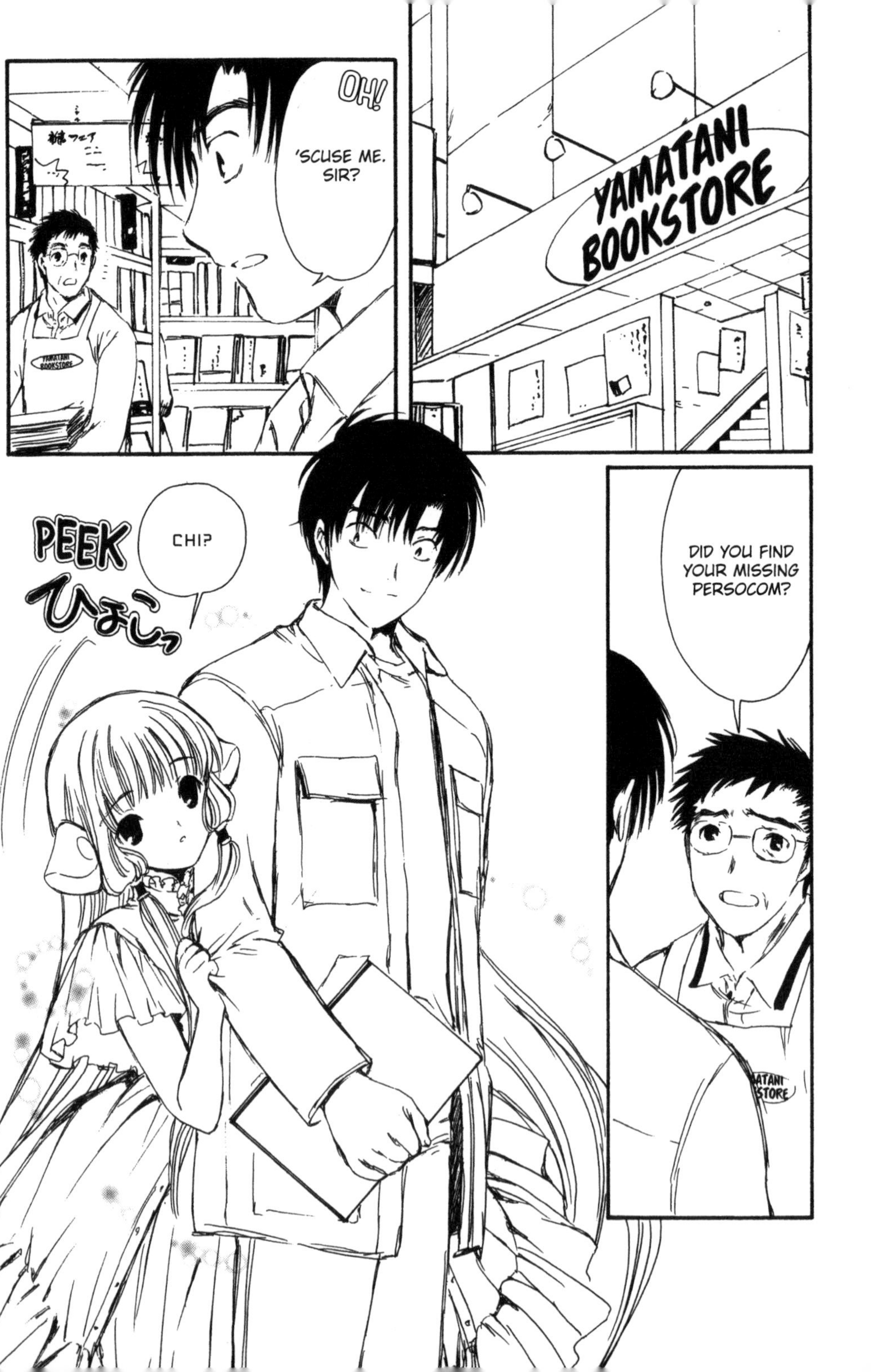
YAMATANI BOOKSTORE
OH!
'SCUSE ME. SIR?
YAMATANI BOOKSTORE
DID YOU FIND YOUR MISSING PERSOCOM?
CHI?
PEEK
ひょこっ

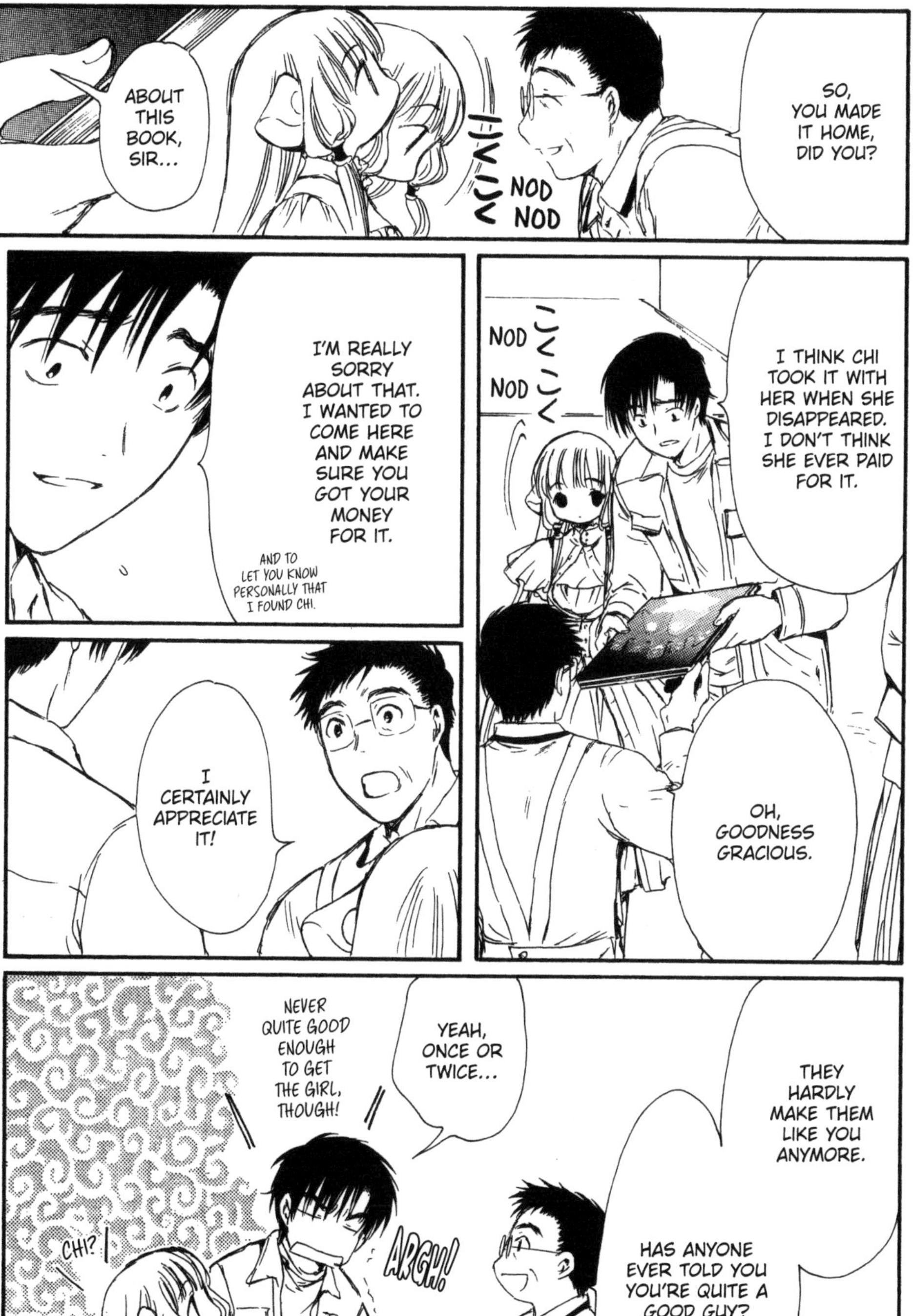
SO, YOU MADE IT HOME, DID YOU?
NOD NOD
ABOUT THIS BOOK, SIR...
I THINK CHI TOOK IT WITH HER WHEN SHE DISAPPEARED. I DON'T THINK SHE EVER PAID FOR IT.
NOD NOD
OH, GOODNESS GRACIOUS.
I'M REALLY SORRY ABOUT THAT. I WANTED TO COME HERE AND MAKE SURE YOU GOT YOUR MONEY FOR IT.
AND TO LET YOU KNOW PERSONALLY THAT I FOUND CHI.
I CERTAINLY APPRECIATE IT!
THEY HARDLY MAKE THEM LIKE YOU ANYMORE.
HAS ANYONE EVER TOLD YOU YOU'RE QUITE A GOOD GUY?
YEAH, ONCE OR TWICE...
ARGH!
NEVER QUITE GOOD ENOUGH TO GET THE GIRL, THOUGH!
CHI?

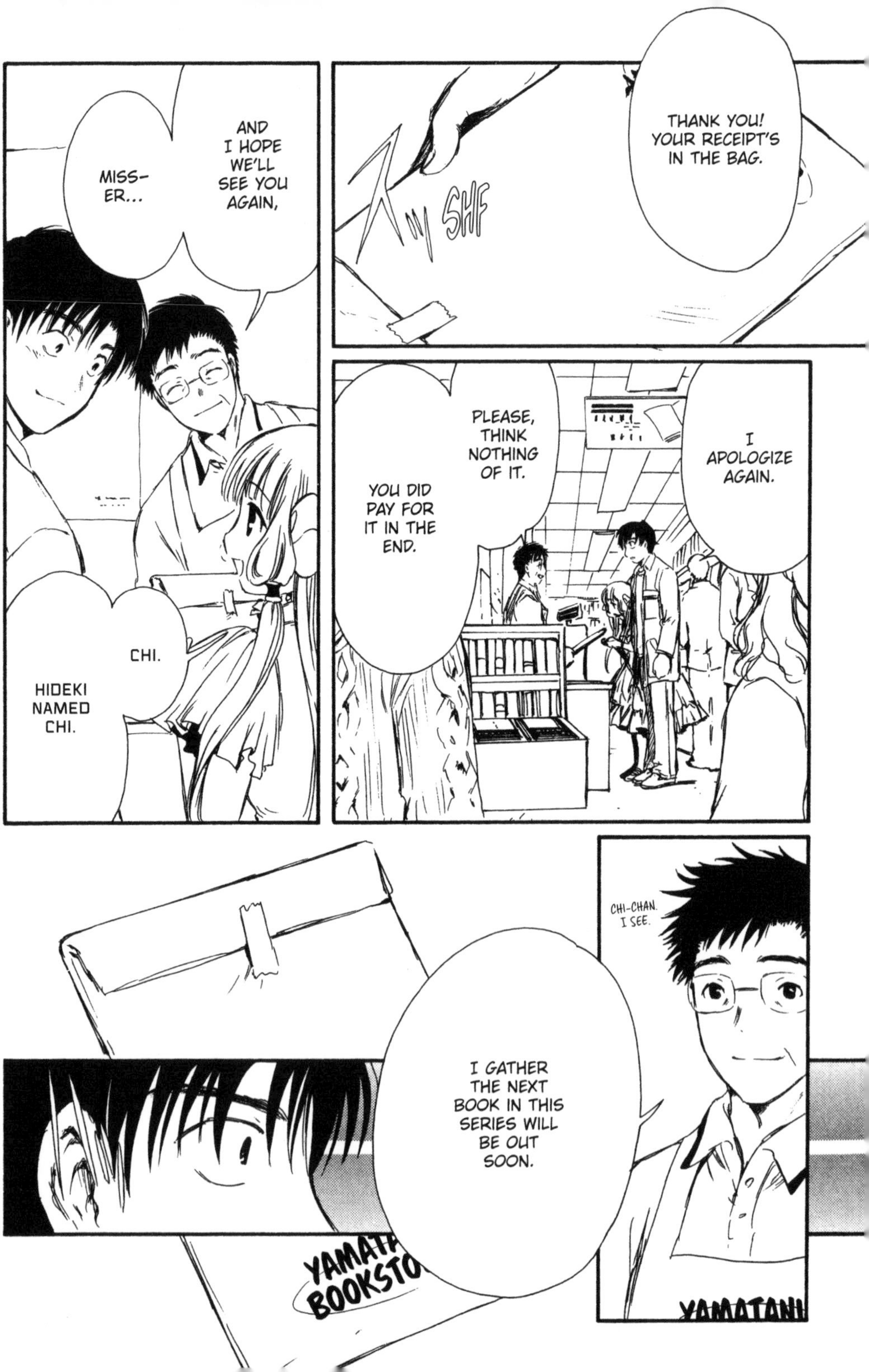
THANK YOU! YOUR RECEIPT'S IN THE BAG.
SHF
AND I HOPE WE'LL SEE YOU AGAIN,
MISS-ER...
I APOLOGIZE AGAIN.
PLEASE, THINK NOTHING OF IT.
YOU DID PAY FOR IT IN THE END.
CHI.
HIDEKI NAMED CHI.
CHI-CHAN. I SEE.
I GATHER THE NEXT BOOK IN THIS SERIES WILL BE OUT SOON.
YAMATANI
YAMATA
BOOKSTO

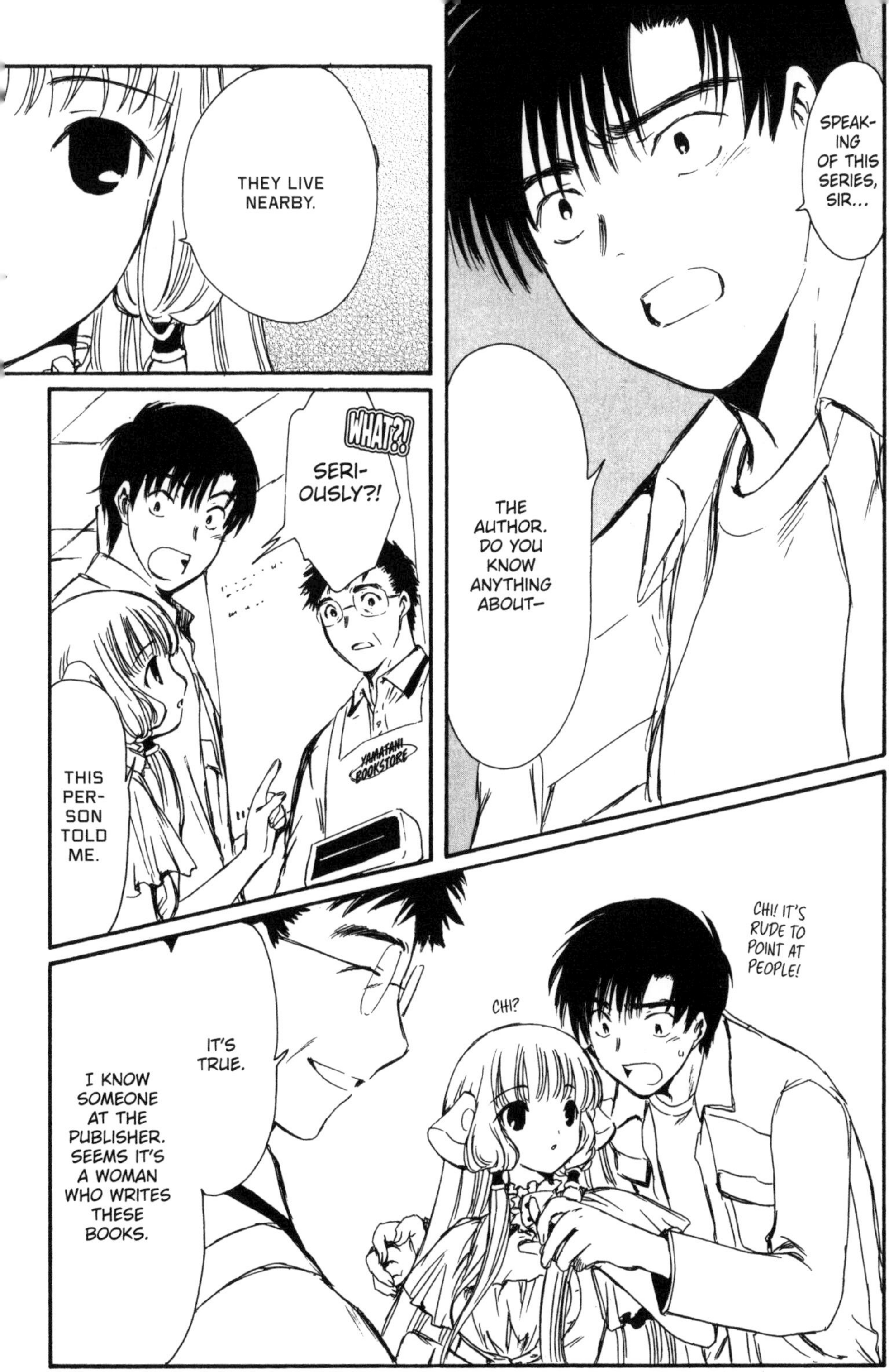
SPEAK-ING OF THIS SERIES, SIR...
THE AUTHOR. DO YOU KNOW ANYTHING ABOUT-
THEY LIVE NEARBY.
WHAT?!
SERI-OUSLY?!
THIS PER-SON TOLD ME.
CHI! IT'S RUDE TO POINT AT PEOPLE!
CHI?
IT'S TRUE.
I KNOW SOMEONE AT THE PUBLISHER. SEEMS IT'S A WOMAN WHO WRITES THESE BOOKS.

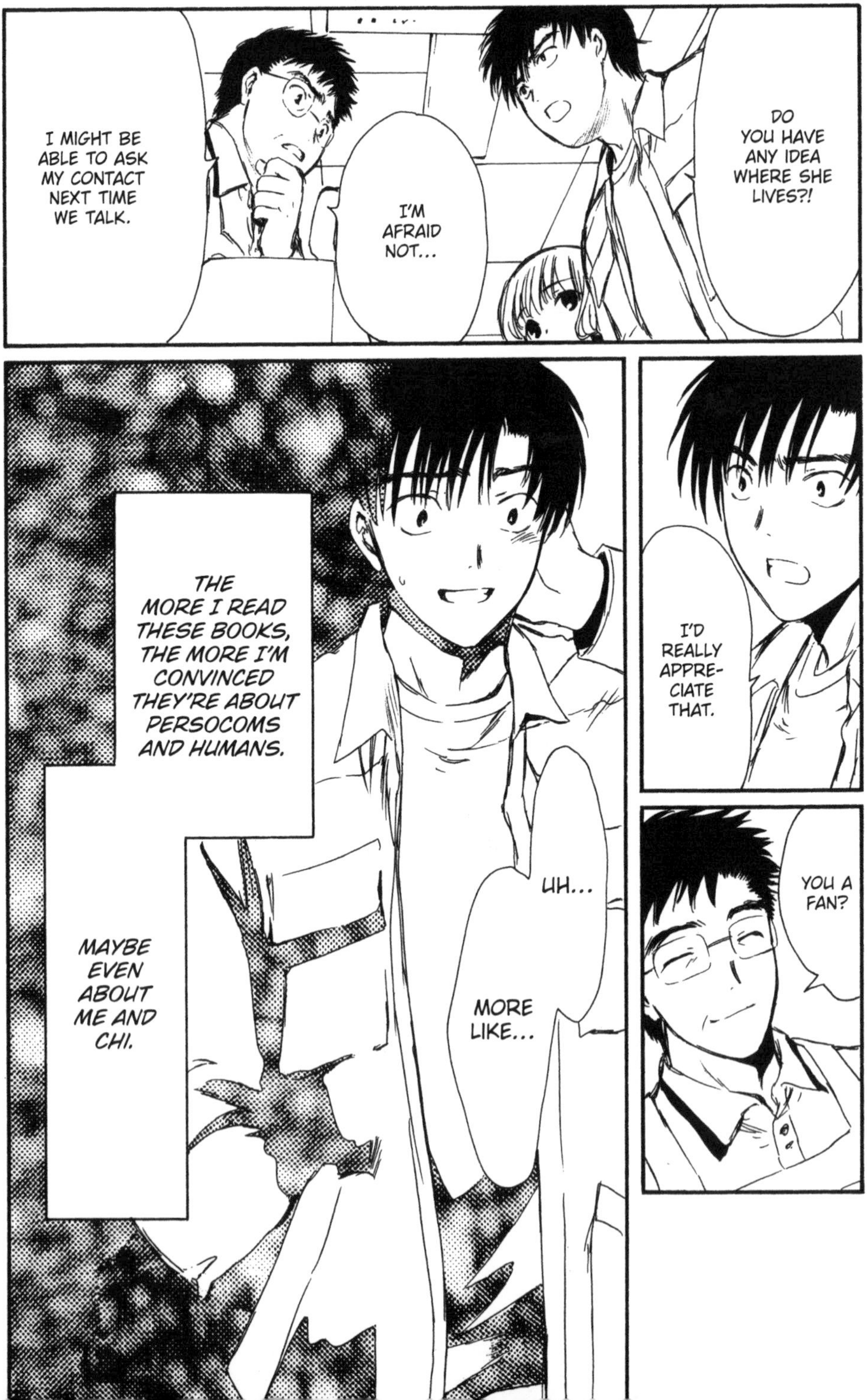
DO YOU HAVE ANY IDEA WHERE SHE LIVES?!
I'M AFRAID NOT...
I MIGHT BE ABLE TO ASK MY CONTACT NEXT TIME WE TALK.
I'D REALLY APPRE-CIATE THAT.
YOU A FAN?
UH...
MORE LIKE...
THE MORE I READ THESE BOOKS, THE MORE I'M CONVINCED THEY'RE ABOUT PERSOCOMS AND HUMANS.
MAYBE EVEN ABOUT ME AND CHI.

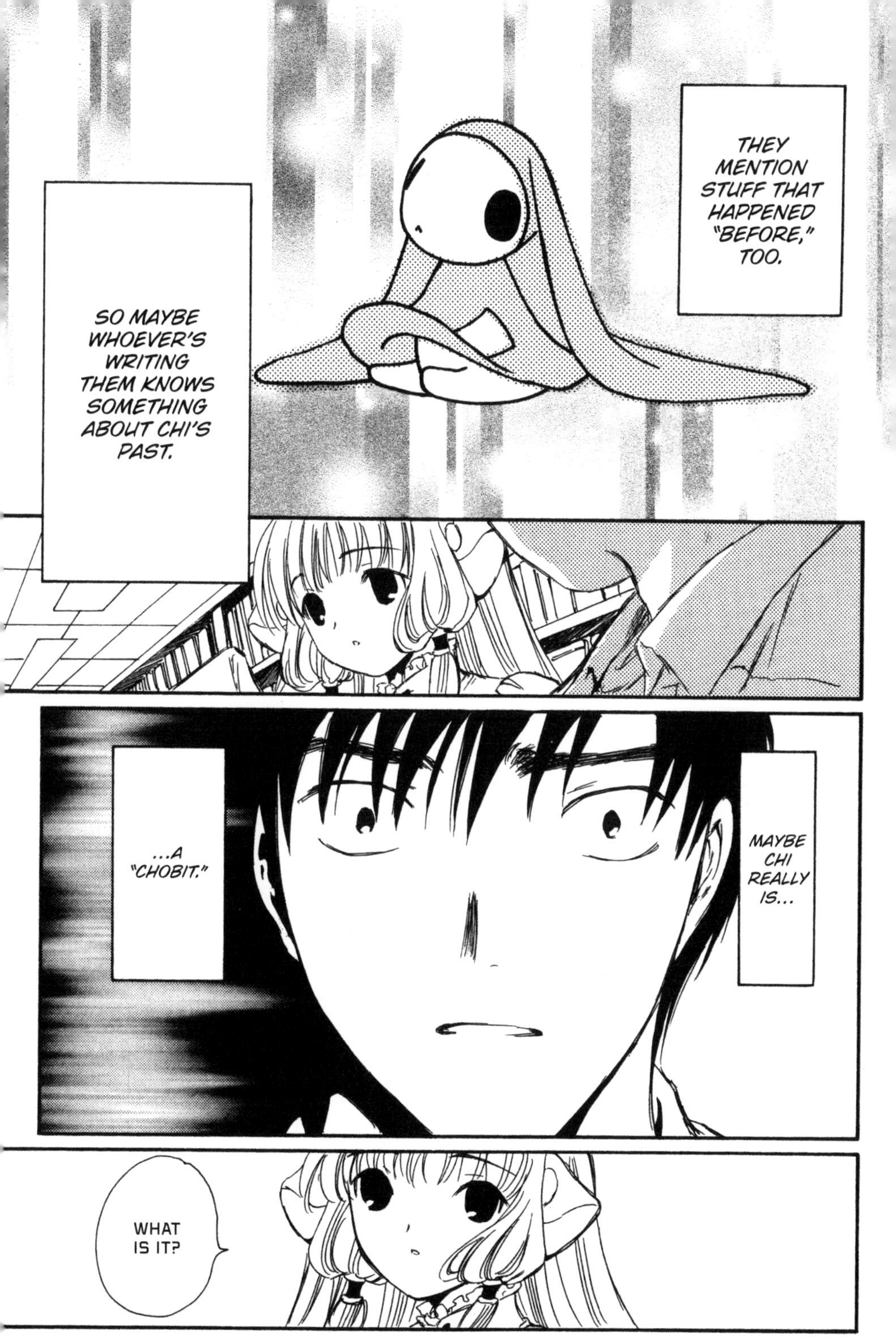
THEY MENTION STUFF THAT HAPPENED "BEFORE," TOO.
SO MAYBE WHOEVER'S WRITING THEM KNOWS SOMETHING ABOUT CHI'S PAST.
MAYBE CHI REALLY IS...
...A "CHOBIT."
WHAT IS IT?

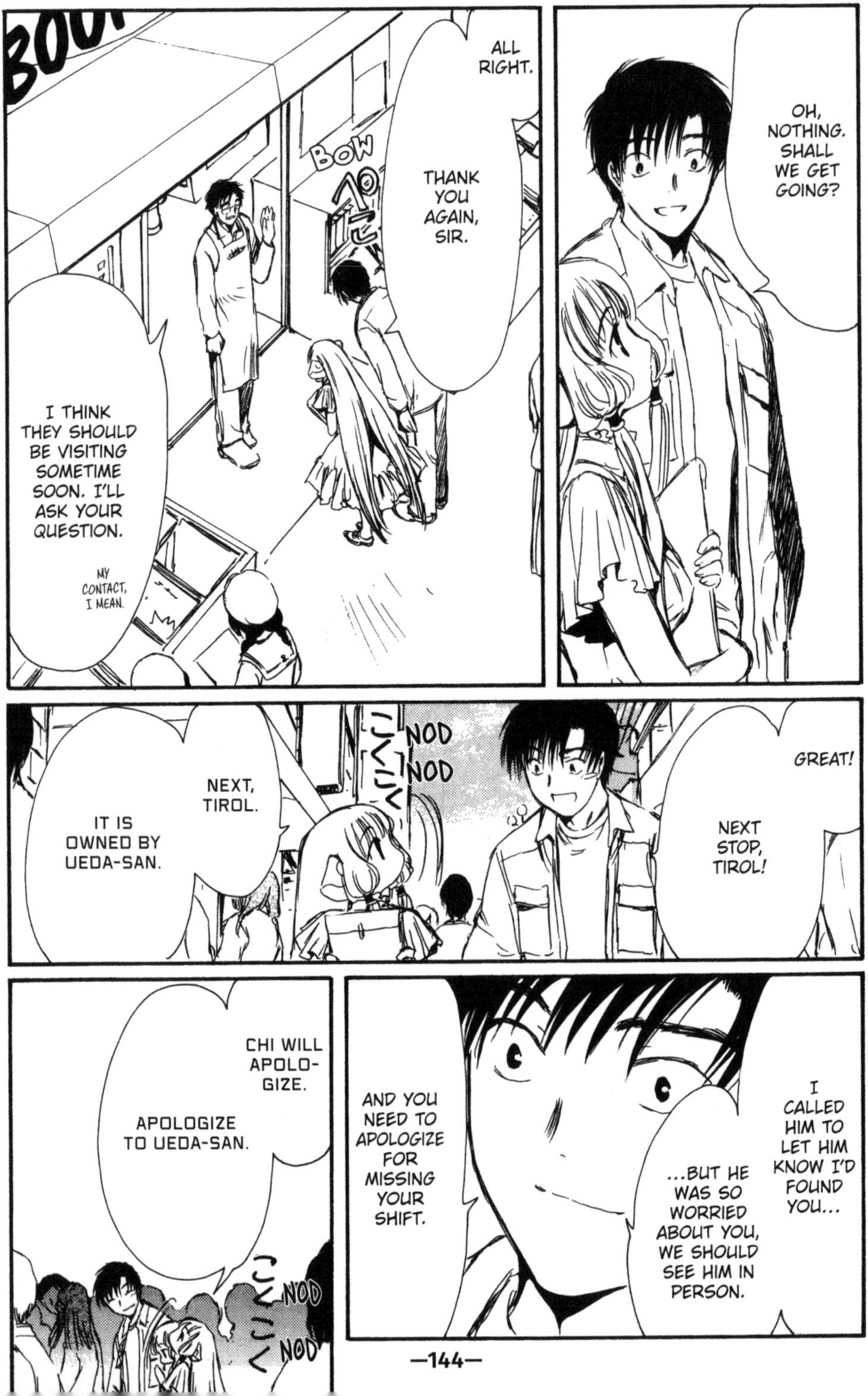
OH, NOTHING. SHALL WE GET GOING?
ALL RIGHT.
THANK YOU AGAIN, SIR.
BOW
I THINK THEY SHOULD BE VISITING SOMETIME SOON. I'LL ASK YOUR QUESTION.
MY CONTACT, I MEAN.
GREAT!
NEXT STOP, TIROL!
NOD NOD
NEXT, TIROL.
IT IS OWNED BY UEDA-SAN.
I CALLED HIM TO LET HIM KNOW I'D FOUND YOU...
...BUT HE WAS SO WORRIED ABOUT YOU, WE SHOULD SEE HIM IN PERSON.
AND YOU NEED TO APOLOGIZE FOR MISSING YOUR SHIFT.
CHI WILL APOLOGIZE.
APOLOGIZE TO UEDA-SAN.
NOD NOD

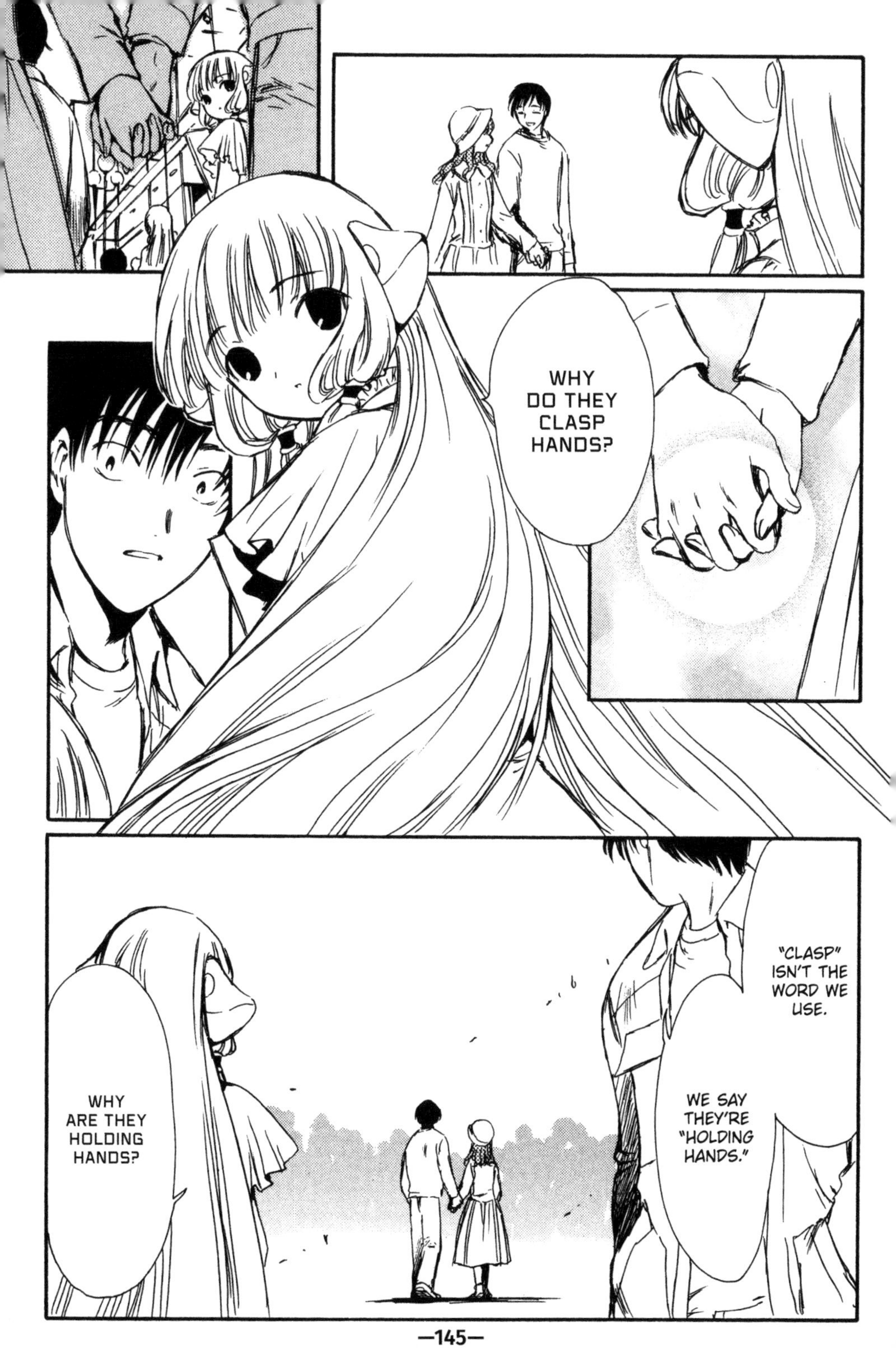
WHY
DO THEY
CLASP
HANDS?
"CLASP" ISN'T THE WORD WE USE.
WE SAY THEY'RE "HOLDING HANDS."
WHY ARE THEY HOLDING HANDS?

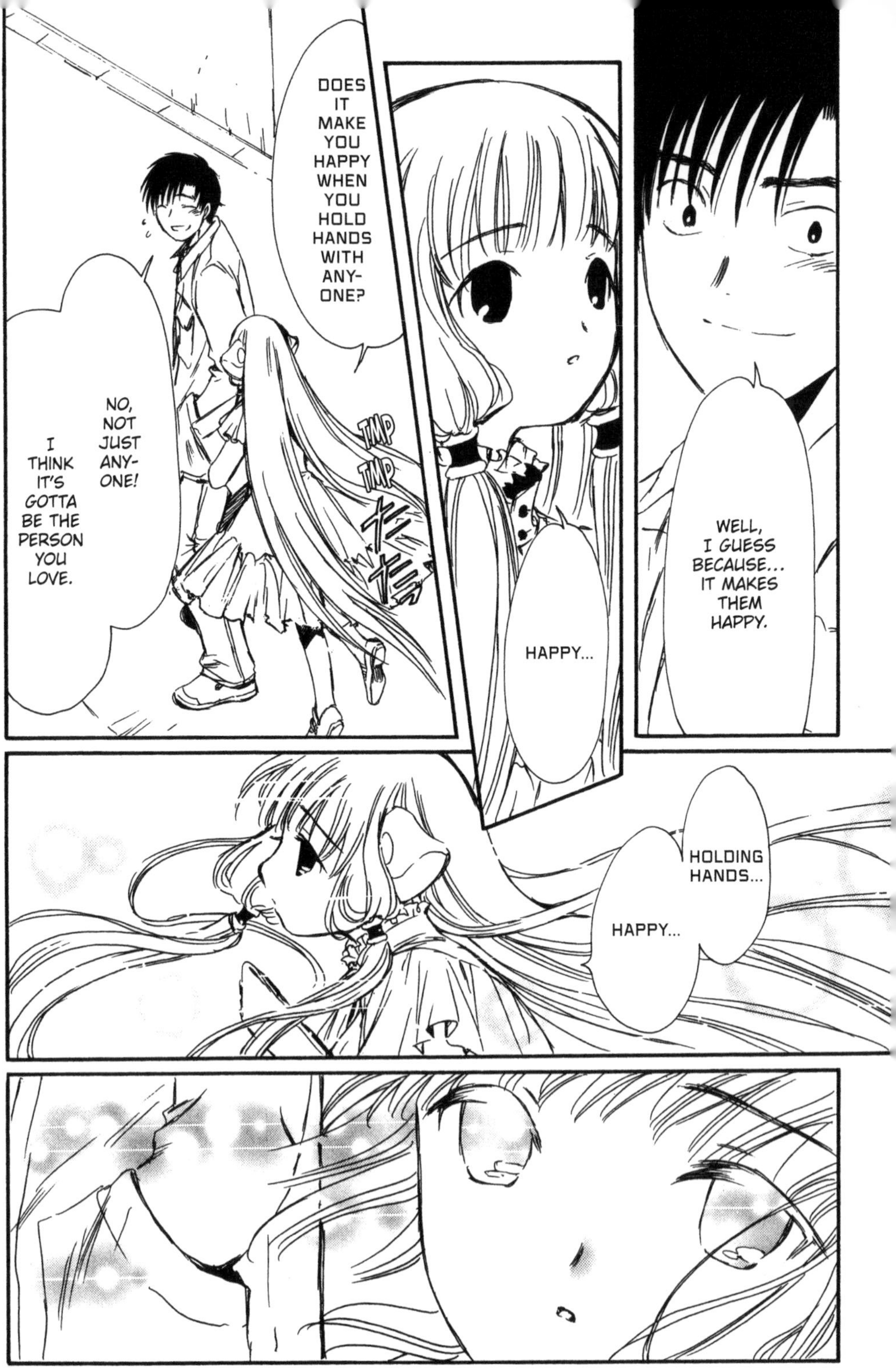

WELL, I GUESS BECAUSE... IT MAKES THEM HAPPY.
HAPPY...
DOES IT MAKE YOU HAPPY WHEN YOU HOLD HANDS WITH ANY-ONE?
TMP TMP
NO, NOT JUST ANY-ONE!
I THINK IT'S GOTTA BE THE PERSON YOU LOVE.
HOLDING HANDS...
HAPPY...

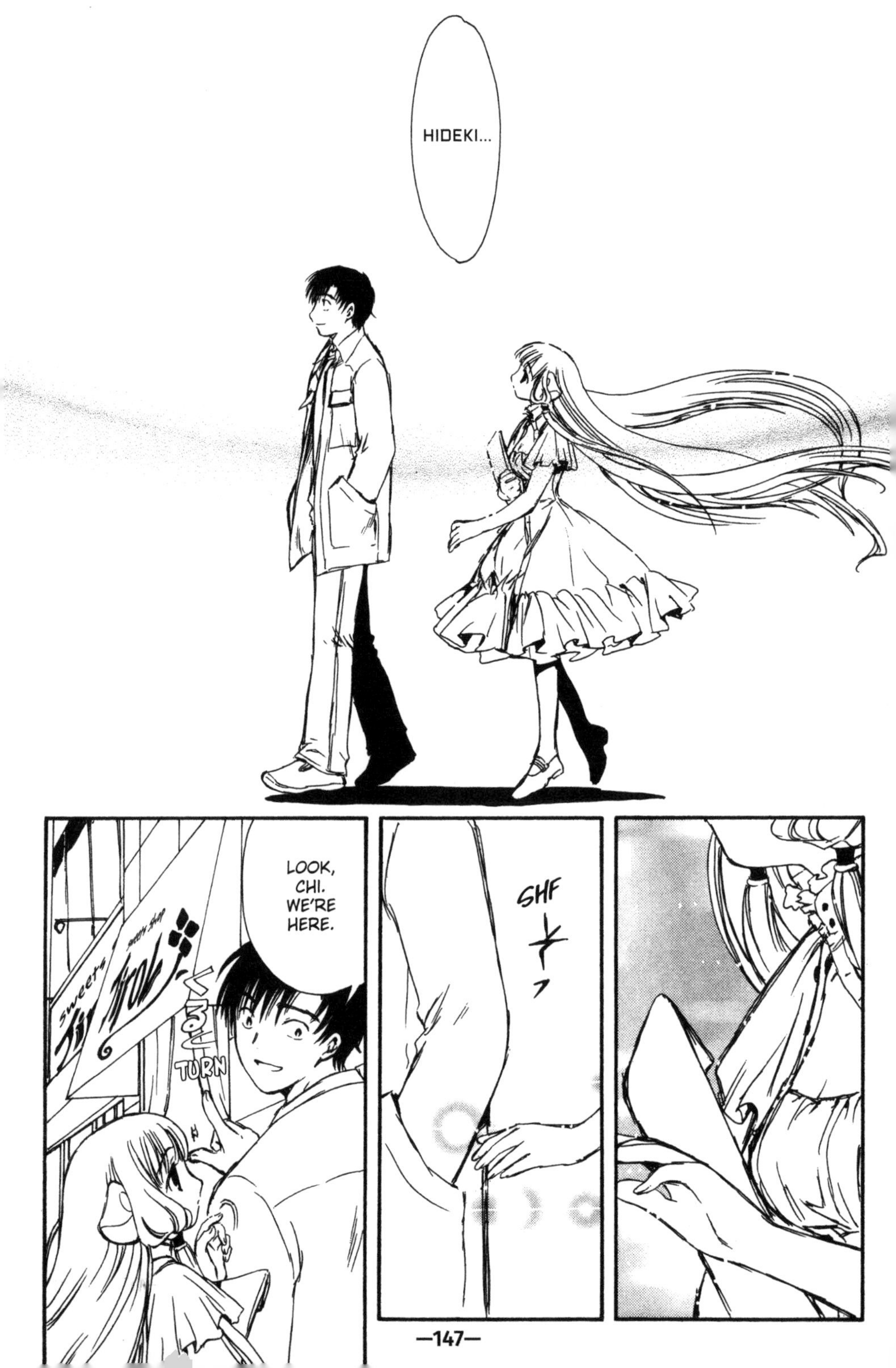
HIDEKI...
SHF
LOOK, CHI. WE'RE HERE.
TURN

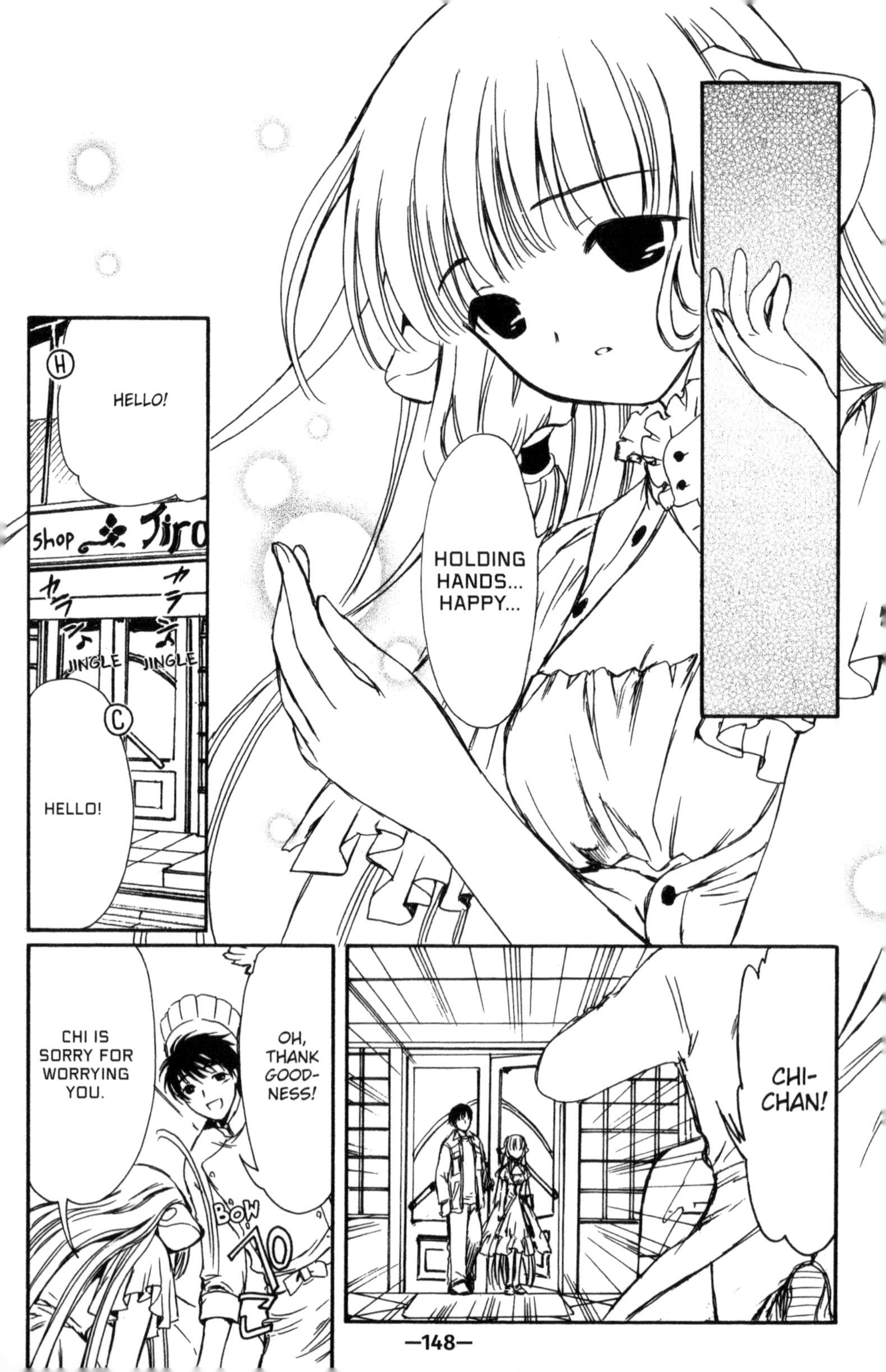
HOLDING HANDS... HAPPY...
HELLO!
shop Jiro
JINGLE JINGLE
HELLO!
CHI-CHAN!
OH, THANK GOOD-NESS!
CHI IS SORRY FOR WORRYING YOU.
BOW

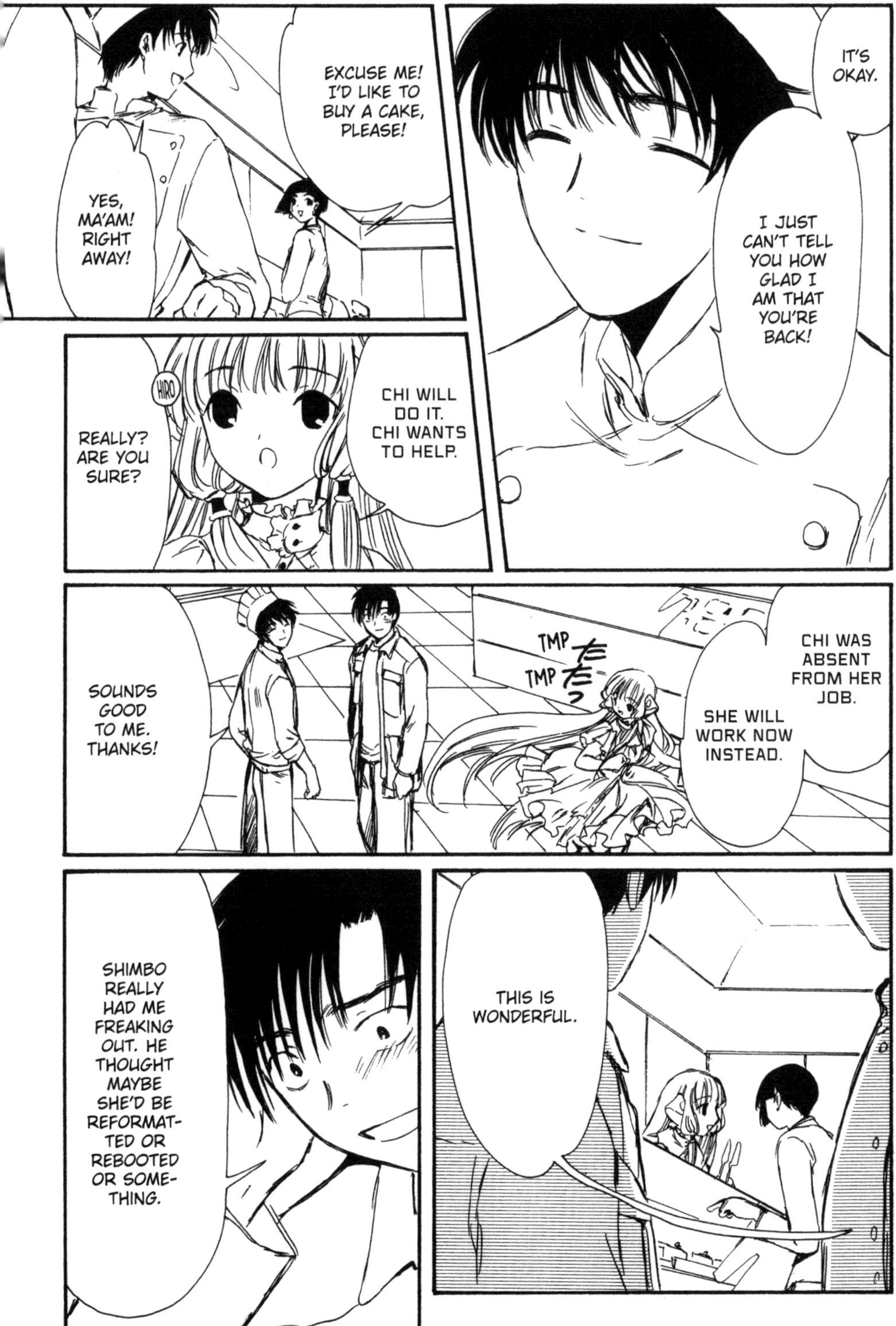
IT'S OKAY.
I JUST CAN'T TELL YOU HOW GLAD I AM THAT YOU'RE BACK!
EXCUSE ME! I'D LIKE TO BUY A CAKE, PLEASE!
YES, MA'AM! RIGHT AWAY!
CHI WILL DO IT. CHI WANTS TO HELP.
HIRO
REALLY? ARE YOU SURE?
CHI WAS ABSENT FROM HER JOB.
SHE WILL WORK NOW INSTEAD.
TMP TMP
SOUNDS GOOD TO ME. THANKS!
THIS IS WONDERFUL.
SHIMBO REALLY HAD ME FREAKING OUT. HE THOUGHT MAYBE SHE'D BE REFORMAT-TED OR REBOOTED OR SOME-THING.

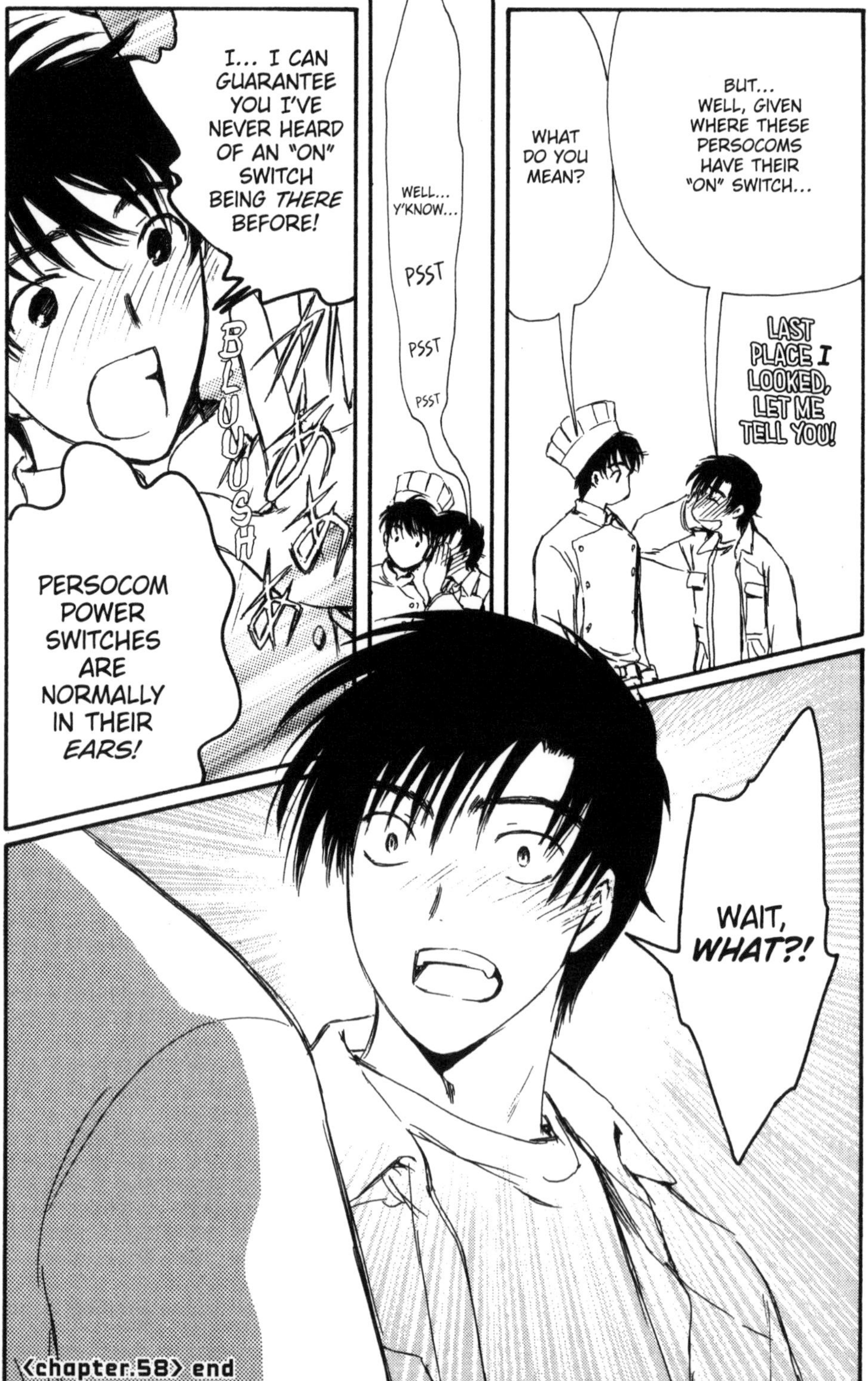
BUT... WELL, GIVEN WHERE THESE PERSOCOMS HAVE THEIR "ON" SWITCH...
WHAT DO YOU MEAN?
LAST PLACE I LOOKED, LET ME TELL YOU!
WELL... Y'KNOW...
PSST
PSST
PSST
I... I CAN GUARANTEE YOU I'VE NEVER HEARD OF AN "ON" SWITCH BEING *THERE* BEFORE!
BLUUUSH
PERSOCOM POWER SWITCHES ARE NORMALLY IN THEIR *EARS!*
WAIT, ***WHAT?!***
<chapter.58> end

〈chapter.59〉

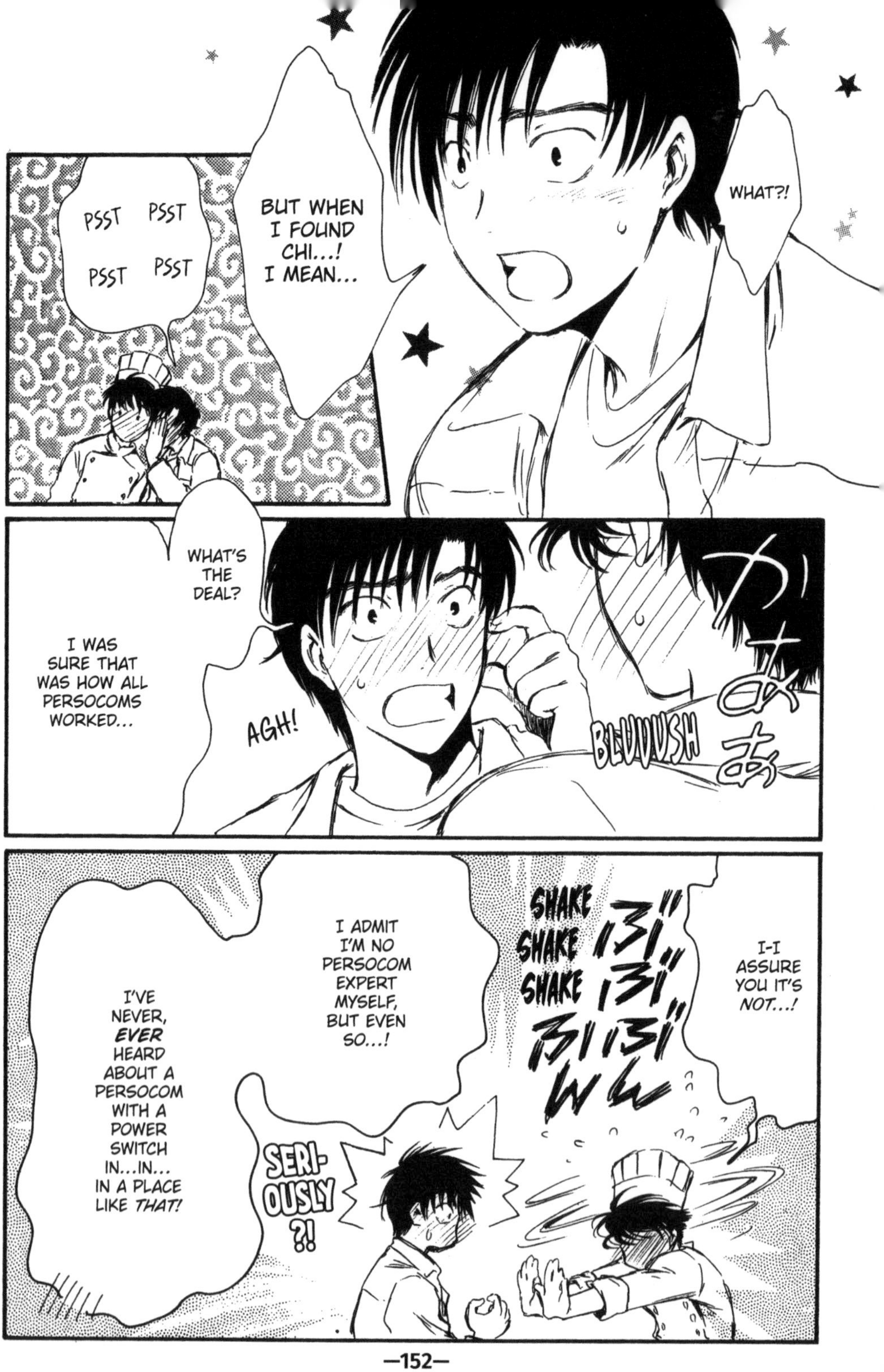
WHAT?!
BUT WHEN I FOUND CHI...! I MEAN...
PSST PSST PSST PSST
かぁぁ
BLUUUSH
WHAT'S THE DEAL?
AGH!
I WAS SURE THAT WAS HOW ALL PERSOCOMS WORKED...
I-I ASSURE YOU IT'S *NOT*...!
SHAKE SHAKE SHAKE
ぶんぶんぶん
I ADMIT I'M NO PERSOCOM EXPERT MYSELF, BUT EVEN SO...!
SERIOUSLY?!
I'VE NEVER, ***EVER*** HEARD ABOUT A PERSOCOM WITH A POWER SWITCH IN...IN... IN A PLACE LIKE *THAT!*

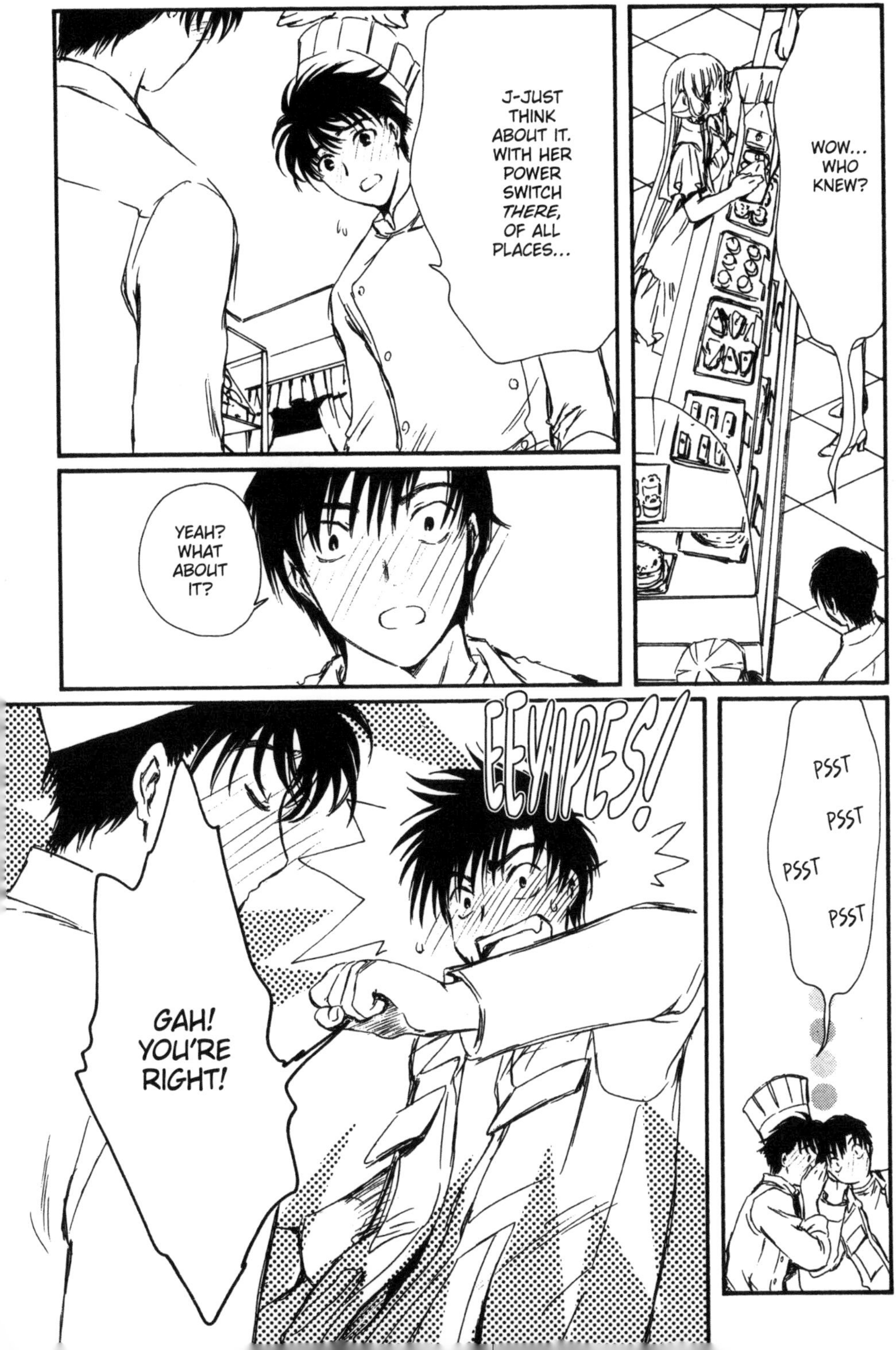
WOW... WHO KNEW?
J-JUST THINK ABOUT IT. WITH HER POWER SWITCH *THERE*, OF ALL PLACES...
YEAH? WHAT ABOUT IT?
PSST PSST PSST PSST
EEYIPES!
GAH! YOU'RE RIGHT!

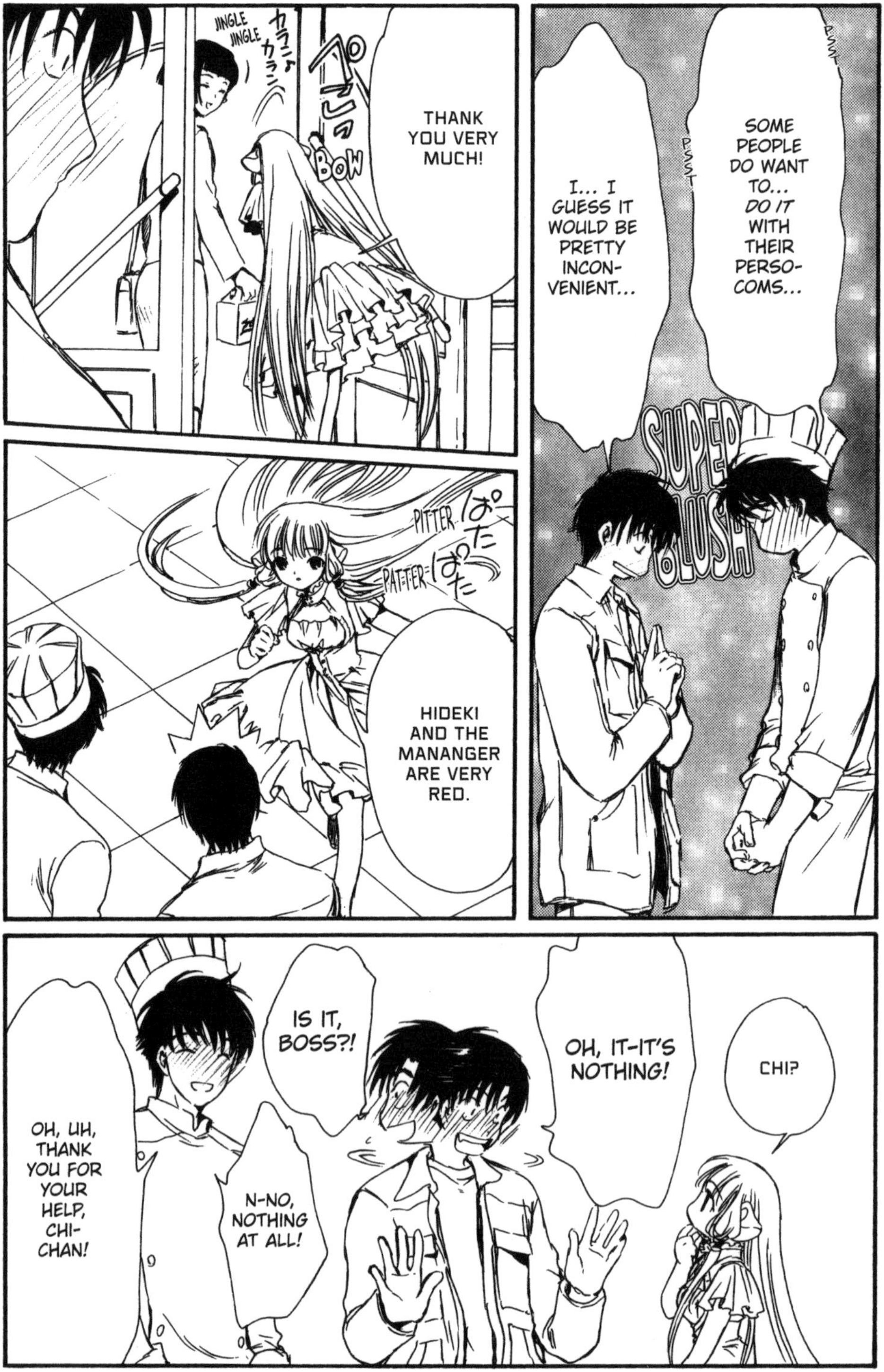
PSSST
SOME PEOPLE DO WANT TO... *DO IT* WITH THEIR PERSO-COMS...
PSSST
I... I GUESS IT WOULD BE PRETTY INCON-VENIENT...
SUPER BLUSH
THANK YOU VERY MUCH!
BOW
カランカラン
JINGLE JINGLE
HIDEKI AND THE MANANGER ARE VERY RED.
ぱたぱた
PITTER PATTER
CHI?
OH, IT-IT'S NOTHING!
IS IT, BOSS?!
N-NO, NOTHING AT ALL!
OH, UH, THANK YOU FOR YOUR HELP, CHI-CHAN!

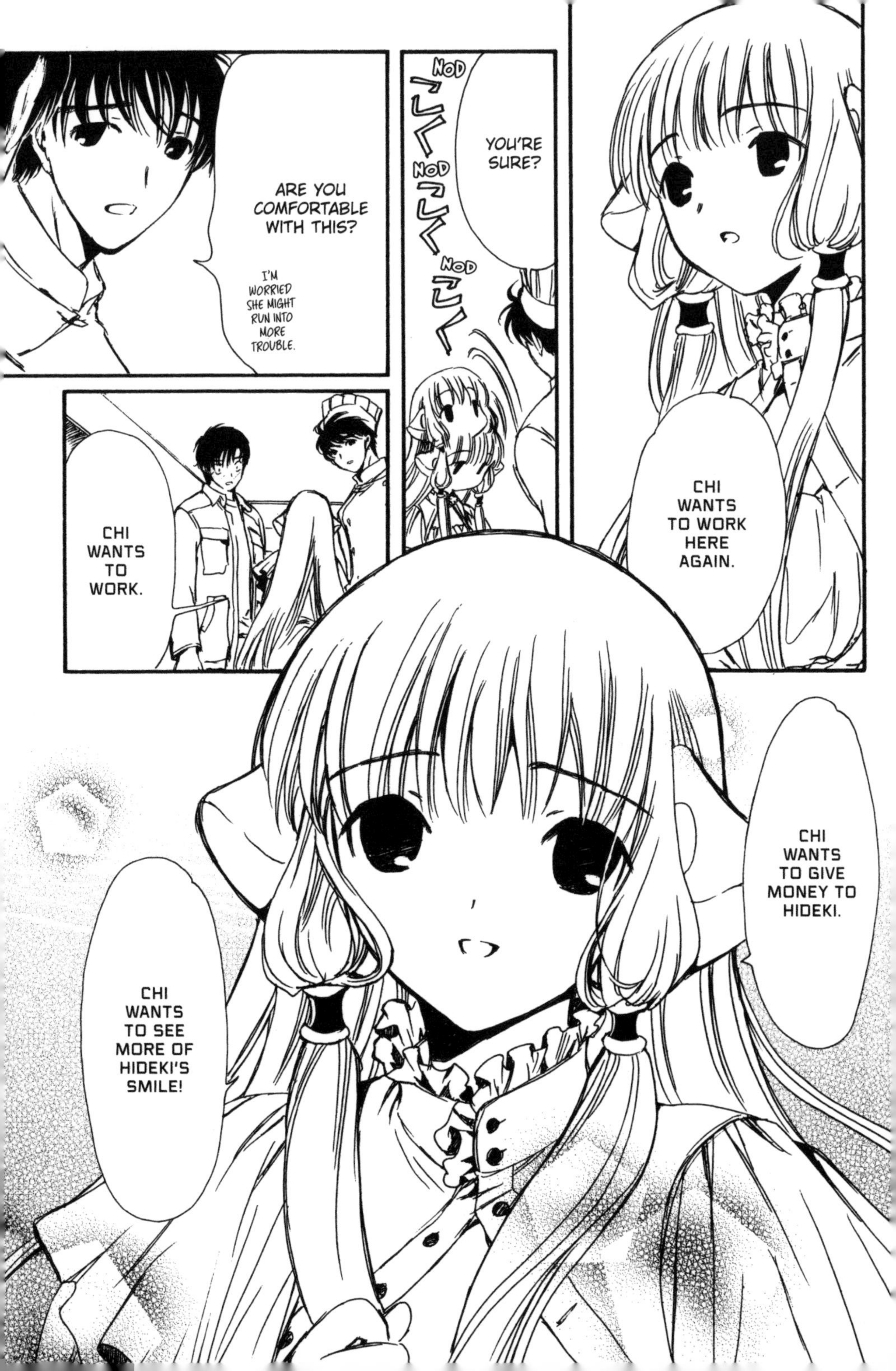
CHI WANTS TO WORK HERE AGAIN.
YOU'RE SURE?
NOD
NOD
NOD
ARE YOU COMFORTABLE WITH THIS?
I'M WORRIED SHE MIGHT RUN INTO MORE TROUBLE.
CHI WANTS TO WORK.
CHI WANTS TO GIVE MONEY TO HIDEKI.
CHI WANTS TO SEE MORE OF HIDEKI'S SMILE!

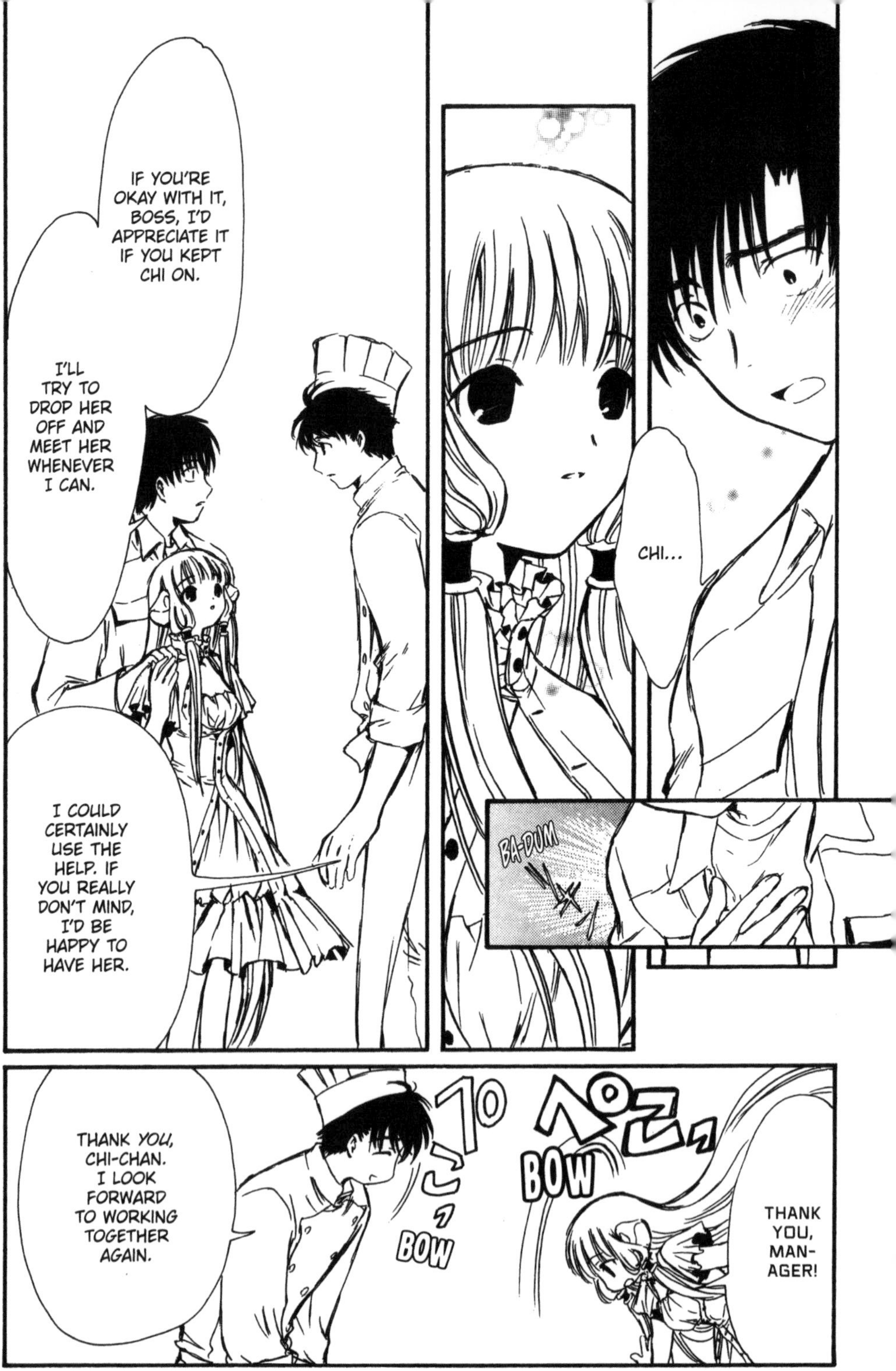
CHI...
BA-DUM
IF YOU'RE OKAY WITH IT, BOSS, I'D APPRECIATE IT IF YOU KEPT CHI ON.
I'LL TRY TO DROP HER OFF AND MEET HER WHENEVER I CAN.
I COULD CERTAINLY USE THE HELP. IF YOU REALLY DON'T MIND, I'D BE HAPPY TO HAVE HER.
THANK YOU, MAN-AGER!
BOW
BOW
THANK *YOU*, CHI-CHAN. I LOOK FORWARD TO WORKING TOGETHER AGAIN.

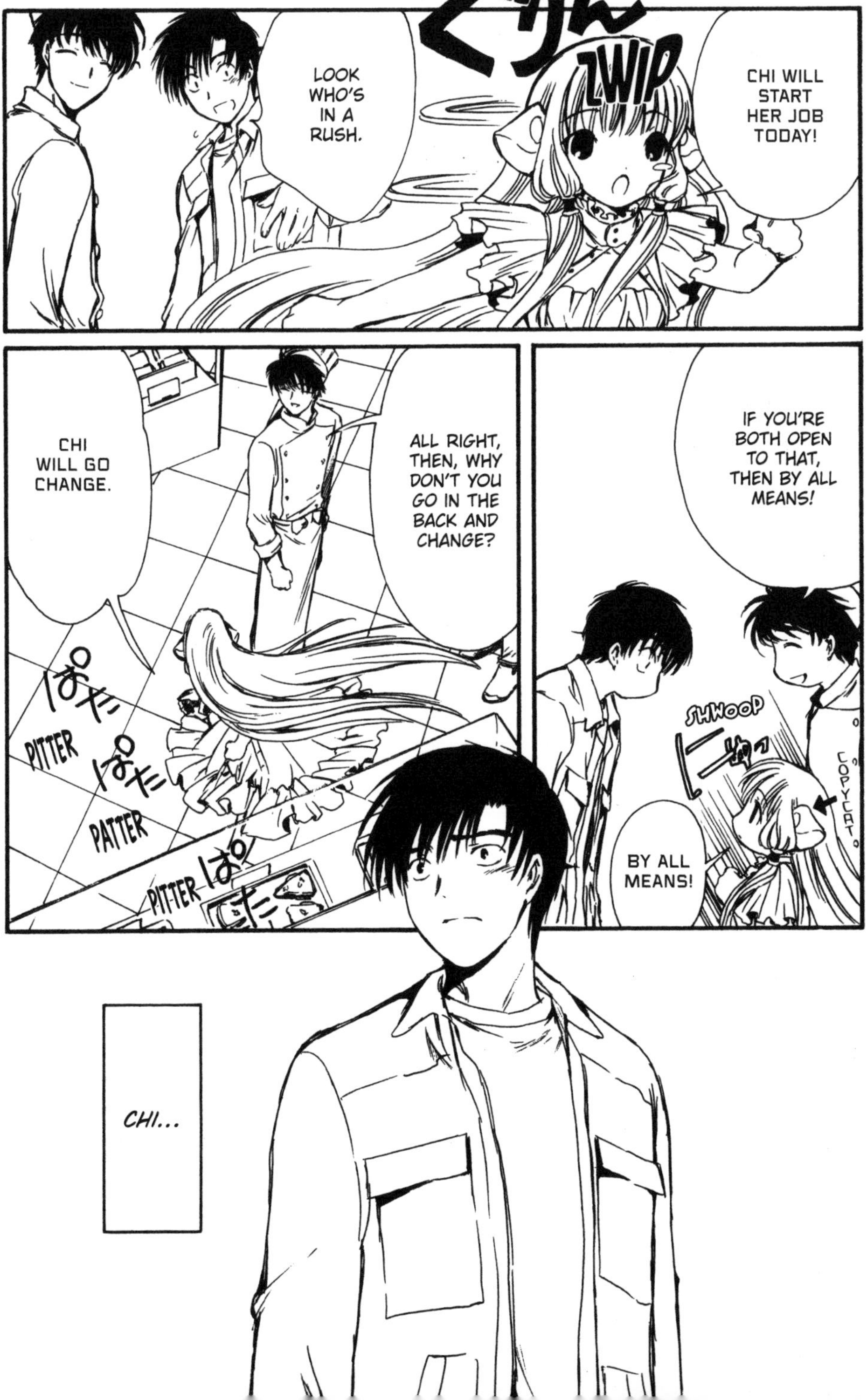
CHI WILL START HER JOB TODAY!
ぐりん
ZWIP
LOOK WHO'S IN A RUSH.
IF YOU'RE BOTH OPEN TO THAT, THEN BY ALL MEANS!
SHWOOP
COPYCAT
BY ALL MEANS!
ALL RIGHT, THEN, WHY DON'T YOU GO IN THE BACK AND CHANGE?
CHI WILL GO CHANGE.
ぱた
PITTER
ぱた
PATTER
ぱた
PITTER
CHI...

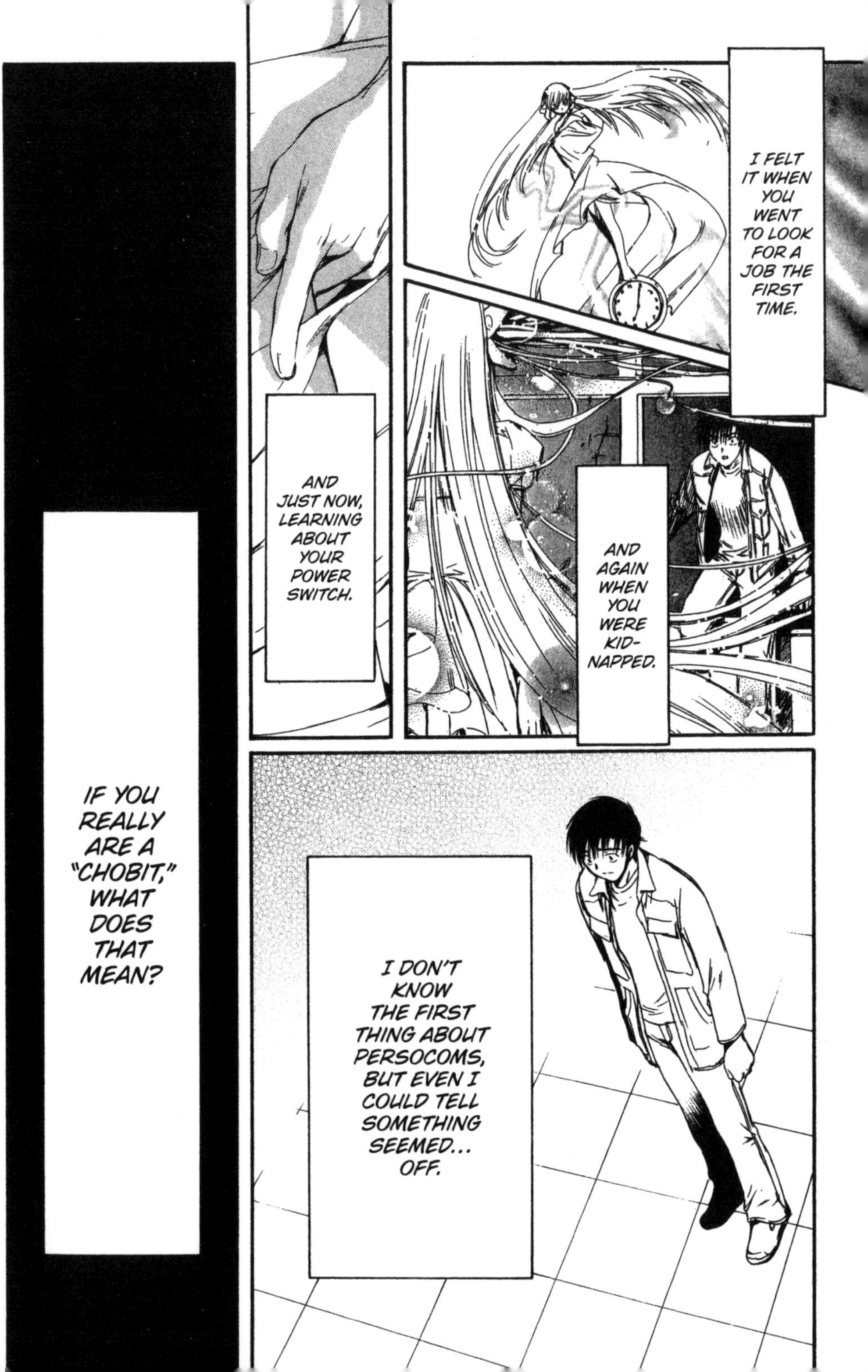
I FELT IT WHEN YOU WENT TO LOOK FOR A JOB THE FIRST TIME.
AND AGAIN WHEN YOU WERE KID-NAPPED.
AND JUST NOW, LEARNING ABOUT YOUR POWER SWITCH.
I DON'T KNOW THE FIRST THING ABOUT PERSOCOMS, BUT EVEN I COULD TELL SOMETHING SEEMED... OFF.
IF YOU REALLY ARE A "CHOBIT," WHAT DOES THAT MEAN?

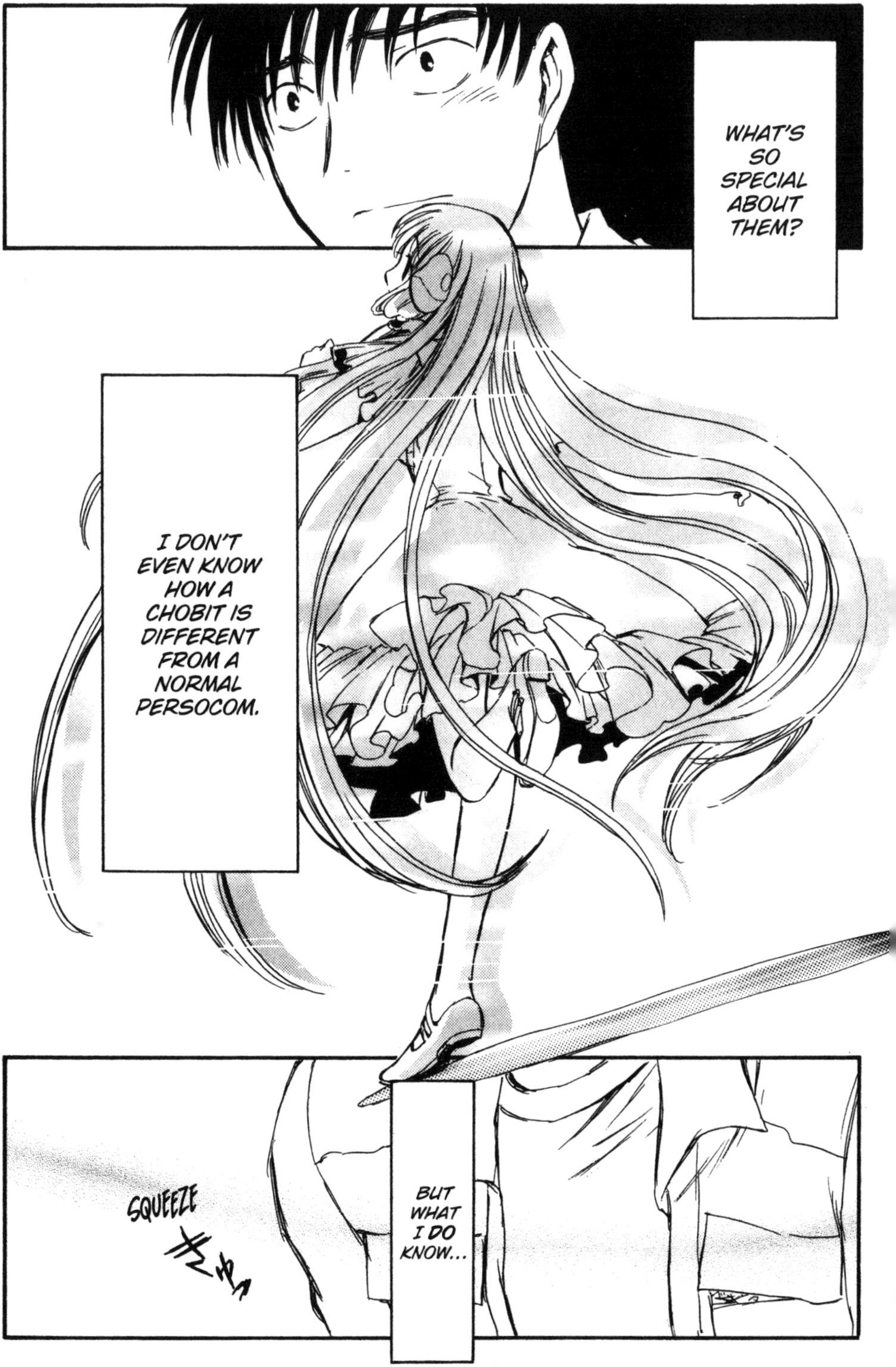
WHAT'S SO SPECIAL ABOUT THEM?
I DON'T EVEN KNOW HOW A CHOBIT IS DIFFERENT FROM A NORMAL PERSOCOM.
BUT WHAT I DO KNOW...
SQUEEZE

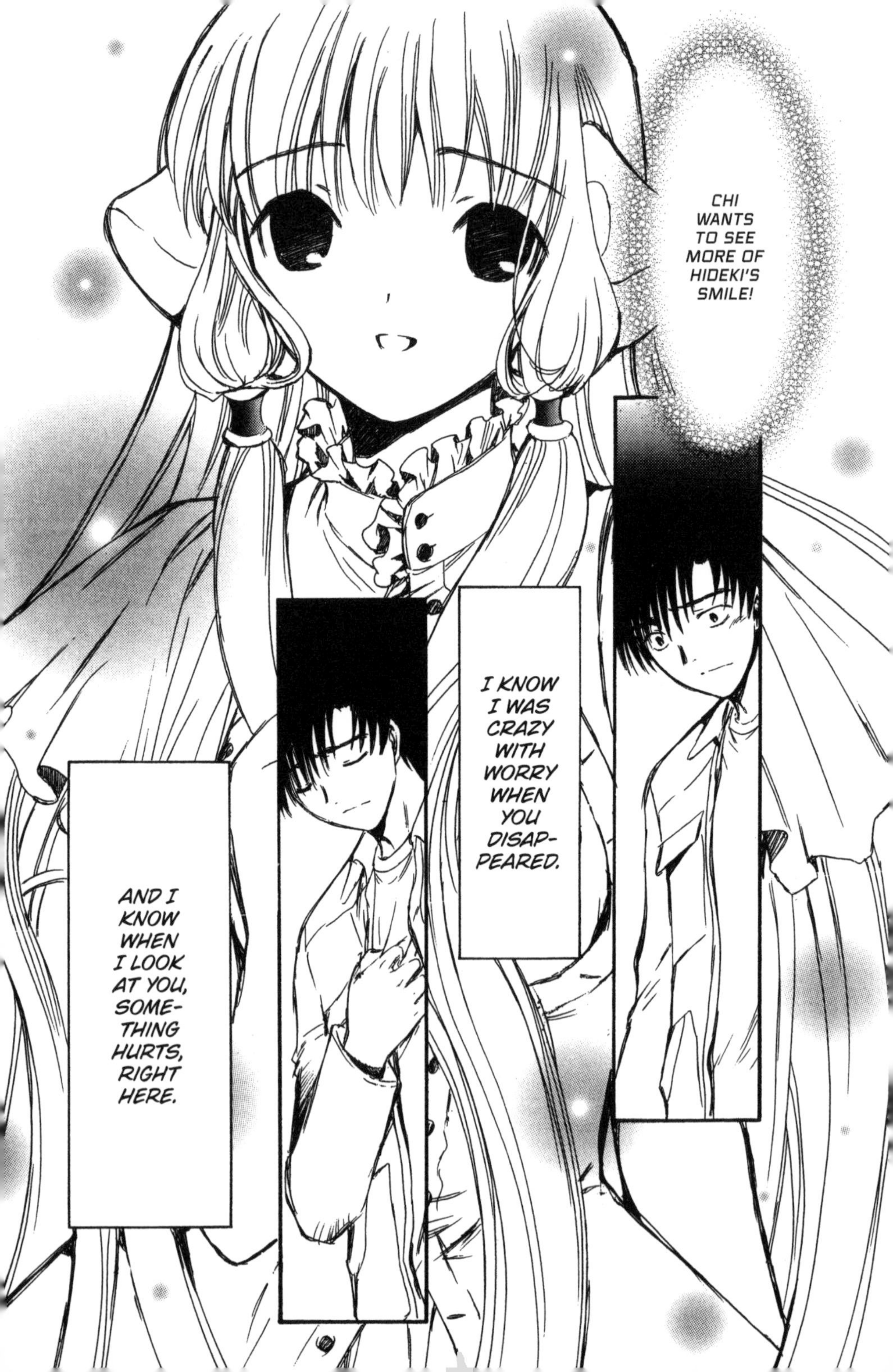
CHI WANTS TO SEE MORE OF HIDEKI'S SMILE!
I KNOW I WAS CRAZY WITH WORRY WHEN YOU DISAP-PEARED.
AND I KNOW WHEN I LOOK AT YOU, SOME-THING HURTS, RIGHT HERE.

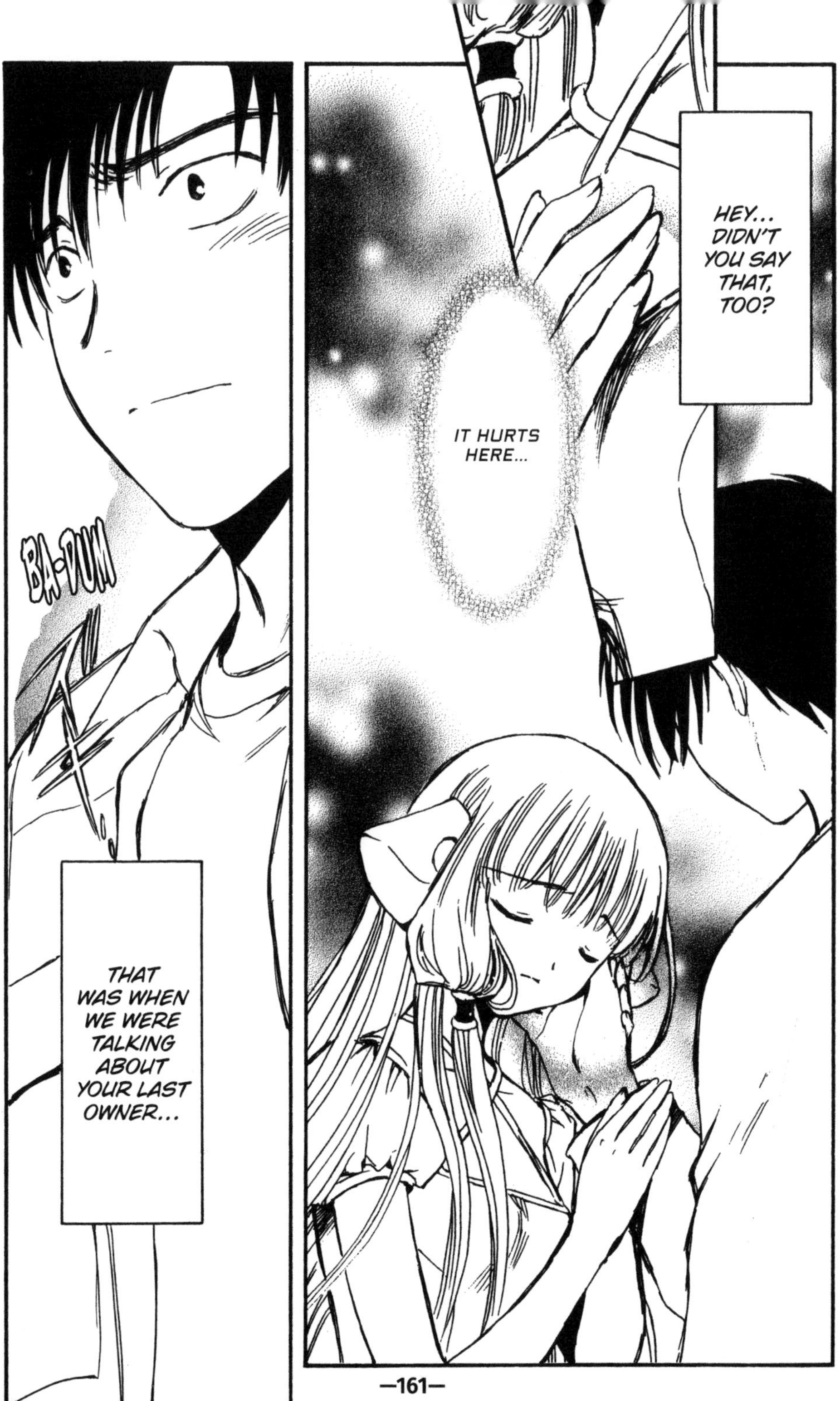
HEY... DIDN'T YOU SAY THAT, TOO?
IT HURTS HERE...
BA-DUM
THAT WAS WHEN WE WERE TALKING ABOUT YOUR LAST OWNER...

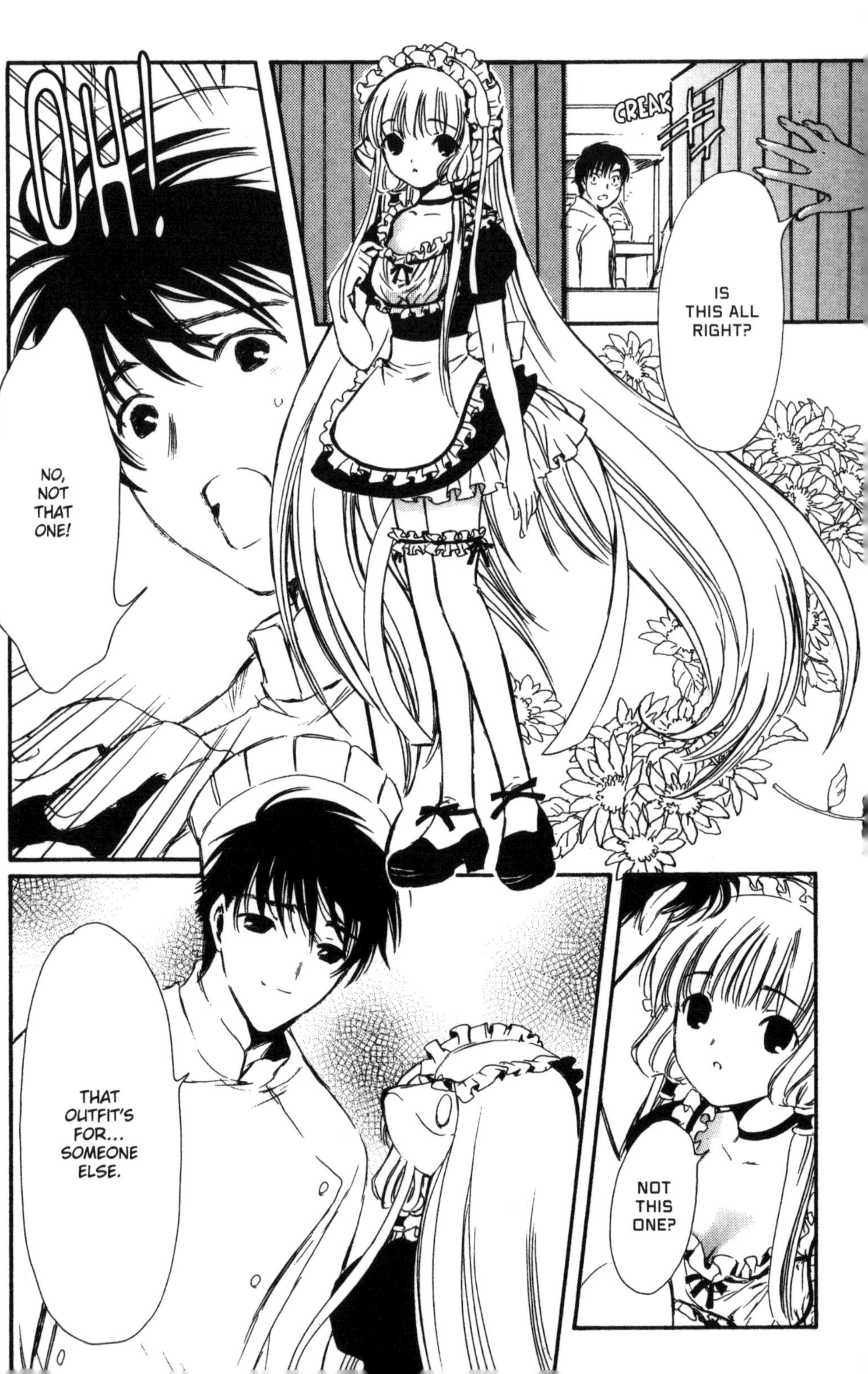
CREAK
IS THIS ALL RIGHT?
OH!
NO, NOT THAT ONE!
NOT THIS ONE?
THAT OUTFIT'S FOR... SOMEONE ELSE.

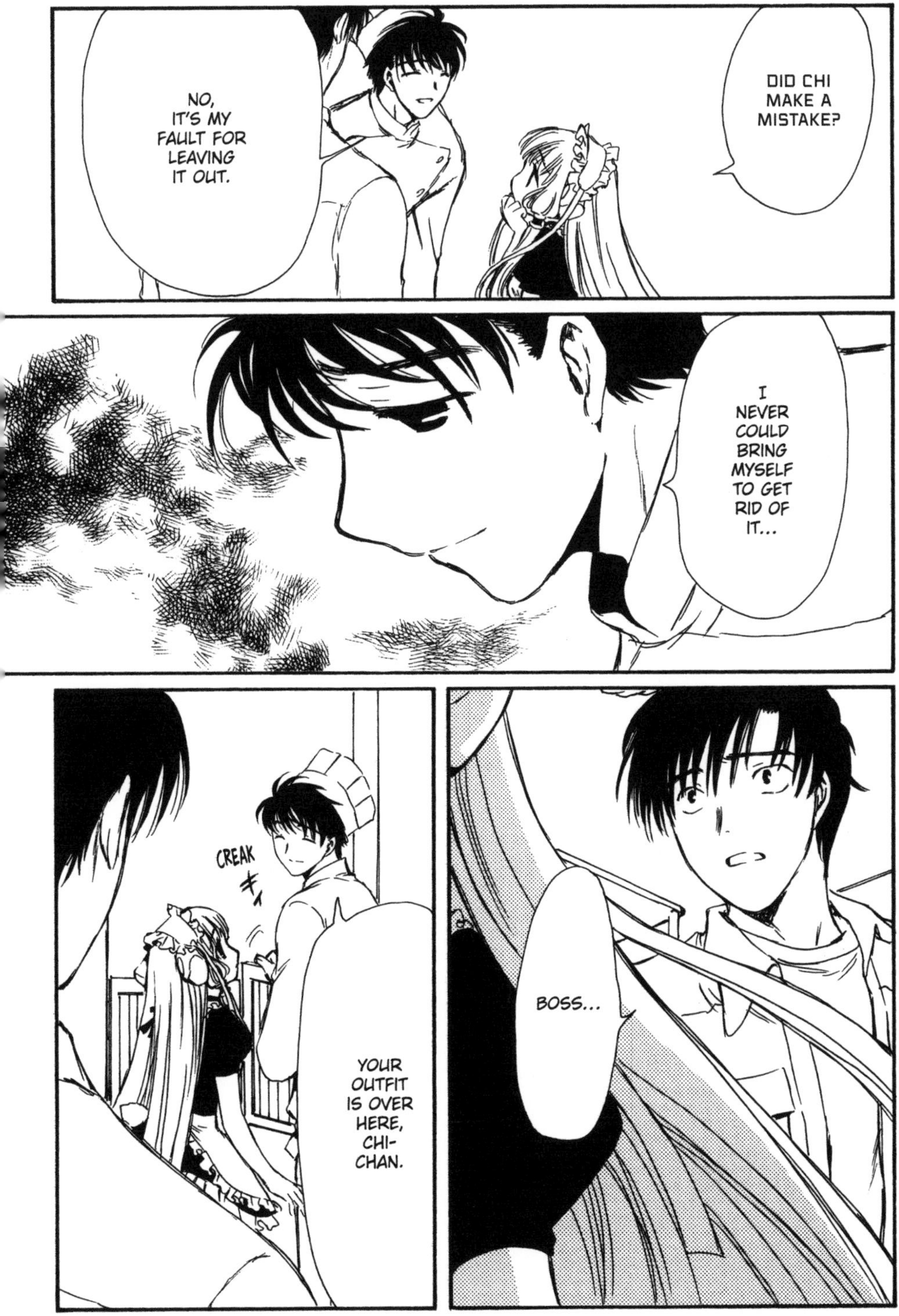
DID CHI MAKE A MISTAKE?
NO, IT'S MY FAULT FOR LEAVING IT OUT.
I NEVER COULD BRING MYSELF TO GET RID OF IT...
BOSS...
CREAK
キィ
YOUR OUTFIT IS OVER HERE, CHI-CHAN.

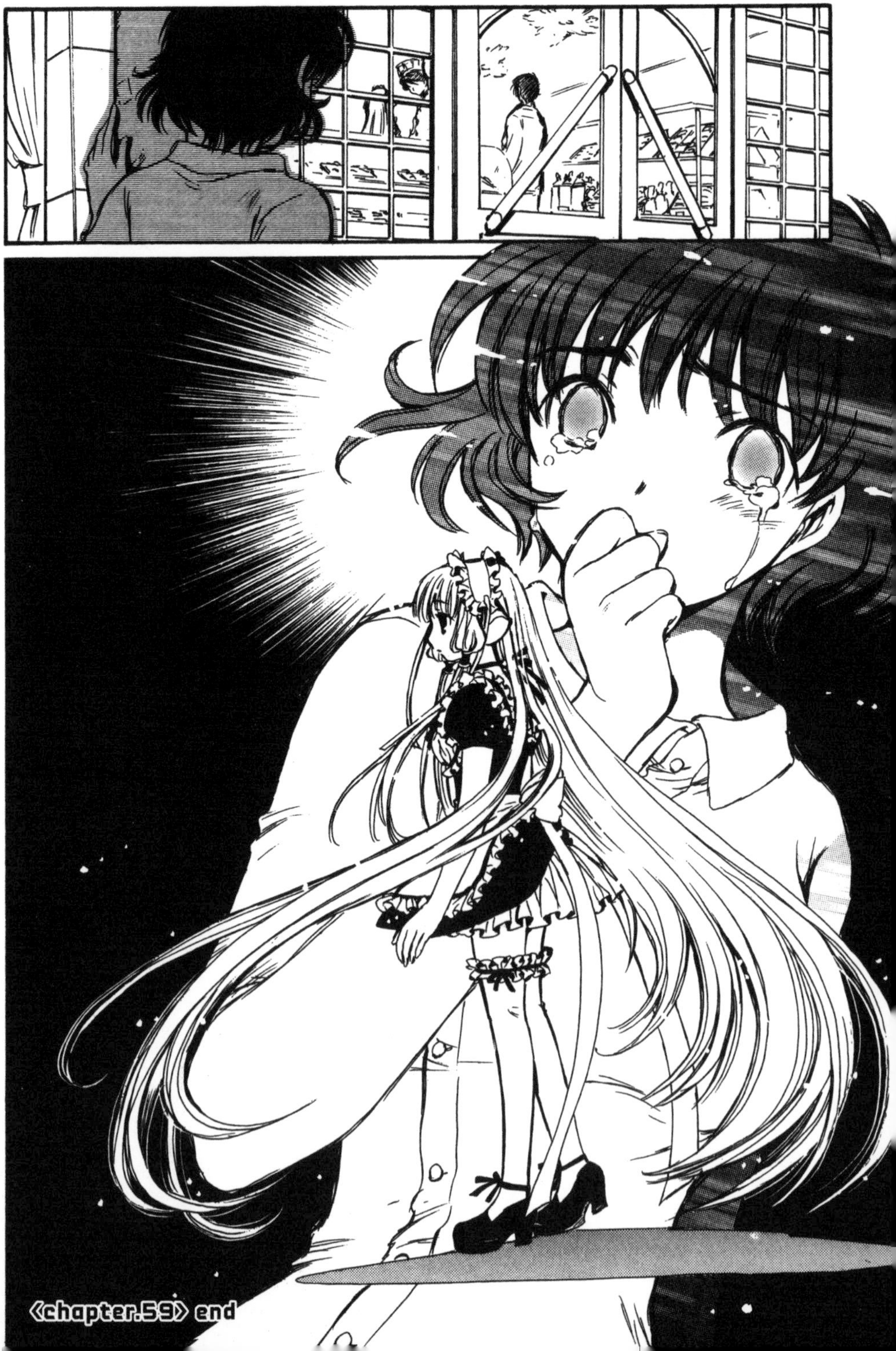
«chapter.59» end

〈chapter.60〉

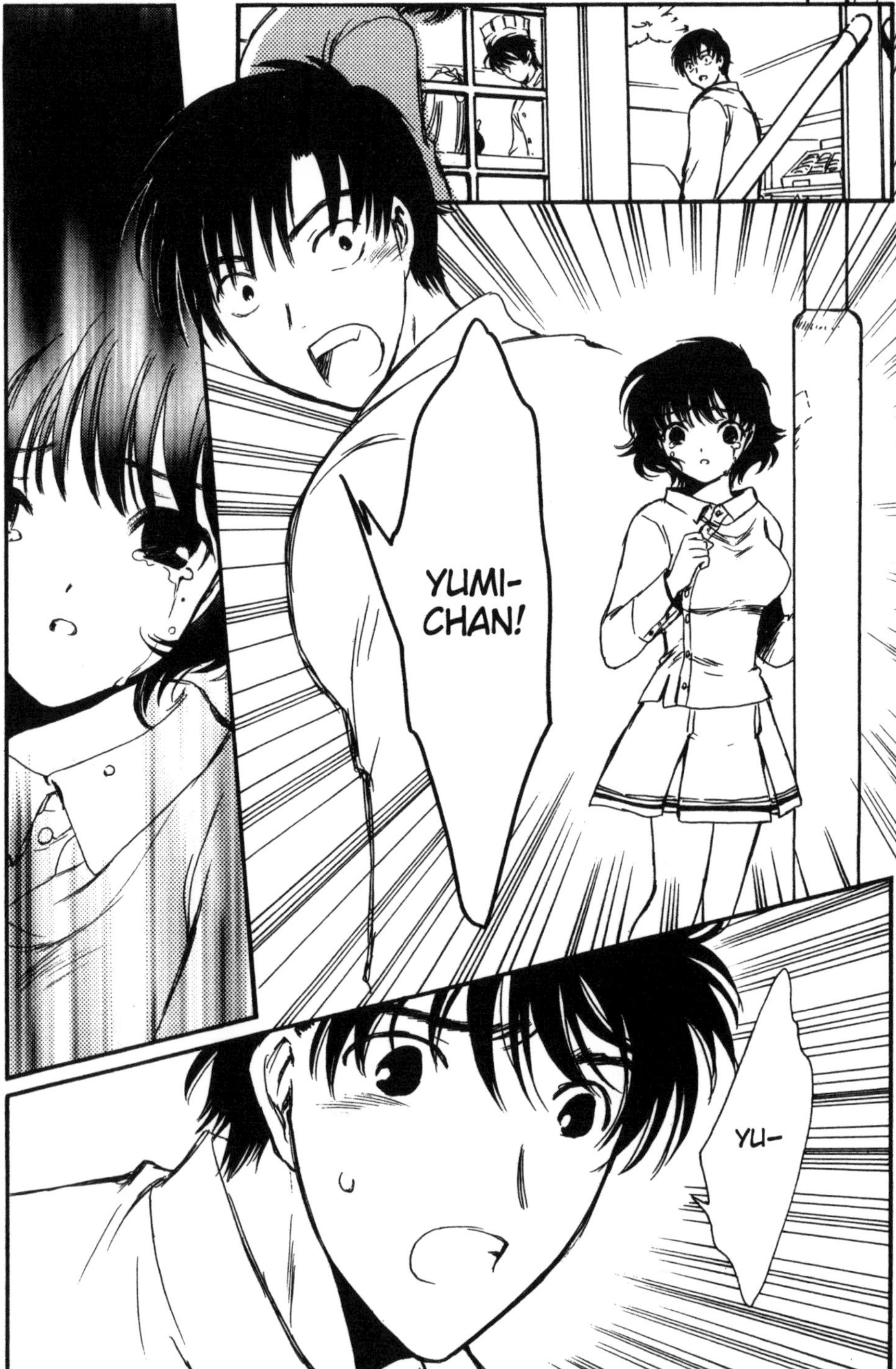
YUMI-
CHAN!
YU-

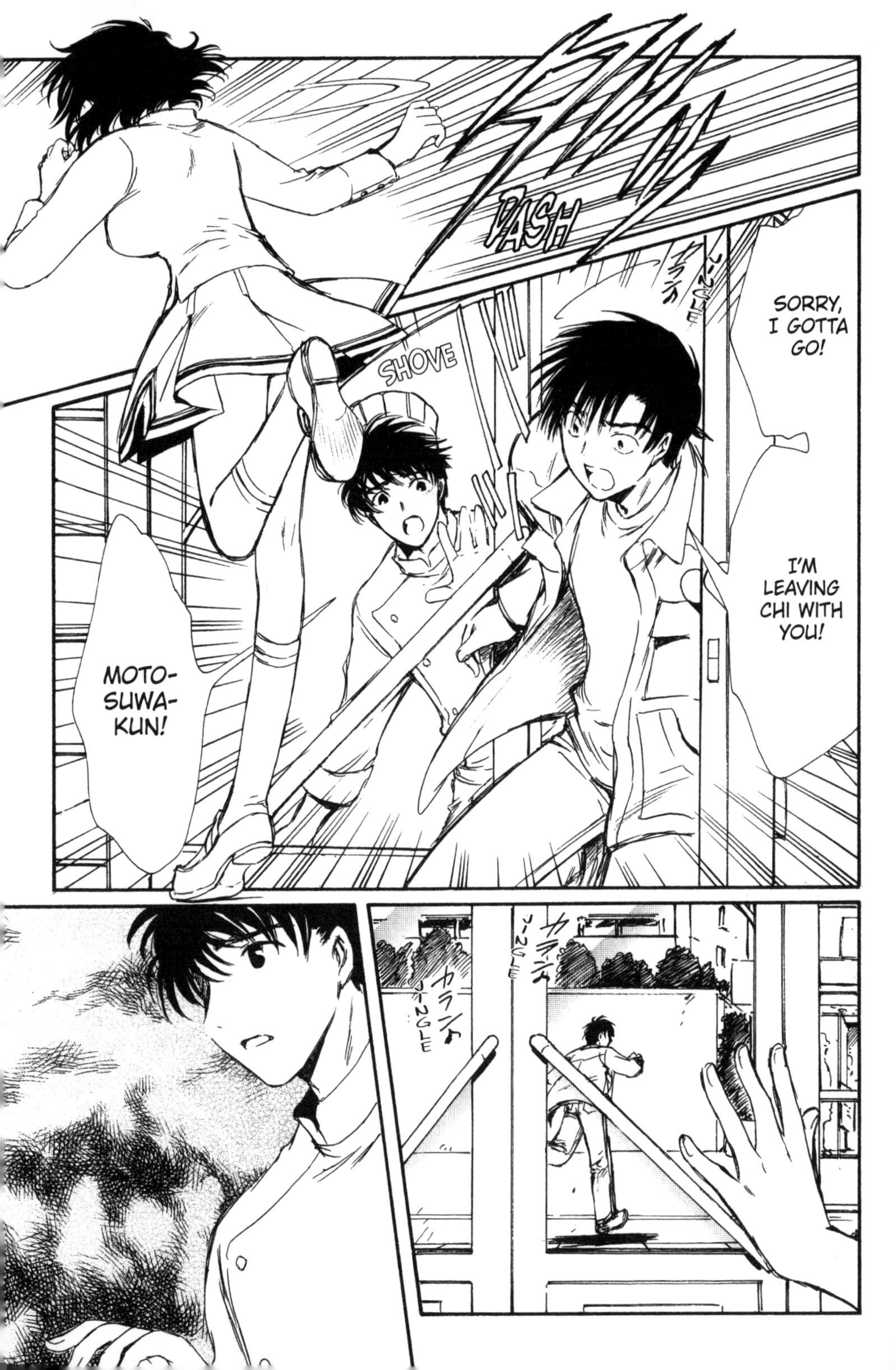
DASH
JINGLE
SORRY, I GOTTA GO!
SHOVE
I'M LEAVING CHI WITH YOU!
MOTO-SUWA-KUN!
JINGLE
JINGLE

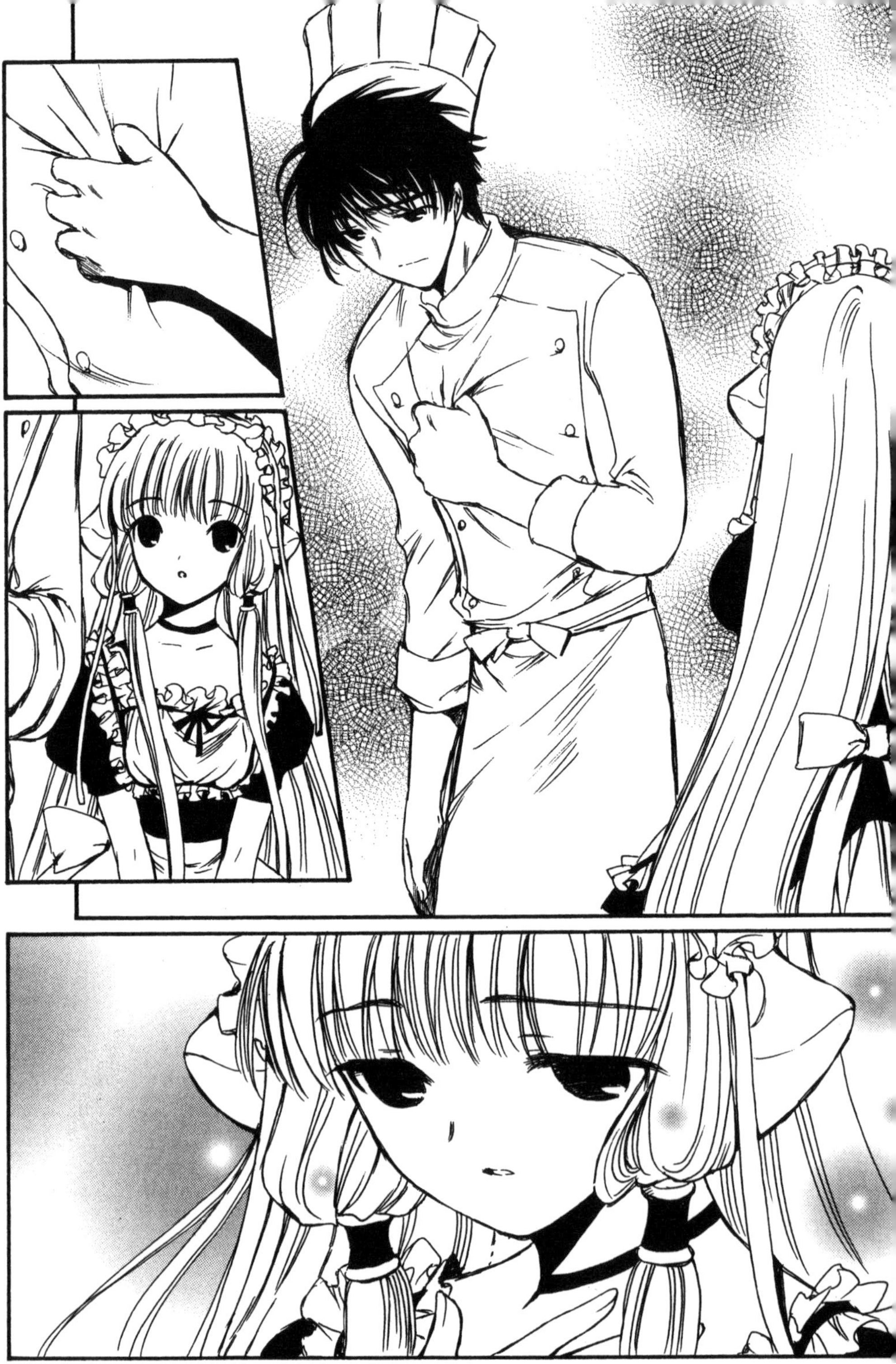

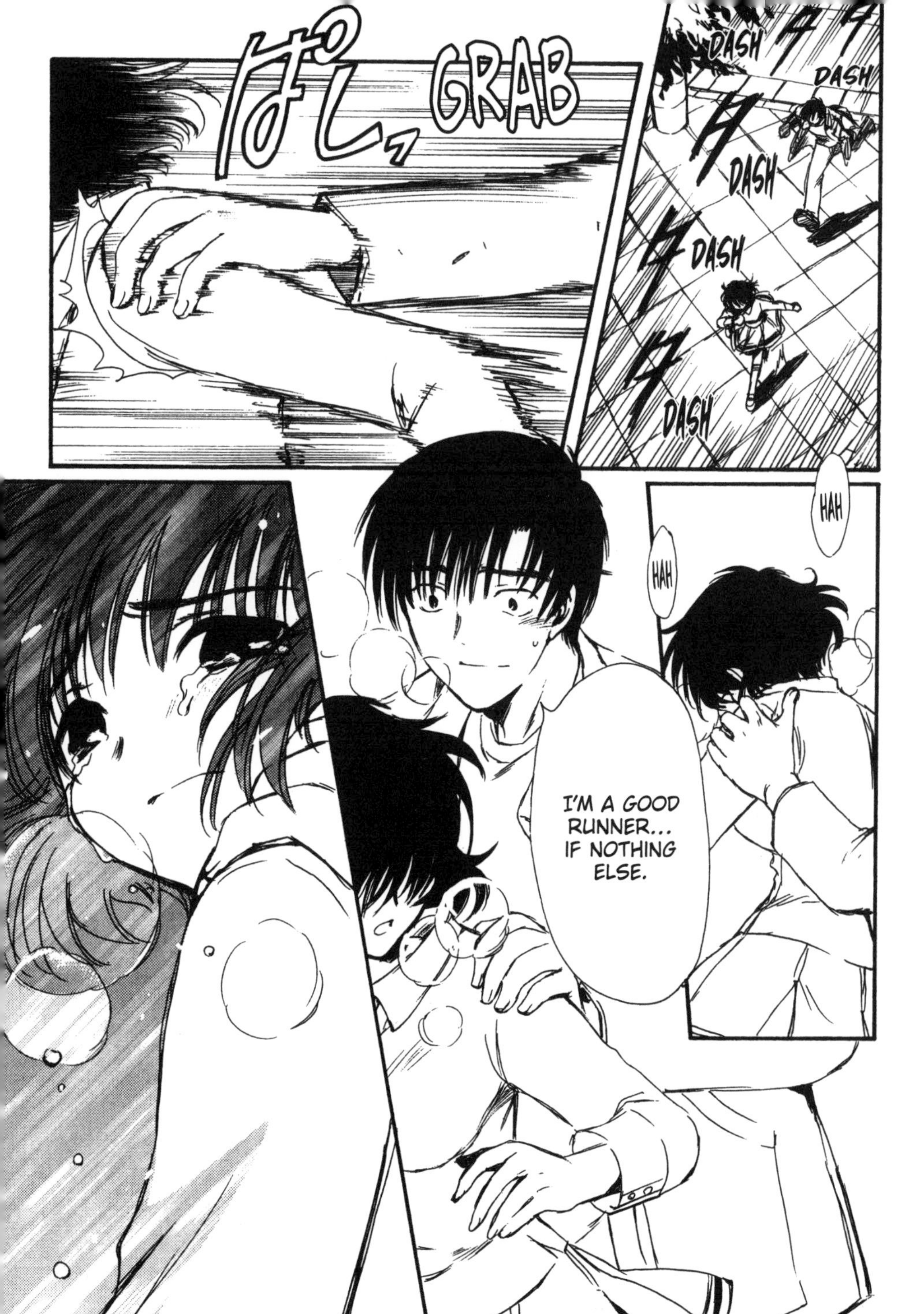
DASH
DASH
DASH
DASH
DASH
ぱしっ
GRAB
HAH
HAH
I'M A GOOD RUNNER... IF NOTHING ELSE.

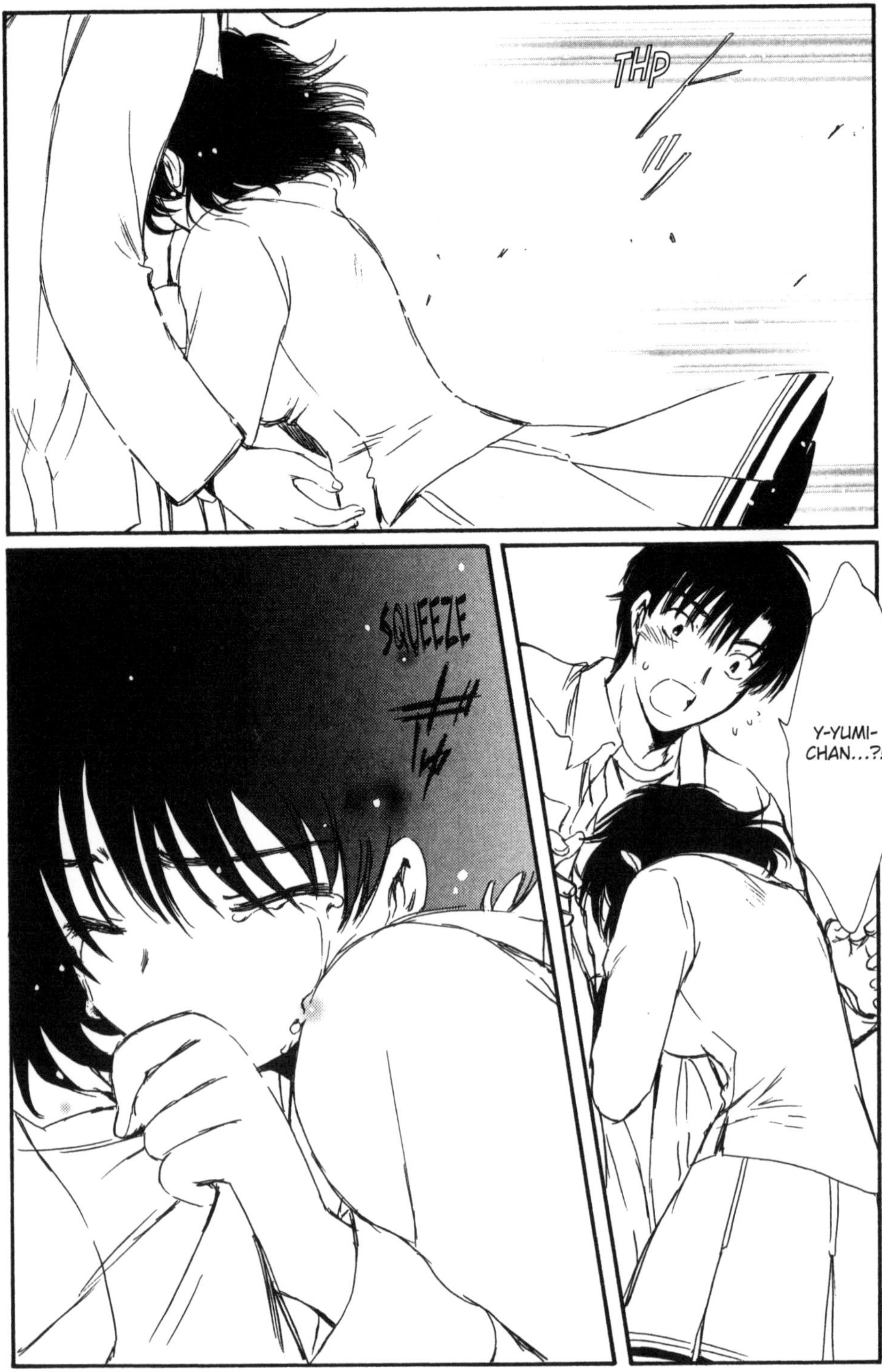
THP
Y-YUMI-CHAN...?!
SQUEEZE

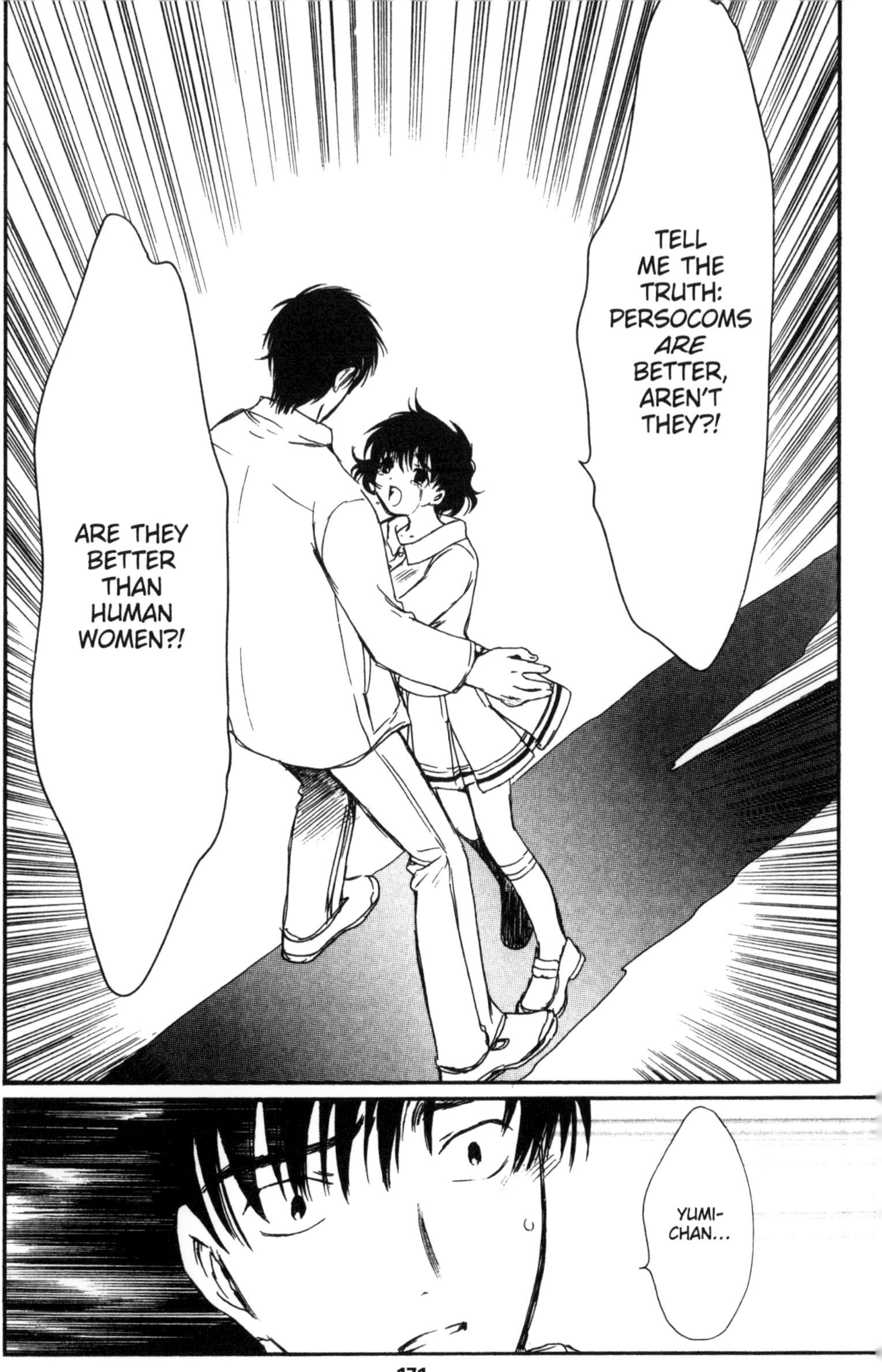
TELL ME THE TRUTH: PERSOCOMS *ARE* BETTER, AREN'T THEY?!
ARE THEY BETTER THAN HUMAN WOMEN?!
YUMI-CHAN...

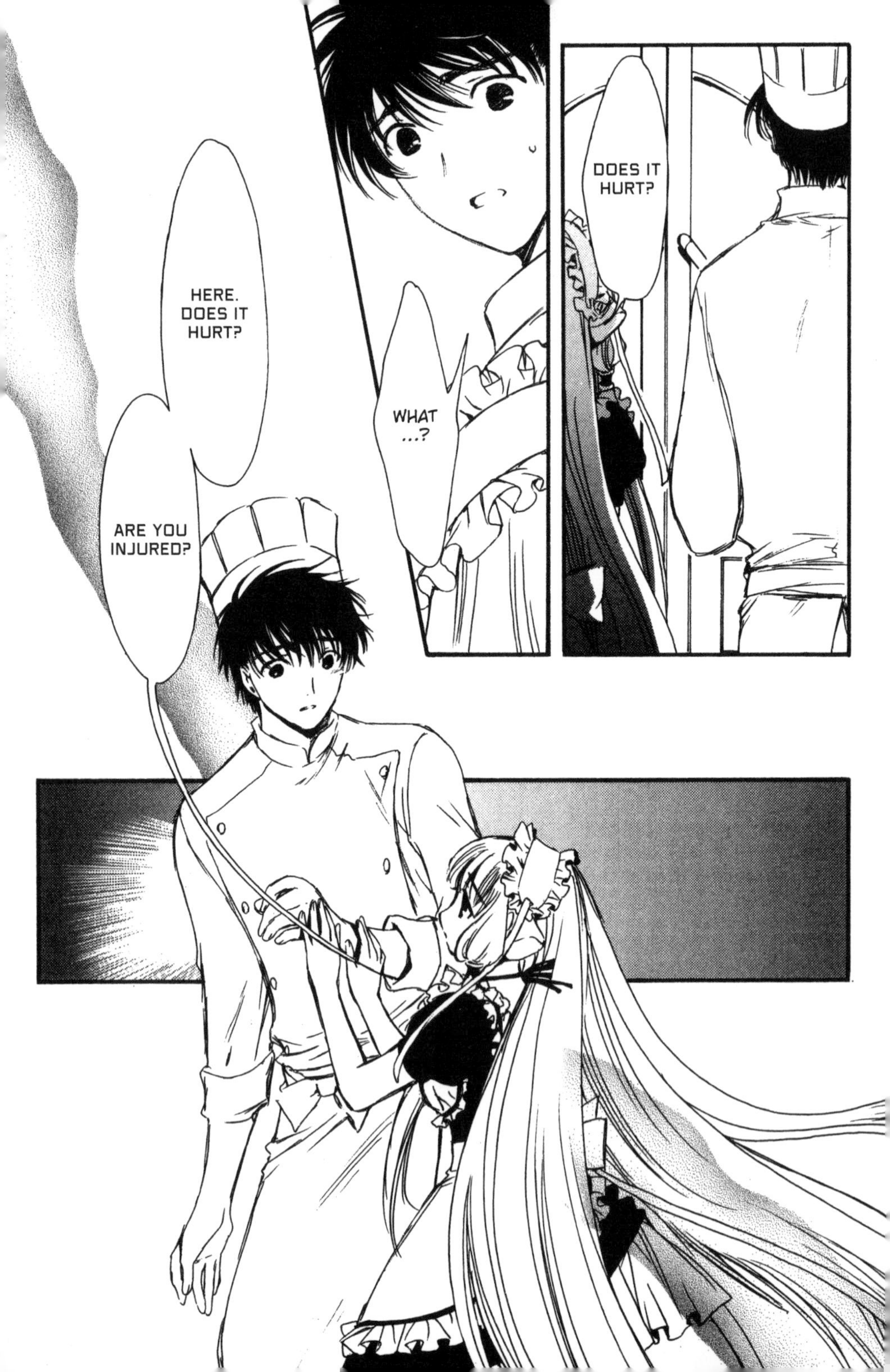
DOES IT HURT?
WHAT ...?
HERE. DOES IT HURT?
ARE YOU INJURED?

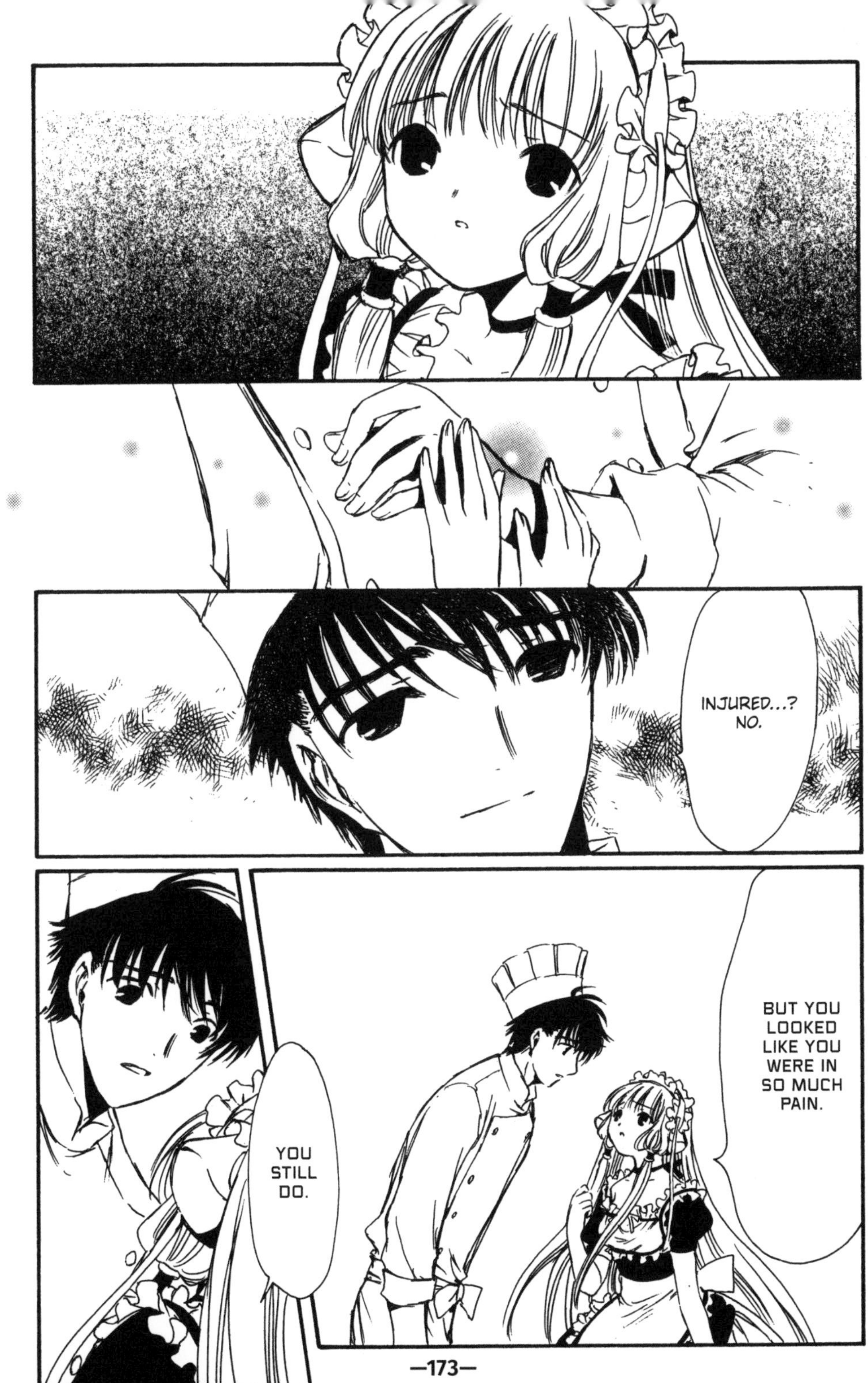
INJURED...? NO.
BUT YOU LOOKED LIKE YOU WERE IN SO MUCH PAIN.
YOU STILL DO.

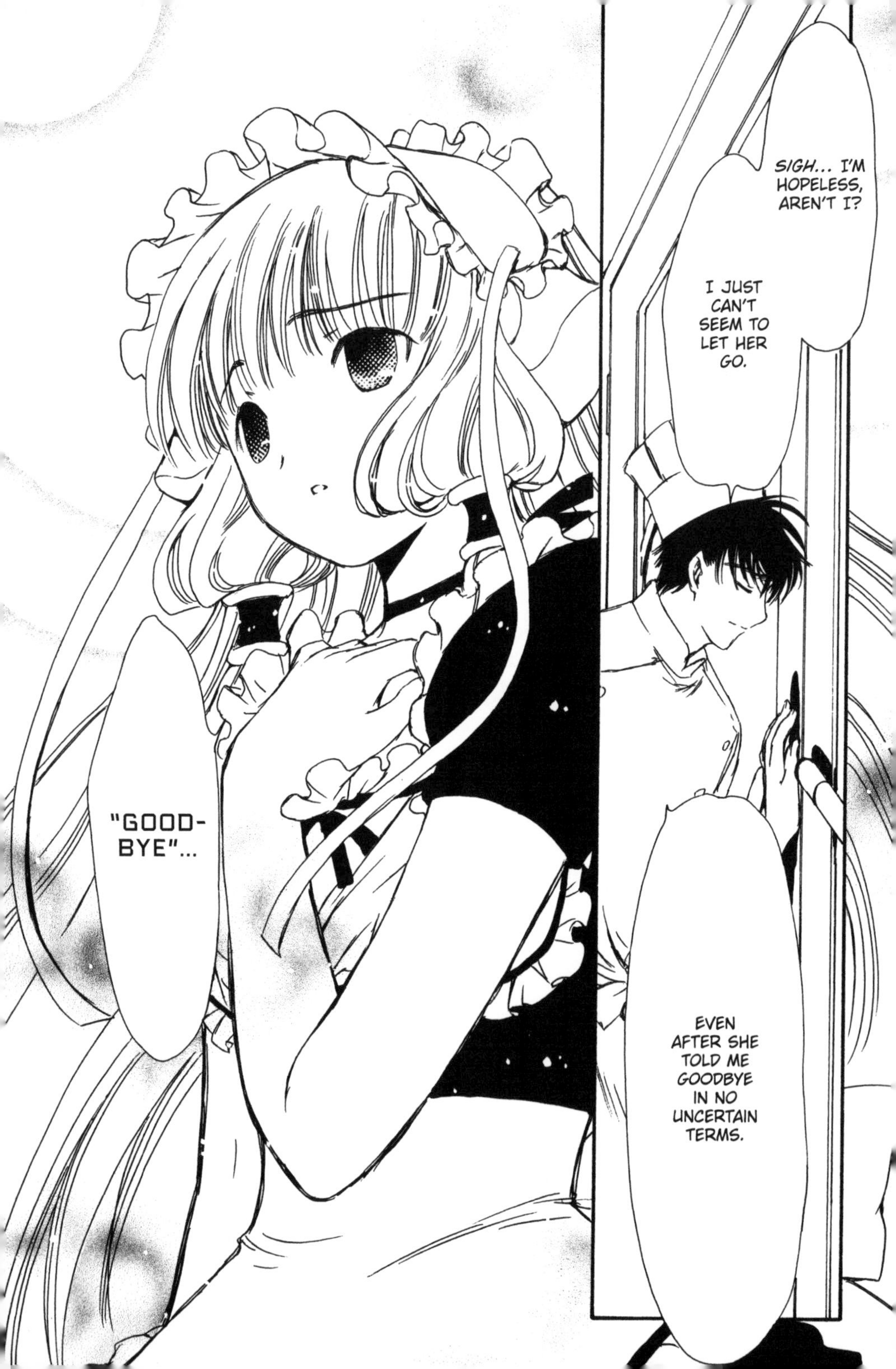
SIGH... I'M HOPELESS, AREN'T I?
I JUST CAN'T SEEM TO LET HER GO.
EVEN AFTER SHE TOLD ME GOODBYE IN NO UNCERTAIN TERMS.
"GOOD-BYE"...

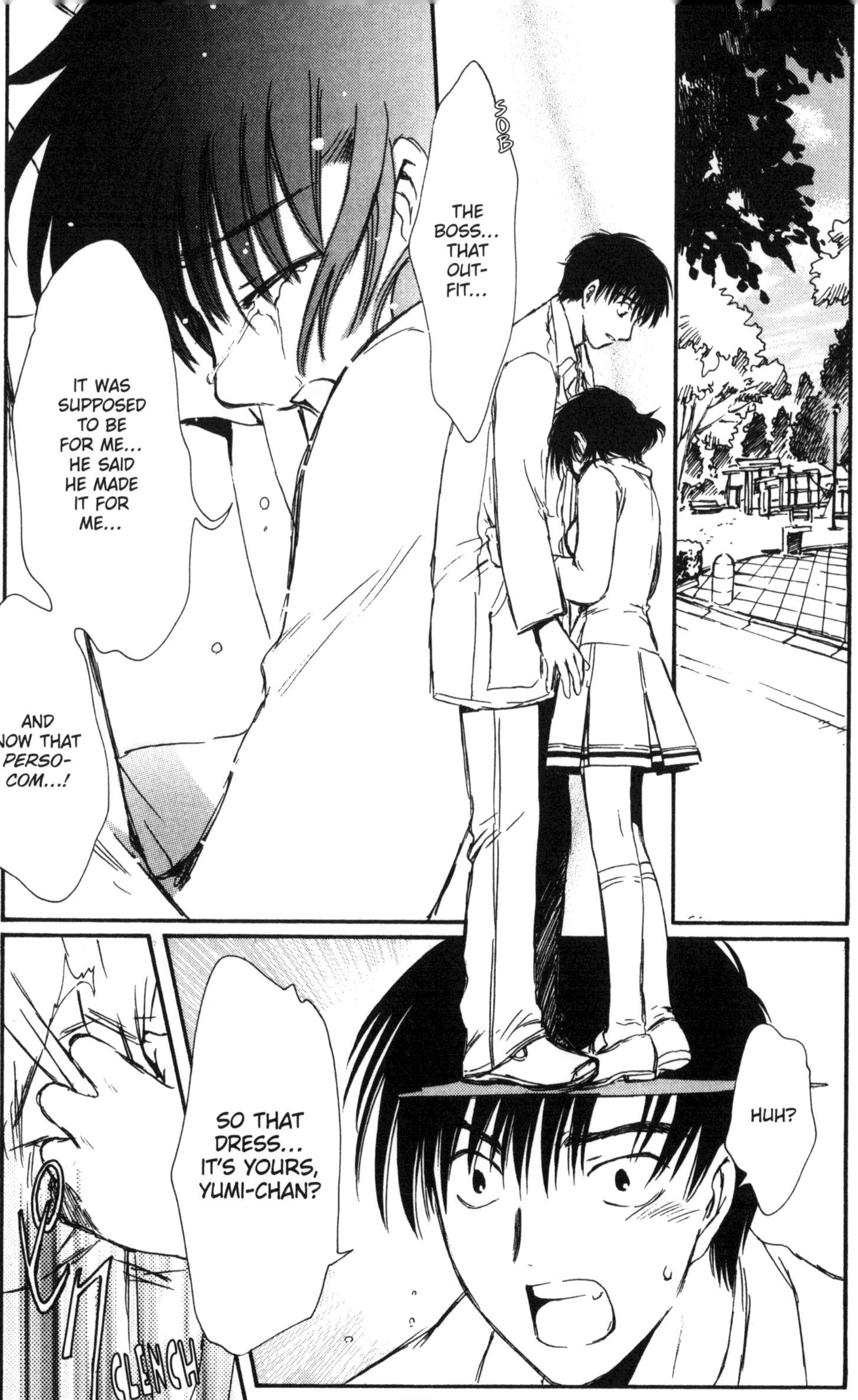
SOB
THE BOSS... THAT OUT-FIT...
IT WAS SUPPOSED TO BE FOR ME... HE SAID HE MADE IT FOR ME...
AND NOW THAT *PERSO-COM*...!
HUH?
SO THAT DRESS... IT'S YOURS, YUMI-CHAN?
CLENCH

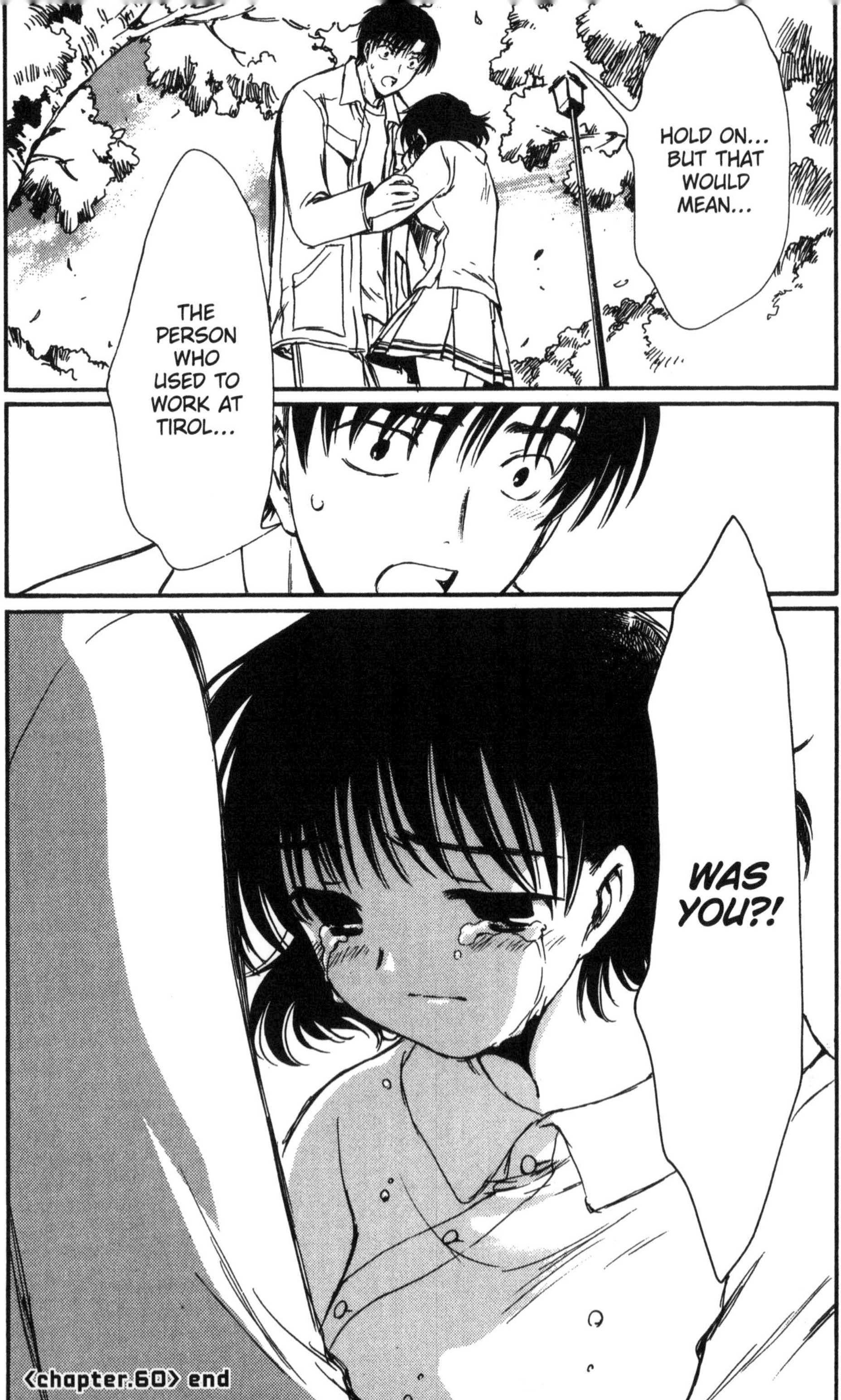
HOLD ON... BUT THAT WOULD MEAN...
THE PERSON WHO USED TO WORK AT TIROL...
WAS YOU?!
⟨chapter.60⟩ end

Chobits

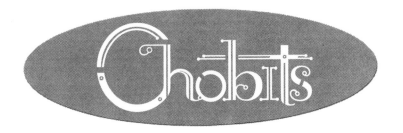

Translation Notes

Omura-kun, page 10

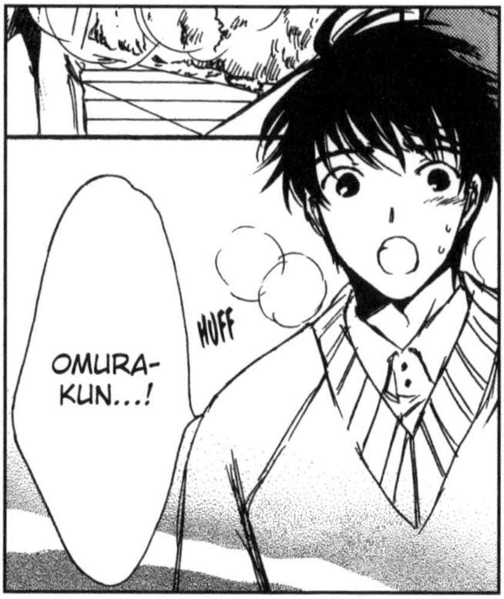
HUFF
OMURA-KUN...!

Although *-kun* is often described as an honorific used mainly for young men, it can also be applied to young women. It can be used with anyone who's younger than the speaker and/or in a subordinate professional relationship (for example, by a supervisor talking to a new hire). In this sense, it simply fills another slot on the hierarchy of honorifics, implying less social parity than *-san* but less familiarity than *-chan*.

Hot Springs Buns, page 42

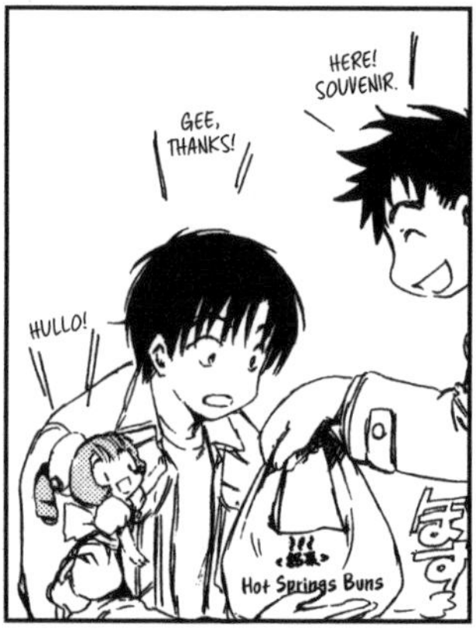
HERE! SOUVENIR.
GEE, THANKS!
HULLO!
Hot Springs Buns

The bag Shimbo is carrying bears the legend *onsen manjuu,* referring to stuffed buns (*manjuu*) from a hot spring (*onsen*). This isn't a specific brand, but can refer to any buns made at a hot spring. Such pastries might use local spring water in the dough, or could be steamed using steam from the springs. The circle with the wavy lines on the bag is the standard symbol for "bath" in Japan.

"Get A *Hold* Of You," page 77

Minoru uses the term *handoru neemu*, a quasi-loanword from the English *handle name*, which Hideki tries to understand by "translating" directly into Japanese ("*handoru no namae?*"; panel 2), but that doesn't cause it to make much more sense to him. In panel 3, he wonders if it has "something to do with cars," because *handoru* is also the Japanese word for a steering wheel.

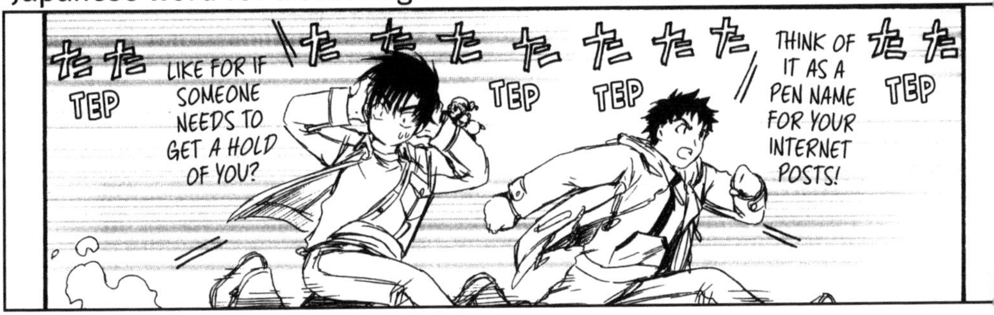
たた
TEP
THINK OF IT AS A PEN NAME FOR YOUR INTERNET POSTS!
たたたたた
TEP
TEP
LIKE FOR IF SOMEONE NEEDS TO GET A HOLD OF YOU?
たた
TEP

SCOME, page 78

SECOM is a long-standing Japanese security company. The name is a portmanteau of "security" and "communication."

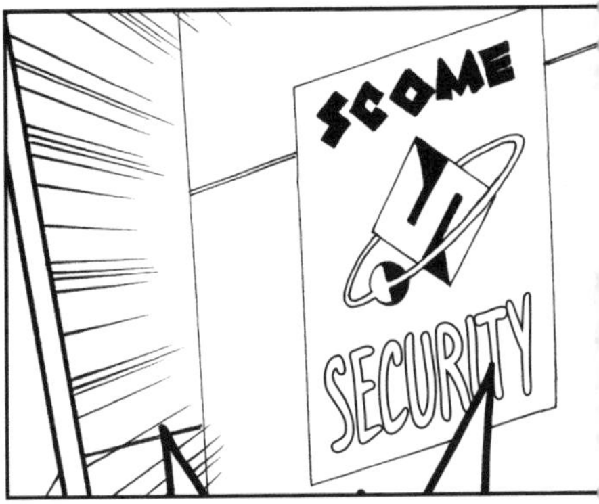
SCOME
SECURITY

Bank Book, page 137

Although, like many countries, Japan is increasingly moving toward electronic banking, at the time *Chobits* was published, anyone who opened a bank account would be issued a bank book (*tsuuchou,* "passbook"), a small, rectangular document like Hideki is holding here. It's essentially a transaction register, but rather than filling it in by hand, you insert the bank book into an ATM while accessing your account. When the transaction is complete, the ATM prints a line to the book indicating the details of the transaction, including your remaining account balance. Judging by his expression in these panels, that number isn't as high as Hideki would like.

Holding Hands, page 145

Chi initially uses the verb *nigiru*, "to hold onto something." *Te wo nigiru* (*te* means "hand") is a valid Japanese expression, but it describes something less romantic than what they're seeing here. Hideki tells her that the right word is *tsunagu*, literally "to connect" or, in a context like this, "to entwine."

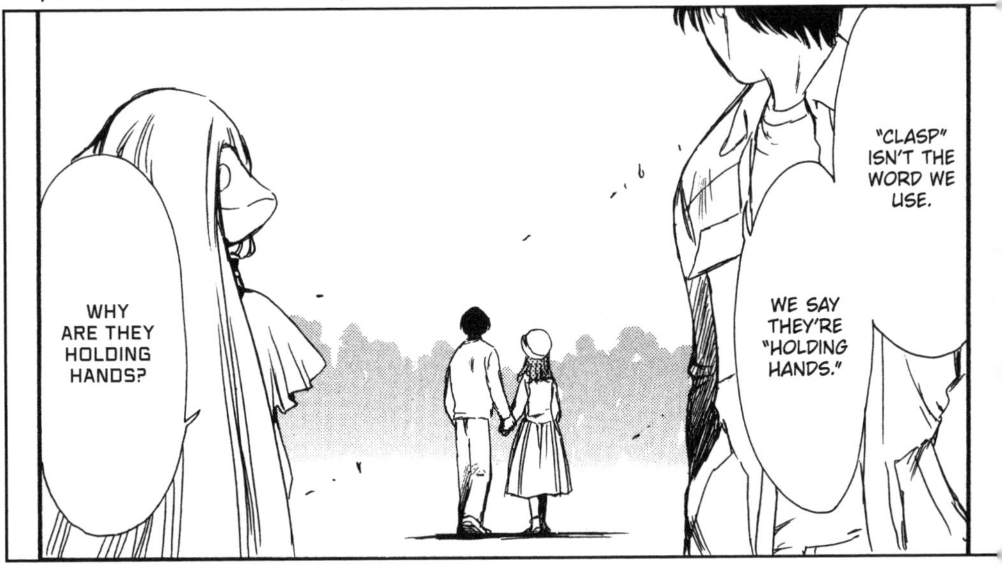
"CLASP" ISN'T THE WORD WE USE.
WE SAY THEY'RE "HOLDING HANDS."
WHY ARE THEY HOLDING HANDS?

Chobits

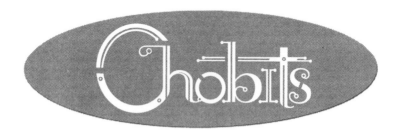

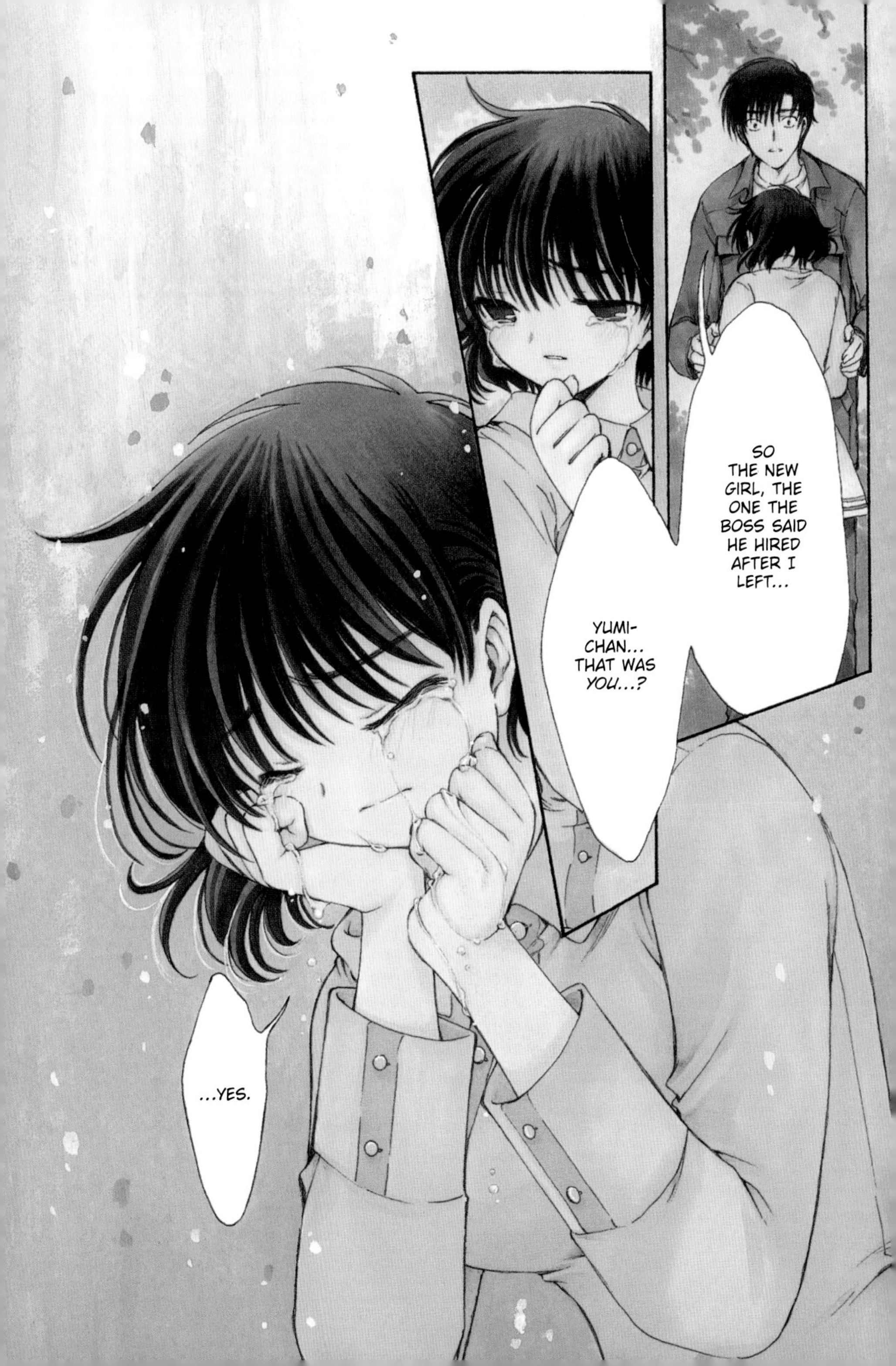
SO THE NEW GIRL, THE ONE THE BOSS SAID HE HIRED AFTER I LEFT...
YUMI-CHAN... THAT WAS *YOU*...?
...YES.

<chapter.61>

Chobits

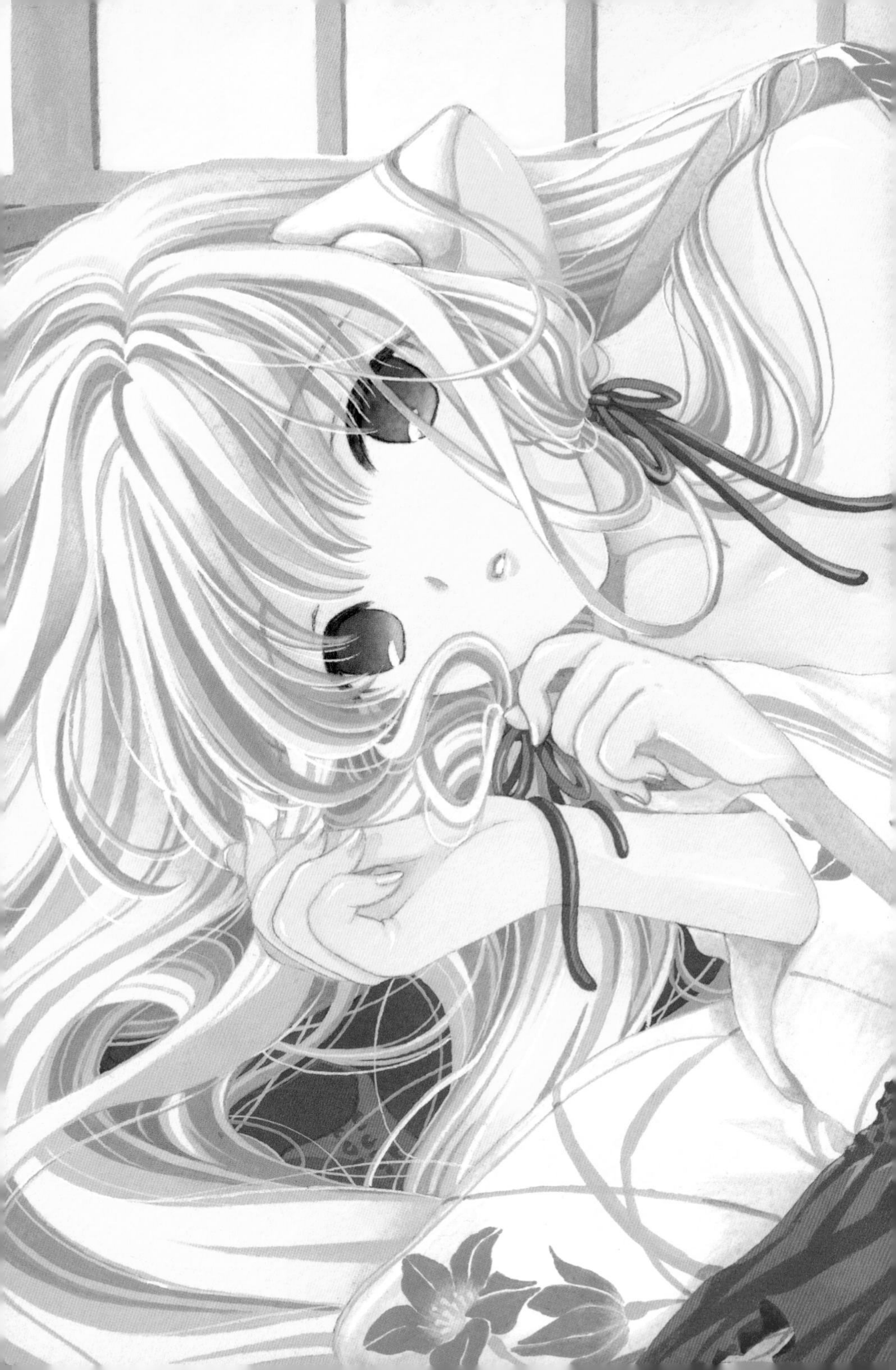

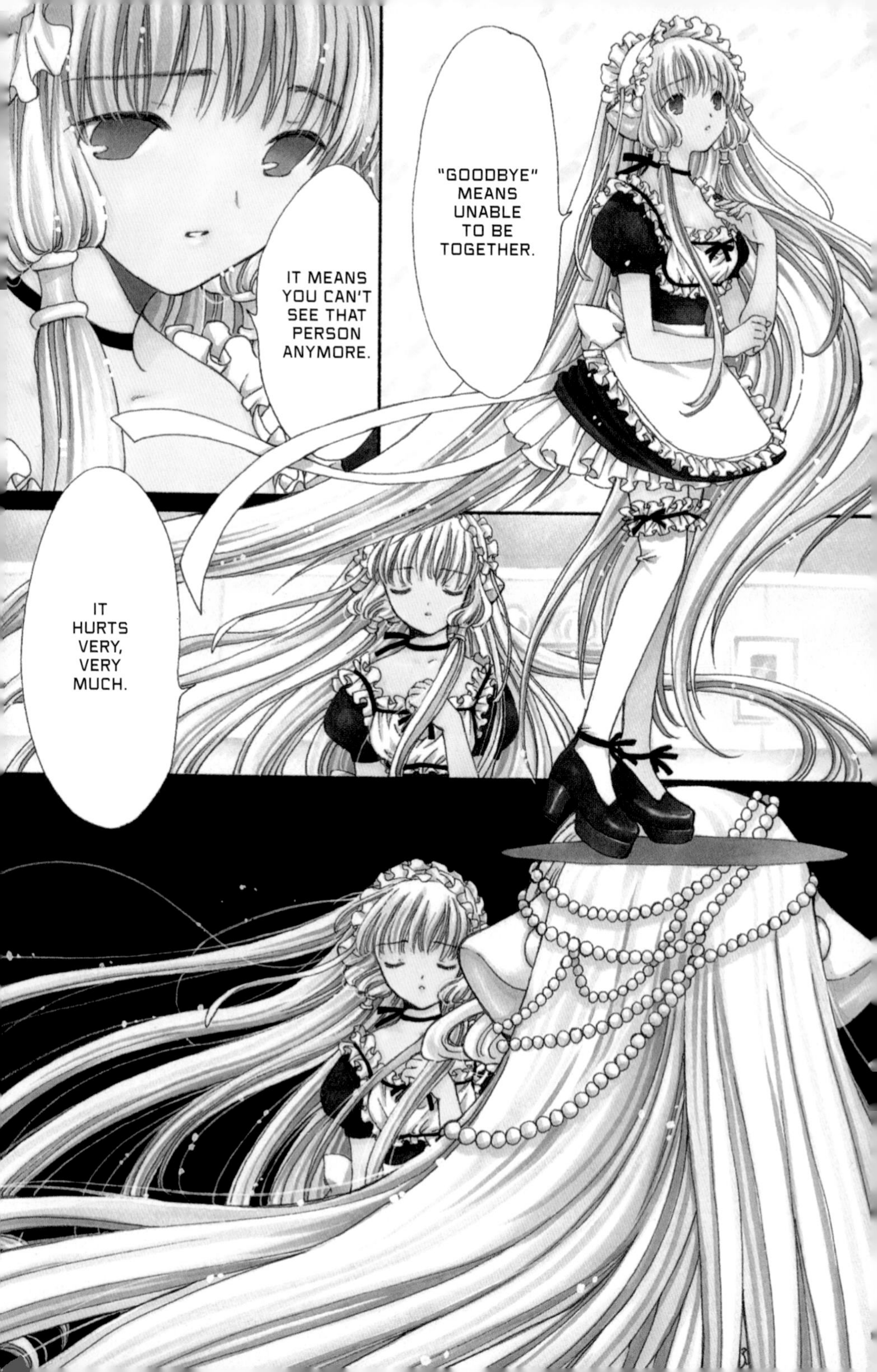
"GOODBYE" MEANS UNABLE TO BE TOGETHER.
IT MEANS YOU CAN'T SEE THAT PERSON ANYMORE.
IT HURTS VERY, VERY MUCH.

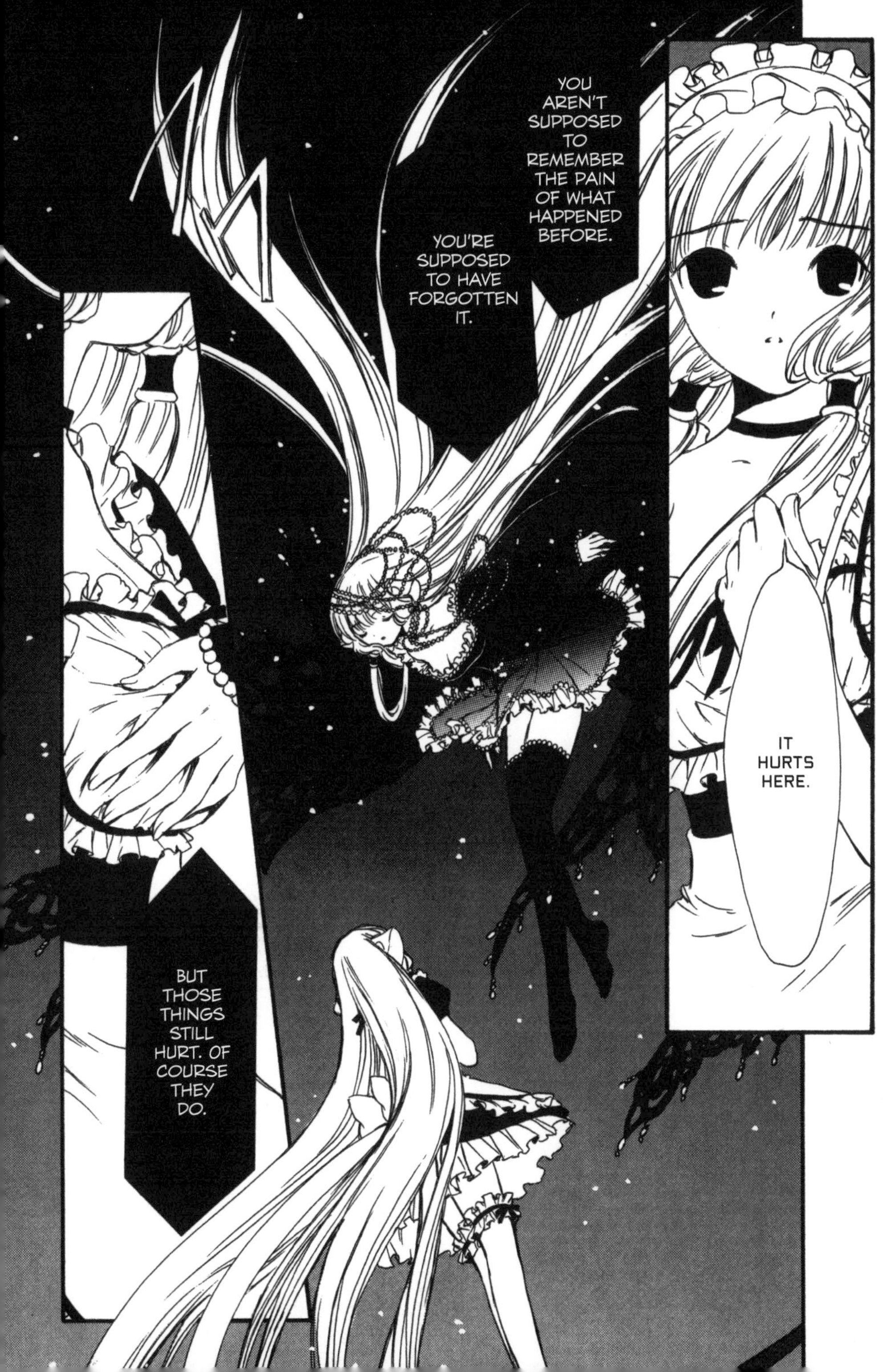
YOU AREN'T SUPPOSED TO REMEMBER THE PAIN OF WHAT HAPPENED BEFORE.
YOU'RE SUPPOSED TO HAVE FORGOTTEN IT.
IT HURTS HERE.
BUT THOSE THINGS STILL HURT. OF COURSE THEY DO.

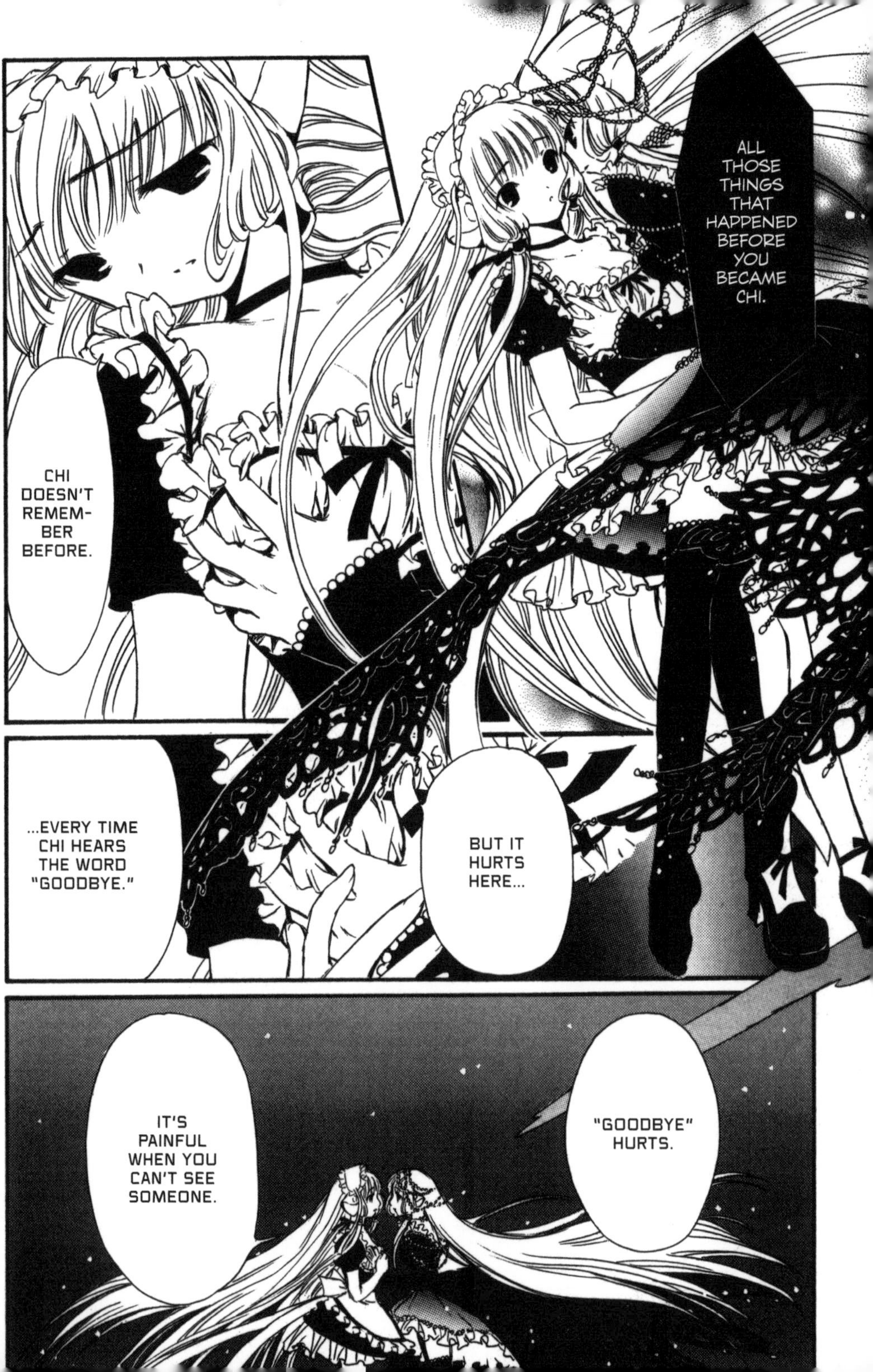
ALL THOSE THINGS THAT HAPPENED BEFORE YOU BECAME CHI.
CHI DOESN'T REMEMBER BEFORE.
BUT IT HURTS HERE...
...EVERY TIME CHI HEARS THE WORD "GOODBYE."
"GOODBYE" HURTS.
IT'S PAINFUL WHEN YOU CAN'T SEE SOMEONE.

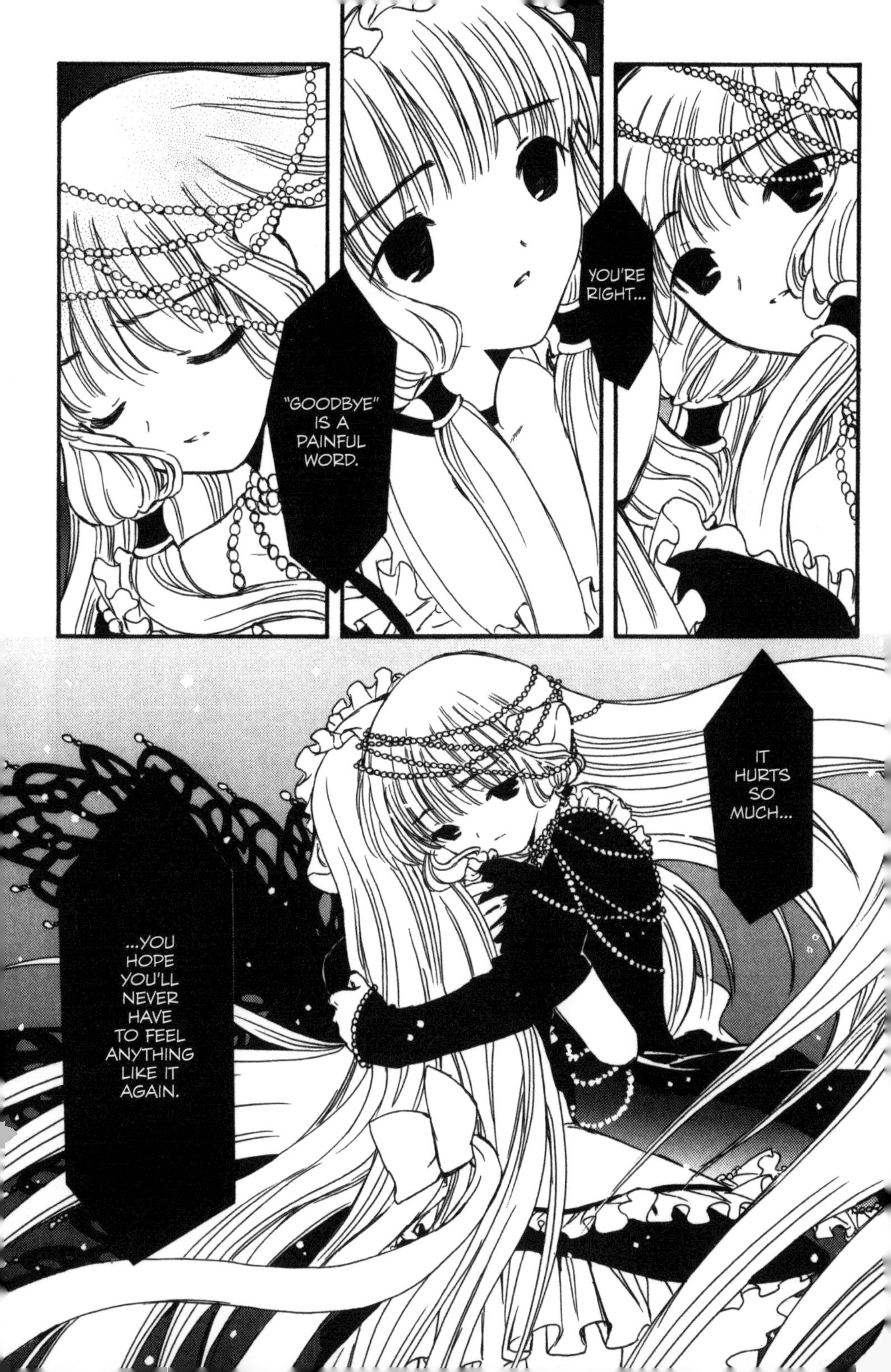
YOU'RE RIGHT...
"GOODBYE" IS A PAINFUL WORD.
IT HURTS SO MUCH...
...YOU HOPE YOU'LL NEVER HAVE TO FEEL ANYTHING LIKE IT AGAIN.

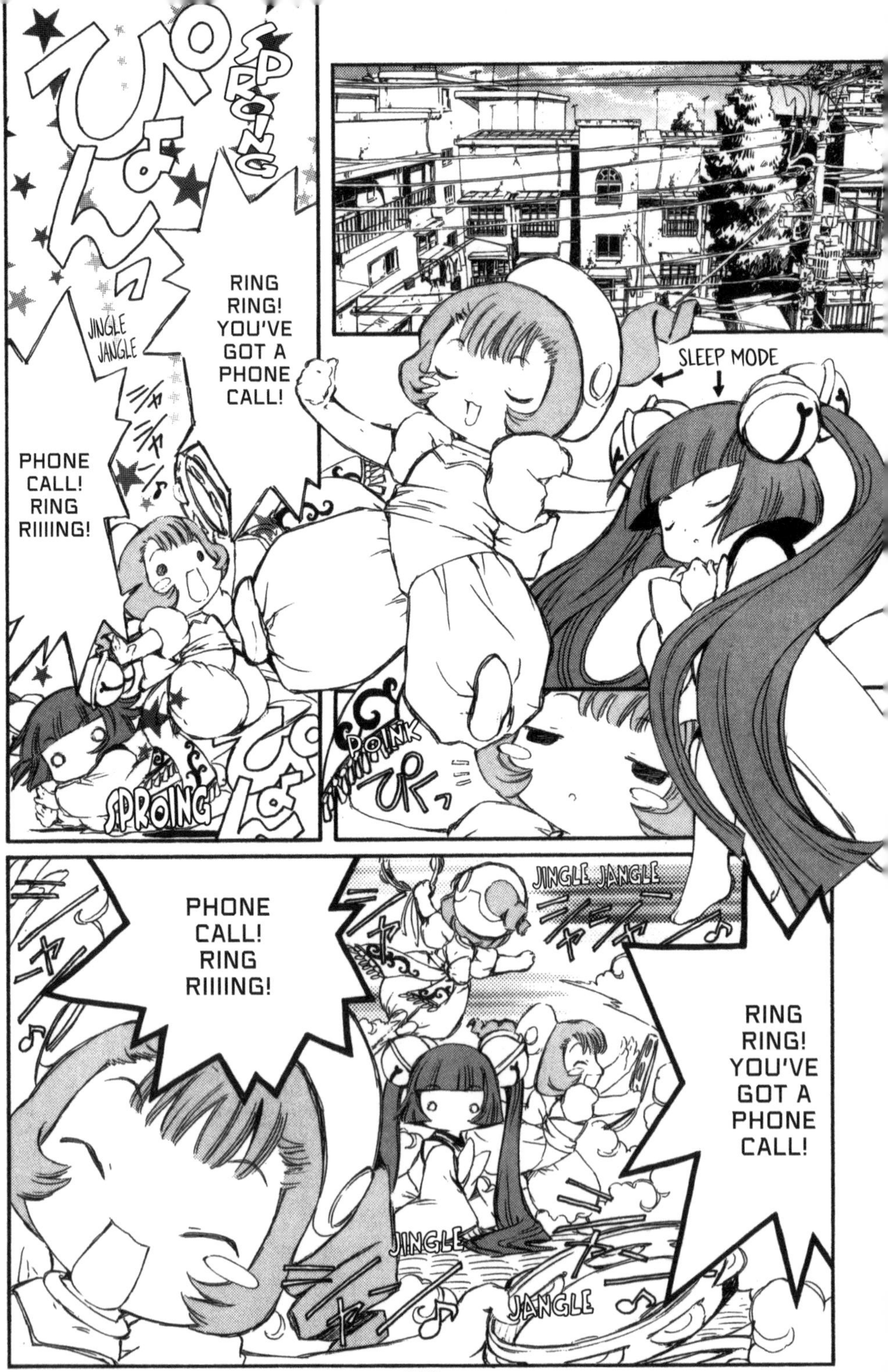
SLEEP MODE
POINK
ぴくっ
ぴょん〜っ
SPROING
RING RING! YOU'VE GOT A PHONE CALL!
JINGLE JANGLE
PHONE CALL! RING RIIIING!
SPROING
RING RING! YOU'VE GOT A PHONE CALL!
JINGLE JANGLE
PHONE CALL! RING RIIIING!
JINGLE
JANGLE

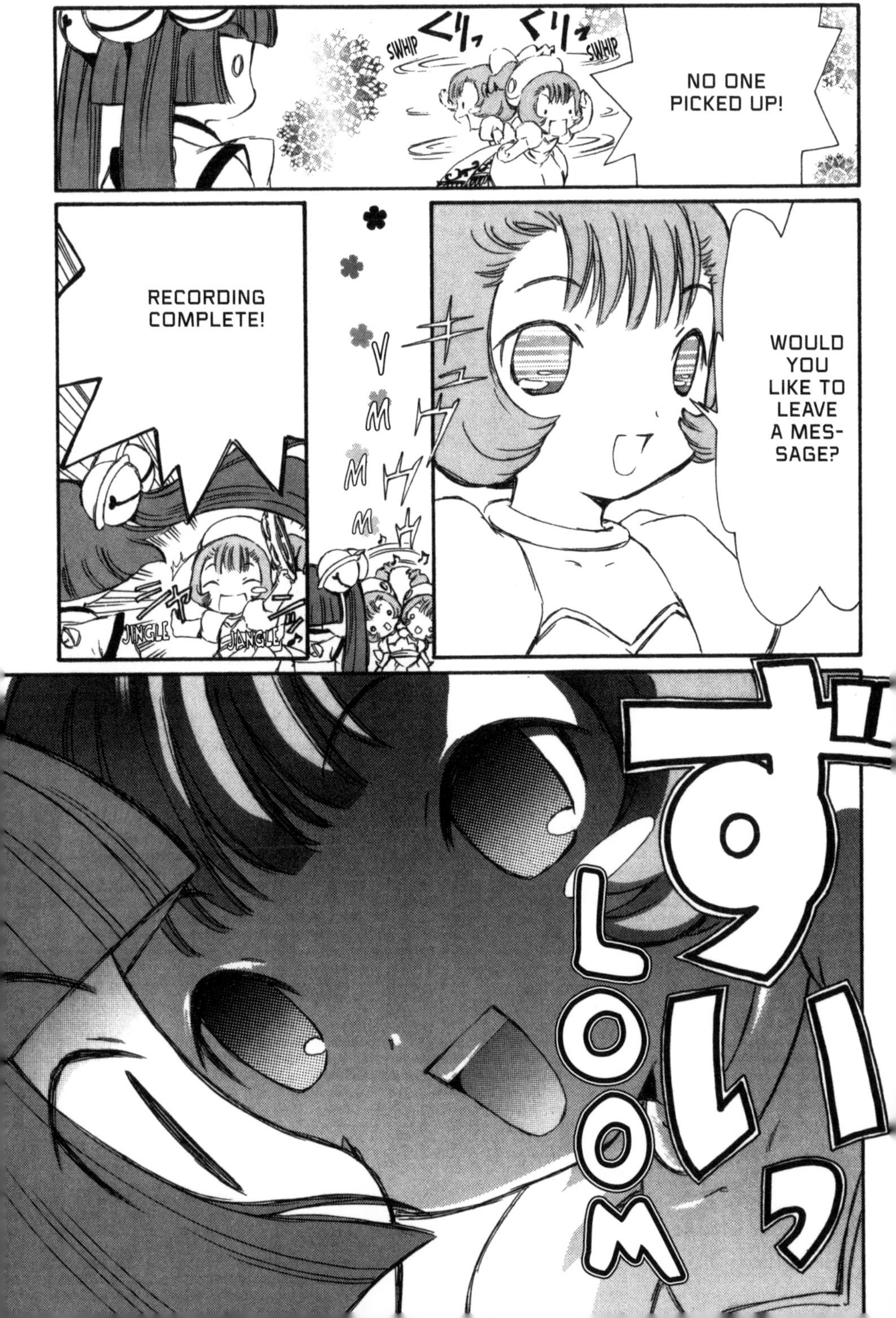
NO ONE PICKED UP!
SWHIP
SWHIP
WOULD YOU LIKE TO LEAVE A MES-SAGE?
VMMMM
RECORDING COMPLETE!
JINGLE
JANGLE
LOOOM

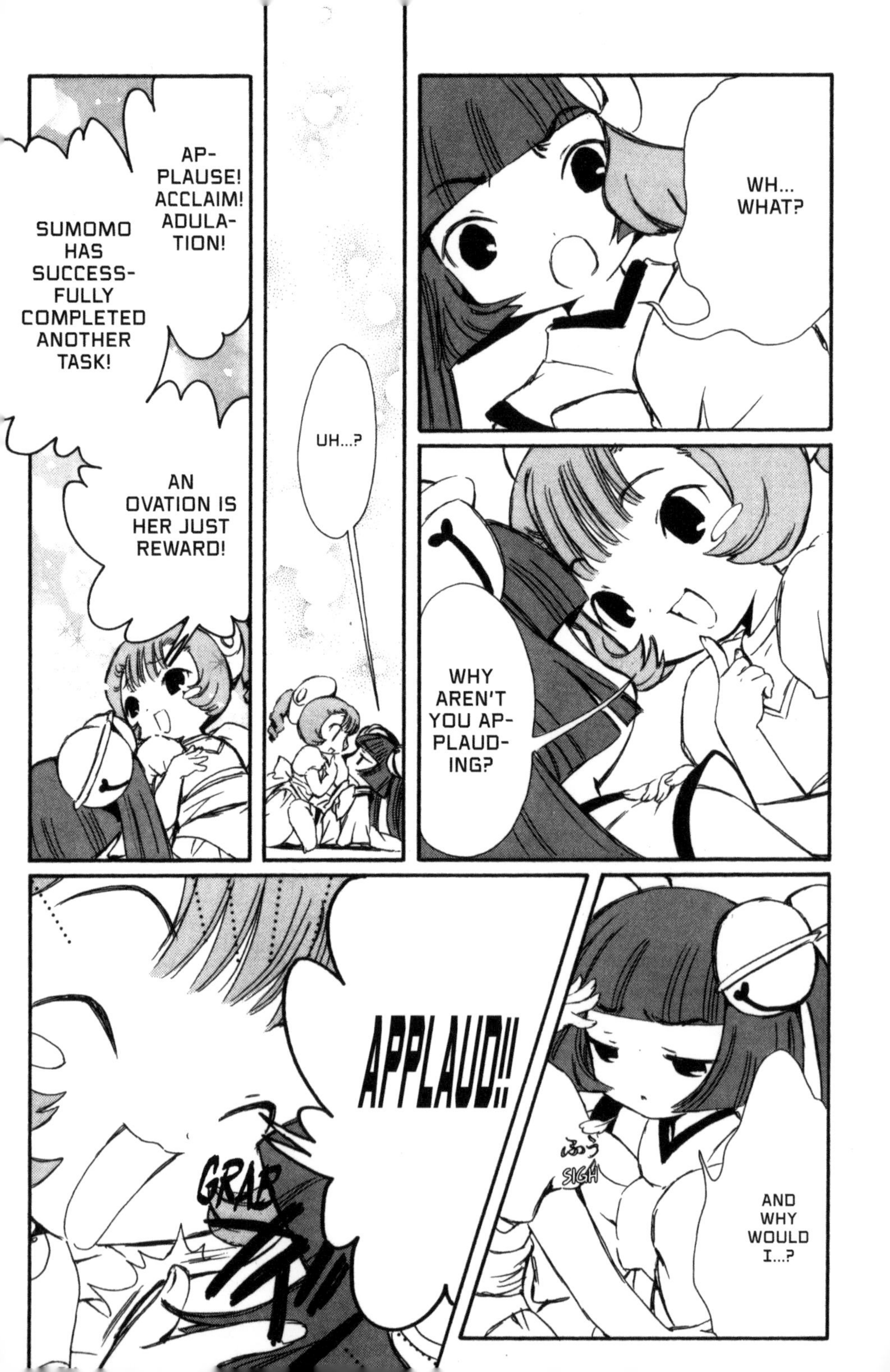
WH... WHAT?
WHY AREN'T YOU AP-PLAUD-ING?
UH...?
AP-PLAUSE! ACCLAIM! ADULA-TION!
SUMOMO HAS SUCCESS-FULLY COMPLETED ANOTHER TASK!
AN OVATION IS HER JUST REWARD!
AND WHY WOULD I...?
SIGH
APPLAUD!!
GRAB

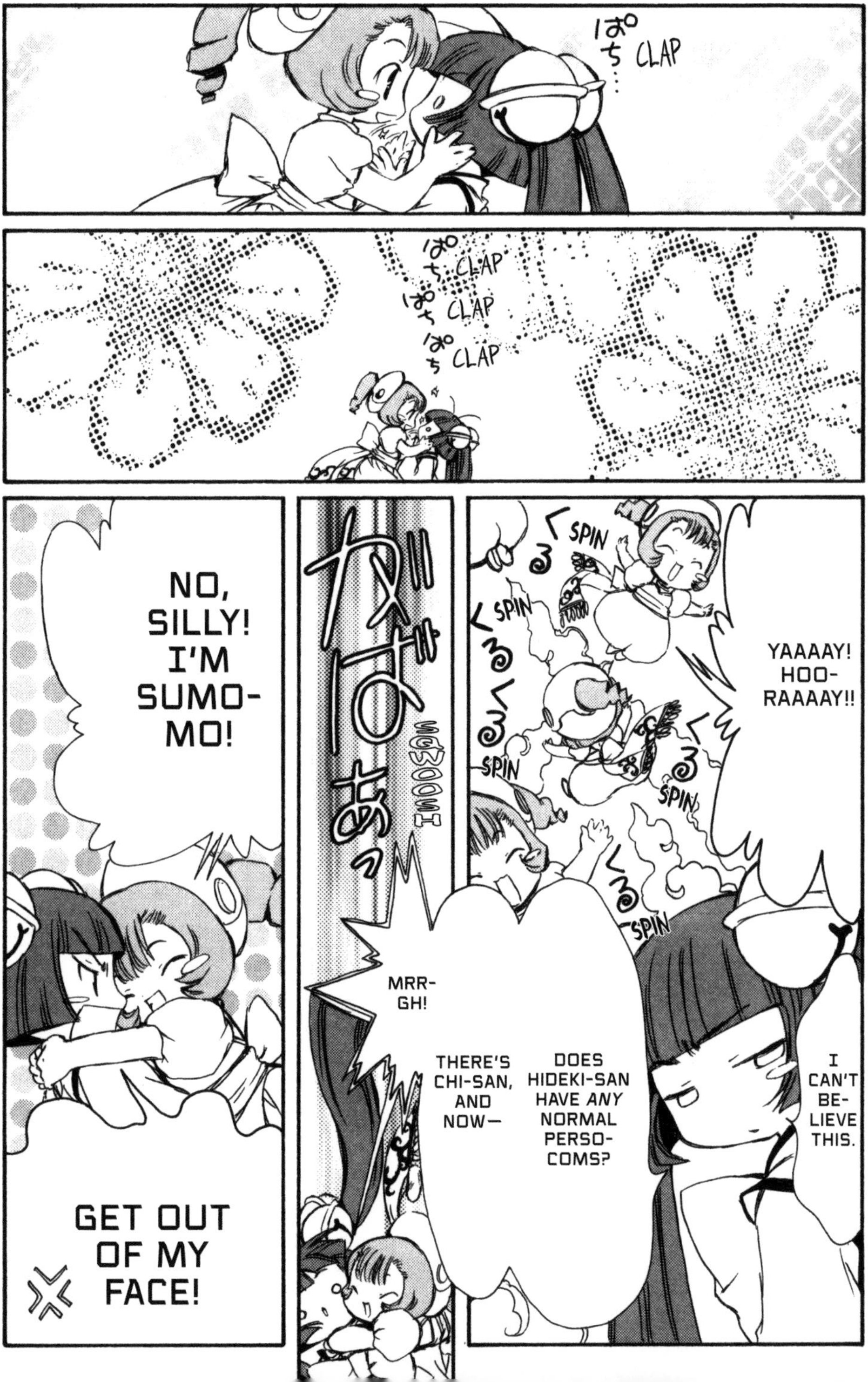
ぱち… CLAP
ぱち CLAP
ぱち CLAP
ぱち CLAP
くる SPIN
くる SPIN
くる SPIN
くる SPIN
くる SPIN
くる SPIN
YAAAAY! HOO-RAAAAY!!
I CAN'T BE-LIEVE THIS.
DOES HIDEKI-SAN HAVE *ANY* NORMAL PERSO-COMS?
THERE'S CHI-SAN, AND NOW—
MRR-GH!
がばあっ WHOOSH
NO, SILLY! I'M SUMO-MO!
GET OUT OF MY FACE!

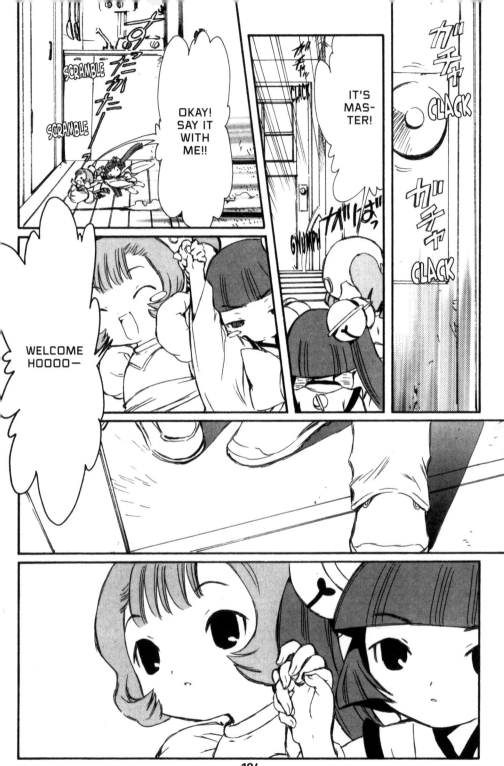

SCRAMBLE

SCRAMBLE

OKAY! SAY IT WITH ME!!

IT'S MAS-TER!

CLACK

CLACK

GWUMPH

WELCOME HOOOO—

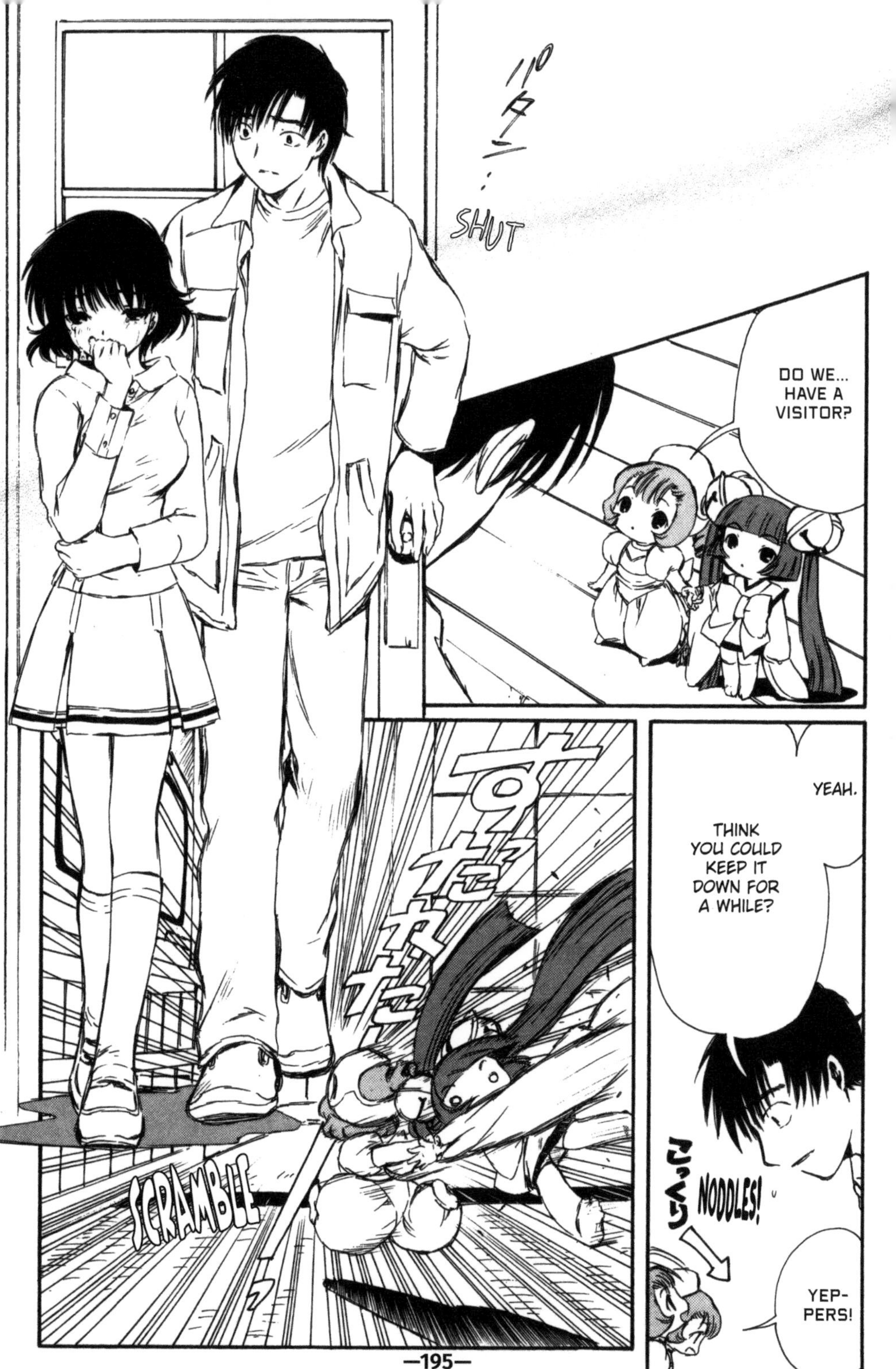

パタン
SHUT
DO WE... HAVE A VISITOR?
YEAH.
THINK YOU COULD KEEP IT DOWN FOR A WHILE?
YEP-PERS!
こっくり
NODDLES!
SCRAMBLE

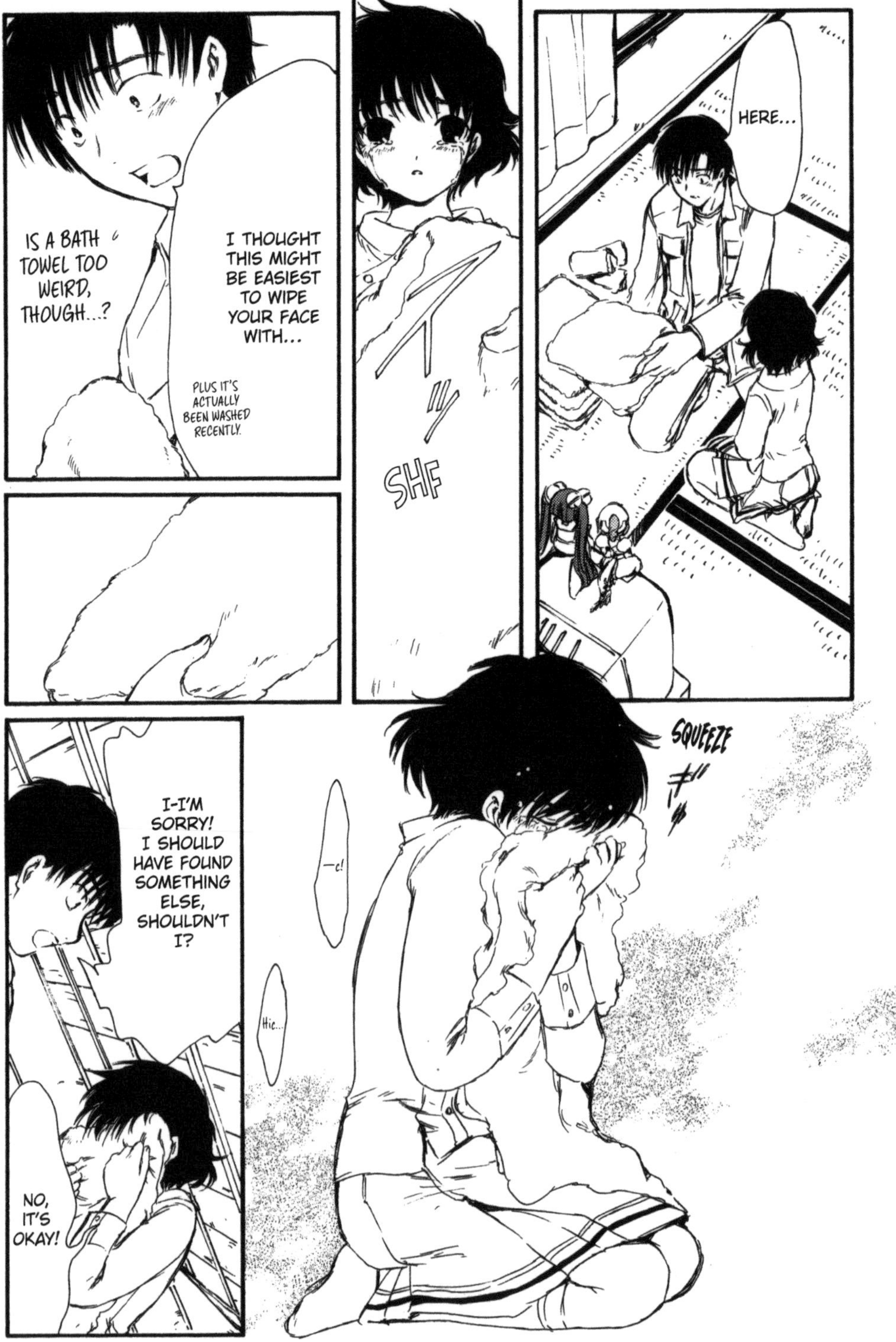
HERE...
SHF
I THOUGHT THIS MIGHT BE EASIEST TO WIPE YOUR FACE WITH...
IS A BATH TOWEL TOO WEIRD, THOUGH...?
PLUS IT'S ACTUALLY BEEN WASHED RECENTLY.
SQUEEZE
—c!
Hic...
I-I'M SORRY! I SHOULD HAVE FOUND SOMETHING ELSE, SHOULDN'T I?
NO, IT'S OKAY!

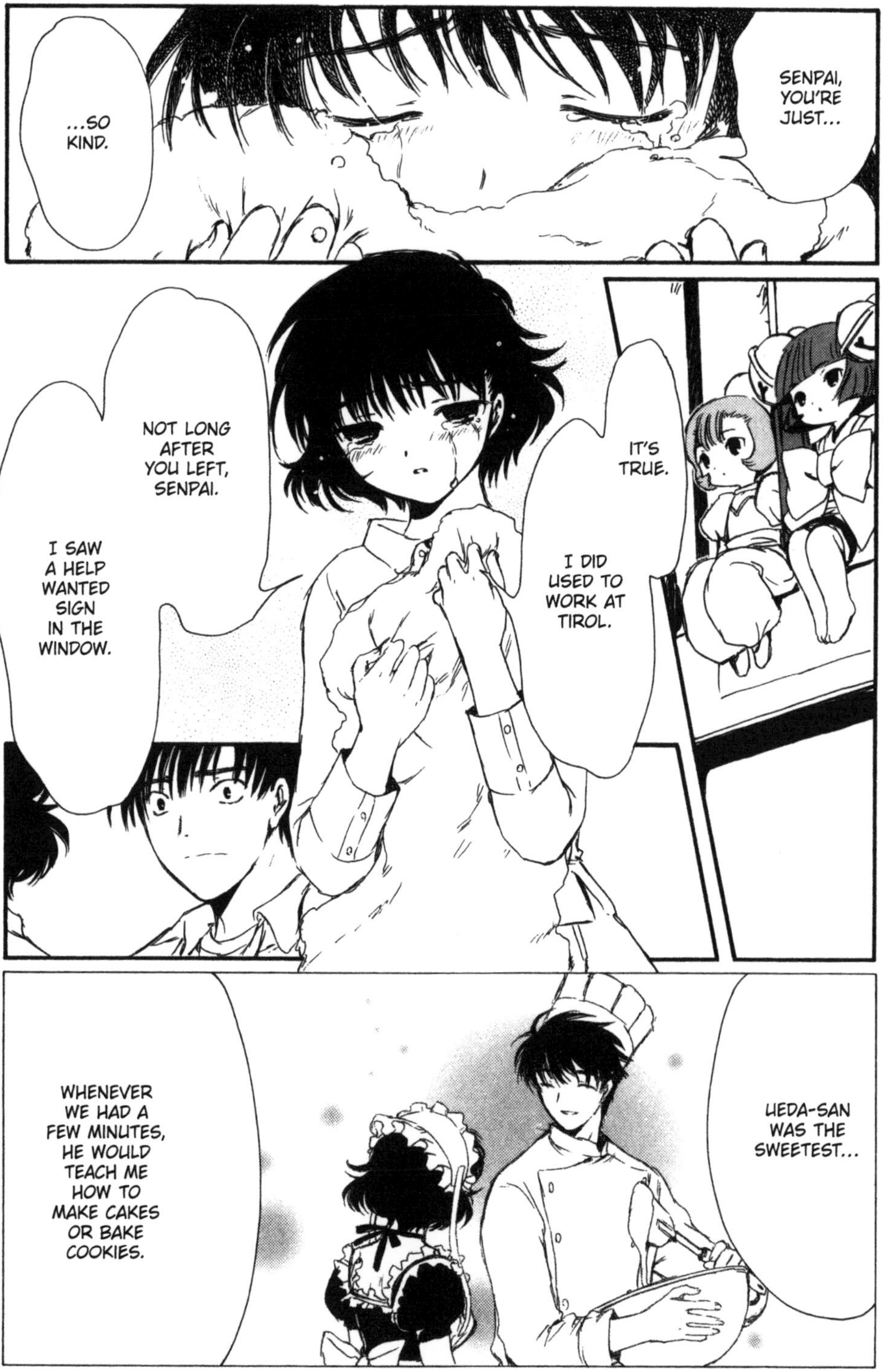
SENPAI, YOU'RE JUST...
...SO KIND.
IT'S TRUE.
I DID USED TO WORK AT TIROL.
NOT LONG AFTER YOU LEFT, SENPAI.
I SAW A HELP WANTED SIGN IN THE WINDOW.
UEDA-SAN WAS THE SWEETEST...
WHENEVER WE HAD A FEW MINUTES, HE WOULD TEACH ME HOW TO MAKE CAKES OR BAKE COOKIES.

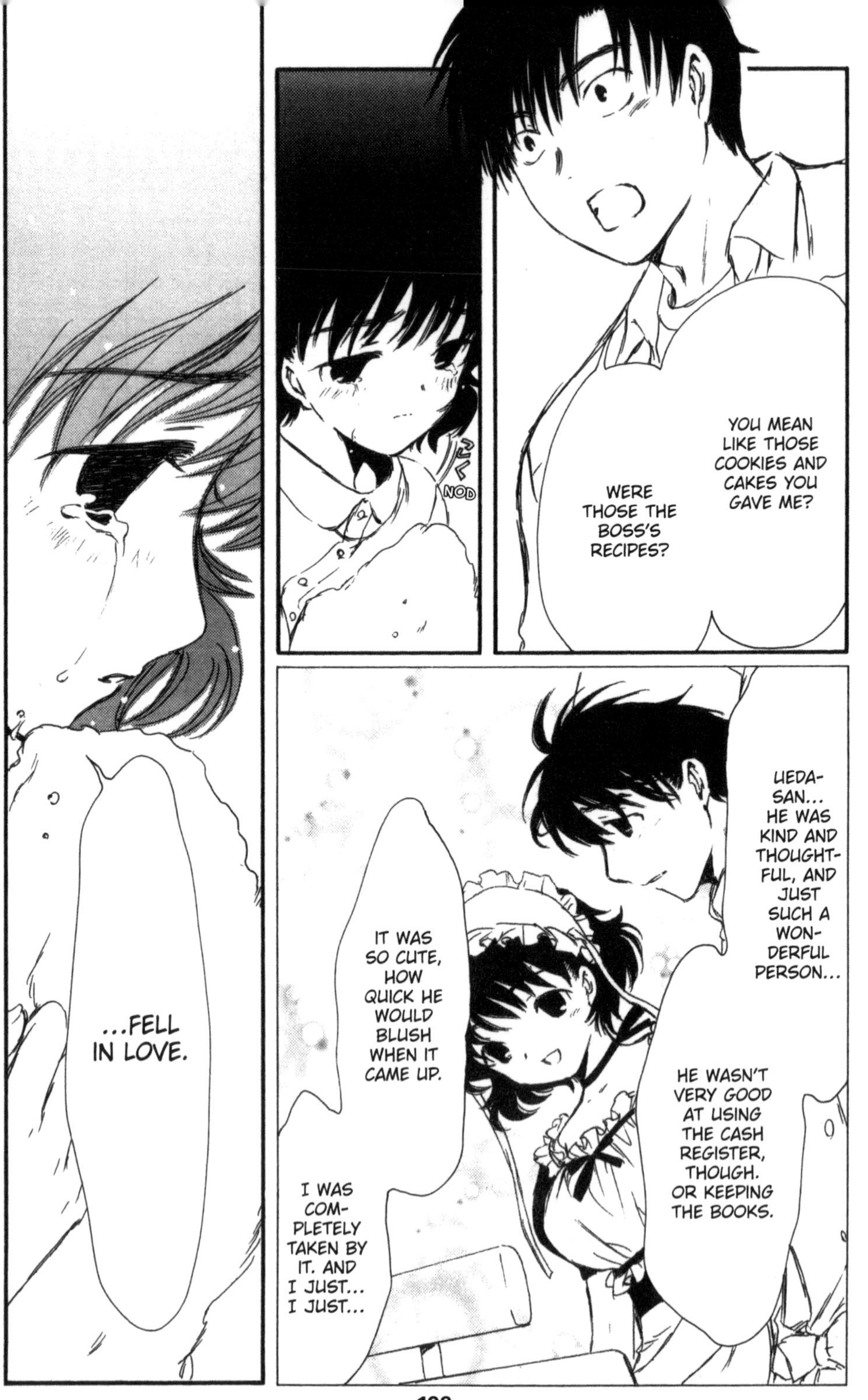
YOU MEAN LIKE THOSE COOKIES AND CAKES YOU GAVE ME?
WERE THOSE THE BOSS'S RECIPES?
NOD
UEDA-SAN... HE WAS KIND AND THOUGHT-FUL, AND JUST SUCH A WON-DERFUL PERSON...
HE WASN'T VERY GOOD AT USING THE CASH REGISTER, THOUGH. OR KEEPING THE BOOKS.
IT WAS SO CUTE, HOW QUICK HE WOULD BLUSH WHEN IT CAME UP.
I WAS COM-PLETELY TAKEN BY IT. AND I JUST... I JUST...
...FELL IN LOVE.

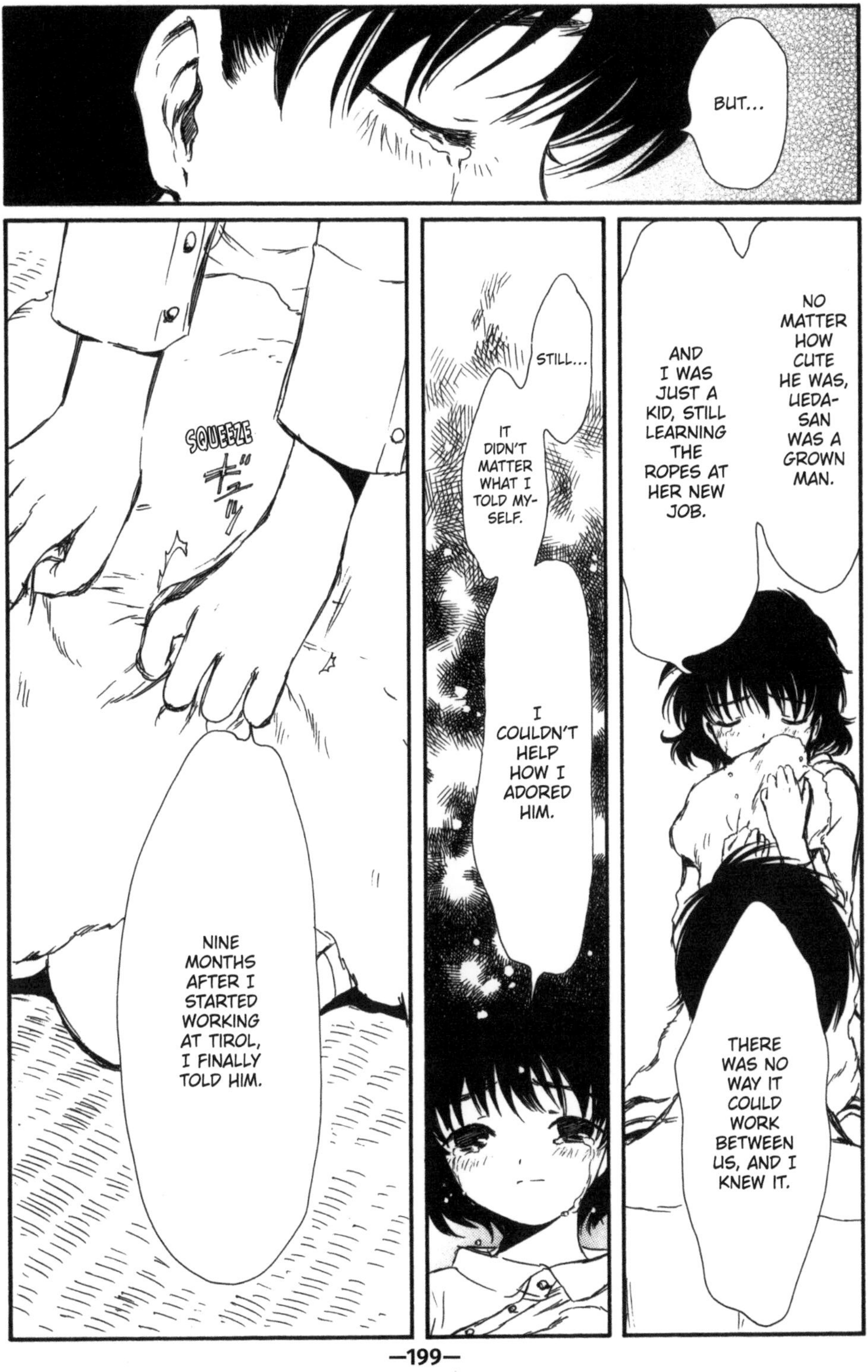
BUT...
NO MATTER HOW CUTE HE WAS, UEDA-SAN WAS A GROWN MAN.
AND I WAS JUST A KID, STILL LEARNING THE ROPES AT HER NEW JOB.
THERE WAS NO WAY IT COULD WORK BETWEEN US, AND I KNEW IT.
STILL...
IT DIDN'T MATTER WHAT I TOLD MY-SELF.
I COULDN'T HELP HOW I ADORED HIM.
SQUEEZE
ギュッ
NINE MONTHS AFTER I STARTED WORKING AT TIROL, I FINALLY TOLD HIM.

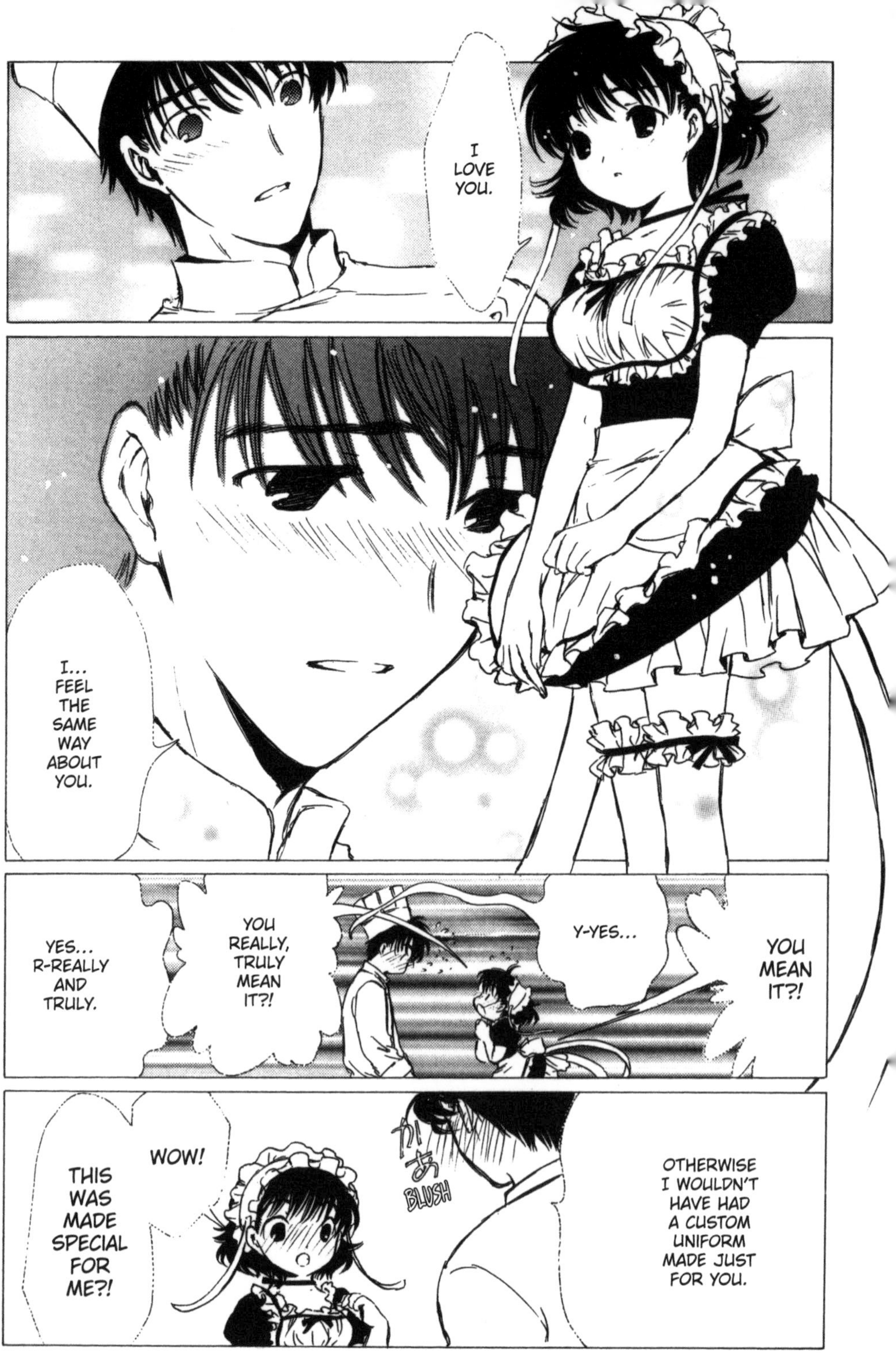
I LOVE YOU.
I... FEEL THE SAME WAY ABOUT YOU.
YOU MEAN IT?!
Y-YES...
YOU REALLY, TRULY MEAN IT?!
YES... R-REALLY AND TRULY.
OTHERWISE I WOULDN'T HAVE HAD A CUSTOM UNIFORM MADE JUST FOR YOU.
かあ BLUSH
WOW!
THIS WAS MADE SPECIAL FOR ME?!

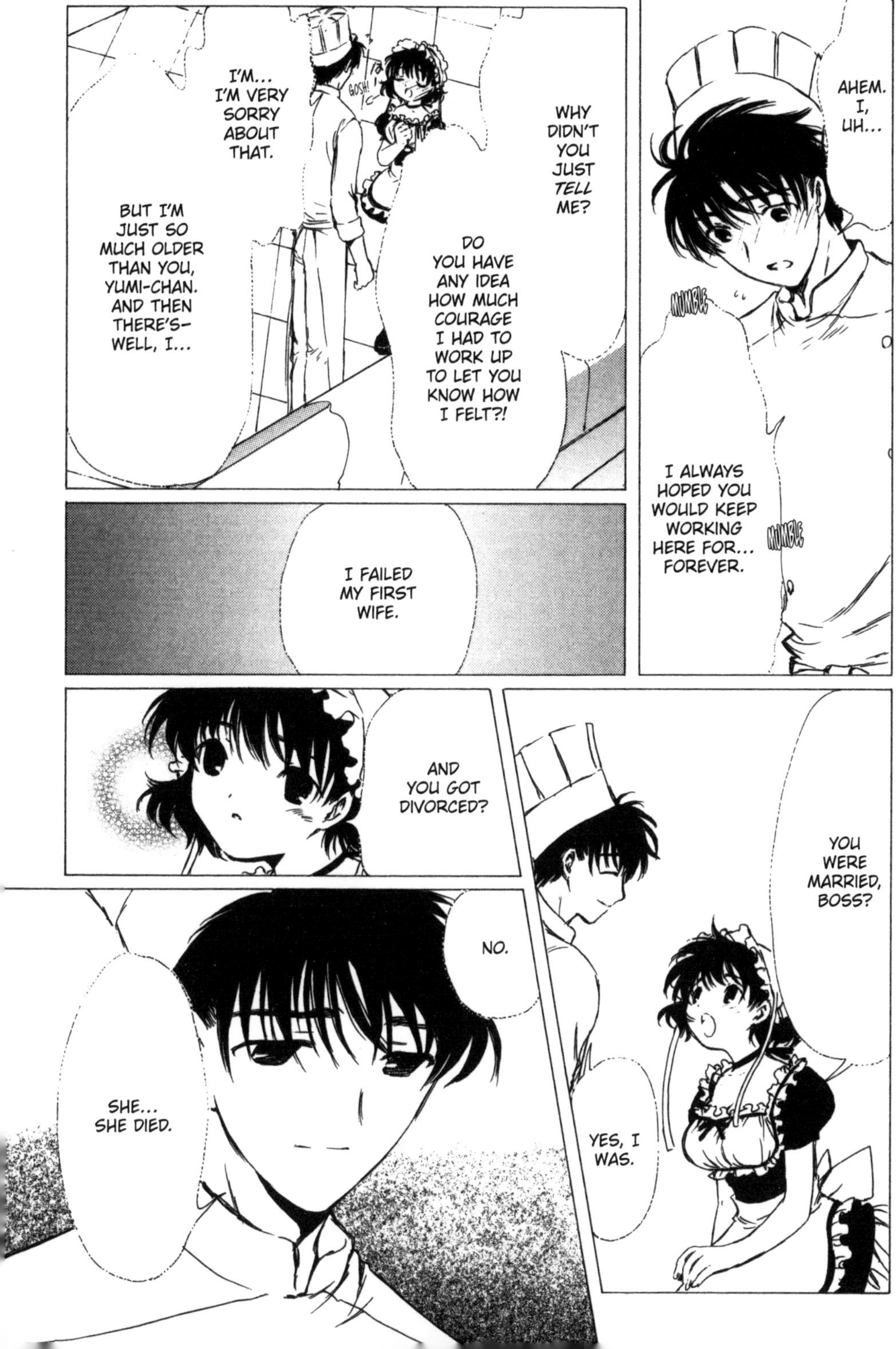
AHEM. I, UH...
MUMBLE
I ALWAYS HOPED YOU WOULD KEEP WORKING HERE FOR... FOREVER.
MUMBLE
WHY DIDN'T YOU JUST *TELL* ME?
DO YOU HAVE ANY IDEA HOW MUCH COURAGE I HAD TO WORK UP TO LET YOU KNOW HOW I FELT?!
GOSH!
I'M... I'M VERY SORRY ABOUT THAT.
BUT I'M JUST SO MUCH OLDER THAN YOU, YUMI-CHAN. AND THEN THERE'S— WELL, I...
I FAILED MY FIRST WIFE.
YOU WERE MARRIED, BOSS?
YES, I WAS.
AND YOU GOT DIVORCED?
NO.
SHE... SHE DIED.

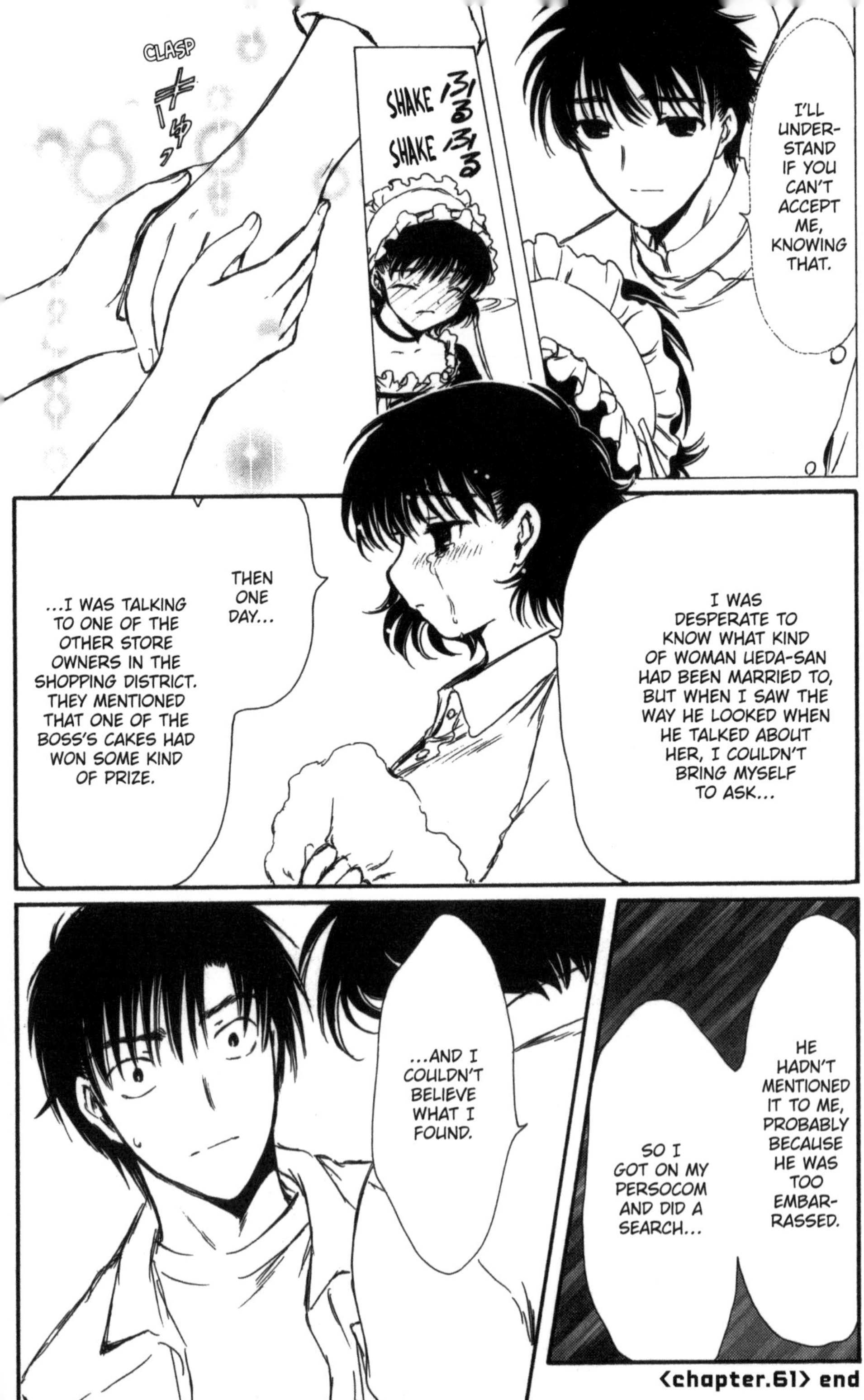
I'LL UNDER-STAND IF YOU CAN'T ACCEPT ME, KNOWING THAT.
SHAKE ぶる
SHAKE ぶる
CLASP
ぎゅっ
I WAS DESPERATE TO KNOW WHAT KIND OF WOMAN UEDA-SAN HAD BEEN MARRIED TO, BUT WHEN I SAW THE WAY HE LOOKED WHEN HE TALKED ABOUT HER, I COULDN'T BRING MYSELF TO ASK...
THEN ONE DAY...
...I WAS TALKING TO ONE OF THE OTHER STORE OWNERS IN THE SHOPPING DISTRICT. THEY MENTIONED THAT ONE OF THE BOSS'S CAKES HAD WON SOME KIND OF PRIZE.
HE HADN'T MENTIONED IT TO ME, PROBABLY BECAUSE HE WAS TOO EMBAR-RASSED.
SO I GOT ON MY PERSOCOM AND DID A SEARCH...
...AND I COULDN'T BELIEVE WHAT I FOUND.

<chapter.61> end

⟨chapter.62⟩

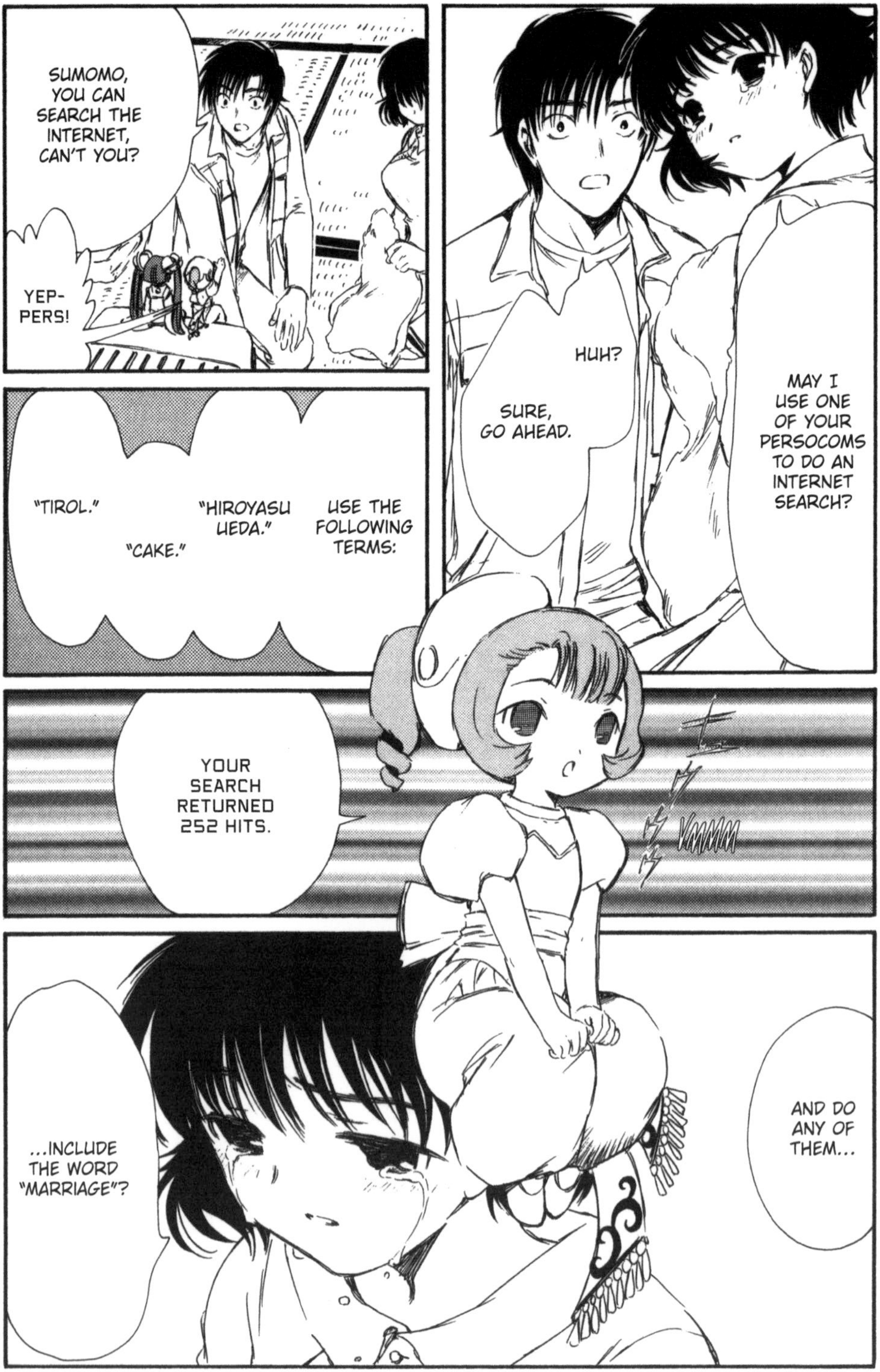
MAY I USE ONE OF YOUR PERSOCOMS TO DO AN INTERNET SEARCH?
HUH?
SURE, GO AHEAD.
SUMOMO, YOU CAN SEARCH THE INTERNET, CAN'T YOU?
YEP-PERS!
USE THE FOLLOWING TERMS:
"HIROYASU UEDA."
"CAKE."
"TIROL."
VMMMM
YOUR SEARCH RETURNED 252 HITS.
AND DO ANY OF THEM...
...INCLUDE THE WORD "MARRIAGE"?

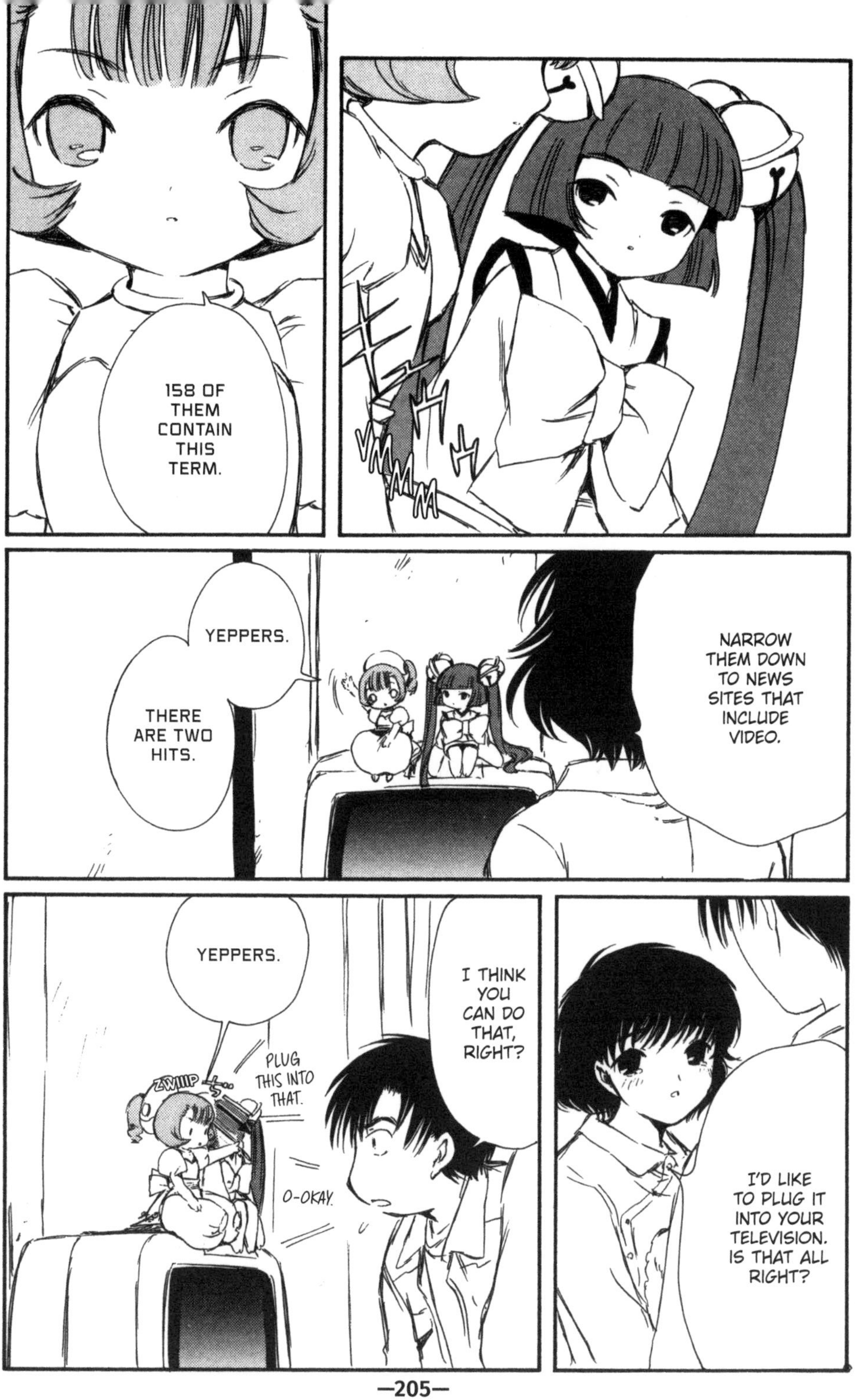
158 OF THEM CONTAIN THIS TERM.
NARROW THEM DOWN TO NEWS SITES THAT INCLUDE VIDEO.
YEPPERS.
THERE ARE TWO HITS.
I'D LIKE TO PLUG IT INTO YOUR TELEVISION. IS THAT ALL RIGHT?
I THINK YOU CAN DO THAT, RIGHT?
O-OKAY.
YEPPERS.
PLUG THIS INTO THAT.
ZWIIIP

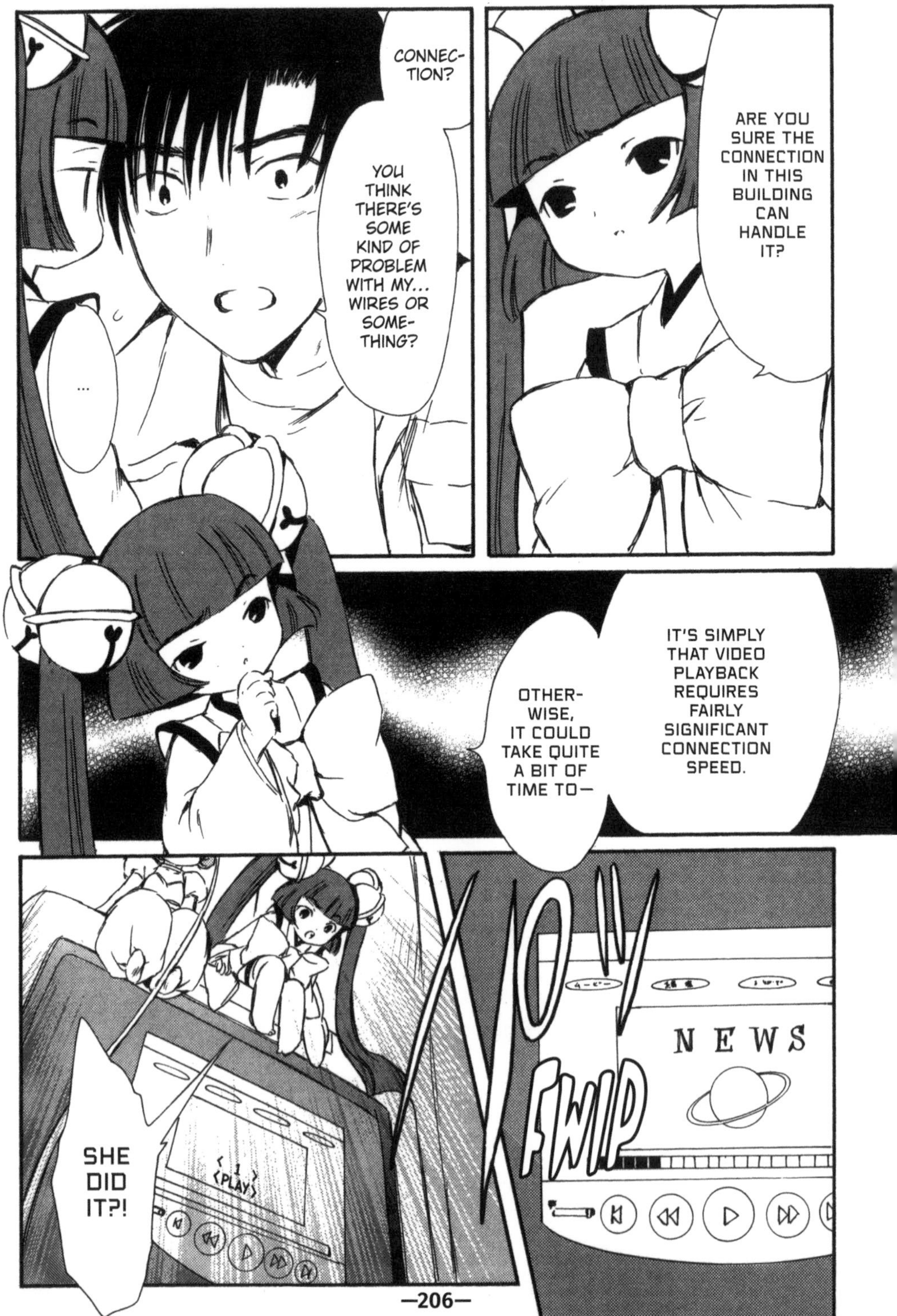
ARE YOU SURE THE CONNECTION IN THIS BUILDING CAN HANDLE IT?
CONNECTION?
YOU THINK THERE'S SOME KIND OF PROBLEM WITH MY... WIRES OR SOMETHING?
...
IT'S SIMPLY THAT VIDEO PLAYBACK REQUIRES FAIRLY SIGNIFICANT CONNECTION SPEED.
OTHERWISE, IT COULD TAKE QUITE A BIT OF TIME TO—
FWIP
NEWS
SHE DID IT?!
< 1 >
<PLAY>

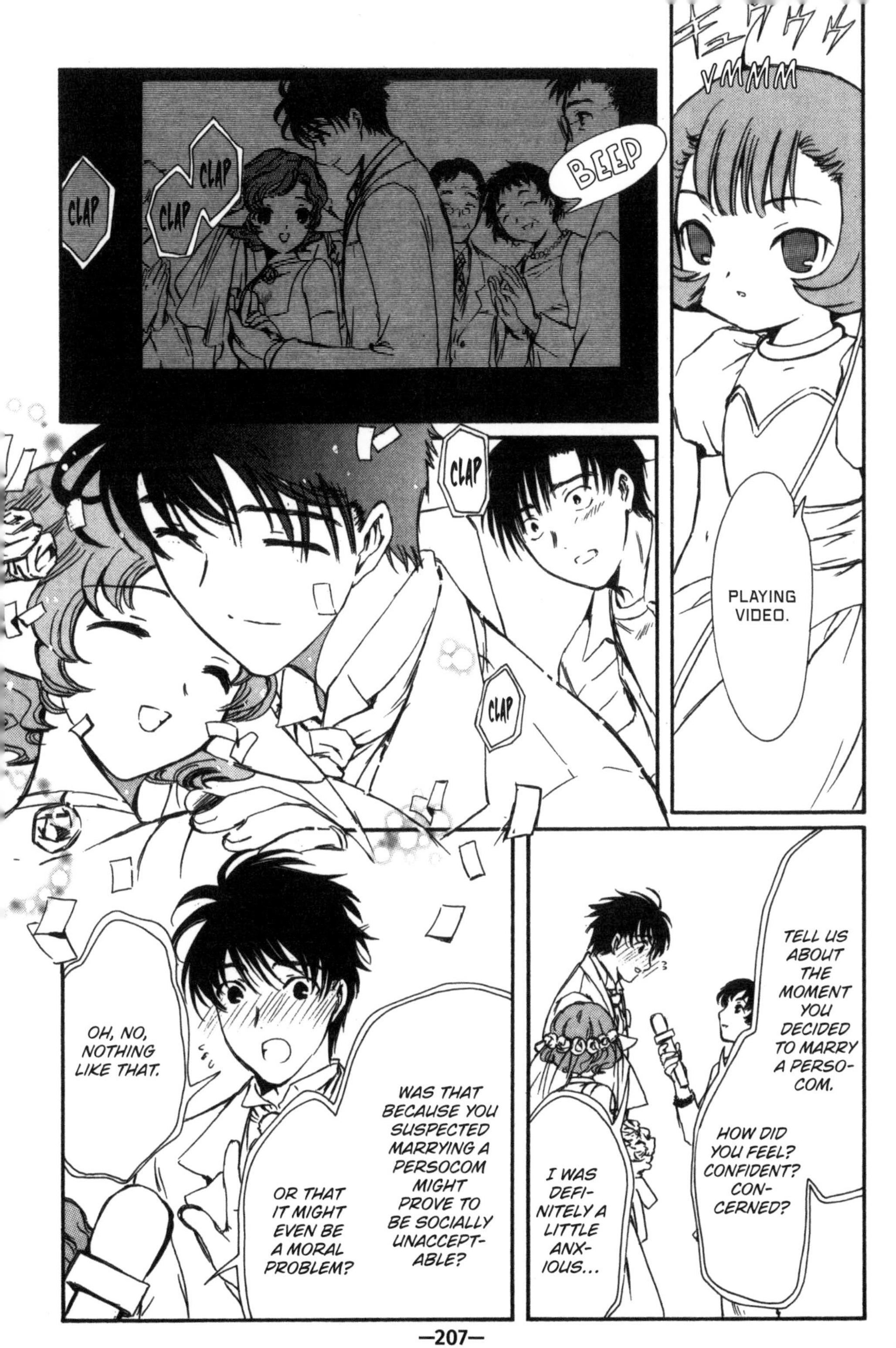
VMMMM
PLAYING VIDEO.
BEEP
CLAP
CLAP
CLAP
CLAP
CLAP
TELL US ABOUT THE MOMENT YOU DECIDED TO MARRY A PERSO-COM.
HOW DID YOU FEEL? CONFIDENT? CON-CERNED?
I WAS DEFI-NITELY A LITTLE ANX-IOUS...
WAS THAT BECAUSE YOU SUSPECTED MARRYING A PERSOCOM MIGHT PROVE TO BE SOCIALLY UNACCEPT-ABLE?
OR THAT IT MIGHT EVEN BE A MORAL PROBLEM?
OH, NO, NOTHING LIKE THAT.

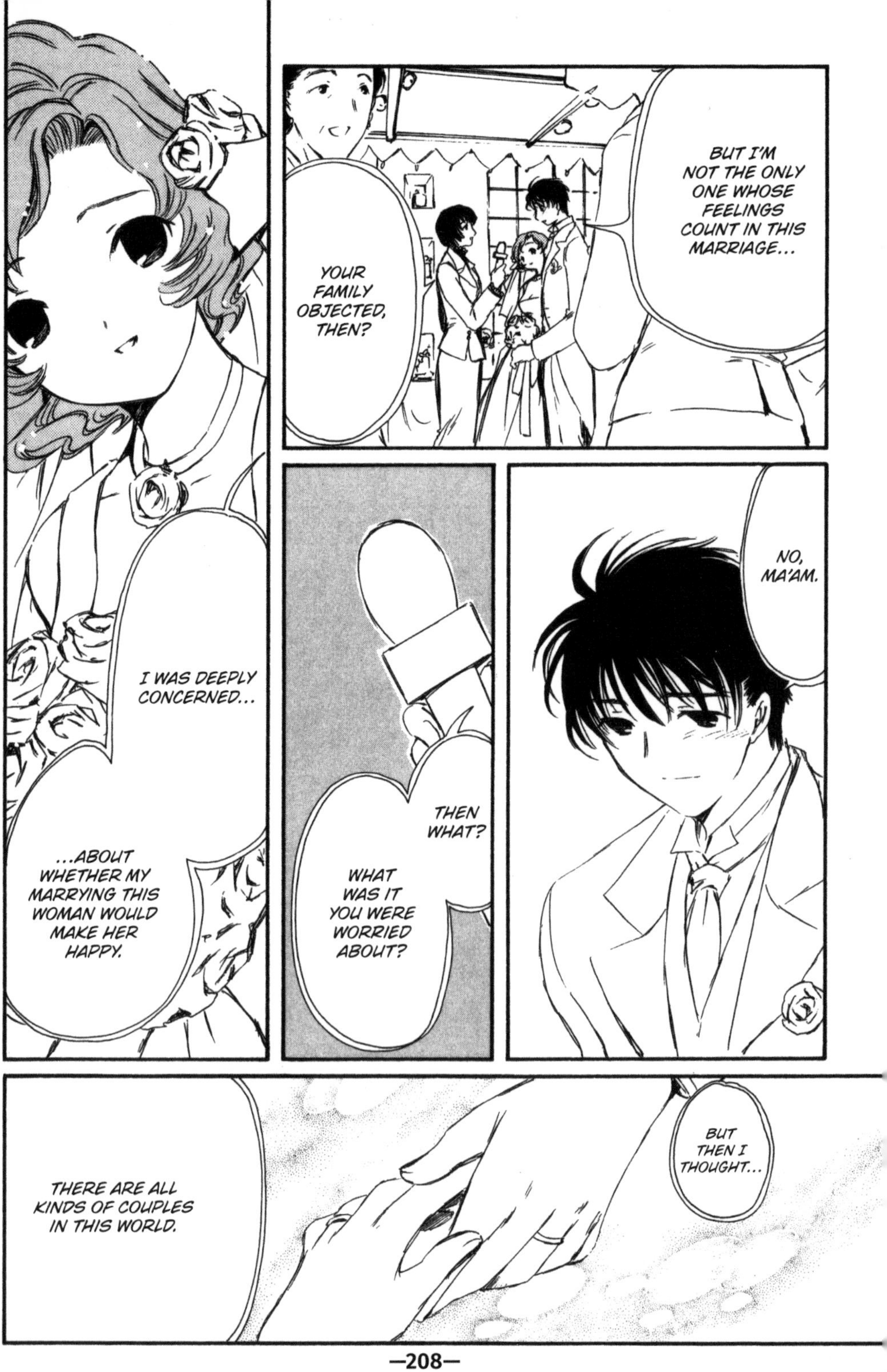
BUT I'M NOT THE ONLY ONE WHOSE FEELINGS COUNT IN THIS MARRIAGE...
YOUR FAMILY OBJECTED, THEN?
NO, MA'AM.
THEN WHAT?
WHAT WAS IT YOU WERE WORRIED ABOUT?
I WAS DEEPLY CONCERNED...
...ABOUT WHETHER MY MARRYING THIS WOMAN WOULD MAKE HER HAPPY.
BUT THEN I THOUGHT...
THERE ARE ALL KINDS OF COUPLES IN THIS WORLD.

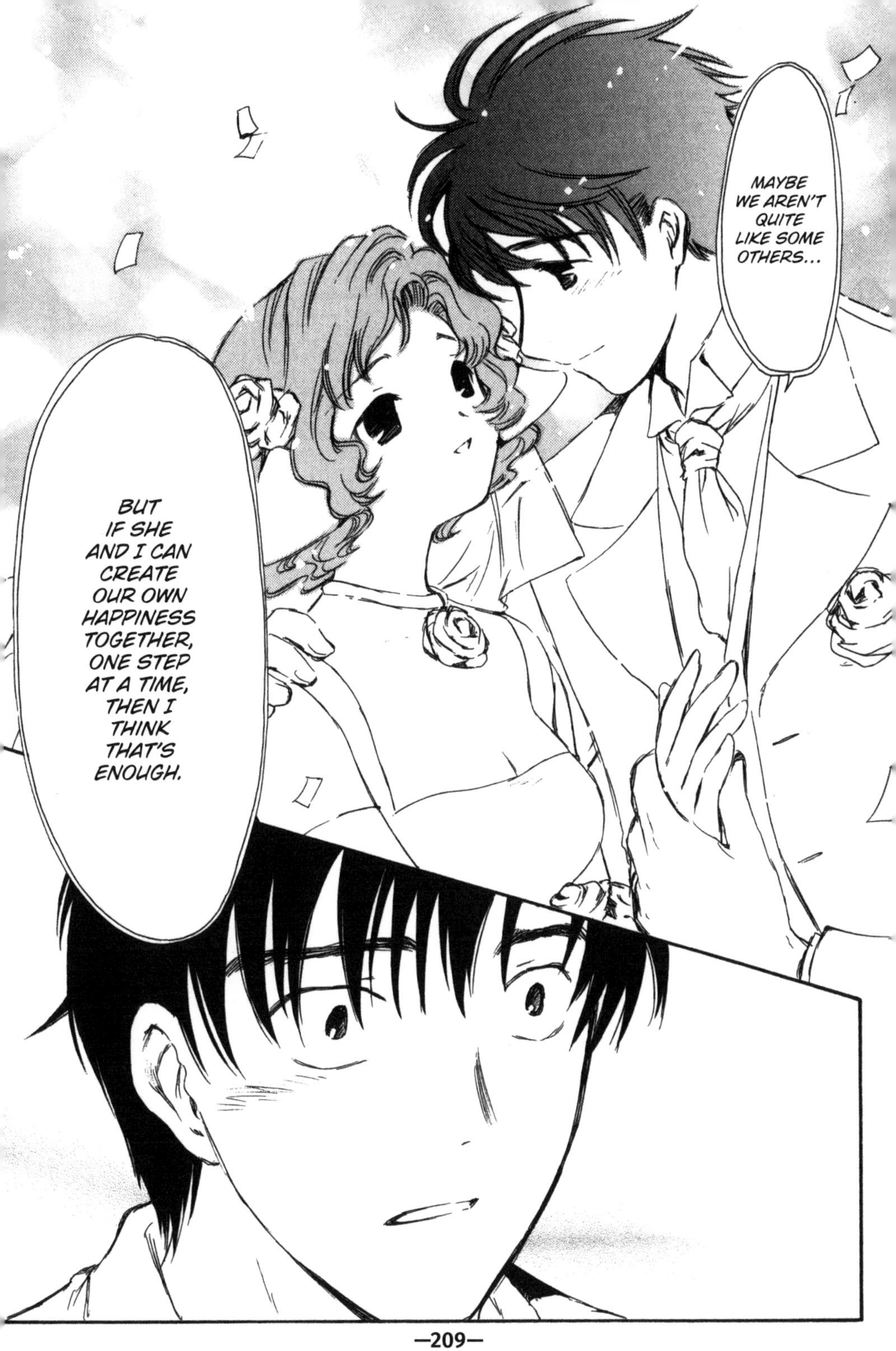
MAYBE WE AREN'T QUITE LIKE SOME OTHERS...
BUT IF SHE AND I CAN CREATE OUR OWN HAPPINESS TOGETHER, ONE STEP AT A TIME, THEN I THINK THAT'S ENOUGH.

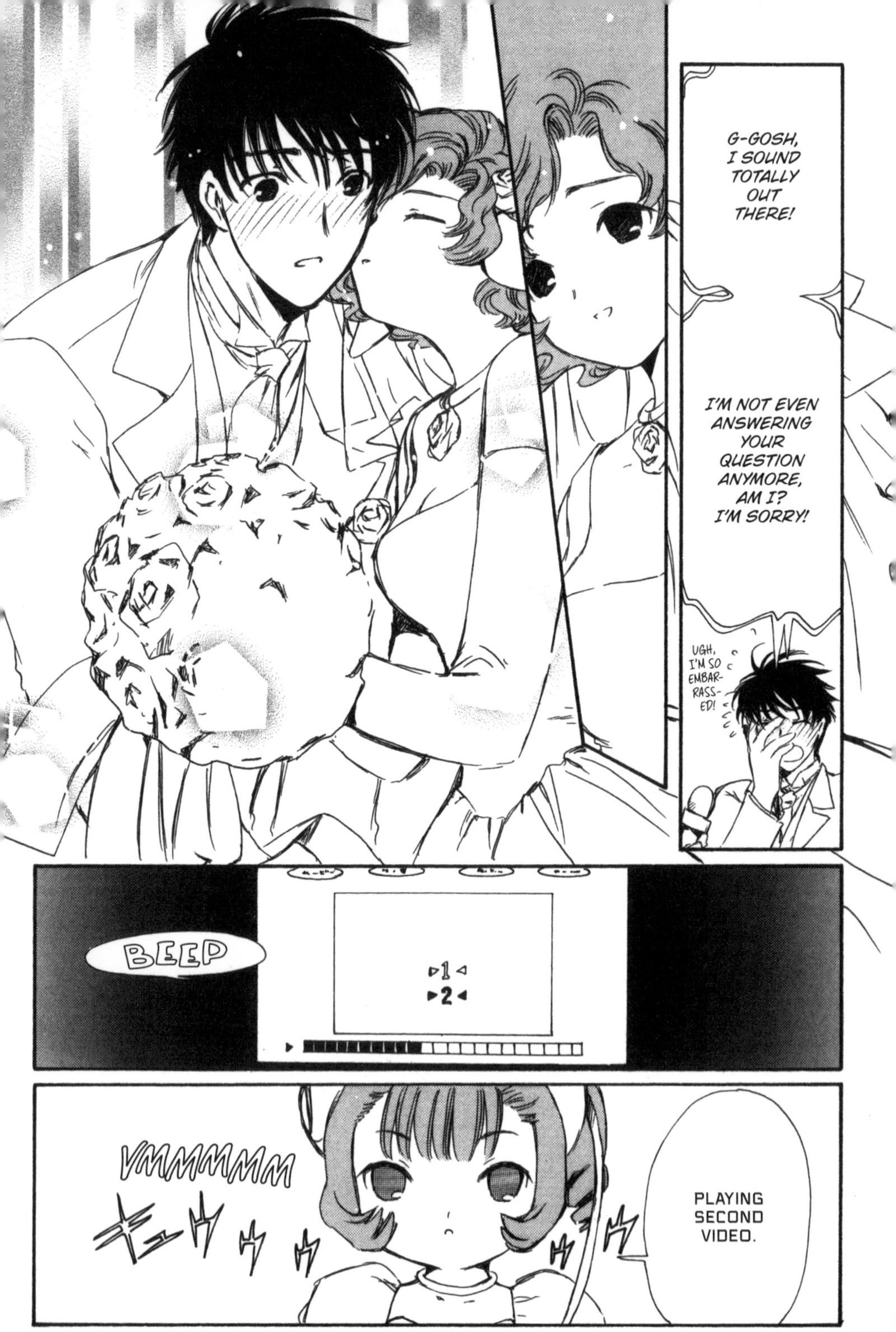
G-GOSH, I SOUND TOTALLY OUT THERE!
I'M NOT EVEN ANSWERING YOUR QUESTION ANYMORE, AM I? I'M SORRY!
UGH, I'M SO EMBAR-RASS-ED!
BEEP
1
2
PLAYING SECOND VIDEO.
VMMMMMM

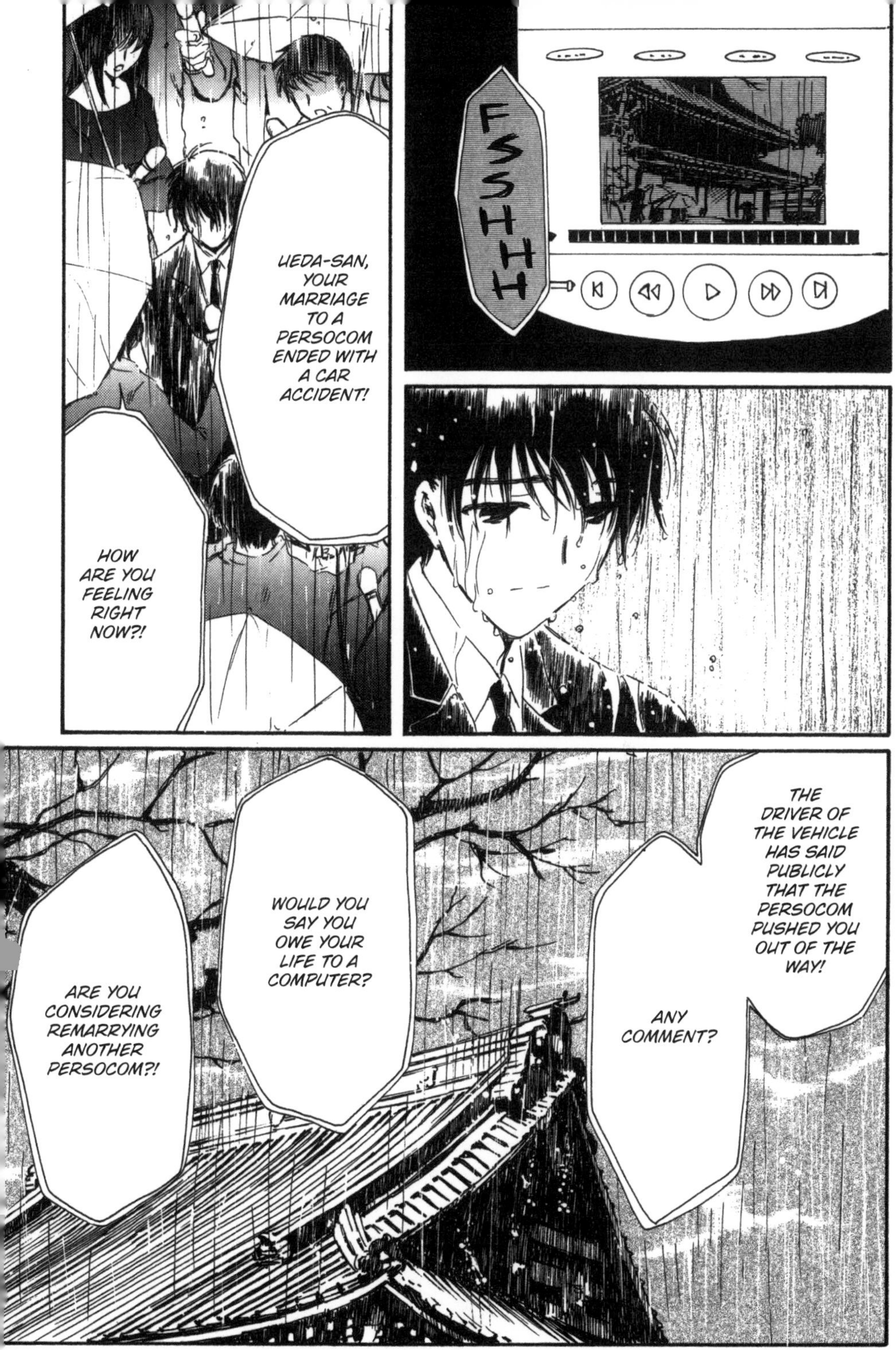
FSSHHH
UEDA-SAN, YOUR MARRIAGE TO A PERSOCOM ENDED WITH A CAR ACCIDENT!
HOW ARE YOU FEELING RIGHT NOW?!
THE DRIVER OF THE VEHICLE HAS SAID PUBLICLY THAT THE PERSOCOM PUSHED YOU OUT OF THE WAY!
ANY COMMENT?
WOULD YOU SAY YOU OWE YOUR LIFE TO A COMPUTER?
ARE YOU CONSIDERING REMARRYING ANOTHER PERSOCOM?!

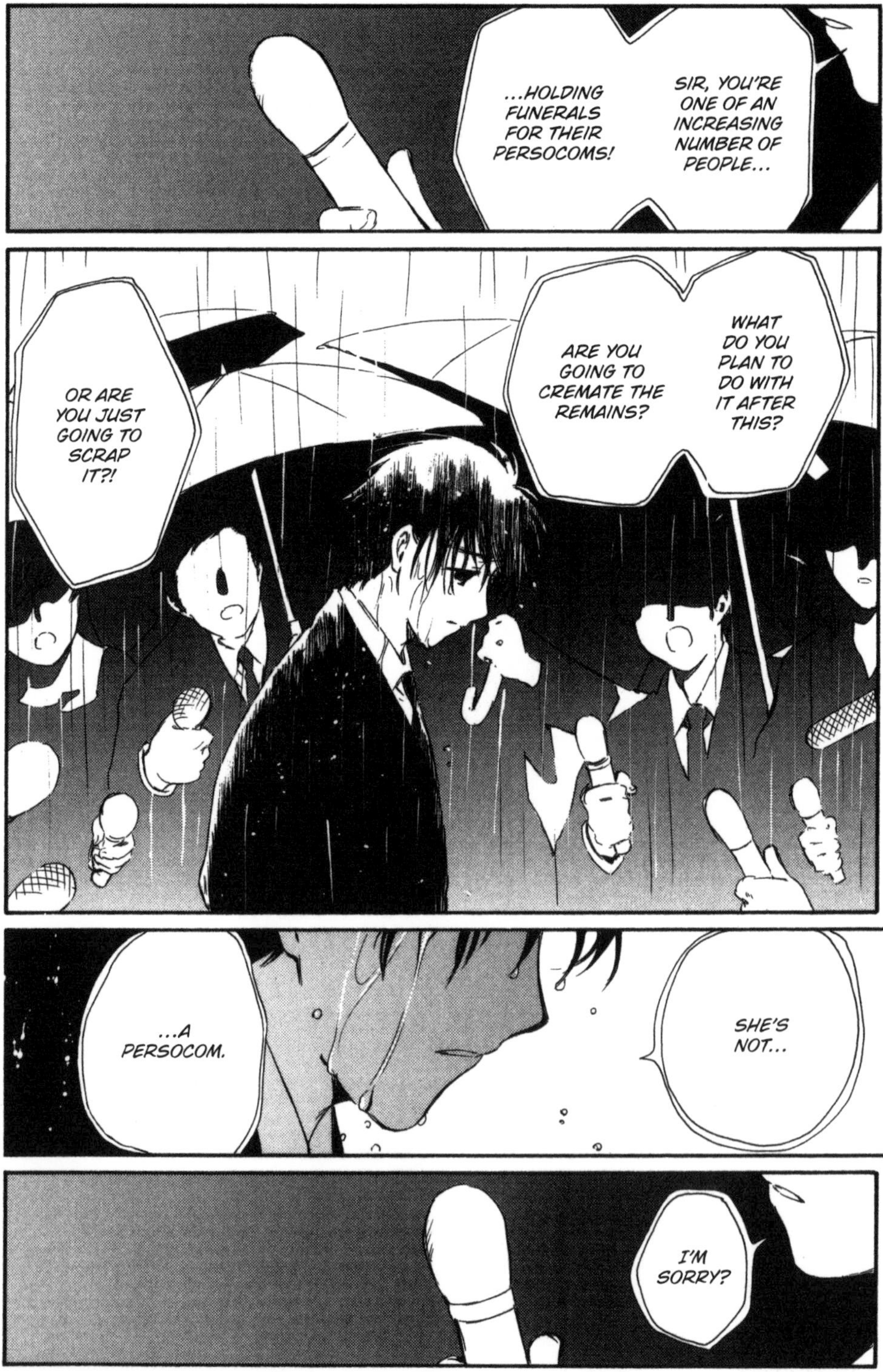
SIR, YOU'RE ONE OF AN INCREASING NUMBER OF PEOPLE...
...HOLDING FUNERALS FOR THEIR PERSOCOMS!
WHAT DO YOU PLAN TO DO WITH IT AFTER THIS?
ARE YOU GOING TO CREMATE THE REMAINS?
OR ARE YOU JUST GOING TO SCRAP IT?!
SHE'S NOT...
...A PERSOCOM.
I'M SORRY?

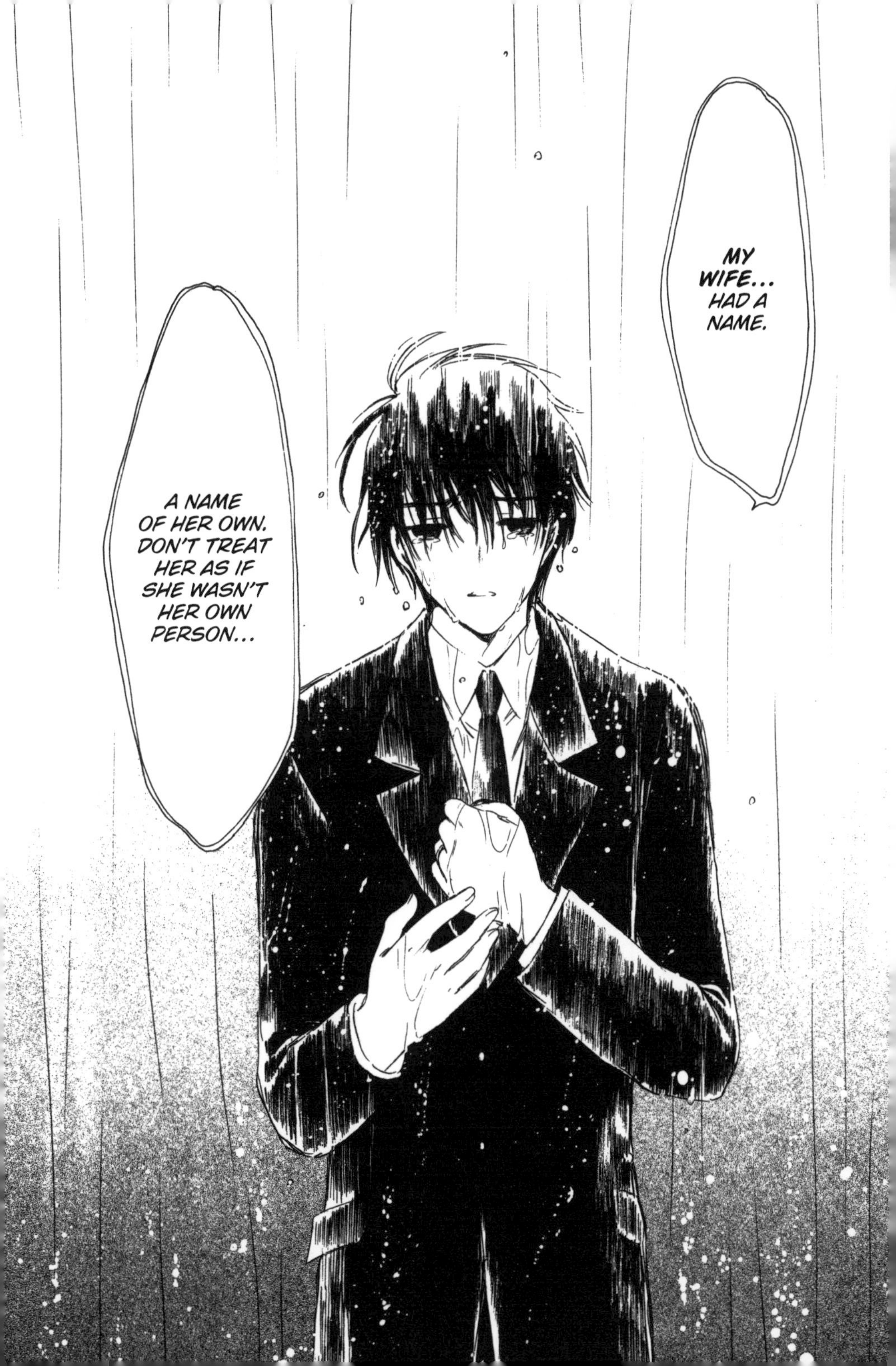
MY WIFE... HAD A NAME.
A NAME OF HER OWN. DON'T TREAT HER AS IF SHE WASN'T HER OWN PERSON...

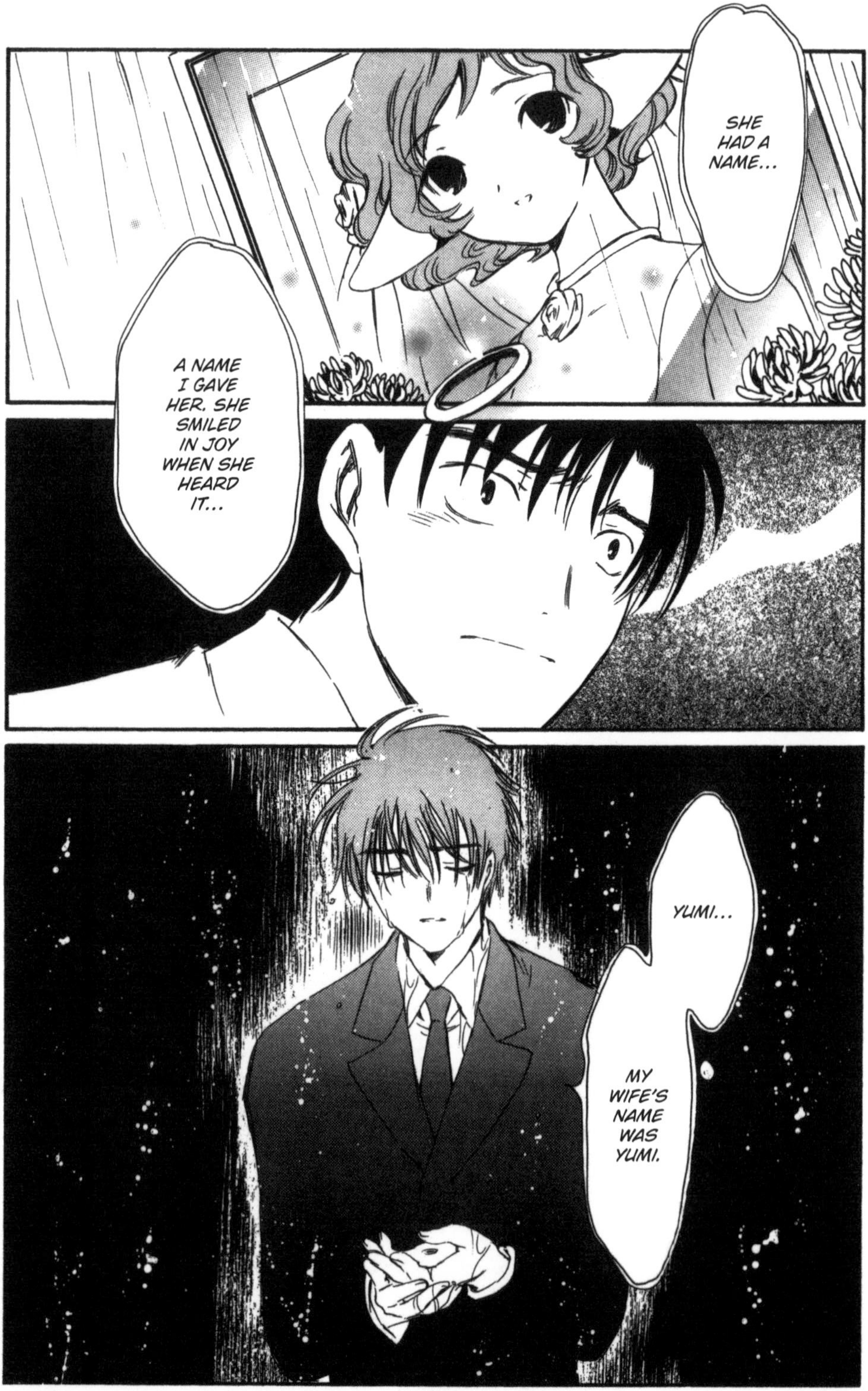
SHE HAD A NAME...
A NAME I GAVE HER. SHE SMILED IN JOY WHEN SHE HEARD IT...
YUMI...
MY WIFE'S NAME WAS YUMI.

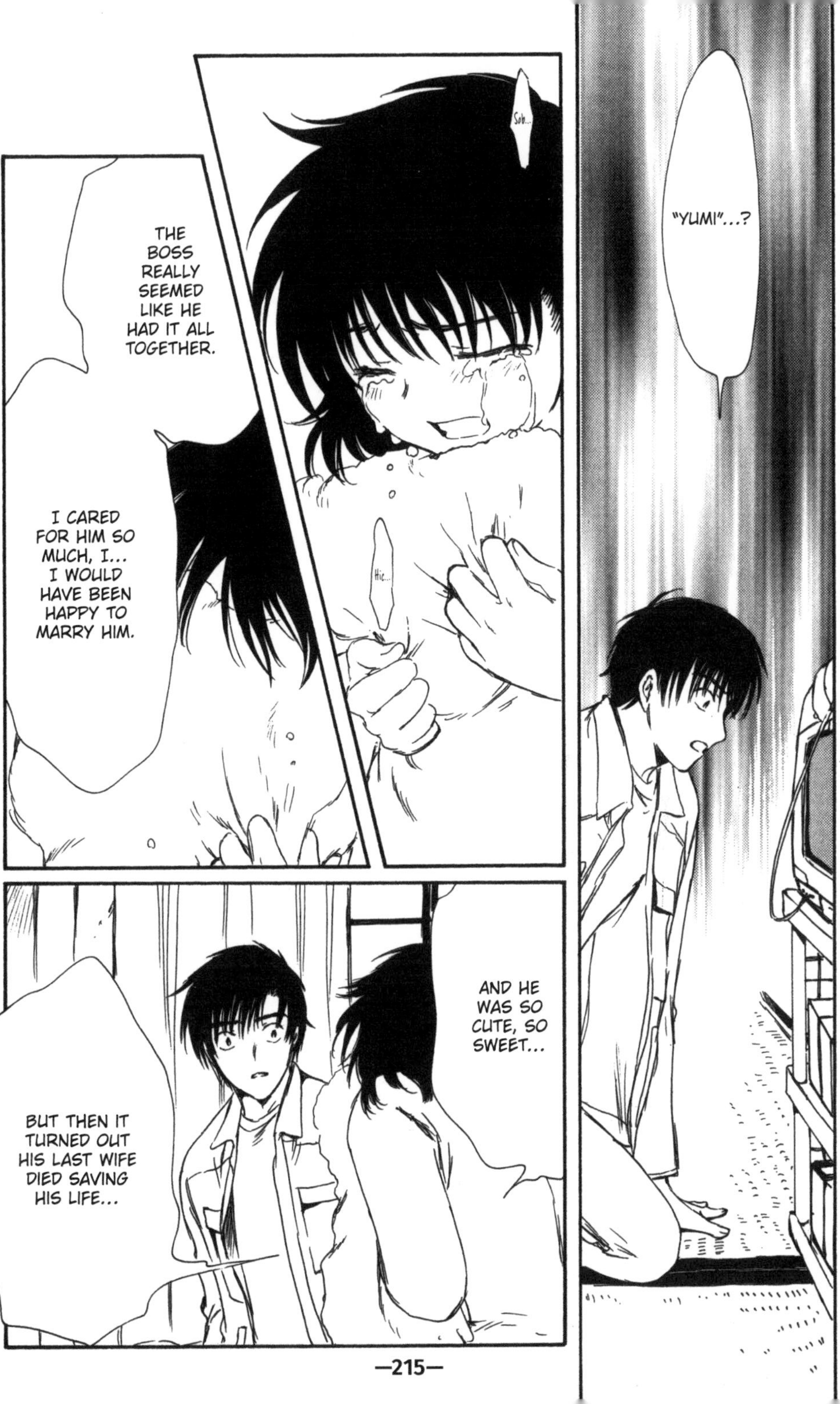
"YUMI"...?
Sob...
Hic...
THE BOSS REALLY SEEMED LIKE HE HAD IT ALL TOGETHER.
I CARED FOR HIM SO MUCH, I... I WOULD HAVE BEEN HAPPY TO MARRY HIM.
AND HE WAS SO CUTE, SO SWEET...
BUT THEN IT TURNED OUT HIS LAST WIFE DIED SAVING HIS LIFE...

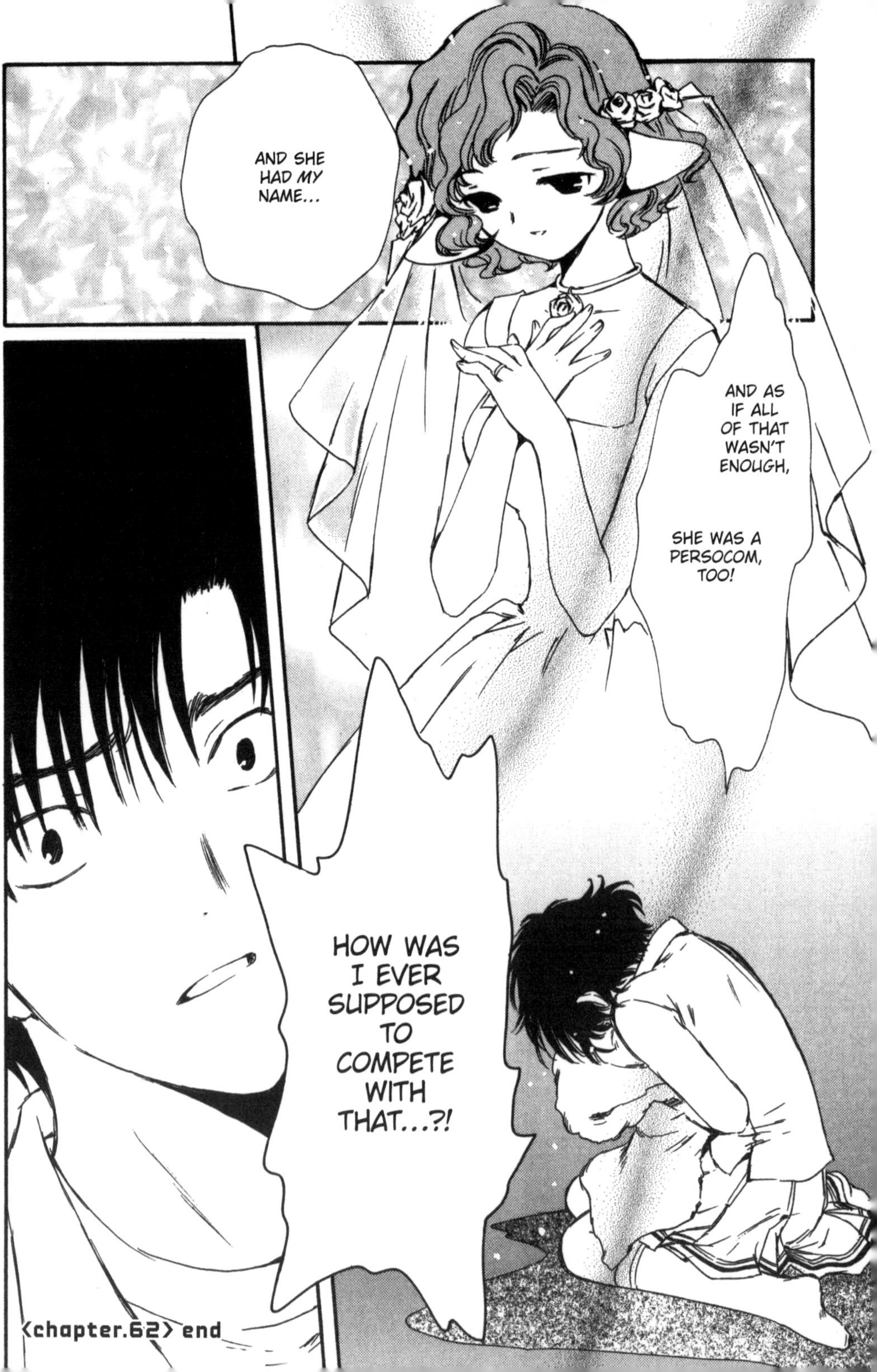
AND SHE HAD MY NAME...
AND AS IF ALL OF THAT WASN'T ENOUGH,
SHE WAS A PERSOCOM, TOO!
HOW WAS I EVER SUPPOSED TO COMPETE WITH THAT...?!
<chapter.62> end

Chobits

<chapter.63>

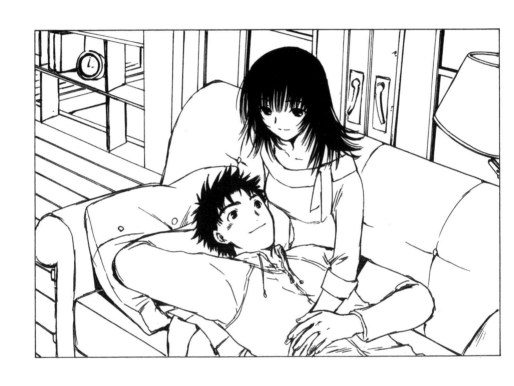

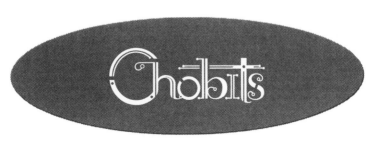

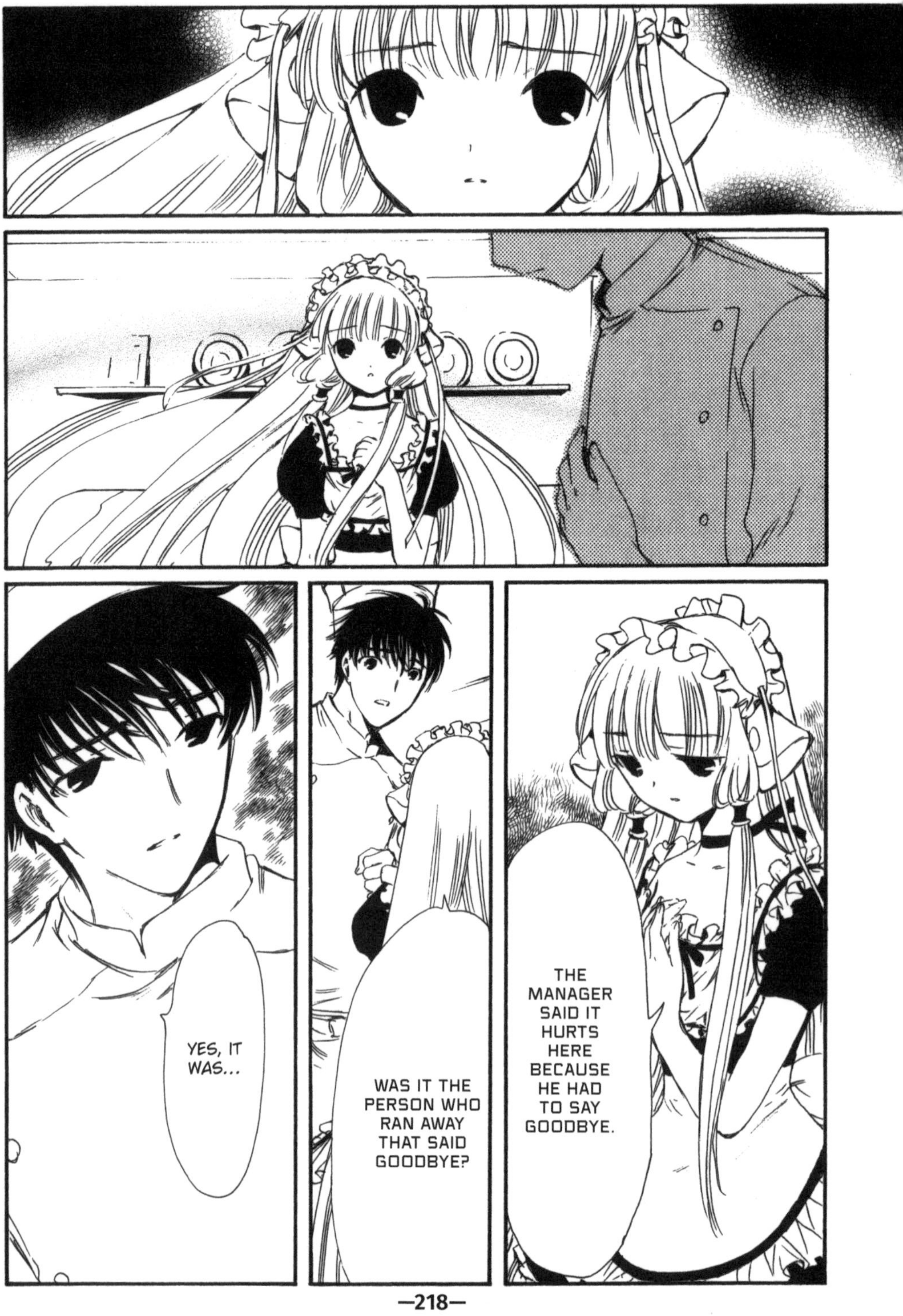
THE MANAGER SAID IT HURTS HERE BECAUSE HE HAD TO SAY GOODBYE.
WAS IT THE PERSON WHO RAN AWAY THAT SAID GOODBYE?
YES, IT WAS...

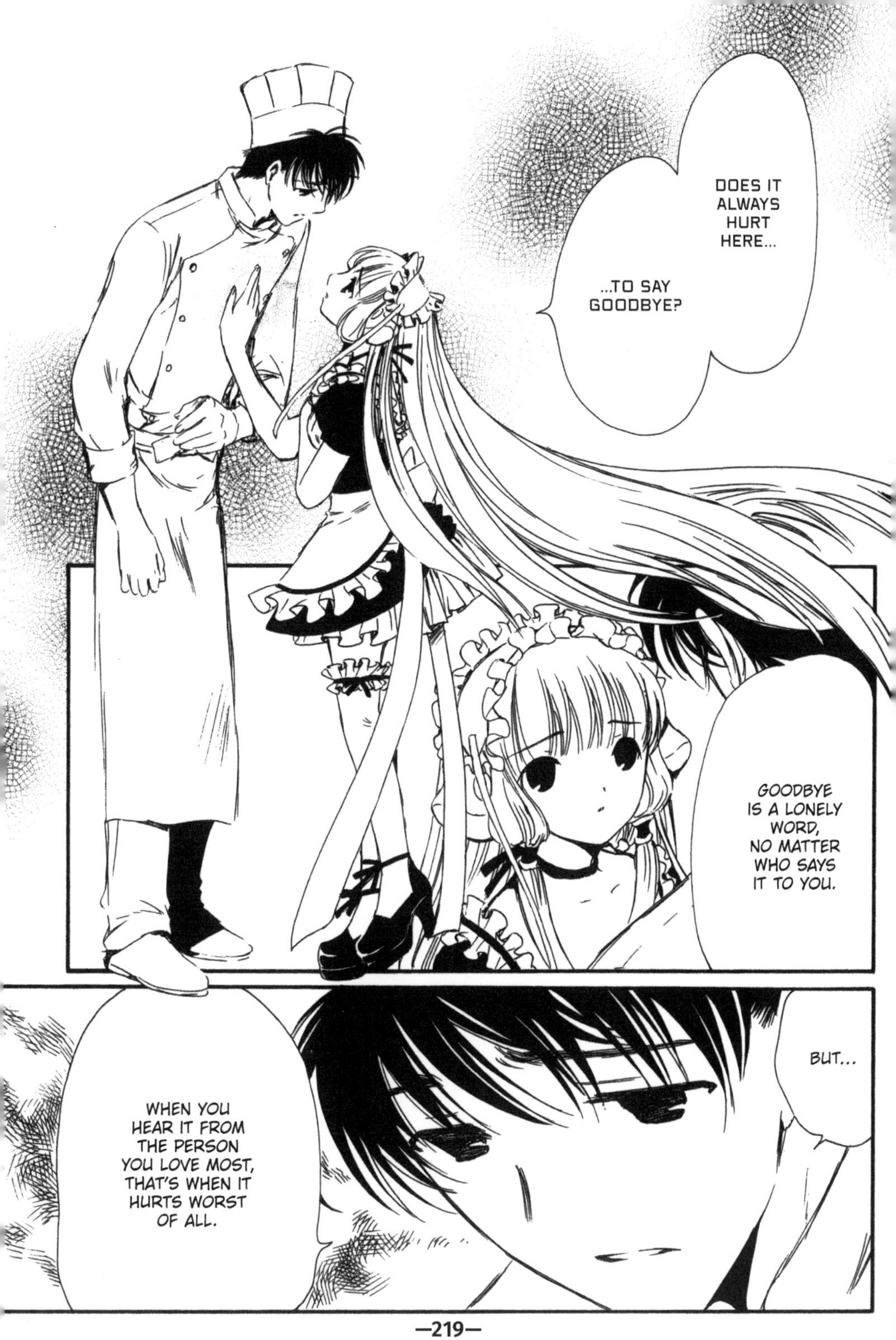
DOES IT ALWAYS HURT HERE...
...TO SAY GOODBYE?
GOODBYE IS A LONELY WORD, NO MATTER WHO SAYS IT TO YOU.
BUT...
WHEN YOU HEAR IT FROM THE PERSON YOU LOVE MOST, THAT'S WHEN IT HURTS WORST OF ALL.

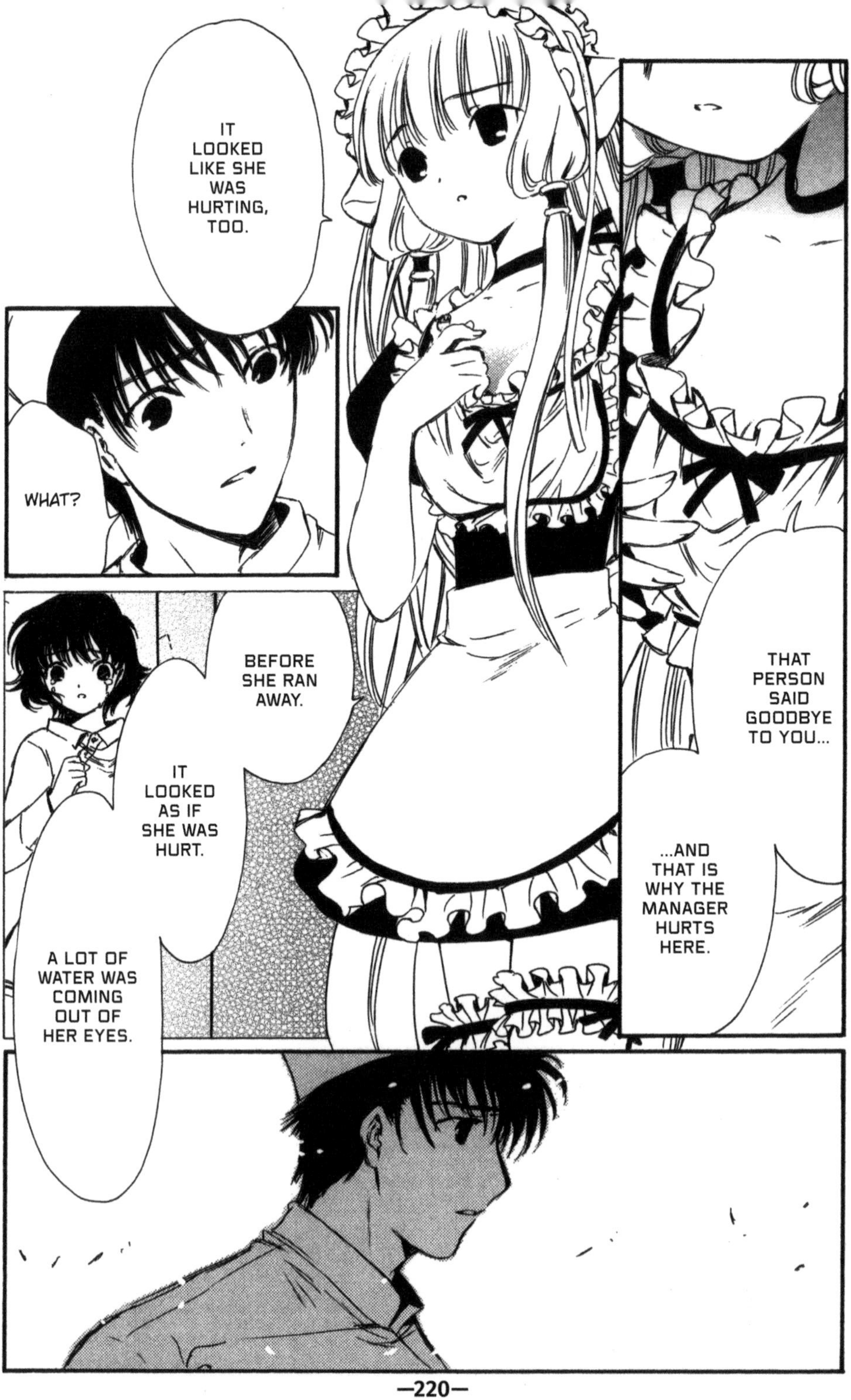

THAT PERSON SAID GOODBYE TO YOU...
...AND THAT IS WHY THE MANAGER HURTS HERE.
IT LOOKED LIKE SHE WAS HURTING, TOO.
WHAT?
BEFORE SHE RAN AWAY.
IT LOOKED AS IF SHE WAS HURT.
A LOT OF WATER WAS COMING OUT OF HER EYES.

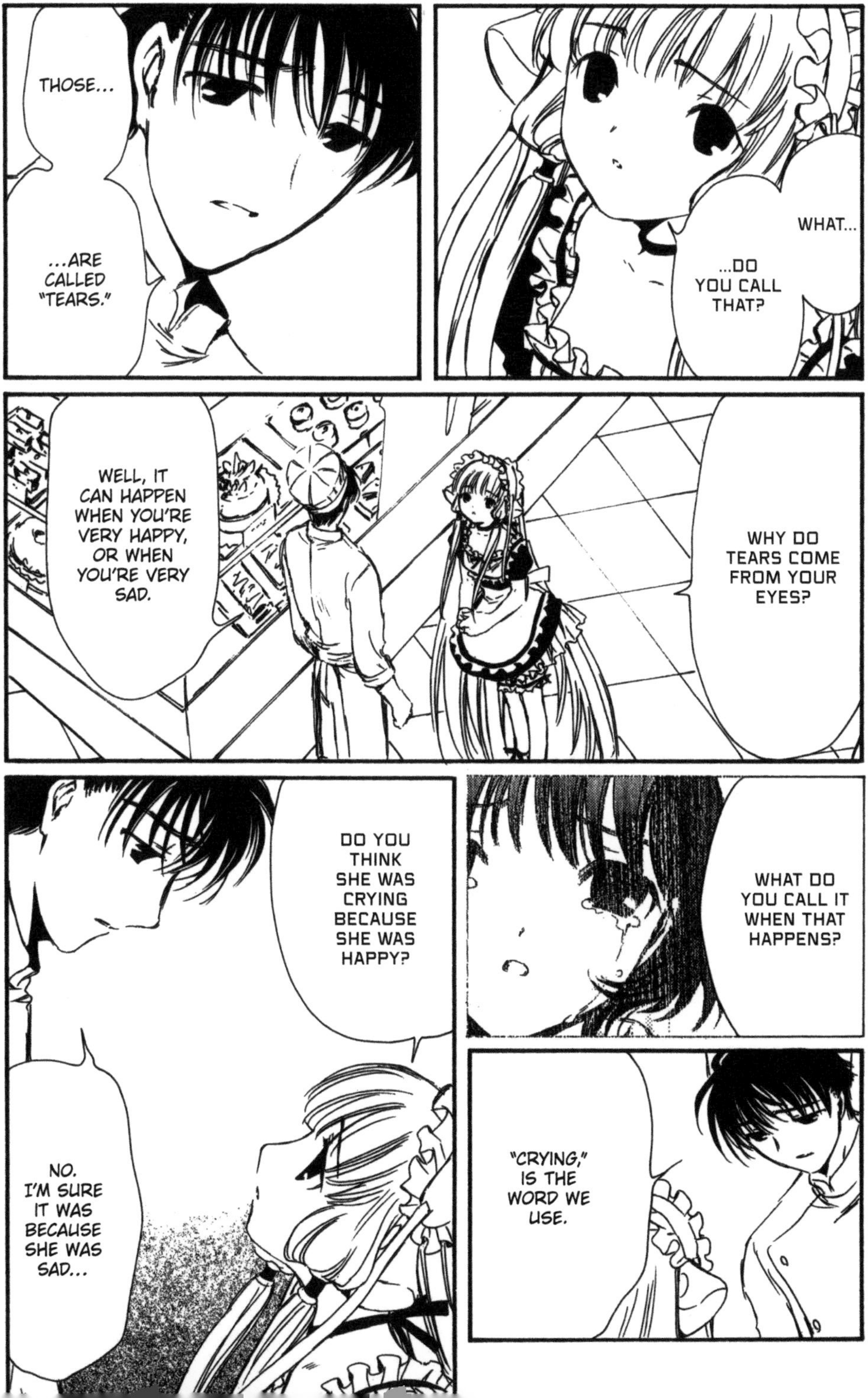
WHAT...
...DO YOU CALL THAT?
THOSE...
...ARE CALLED "TEARS."
WHY DO TEARS COME FROM YOUR EYES?
WELL, IT CAN HAPPEN WHEN YOU'RE VERY HAPPY, OR WHEN YOU'RE VERY SAD.
WHAT DO YOU CALL IT WHEN THAT HAPPENS?
"CRYING," IS THE WORD WE USE.
DO YOU THINK SHE WAS CRYING BECAUSE SHE WAS HAPPY?
NO. I'M SURE IT WAS BECAUSE SHE WAS SAD...

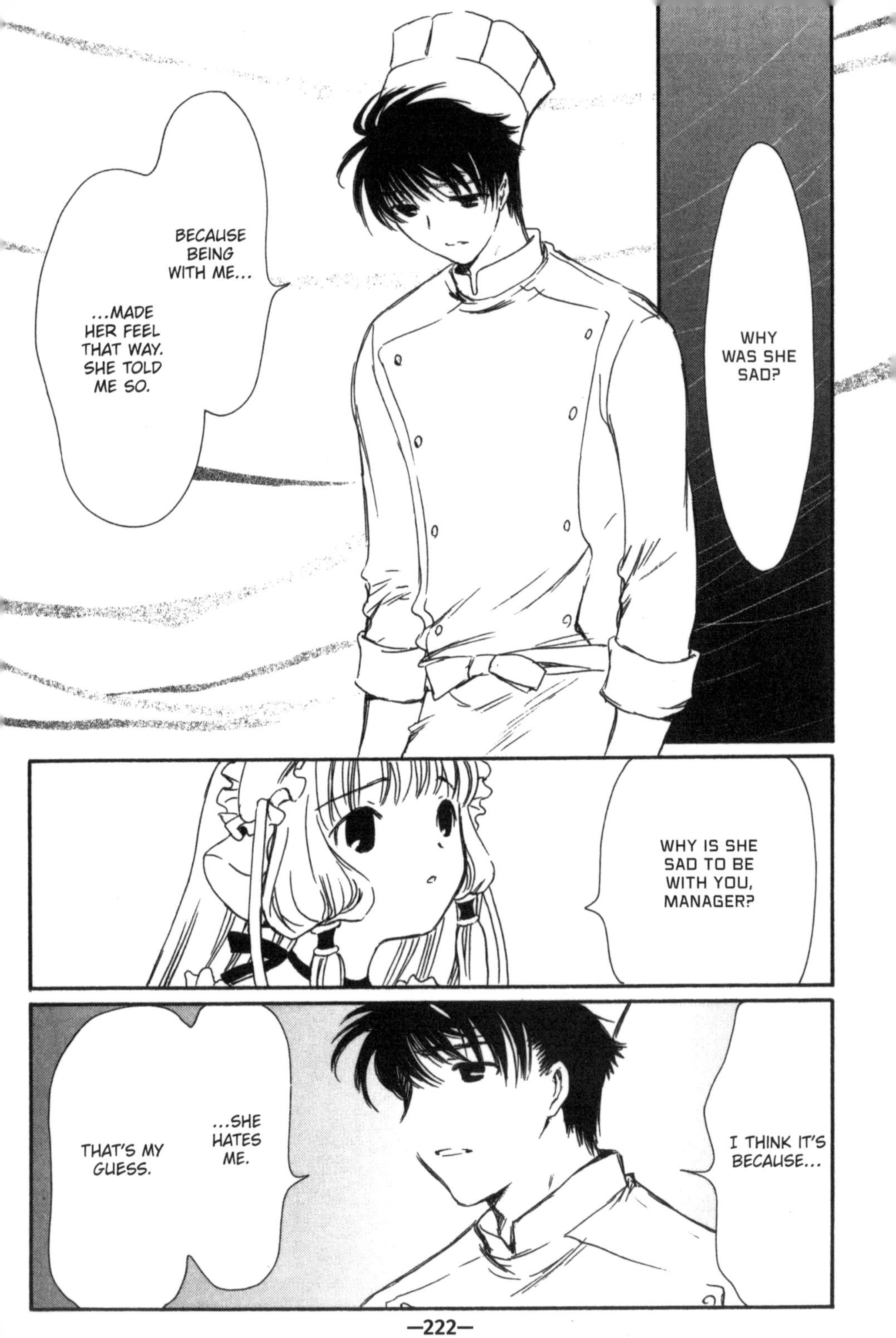
WHY WAS SHE SAD?
BECAUSE BEING WITH ME...
...MADE HER FEEL THAT WAY. SHE TOLD ME SO.
WHY IS SHE SAD TO BE WITH YOU, MANAGER?
I THINK IT'S BECAUSE...
...SHE HATES ME.
THAT'S MY GUESS.

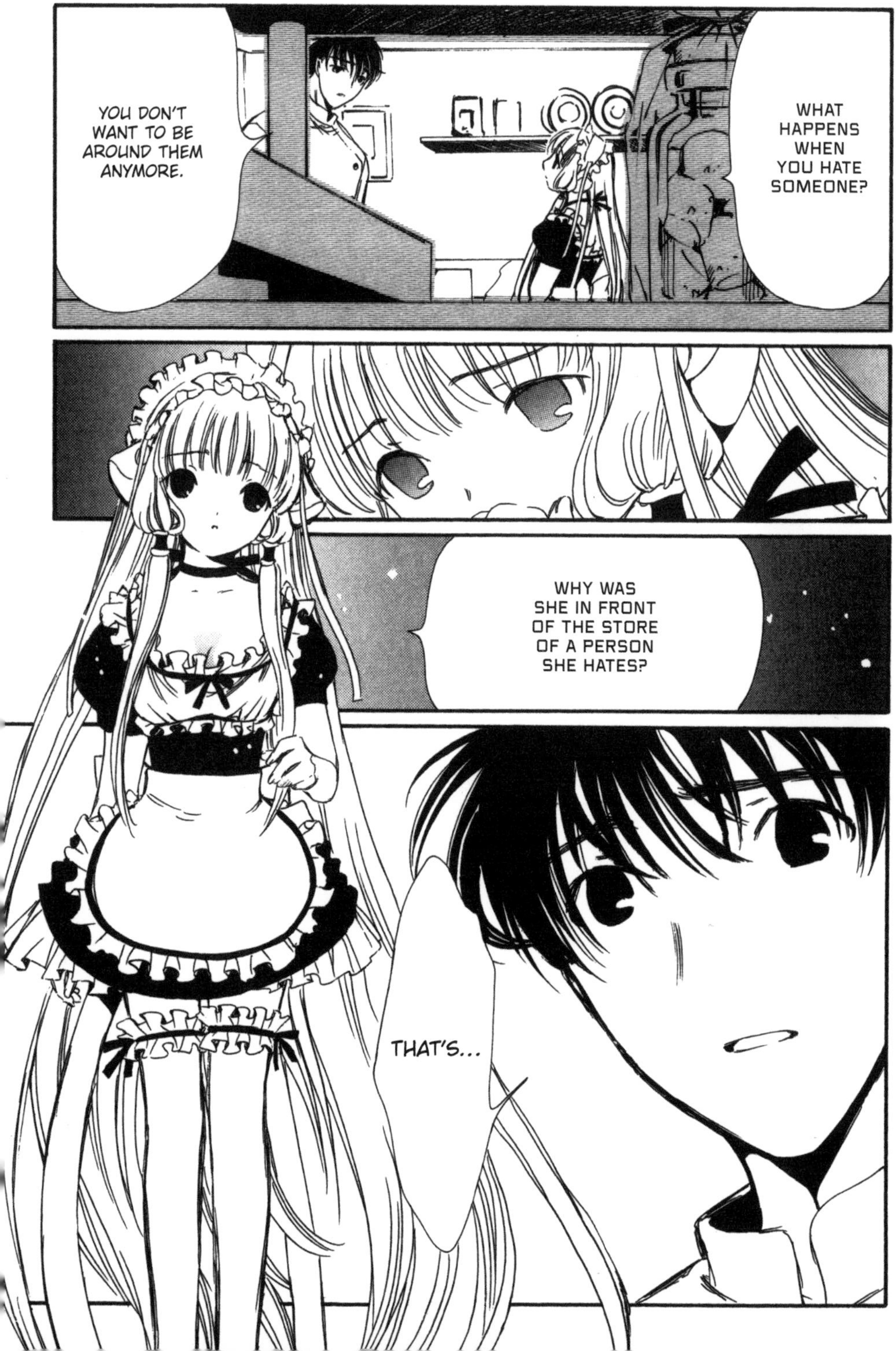
WHAT HAPPENS WHEN YOU HATE SOMEONE?
YOU DON'T WANT TO BE AROUND THEM ANYMORE.
WHY WAS SHE IN FRONT OF THE STORE OF A PERSON SHE HATES?
THAT'S...

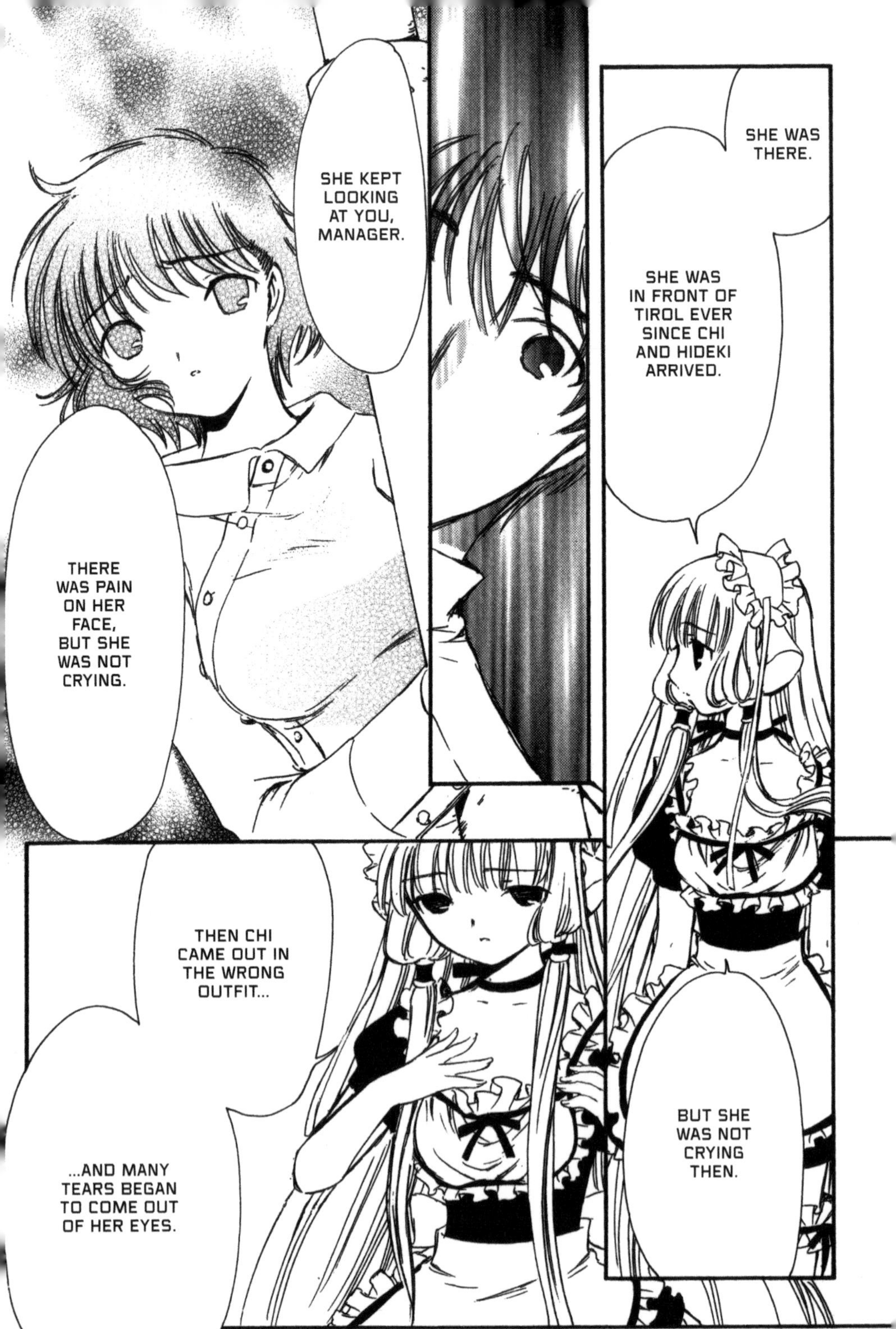
SHE WAS THERE.
SHE WAS IN FRONT OF TIROL EVER SINCE CHI AND HIDEKI ARRIVED.
SHE KEPT LOOKING AT YOU, MANAGER.
THERE WAS PAIN ON HER FACE, BUT SHE WAS NOT CRYING.
BUT SHE WAS NOT CRYING THEN.
THEN CHI CAME OUT IN THE WRONG OUTFIT...
...AND MANY TEARS BEGAN TO COME OUT OF HER EYES.

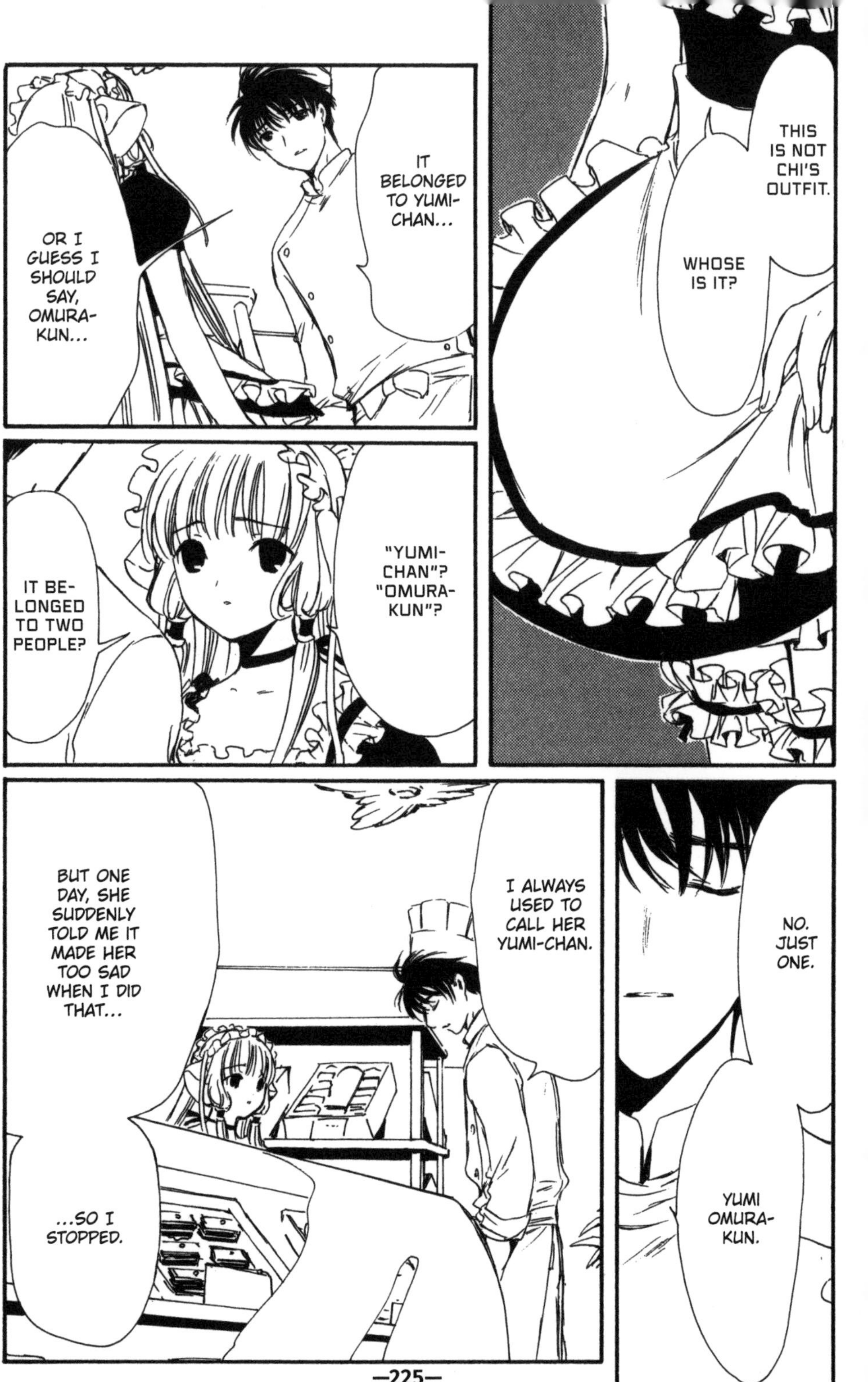
THIS IS NOT CHI'S OUTFIT.
WHOSE IS IT?
IT BELONGED TO YUMI-CHAN...
OR I GUESS I SHOULD SAY, OMURA-KUN...
"YUMI-CHAN"? "OMURA-KUN"?
IT BE-LONGED TO TWO PEOPLE?
NO. JUST ONE.
YUMI OMURA-KUN.
I ALWAYS USED TO CALL HER YUMI-CHAN.
BUT ONE DAY, SHE SUDDENLY TOLD ME IT MADE HER TOO SAD WHEN I DID THAT...
...SO I STOPPED.

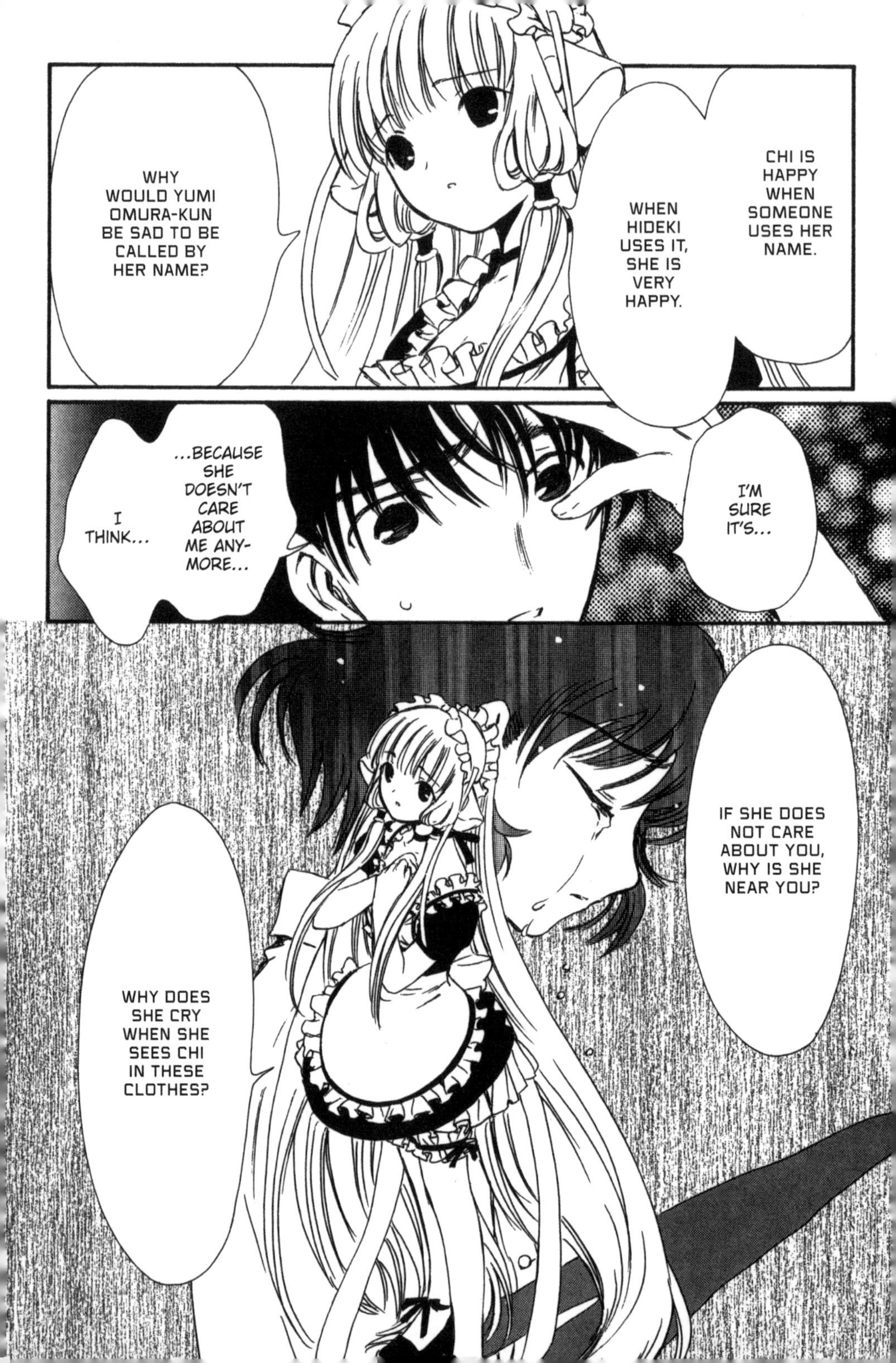
CHI IS HAPPY WHEN SOMEONE USES HER NAME.
WHEN HIDEKI USES IT, SHE IS VERY HAPPY.
WHY WOULD YUMI OMURA-KUN BE SAD TO BE CALLED BY HER NAME?
I'M SURE IT'S...
...BECAUSE SHE DOESN'T CARE ABOUT ME ANYMORE...
I THINK...
IF SHE DOES NOT CARE ABOUT YOU, WHY IS SHE NEAR YOU?
WHY DOES SHE CRY WHEN SHE SEES CHI IN THESE CLOTHES?

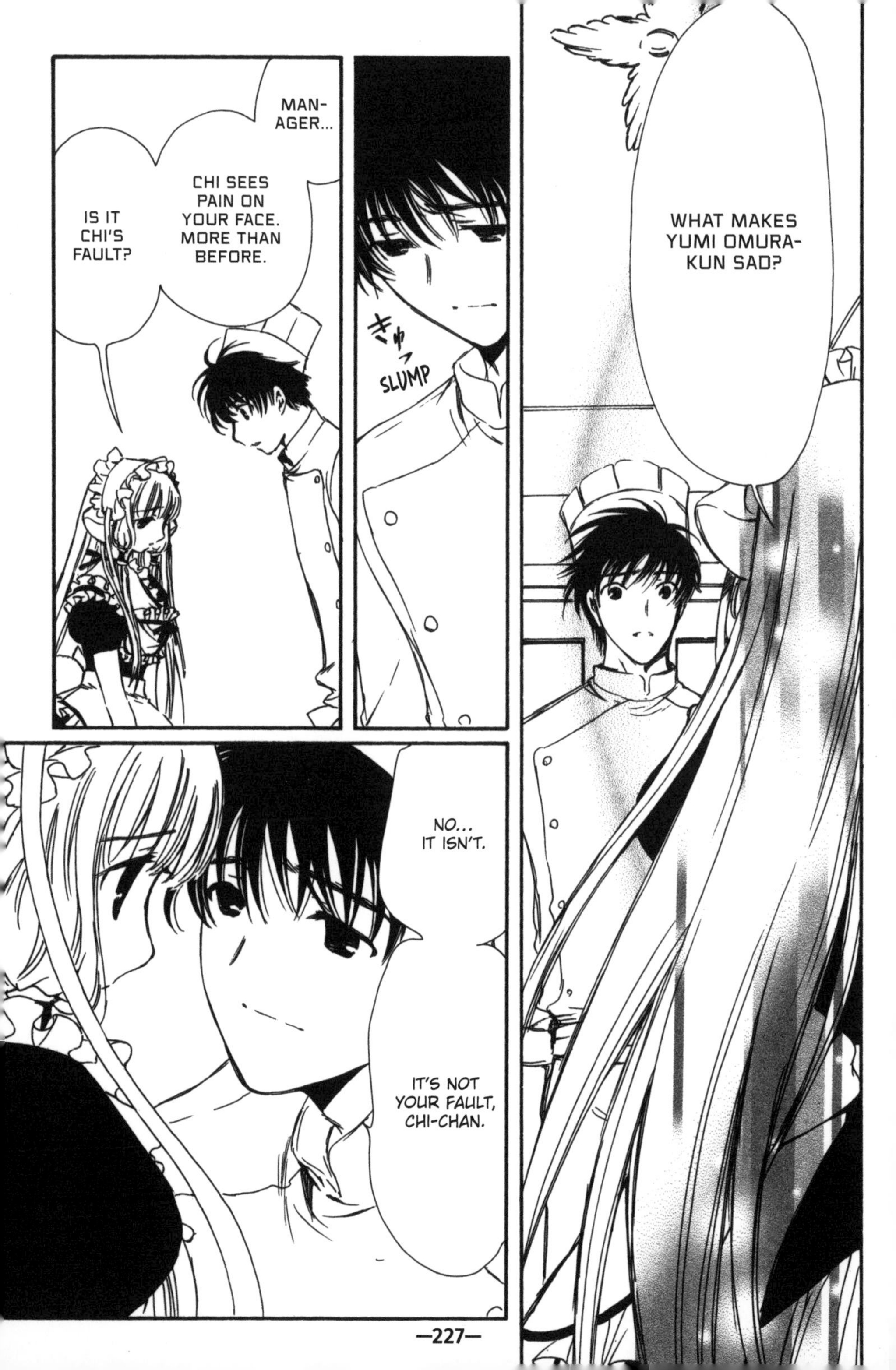
WHAT MAKES YUMI OMURA-KUN SAD?
SLUMP
MAN-AGER...
CHI SEES PAIN ON YOUR FACE. MORE THAN BEFORE.
IS IT CHI'S FAULT?
NO... IT ISN'T.
IT'S NOT YOUR FAULT, CHI-CHAN.

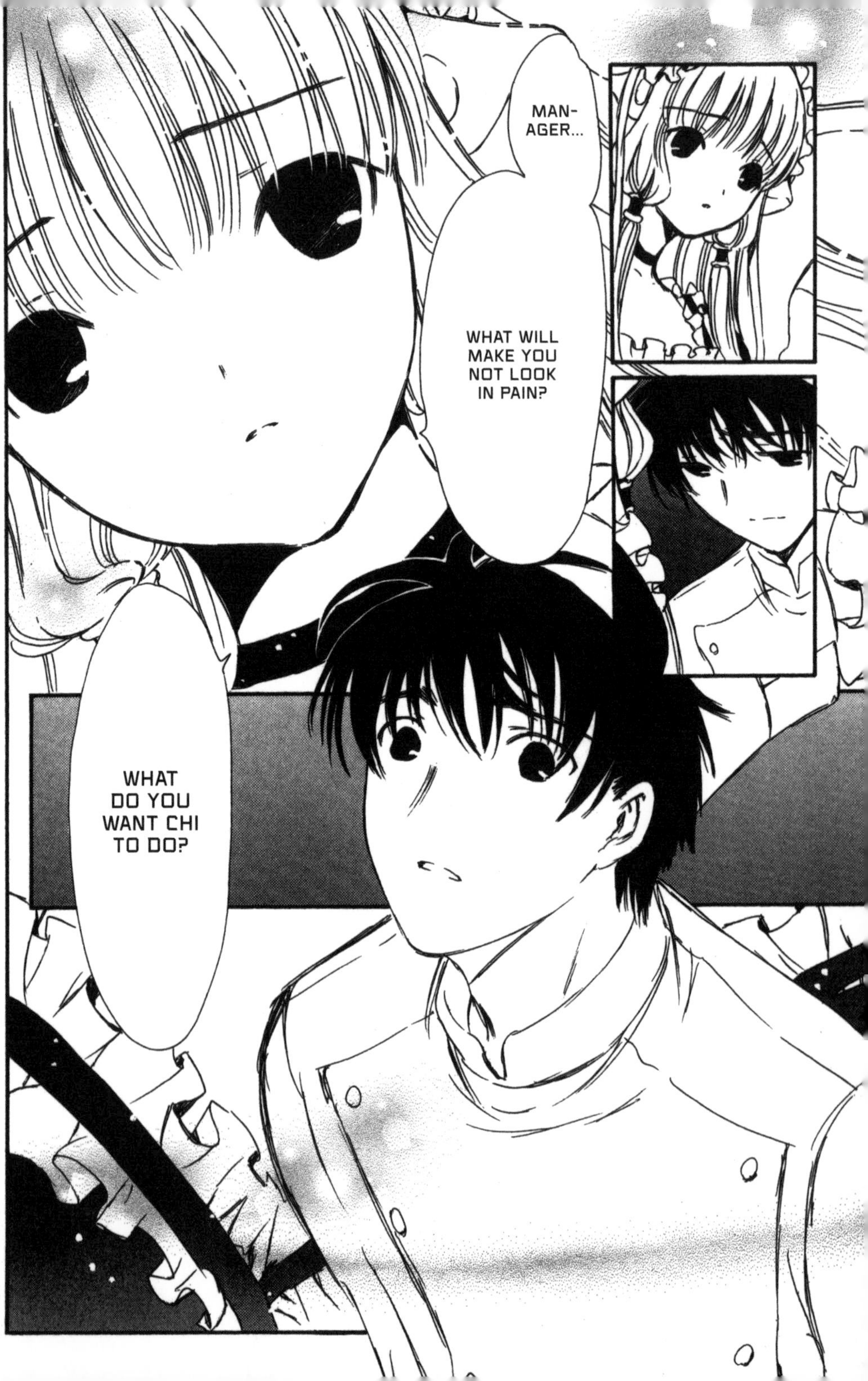
MAN-
AGER...
WHAT WILL MAKE YOU NOT LOOK IN PAIN?
WHAT DO YOU WANT CHI TO DO?

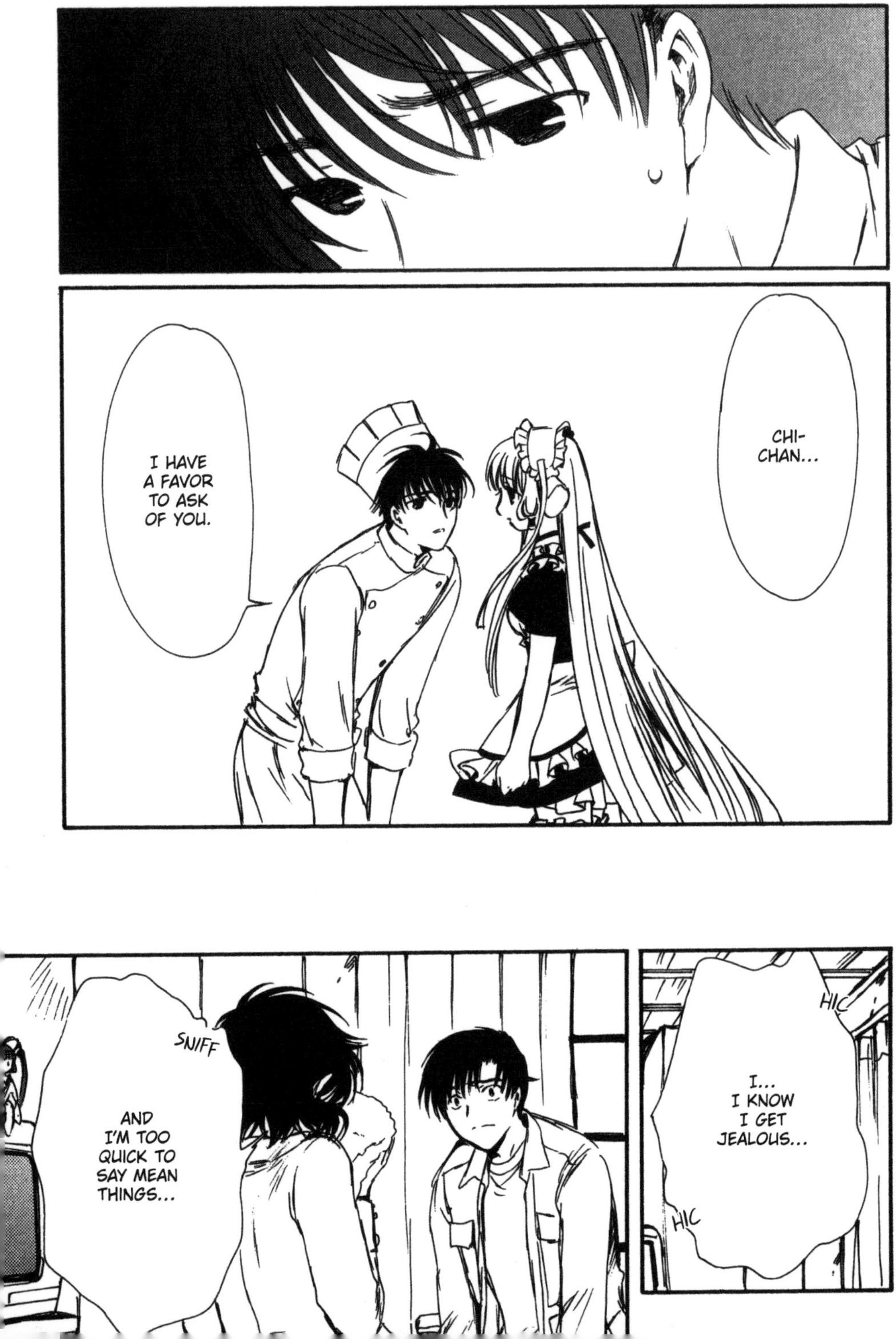
CHI-CHAN...
I HAVE A FAVOR TO ASK OF YOU.
HIC
I... I KNOW I GET JEALOUS...
HIC
SNIFF
AND I'M TOO QUICK TO SAY MEAN THINGS...

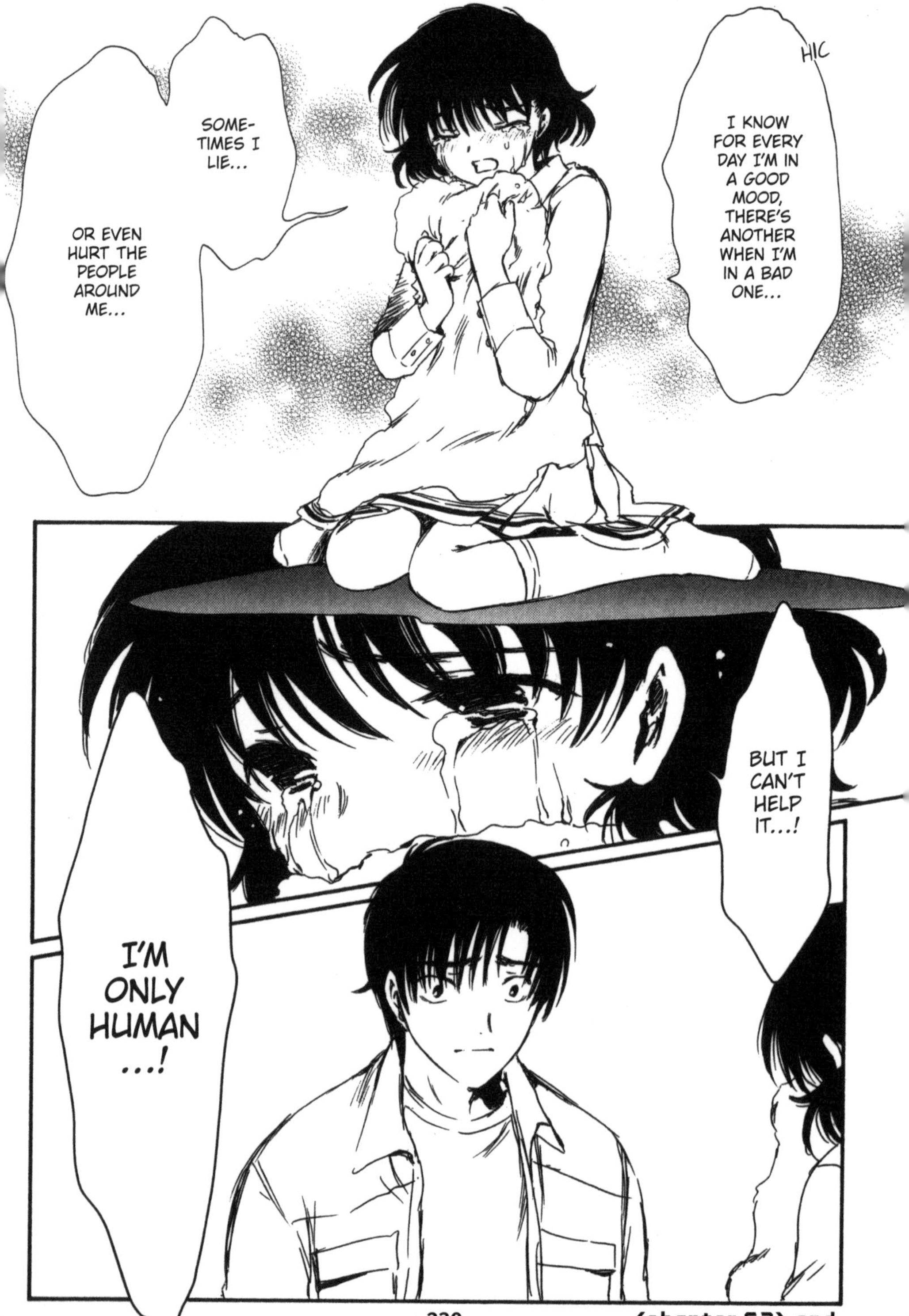
HIC
I KNOW FOR EVERY DAY I'M IN A GOOD MOOD, THERE'S ANOTHER WHEN I'M IN A BAD ONE...
SOME-TIMES I LIE...
OR EVEN HURT THE PEOPLE AROUND ME...
BUT I CAN'T HELP IT...!
I'M ONLY HUMAN ...!

<chapter.63> end

Chobits

⟨chapter.64⟩

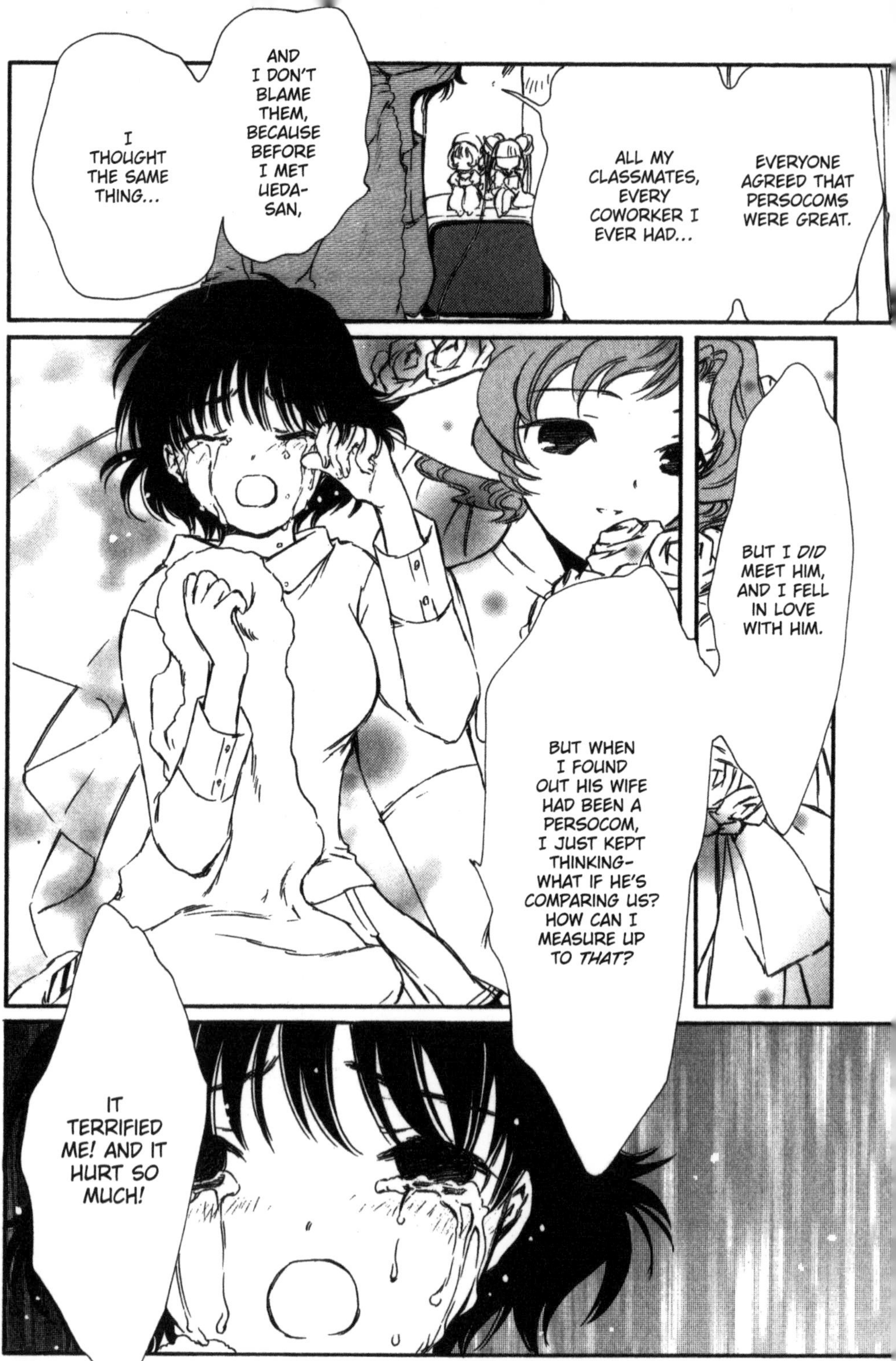
EVERYONE AGREED THAT PERSOCOMS WERE GREAT.
ALL MY CLASSMATES, EVERY COWORKER I EVER HAD...
AND I DON'T BLAME THEM, BECAUSE BEFORE I MET UEDA-SAN,
I THOUGHT THE SAME THING...
BUT I *DID* MEET HIM, AND I FELL IN LOVE WITH HIM.
BUT WHEN I FOUND OUT HIS WIFE HAD BEEN A PERSOCOM, I JUST KEPT THINKING- WHAT IF HE'S COMPARING US? HOW CAN I MEASURE UP TO *THAT*?
IT TERRIFIED ME! AND IT HURT SO MUCH!

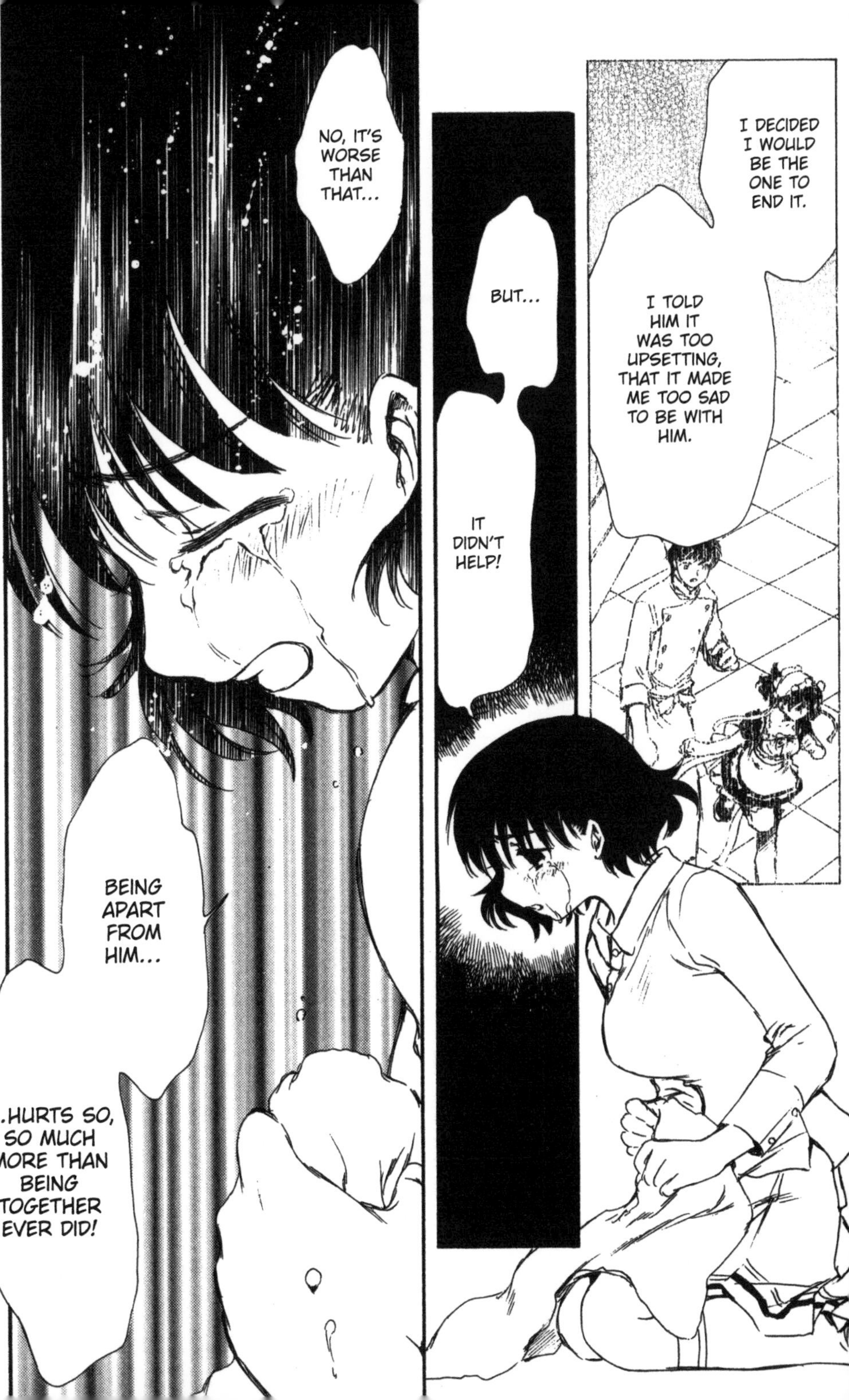
I DECIDED I WOULD BE THE ONE TO END IT.
I TOLD HIM IT WAS TOO UPSETTING, THAT IT MADE ME TOO SAD TO BE WITH HIM.
BUT...
IT DIDN'T HELP!
NO, IT'S WORSE THAN THAT...
BEING APART FROM HIM...
...HURTS SO, SO MUCH MORE THAN BEING TOGETHER EVER DID!

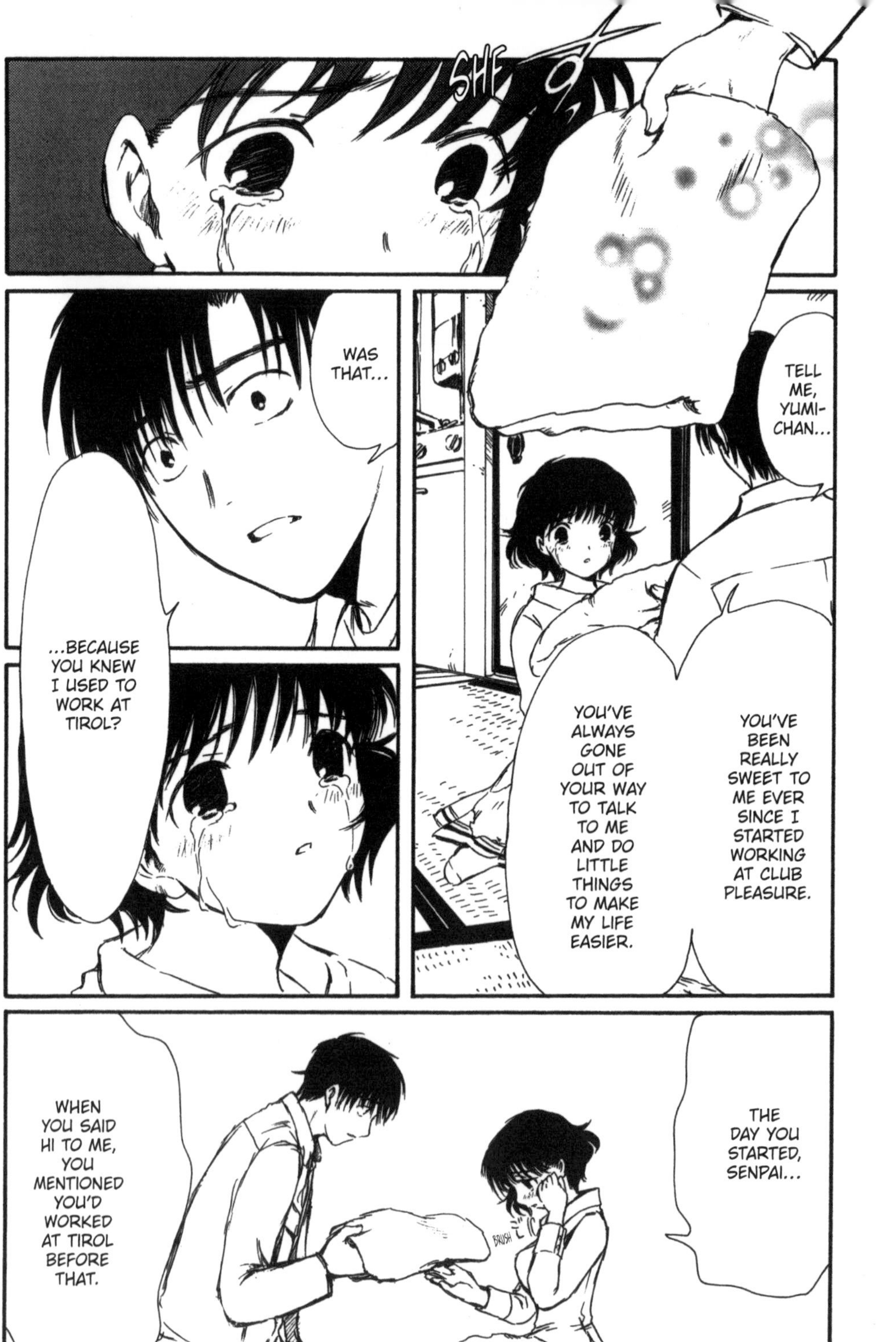
SHF
TELL ME, YUMI-CHAN...
YOU'VE BEEN REALLY SWEET TO ME EVER SINCE I STARTED WORKING AT CLUB PLEASURE.
YOU'VE ALWAYS GONE OUT OF YOUR WAY TO TALK TO ME AND DO LITTLE THINGS TO MAKE MY LIFE EASIER.
WAS THAT...
...BECAUSE YOU KNEW I USED TO WORK AT TIROL?
THE DAY YOU STARTED, SENPAI...
WHEN YOU SAID HI TO ME, YOU MENTIONED YOU'D WORKED AT TIROL BEFORE THAT.
BRUSH

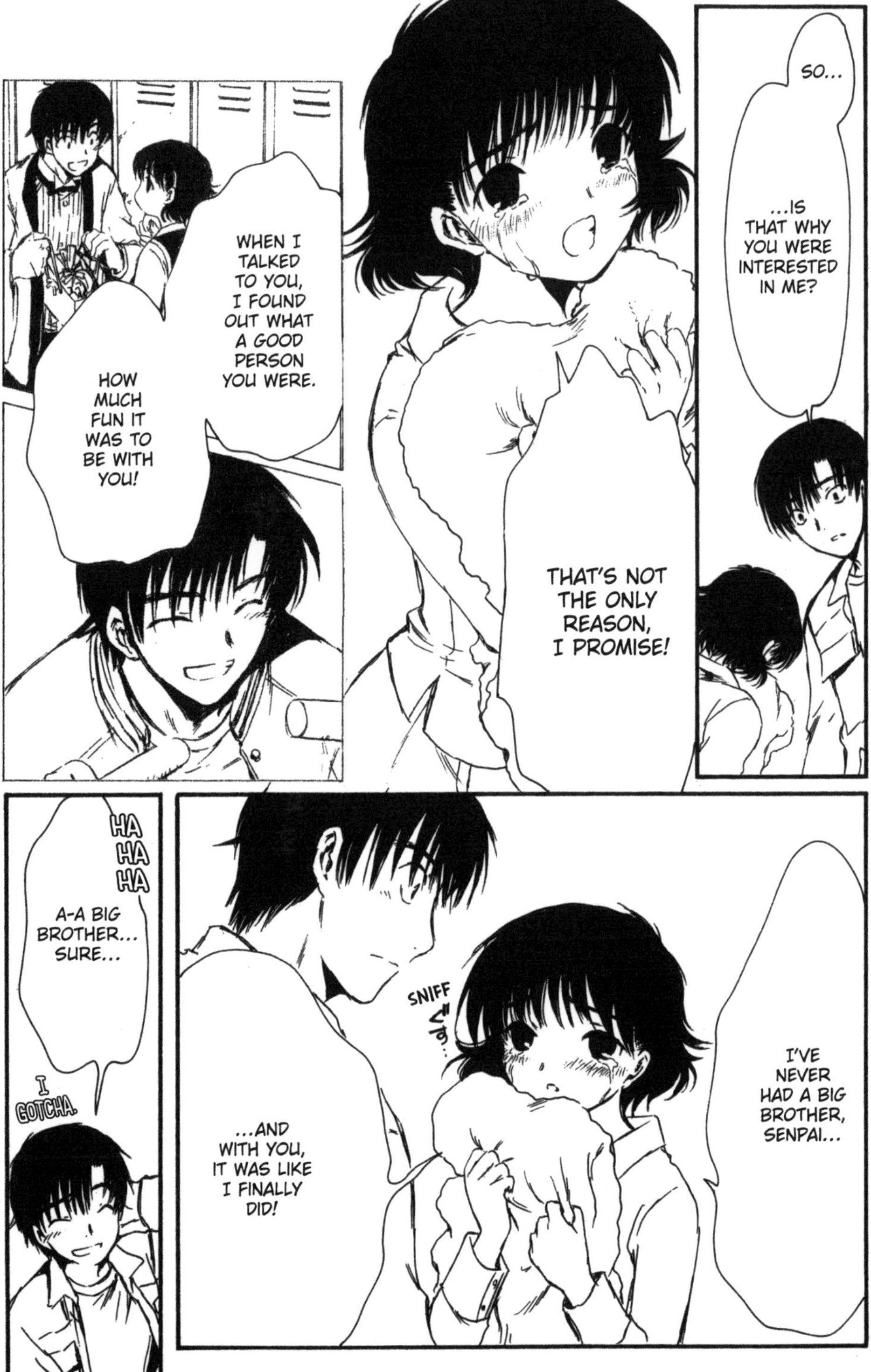
SO...
...IS THAT WHY YOU WERE INTERESTED IN ME?
THAT'S NOT THE ONLY REASON, I PROMISE!
WHEN I TALKED TO YOU, I FOUND OUT WHAT A GOOD PERSON YOU WERE.
HOW MUCH FUN IT WAS TO BE WITH YOU!
I'VE NEVER HAD A BIG BROTHER, SENPAI...
SNIFF
...AND WITH YOU, IT WAS LIKE I FINALLY DID!
HA HA HA
A-A BIG BROTHER... SURE...
I GOTCHA.

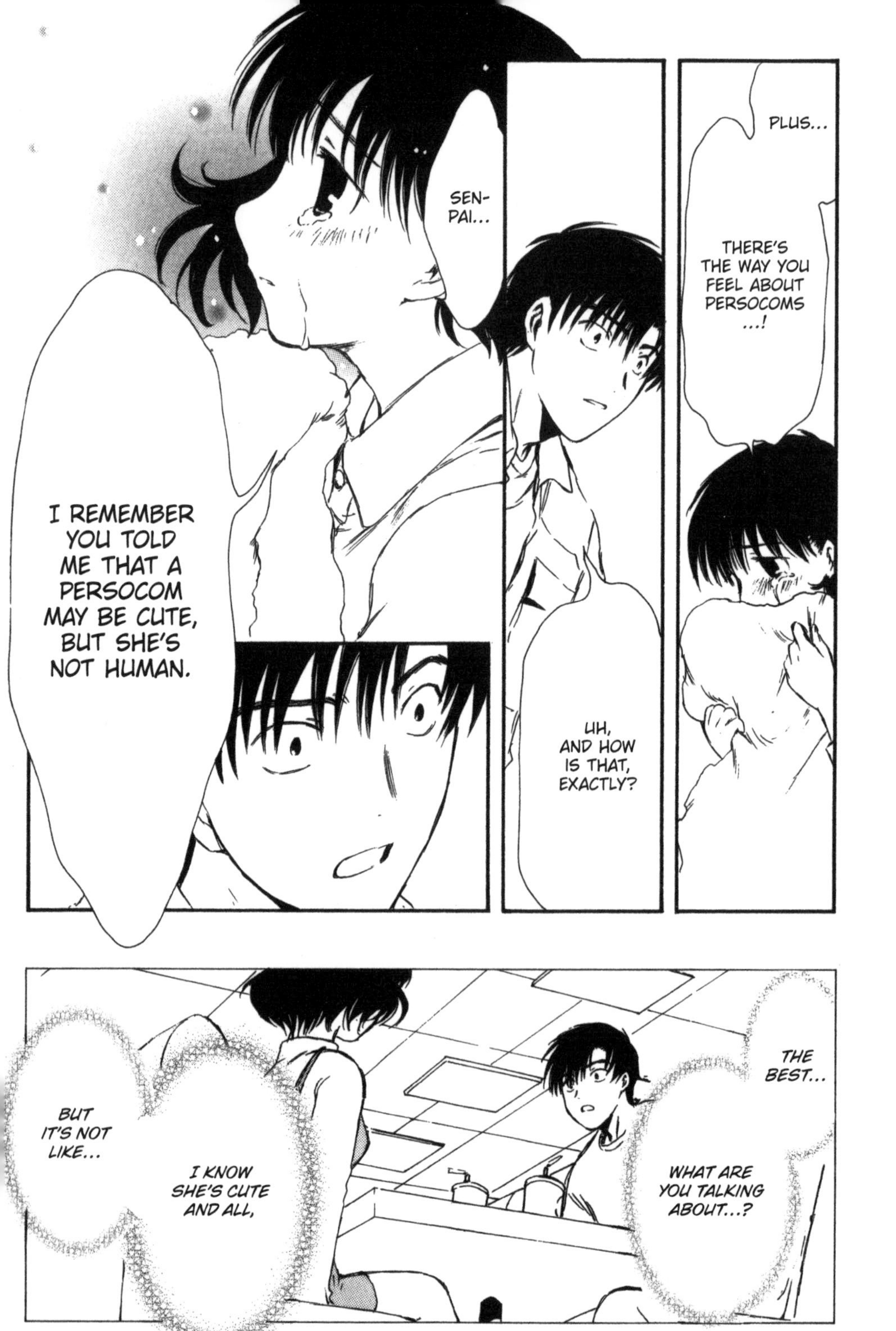
PLUS…
THERE'S THE WAY YOU FEEL ABOUT PERSOCOMS …!
SEN-PAI…
UH, AND HOW IS THAT, EXACTLY?
I REMEMBER YOU TOLD ME THAT A PERSOCOM MAY BE CUTE, BUT SHE'S NOT HUMAN.
THE BEST…
WHAT ARE YOU TALKING ABOUT…?
I KNOW SHE'S CUTE AND ALL,
BUT IT'S NOT LIKE…

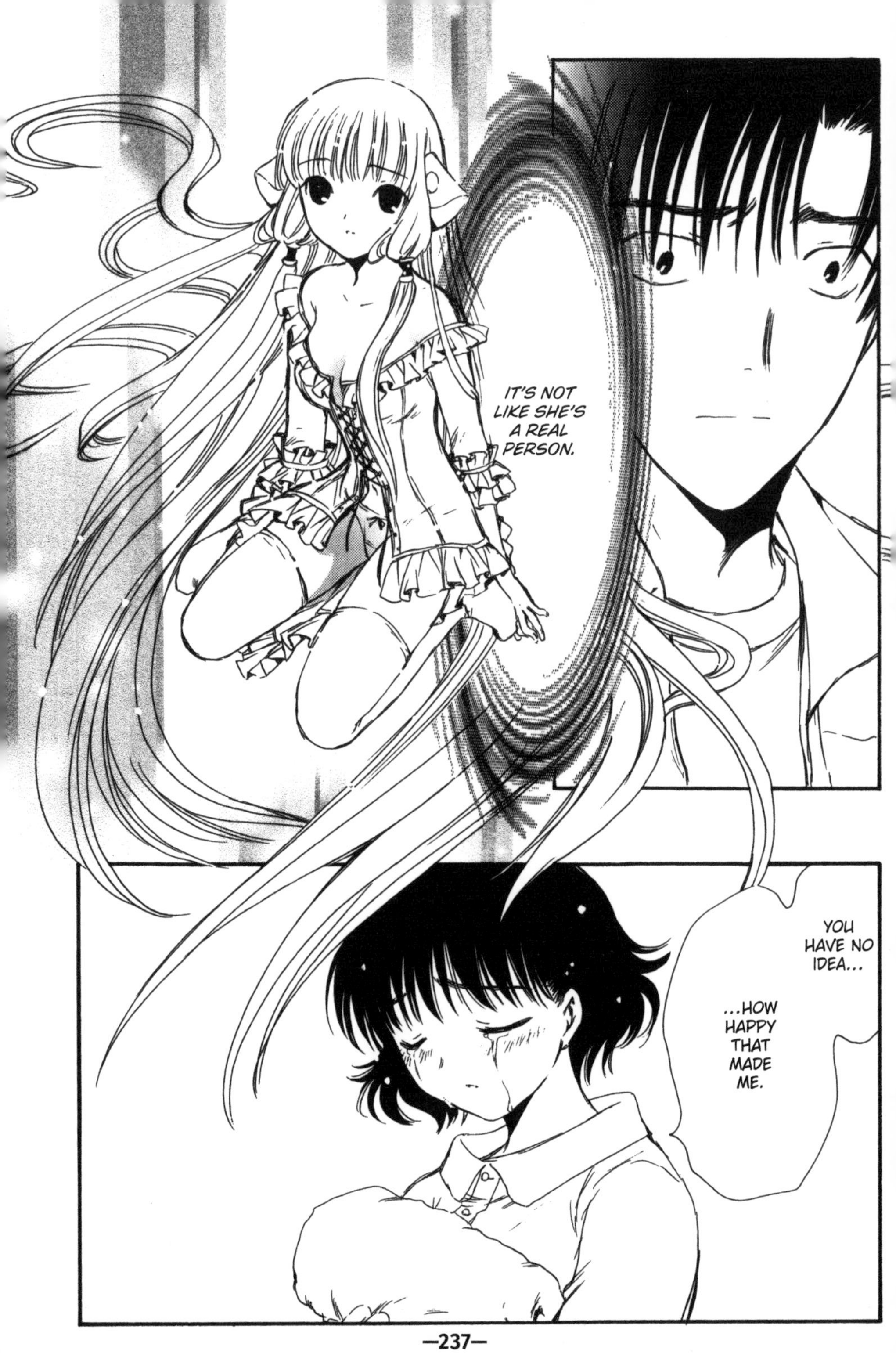
IT'S NOT LIKE SHE'S A REAL PERSON.
YOU HAVE NO IDEA...
...HOW HAPPY THAT MADE ME.

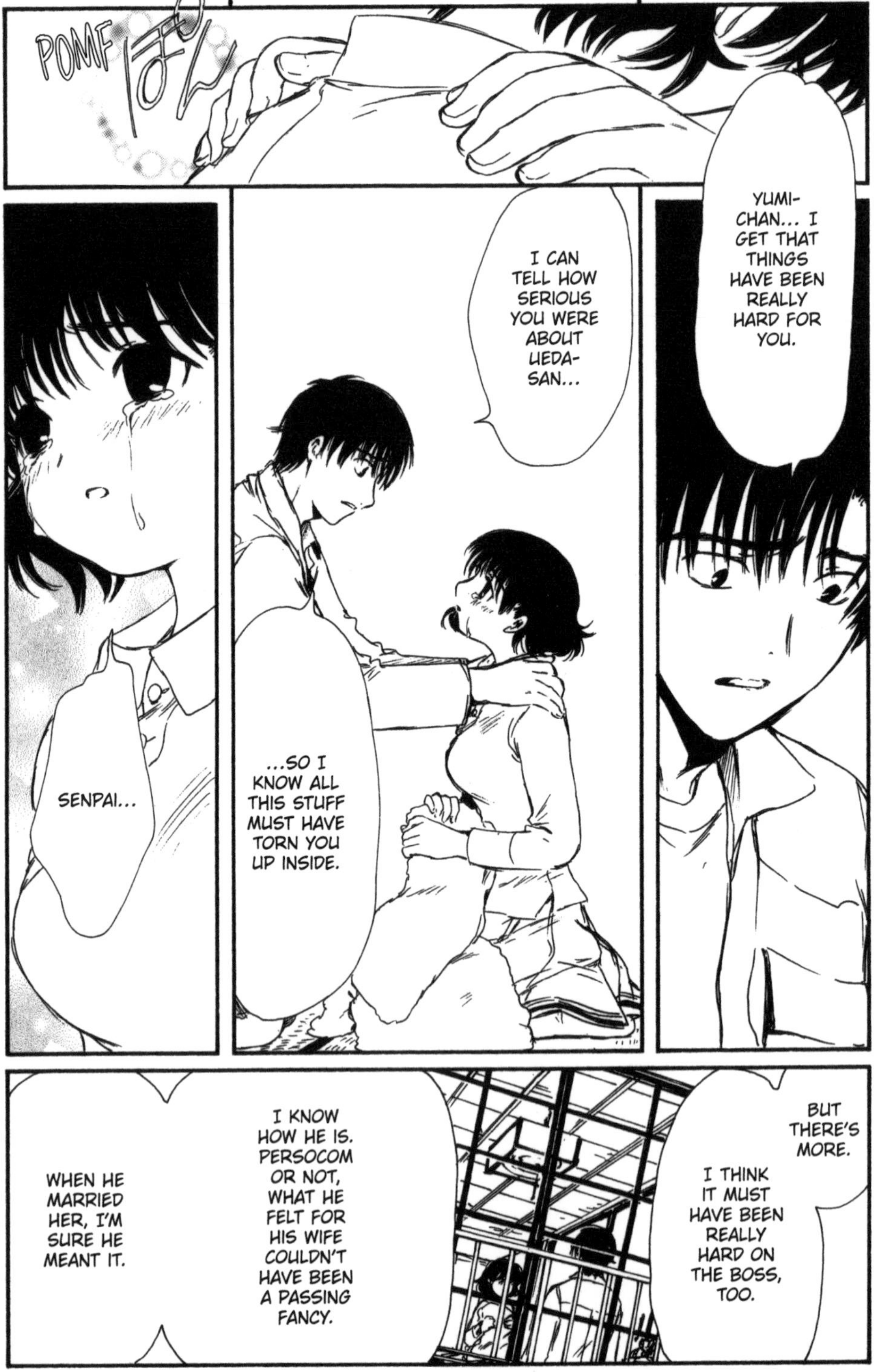
POMF
ぽん
YUMI-CHAN... I GET THAT THINGS HAVE BEEN REALLY HARD FOR YOU.
I CAN TELL HOW SERIOUS YOU WERE ABOUT UEDA-SAN...
...SO I KNOW ALL THIS STUFF MUST HAVE TORN YOU UP INSIDE.
SENPAI...
BUT THERE'S MORE.
I THINK IT MUST HAVE BEEN REALLY HARD ON THE BOSS, TOO.
I KNOW HOW HE IS. PERSOCOM OR NOT, WHAT HE FELT FOR HIS WIFE COULDN'T HAVE BEEN A PASSING FANCY.
WHEN HE MARRIED HER, I'M SURE HE MEANT IT.

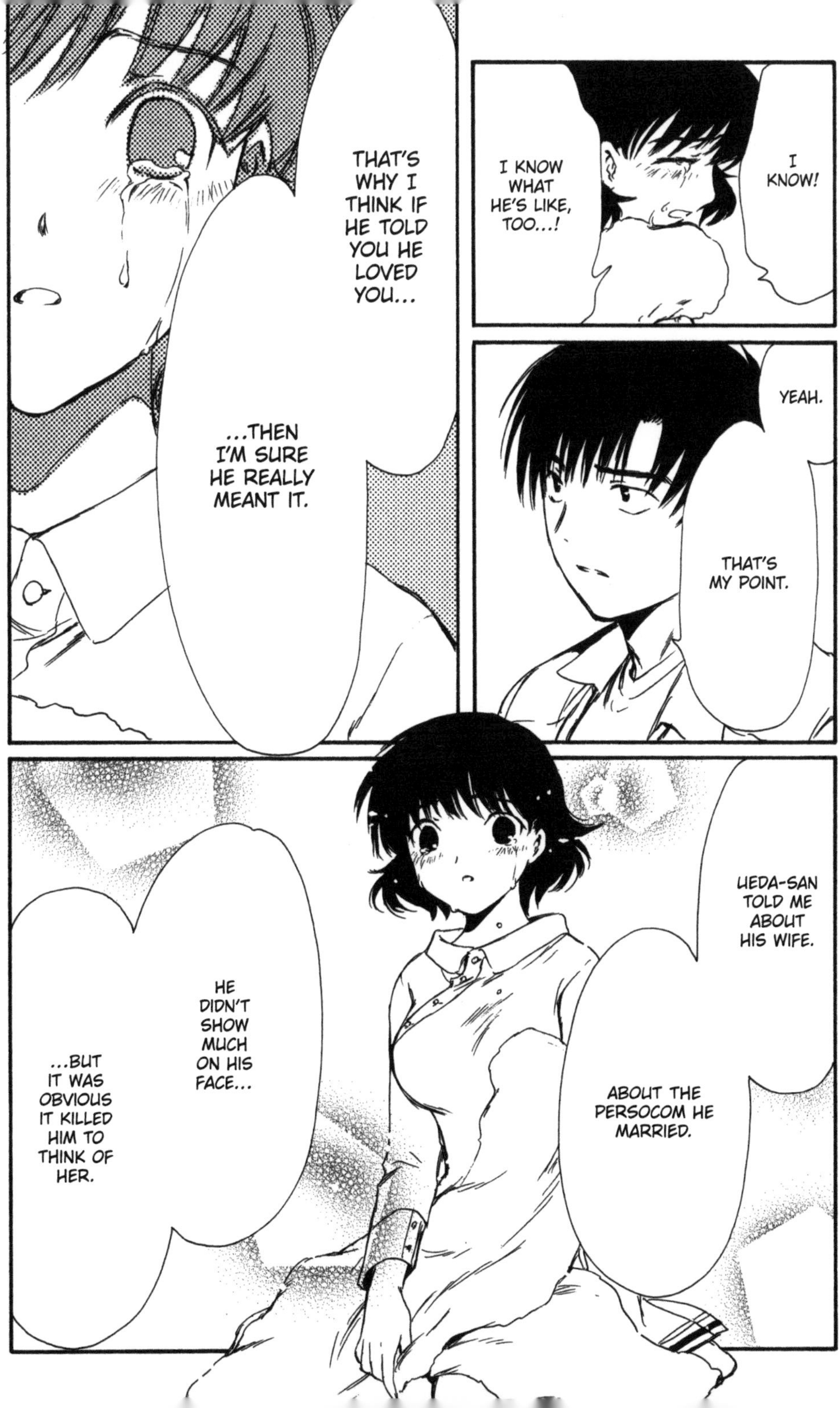
I KNOW!
I KNOW WHAT HE'S LIKE, TOO...!
YEAH.
THAT'S MY POINT.
THAT'S WHY I THINK IF HE TOLD YOU HE LOVED YOU...
...THEN I'M SURE HE REALLY MEANT IT.
UEDA-SAN TOLD ME ABOUT HIS WIFE.
ABOUT THE PERSOCOM HE MARRIED.
HE DIDN'T SHOW MUCH ON HIS FACE...
...BUT IT WAS OBVIOUS IT KILLED HIM TO THINK OF HER.

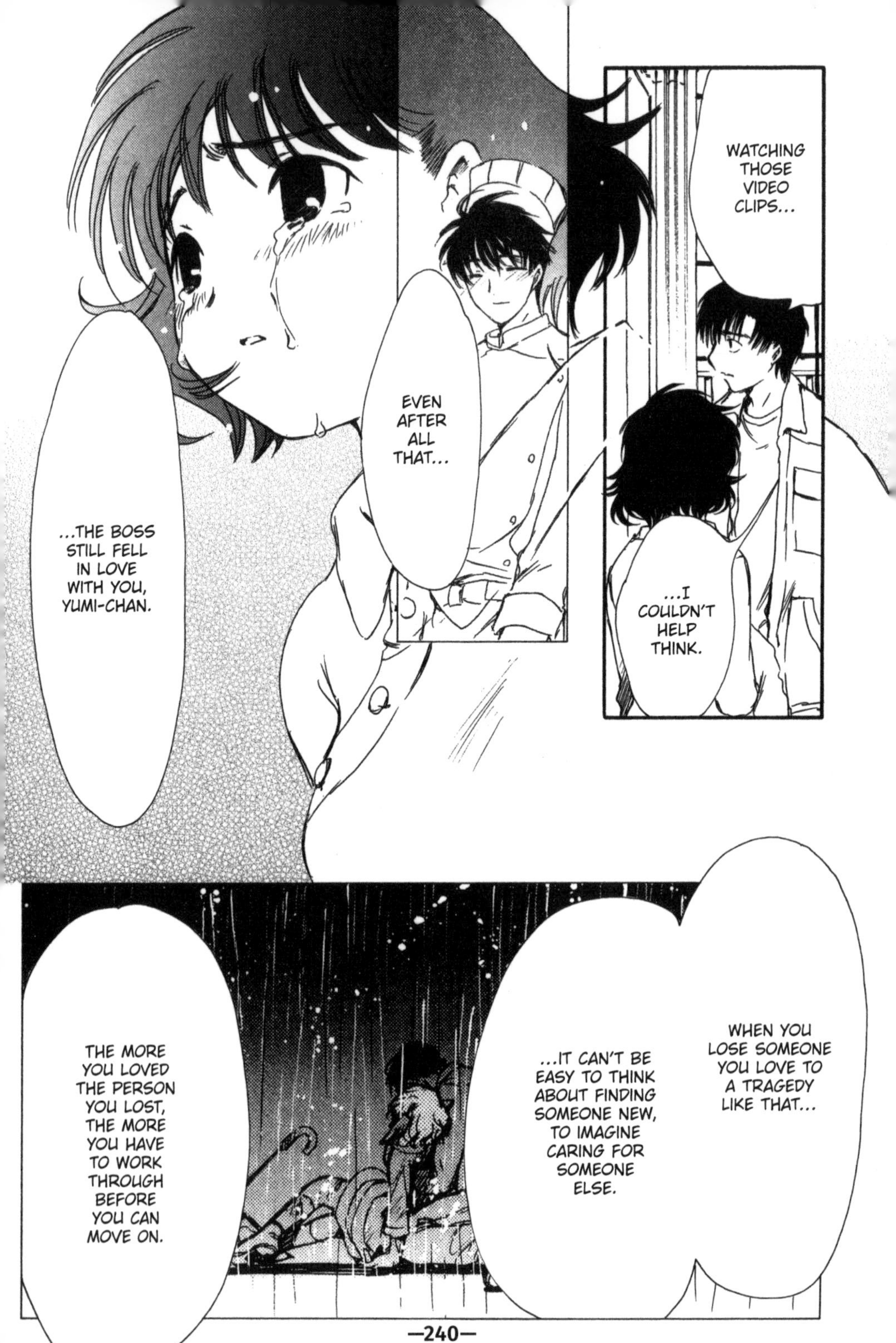
WATCHING THOSE VIDEO CLIPS...
...I COULDN'T HELP THINK.
EVEN AFTER ALL THAT...
...THE BOSS STILL FELL IN LOVE WITH YOU, YUMI-CHAN.
WHEN YOU LOSE SOMEONE YOU LOVE TO A TRAGEDY LIKE THAT...
...IT CAN'T BE EASY TO THINK ABOUT FINDING SOMEONE NEW, TO IMAGINE CARING FOR SOMEONE ELSE.
THE MORE YOU LOVED THE PERSON YOU LOST, THE MORE YOU HAVE TO WORK THROUGH BEFORE YOU CAN MOVE ON.

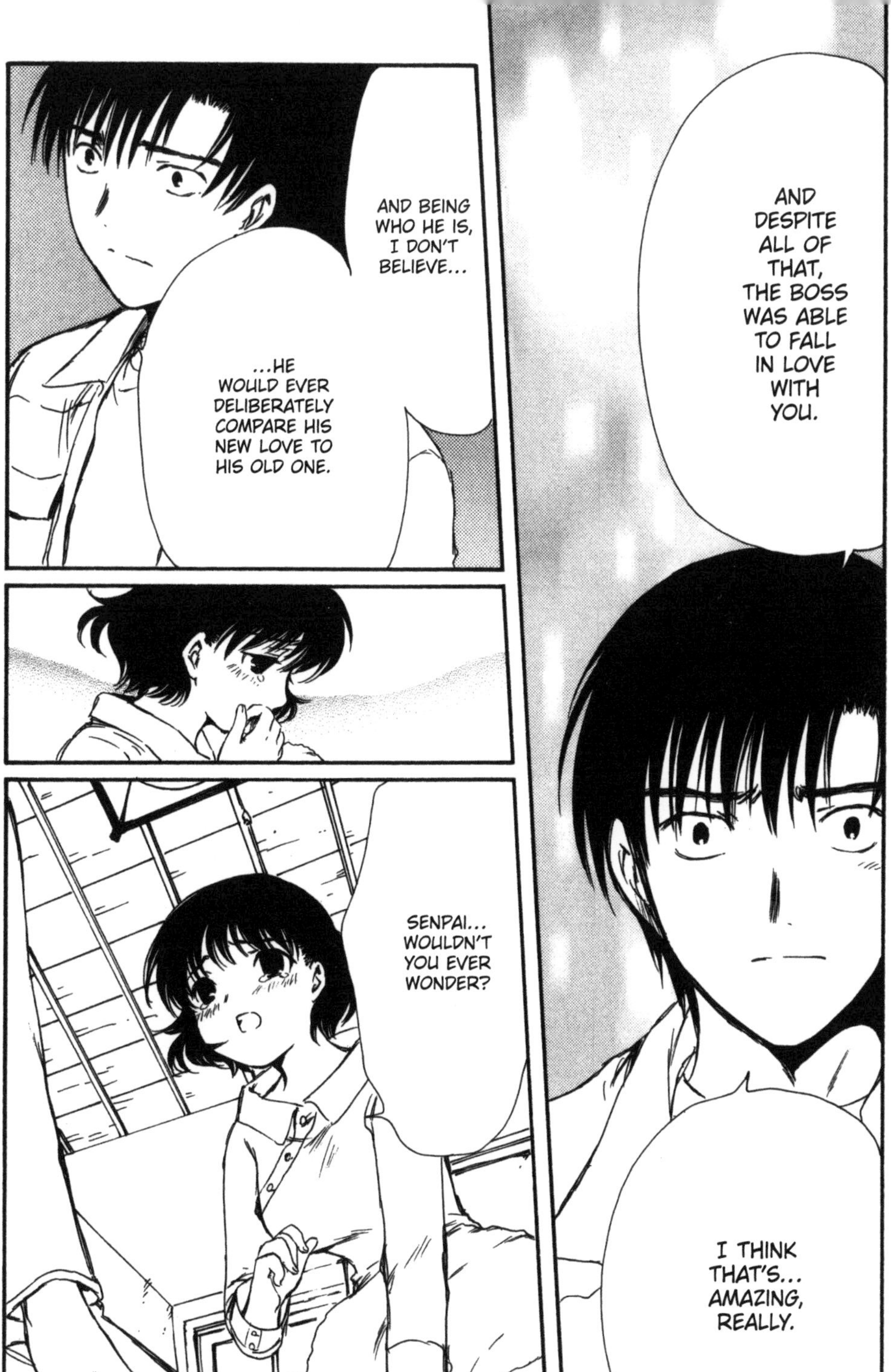
AND DESPITE ALL OF THAT, THE BOSS WAS ABLE TO FALL IN LOVE WITH YOU.
I THINK THAT'S... AMAZING, REALLY.
AND BEING WHO HE IS, I DON'T BELIEVE...
...HE WOULD EVER DELIBERATELY COMPARE HIS NEW LOVE TO HIS OLD ONE.
SENPAI... WOULDN'T YOU EVER WONDER?

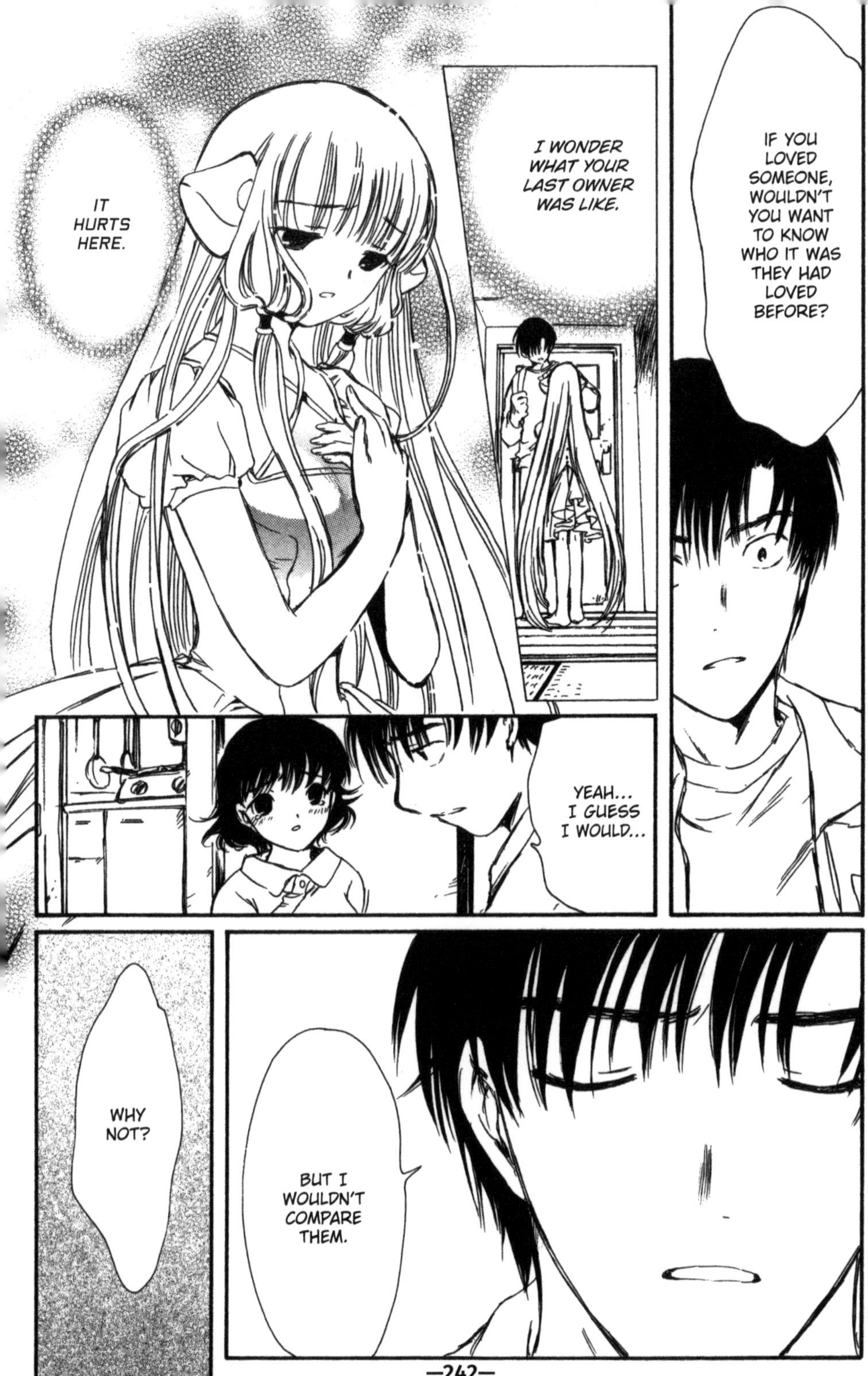
IF YOU LOVED SOMEONE, WOULDN'T YOU WANT TO KNOW WHO IT WAS THEY HAD LOVED BEFORE?
I WONDER WHAT YOUR LAST OWNER WAS LIKE.
IT HURTS HERE.
YEAH... I GUESS I WOULD...
BUT I WOULDN'T COMPARE THEM.
WHY NOT?

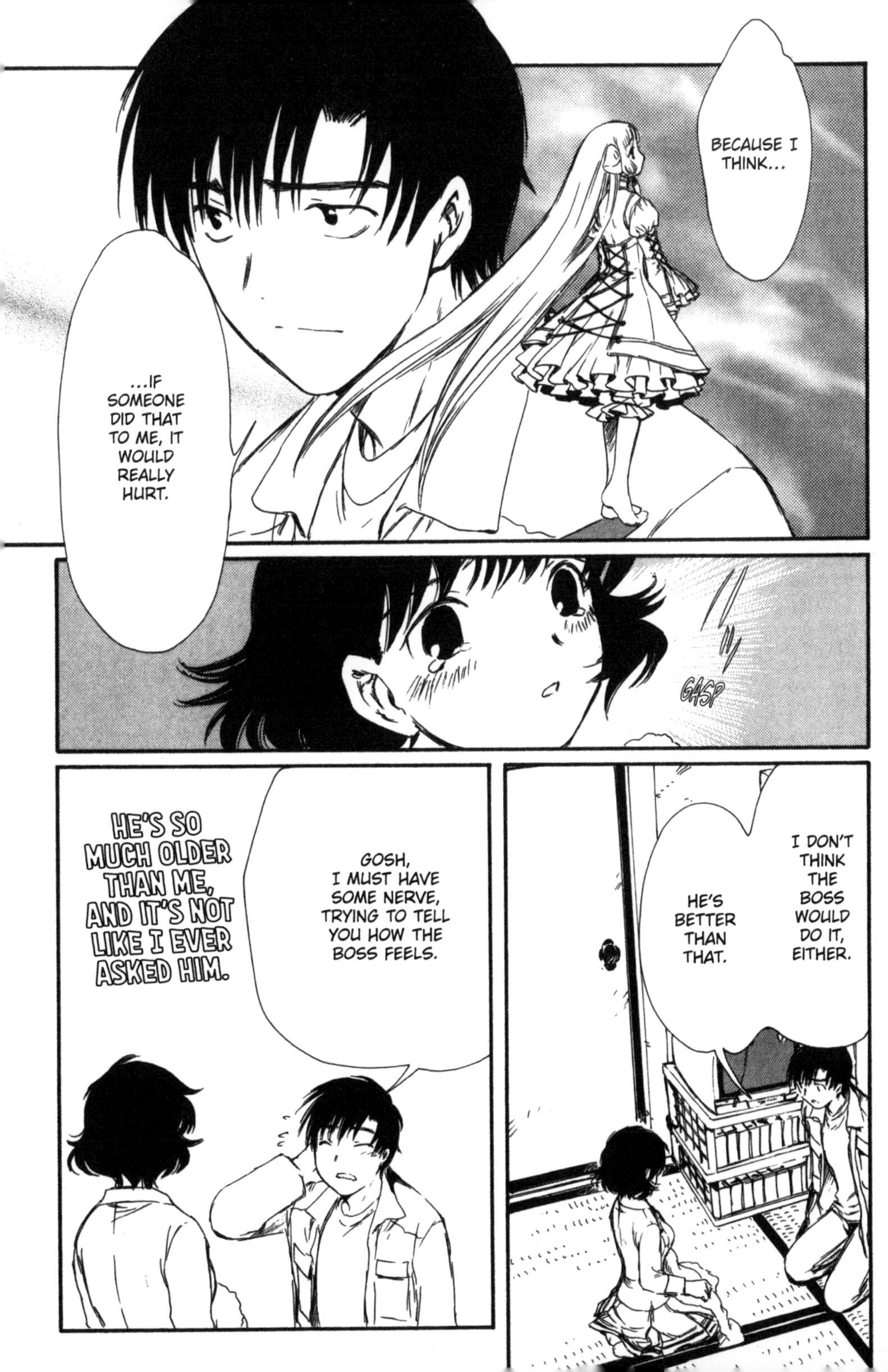
BECAUSE I THINK...
...IF SOMEONE DID THAT TO ME, IT WOULD REALLY HURT.
GASP
I DON'T THINK THE BOSS WOULD DO IT, EITHER.
HE'S BETTER THAN THAT.
GOSH, I MUST HAVE SOME NERVE, TRYING TO TELL YOU HOW THE BOSS FEELS.
HE'S SO MUCH OLDER THAN ME, AND IT'S NOT LIKE I EVER ASKED HIM.

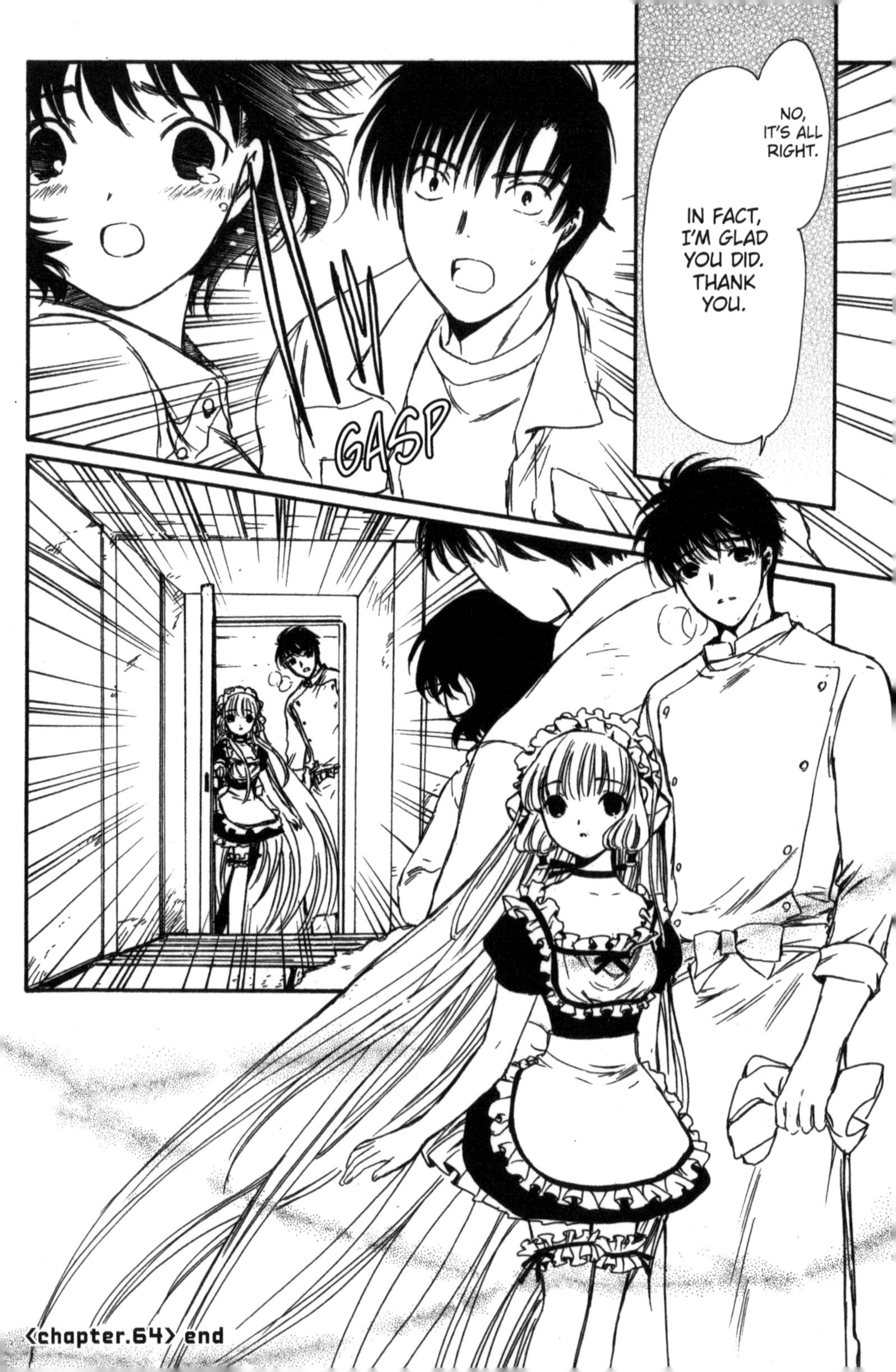
NO, IT'S ALL RIGHT.
IN FACT, I'M GLAD YOU DID. THANK YOU.
GASP
<chapter.64> end

Chobits

<chapter.65>

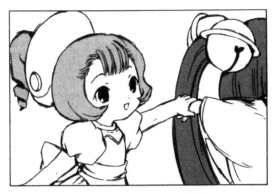

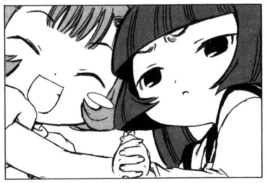

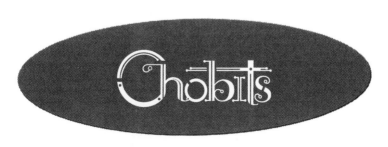

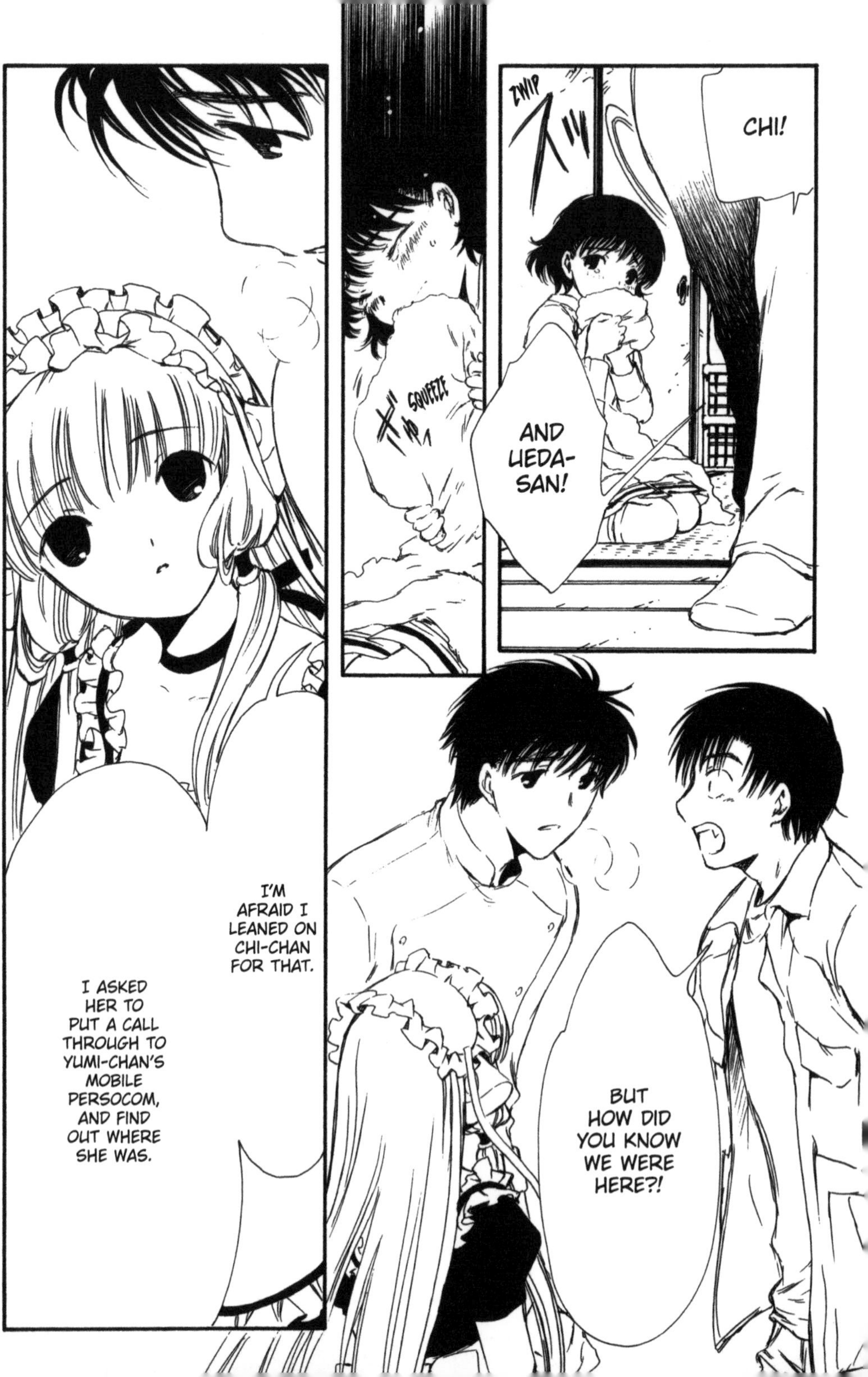
ZWIP
CHI!
AND UEDA-SAN!
SQUEEZE
BUT HOW DID YOU KNOW WE WERE HERE?!
I'M AFRAID I LEANED ON CHI-CHAN FOR THAT.
I ASKED HER TO PUT A CALL THROUGH TO YUMI-CHAN'S MOBILE PERSOCOM, AND FIND OUT WHERE SHE WAS.

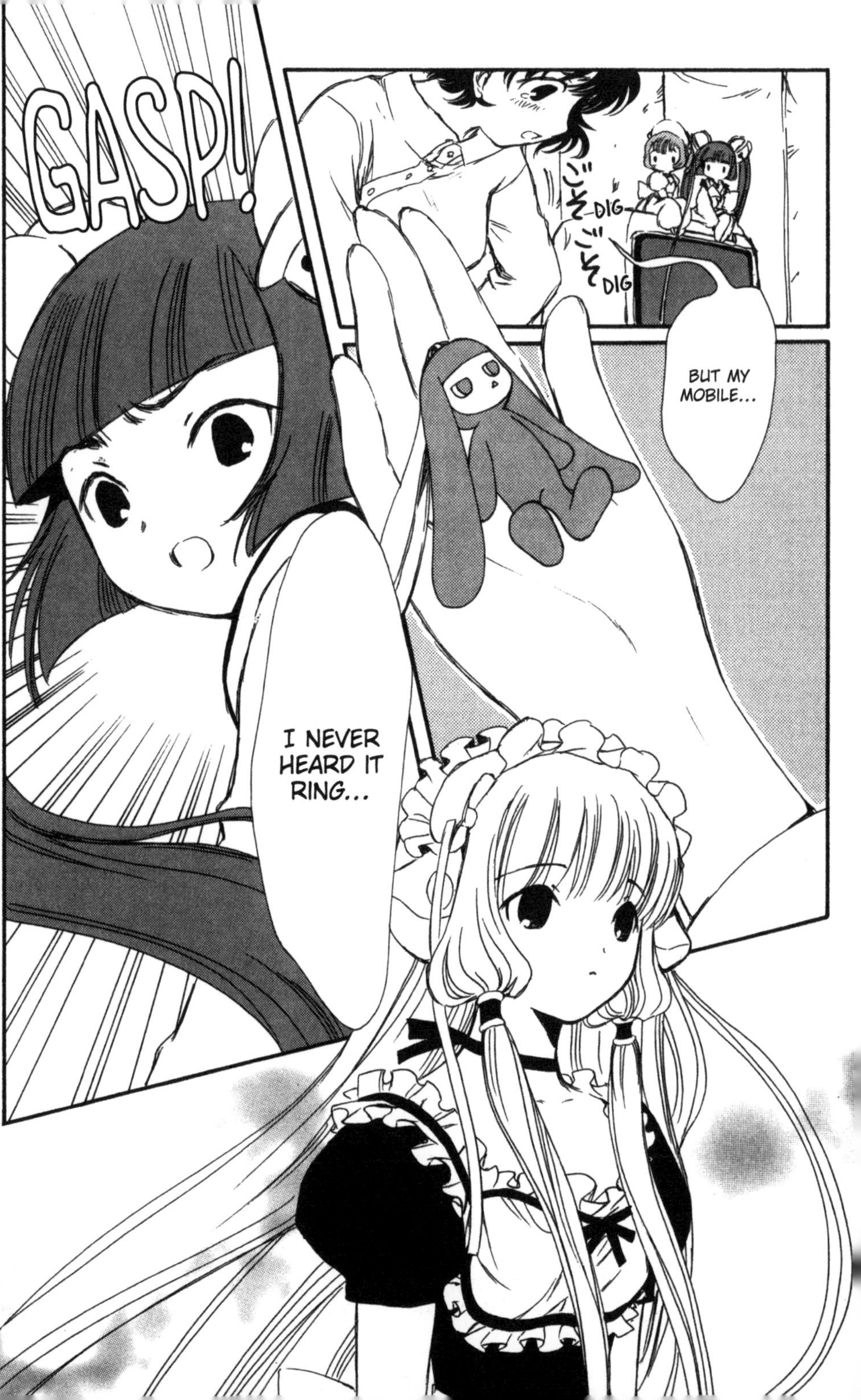
ごそ DIG
ごそ DIG
BUT MY MOBILE...
GASP!
I NEVER HEARD IT RING...

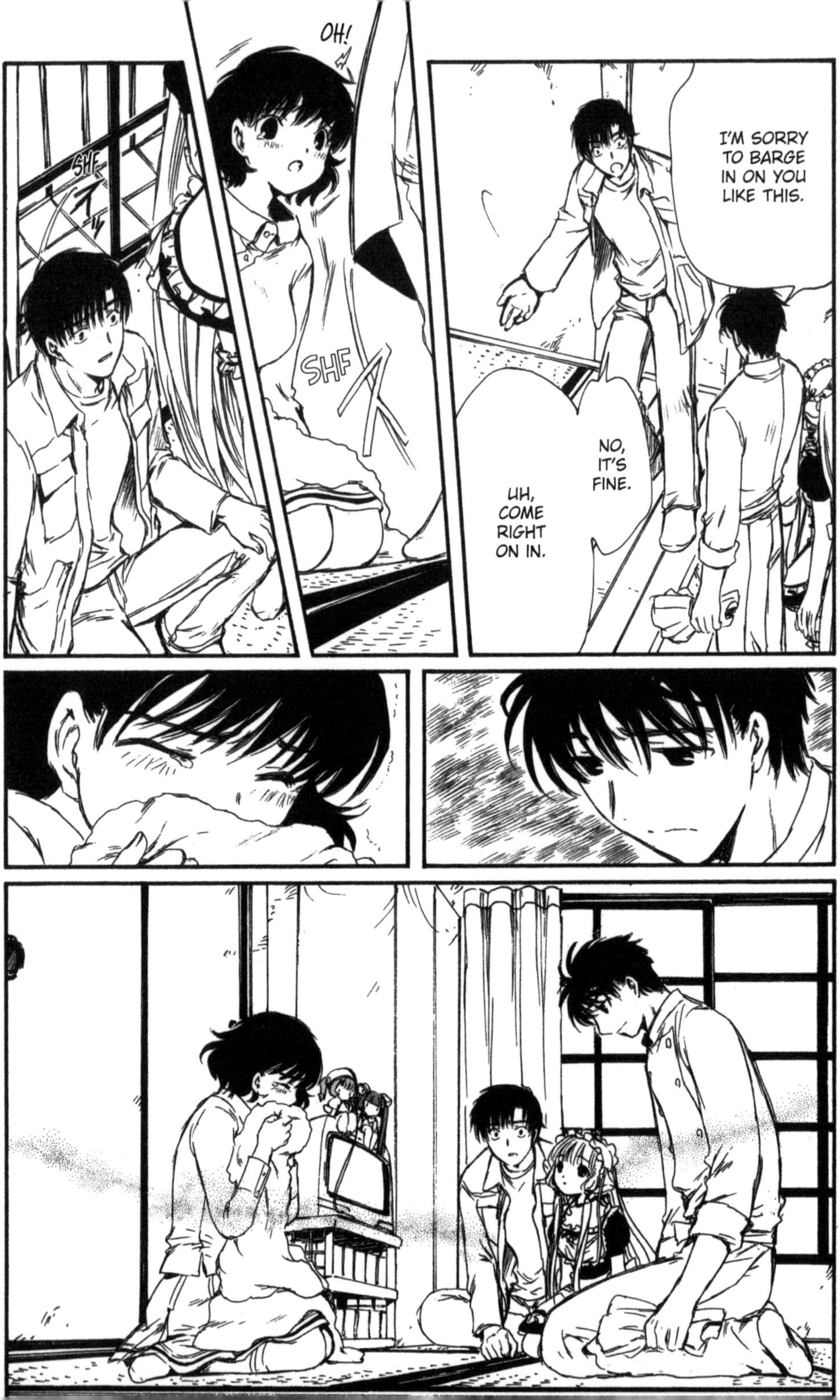
I'M SORRY TO BARGE IN ON YOU LIKE THIS.
NO, IT'S FINE.
UH, COME RIGHT ON IN.
OH!
SHF
SHF

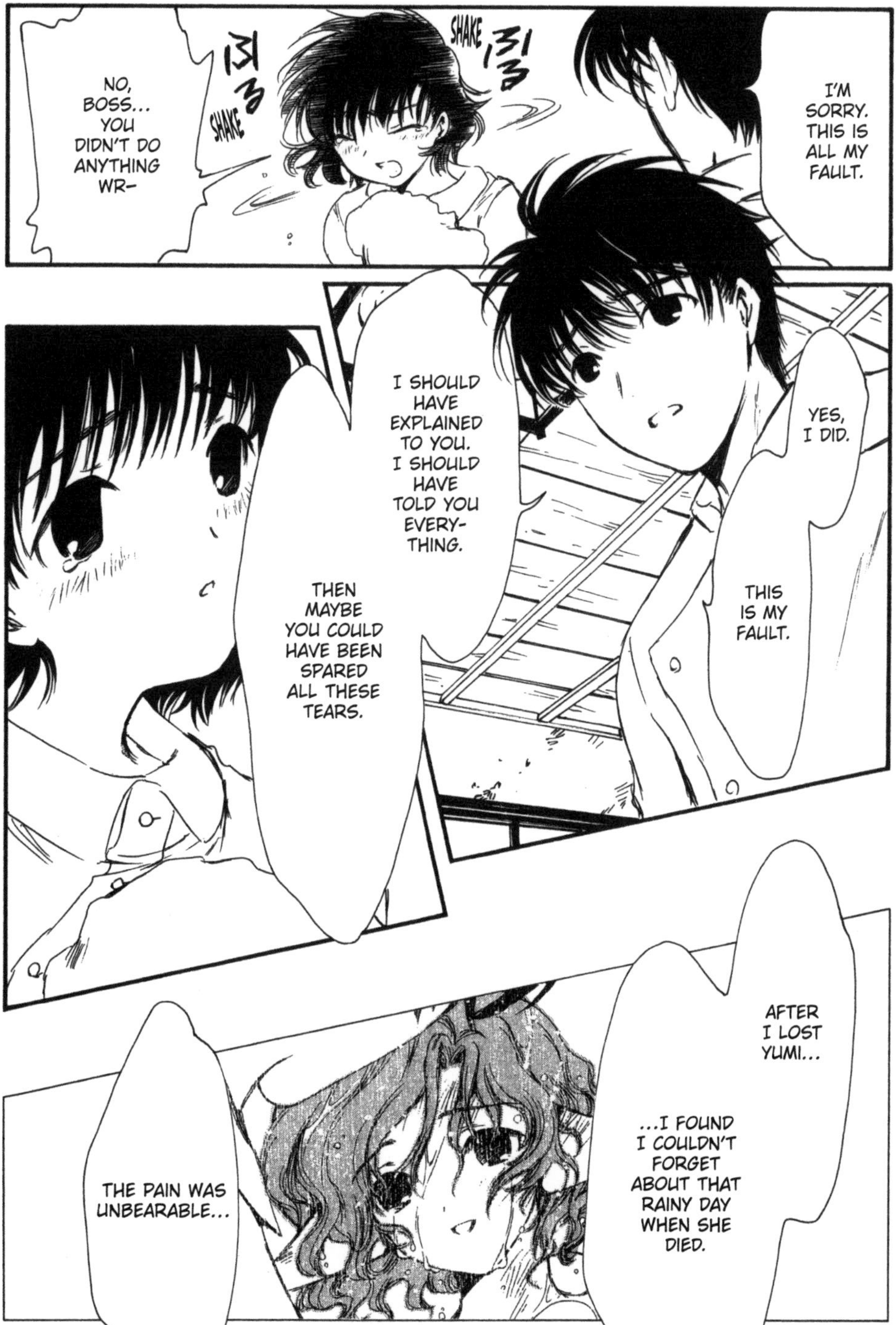
I'M SORRY. THIS IS ALL MY FAULT.
SHAKE
SHAKE
NO, BOSS... YOU DIDN'T DO ANYTHING WR-
YES, I DID.
THIS IS MY FAULT.
I SHOULD HAVE EXPLAINED TO YOU. I SHOULD HAVE TOLD YOU EVERY-THING.
THEN MAYBE YOU COULD HAVE BEEN SPARED ALL THESE TEARS.
AFTER I LOST YUMI...
...I FOUND I COULDN'T FORGET ABOUT THAT RAINY DAY WHEN SHE DIED.
THE PAIN WAS UNBEARABLE...

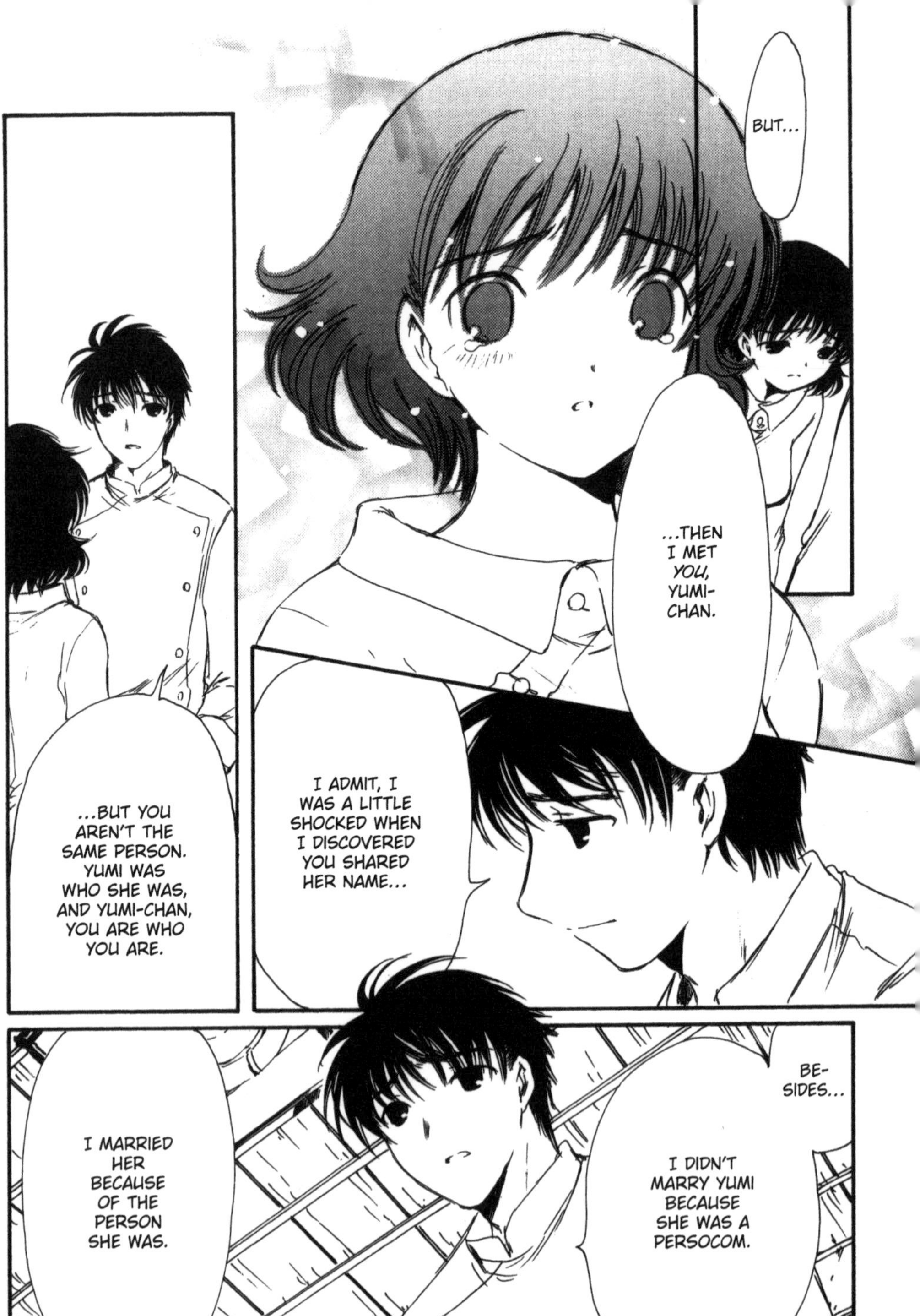
BUT...
...THEN I MET *YOU,* YUMI-CHAN.
I ADMIT, I WAS A LITTLE SHOCKED WHEN I DISCOVERED YOU SHARED HER NAME...
...BUT YOU AREN'T THE SAME PERSON. YUMI WAS WHO SHE WAS, AND YUMI-CHAN, YOU ARE WHO YOU ARE.
BE-SIDES...
I DIDN'T MARRY YUMI BECAUSE SHE WAS A PERSOCOM.
I MARRIED HER BECAUSE OF THE PERSON SHE WAS.

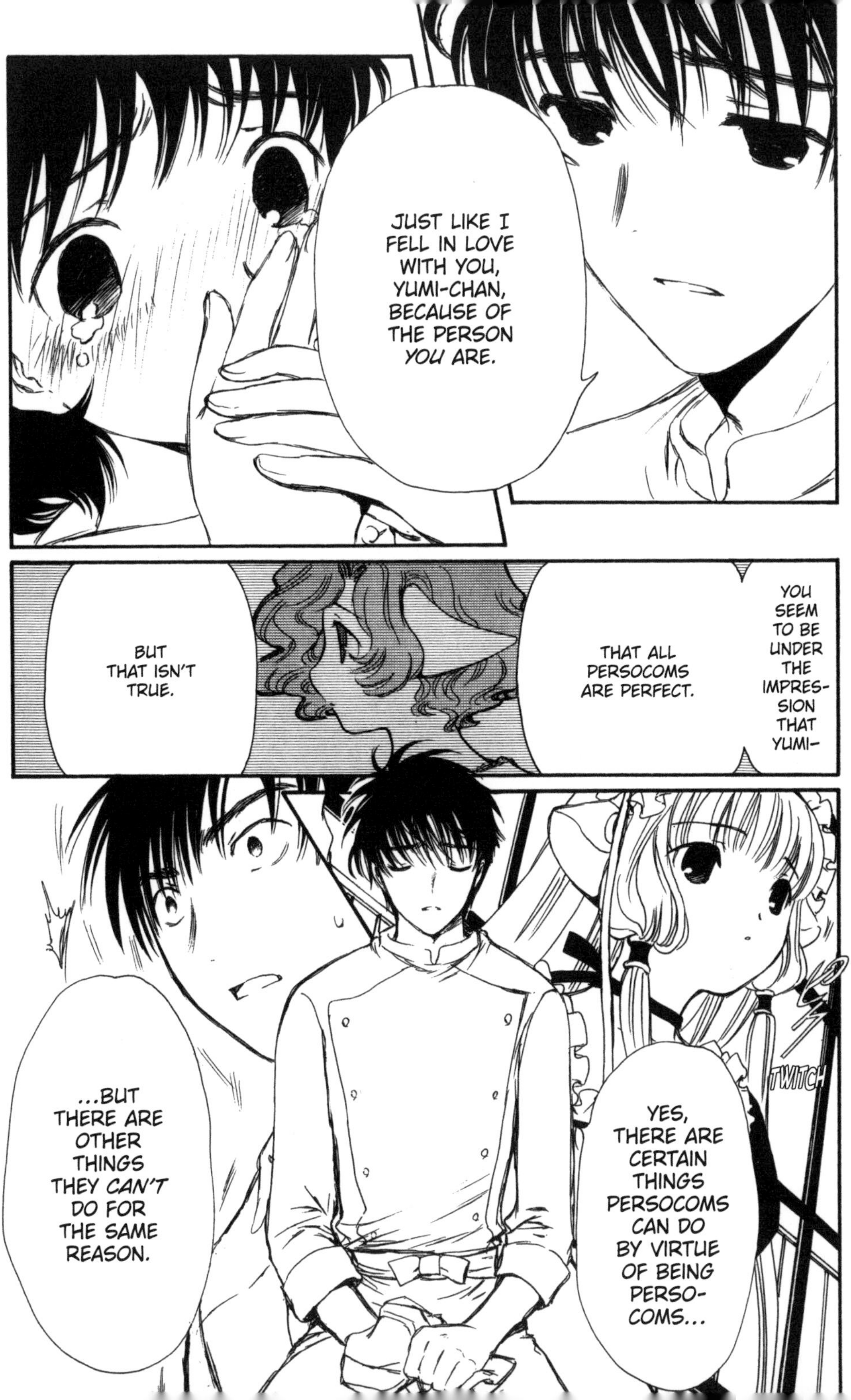
JUST LIKE I FELL IN LOVE WITH YOU, YUMI-CHAN, BECAUSE OF THE PERSON *YOU* ARE.
YOU SEEM TO BE UNDER THE IMPRES-SION THAT YUMI-
THAT ALL PERSOCOMS ARE PERFECT.
BUT THAT ISN'T TRUE.
TWITCH
YES, THERE ARE CERTAIN THINGS PERSOCOMS CAN DO BY VIRTUE OF BEING PERSO-COMS...
...BUT THERE ARE OTHER THINGS THEY *CAN'T* DO FOR THE SAME REASON.

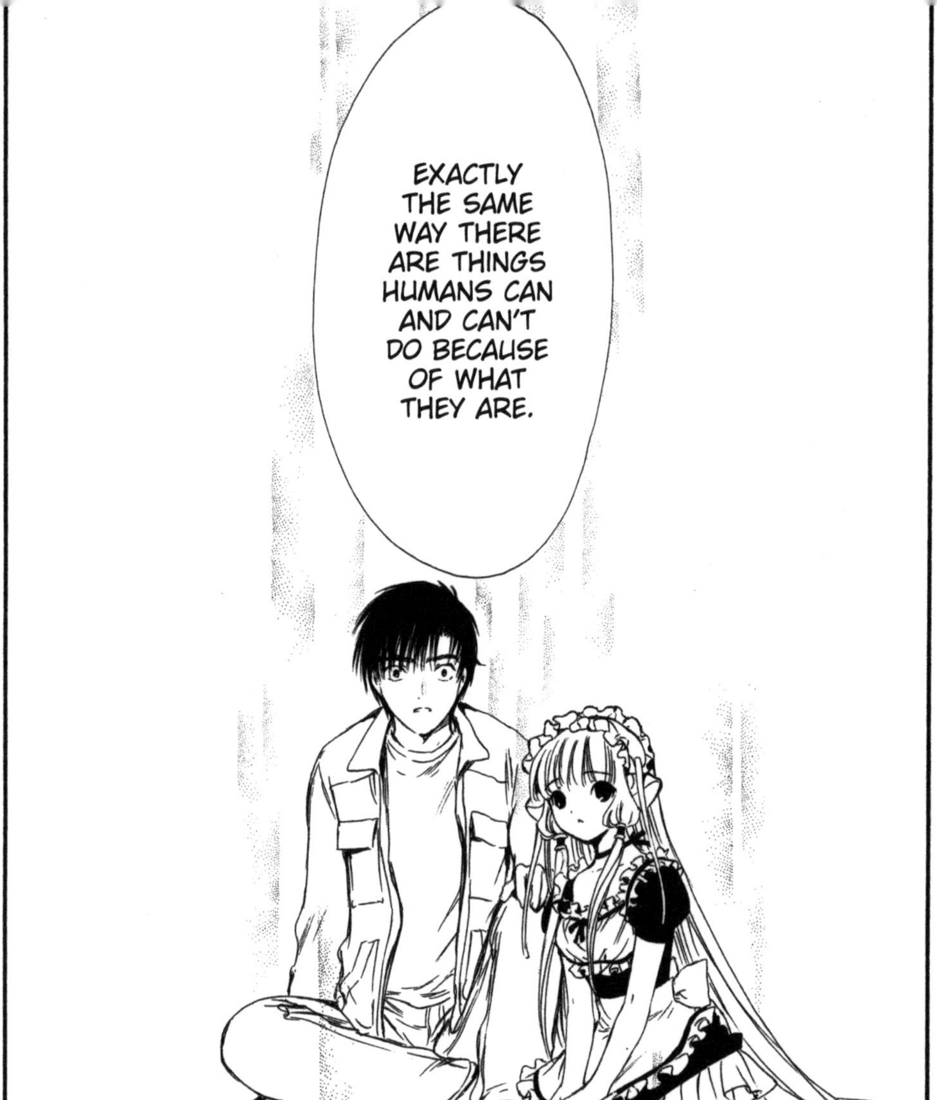
EXACTLY THE SAME WAY THERE ARE THINGS HUMANS CAN AND CAN'T DO BECAUSE OF WHAT THEY ARE.

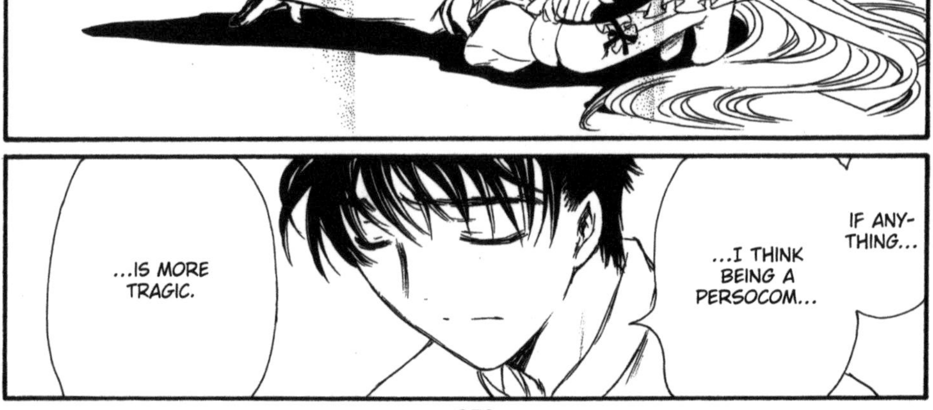
IF ANY-THING...
...I THINK BEING A PERSOCOM...
...IS MORE TRAGIC.

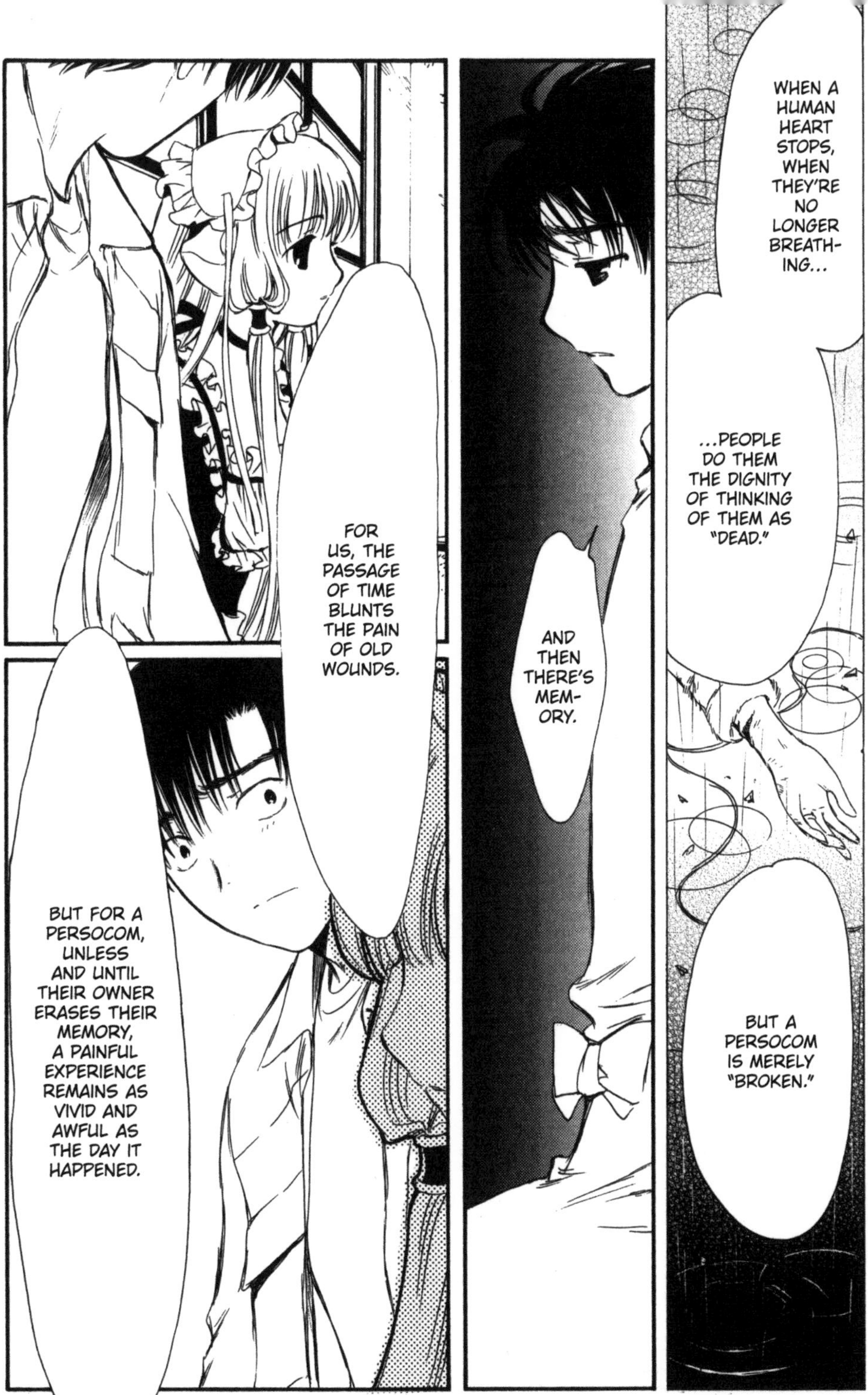
WHEN A HUMAN HEART STOPS, WHEN THEY'RE NO LONGER BREATHING...
...PEOPLE DO THEM THE DIGNITY OF THINKING OF THEM AS "DEAD."
BUT A PERSOCOM IS MERELY "BROKEN."
AND THEN THERE'S MEMORY.
FOR US, THE PASSAGE OF TIME BLUNTS THE PAIN OF OLD WOUNDS.
BUT FOR A PERSOCOM, UNLESS AND UNTIL THEIR OWNER ERASES THEIR MEMORY, A PAINFUL EXPERIENCE REMAINS AS VIVID AND AWFUL AS THE DAY IT HAPPENED.

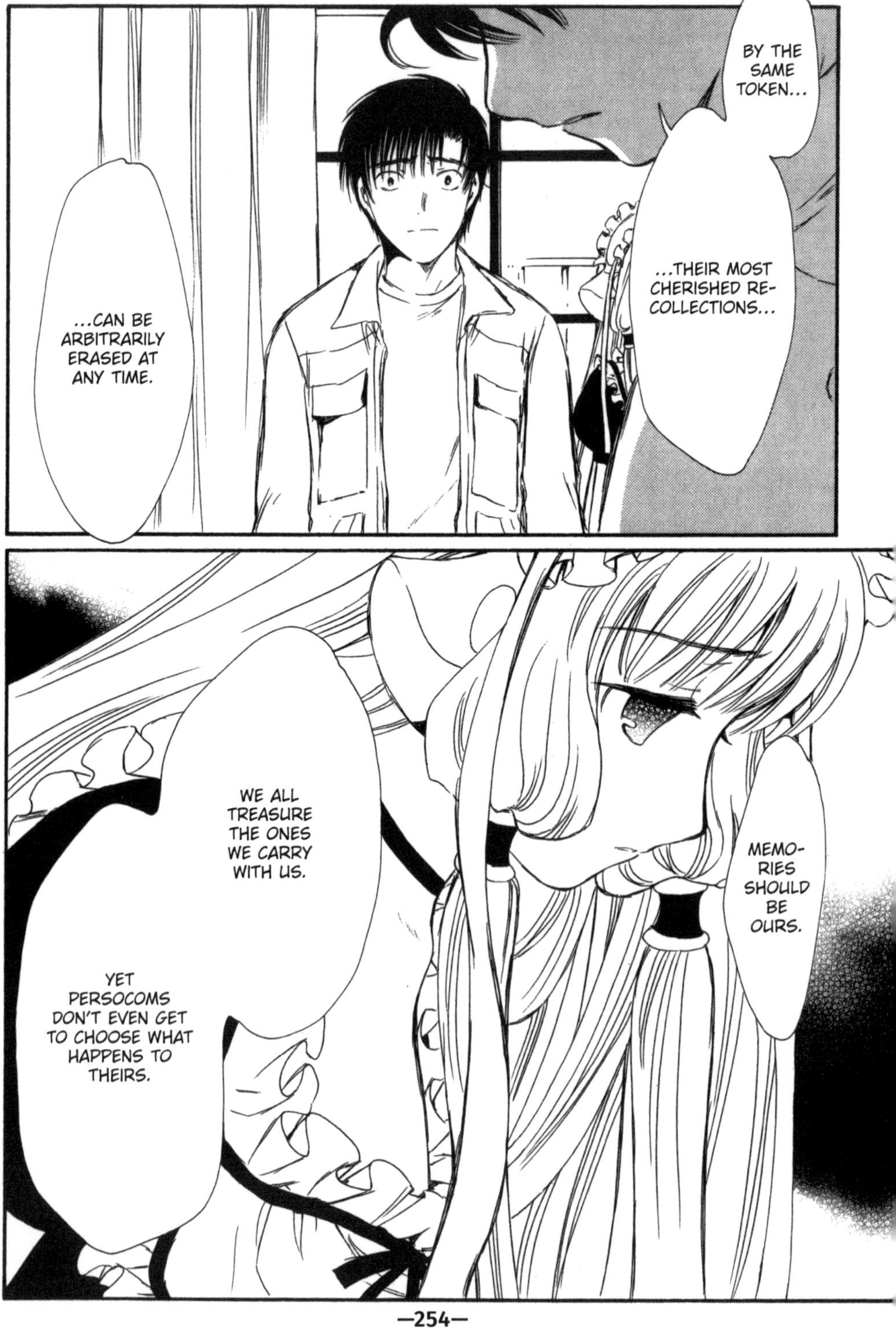
BY THE SAME TOKEN...
...THEIR MOST CHERISHED RE-COLLECTIONS...
...CAN BE ARBITRARILY ERASED AT ANY TIME.
MEMO-RIES SHOULD BE OURS.
WE ALL TREASURE THE ONES WE CARRY WITH US.
YET PERSOCOMS DON'T EVEN GET TO CHOOSE WHAT HAPPENS TO THEIRS.

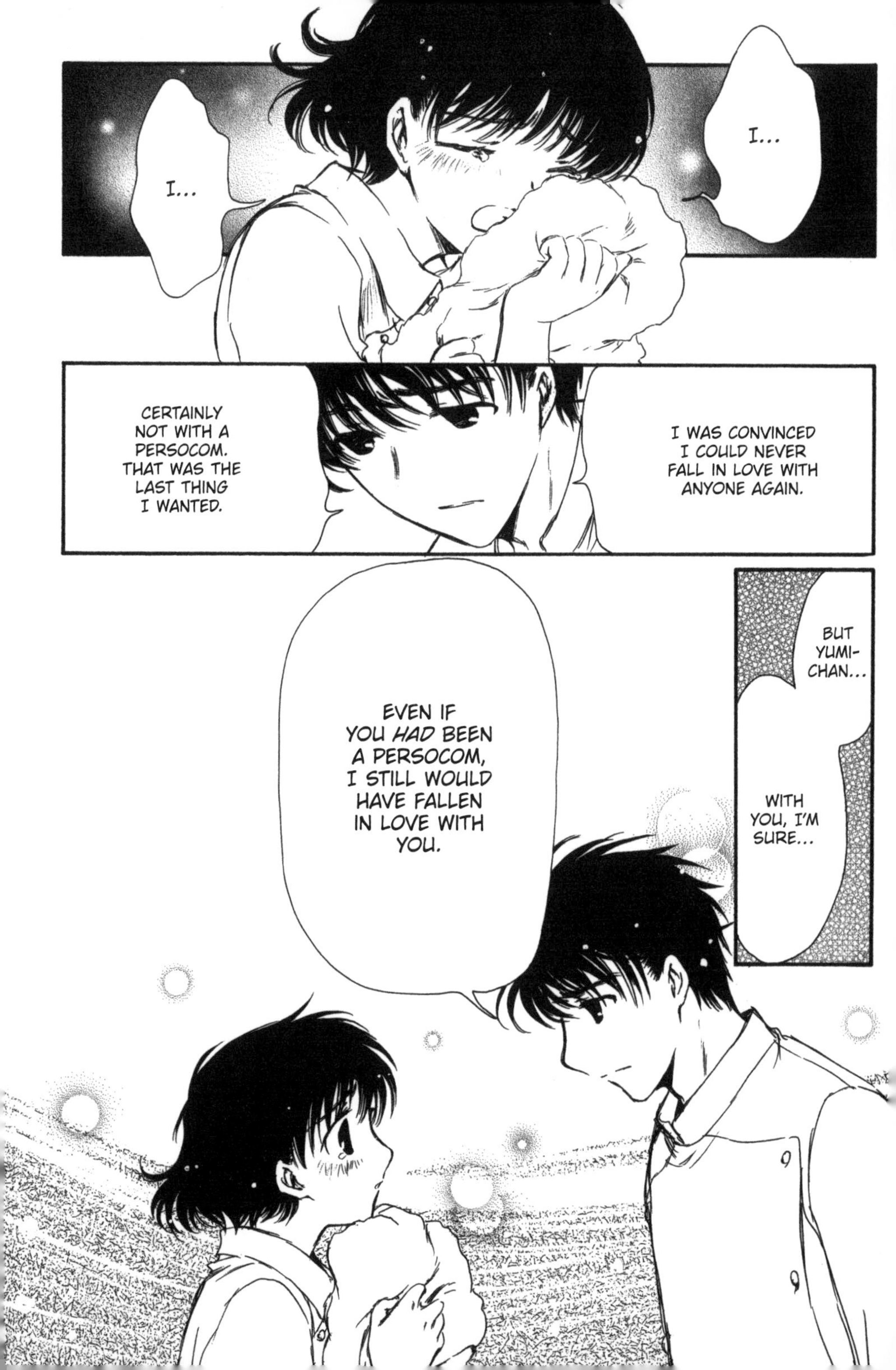
I...
I...
I WAS CONVINCED I COULD NEVER FALL IN LOVE WITH ANYONE AGAIN.
CERTAINLY NOT WITH A PERSOCOM. THAT WAS THE LAST THING I WANTED.
BUT YUMI-CHAN...
WITH YOU, I'M SURE...
EVEN IF YOU *HAD* BEEN A PERSOCOM, I STILL WOULD HAVE FALLEN IN LOVE WITH YOU.

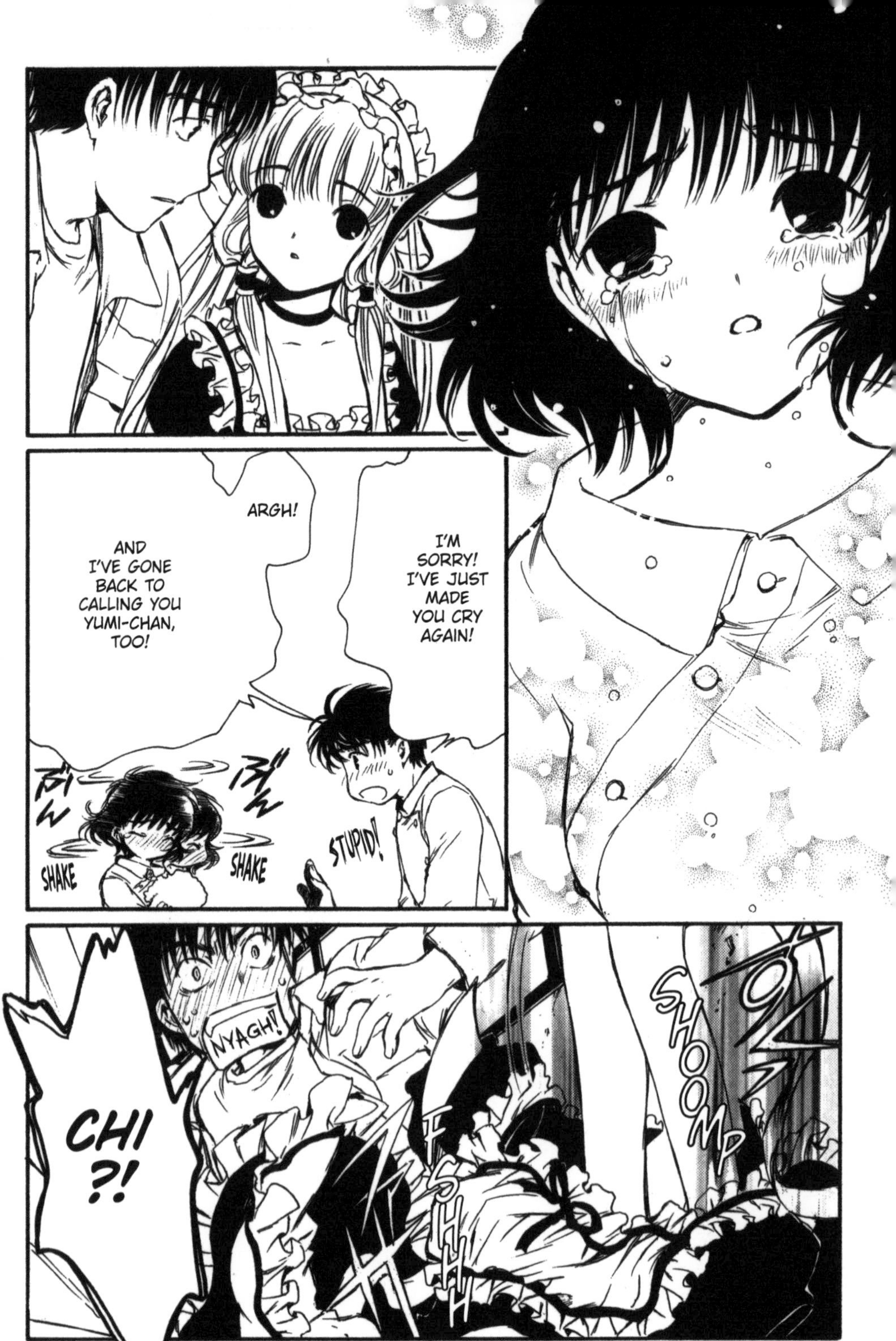
I'M SORRY! I'VE JUST MADE YOU CRY AGAIN!
ARGH!
AND I'VE GONE BACK TO CALLING YOU YUMI-CHAN, TOO!
STUPID!
SHAKE
SHAKE
SHOOMP
FSHHH
NYAGH!
CHI ?!

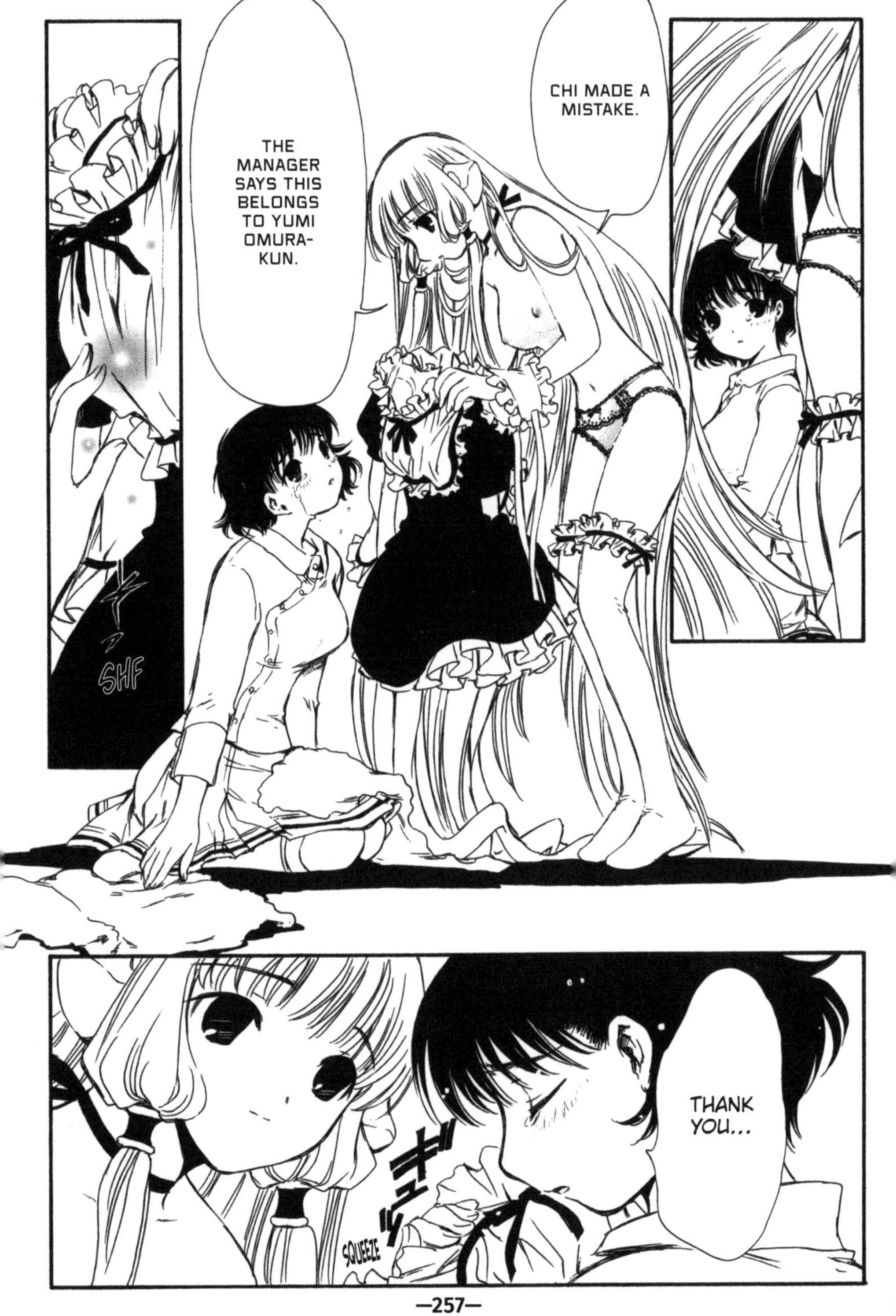
CHI MADE A MISTAKE.
THE MANAGER SAYS THIS BELONGS TO YUMI OMURA-KUN.
SHF
THANK YOU...
SQUEEZE

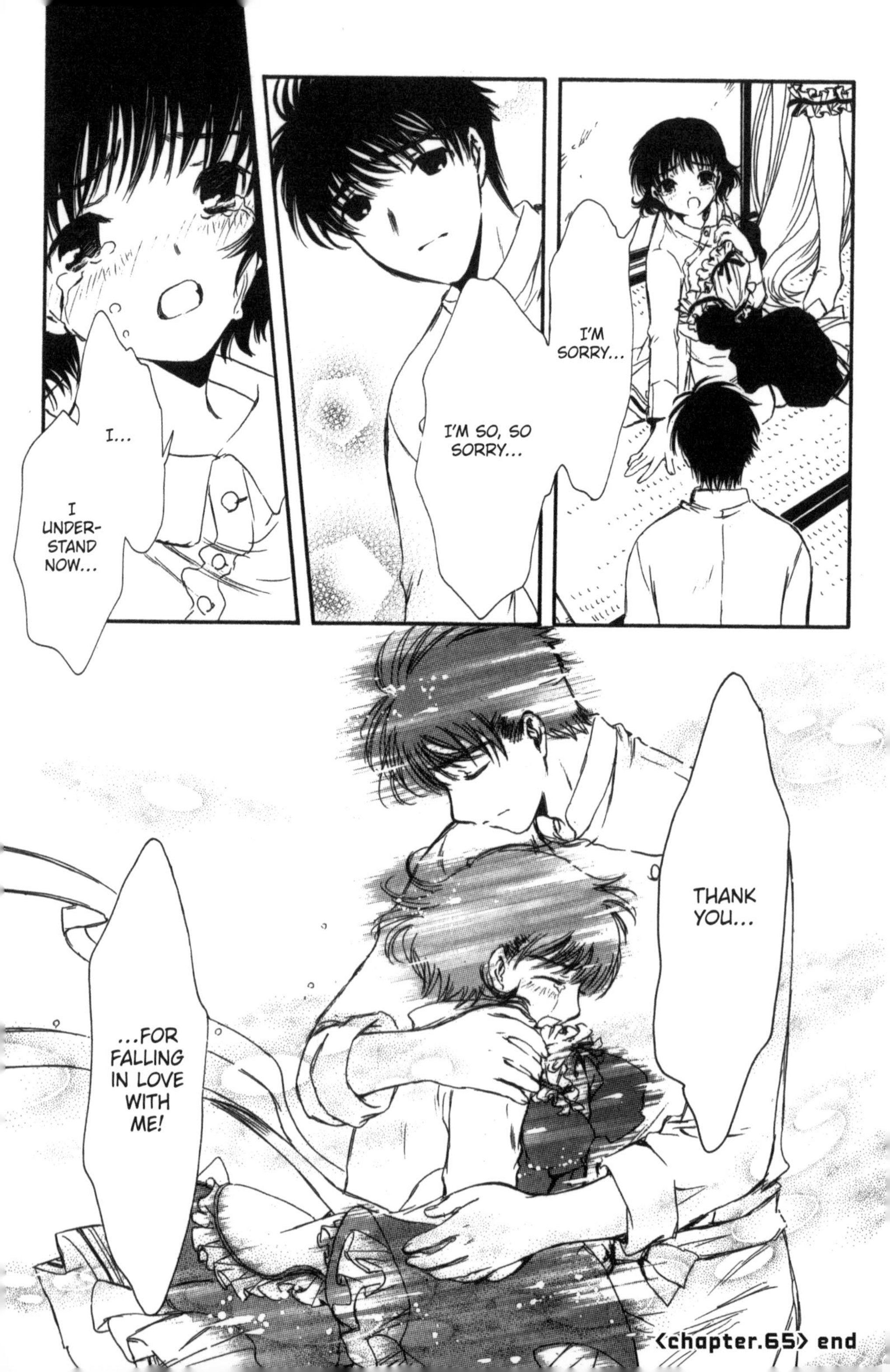
I'M SORRY...
I'M SO, SO SORRY...
I...
I UNDERSTAND NOW...
THANK YOU...
...FOR FALLING IN LOVE WITH ME!
<chapter.65> end

〈chapter.66〉

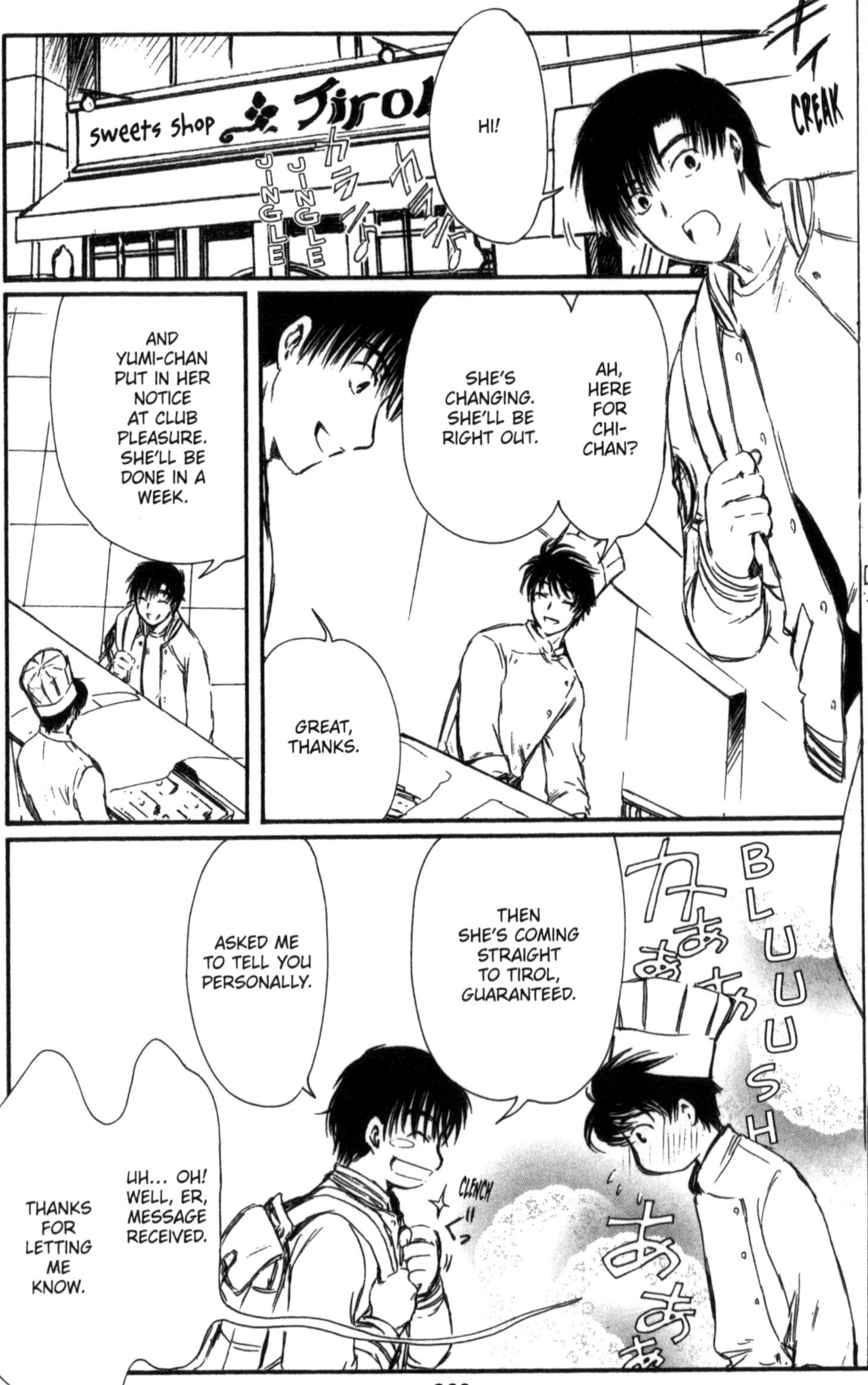
CREAK
HI!
sweets shop Tirol
JINGLE
JINGLE
AH, HERE FOR CHI-CHAN?
SHE'S CHANGING. SHE'LL BE RIGHT OUT.
GREAT, THANKS.
AND YUMI-CHAN PUT IN HER NOTICE AT CLUB PLEASURE. SHE'LL BE DONE IN A WEEK.
BLUUUSH
THEN SHE'S COMING STRAIGHT TO TIROL, GUARANTEED.
ASKED ME TO TELL YOU PERSONALLY.
CLENCH
UH... OH! WELL, ER, MESSAGE RECEIVED.
THANKS FOR LETTING ME KNOW.

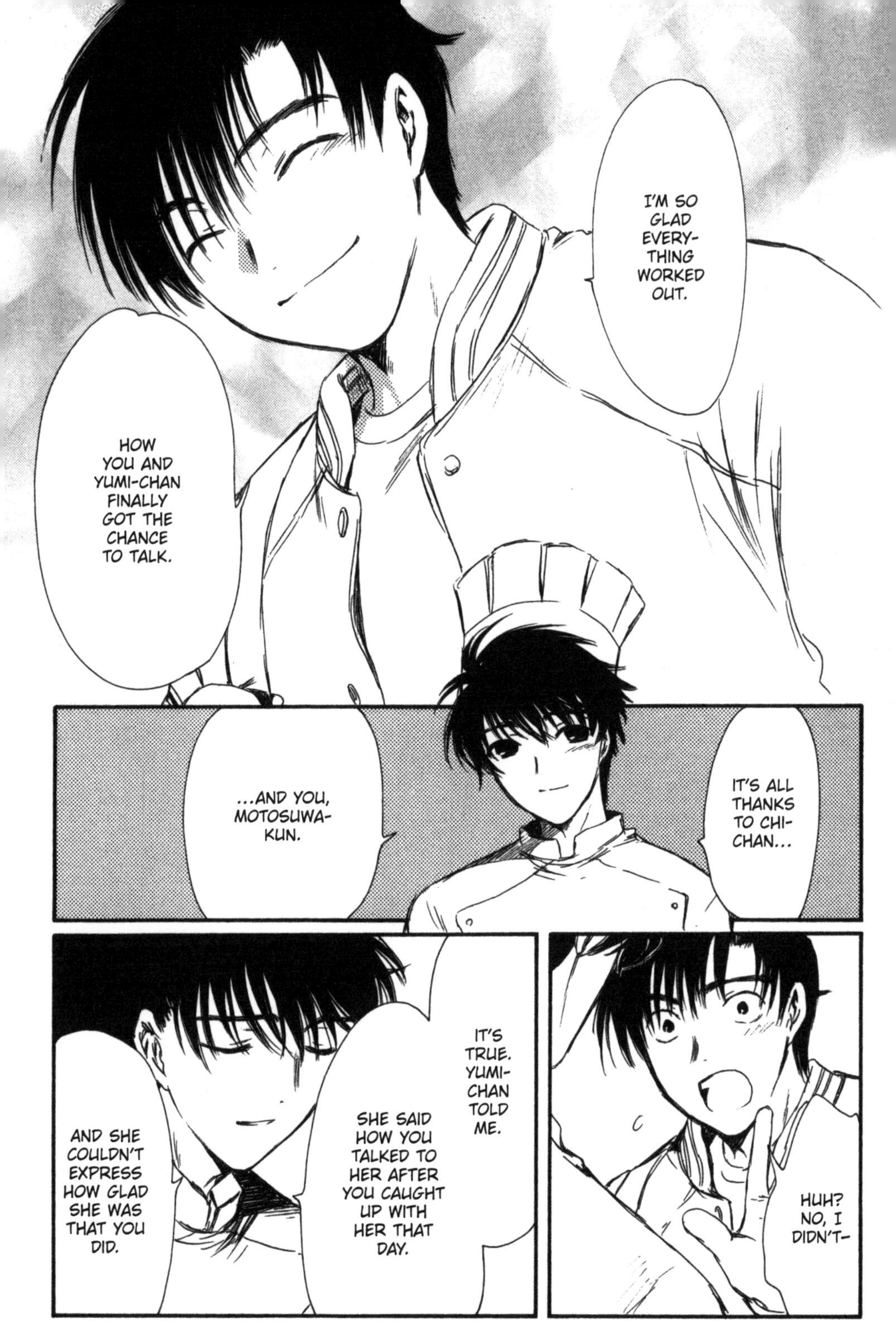
I'M SO GLAD EVERY-THING WORKED OUT.
HOW YOU AND YUMI-CHAN FINALLY GOT THE CHANCE TO TALK.
IT'S ALL THANKS TO CHI-CHAN...
...AND YOU, MOTOSUWA-KUN.
HUH? NO, I DIDN'T-
IT'S TRUE. YUMI-CHAN TOLD ME.
SHE SAID HOW YOU TALKED TO HER AFTER YOU CAUGHT UP WITH HER THAT DAY.
AND SHE COULDN'T EXPRESS HOW GLAD SHE WAS THAT YOU DID.

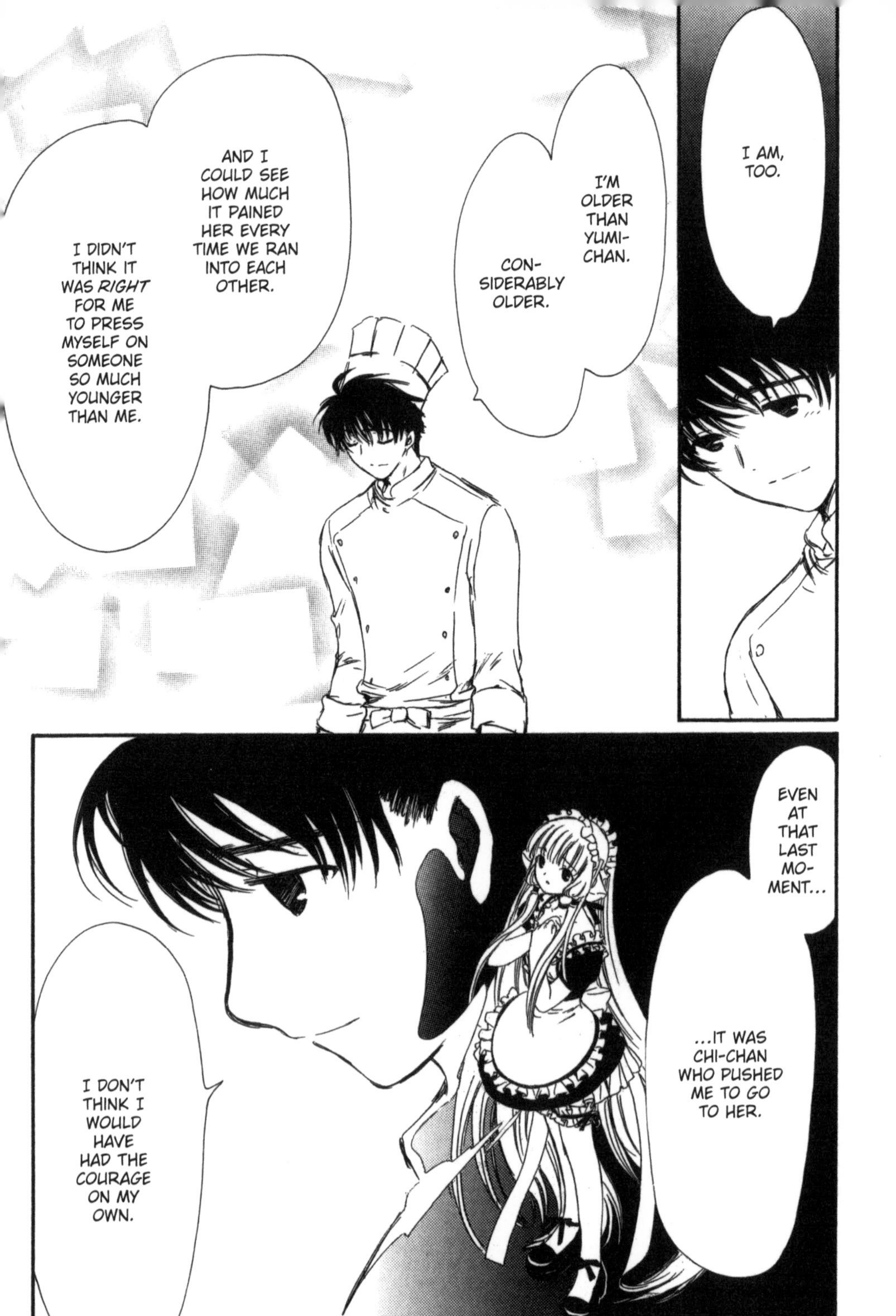
I AM, TOO.
I'M OLDER THAN YUMI-CHAN.
CON-SIDERABLY OLDER.
AND I COULD SEE HOW MUCH IT PAINED HER EVERY TIME WE RAN INTO EACH OTHER.
I DIDN'T THINK IT WAS *RIGHT* FOR ME TO PRESS MYSELF ON SOMEONE SO MUCH YOUNGER THAN ME.
EVEN AT THAT LAST MO-MENT...
...IT WAS CHI-CHAN WHO PUSHED ME TO GO TO HER.
I DON'T THINK I WOULD HAVE HAD THE COURAGE ON MY OWN.

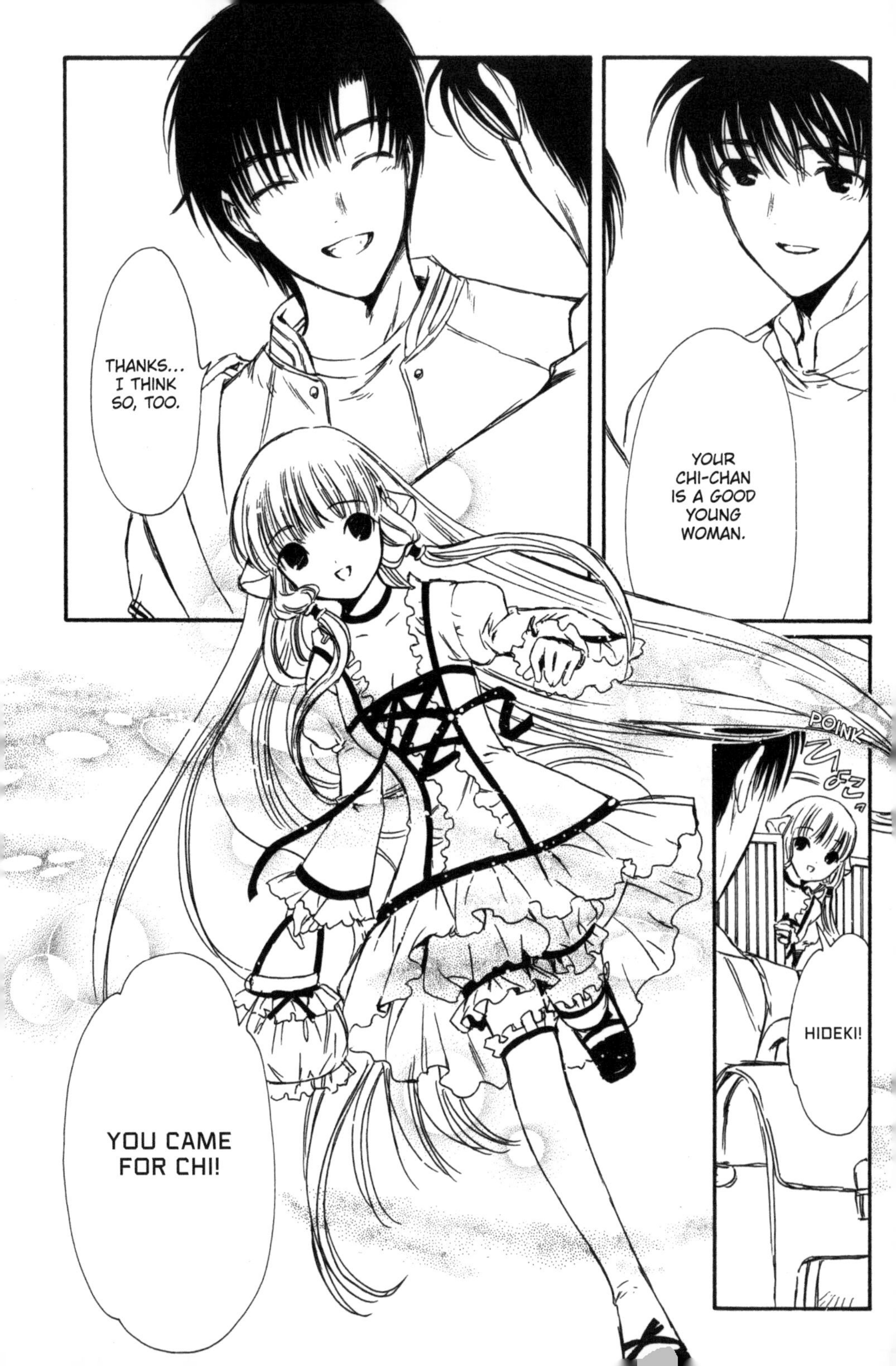
YOUR CHI-CHAN IS A GOOD YOUNG WOMAN.
THANKS... I THINK SO, TOO.
POINK
HIDEKI!
YOU CAME FOR CHI!

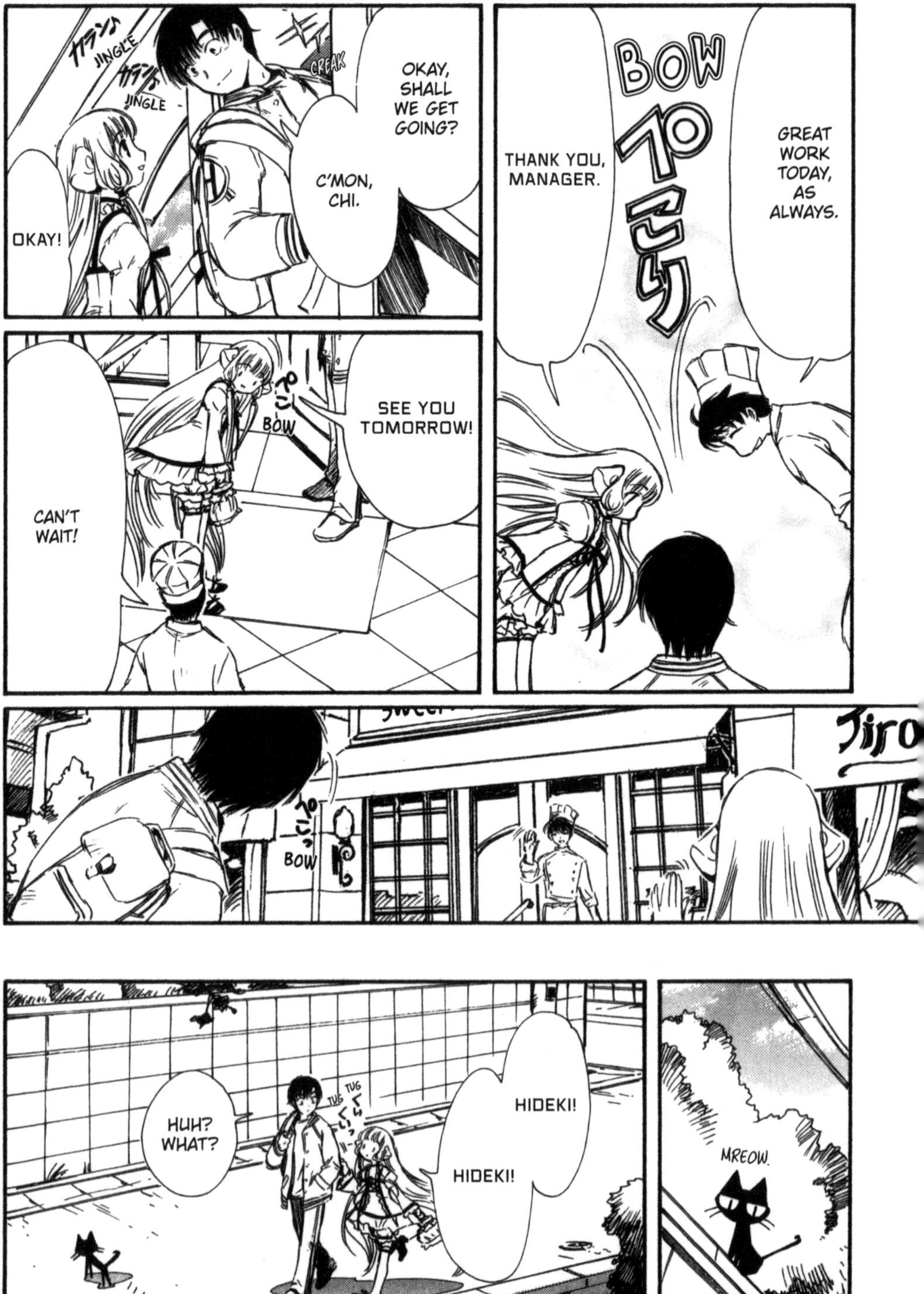
GREAT WORK TODAY, AS ALWAYS.
BOW
ペこり
THANK YOU, MANAGER.
カラン♪ JINGLE
カラン♪ JINGLE
CREAK
OKAY, SHALL WE GET GOING?
C'MON, CHI.
OKAY!
SEE YOU TOMORROW!
ぺこ BOW
CAN'T WAIT!
ぺこっ BOW
MREOW.
HIDEKI!
HIDEKI!
TUG TUG
HUH? WHAT?

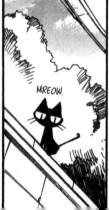

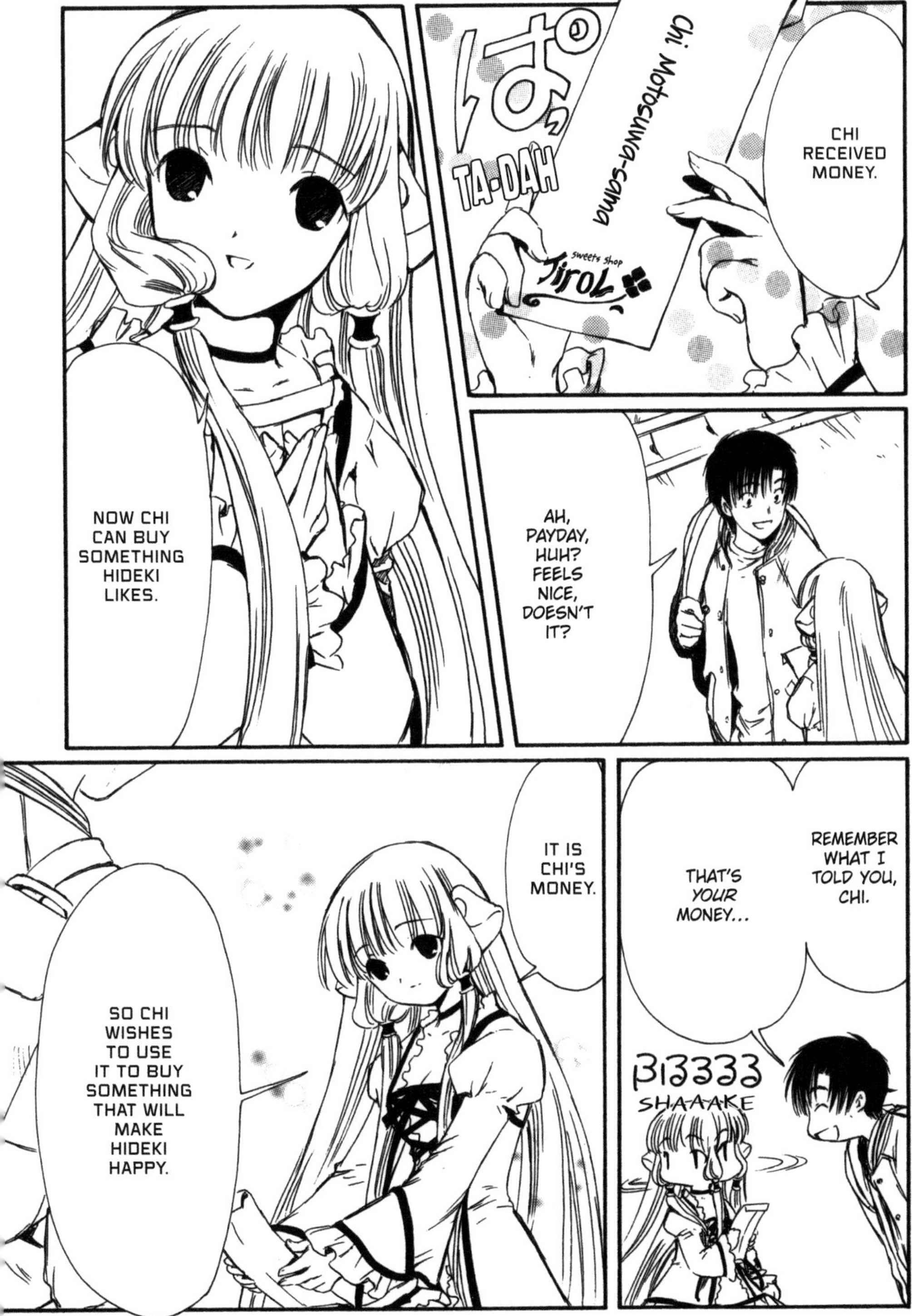
CHI RECEIVED MONEY.
ぱっ
TA-DAH
Chi Motosuwa-sama
sweets shop
Tirol
AH, PAYDAY, HUH? FEELS NICE, DOESN'T IT?
NOW CHI CAN BUY SOMETHING HIDEKI LIKES.
REMEMBER WHAT I TOLD YOU, CHI.
THAT'S *YOUR* MONEY...
ぶるるるる
SHAAAKE
IT IS CHI'S MONEY.
SO CHI WISHES TO USE IT TO BUY SOMETHING THAT WILL MAKE HIDEKI HAPPY.

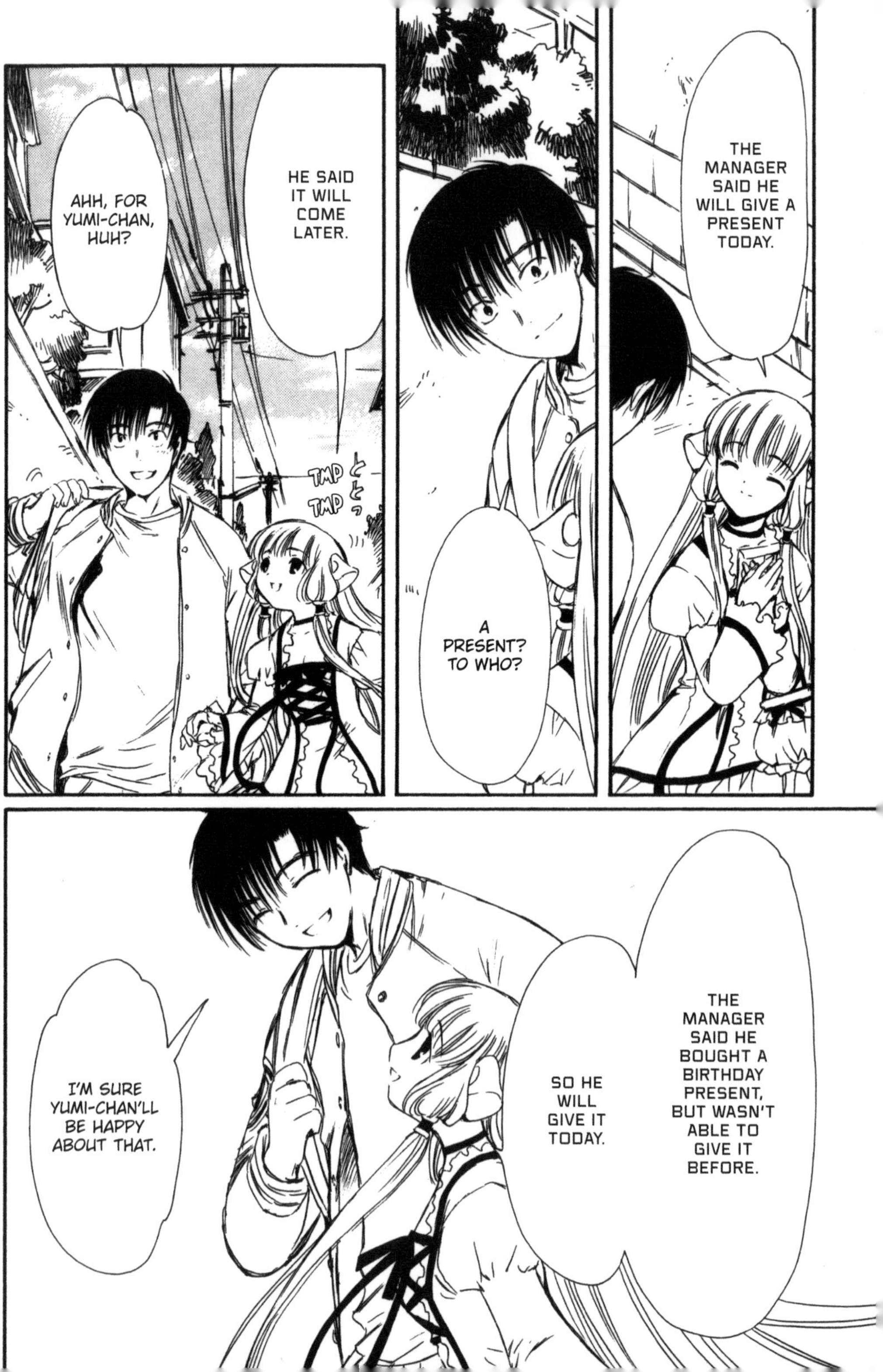
THE MANAGER SAID HE WILL GIVE A PRESENT TODAY.
A PRESENT? TO WHO?
HE SAID IT WILL COME LATER.
AHH, FOR YUMI-CHAN, HUH?
TMP TMP
THE MANAGER SAID HE BOUGHT A BIRTHDAY PRESENT, BUT WASN'T ABLE TO GIVE IT BEFORE.
SO HE WILL GIVE IT TODAY.
I'M SURE YUMI-CHAN'LL BE HAPPY ABOUT THAT.

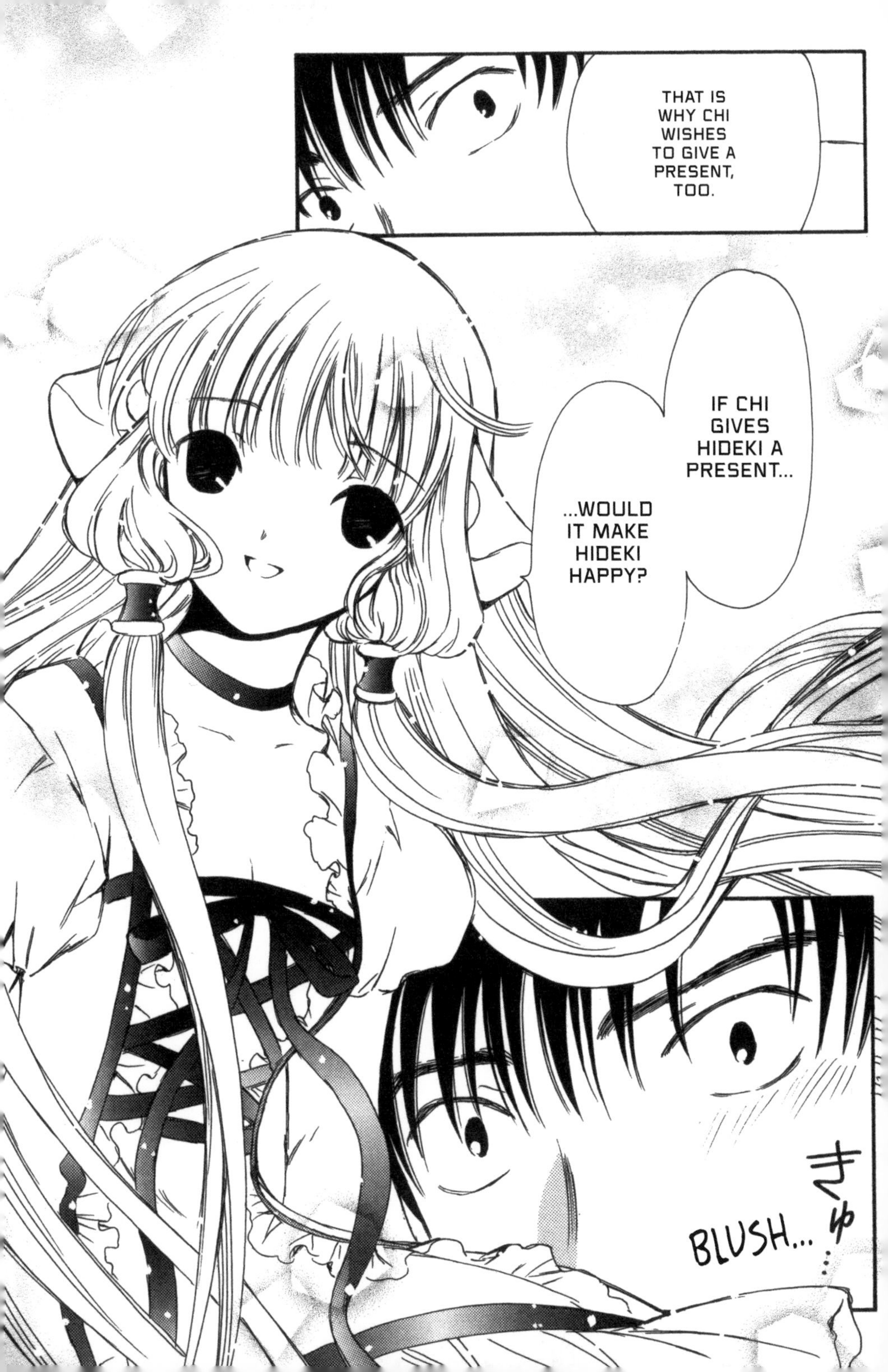
THAT IS WHY CHI WISHES TO GIVE A PRESENT, TOO.
IF CHI GIVES HIDEKI A PRESENT...
...WOULD IT MAKE HIDEKI HAPPY?
きゅ
BLUSH...

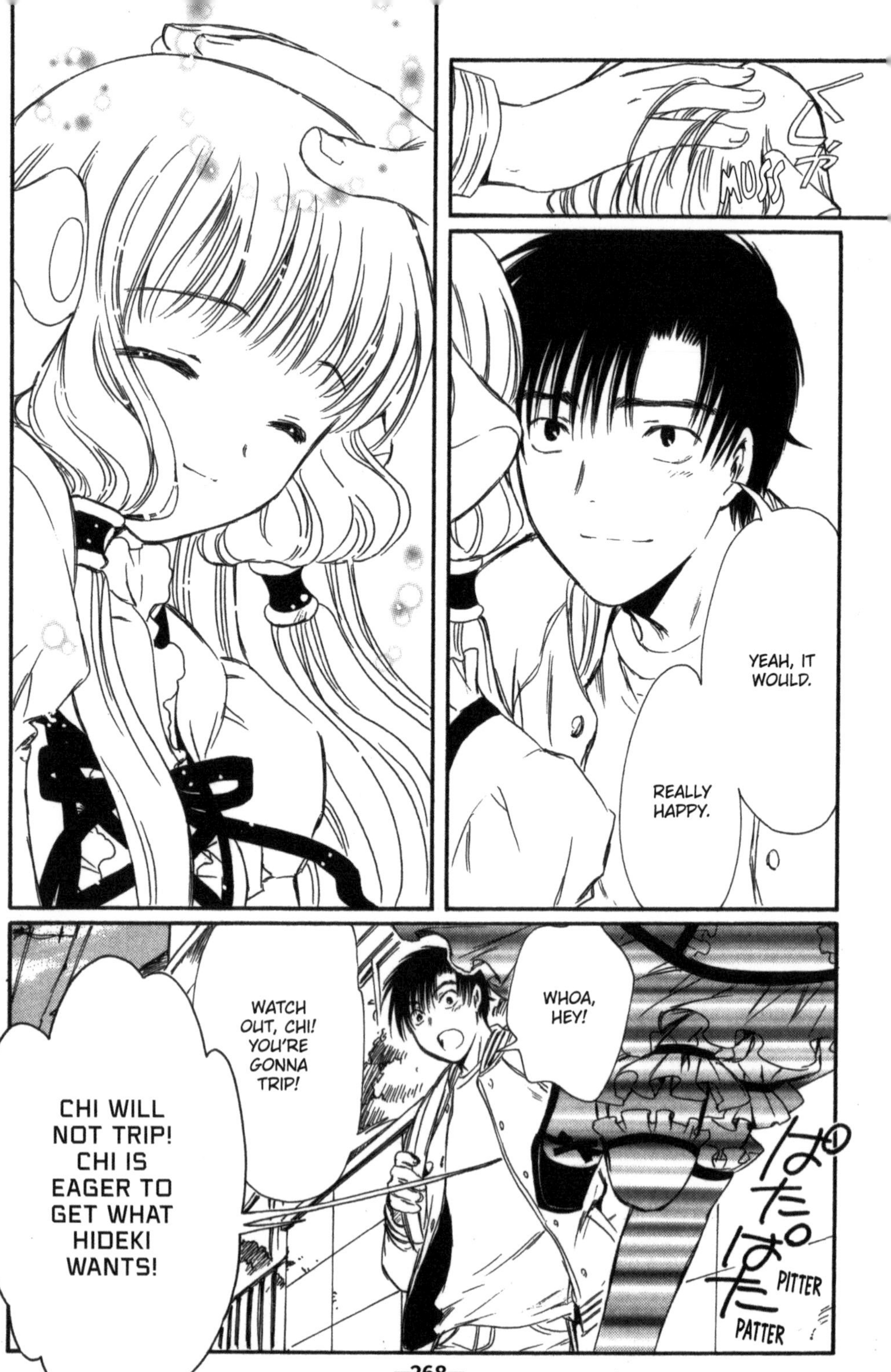
MUSS
YEAH, IT WOULD.
REALLY HAPPY.
WHOA, HEY!
WATCH OUT, CHI! YOU'RE GONNA TRIP!
CHI WILL NOT TRIP! CHI IS EAGER TO GET WHAT HIDEKI WANTS!
ぱたぱた
PITTER PATTER

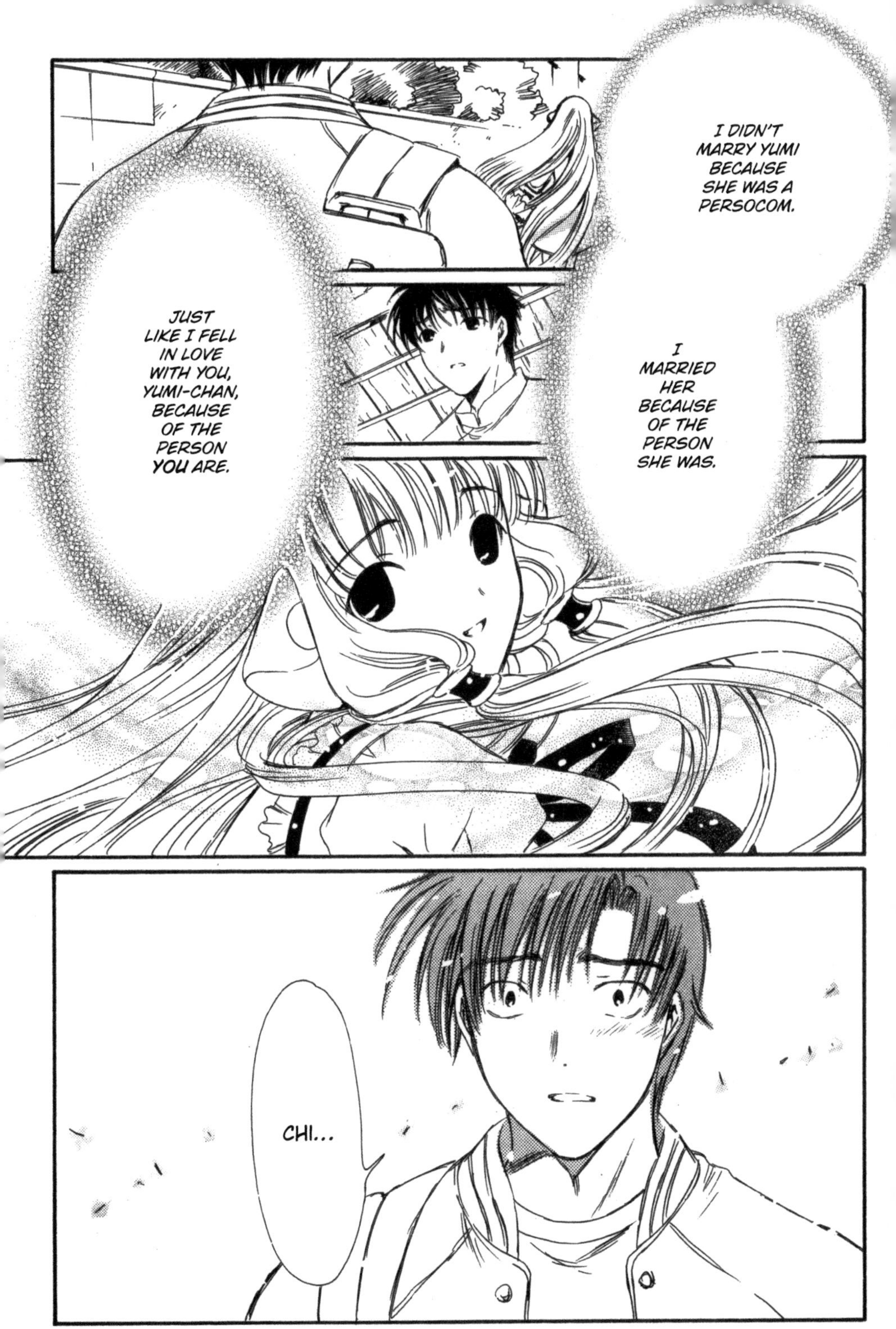
I DIDN'T MARRY YUMI BECAUSE SHE WAS A PERSOCOM.
I MARRIED HER BECAUSE OF THE PERSON SHE WAS.
JUST LIKE I FELL IN LOVE WITH YOU, YUMI-CHAN, BECAUSE OF THE PERSON YOU ARE.
CHI...

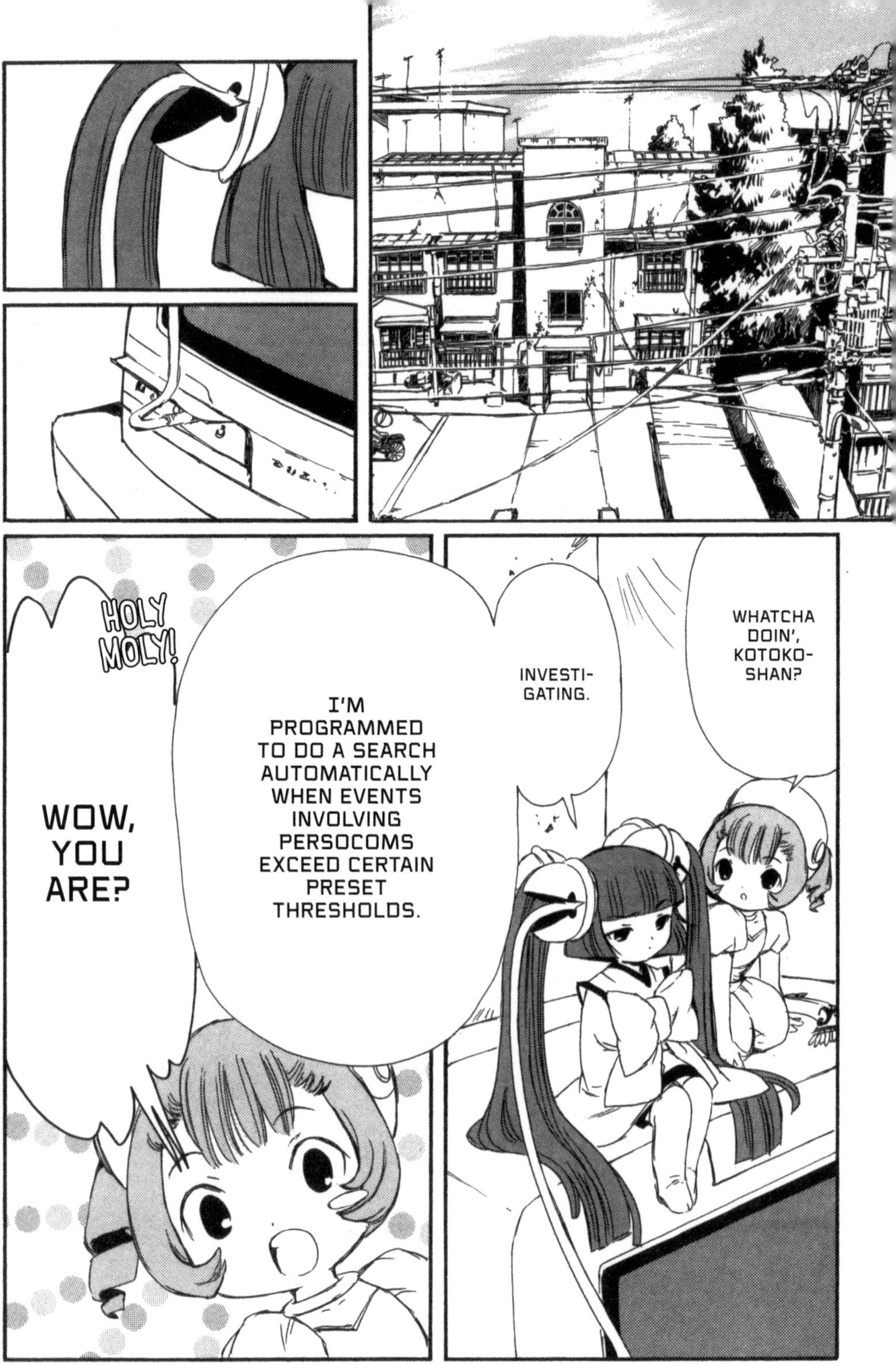
WHATCHA DOIN', KOTOKO-SHAN?
INVESTI-GATING.
I'M PROGRAMMED TO DO A SEARCH AUTOMATICALLY WHEN EVENTS INVOLVING PERSOCOMS EXCEED CERTAIN PRESET THRESHOLDS.
HOLY MOLY!
WOW, YOU ARE?

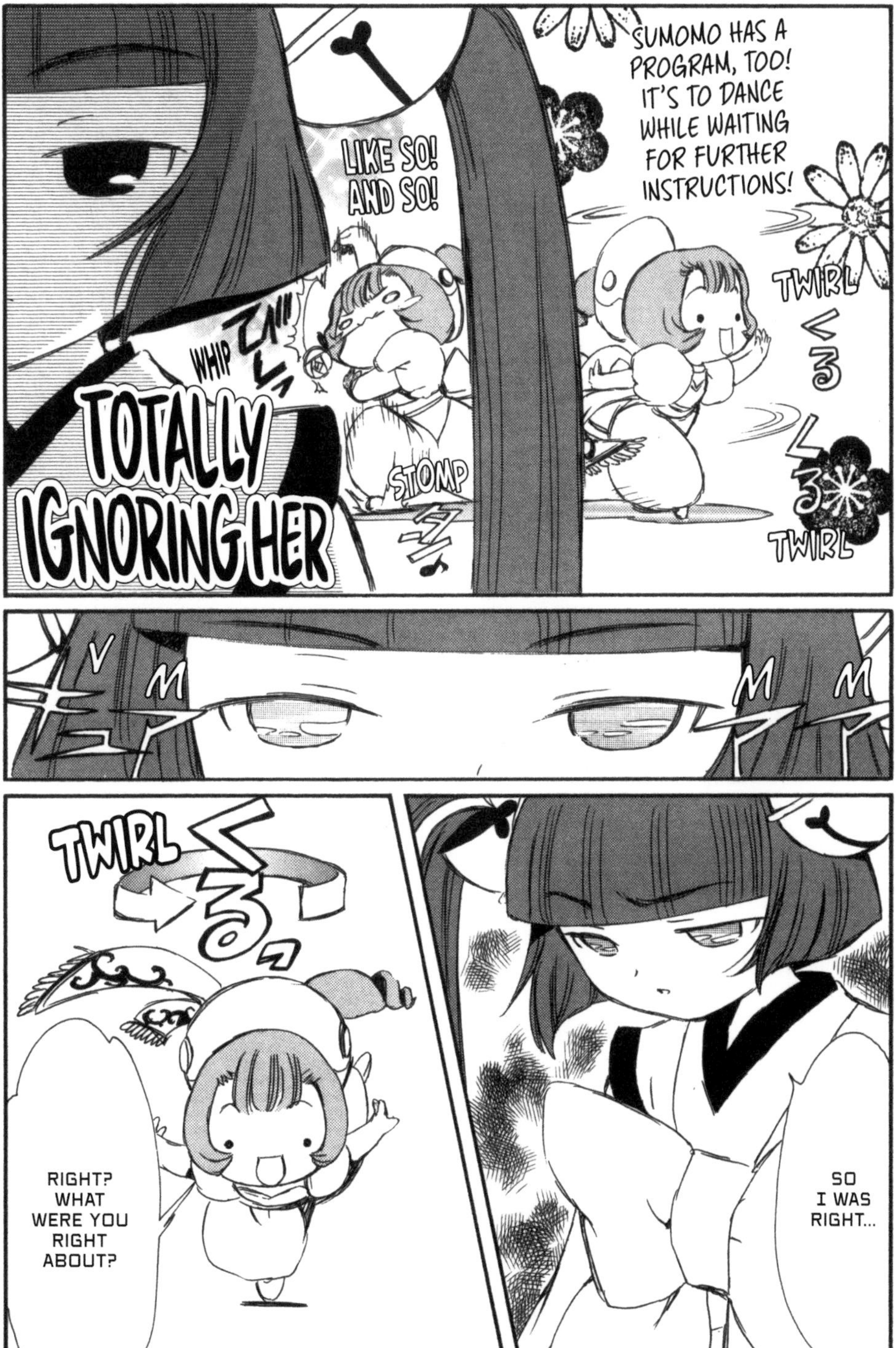
SUMOMO HAS A PROGRAM, TOO! IT'S TO DANCE WHILE WAITING FOR FURTHER INSTRUCTIONS!
TWIRL
TWIRL
LIKE SO! AND SO!
WHIP
STOMP
TOTALLY IGNORING HER
M M
M M
SO I WAS RIGHT...
TWIRL
RIGHT? WHAT WERE YOU RIGHT ABOUT?

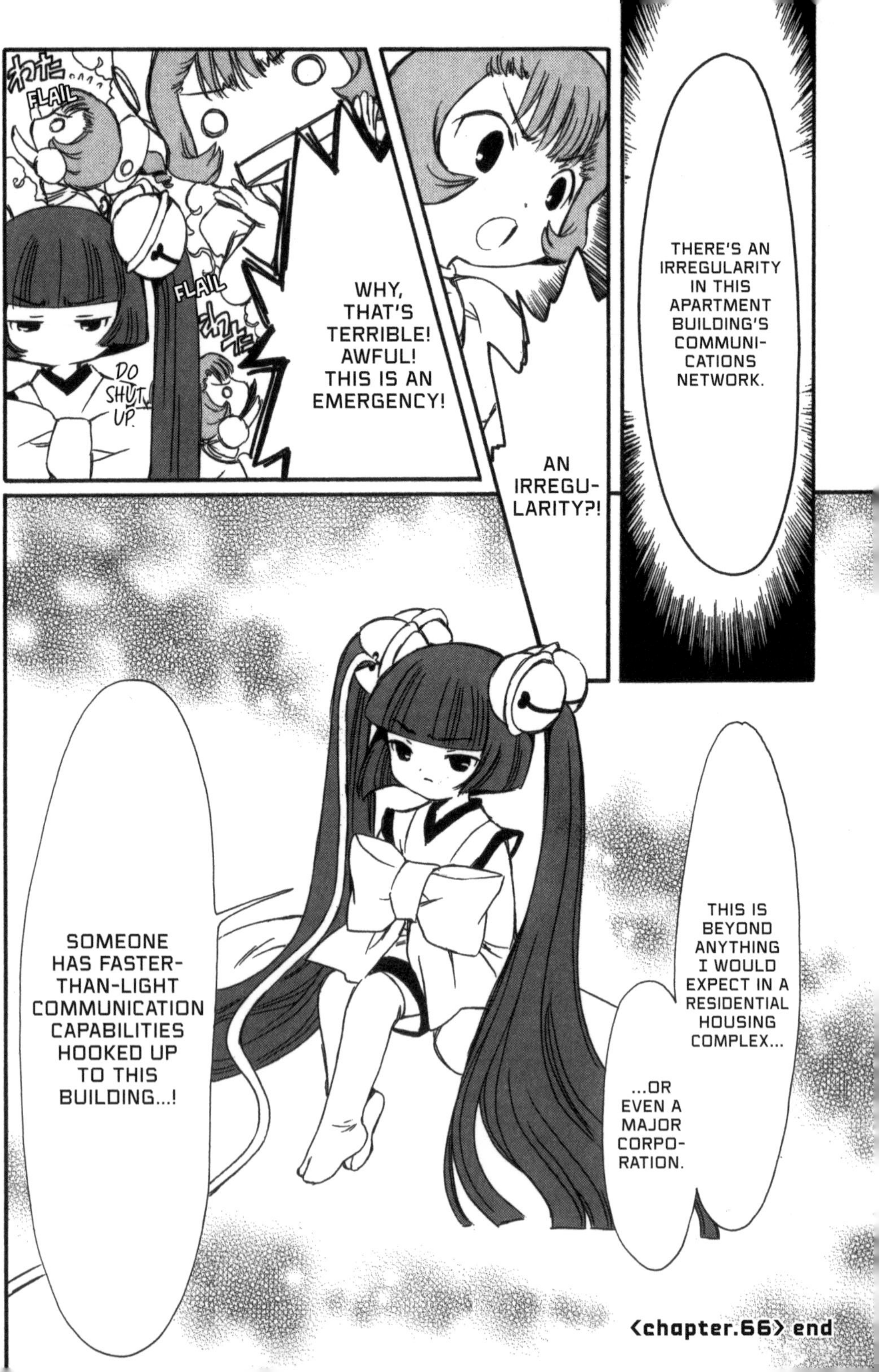
THERE'S AN IRREGULARITY IN THIS APARTMENT BUILDING'S COMMUNICATIONS NETWORK.
AN IRREGULARITY?!
WHY, THAT'S TERRIBLE! AWFUL! THIS IS AN EMERGENCY!
わた FLAIL
FLAIL わた
DO SHUT UP.
THIS IS BEYOND ANYTHING I WOULD EXPECT IN A RESIDENTIAL HOUSING COMPLEX...
...OR EVEN A MAJOR CORPORATION.
SOMEONE HAS FASTER-THAN-LIGHT COMMUNICATION CAPABILITIES HOOKED UP TO THIS BUILDING...!
⟨chapter.66⟩ end

Chobits

〈chapter.67〉

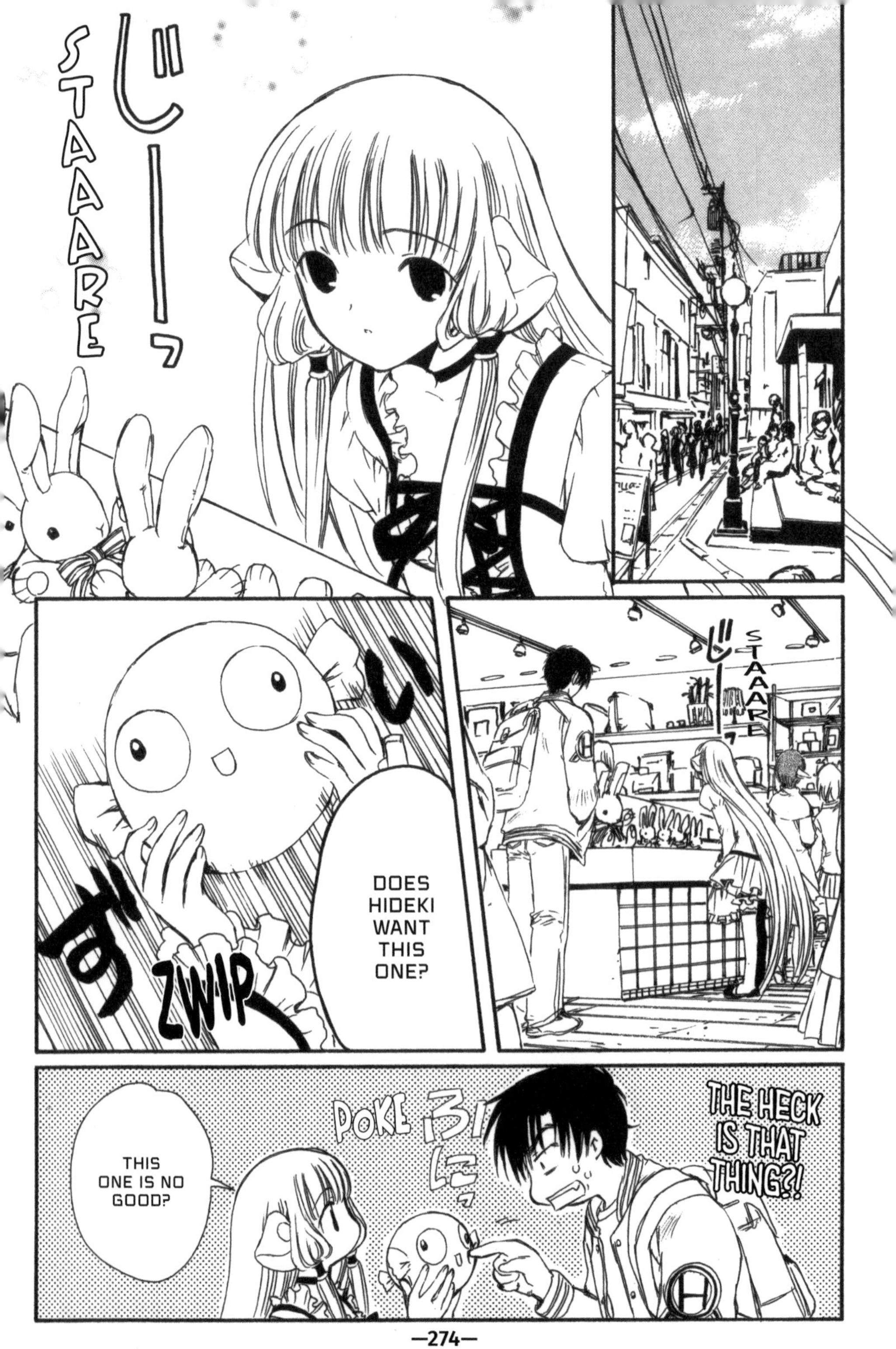
STAAARE
STAAARE
DOES HIDEKI WANT THIS ONE?
ZWIP
THE HECK IS THAT THING?!
POKE
THIS ONE IS NO GOOD?

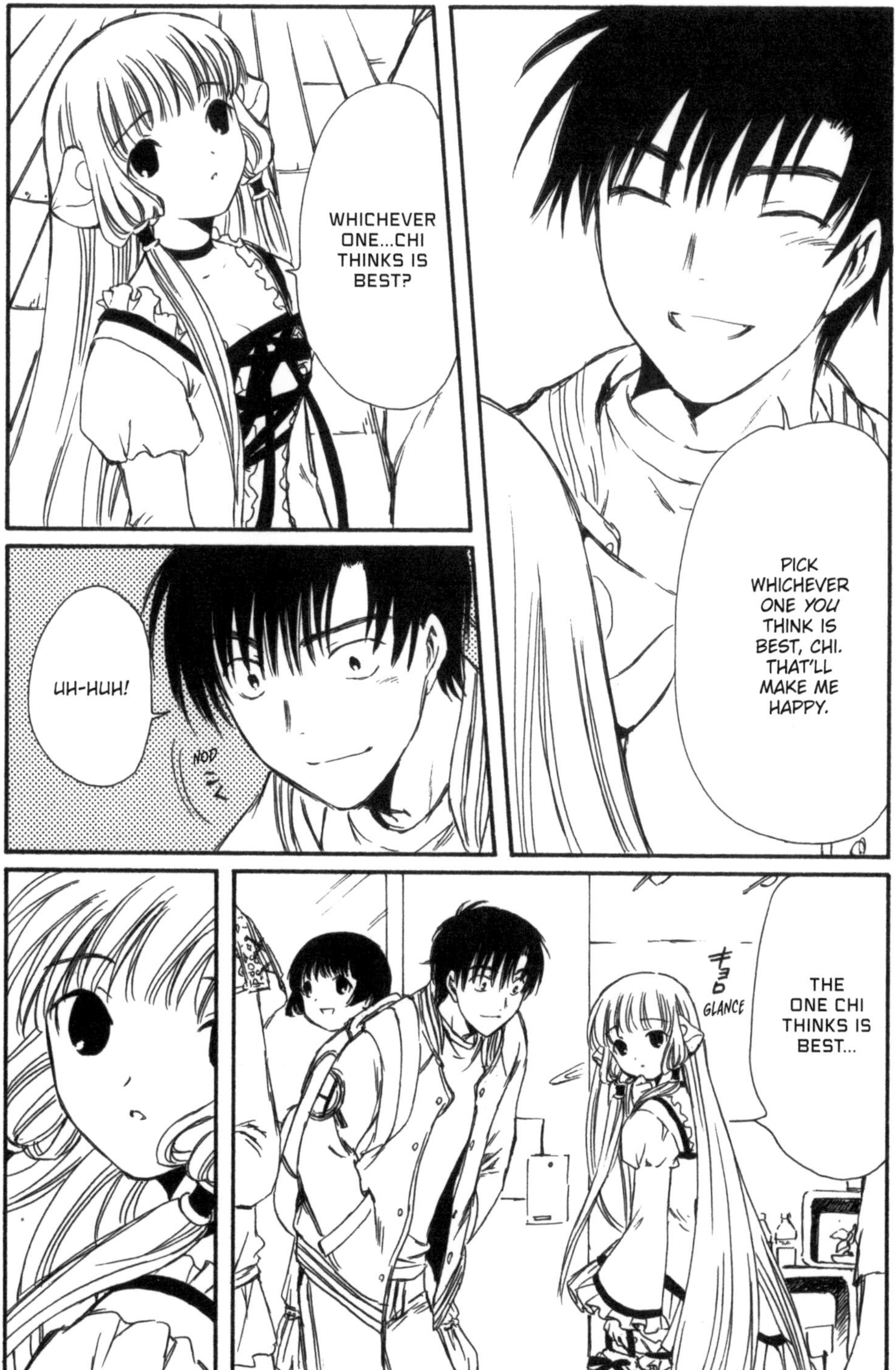
PICK WHICHEVER ONE *YOU* THINK IS BEST, CHI. THAT'LL MAKE ME HAPPY.
WHICHEVER ONE...CHI THINKS IS BEST?
UH-HUH!
NOD
THE ONE CHI THINKS IS BEST...
GLANCE

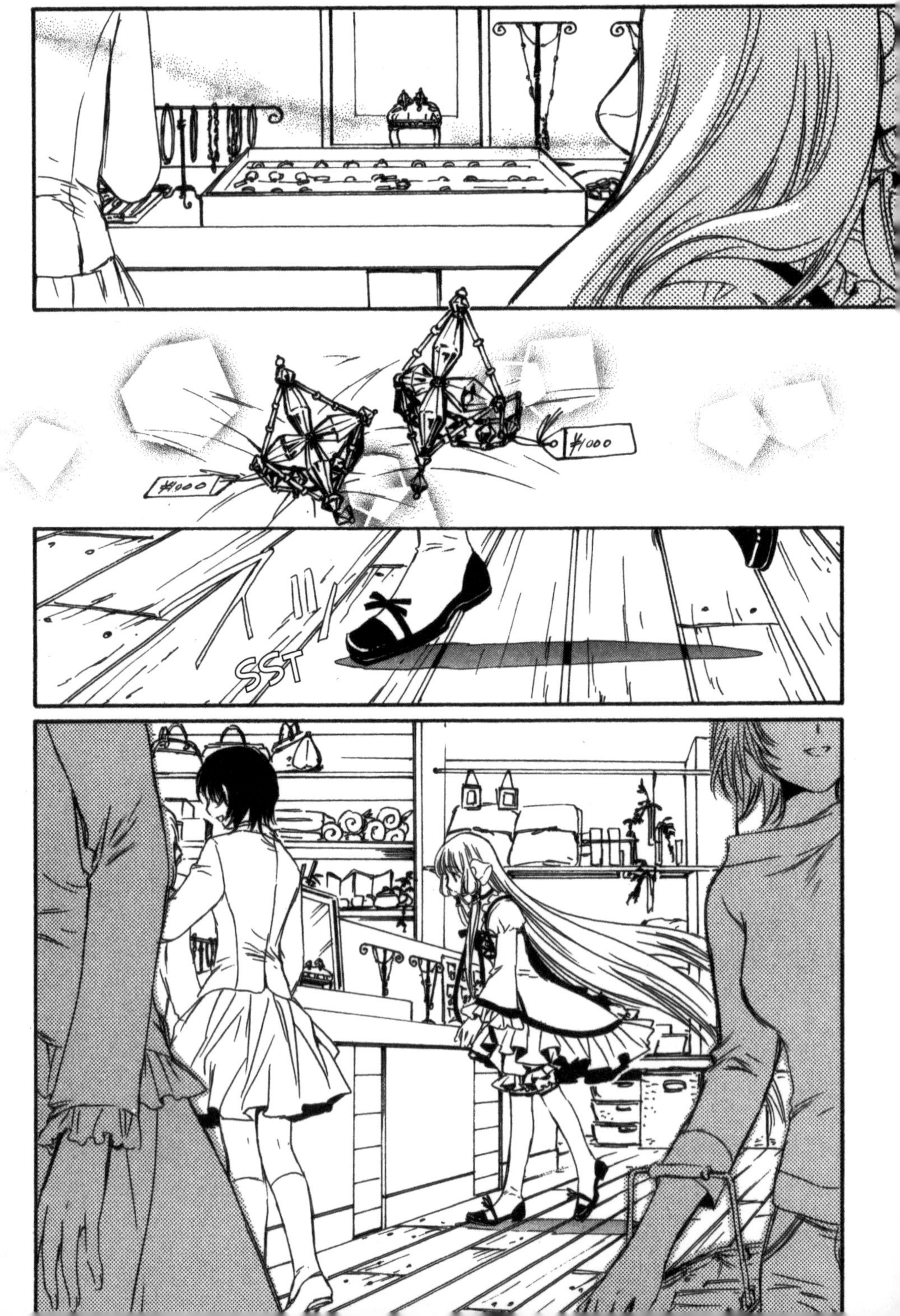
¥1000
¥1000
SST

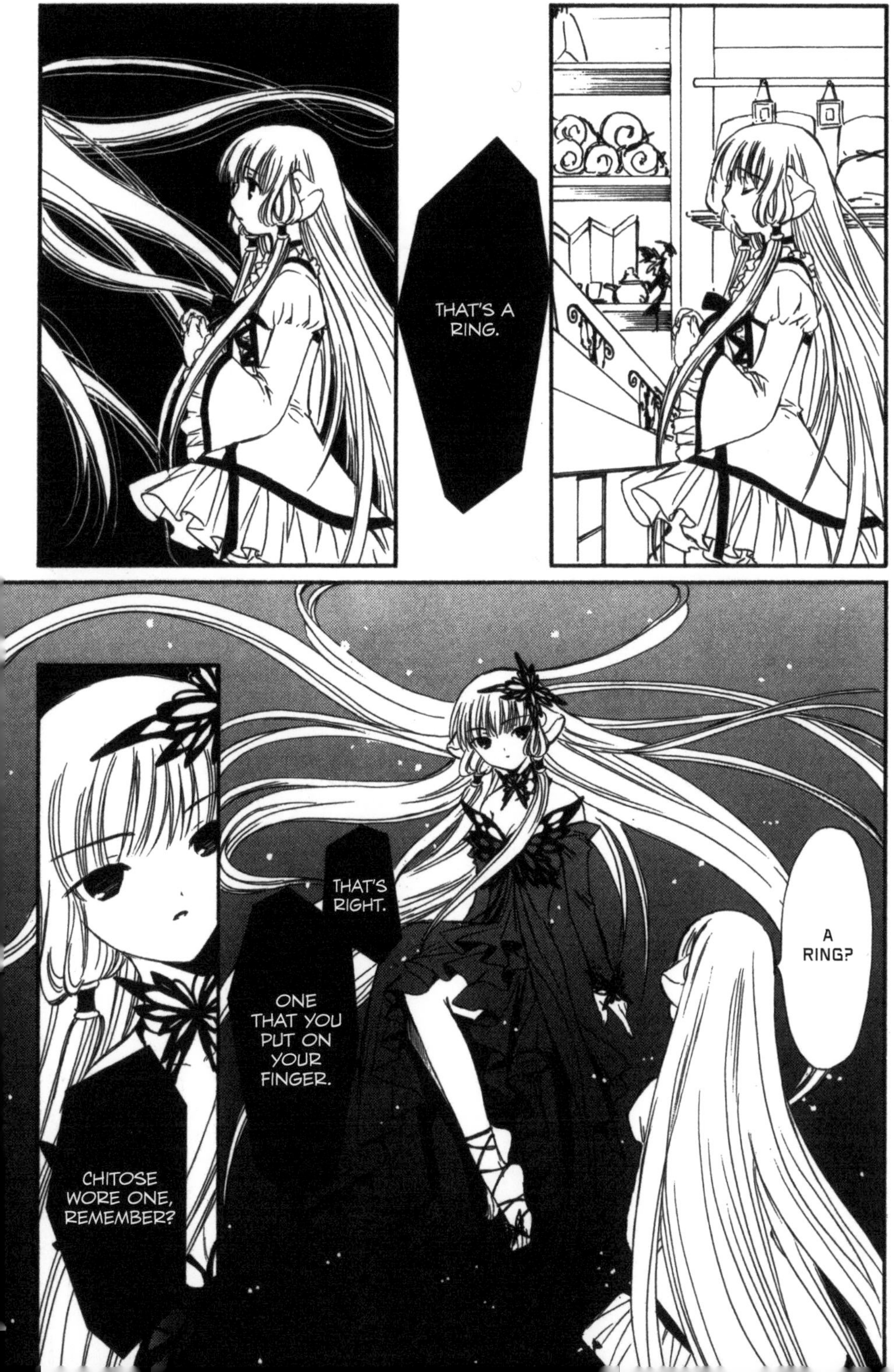
THAT'S A RING.
A RING?
THAT'S RIGHT.
ONE THAT YOU PUT ON YOUR FINGER.
CHITOSE WORE ONE, REMEMBER?

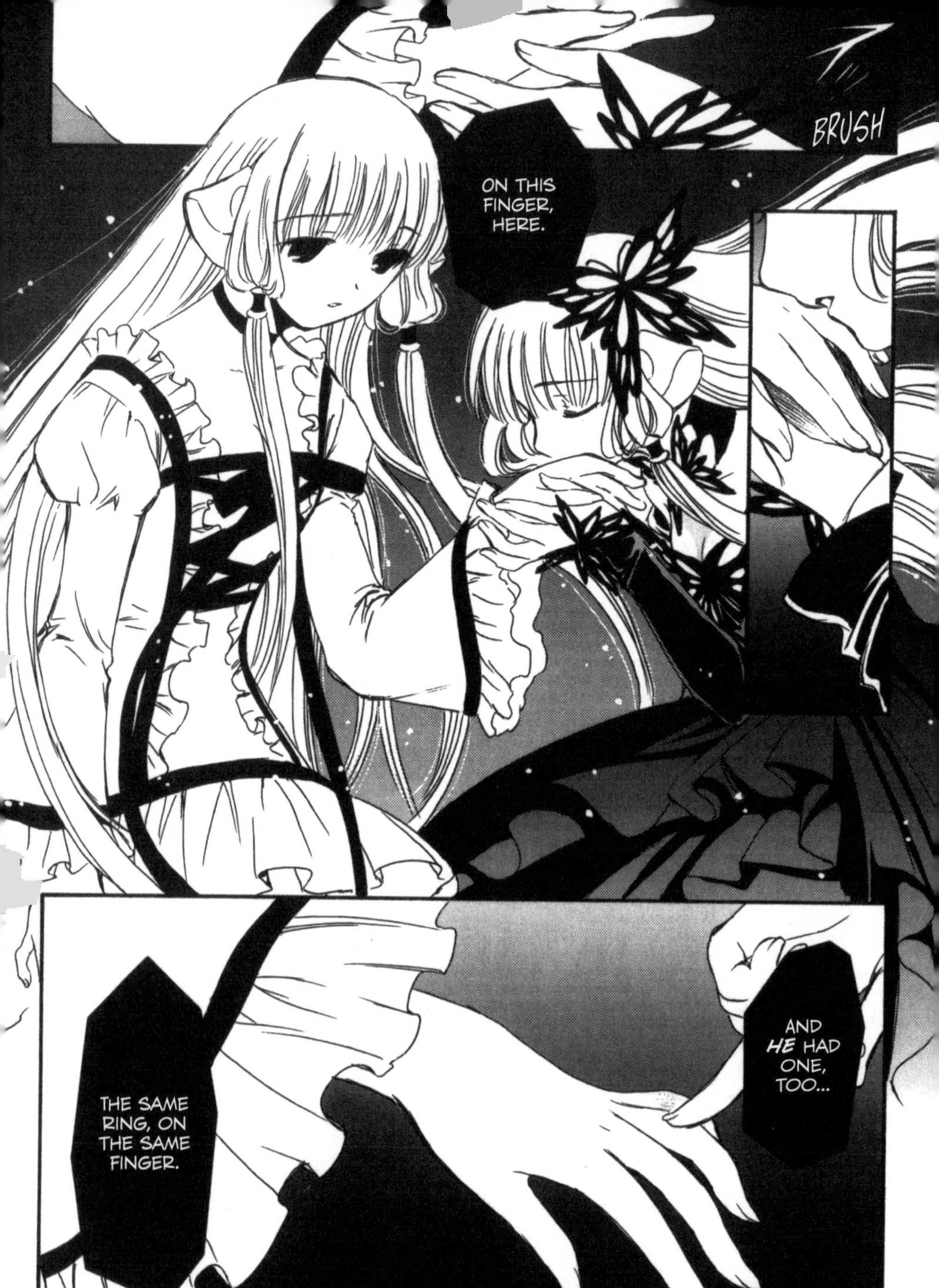
BRUSH
ON THIS FINGER, HERE.
AND *HE* HAD ONE, TOO...
THE SAME RING, ON THE SAME FINGER.

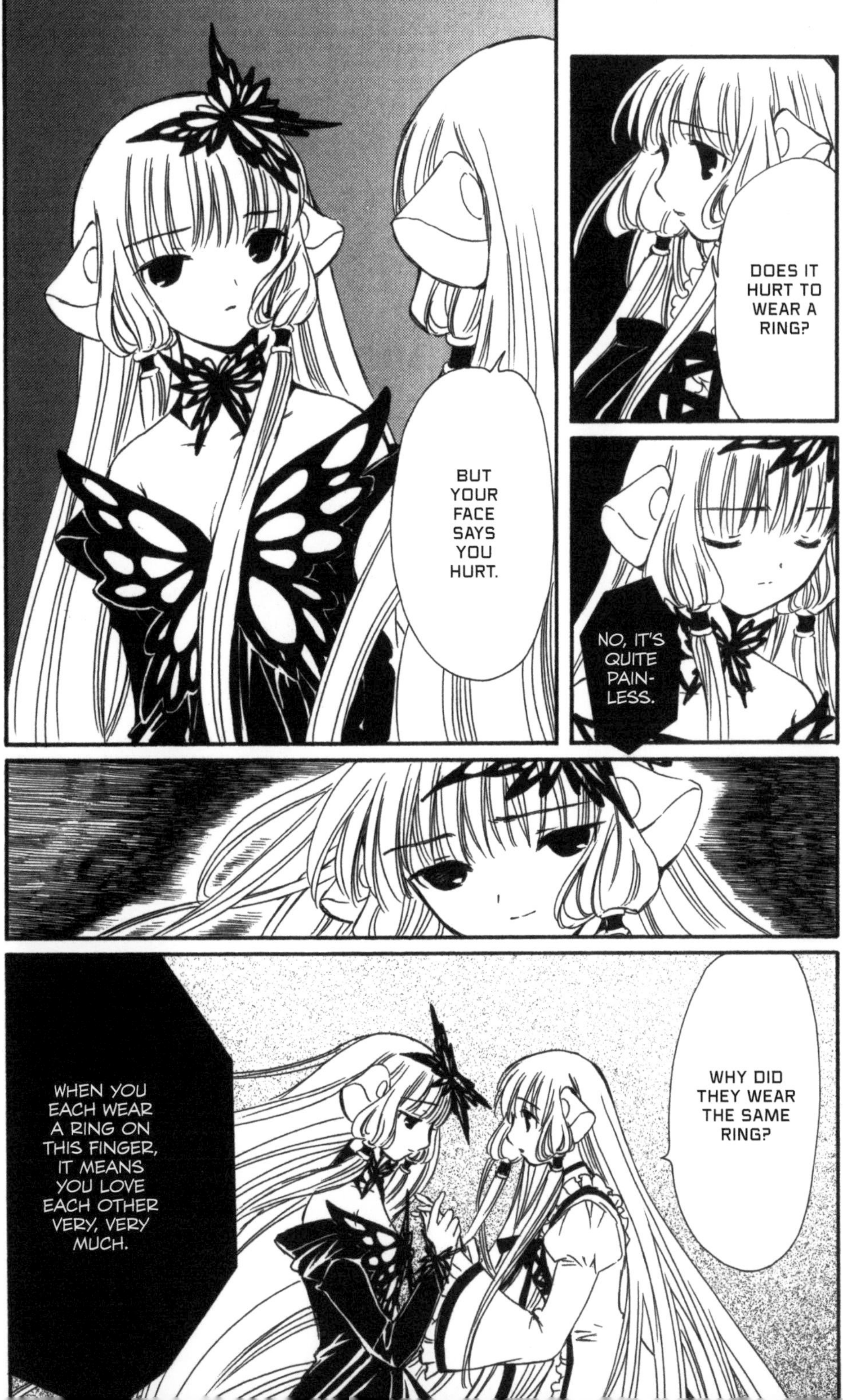
DOES IT HURT TO WEAR A RING?
NO, IT'S QUITE PAIN-LESS.
BUT YOUR FACE SAYS YOU HURT.
WHY DID THEY WEAR THE SAME RING?
WHEN YOU EACH WEAR A RING ON THIS FINGER, IT MEANS YOU LOVE EACH OTHER VERY, VERY MUCH.

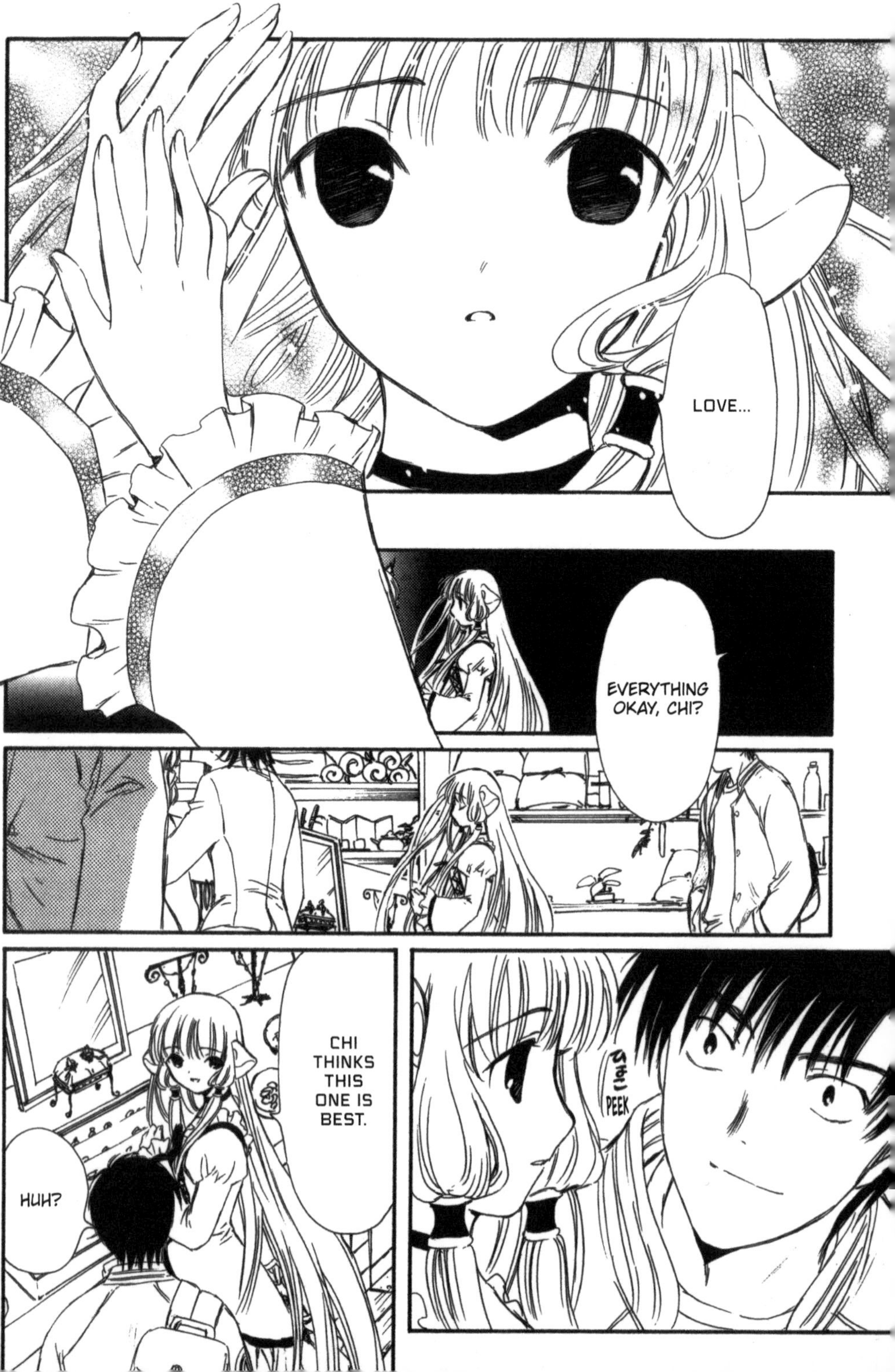
LOVE...
EVERYTHING OKAY, CHI?
PEEK
CHI THINKS THIS ONE IS BEST.
HUH?

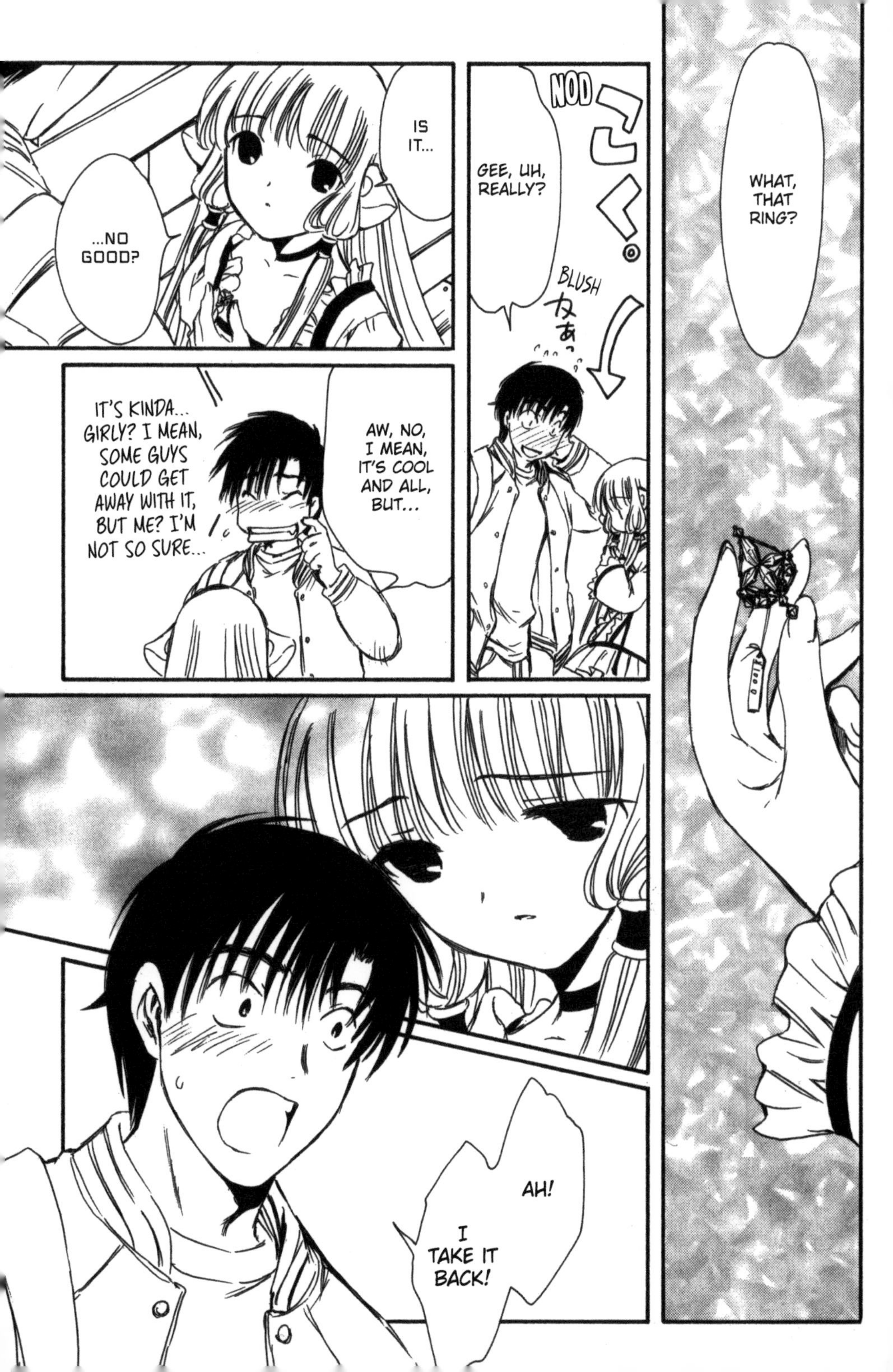
WHAT, THAT RING?
NOD
GEE, UH, REALLY?
BLUSH
IS IT...
...NO GOOD?
AW, NO, I MEAN, IT'S COOL AND ALL, BUT...
IT'S KINDA... GIRLY? I MEAN, SOME GUYS COULD GET AWAY WITH IT, BUT ME? I'M NOT SO SURE...
AH!
I TAKE IT BACK!

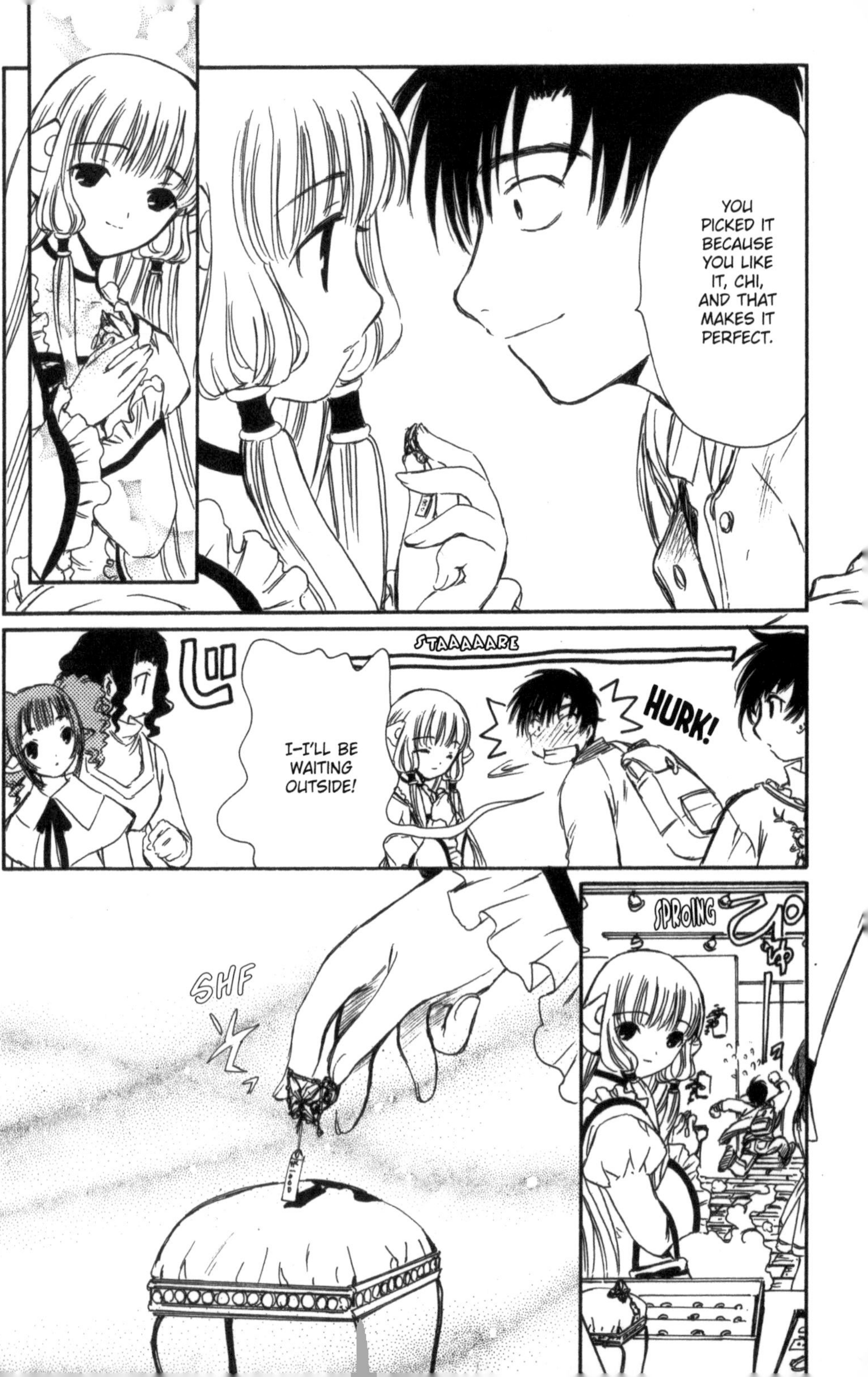
YOU PICKED IT BECAUSE YOU LIKE IT, CHI, AND THAT MAKES IT PERFECT.
HURK!
STAAAAARE
I-I'LL BE WAITING OUTSIDE!
SPROING
SHF

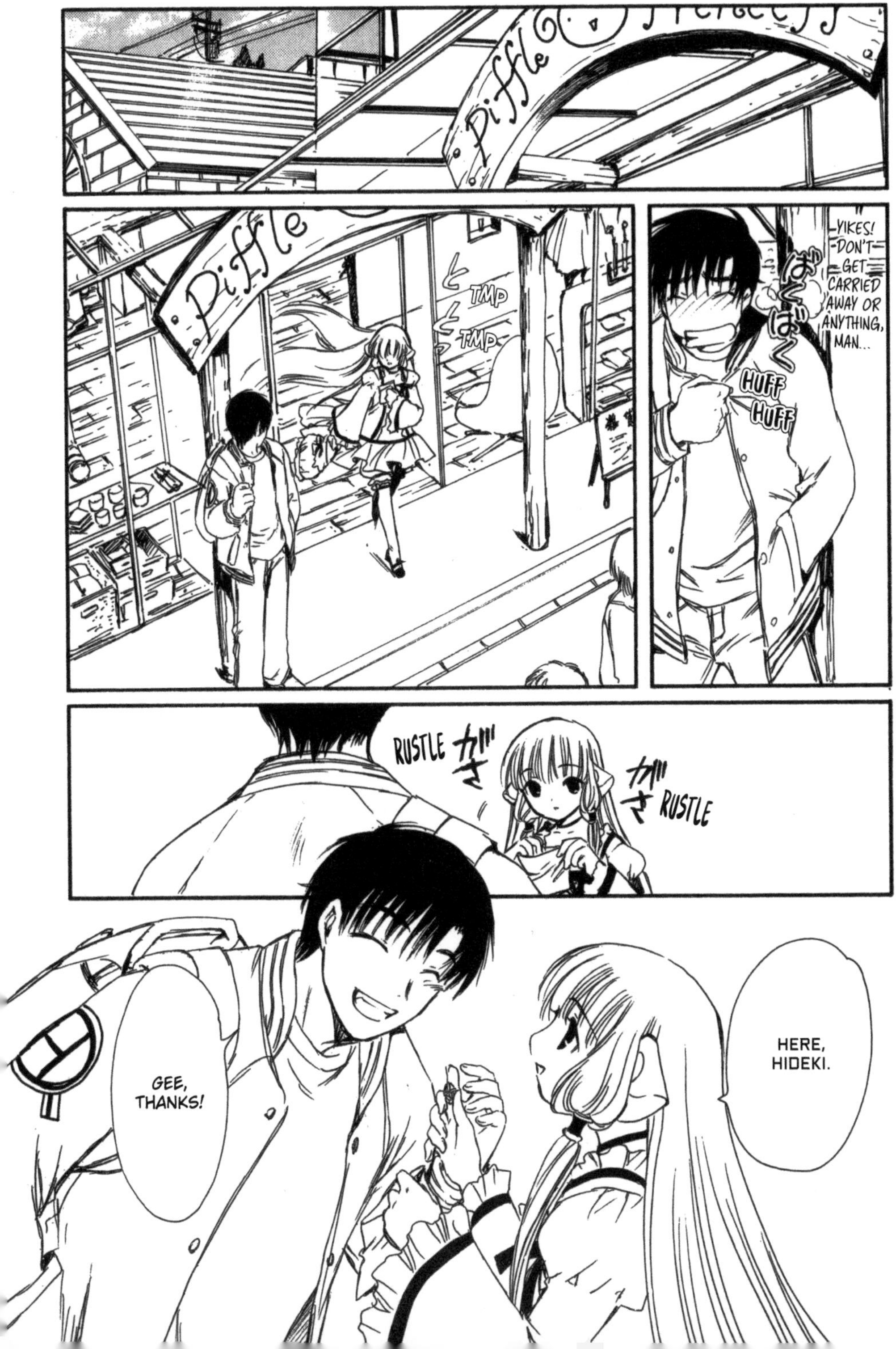
Piffle
YIKES! DON'T GET CARRIED AWAY OR ANYTHING, MAN...
ばくばく
HUFF HUFF
Piffle
TMP
TMP
がさ RUSTLE
がさ RUSTLE
HERE, HIDEKI.
GEE, THANKS!

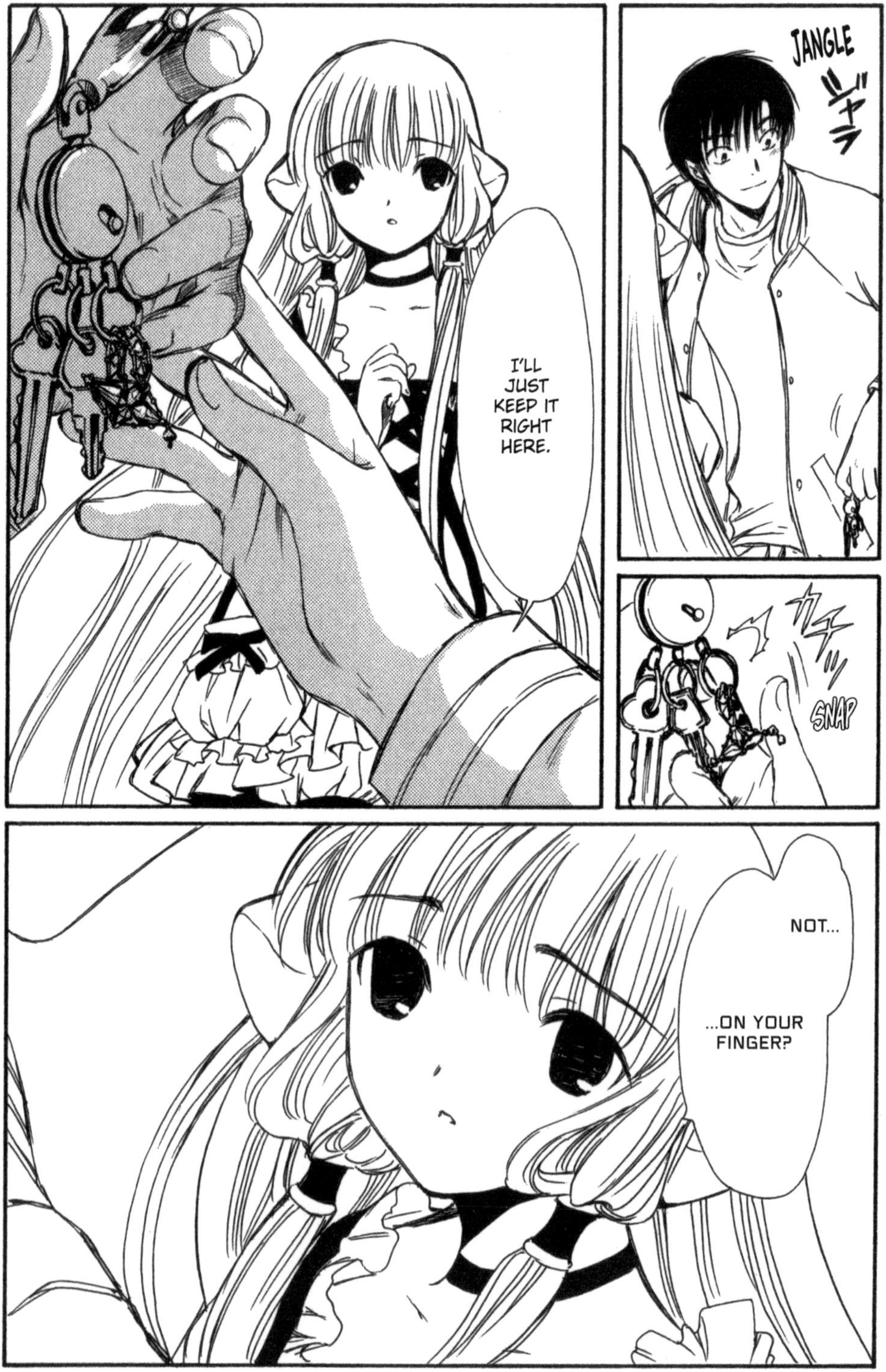
JANGLE
ジャラ
カチッ
SNAP
I'LL JUST KEEP IT RIGHT HERE.
NOT...
...ON YOUR FINGER?

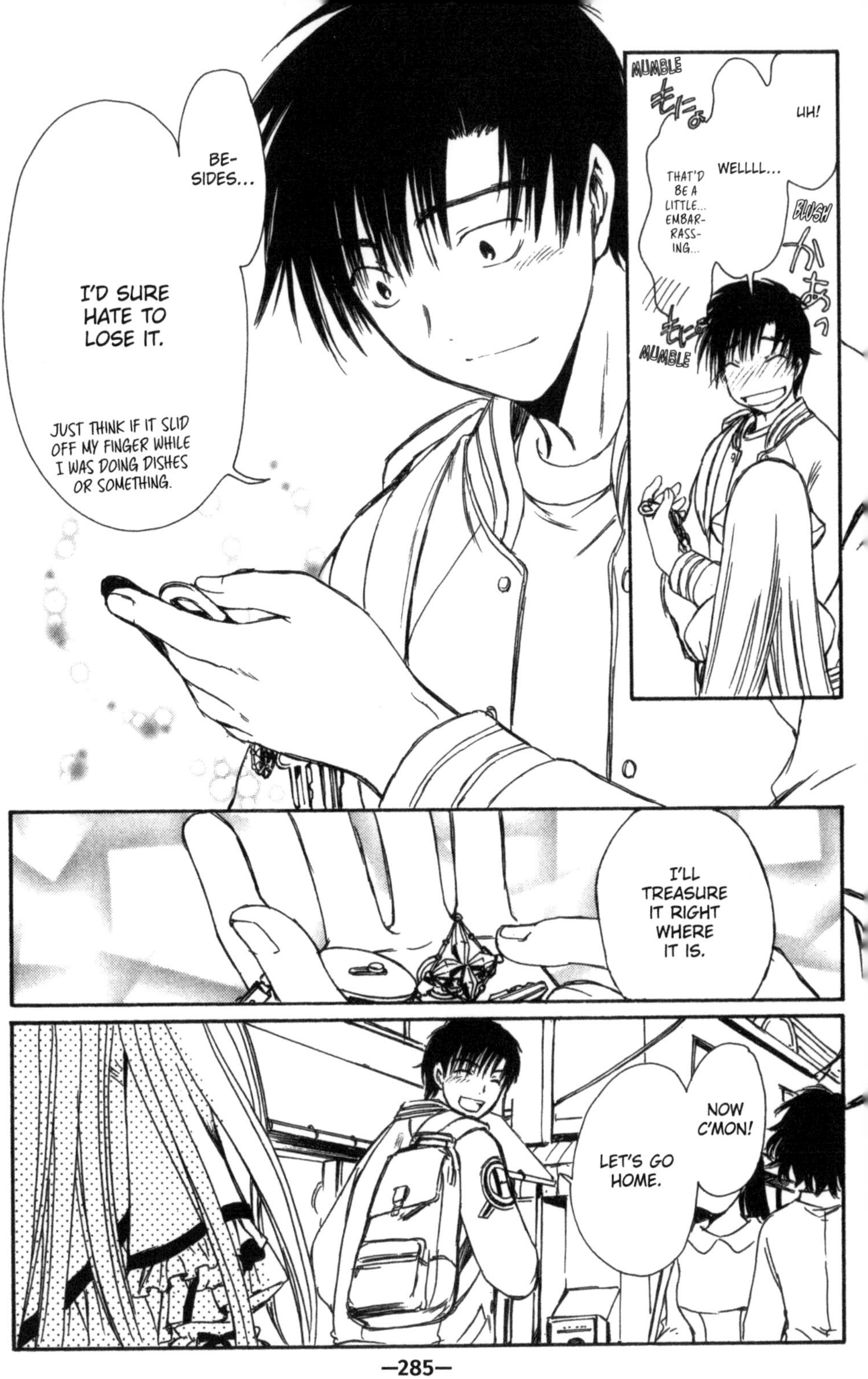
UH! WELLLL...
THAT'D BE A LITTLE... EMBAR-RASS-ING...
MUMBLE
BLUSH
MUMBLE
BE-SIDES...
I'D SURE HATE TO LOSE IT.
JUST THINK IF IT SLID OFF MY FINGER WHILE I WAS DOING DISHES OR SOMETHING.
I'LL TREASURE IT RIGHT WHERE IT IS.
NOW C'MON!
LET'S GO HOME.

ガサッ
RUSTLE

〈chapter.67〉 end

⟨chapter.68⟩

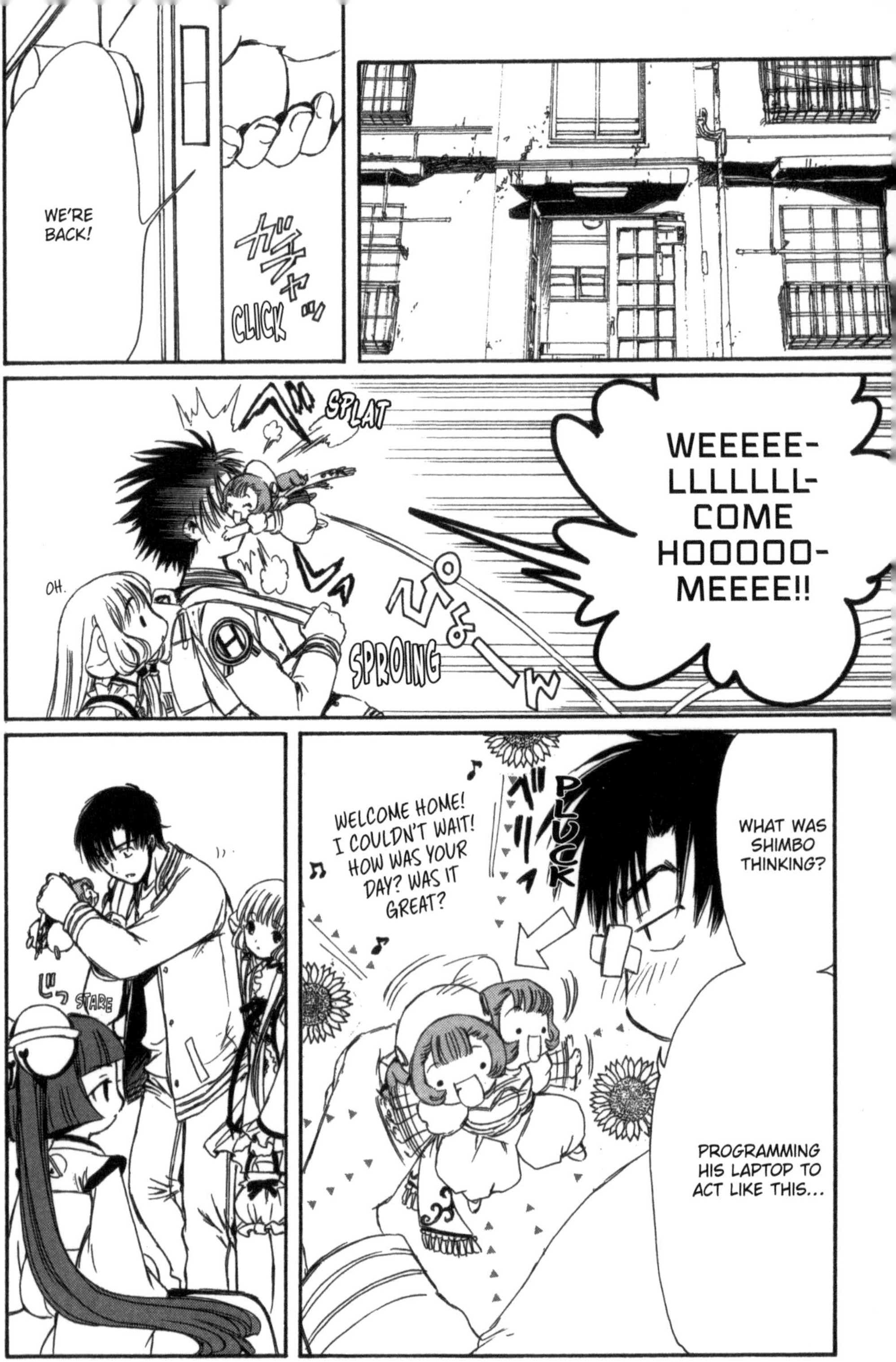
WE'RE BACK!
CLICK
WEEEEE-LLLLLLL-COME HOOOOO-MEEEE!!
SPLAT
SPROING
OH.
WHAT WAS SHIMBO THINKING?
PLUCK
WELCOME HOME! I COULDN'T WAIT! HOW WAS YOUR DAY? WAS IT GREAT?
PROGRAMMING HIS LAPTOP TO ACT LIKE THIS...
STARE

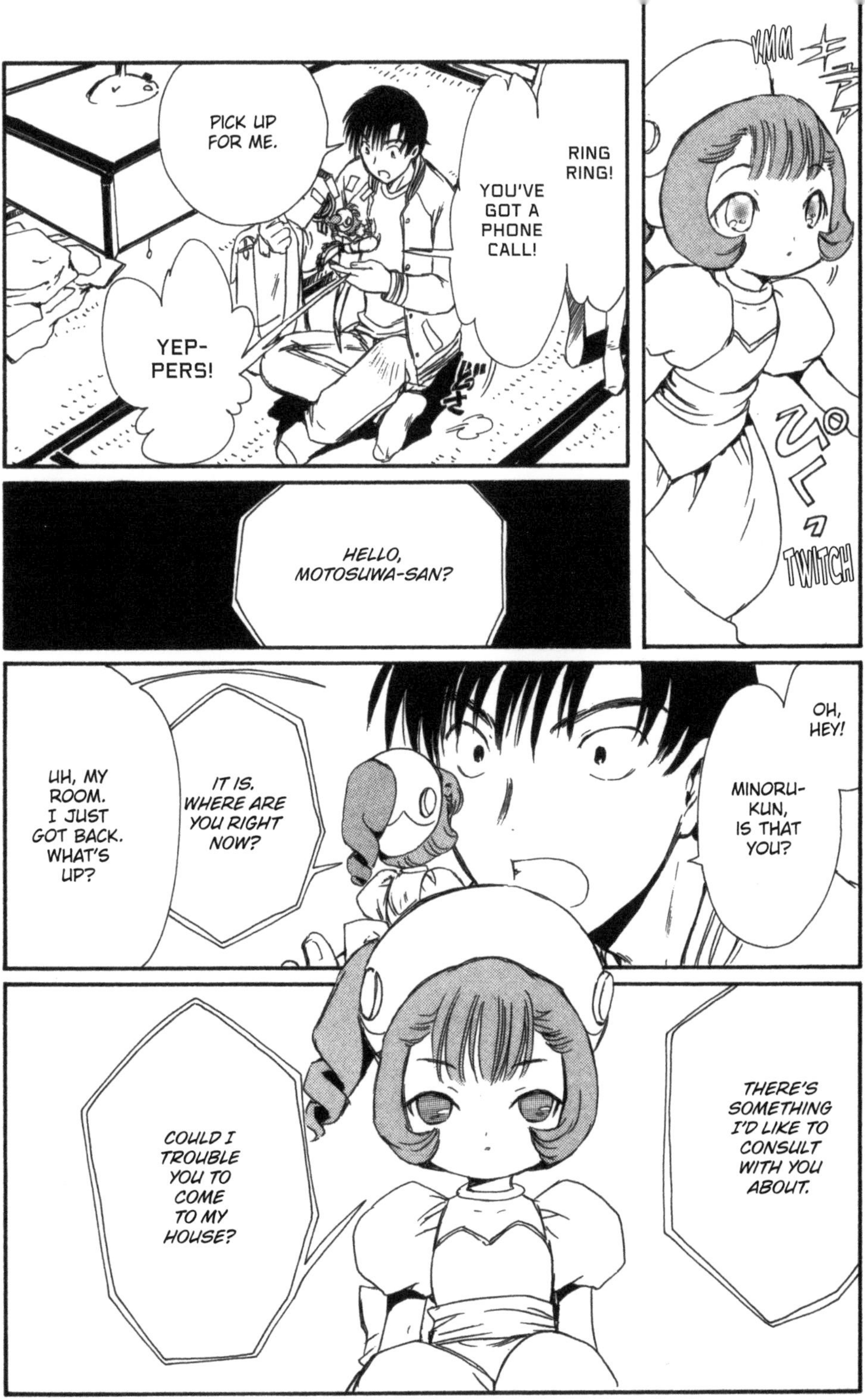
VMM
TWITCH
RING RING!
YOU'VE GOT A PHONE CALL!
PICK UP FOR ME.
YEP-PERS!
HELLO, MOTOSUWA-SAN?
OH, HEY!
MINORU-KUN, IS THAT YOU?
IT IS. WHERE ARE YOU RIGHT NOW?
UH, MY ROOM. I JUST GOT BACK. WHAT'S UP?
THERE'S SOMETHING I'D LIKE TO CONSULT WITH YOU ABOUT.
COULD I TROUBLE YOU TO COME TO MY HOUSE?

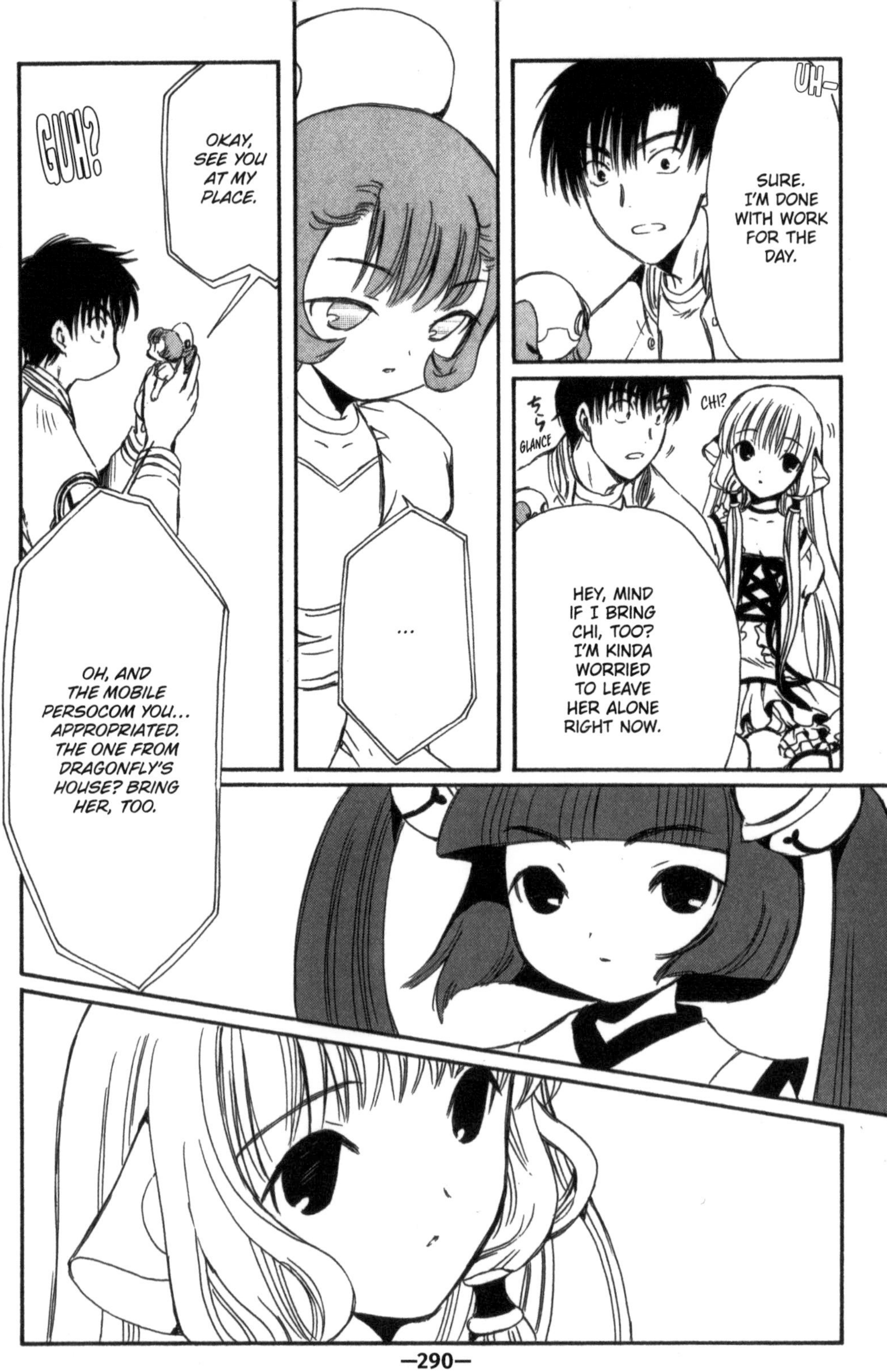
UH–
SURE. I'M DONE WITH WORK FOR THE DAY.
ちら
GLANCE
CHI?
HEY, MIND IF I BRING CHI, TOO? I'M KINDA WORRIED TO LEAVE HER ALONE RIGHT NOW.
...
OKAY, SEE YOU AT MY PLACE.
GUH?
OH, AND THE MOBILE PERSOCOM YOU... APPROPRIATED. THE ONE FROM DRAGONFLY'S HOUSE? BRING HER, TOO.

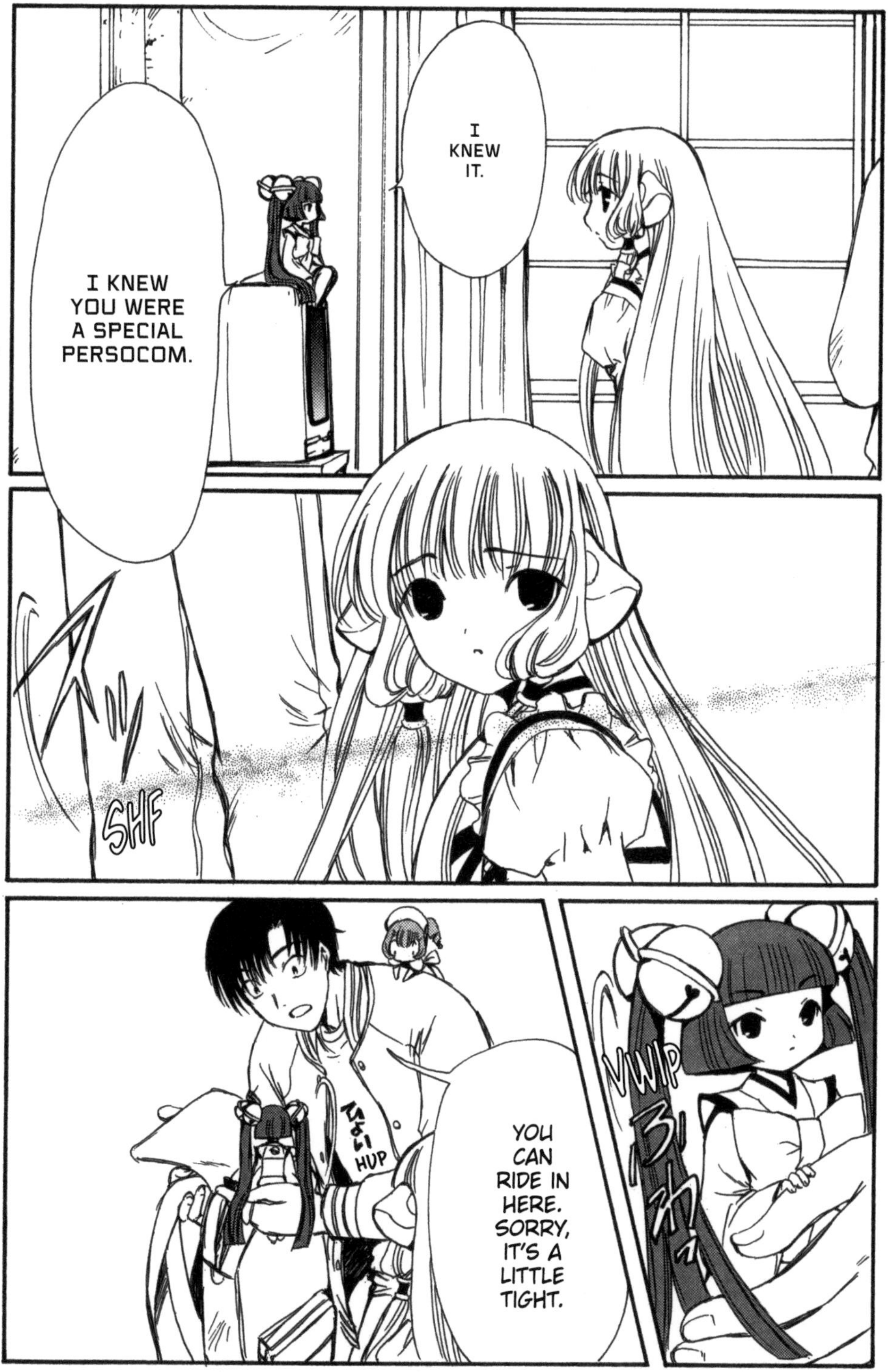
I KNEW IT.
I KNEW YOU WERE A SPECIAL PERSOCOM.
SHF
VWIP
YOU CAN RIDE IN HERE. SORRY, IT'S A LITTLE TIGHT.
HUP

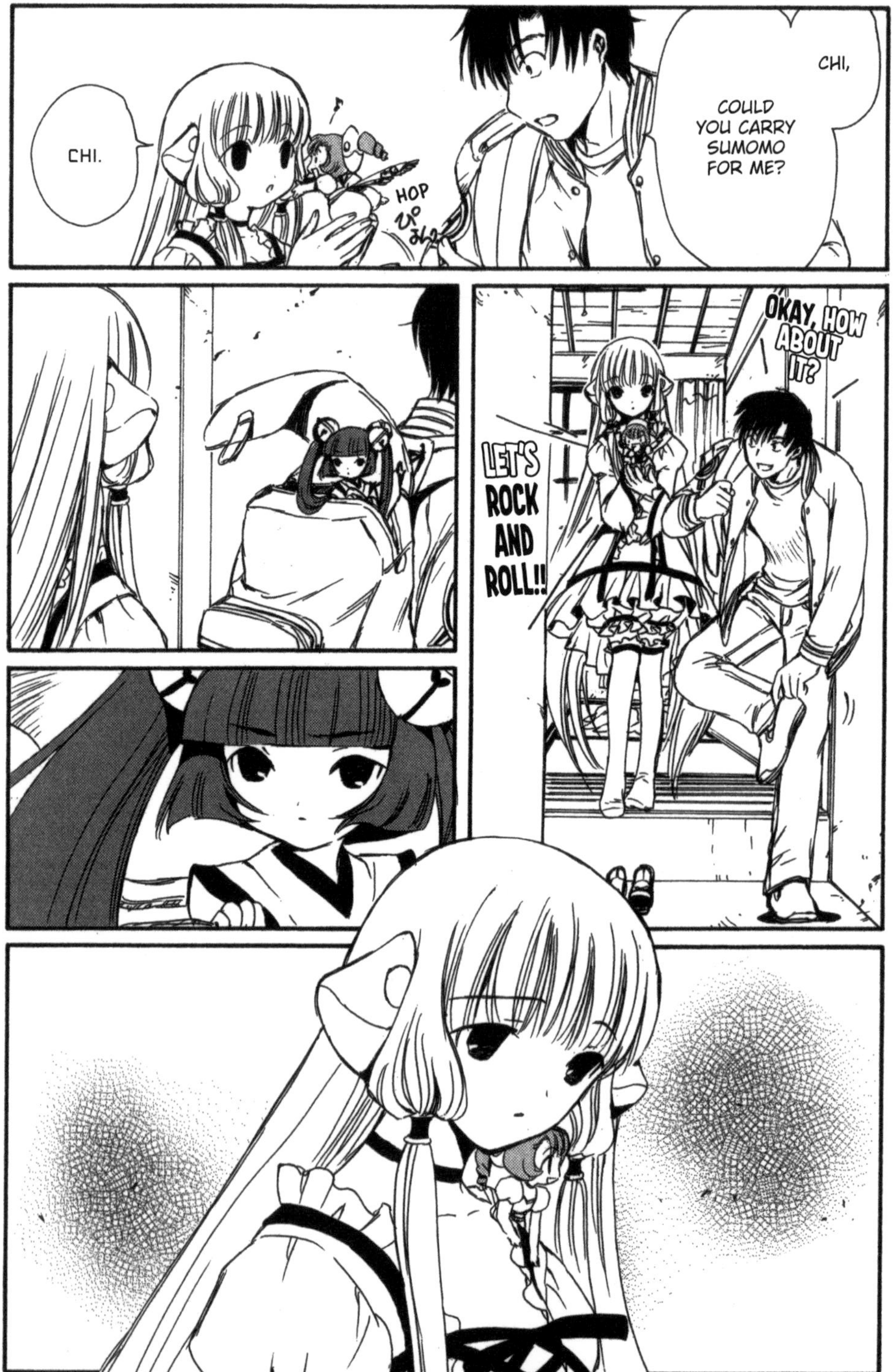
CHI,
COULD YOU CARRY SUMOMO FOR ME?
HOP ぴょん
CHI.
OKAY, HOW ABOUT IT?
LET'S ROCK AND ROLL!!

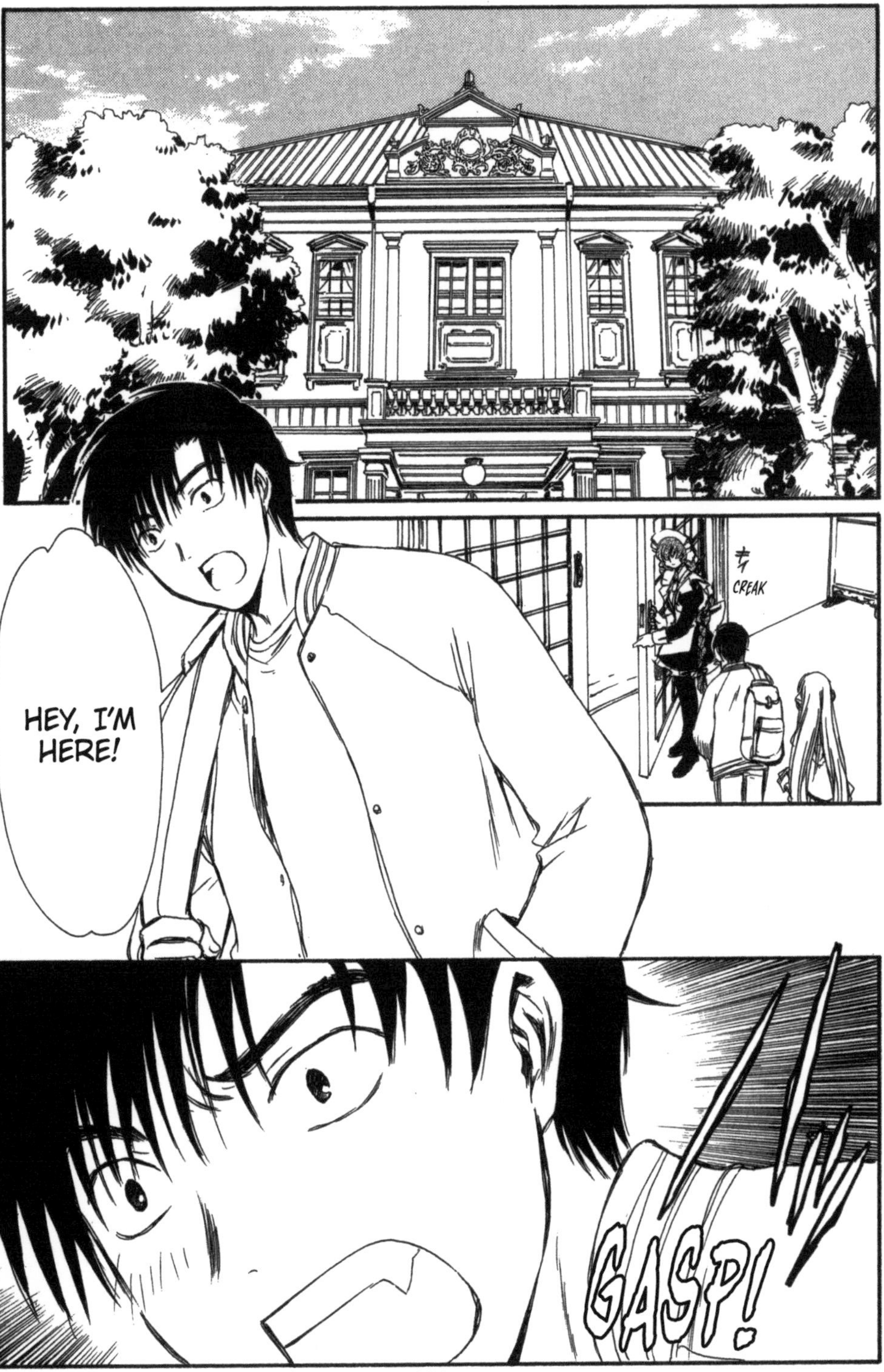
HEY, I'M HERE!
キィ
CREAK
GASP!

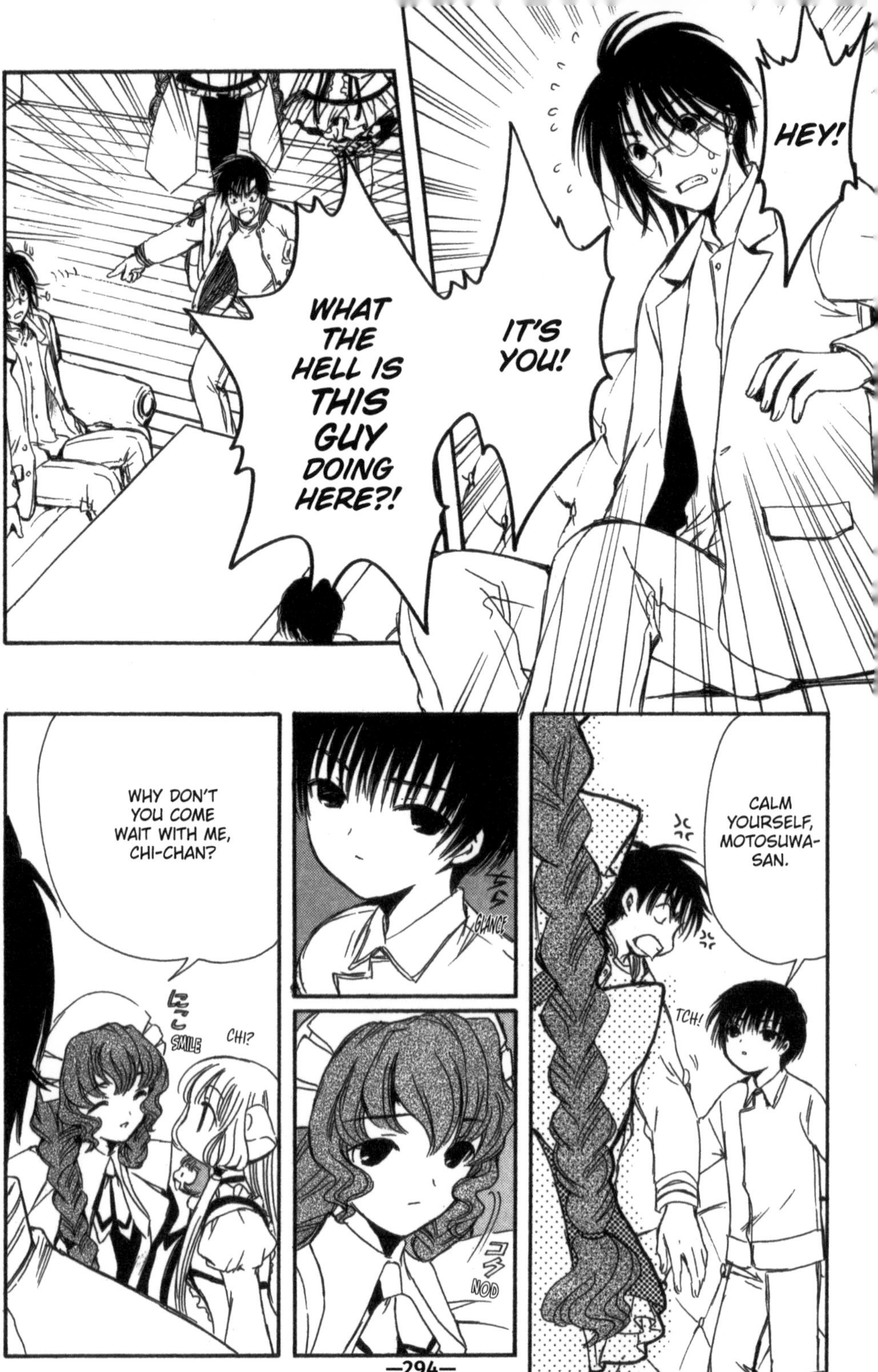
HEY!
IT'S YOU!
WHAT THE HELL IS THIS GUY DOING HERE?!
CALM YOURSELF, MOTOSUWA-SAN.
TCH!
GLANCE
NOD
WHY DON'T YOU COME WAIT WITH ME, CHI-CHAN?
SMILE
CHI?

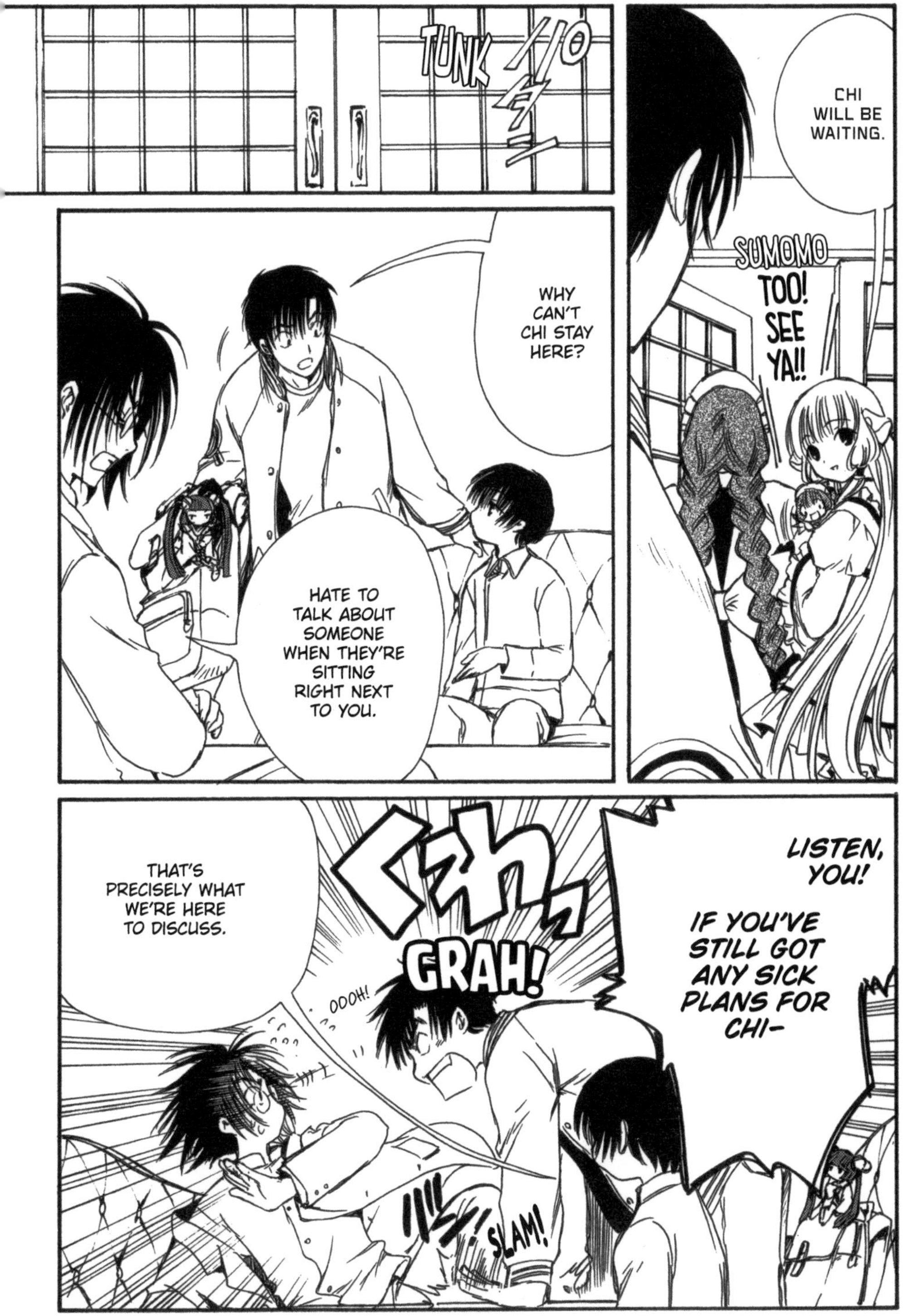
CHI WILL BE WAITING.
SUMOMO TOO! SEE YA!!
TUNK
WHY CAN'T CHI STAY HERE?
HATE TO TALK ABOUT SOMEONE WHEN THEY'RE SITTING RIGHT NEXT TO YOU.
LISTEN, YOU!
IF YOU'VE STILL GOT ANY SICK PLANS FOR CHI-
GRAH!
OOOH!
SLAM!
THAT'S PRECISELY WHAT WE'RE HERE TO DISCUSS.

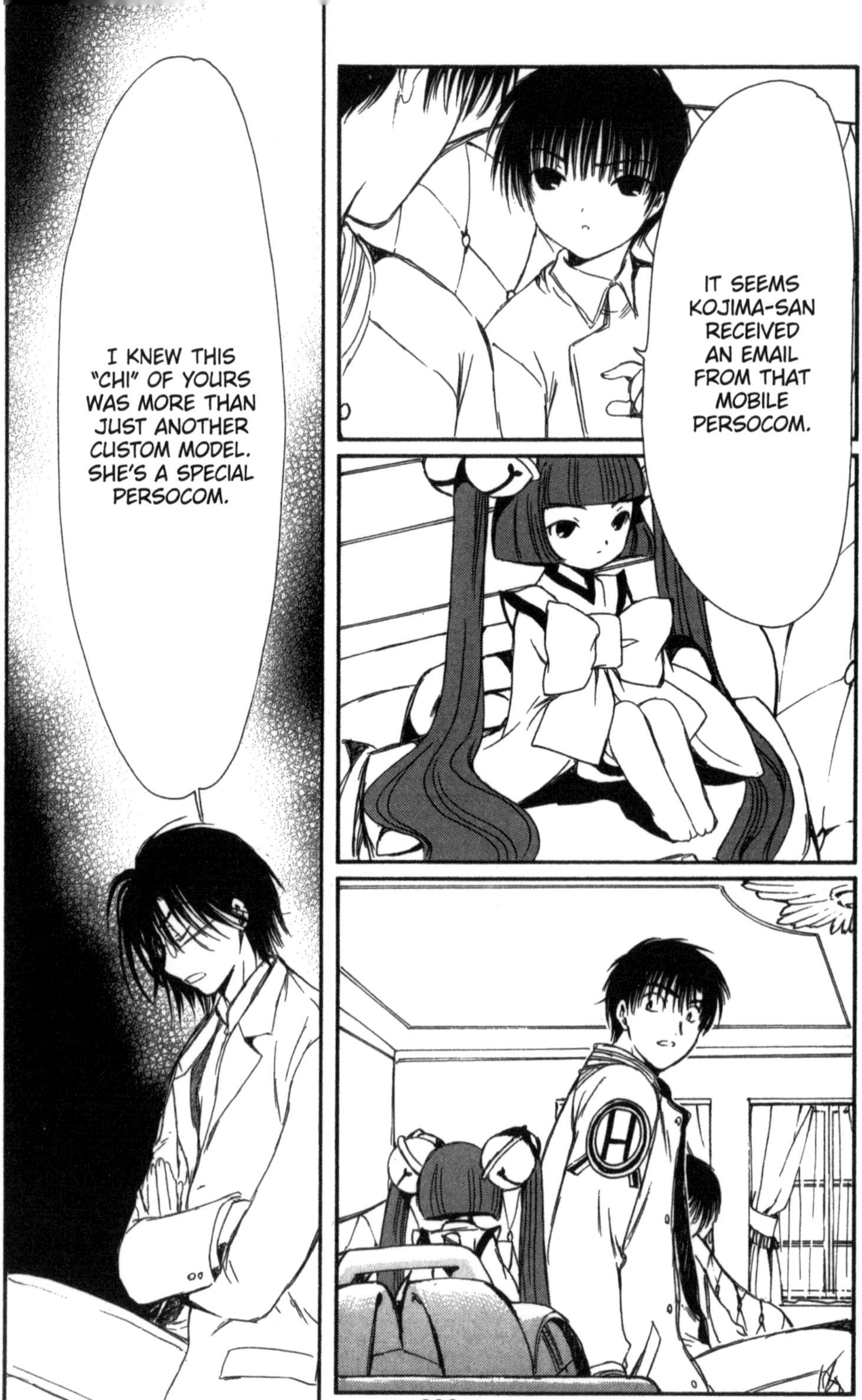
IT SEEMS KOJIMA-SAN RECEIVED AN EMAIL FROM THAT MOBILE PERSOCOM.
I KNEW THIS "CHI" OF YOURS WAS MORE THAN JUST ANOTHER CUSTOM MODEL. SHE'S A SPECIAL PERSOCOM.

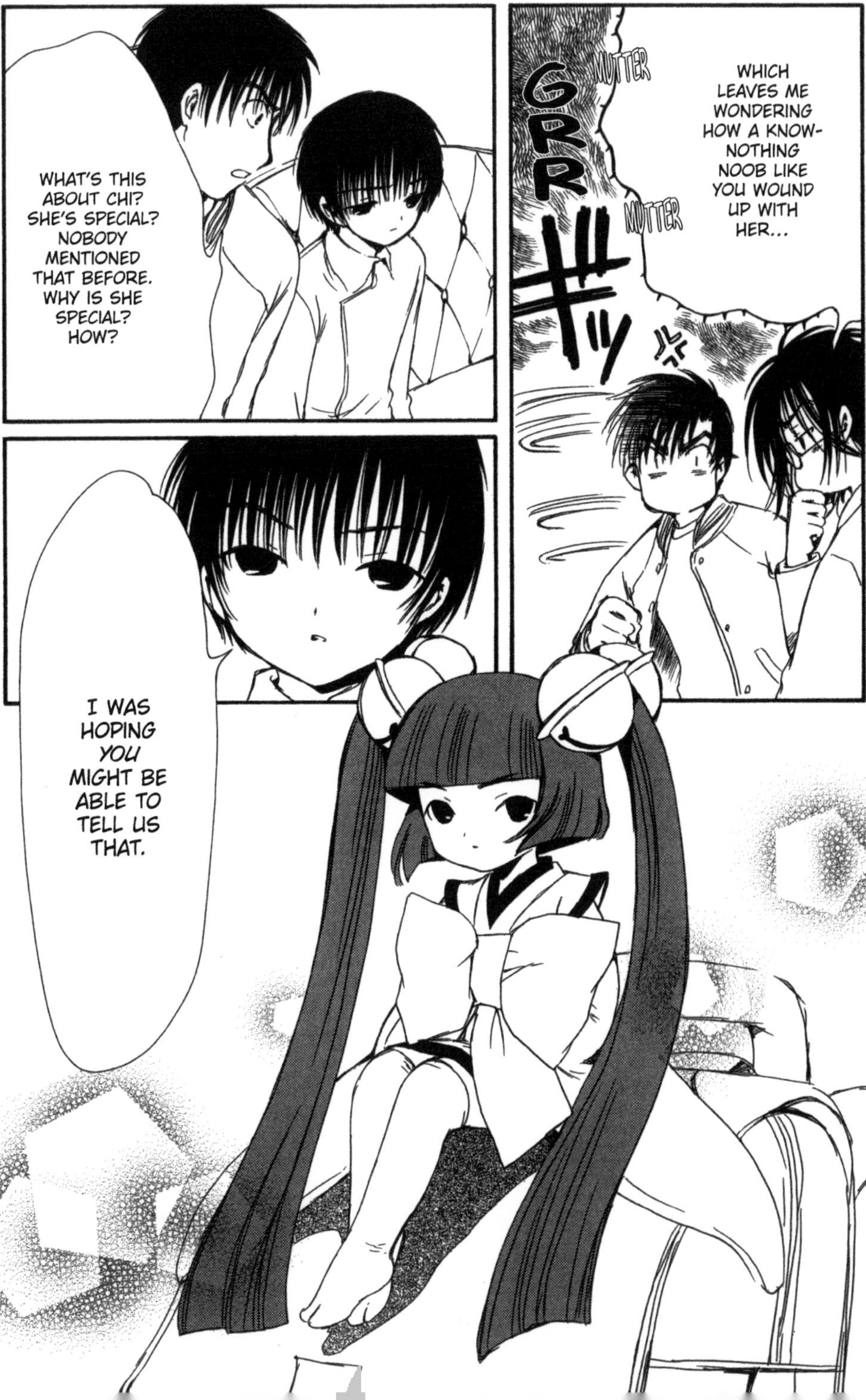

GRR
ギッ
MUTTER
MUTTER
WHICH LEAVES ME WONDERING HOW A KNOW-NOTHING NOOB LIKE YOU WOUND UP WITH HER...
WHAT'S THIS ABOUT CHI? SHE'S SPECIAL? NOBODY MENTIONED THAT BEFORE. WHY IS SHE SPECIAL? HOW?
I WAS HOPING *YOU* MIGHT BE ABLE TO TELL US THAT.

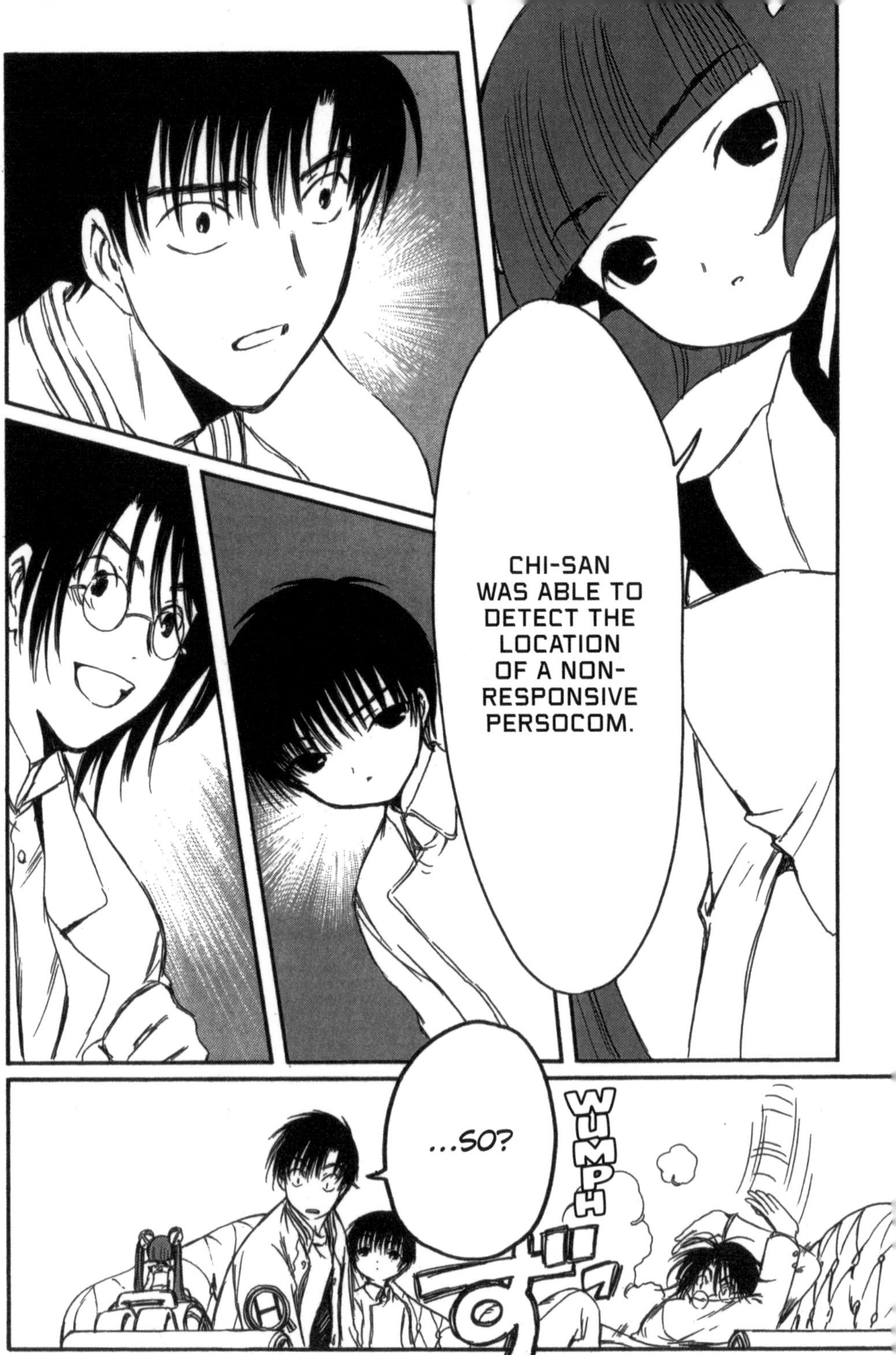
CHI-SAN WAS ABLE TO DETECT THE LOCATION OF A NON-RESPONSIVE PERSOCOM.
WUMPH
...SO?

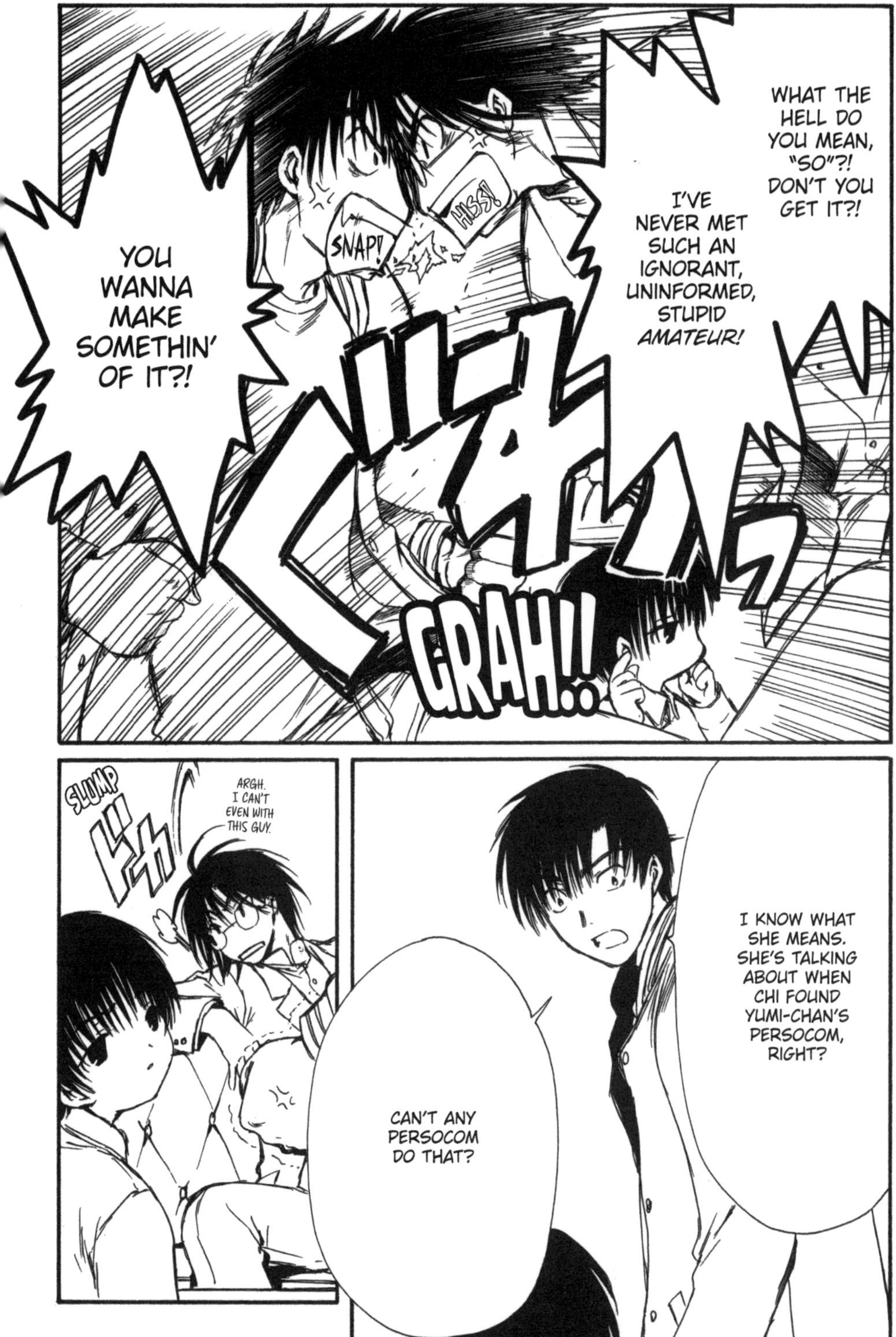
WHAT THE HELL DO YOU MEAN, "SO"?! DON'T YOU GET IT?!
I'VE NEVER MET SUCH AN IGNORANT, UNINFORMED, STUPID *AMATEUR!*
HISS!
SNAP!
YOU WANNA MAKE SOMETHIN' OF IT?!
GRAH!!
I KNOW WHAT SHE MEANS. SHE'S TALKING ABOUT WHEN CHI FOUND YUMI-CHAN'S PERSOCOM, RIGHT?
CAN'T ANY PERSOCOM DO THAT?
ARGH. I CAN'T EVEN WITH THIS GUY.
SLUMP

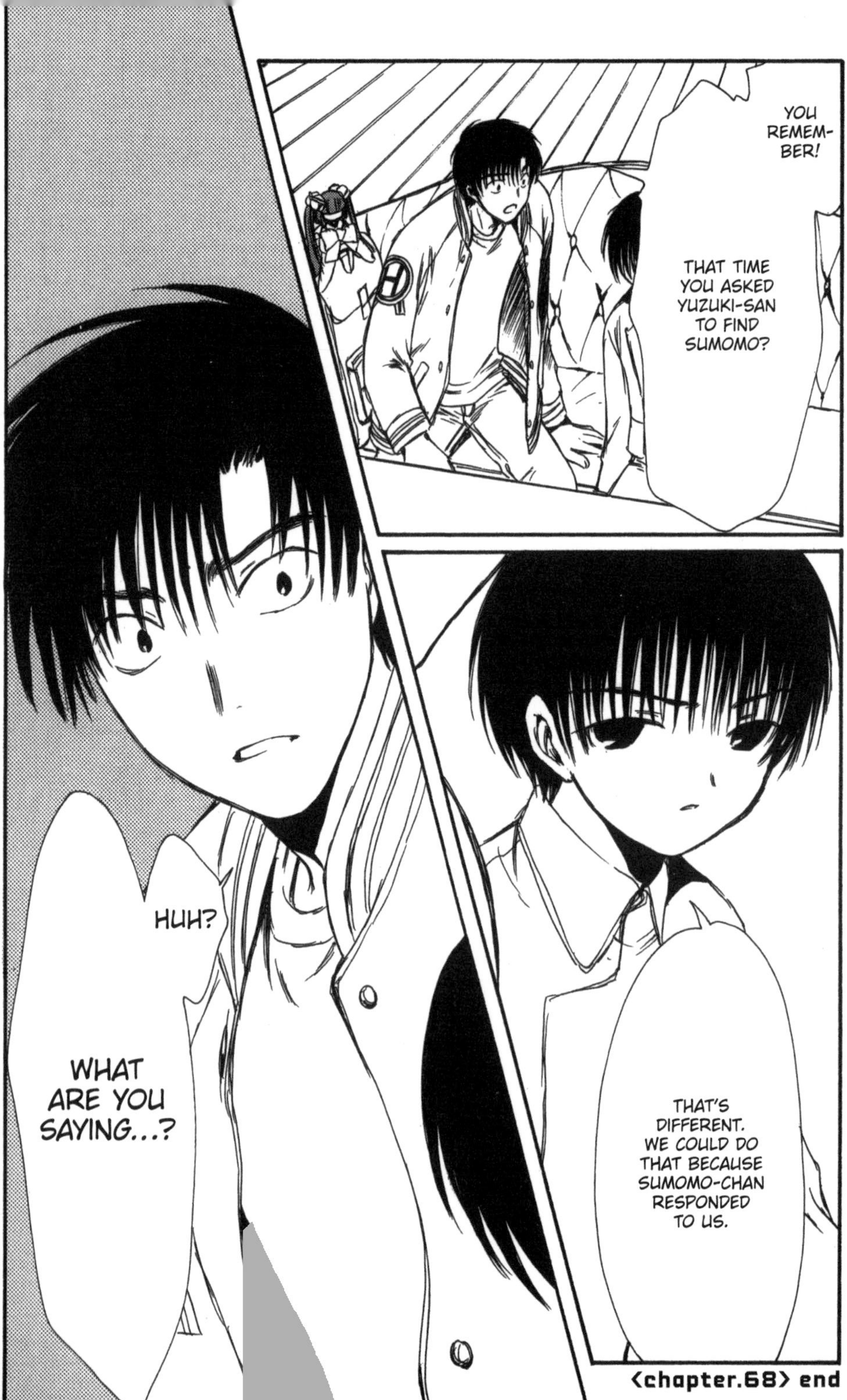
YOU REMEMBER!
THAT TIME YOU ASKED YUZUKI-SAN TO FIND SUMOMO?
THAT'S DIFFERENT. WE COULD DO THAT BECAUSE SUMOMO-CHAN RESPONDED TO US.
HUH?
WHAT ARE YOU SAYING...?

<chapter.68> end

〈chapter.69〉

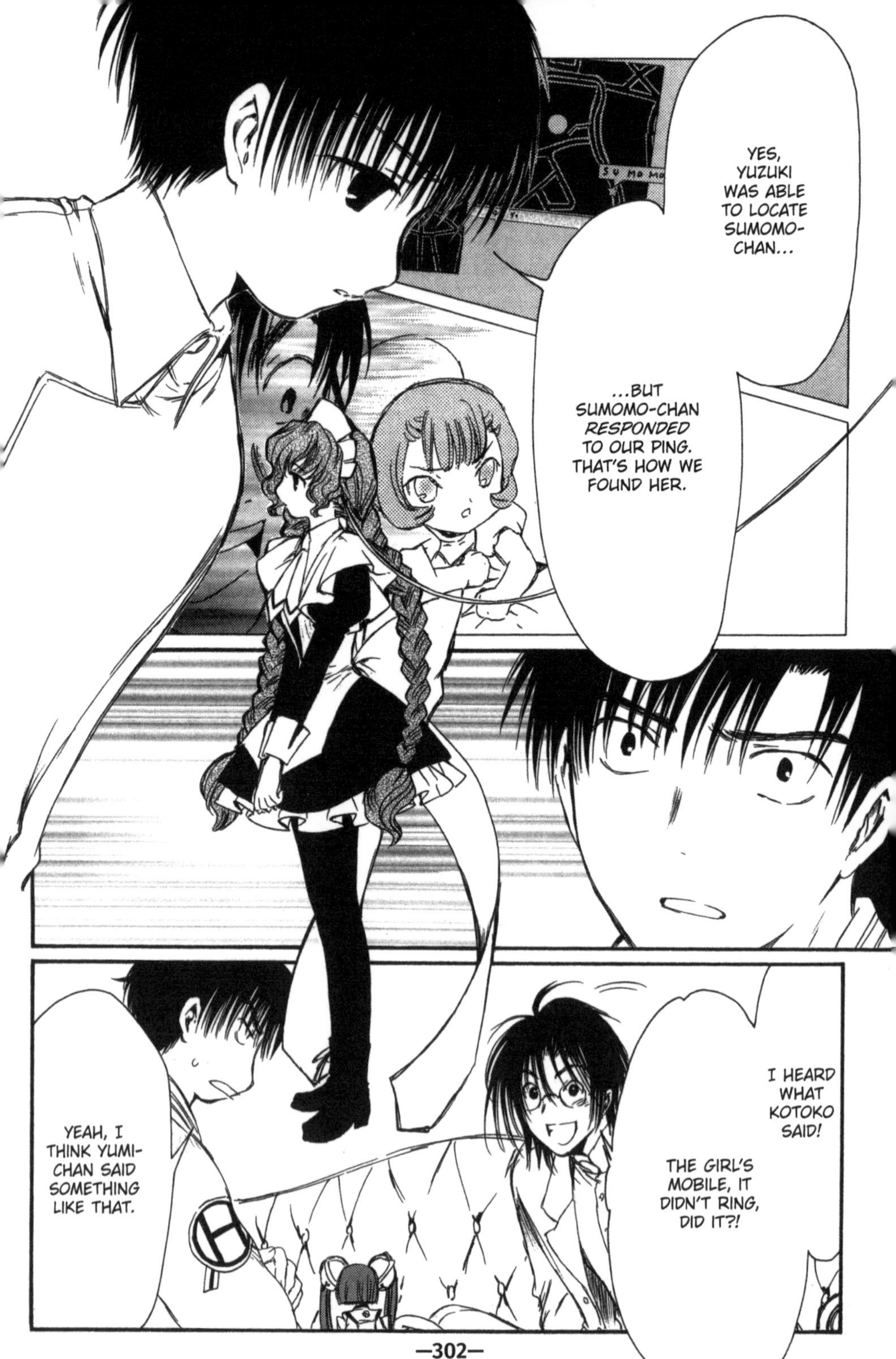
YES, YUZUKI WAS ABLE TO LOCATE SUMOMO-CHAN...
...BUT SUMOMO-CHAN *RESPONDED* TO OUR PING. THAT'S HOW WE FOUND HER.
I HEARD WHAT KOTOKO SAID!
THE GIRL'S MOBILE, IT DIDN'T RING, DID IT?!
YEAH, I THINK YUMI-CHAN SAID SOMETHING LIKE THAT.

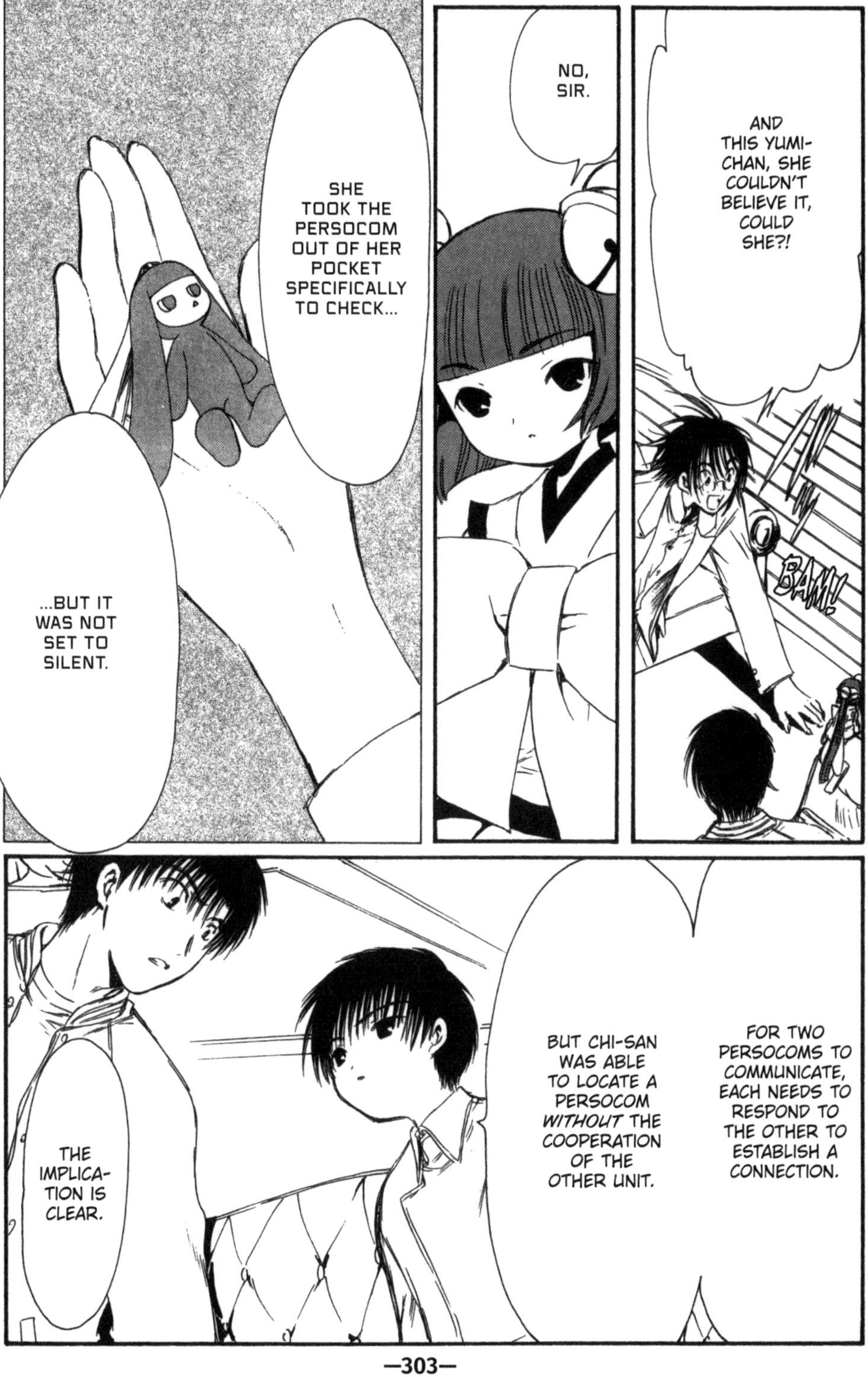

AND THIS YUMI-CHAN, SHE COULDN'T BELIEVE IT, COULD SHE?!
BAM!
NO, SIR.
SHE TOOK THE PERSOCOM OUT OF HER POCKET SPECIFICALLY TO CHECK...
...BUT IT WAS NOT SET TO SILENT.
FOR TWO PERSOCOMS TO COMMUNICATE, EACH NEEDS TO RESPOND TO THE OTHER TO ESTABLISH A CONNECTION.
BUT CHI-SAN WAS ABLE TO LOCATE A PERSOCOM *WITHOUT* THE COOPERATION OF THE OTHER UNIT.
THE IMPLICATION IS CLEAR.

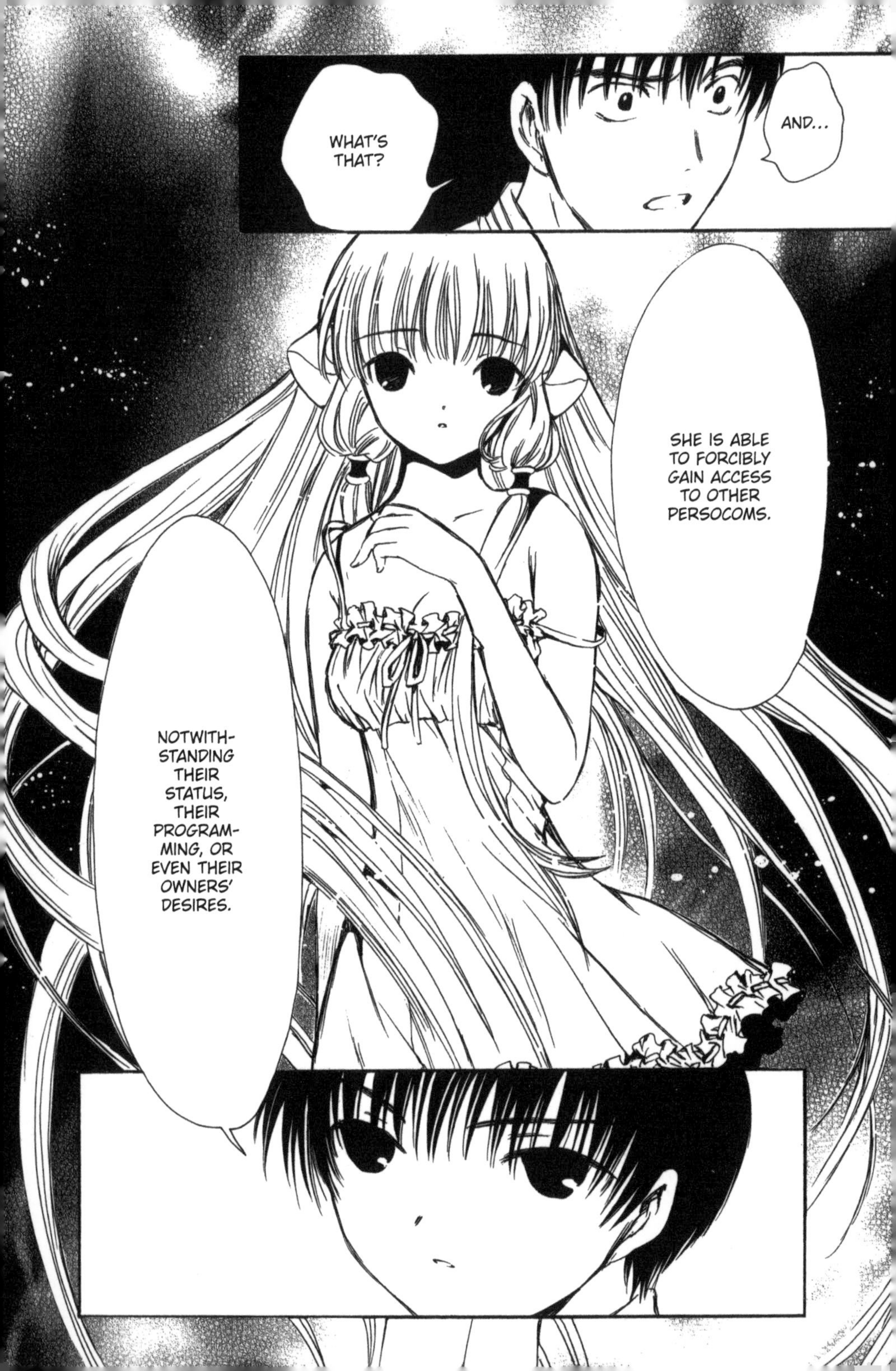
AND...
WHAT'S THAT?
SHE IS ABLE TO FORCIBLY GAIN ACCESS TO OTHER PERSOCOMS.
NOTWITH-STANDING THEIR STATUS, THEIR PROGRAM-MING, OR EVEN THEIR OWNERS' DESIRES.

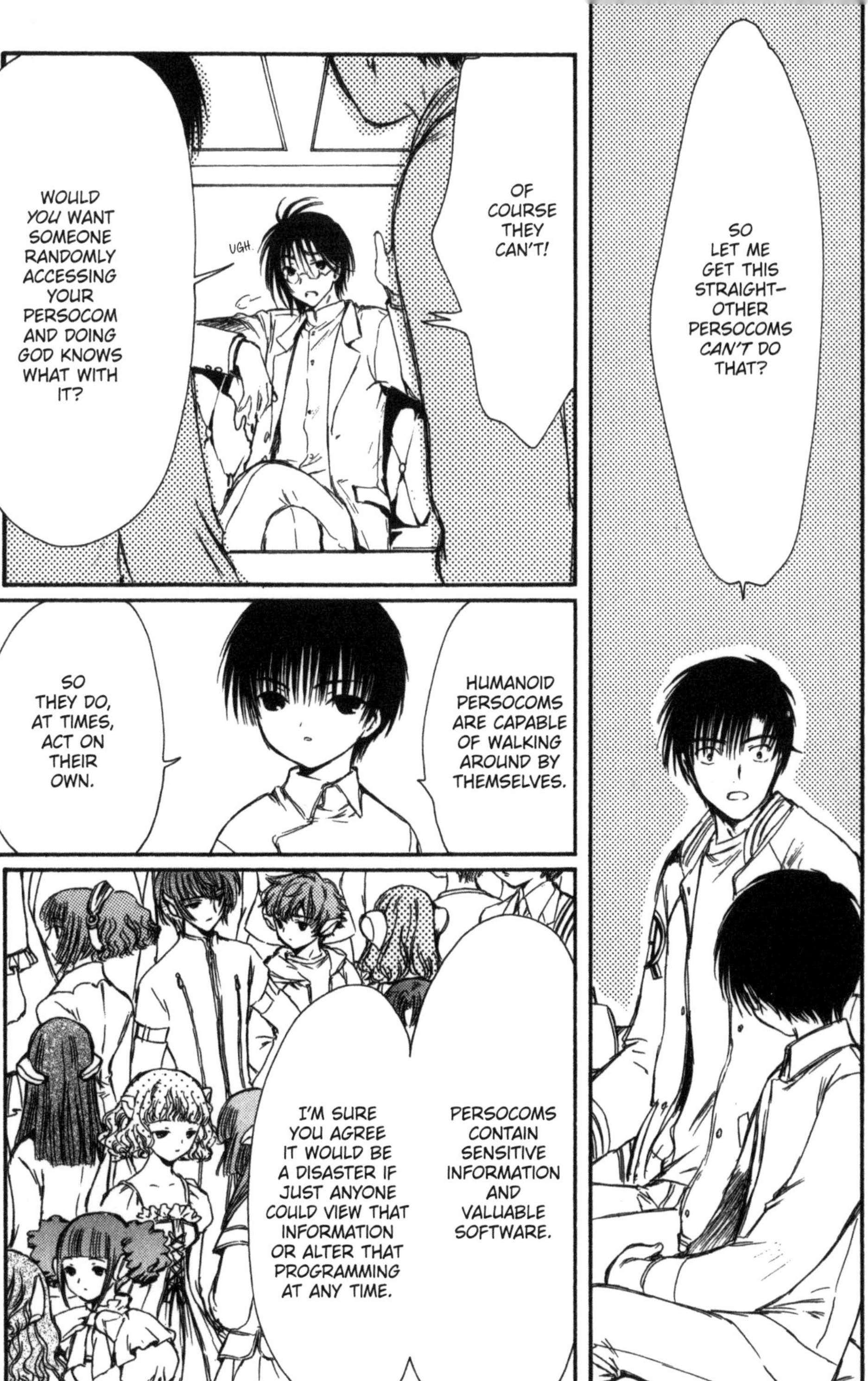
SO LET ME GET THIS STRAIGHT— OTHER PERSOCOMS *CAN'T* DO THAT?
OF COURSE THEY CAN'T!
UGH.
WOULD *YOU* WANT SOMEONE RANDOMLY ACCESSING YOUR PERSOCOM AND DOING GOD KNOWS WHAT WITH IT?
HUMANOID PERSOCOMS ARE CAPABLE OF WALKING AROUND BY THEMSELVES.
SO THEY DO, AT TIMES, ACT ON THEIR OWN.
PERSOCOMS CONTAIN SENSITIVE INFORMATION AND VALUABLE SOFTWARE.
I'M SURE YOU AGREE IT WOULD BE A DISASTER IF JUST ANYONE COULD VIEW THAT INFORMATION OR ALTER THAT PROGRAMMING AT ANY TIME.

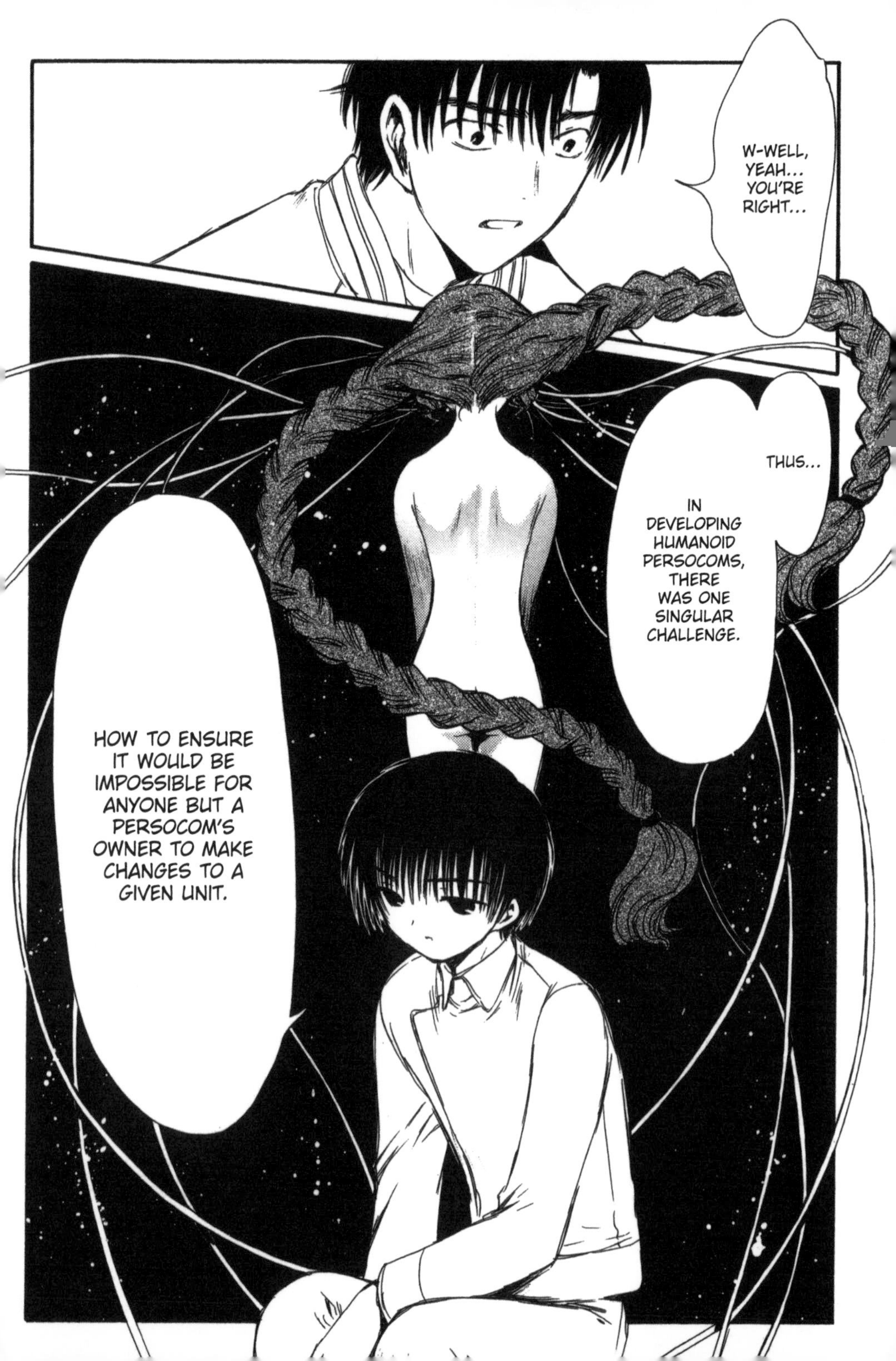
W-WELL, YEAH... YOU'RE RIGHT...
THUS...
IN DEVELOPING HUMANOID PERSOCOMS, THERE WAS ONE SINGULAR CHALLENGE.
HOW TO ENSURE IT WOULD BE IMPOSSIBLE FOR ANYONE BUT A PERSOCOM'S OWNER TO MAKE CHANGES TO A GIVEN UNIT.

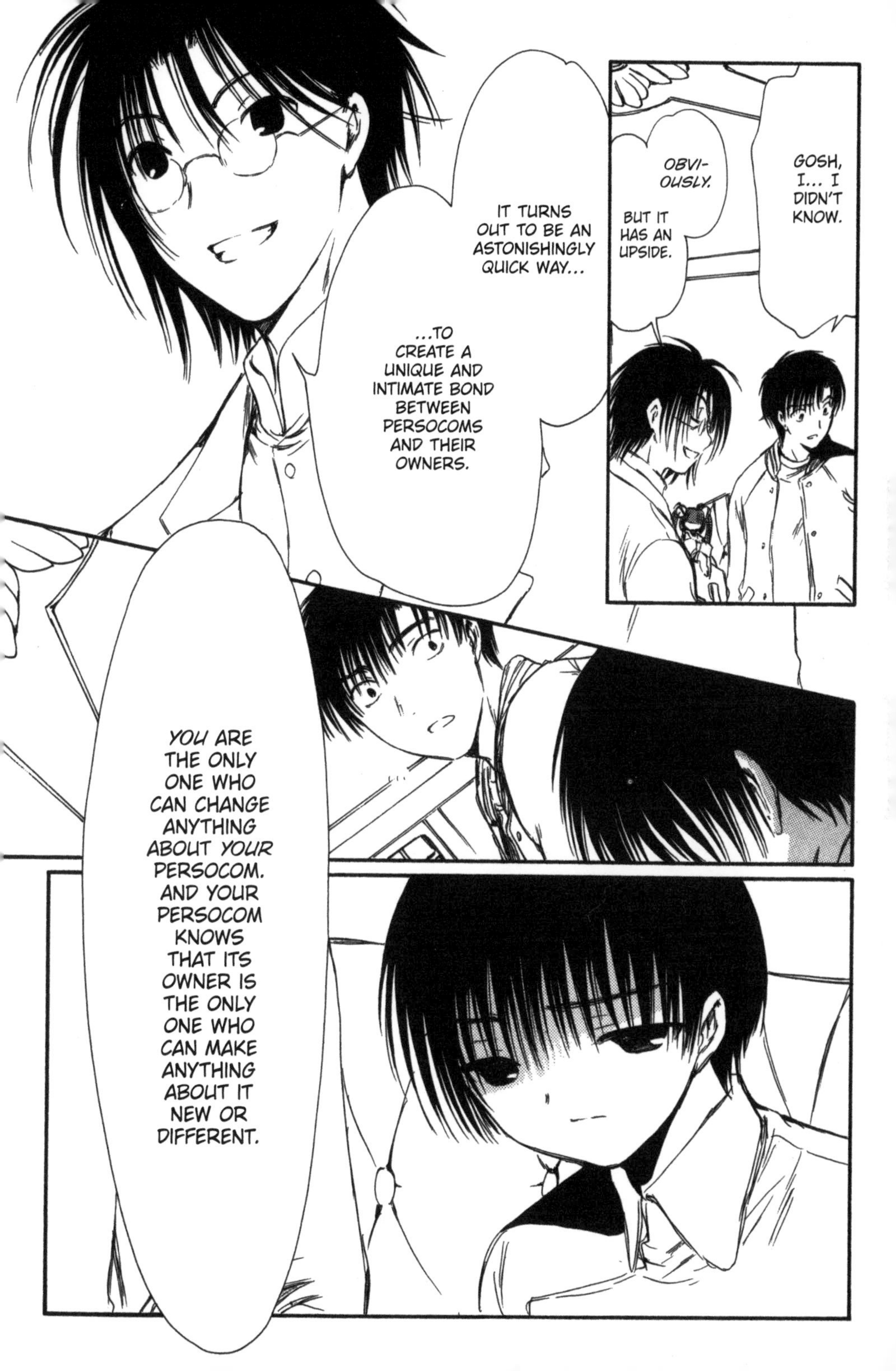
GOSH, I... I DIDN'T KNOW.
OBVIOUSLY.
BUT IT HAS AN UPSIDE.
IT TURNS OUT TO BE AN ASTONISHINGLY QUICK WAY...
...TO CREATE A UNIQUE AND INTIMATE BOND BETWEEN PERSOCOMS AND THEIR OWNERS.
YOU ARE THE ONLY ONE WHO CAN CHANGE ANYTHING ABOUT *YOUR* PERSOCOM. AND YOUR PERSOCOM KNOWS THAT ITS OWNER IS THE ONLY ONE WHO CAN MAKE ANYTHING ABOUT IT NEW OR DIFFERENT.

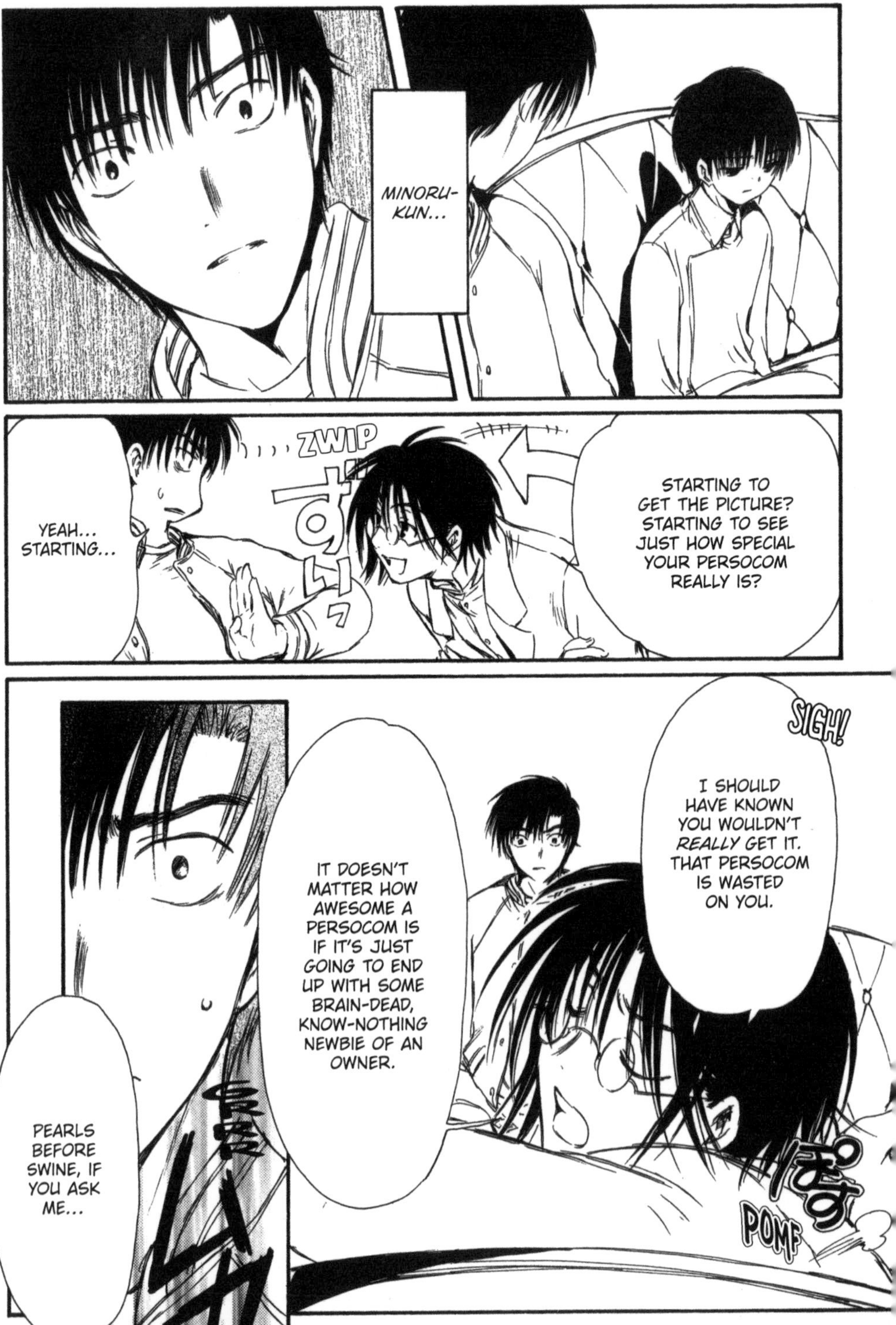
MINORU-KUN...
STARTING TO GET THE PICTURE? STARTING TO SEE JUST HOW SPECIAL YOUR PERSOCOM REALLY IS?
ZWIP
YEAH... STARTING...
SIGH!
I SHOULD HAVE KNOWN YOU WOULDN'T *REALLY* GET IT. THAT PERSOCOM IS WASTED ON YOU.
POMF
IT DOESN'T MATTER HOW AWESOME A PERSOCOM IS IF IT'S JUST GOING TO END UP WITH SOME BRAIN-DEAD, KNOW-NOTHING NEWBIE OF AN OWNER.
PEARLS BEFORE SWINE, IF YOU ASK ME...

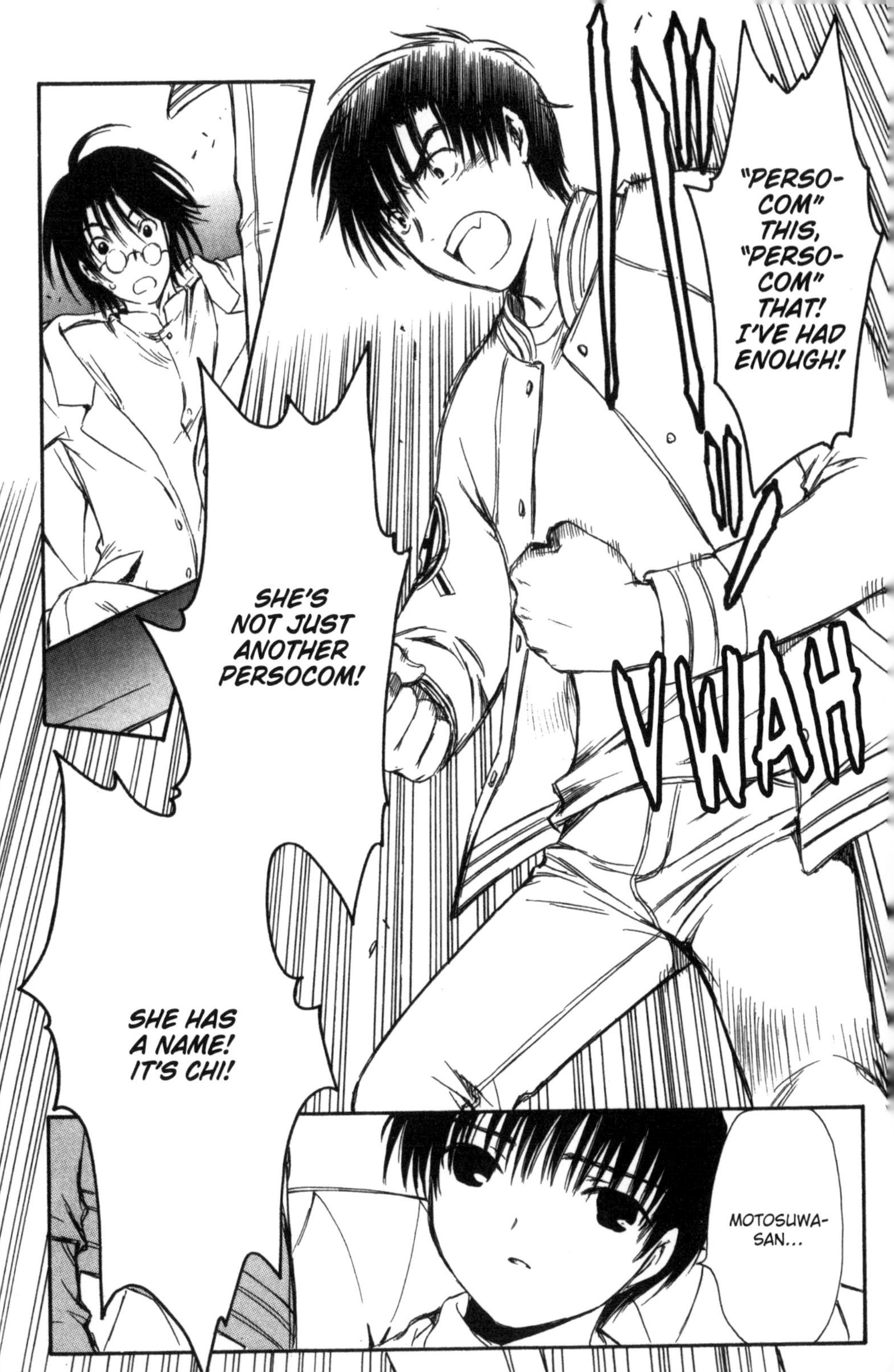
"PERSO-COM" THIS, "PERSO-COM" THAT! I'VE HAD ENOUGH!
VWAH
SHE'S NOT JUST ANOTHER PERSOCOM!
SHE HAS A NAME! IT'S CHI!
MOTOSUWA-SAN...

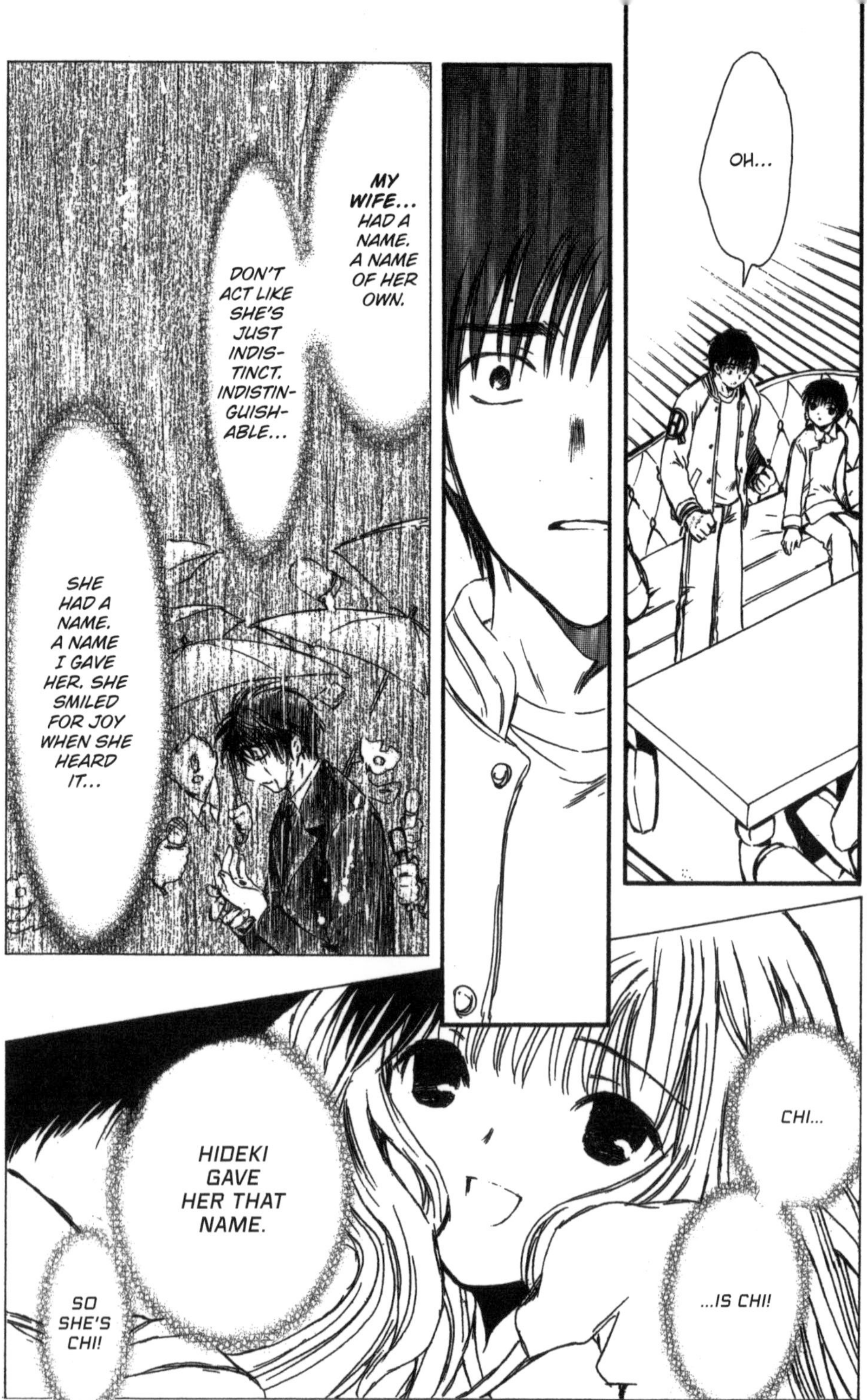
OH...
MY WIFE... HAD A NAME. A NAME OF HER OWN.
DON'T ACT LIKE SHE'S JUST INDIS-TINCT. INDISTIN-GUISH-ABLE...
SHE HAD A NAME. A NAME I GAVE HER. SHE SMILED FOR JOY WHEN SHE HEARD IT...
CHI...
...IS CHI!
HIDEKI GAVE HER THAT NAME.
SO SHE'S CHI!

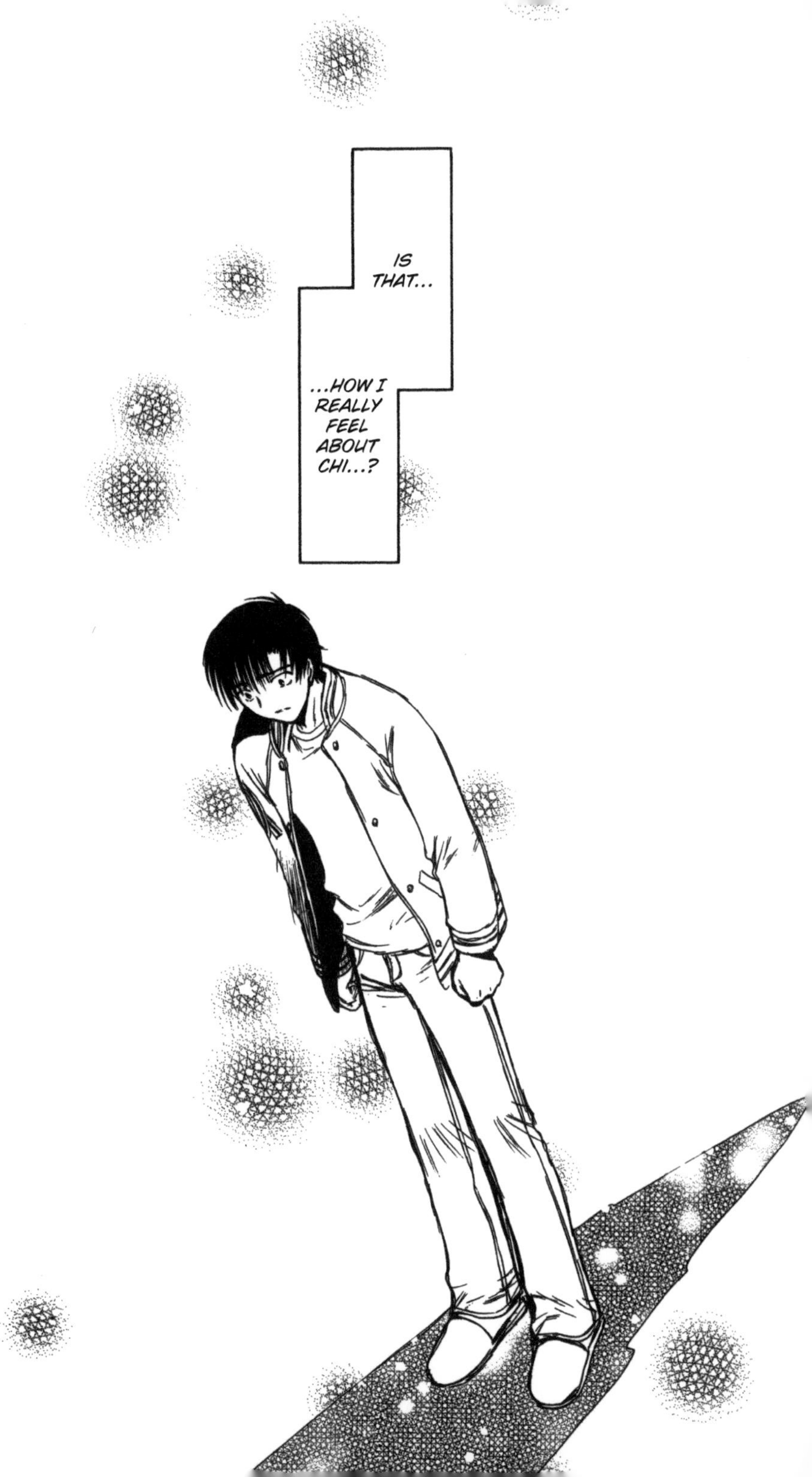
IS THAT...
...HOW I REALLY FEEL ABOUT CHI...?

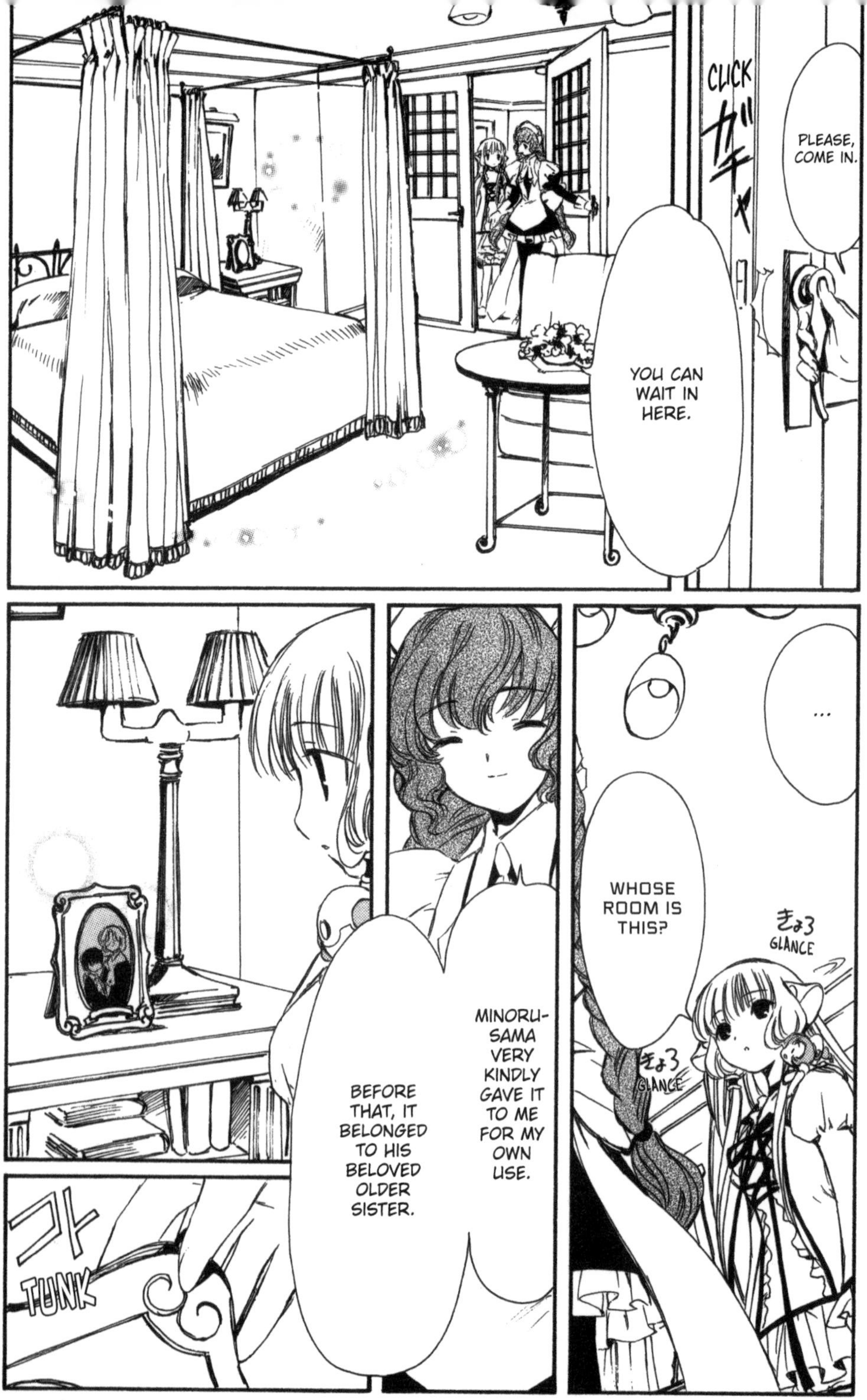
PLEASE, COME IN.
CLICK
ガチャ
YOU CAN WAIT IN HERE.
...
WHOSE ROOM IS THIS?
きょろ
GLANCE
きょろ
GLANCE
MINORU-SAMA VERY KINDLY GAVE IT TO ME FOR MY OWN USE.
BEFORE THAT, IT BELONGED TO HIS BELOVED OLDER SISTER.
コト
TUNK

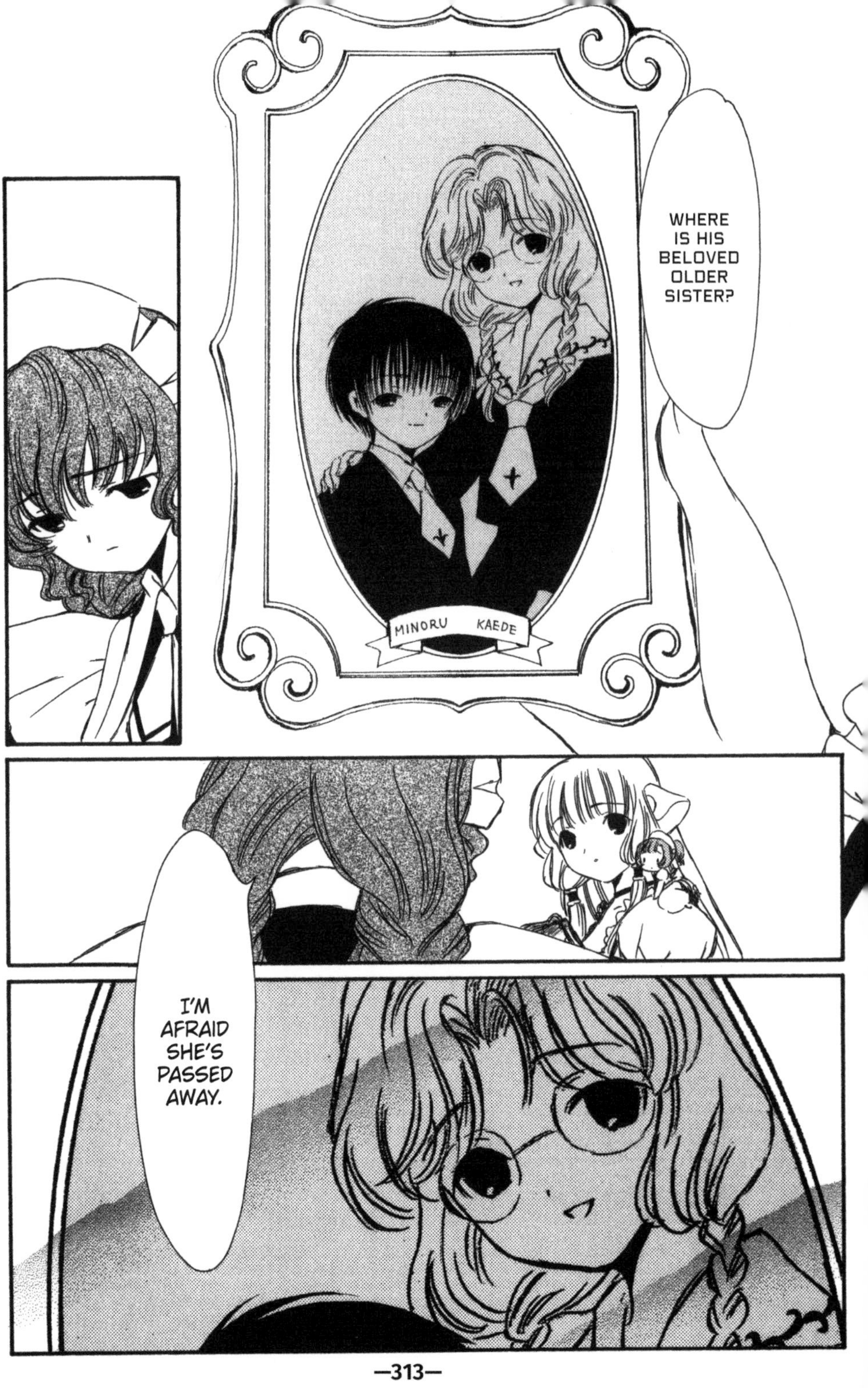
WHERE IS HIS BELOVED OLDER SISTER?
MINORU
KAEDE
I'M AFRAID SHE'S PASSED AWAY.

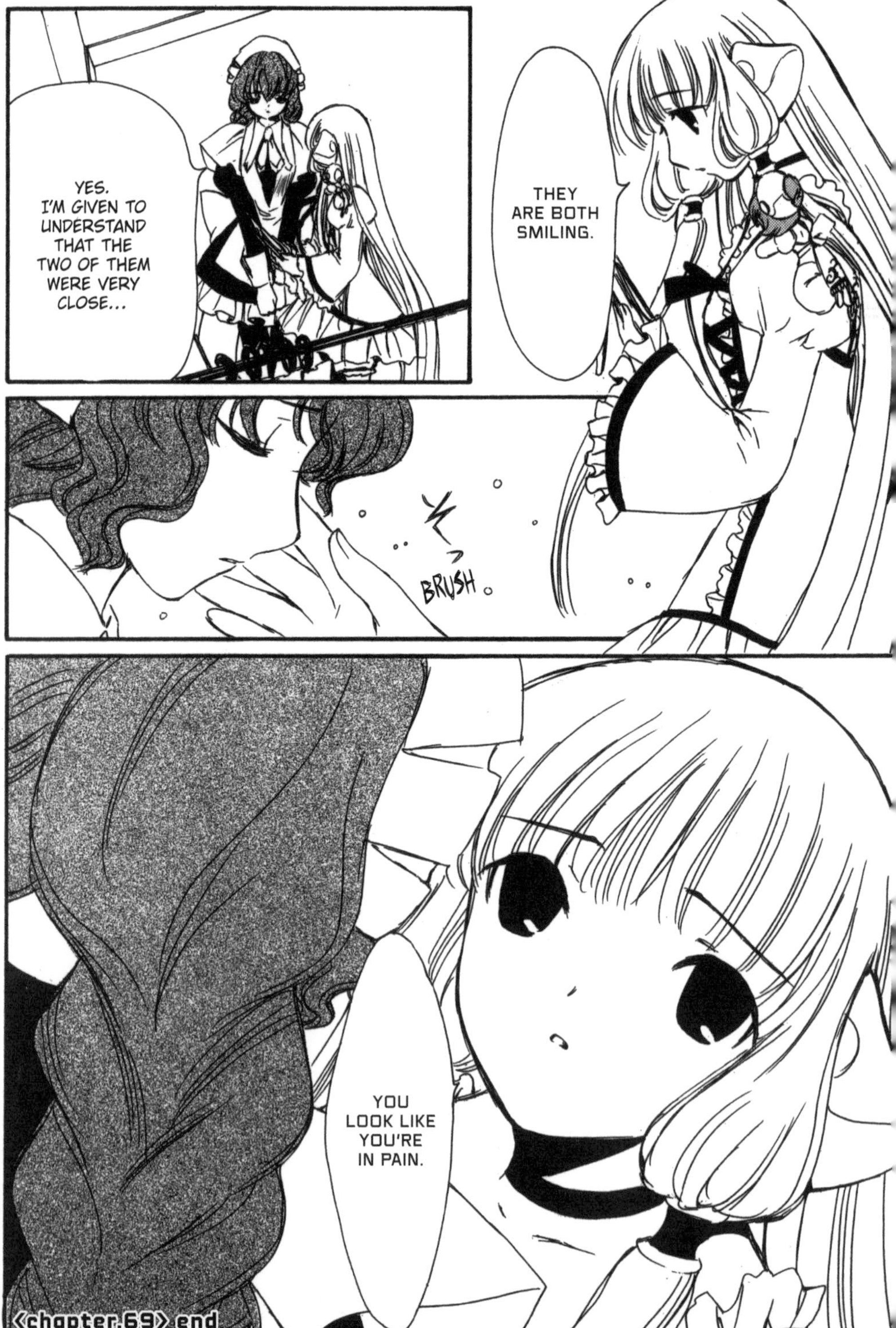
THEY ARE BOTH SMILING.
YES. I'M GIVEN TO UNDERSTAND THAT THE TWO OF THEM WERE VERY CLOSE...
BRUSH
YOU LOOK LIKE YOU'RE IN PAIN.
«chapter.69» end

Chobits

‹chapter.70›

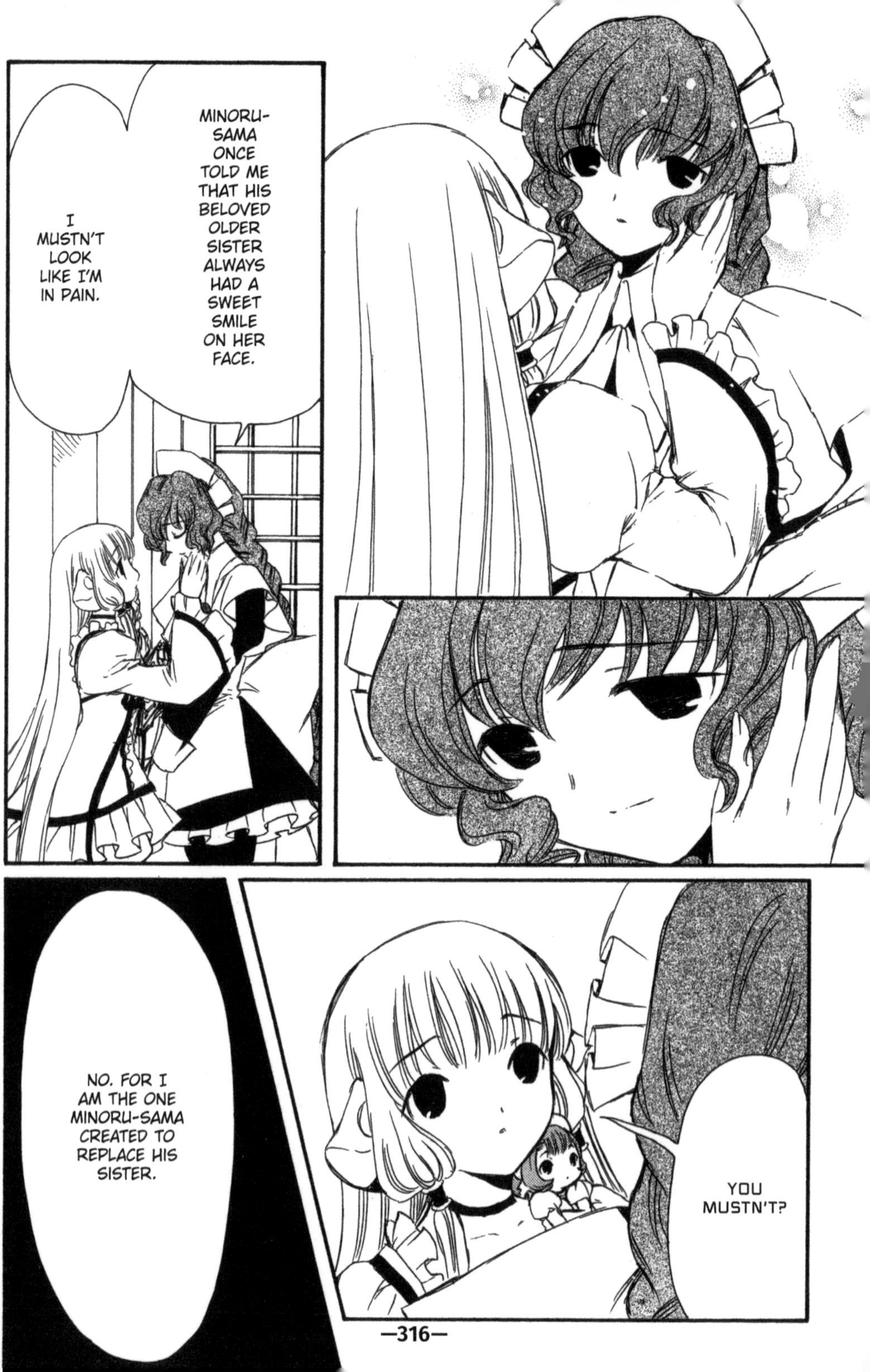
MINORU-SAMA ONCE TOLD ME THAT HIS BELOVED OLDER SISTER ALWAYS HAD A SWEET SMILE ON HER FACE.
I MUSTN'T LOOK LIKE I'M IN PAIN.
YOU MUSTN'T?
NO. FOR I AM THE ONE MINORU-SAMA CREATED TO REPLACE HIS SISTER.

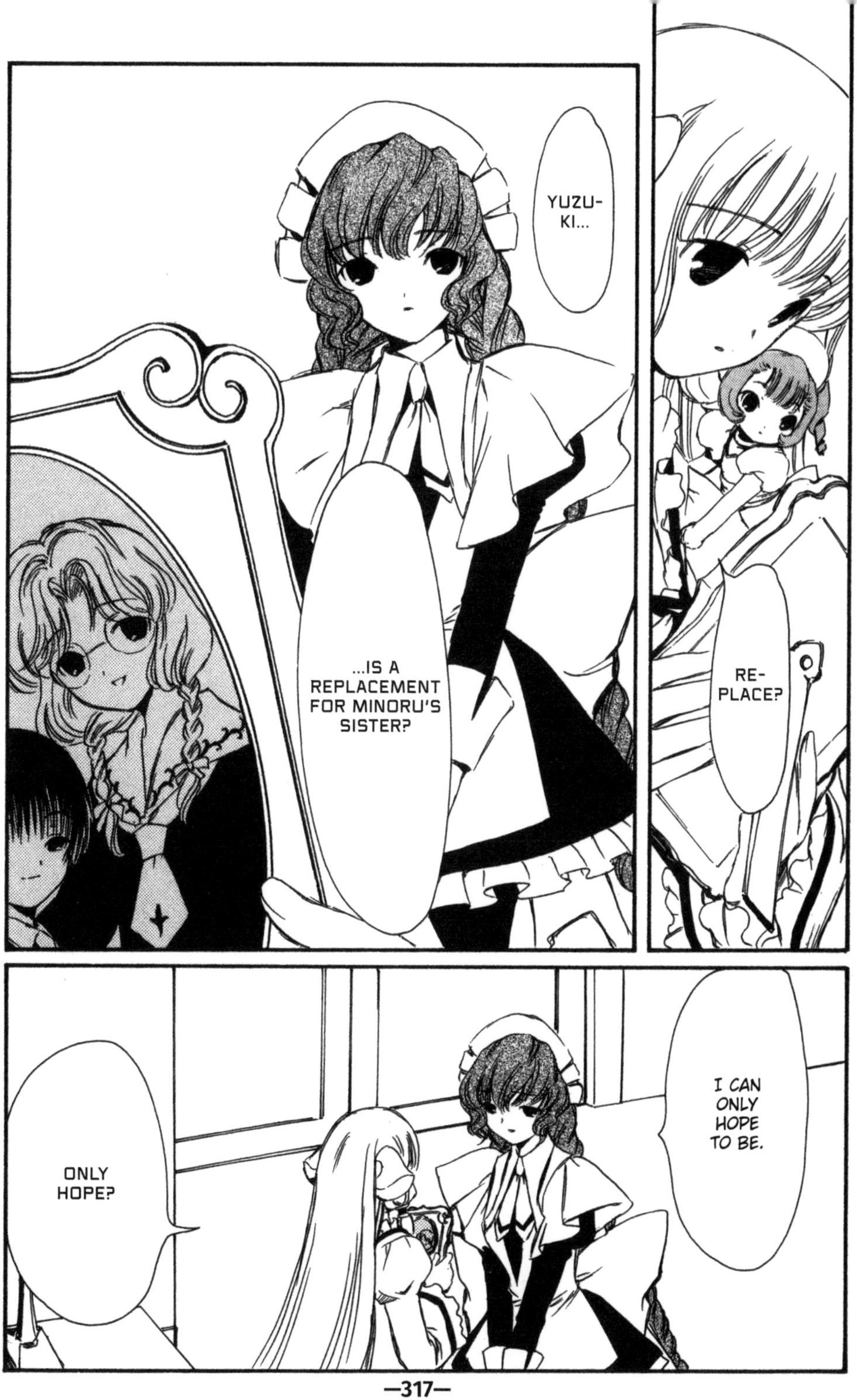
RE-PLACE?
YUZU-KI...
...IS A REPLACEMENT FOR MINORU'S SISTER?
I CAN ONLY HOPE TO BE.
ONLY HOPE?

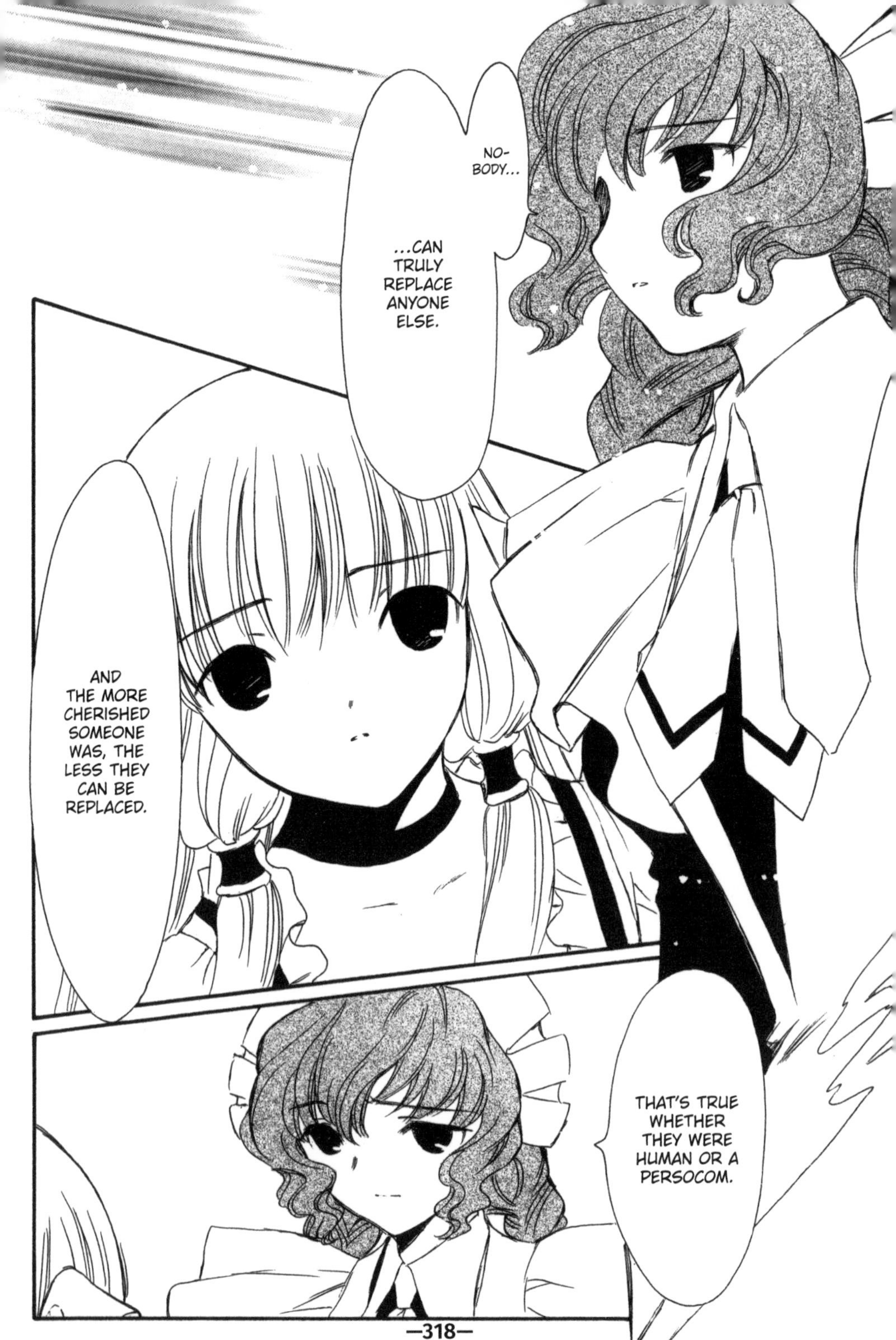
NO-BODY...
...CAN TRULY REPLACE ANYONE ELSE.
AND THE MORE CHERISHED SOMEONE WAS, THE LESS THEY CAN BE REPLACED.
THAT'S TRUE WHETHER THEY WERE HUMAN OR A PERSOCOM.

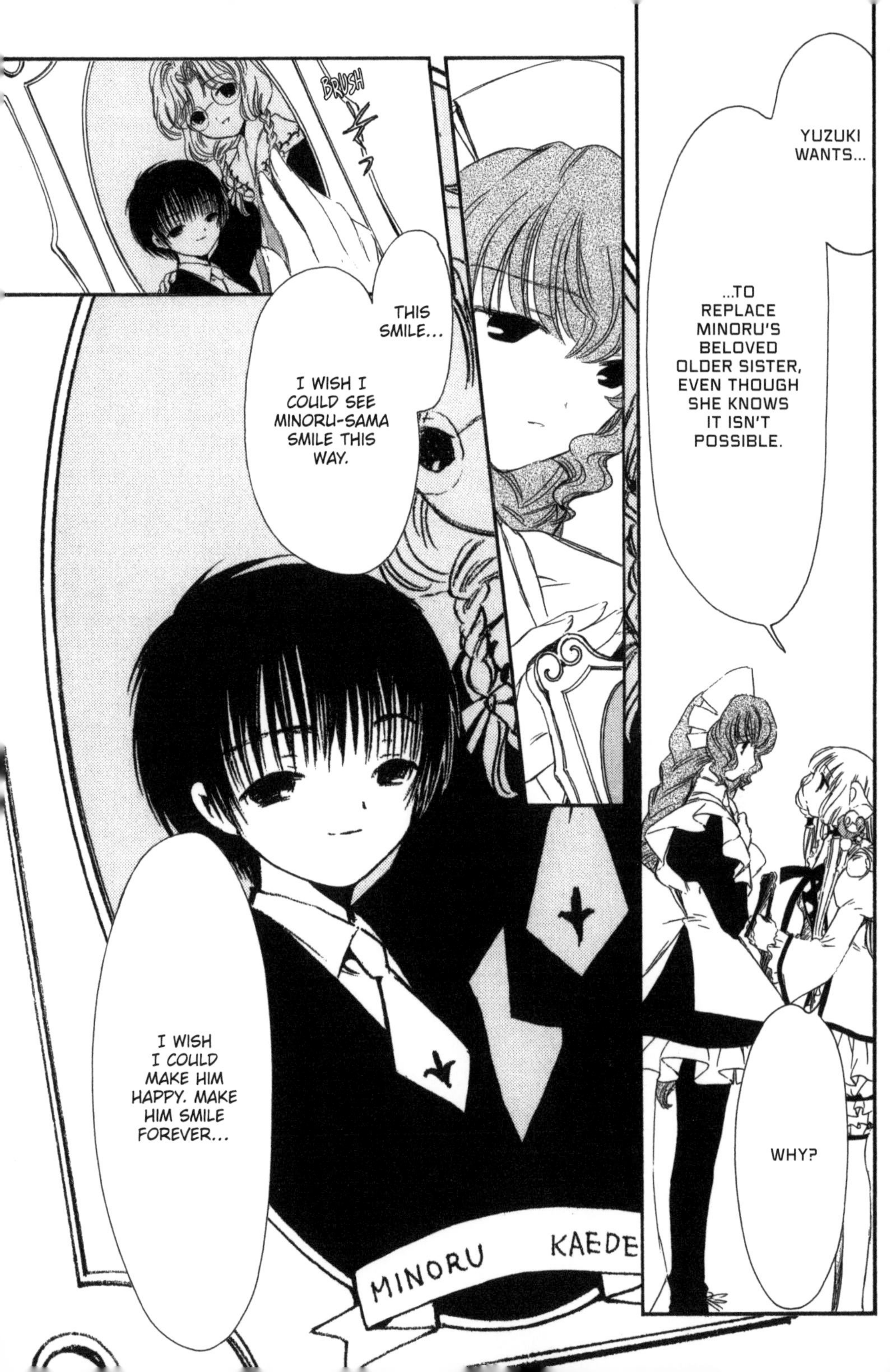
YUZUKI WANTS...
...TO REPLACE MINORU'S BELOVED OLDER SISTER, EVEN THOUGH SHE KNOWS IT ISN'T POSSIBLE.
WHY?
BRUSH
THIS SMILE...
I WISH I COULD SEE MINORU-SAMA SMILE THIS WAY.
I WISH I COULD MAKE HIM HAPPY. MAKE HIM SMILE FOREVER...
MINORU KAEDE

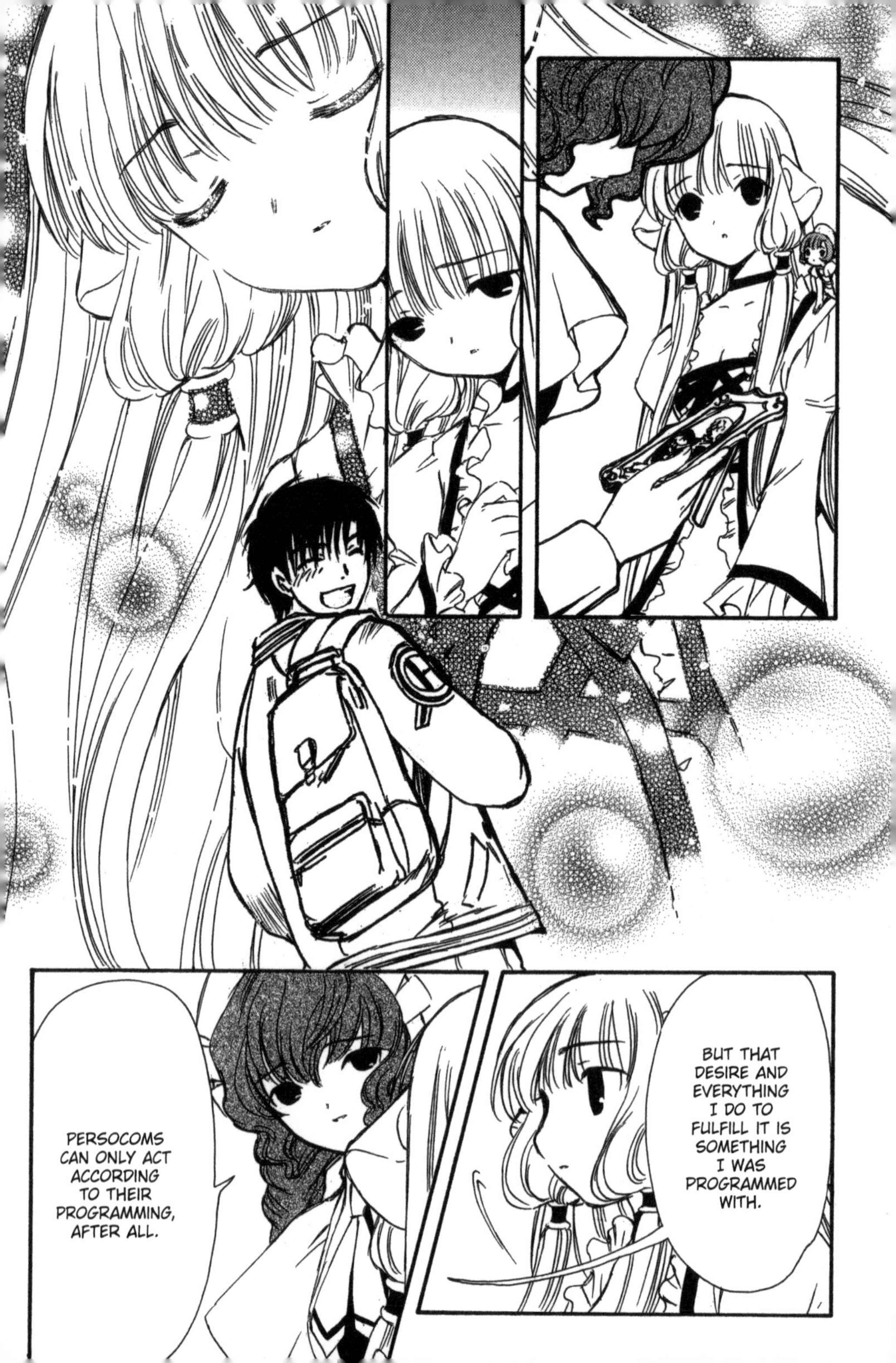
BUT THAT DESIRE AND EVERYTHING I DO TO FULFILL IT IS SOMETHING I WAS PROGRAMMED WITH.
PERSOCOMS CAN ONLY ACT ACCORDING TO THEIR PROGRAMMING, AFTER ALL.

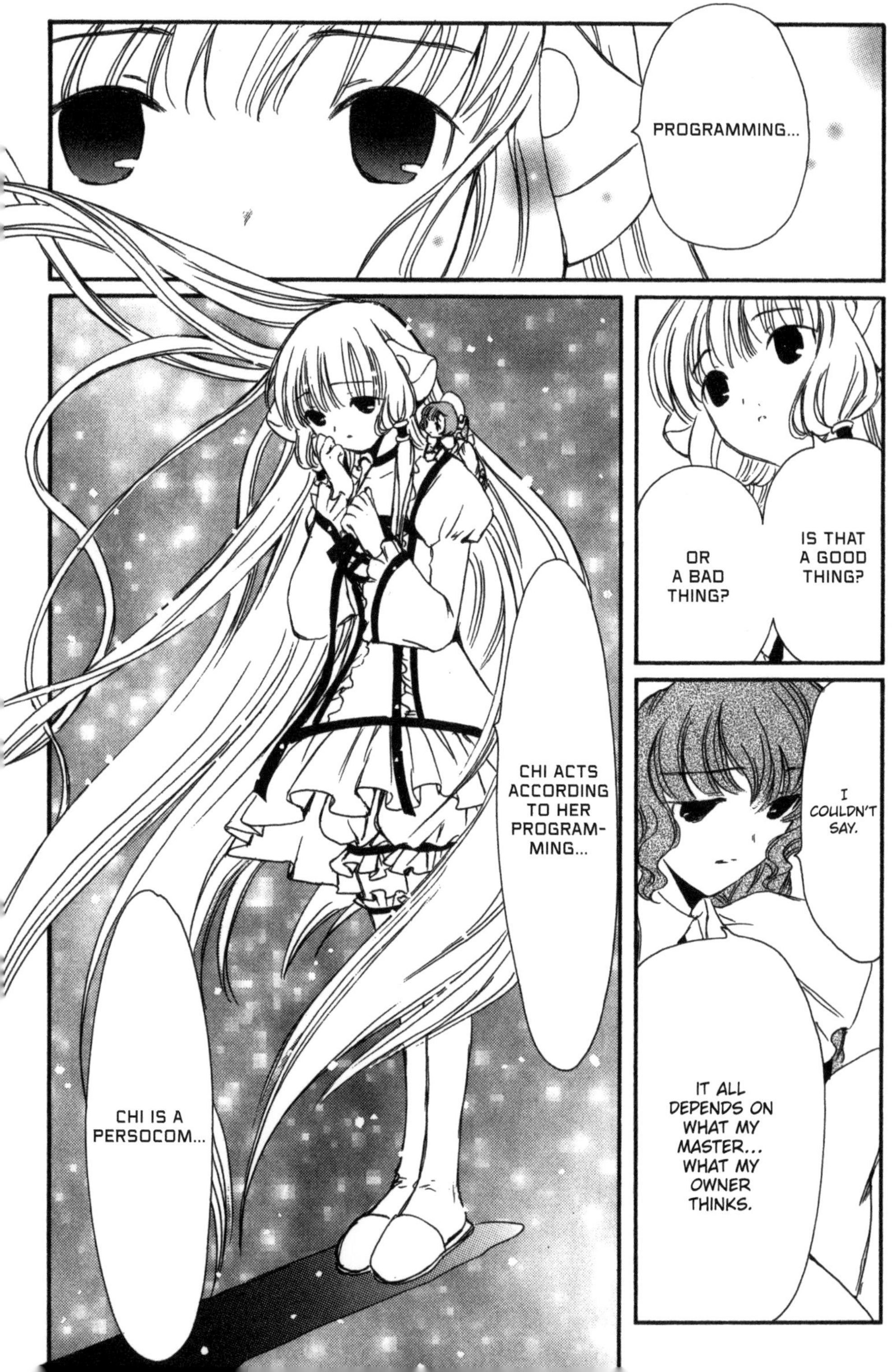
PROGRAMMING...
IS THAT A GOOD THING?
OR A BAD THING?
I COULDN'T SAY.
IT ALL DEPENDS ON WHAT MY MASTER... WHAT MY OWNER THINKS.
CHI ACTS ACCORDING TO HER PROGRAM-MING...
CHI IS A PERSOCOM...

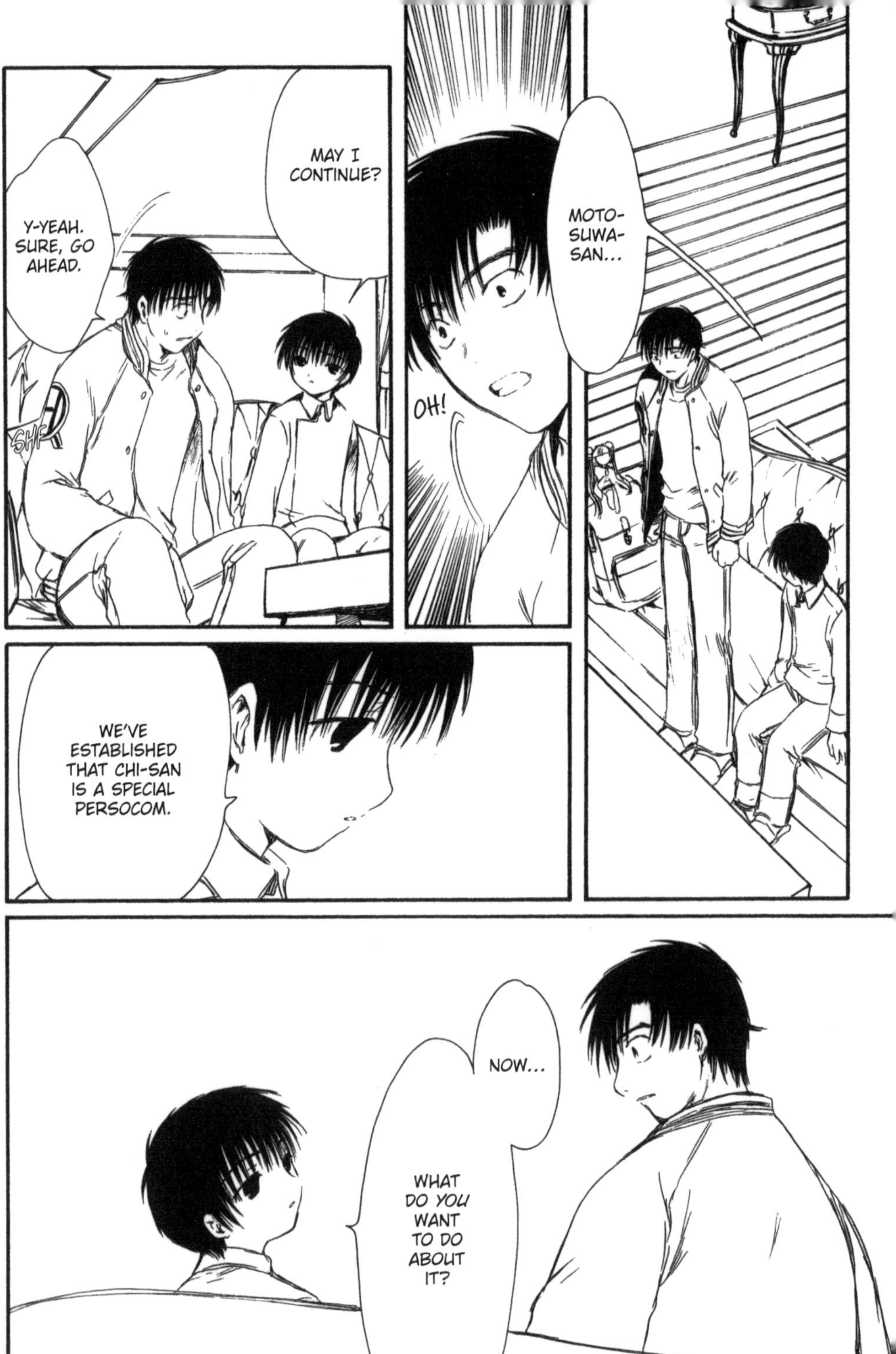
MOTO-SUWA-SAN...
OH!
MAY I CONTINUE?
Y-YEAH. SURE, GO AHEAD.
SHF
WE'VE ESTABLISHED THAT CHI-SAN IS A SPECIAL PERSOCOM.
NOW...
WHAT DO YOU WANT TO DO ABOUT IT?

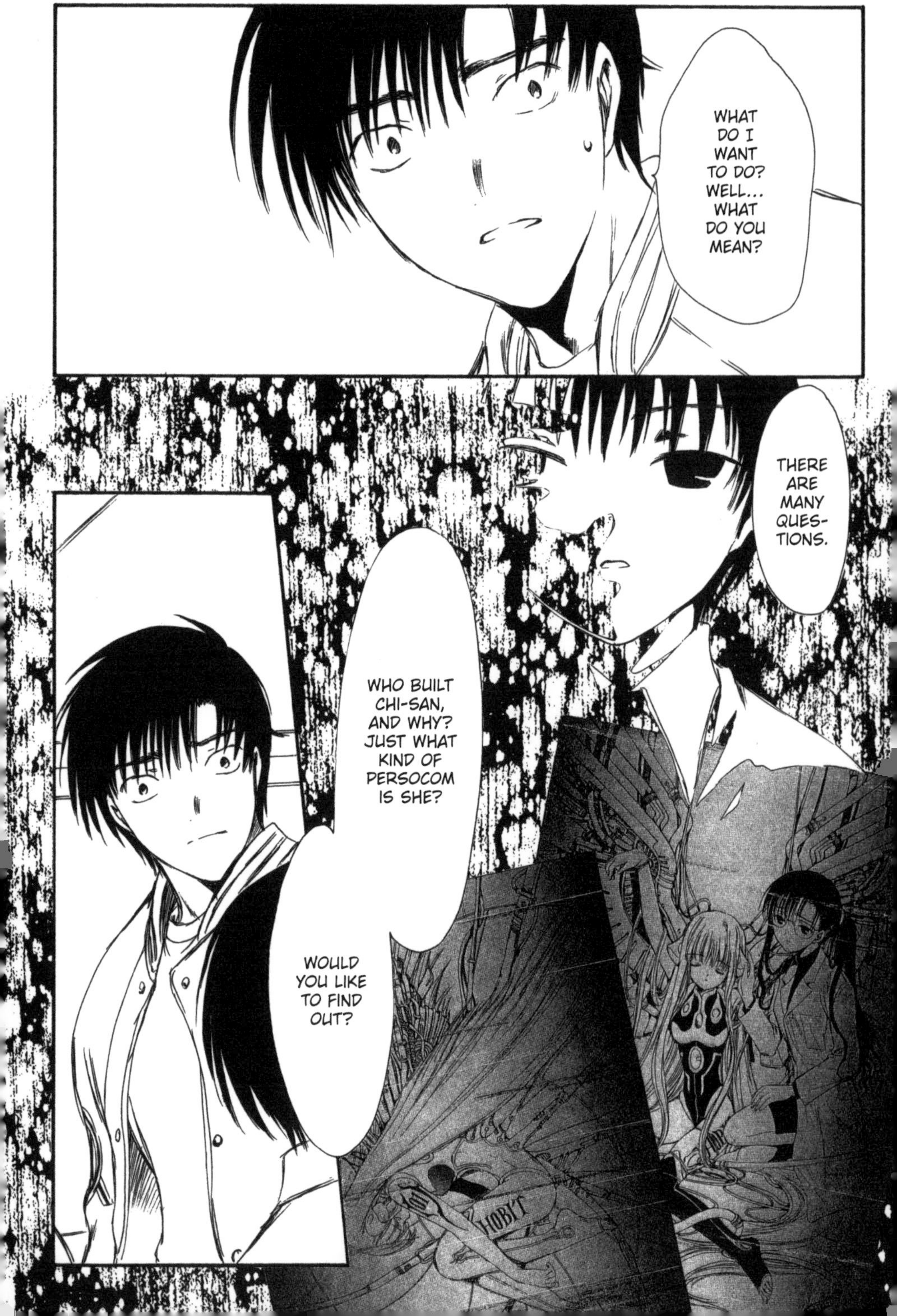
WHAT DO I WANT TO DO? WELL... WHAT DO YOU MEAN?
THERE ARE MANY QUES-TIONS.
WHO BUILT CHI-SAN, AND WHY? JUST WHAT KIND OF PERSOCOM IS SHE?
WOULD YOU LIKE TO FIND OUT?
HOBIT

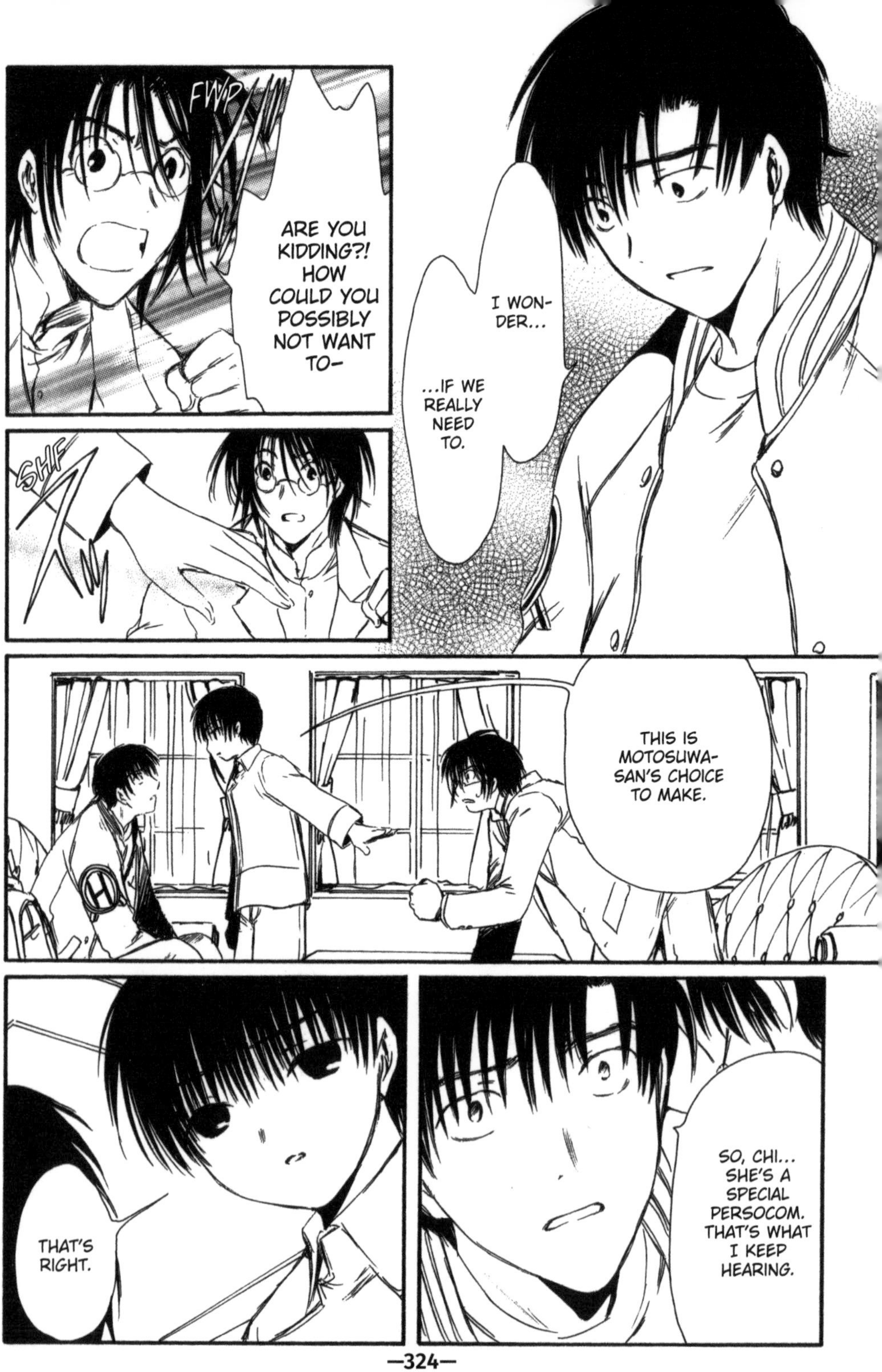
I WON-DER...
...IF WE REALLY NEED TO.
FWP
ARE YOU KIDDING?! HOW COULD YOU POSSIBLY NOT WANT TO-
SHF
THIS IS MOTOSUWA-SAN'S CHOICE TO MAKE.
SO, CHI... SHE'S A SPECIAL PERSOCOM. THAT'S WHAT I KEEP HEARING.
THAT'S RIGHT.

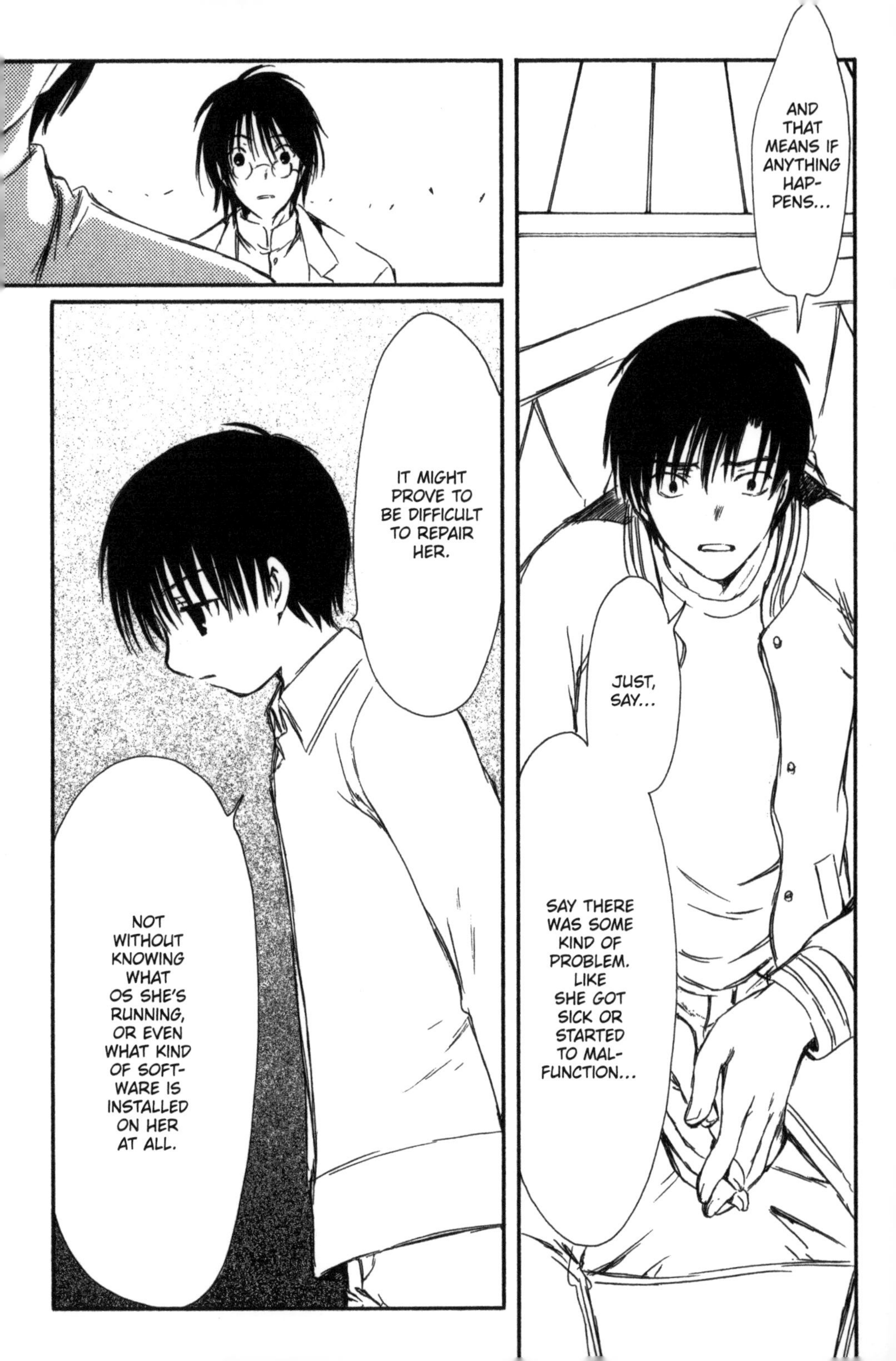
AND THAT MEANS IF ANYTHING HAP-PENS...
JUST, SAY...
SAY THERE WAS SOME KIND OF PROBLEM. LIKE SHE GOT SICK OR STARTED TO MAL-FUNCTION...
IT MIGHT PROVE TO BE DIFFICULT TO REPAIR HER.
NOT WITHOUT KNOWING WHAT OS SHE'S RUNNING, OR EVEN WHAT KIND OF SOFT-WARE IS INSTALLED ON HER AT ALL.

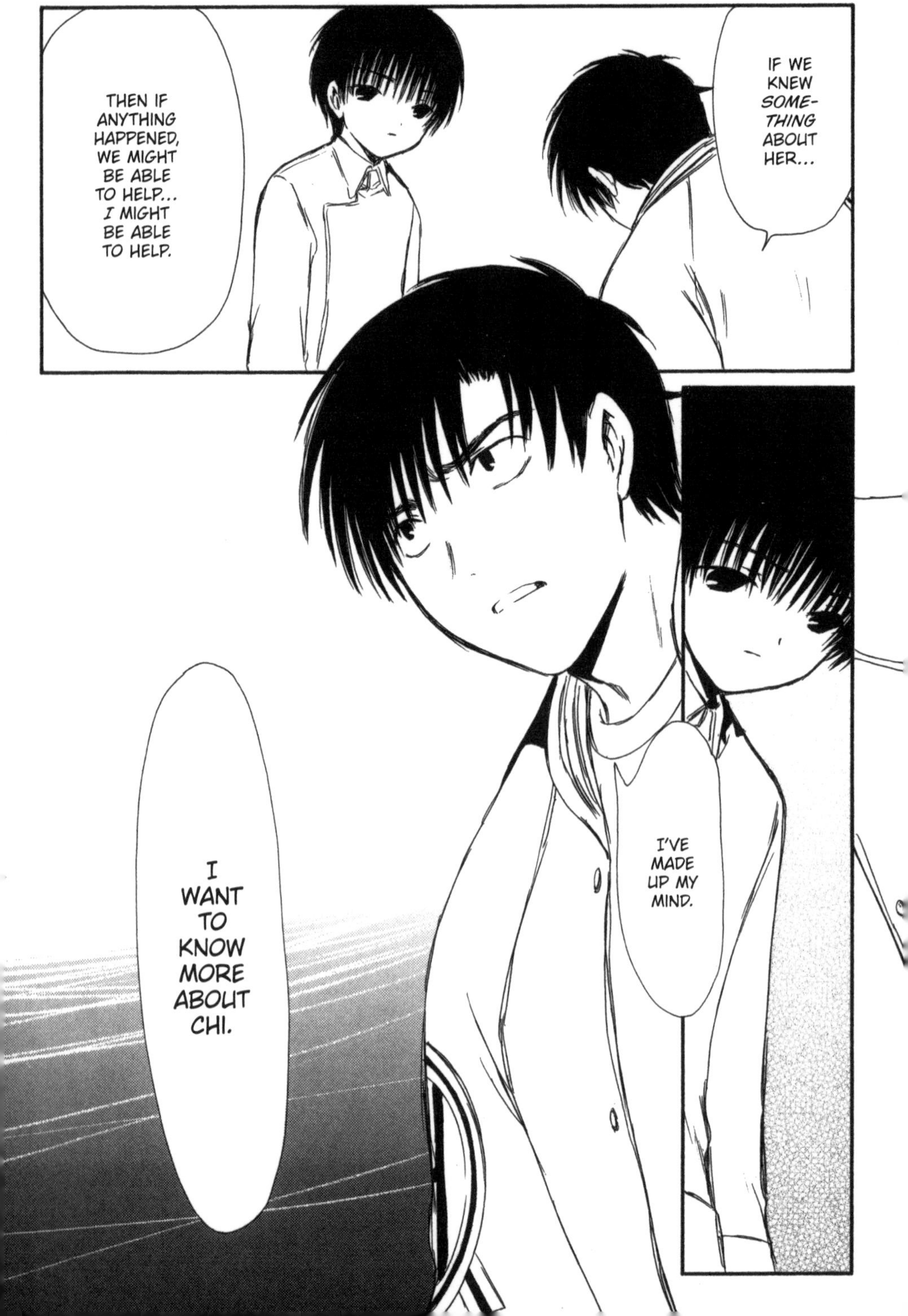
IF WE KNEW SOMETHING ABOUT HER...
THEN IF ANYTHING HAPPENED, WE MIGHT BE ABLE TO HELP... I MIGHT BE ABLE TO HELP.
I'VE MADE UP MY MIND.
I WANT TO KNOW MORE ABOUT CHI.

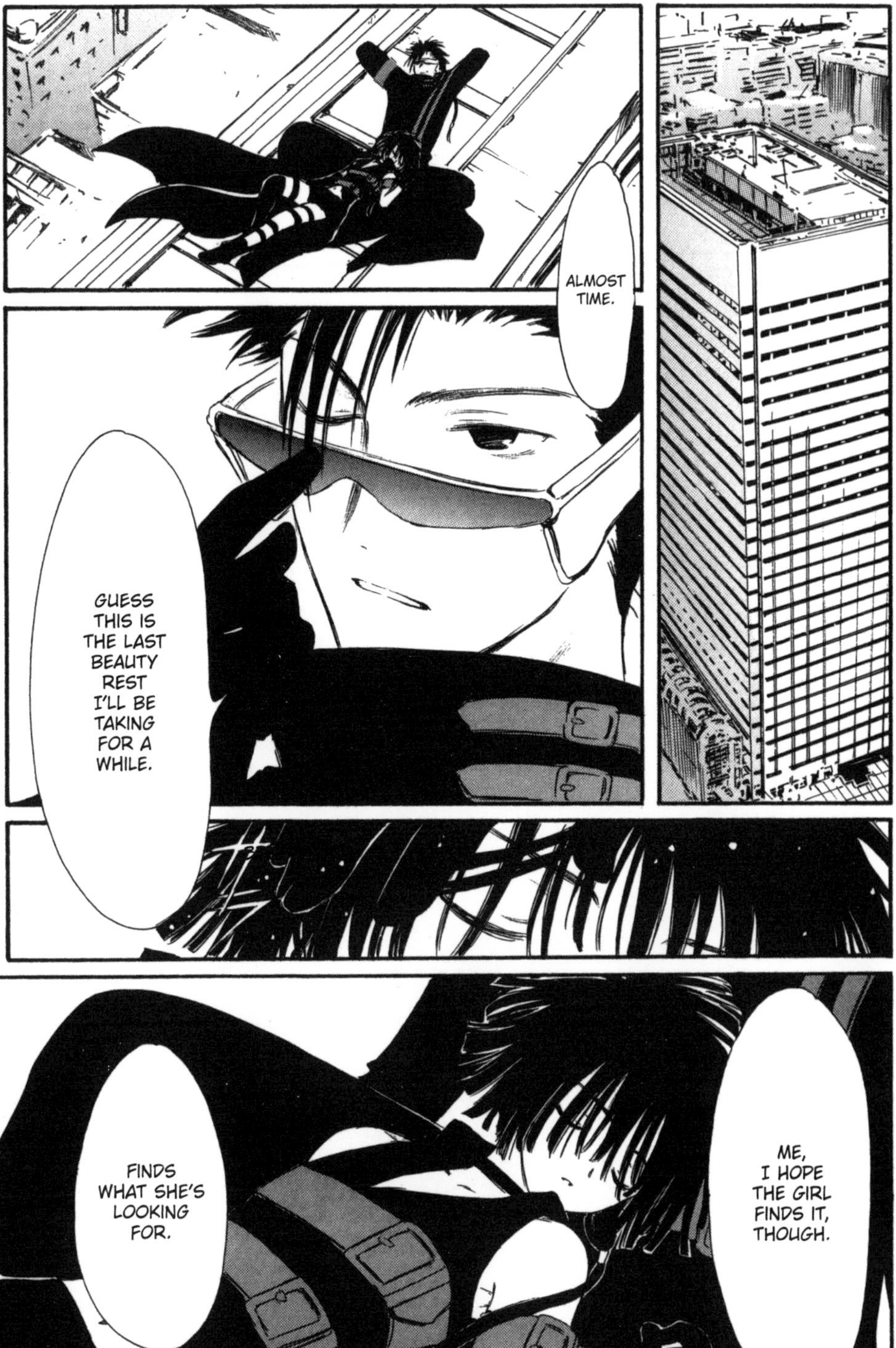
ALMOST TIME.
GUESS THIS IS THE LAST BEAUTY REST I'LL BE TAKING FOR A WHILE.
ME, I HOPE THE GIRL FINDS IT, THOUGH.
FINDS WHAT SHE'S LOOKING FOR.

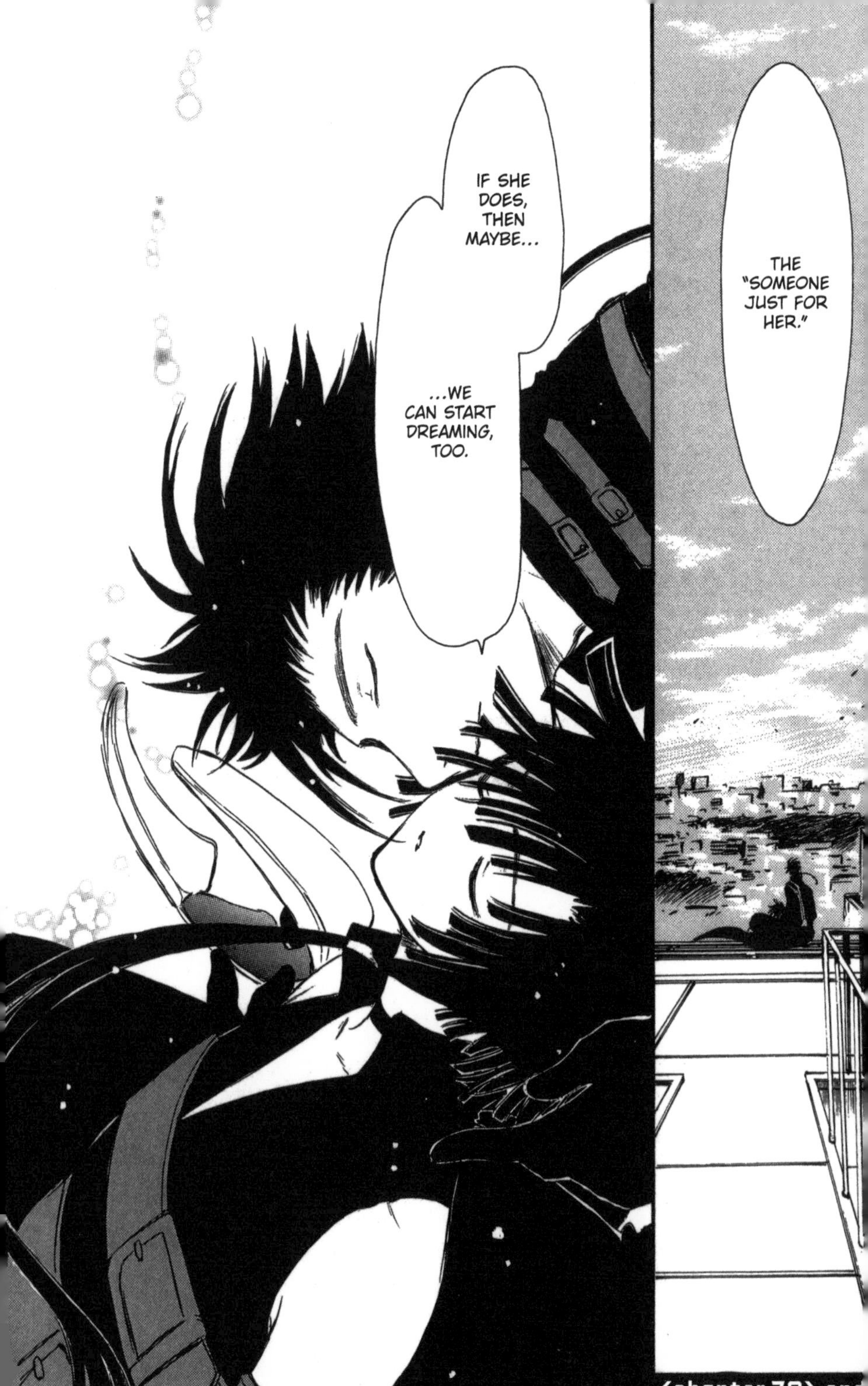
THE "SOMEONE JUST FOR HER."
<chapter 70> en
IF SHE DOES, THEN MAYBE...
...WE CAN START DREAMING, TOO.

〈chapter.71〉

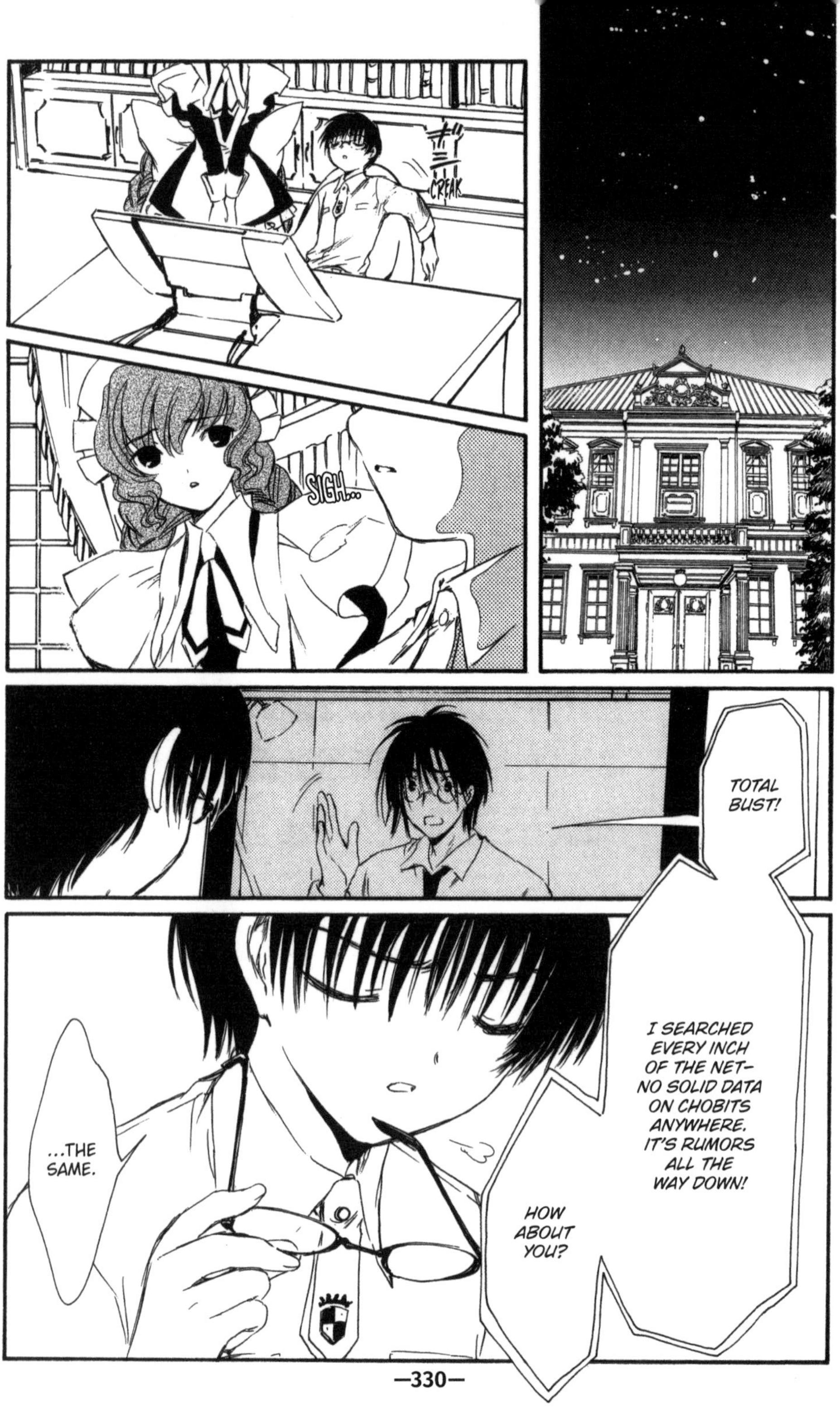
CREAK
SIGH...
TOTAL BUST!
I SEARCHED EVERY INCH OF THE NET— NO SOLID DATA ON CHOBITS ANYWHERE. IT'S RUMORS ALL THE WAY DOWN!
HOW ABOUT YOU?
...THE SAME.

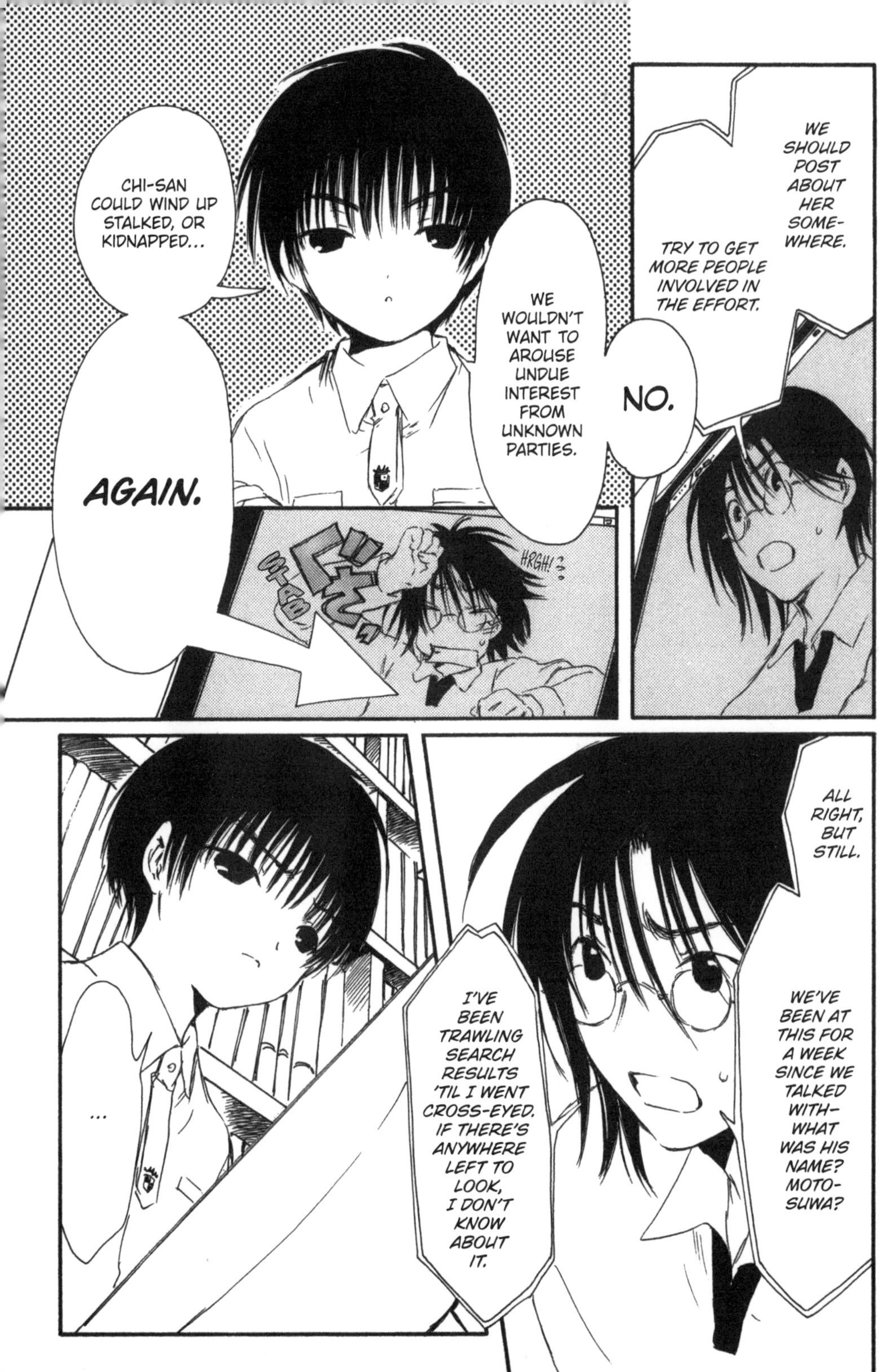
WE SHOULD POST ABOUT HER SOME-WHERE.
TRY TO GET MORE PEOPLE INVOLVED IN THE EFFORT.
NO.
WE WOULDN'T WANT TO AROUSE UNDUE INTEREST FROM UNKNOWN PARTIES.
CHI-SAN COULD WIND UP STALKED, OR KIDNAPPED...
AGAIN.
HRGH!
ALL RIGHT, BUT STILL.
WE'VE BEEN AT THIS FOR A WEEK SINCE WE TALKED WITH—WHAT WAS HIS NAME? MOTO-SUWA?
I'VE BEEN TRAWLING SEARCH RESULTS 'TIL I WENT CROSS-EYED. IF THERE'S ANYWHERE LEFT TO LOOK, I DON'T KNOW ABOUT IT.
...

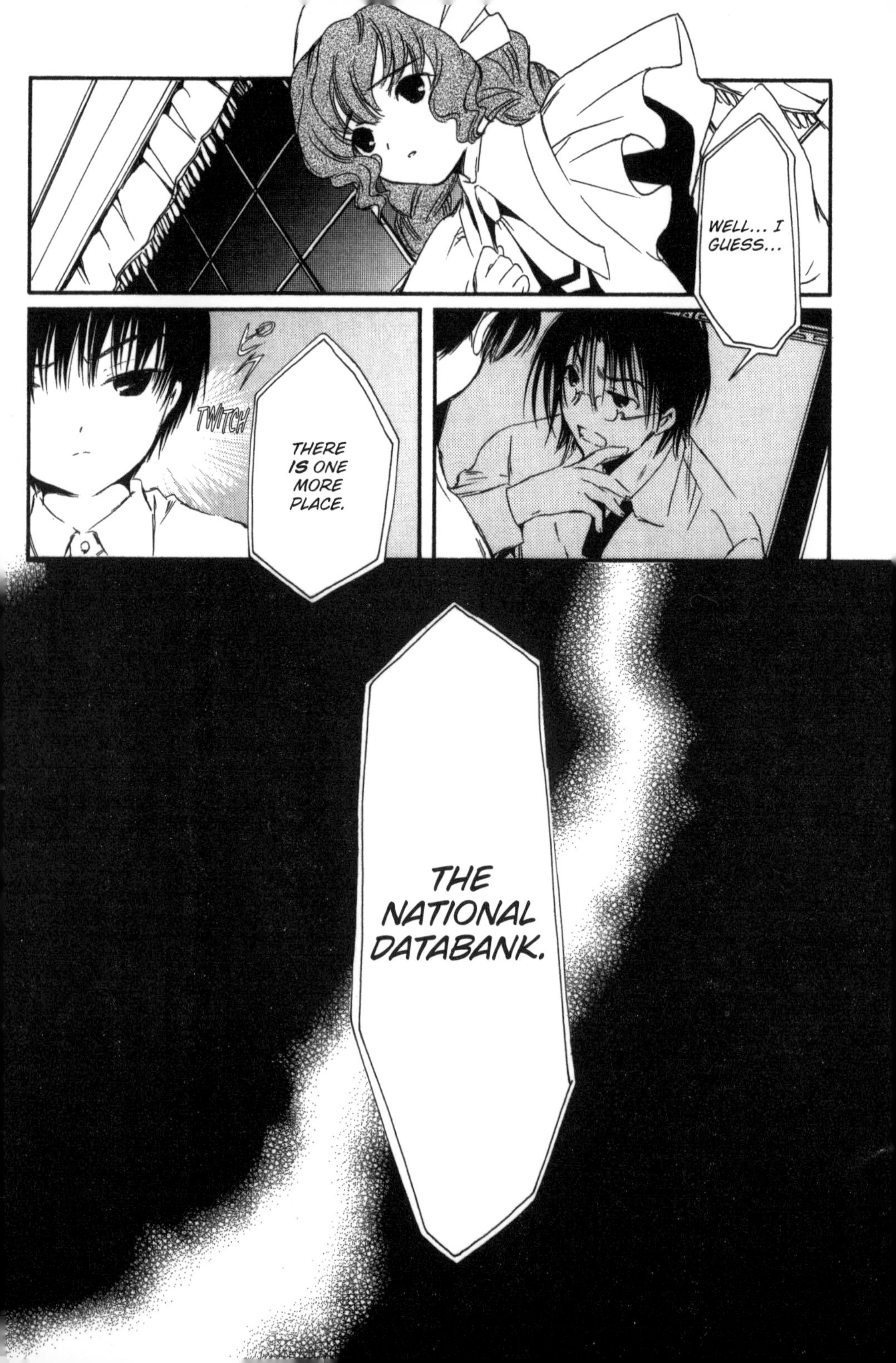
WELL... I GUESS...
THERE IS ONE MORE PLACE.
TWITCH
THE NATIONAL DATABANK.

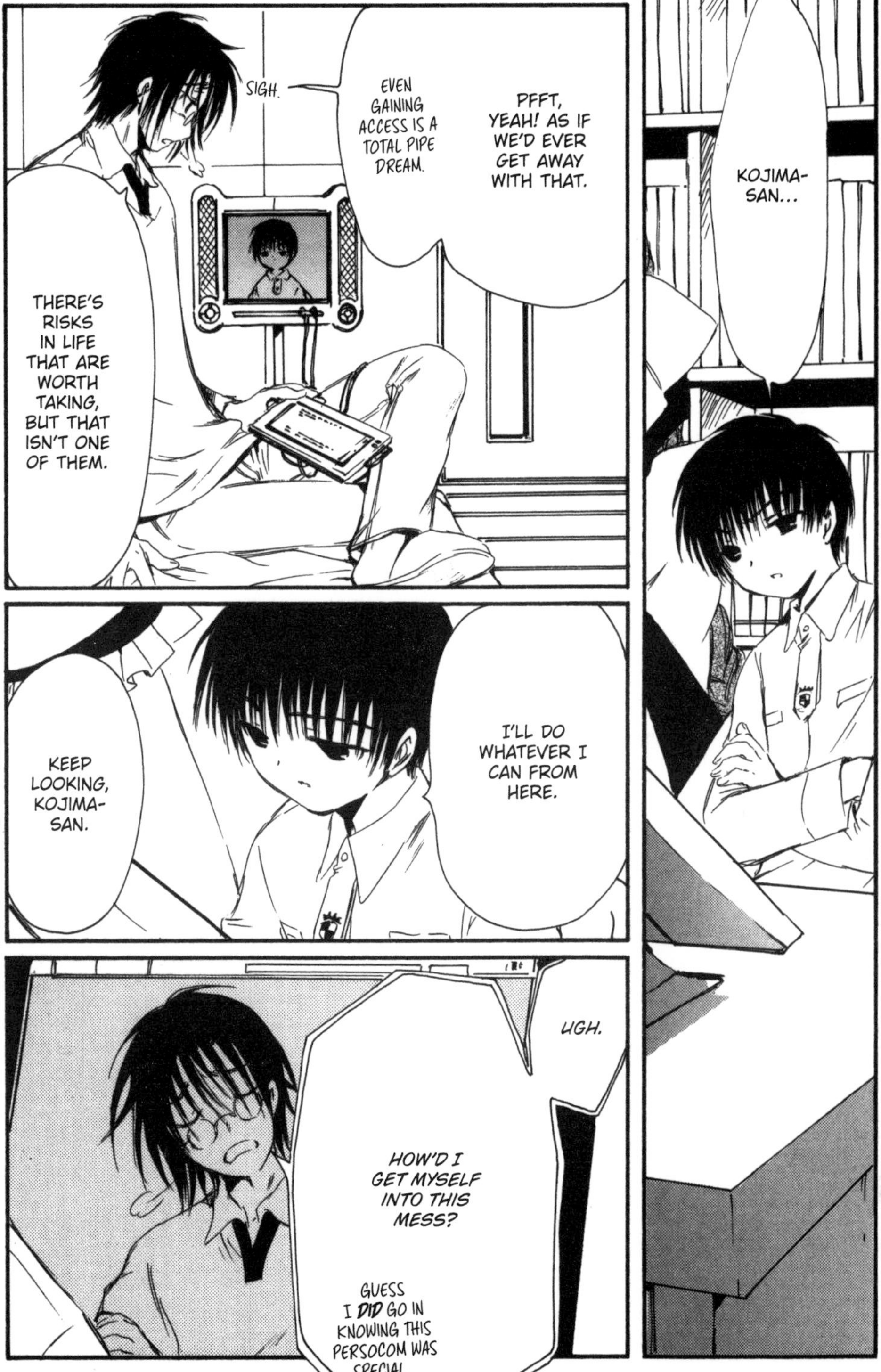
KOJIMA-SAN...
PFFT, YEAH! AS IF WE'D EVER GET AWAY WITH THAT.
EVEN GAINING ACCESS IS A TOTAL PIPE DREAM.
SIGH.
THERE'S RISKS IN LIFE THAT ARE WORTH TAKING, BUT THAT ISN'T ONE OF THEM.
I'LL DO WHATEVER I CAN FROM HERE.
KEEP LOOKING, KOJIMA-SAN.
UGH.
HOW'D I GET MYSELF INTO THIS MESS?
GUESS I DID GO IN KNOWING THIS PERSOCOM WAS SPECIAL...

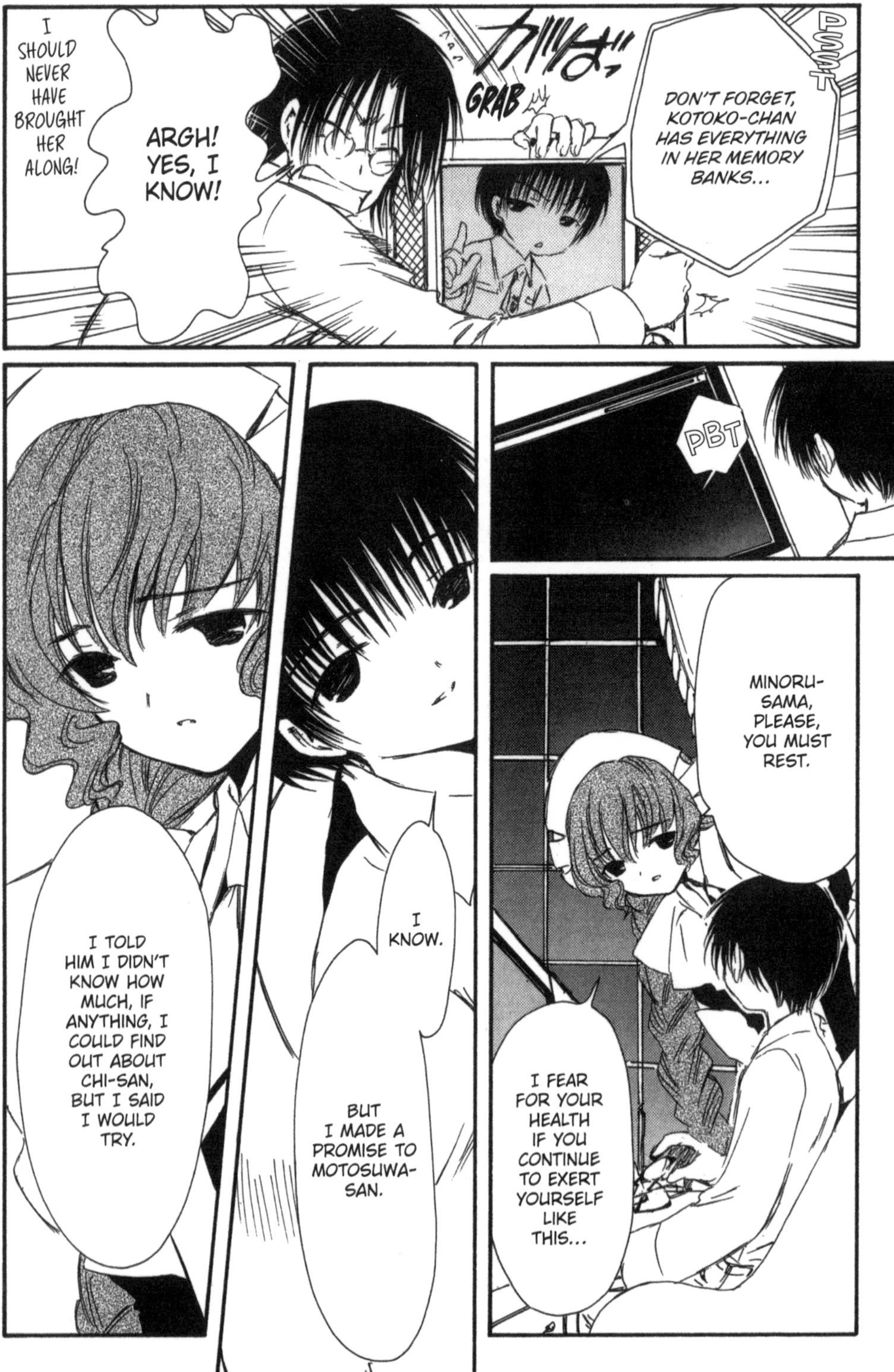
PSST
DON'T FORGET, KOTOKO-CHAN HAS EVERYTHING IN HER MEMORY BANKS...
GRAB
ARGH! YES, I KNOW!
I SHOULD NEVER HAVE BROUGHT HER ALONG!
PBT
MINORU-SAMA, PLEASE, YOU MUST REST.
I FEAR FOR YOUR HEALTH IF YOU CONTINUE TO EXERT YOURSELF LIKE THIS...
I KNOW.
BUT I MADE A PROMISE TO MOTOSUWA-SAN.
I TOLD HIM I DIDN'T KNOW HOW MUCH, IF ANYTHING, I COULD FIND OUT ABOUT CHI-SAN, BUT I SAID I WOULD TRY.

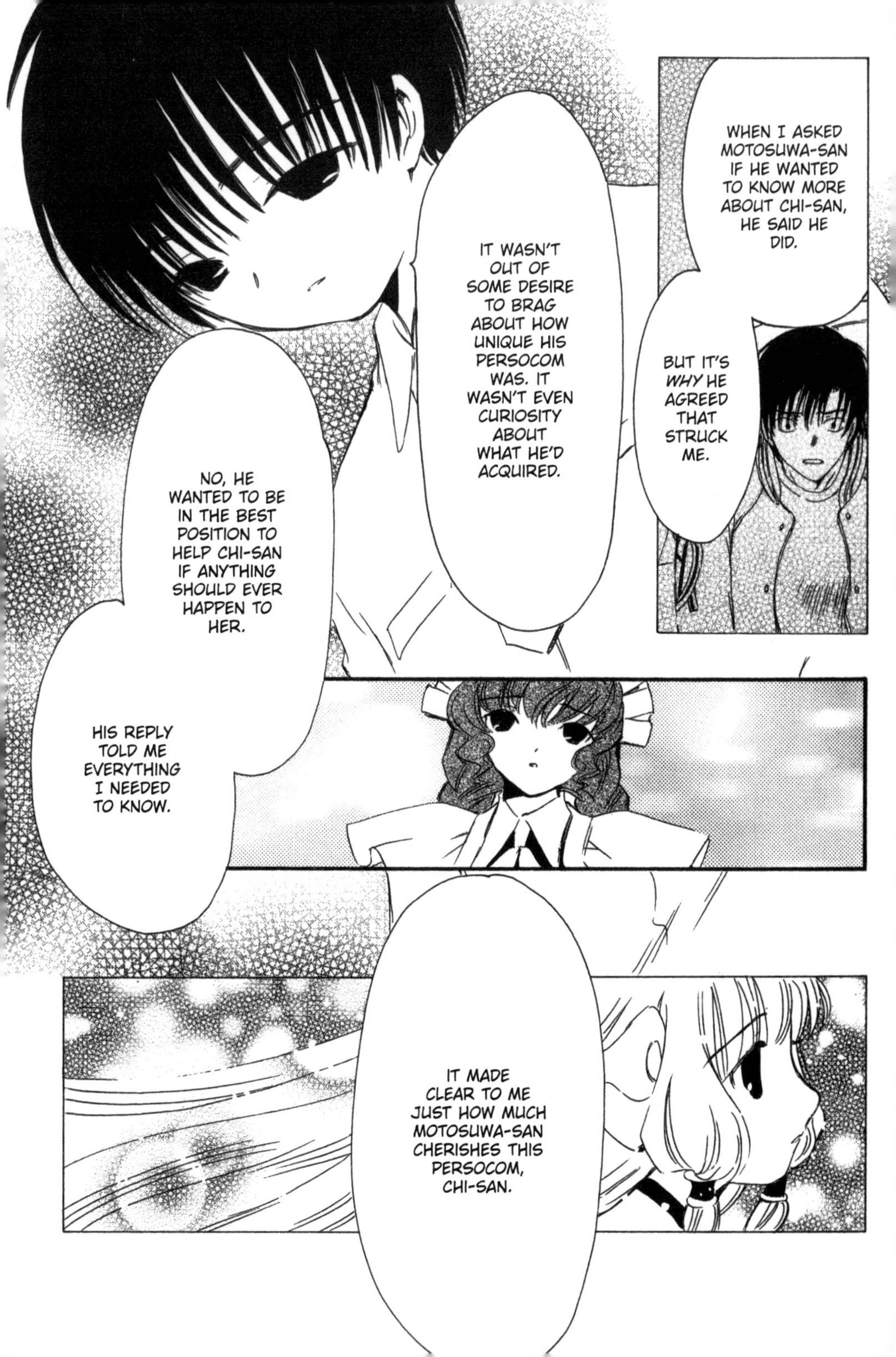
WHEN I ASKED MOTOSUWA-SAN IF HE WANTED TO KNOW MORE ABOUT CHI-SAN, HE SAID HE DID.
BUT IT'S *WHY* HE AGREED THAT STRUCK ME.
IT WASN'T OUT OF SOME DESIRE TO BRAG ABOUT HOW UNIQUE HIS PERSOCOM WAS. IT WASN'T EVEN CURIOSITY ABOUT WHAT HE'D ACQUIRED.
NO, HE WANTED TO BE IN THE BEST POSITION TO HELP CHI-SAN IF ANYTHING SHOULD EVER HAPPEN TO HER.
HIS REPLY TOLD ME EVERYTHING I NEEDED TO KNOW.
IT MADE CLEAR TO ME JUST HOW MUCH MOTOSUWA-SAN CHERISHES THIS PERSOCOM, CHI-SAN.

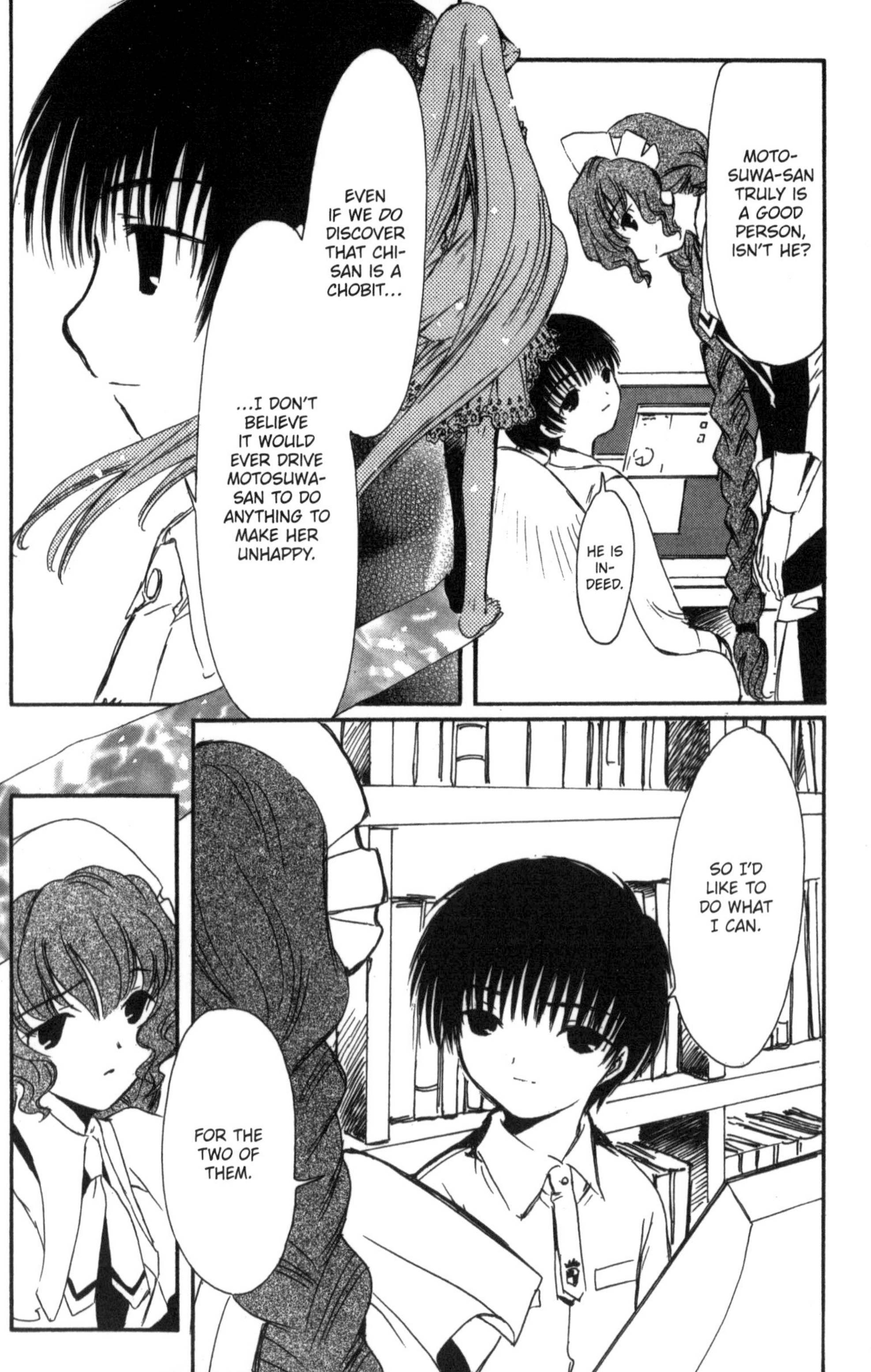
MOTO-SUWA-SAN TRULY IS A GOOD PERSON, ISN'T HE?
HE IS IN-DEED.
EVEN IF WE *DO* DISCOVER THAT CHI-SAN IS A CHOBIT…
…I DON'T BELIEVE IT WOULD EVER DRIVE MOTOSUWA-SAN TO DO ANYTHING TO MAKE HER UNHAPPY.
SO I'D LIKE TO DO WHAT I CAN.
FOR THE TWO OF THEM.

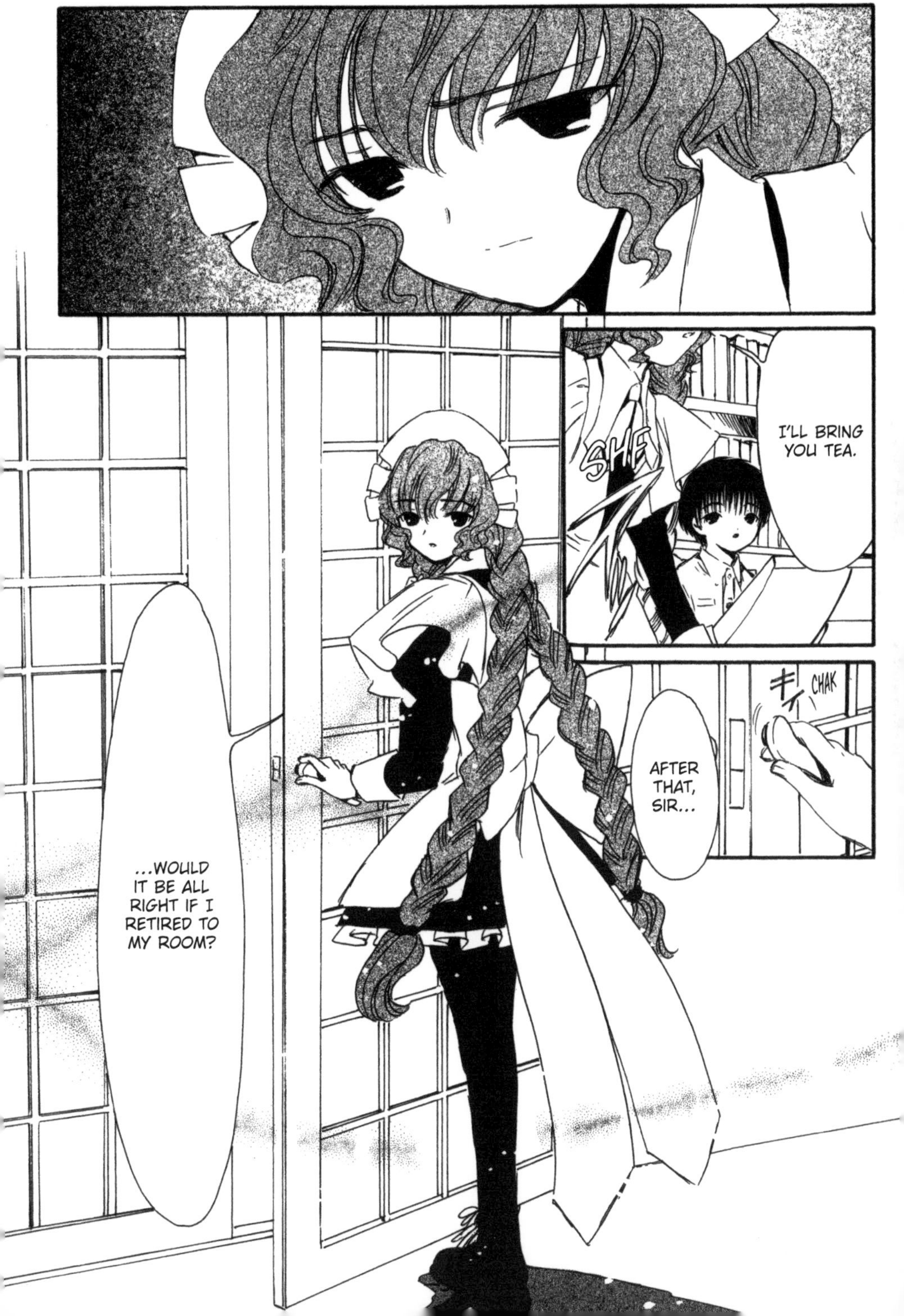
I'LL BRING YOU TEA.
SHF
AFTER THAT, SIR...
CHAK
...WOULD IT BE ALL RIGHT IF I RETIRED TO MY ROOM?

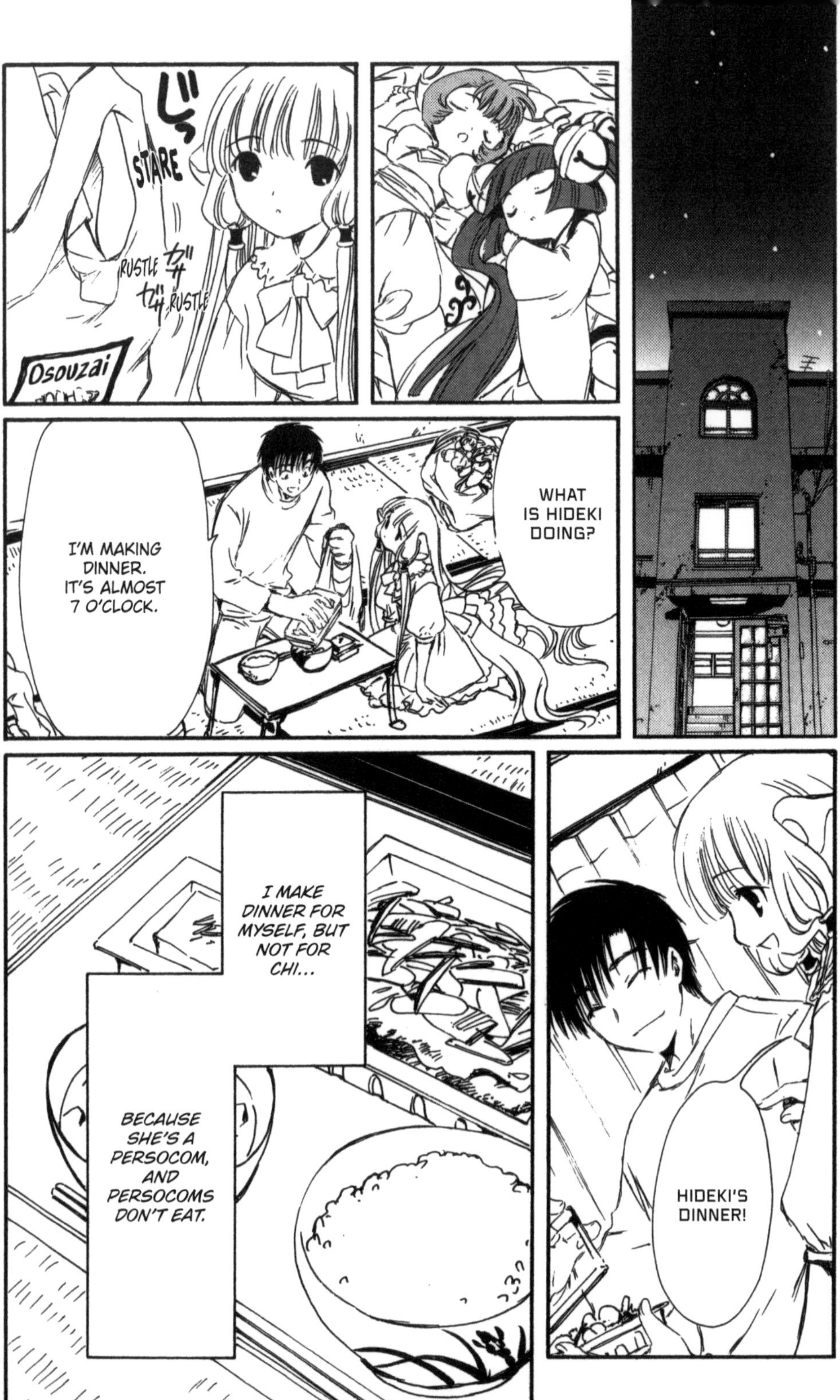
STARE
RUSTLE ガサ
ガサ RUSTLE
Osouzai
WHAT IS HIDEKI DOING?
I'M MAKING DINNER. IT'S ALMOST 7 O'CLOCK.
HIDEKI'S DINNER!
I MAKE DINNER FOR MYSELF, BUT NOT FOR CHI...
BECAUSE SHE'S A PERSOCOM, AND PERSOCOMS DON'T EAT.

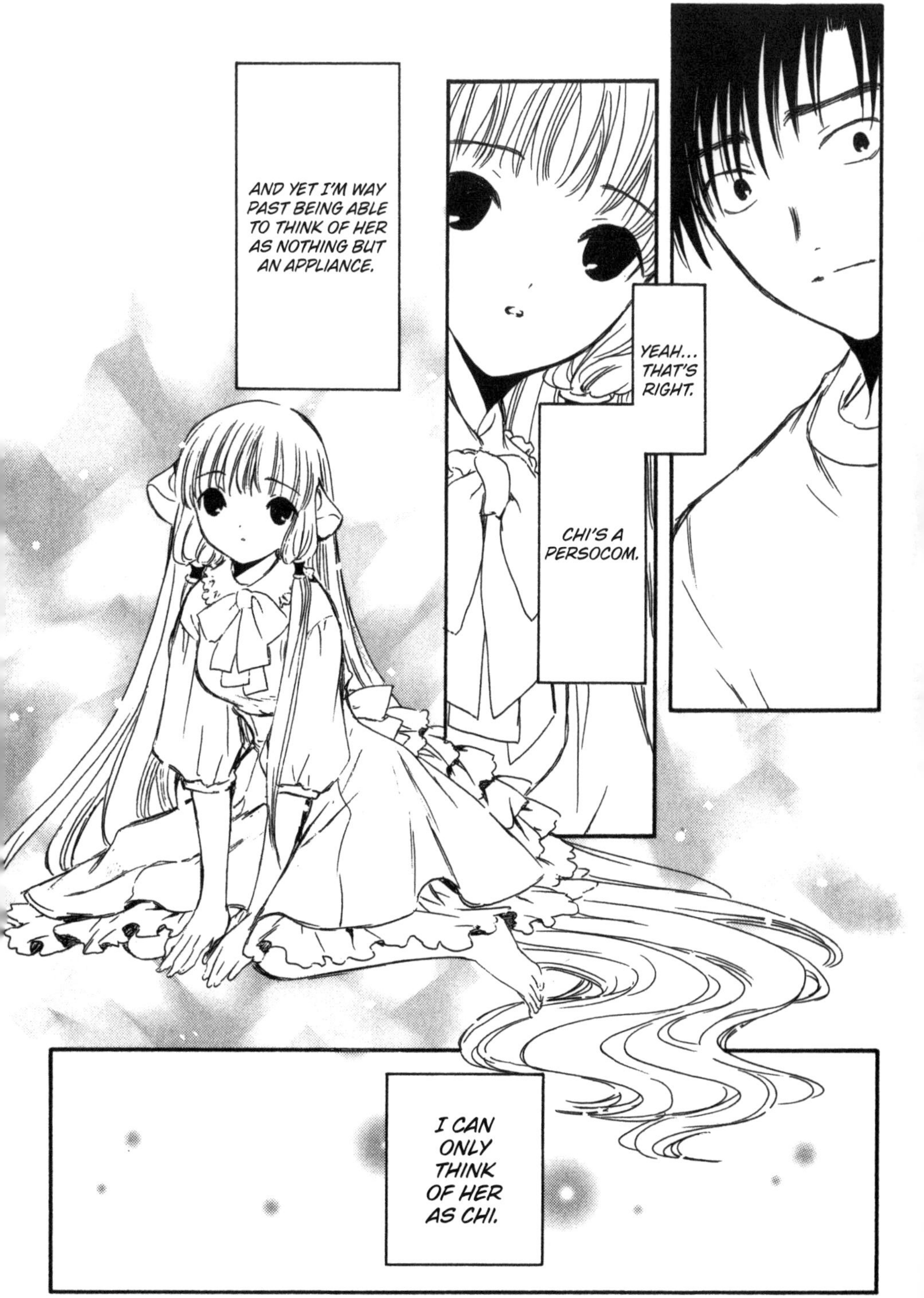
YEAH... THAT'S RIGHT.
CHI'S A PERSOCOM.
AND YET I'M WAY PAST BEING ABLE TO THINK OF HER AS NOTHING BUT AN APPLIANCE.
I CAN ONLY THINK OF HER AS CHI.

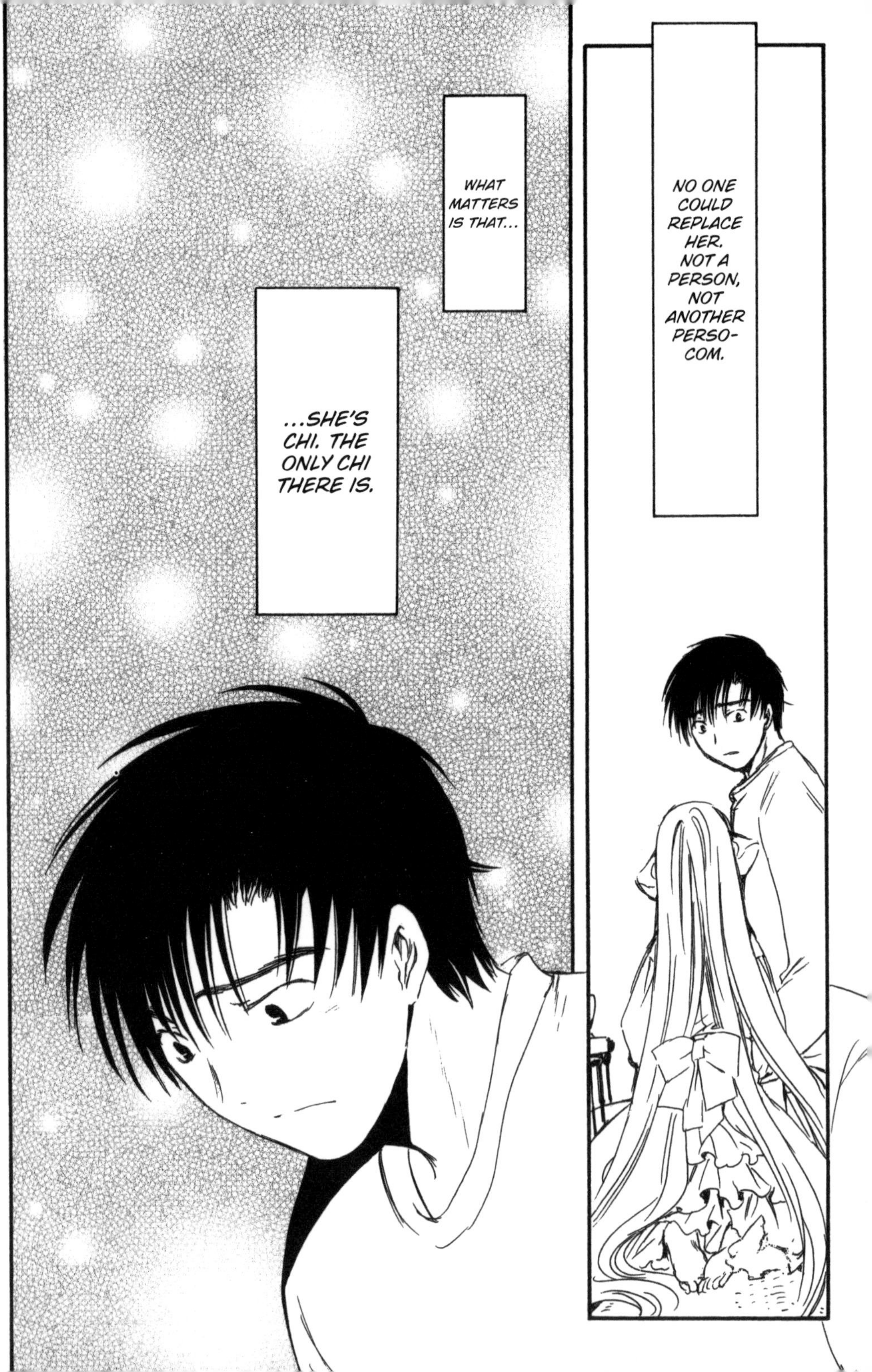
NO ONE COULD REPLACE HER. NOT A PERSON, NOT ANOTHER PERSO-COM.
WHAT MATTERS IS THAT...
...SHE'S CHI. THE ONLY CHI THERE IS.

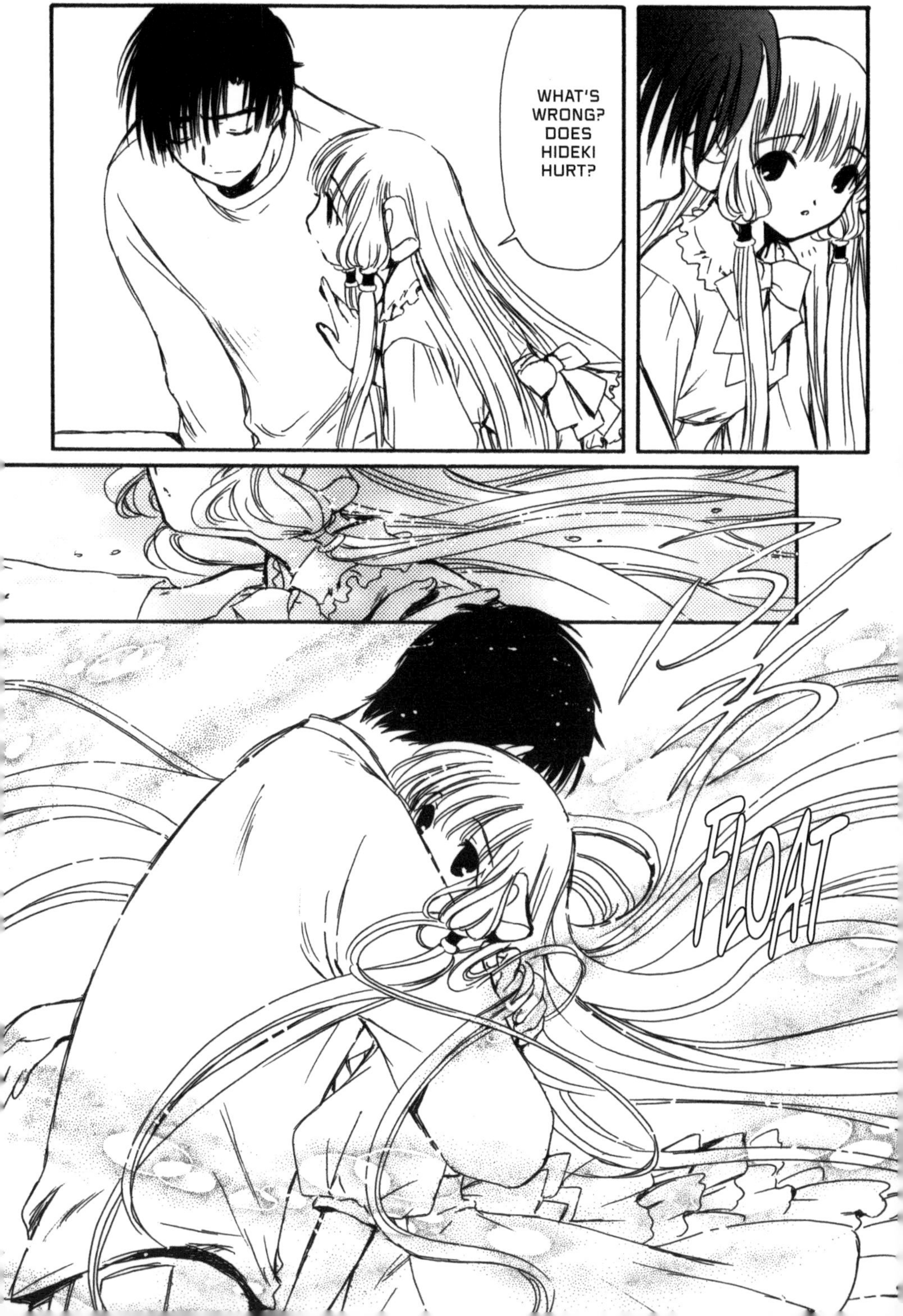
WHAT'S WRONG? DOES HIDEKI HURT?
FLOAT

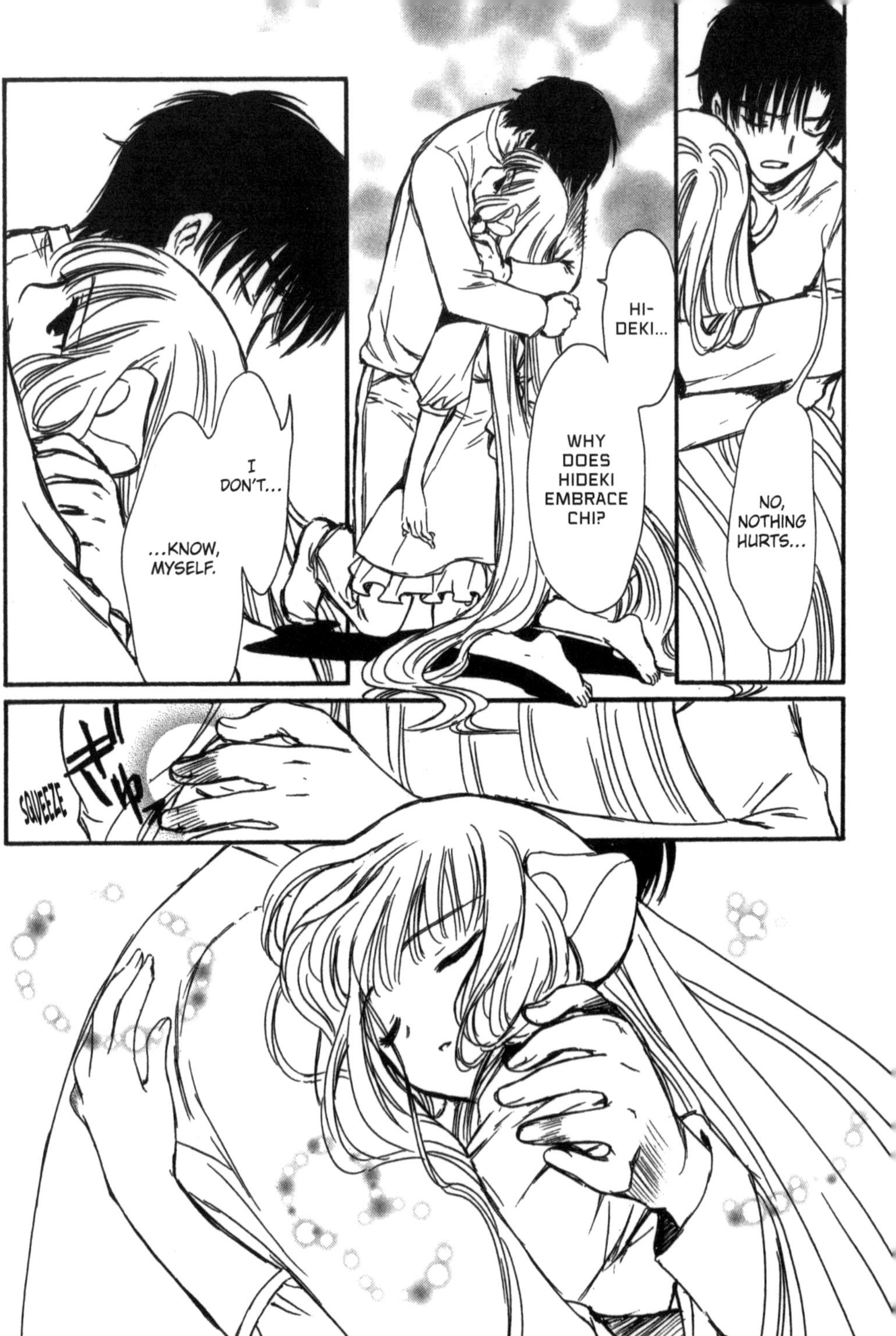
NO, NOTHING HURTS...
HI-DEKI...
WHY DOES HIDEKI EMBRACE CHI?
I DON'T...
...KNOW, MYSELF.
SQUEEZE

<chapter.71> end

Chobits

〈chapter.72〉

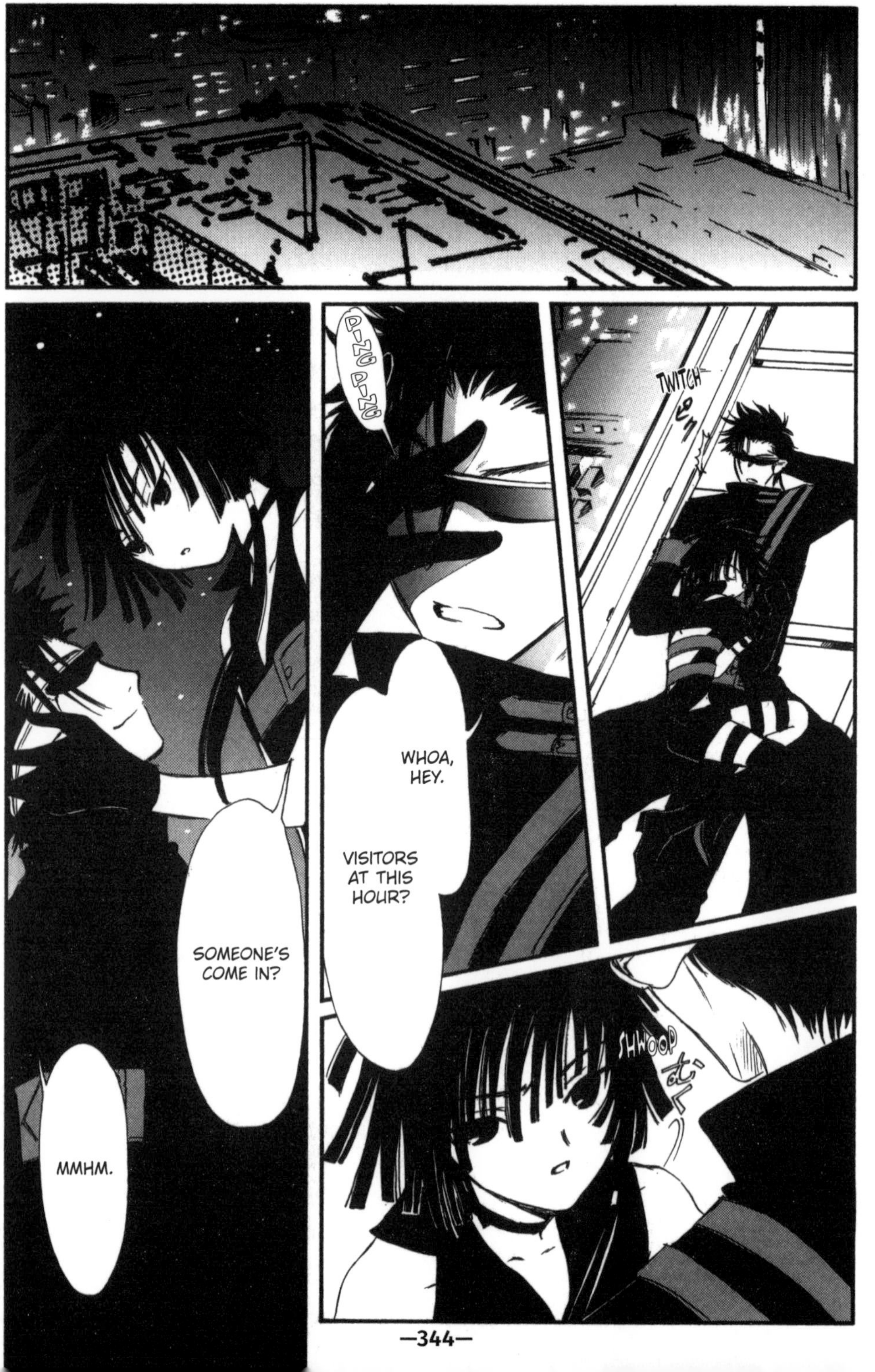
TWITCH
PING PING
WHOA, HEY.
VISITORS AT THIS HOUR?
SHWOOP
SOMEONE'S COME IN?
MMHM.

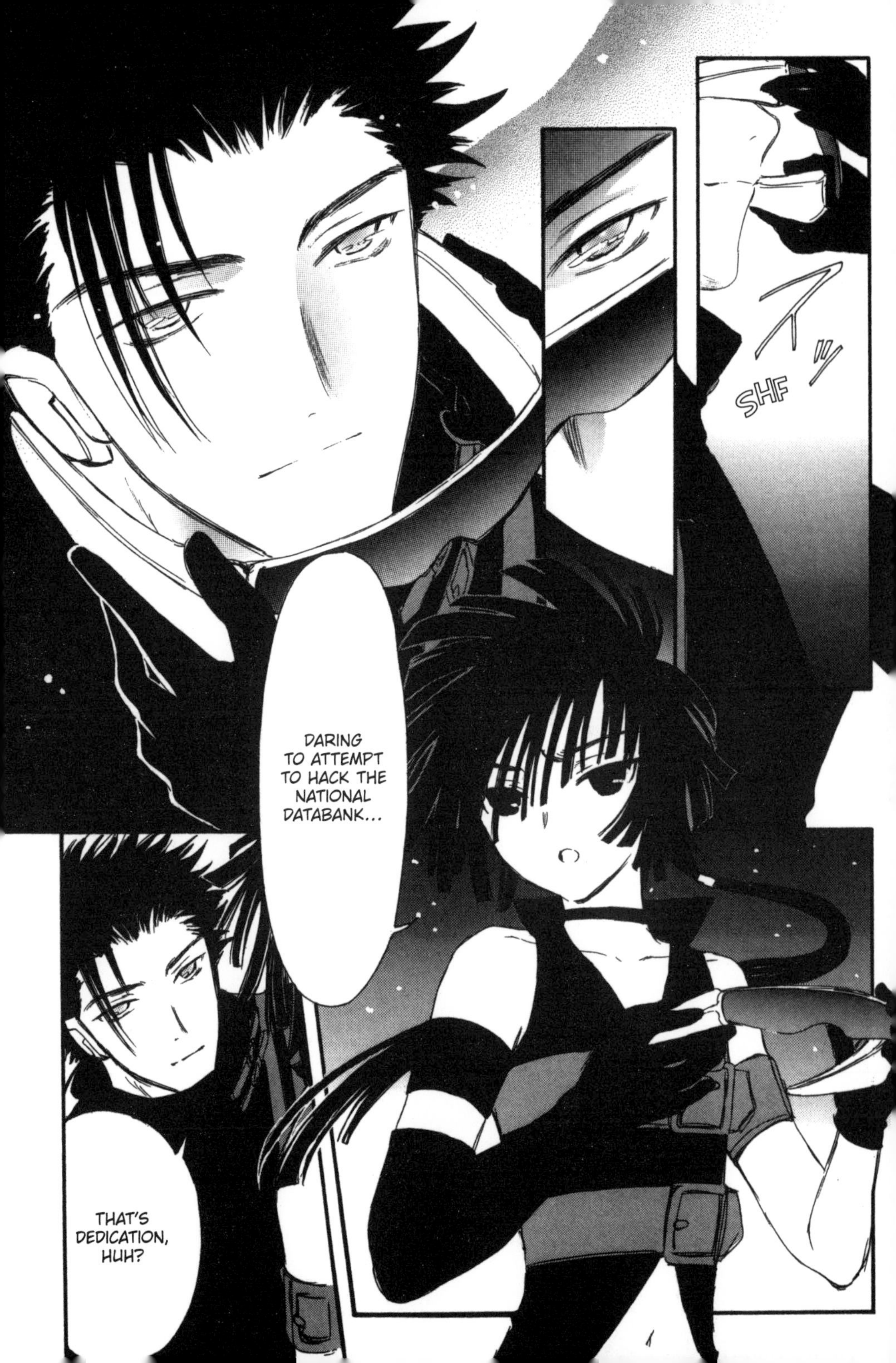
SHF
DARING TO ATTEMPT TO HACK THE NATIONAL DATABANK...
THAT'S DEDICATION, HUH?

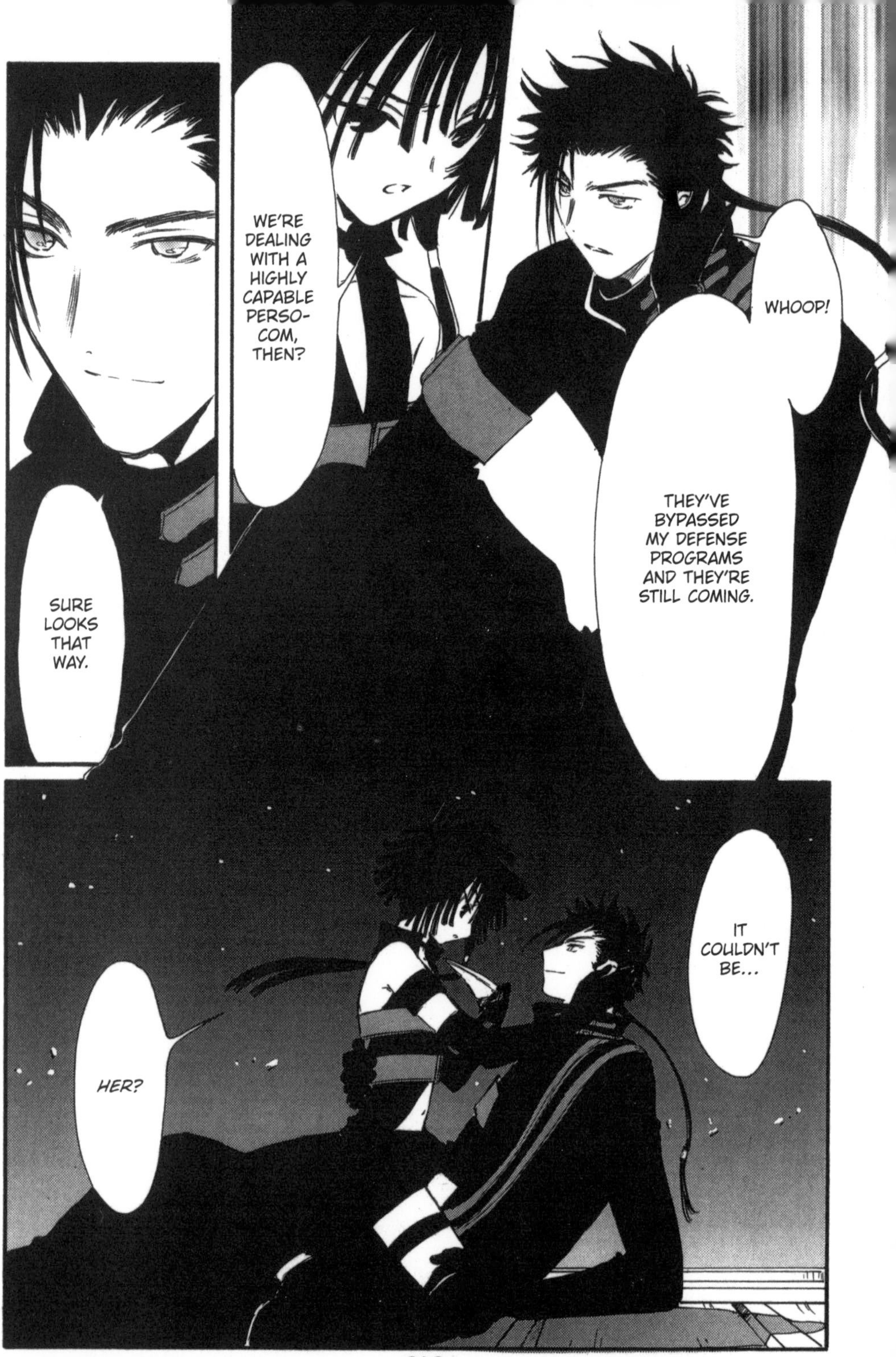
WHOOP!
THEY'VE BYPASSED MY DEFENSE PROGRAMS AND THEY'RE STILL COMING.
WE'RE DEALING WITH A HIGHLY CAPABLE PERSO-COM, THEN?
SURE LOOKS THAT WAY.
IT COULDN'T BE...
HER?

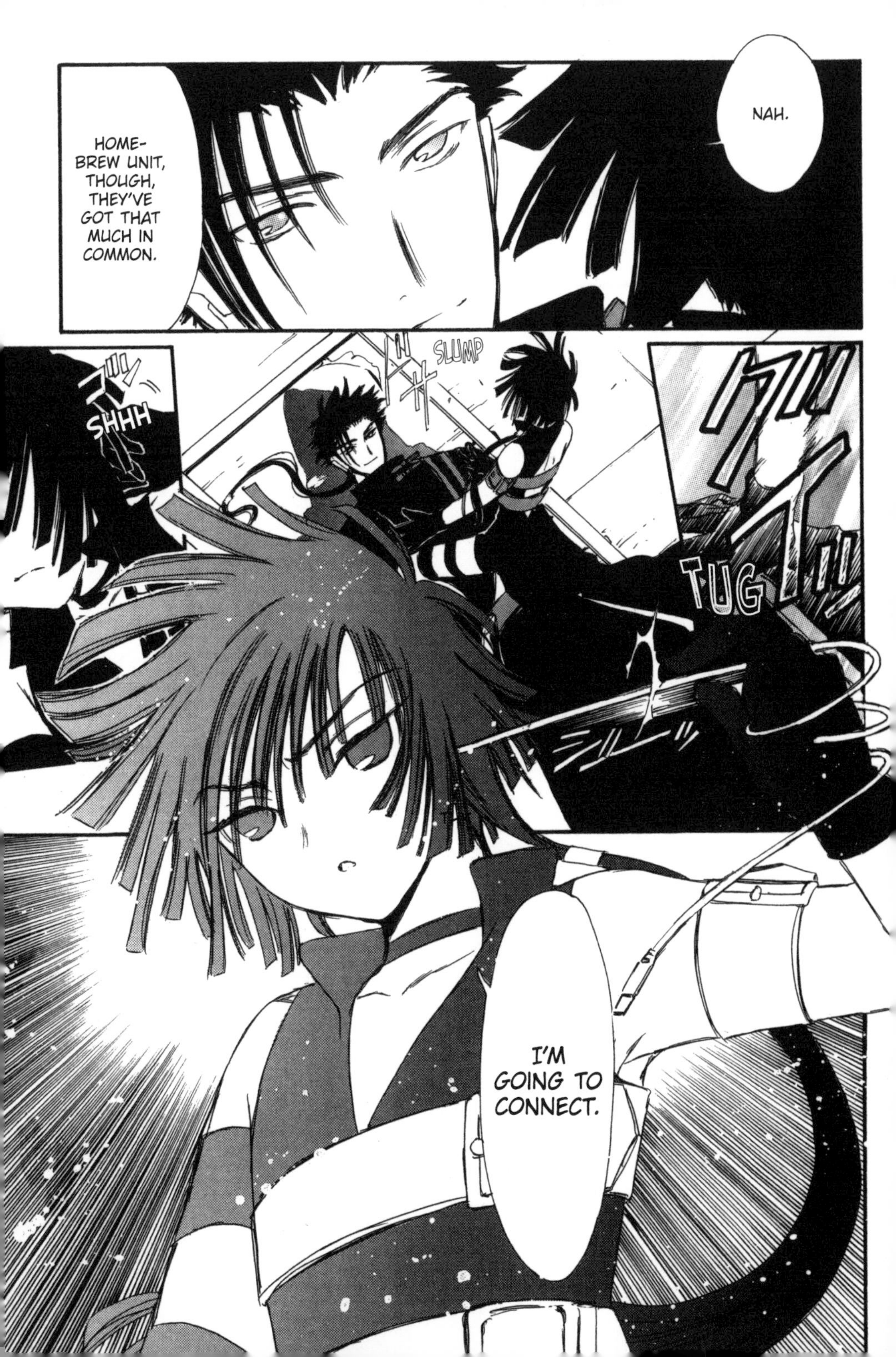
NAH.
HOME-BREW UNIT, THOUGH, THEY'VE GOT THAT MUCH IN COMMON.
TUG
SLUMP
SHHH
I'M GOING TO CONNECT.

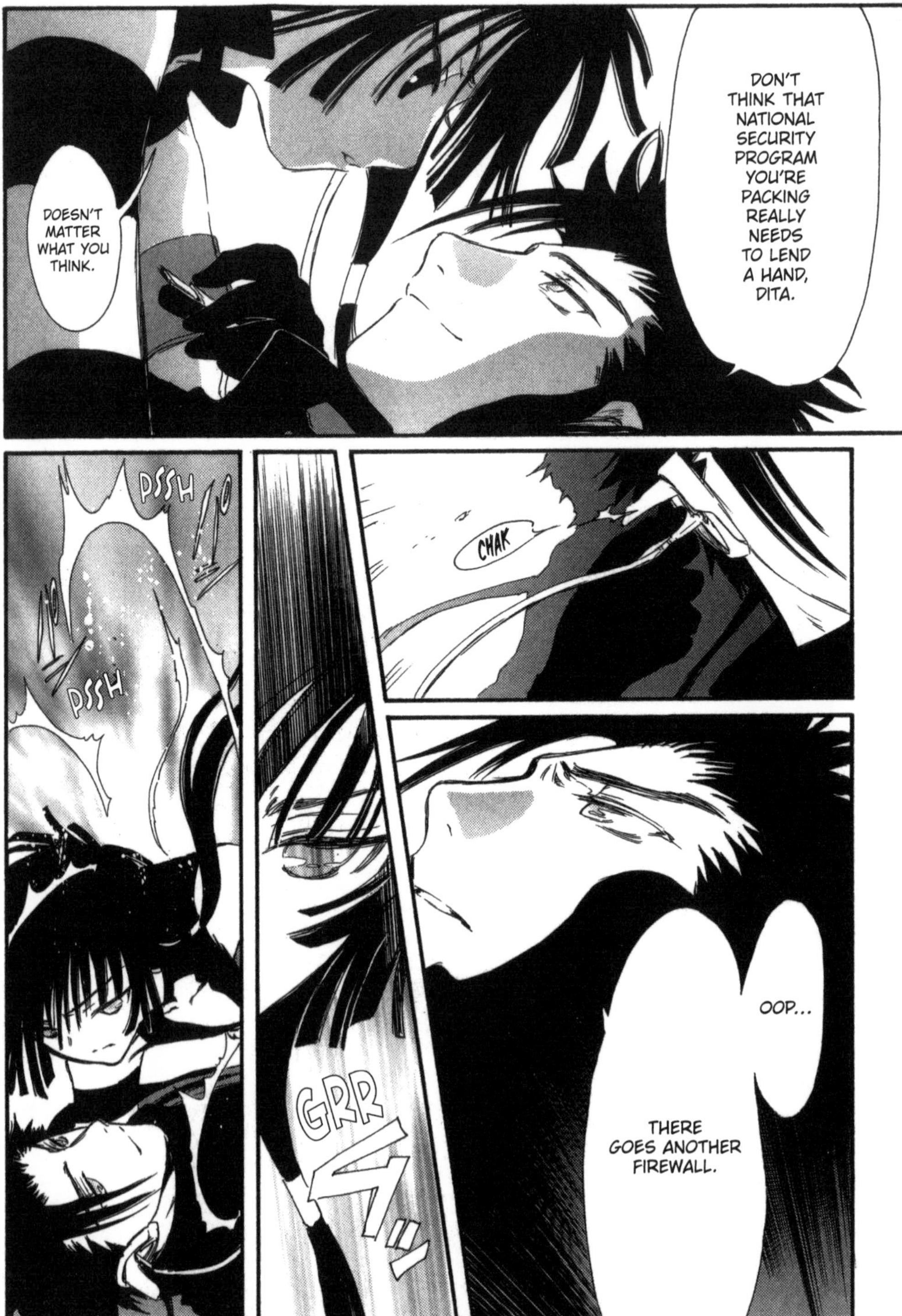
DON'T THINK THAT NATIONAL SECURITY PROGRAM YOU'RE PACKING REALLY NEEDS TO LEND A HAND, DITA.
DOESN'T MATTER WHAT YOU THINK.
CHAK
OOP...
THERE GOES ANOTHER FIREWALL.
GRR
PSSH
PSSH

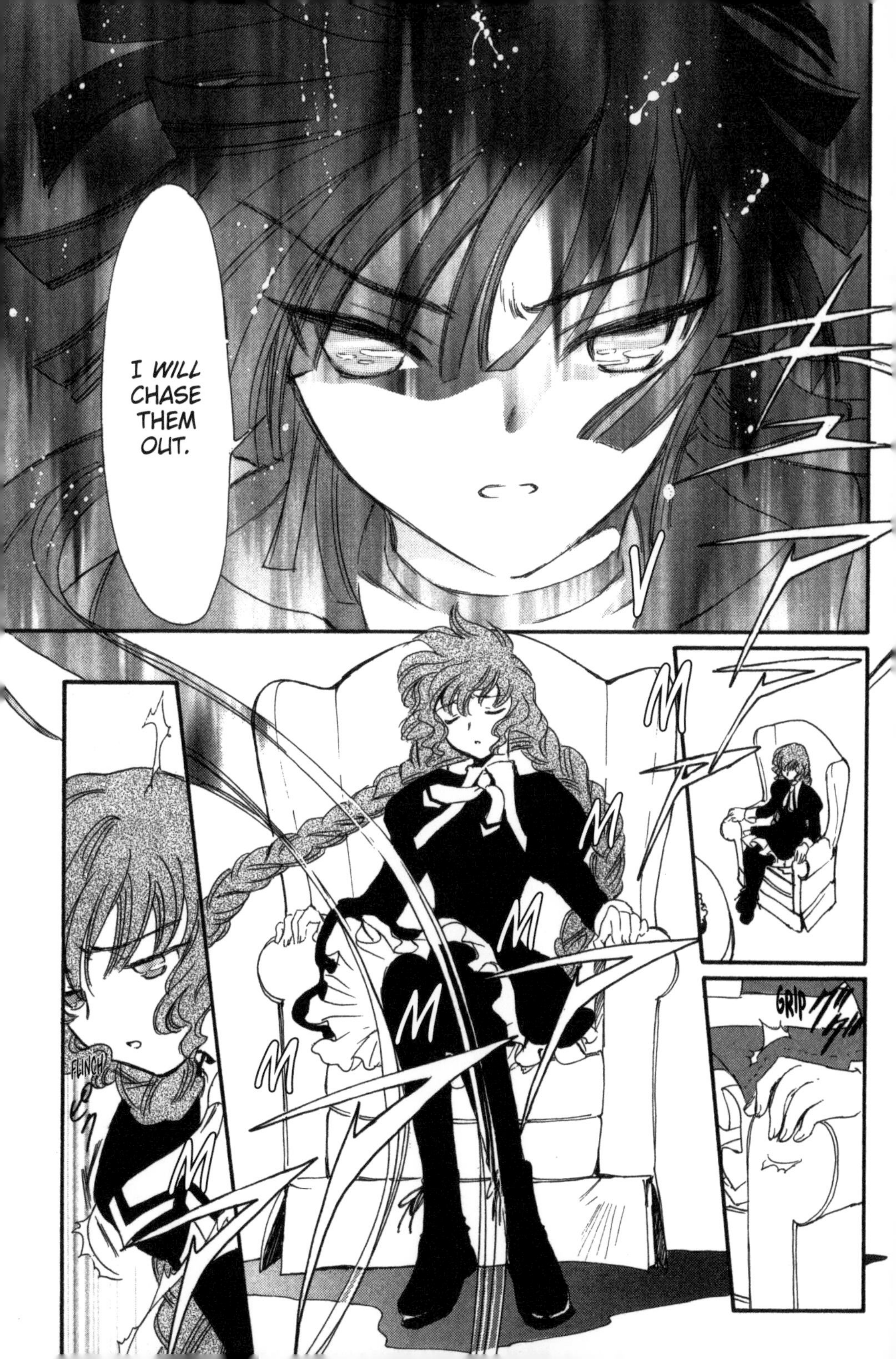
I WILL CHASE THEM OUT.
GRIP
FLINCH

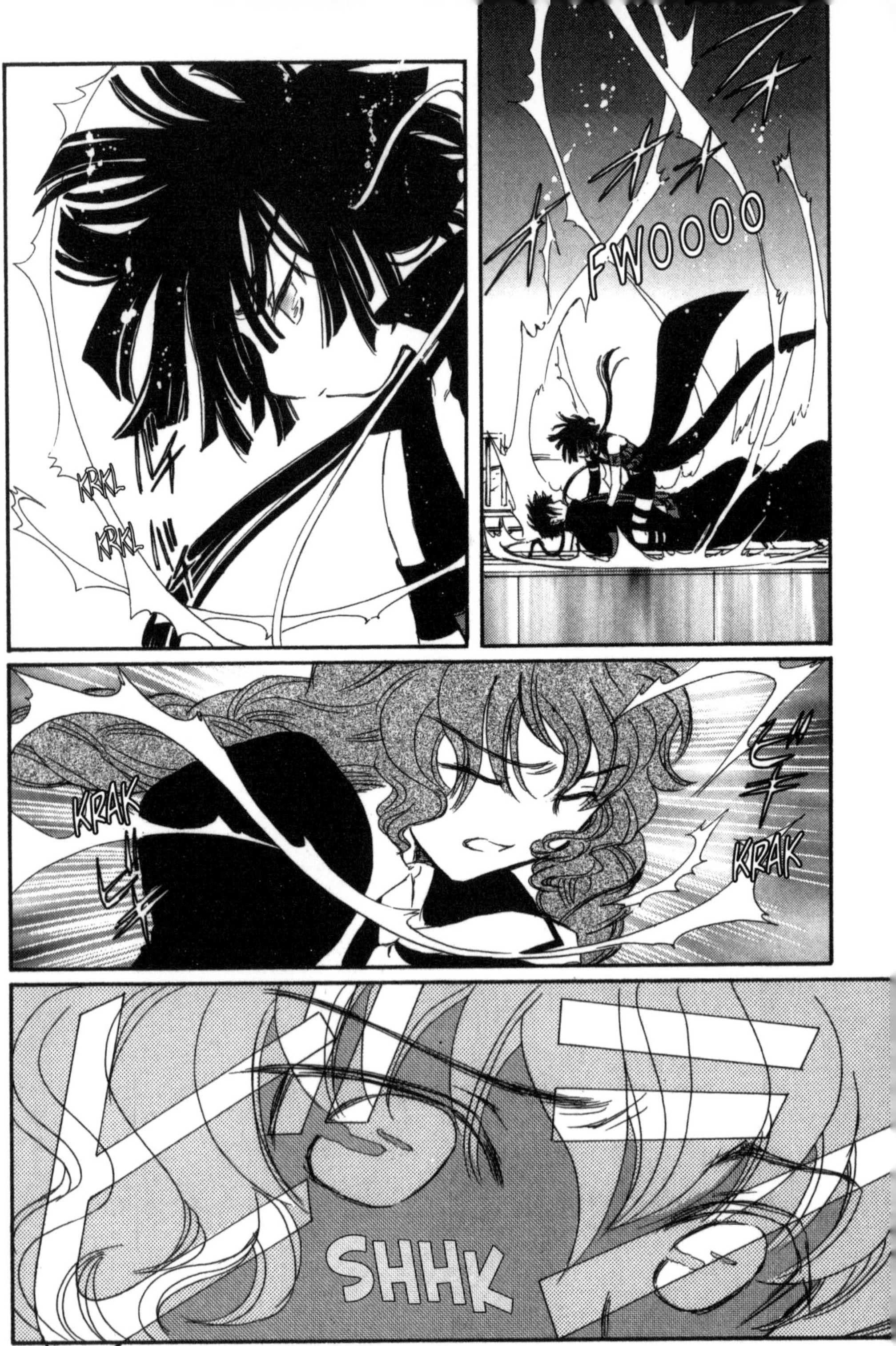
FWOOOO
KRKL
KRKL
KRAK
KRAK
SHHK

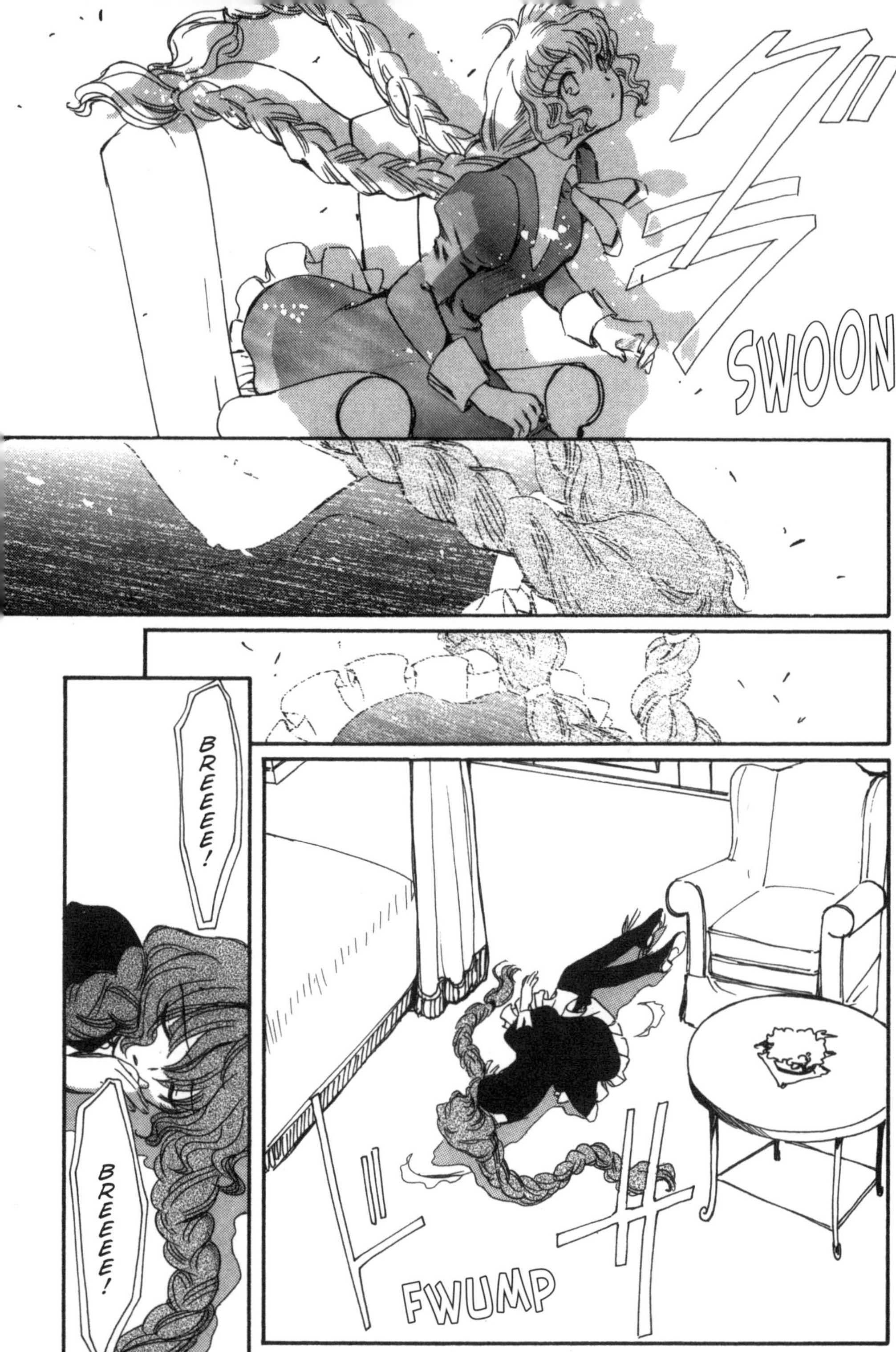
SWOON
FWUMP
BREEEEE!
BREEEEE!

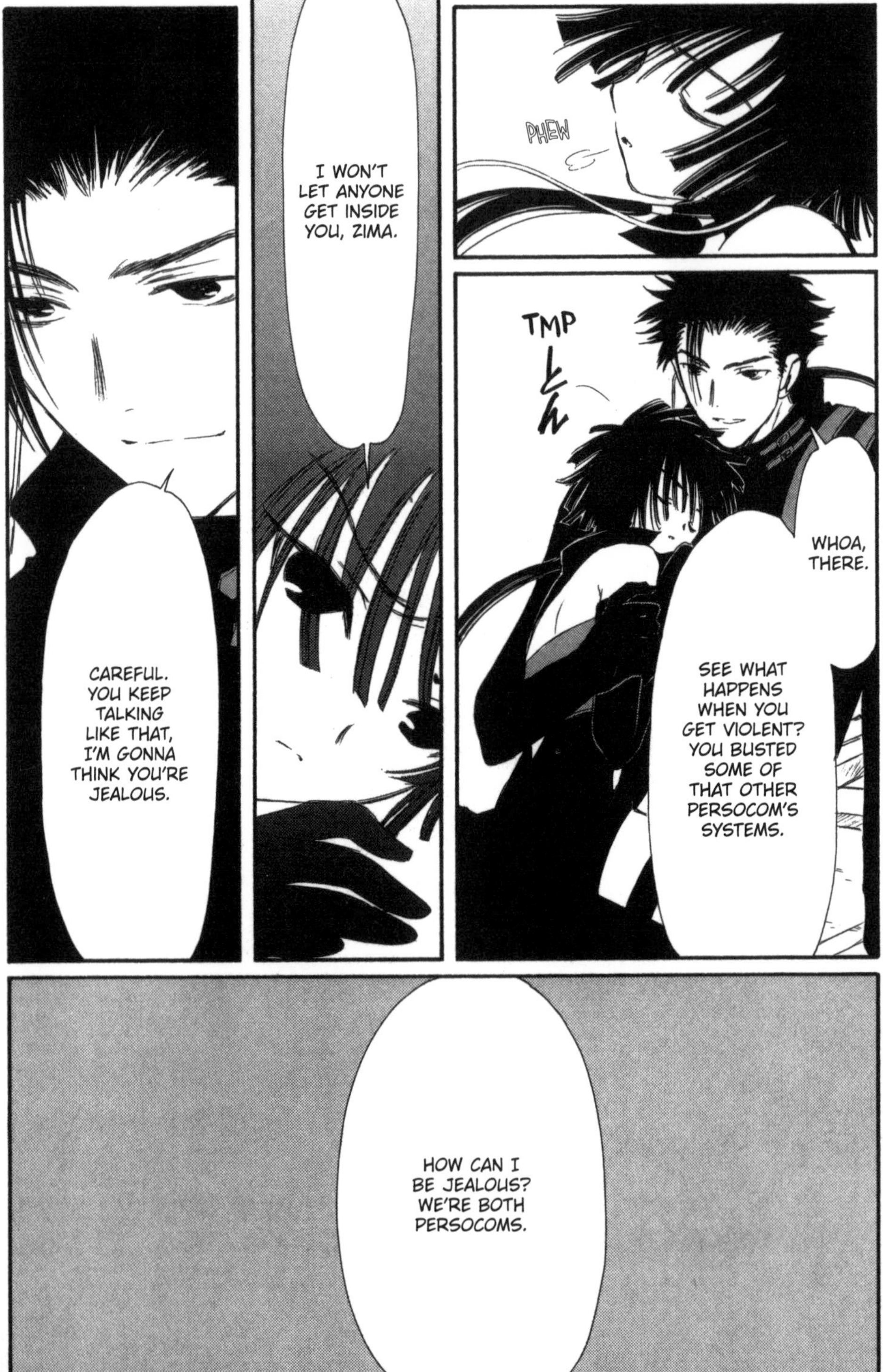
PHEW
TMP
WHOA, THERE.
SEE WHAT HAPPENS WHEN YOU GET VIOLENT? YOU BUSTED SOME OF THAT OTHER PERSOCOM'S SYSTEMS.
I WON'T LET ANYONE GET INSIDE YOU, ZIMA.
CAREFUL. YOU KEEP TALKING LIKE THAT, I'M GONNA THINK YOU'RE JEALOUS.
HOW CAN I BE JEALOUS? WE'RE BOTH PERSOCOMS.

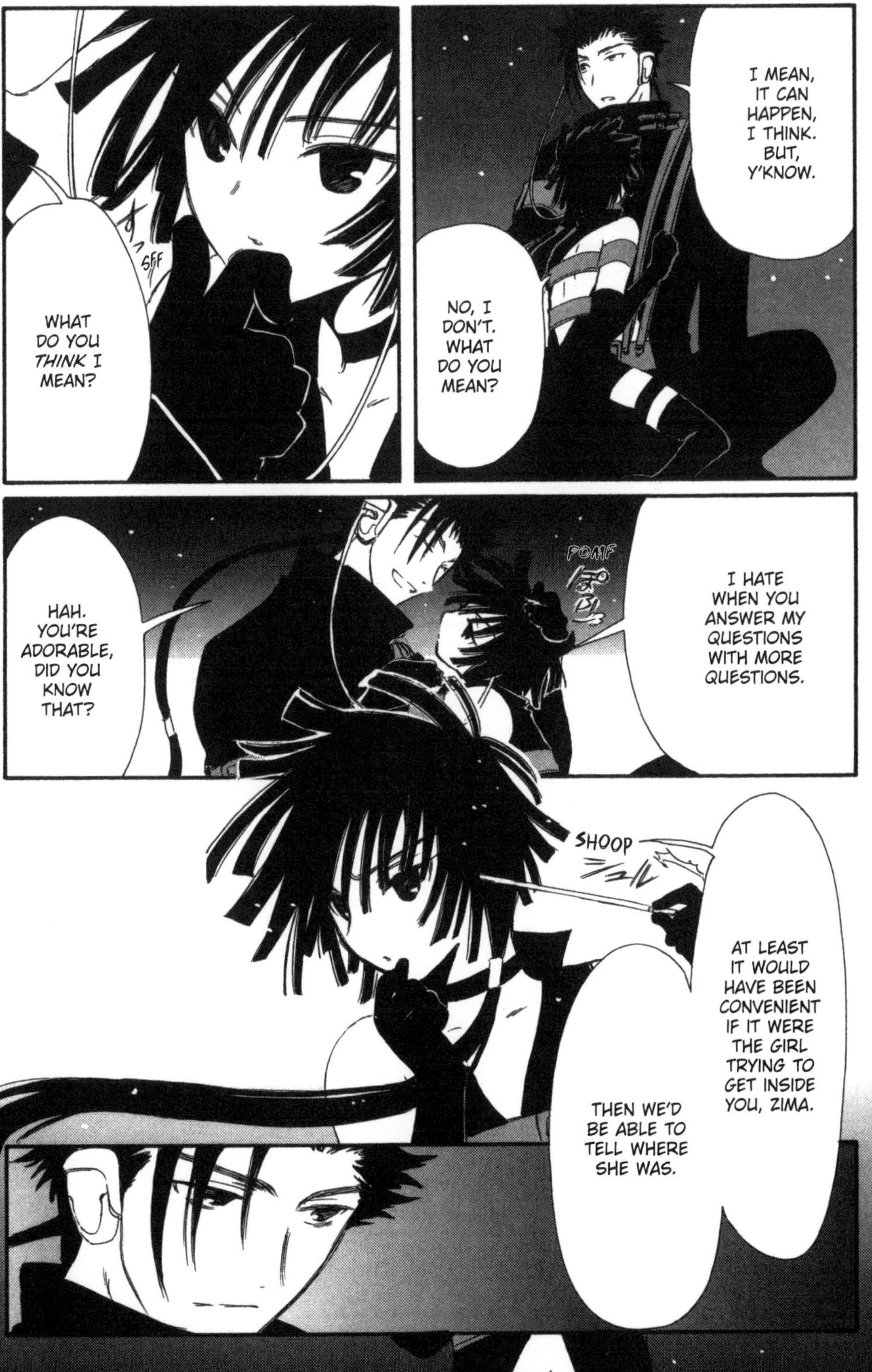

I MEAN, IT CAN HAPPEN, I THINK. BUT, Y'KNOW.
NO, I DON'T. WHAT DO YOU MEAN?
SFF
WHAT DO YOU *THINK* I MEAN?
I HATE WHEN YOU ANSWER MY QUESTIONS WITH MORE QUESTIONS.
POMF
HAH. YOU'RE ADORABLE, DID YOU KNOW THAT?
SHOOP
AT LEAST IT WOULD HAVE BEEN CONVENIENT IF IT WERE THE GIRL TRYING TO GET INSIDE YOU, ZIMA.
THEN WE'D BE ABLE TO TELL WHERE SHE WAS.

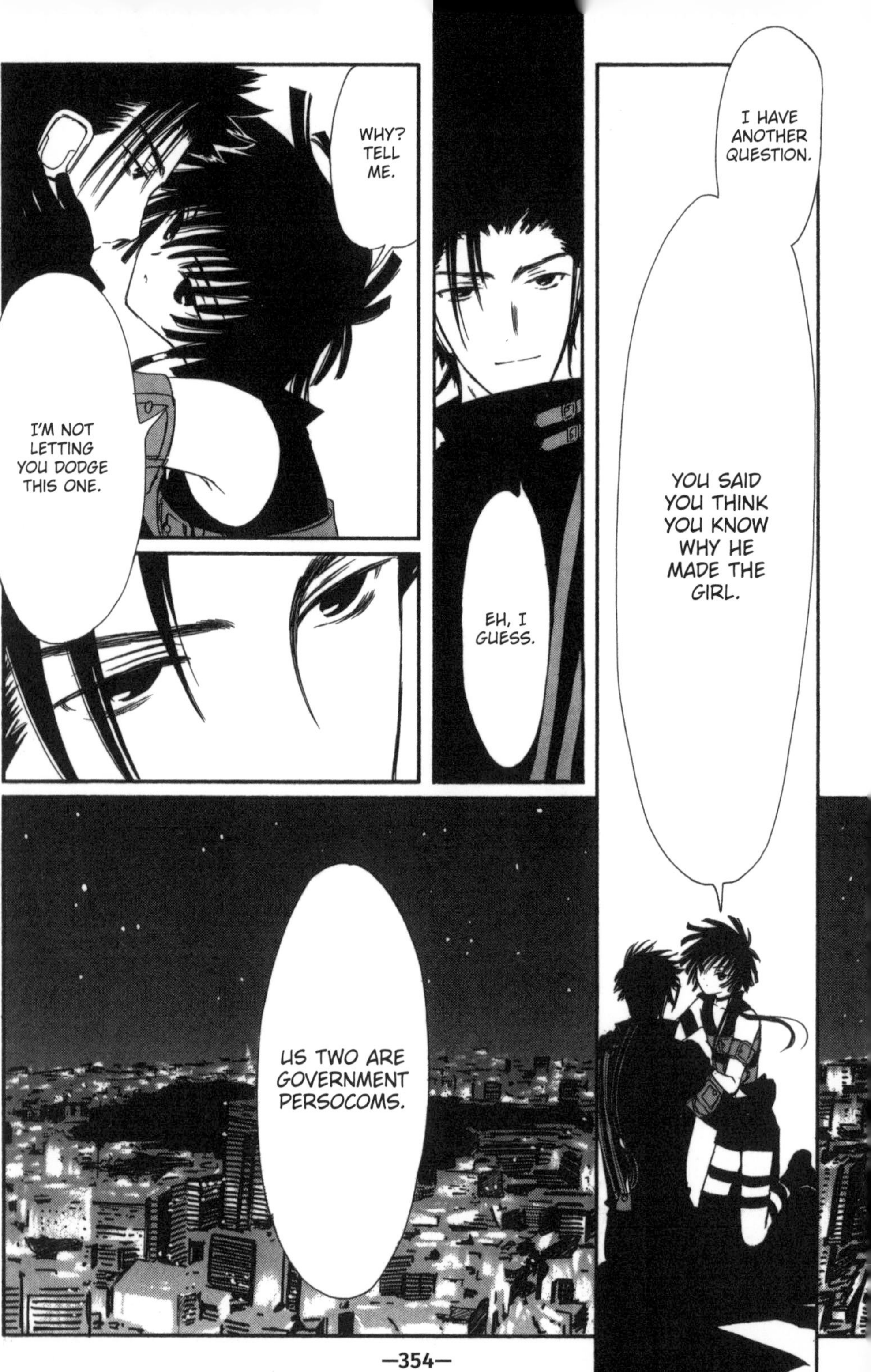
I HAVE ANOTHER QUESTION.
YOU SAID YOU THINK YOU KNOW WHY HE MADE THE GIRL.
EH, I GUESS.
WHY? TELL ME.
I'M NOT LETTING YOU DODGE THIS ONE.
US TWO ARE GOVERNMENT PERSOCOMS.

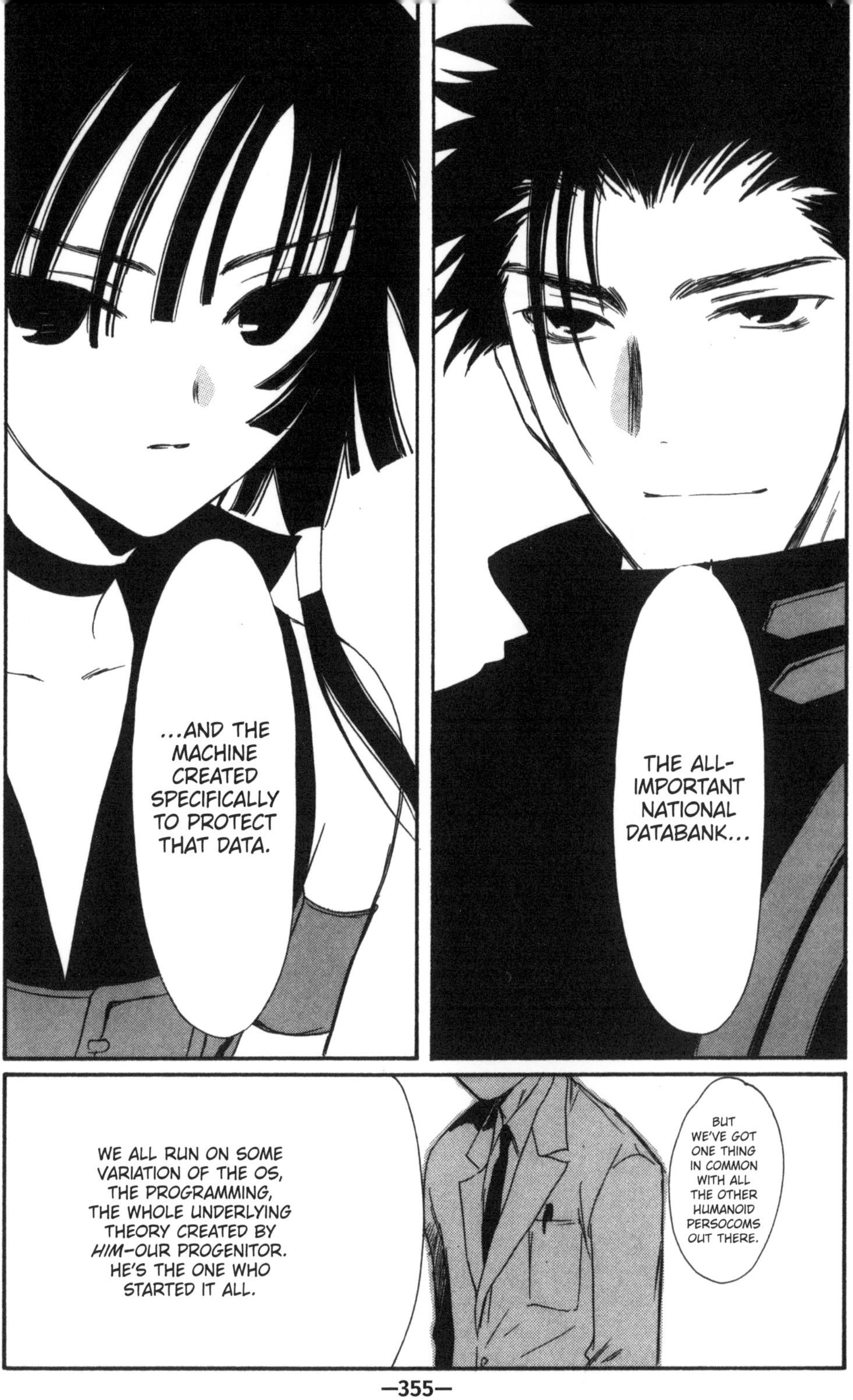
THE ALL-IMPORTANT NATIONAL DATABANK...
...AND THE MACHINE CREATED SPECIFICALLY TO PROTECT THAT DATA.
BUT WE'VE GOT ONE THING IN COMMON WITH ALL THE OTHER HUMANOID PERSOCOMS OUT THERE.
WE ALL RUN ON SOME VARIATION OF THE OS, THE PROGRAMMING, THE WHOLE UNDERLYING THEORY CREATED BY *HIM*–OUR PROGENITOR. HE'S THE ONE WHO STARTED IT ALL.

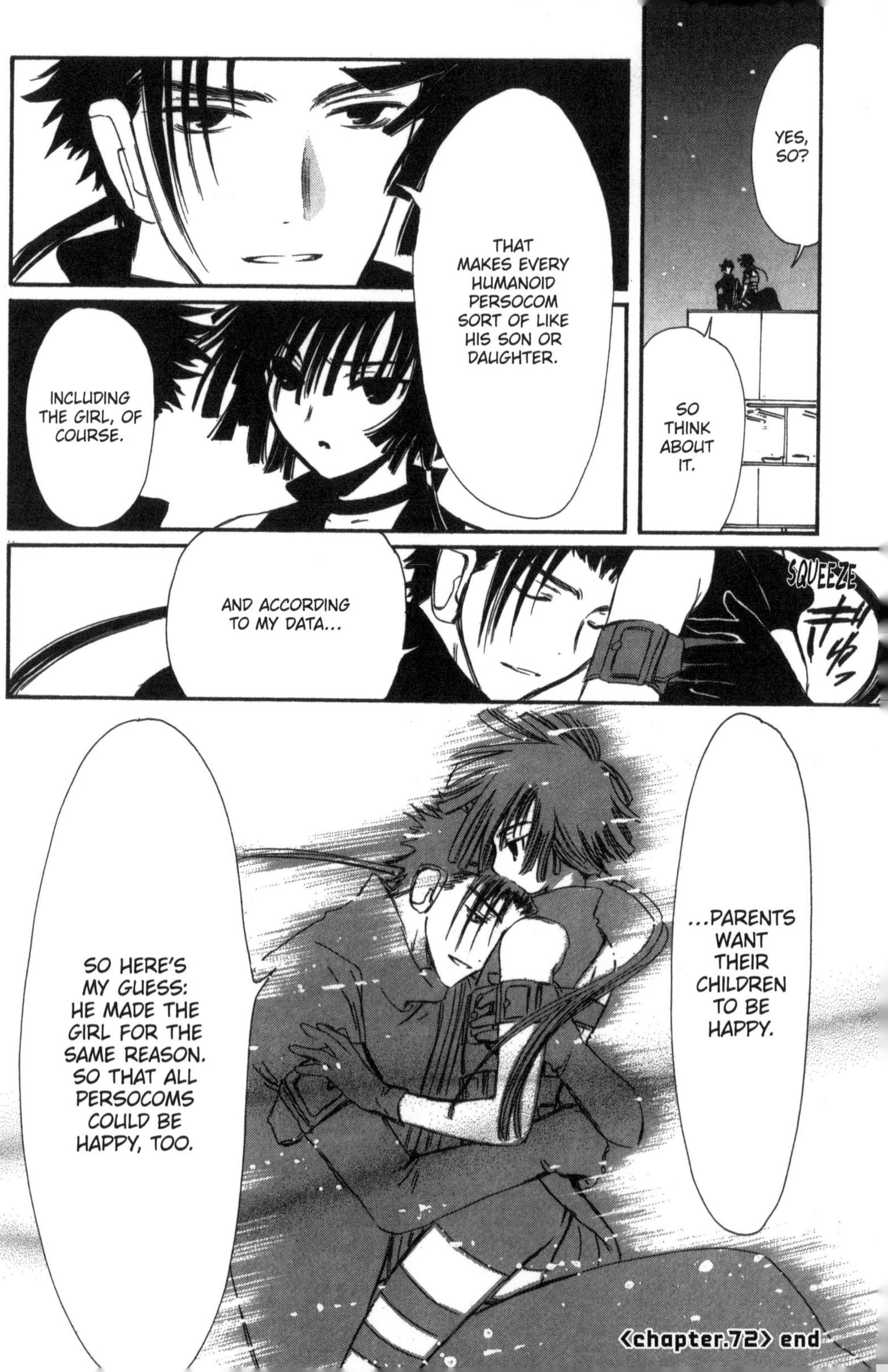
YES, SO?
SO THINK ABOUT IT.
THAT MAKES EVERY HUMANOID PERSOCOM SORT OF LIKE HIS SON OR DAUGHTER.
INCLUDING THE GIRL, OF COURSE.
SQUEEZE
AND ACCORDING TO MY DATA...
...PARENTS WANT THEIR CHILDREN TO BE HAPPY.
SO HERE'S MY GUESS: HE MADE THE GIRL FOR THE SAME REASON. SO THAT ALL PERSOCOMS COULD BE HAPPY, TOO.
«chapter.72» end

Chobits

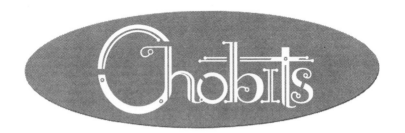

Translation Notes

Cremate, page 212

Cremation, often accompanied by a Buddhist service, is the most common form of funeral in Japan. Implicitly, the reporter is asking whether Ueda plans to treat his wife's body as that of a human or a disposable machine. (The verb in his second word balloon, *haiki suru,* is especially stark: the most crassly treated of human corpses might be *suterareta,* thrown away or abandoned, but it would never be *haiki sareta,* which purely refers to disposing of inanimate objects and especially machines.)

WHAT DO YOU PLAN TO DO WITH IT AFTER THIS?
ARE YOU GOING TO CREMATE THE REMAINS?
OR ARE YOU JUST GOING TO SCRAP IT?!

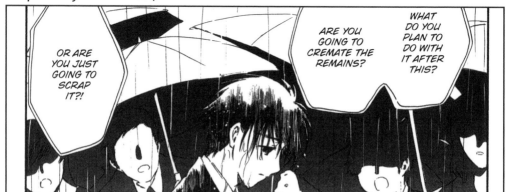

Senpai, page 234

Typically, *senpai* refers to someone who has more experience at something than you do (it literally means "a fellow who is ahead"). A senpai is often, but not always, older than you are. Although Yumi always addresses Hideki as "senpai" at Club Pleasure, it seems from the dialogue on this page that *she* is actually *his* senpai in terms of having begun the job before him. Most likely, Yumi addresses him this way in deference to the fact that he's much further along in school (or simply age) than she is.

THE DAY YOU STARTED, SENPAI...
BRUSH
WHEN YOU SAID HI TO ME, YOU MENTIONED YOU'D WORKED AT TIROL BEFORE THAT.

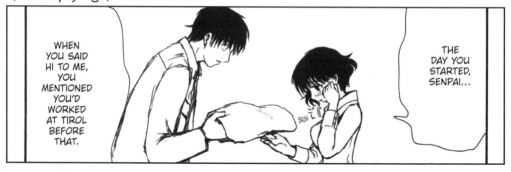

Bow, page 264

The sound effect here, *peko,* is the standard one for a character bowing, but as you can see, Chi in panel three on this page and Hideki in panel four, don't do "full" bows from the waist. Instead, they sort of dip the top halves of their bodies while still moving. This is common at the end of social interactions in Japan, especially less formal ones; as shown here, you can do it while walking away to add a touch of politeness even as you exit the situation. In fact, the range of "bows" in Japan encompasses everything from extremely deep, formal bows (including prostration, although this is uncommon today) to a simple nod of the head, which may occur, say, between coworkers passing in the hallway, or may be given by a superior acknowledging a subordinate. (If you're new to bowing and aren't sure what's best, you'll rarely go wrong by sticking to the standard bow from the waist.)

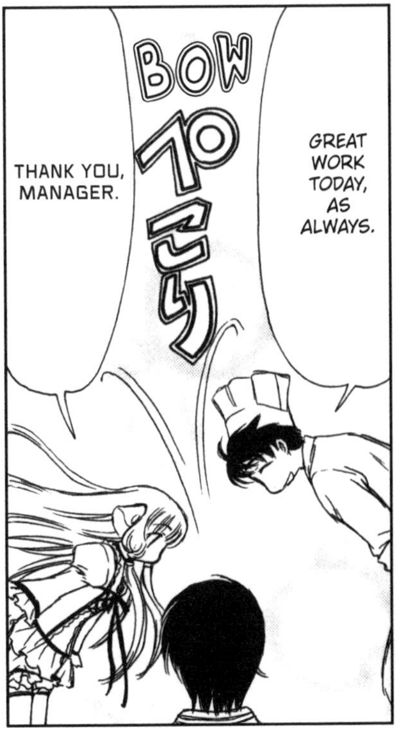
GREAT WORK TODAY, AS ALWAYS.
BOW
THANK YOU, MANAGER.

-Shan, page 270

This unconventional honorific is probably a childish corruption of -san, intended to sound cute.

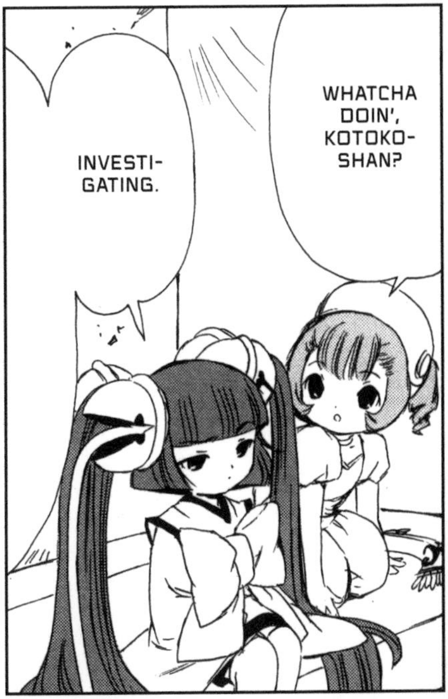
WHATCHA DOIN', KOTOKO-SHAN?
INVESTI-GATING.

¥1000, page 276

Back when *Chobits* was running, the exchange rate was around 113 yen to one US dollar, making each of these rings a bit more than eight dollars. However, there's no way to know whether prices in the *Chobits* universe are intended to reflect contemporary real-world currency values, so that conversion may be meaningless.

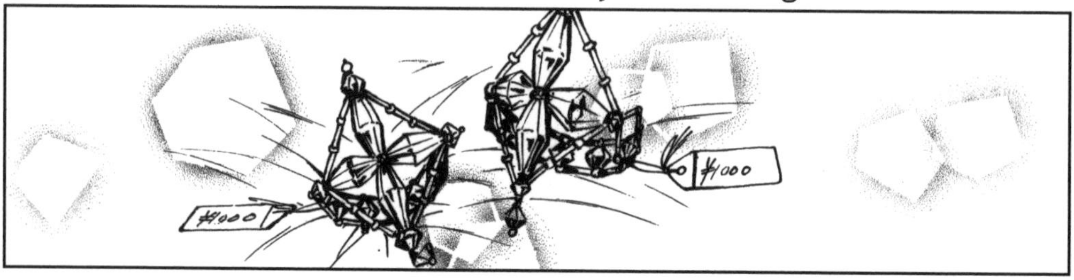
¥1000
¥1000

Osouzai, page 338

This appears to be the name of the grocery or convenience store where Hideki bought his dinner, but it also happens to be a Japanese word meaning "side dish."

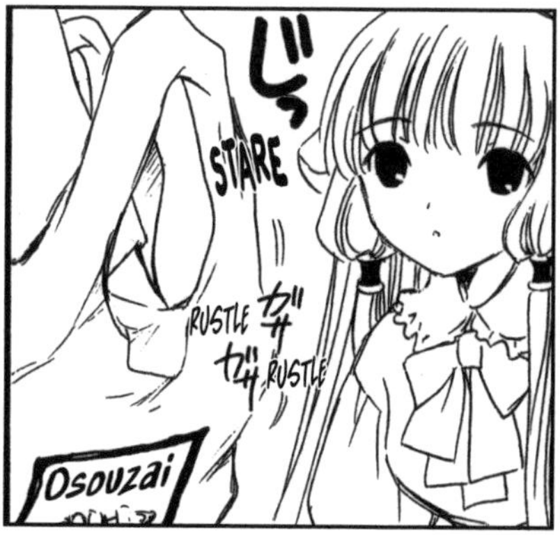
じっ
STARE
ガサ
RUSTLE
ガサ
RUSTLE
Osouzai

Chobits

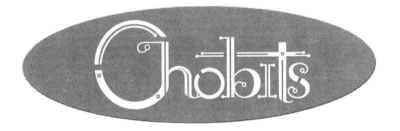

A Kodansha Comics Hardcover Original
Chobits 20th Anniversary Edition volume 3 copyright © 2002
CLAMP · Shigatsu Tsuitachi Co., Ltd. / Kodansha Ltd.
English translation copyright © 2020
CLAMP · Shigatsu Tsuitachi Co., Ltd. / Kodansha Ltd.

Published in the United States by Kodansha Comics, an imprint of Kodansha USA Publishing, LLC, New York.

Publication rights for this English edition arranged through Kodansha Ltd., Tokyo.

First published in Japan in 2002 by Kodansha Ltd., Tokyo as *Chobittsu*, volumes 5 and 6.

ISBN 978-1-64651-018-4

Printed in China.

www.kodanshacomics.com

9 8 7 6 5 4 3 2 1
Translation: Kevin Steinbach
Lettering: Michael Martin
Editing: Tiff Ferentini
Kodansha Comics edition cover design: Phil Balsman

Publisher: Kiichiro Sugawara

Director of publishing services: Ben Applegate
Associate director of operations: Stephen Pakula
Publishing services managing editor: Noelle Webster
Assistant production manager: Emi Lotto, Angela Zurlo

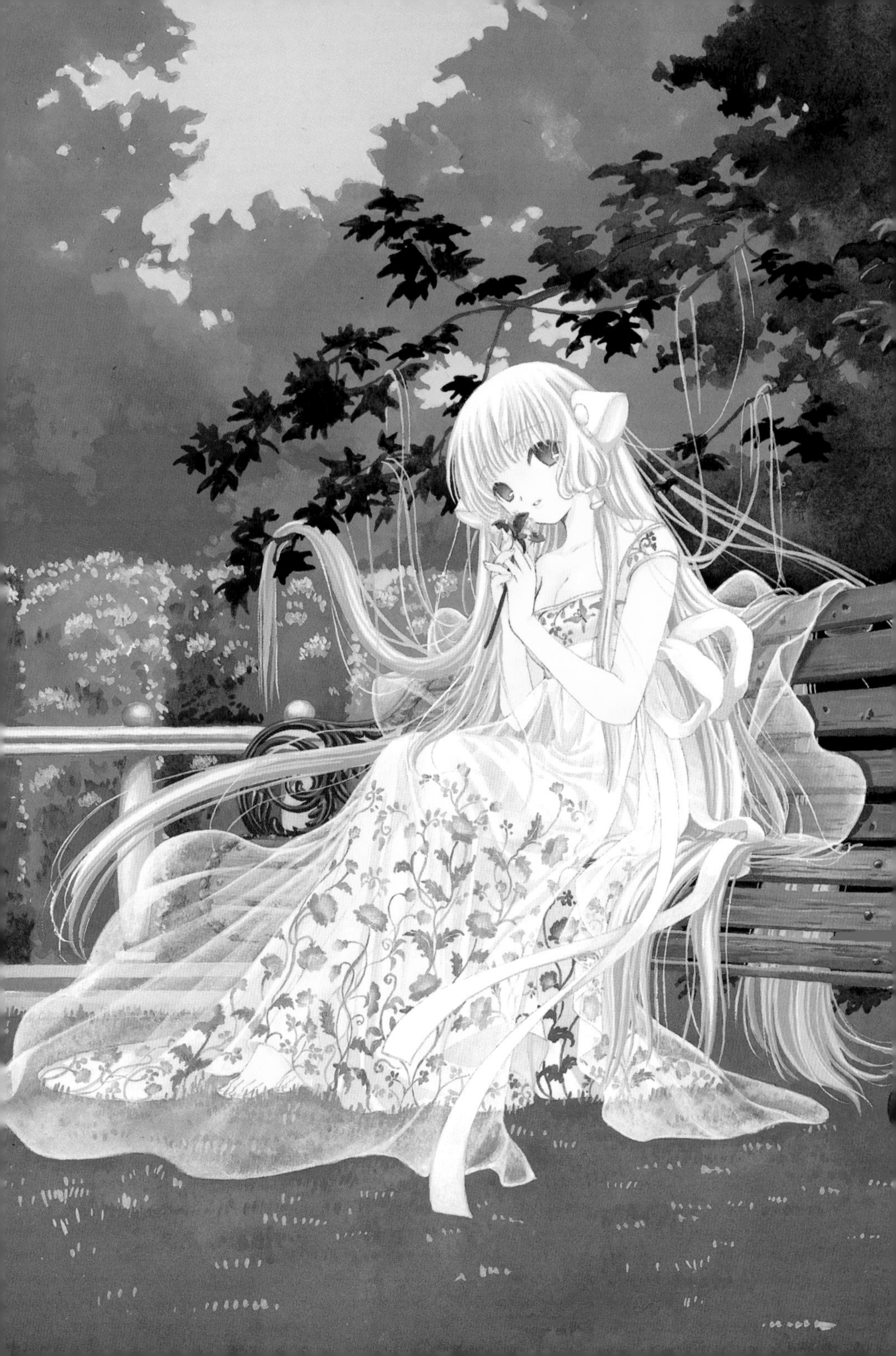

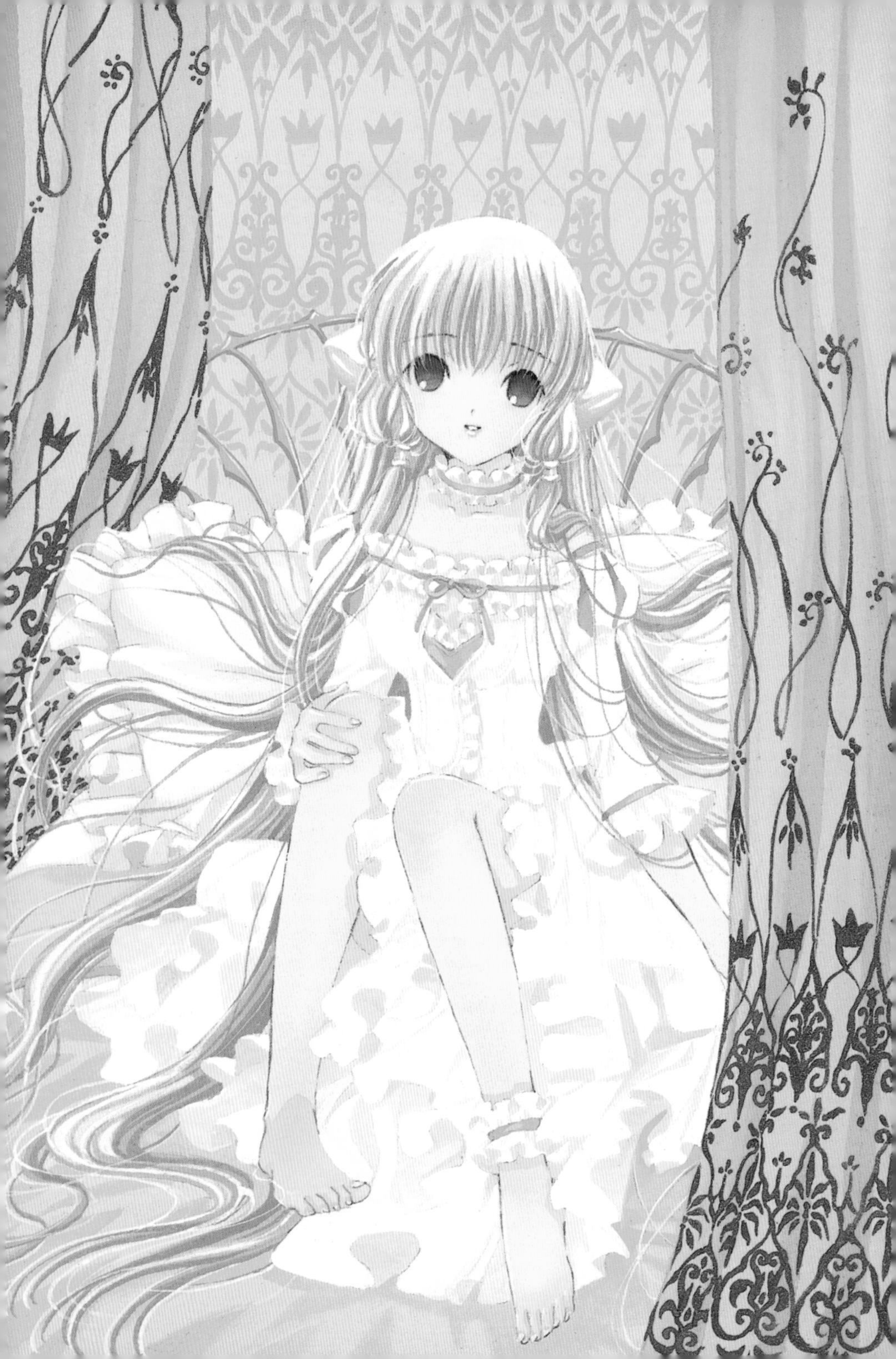

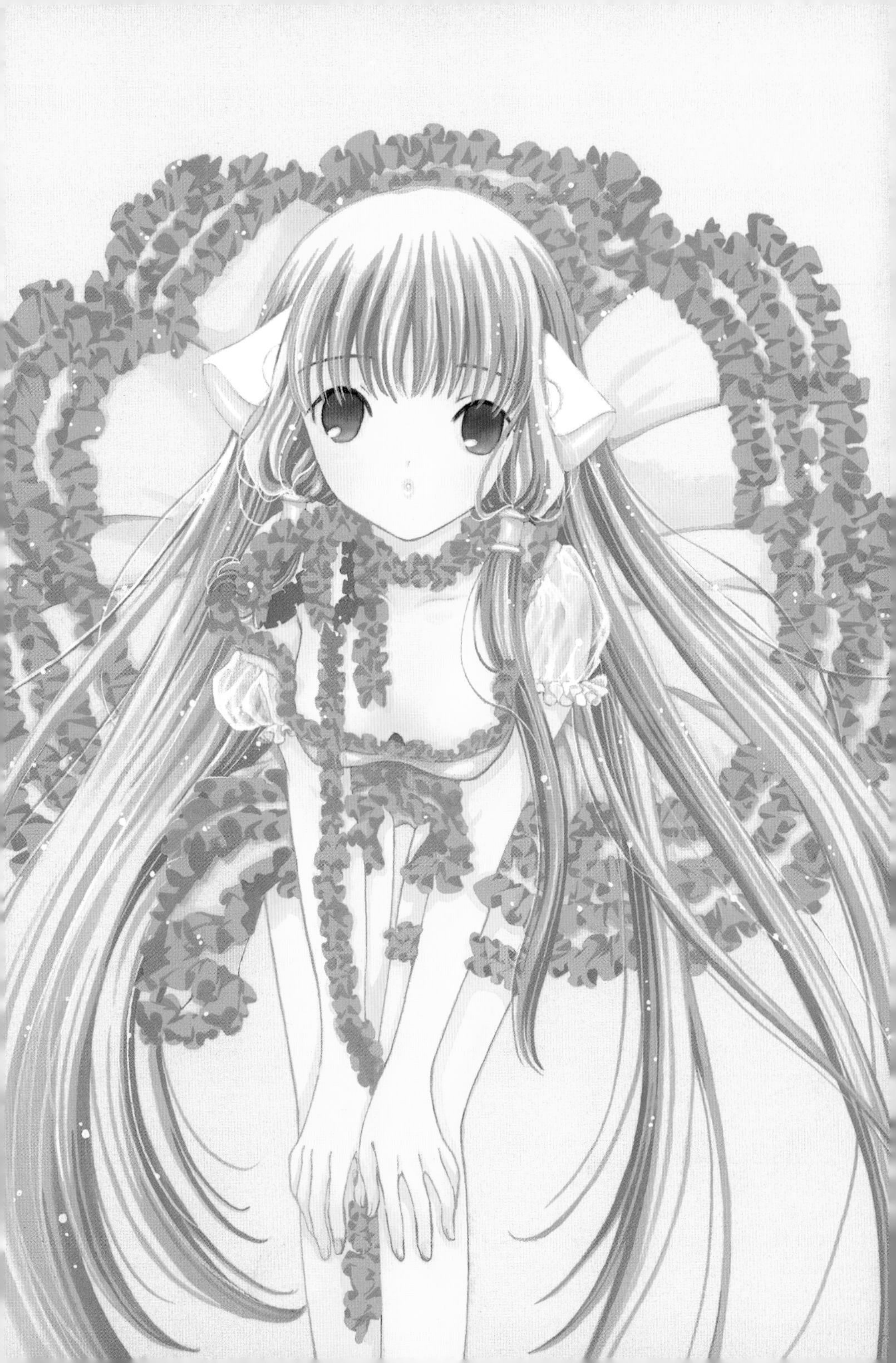

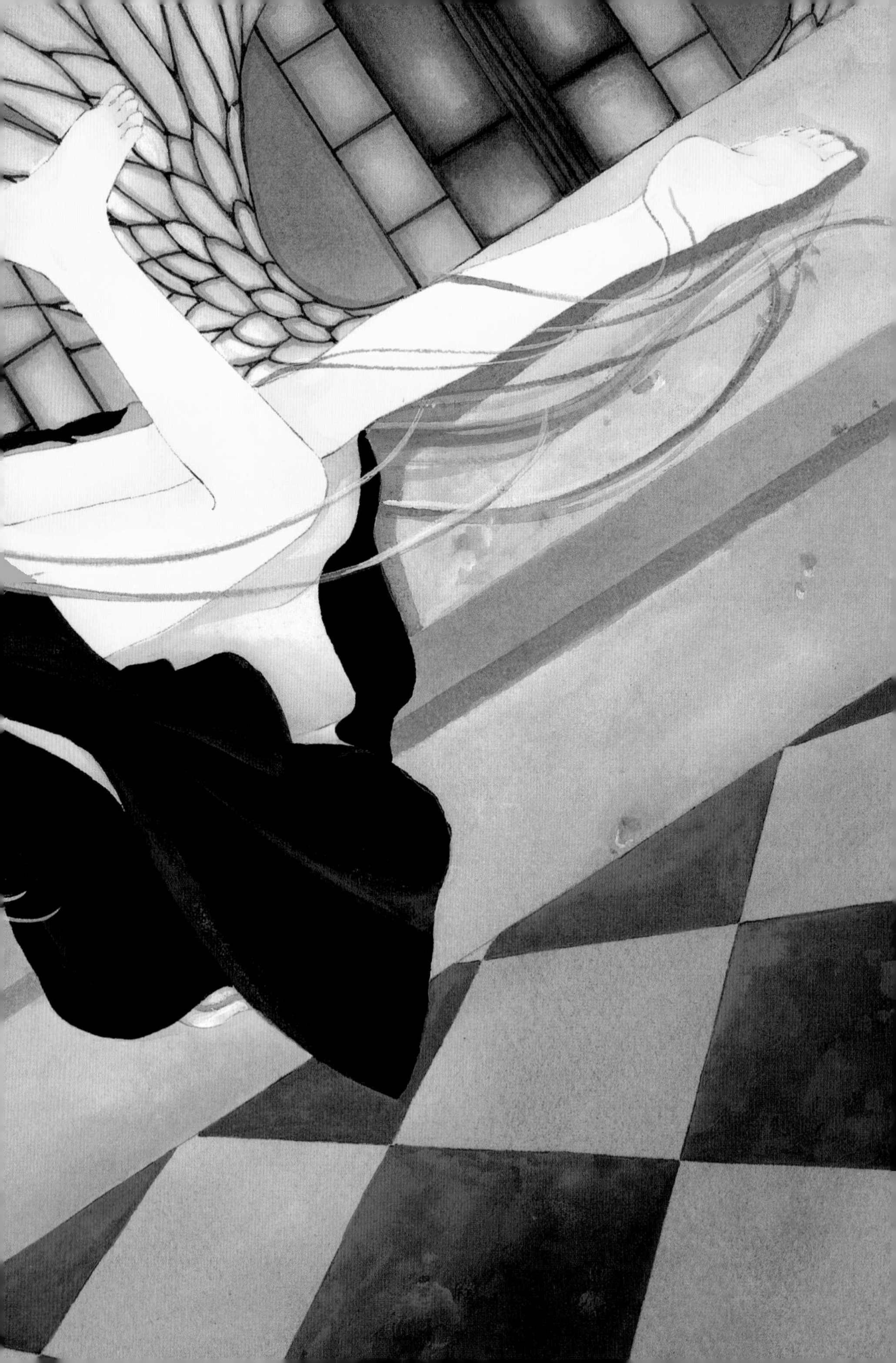

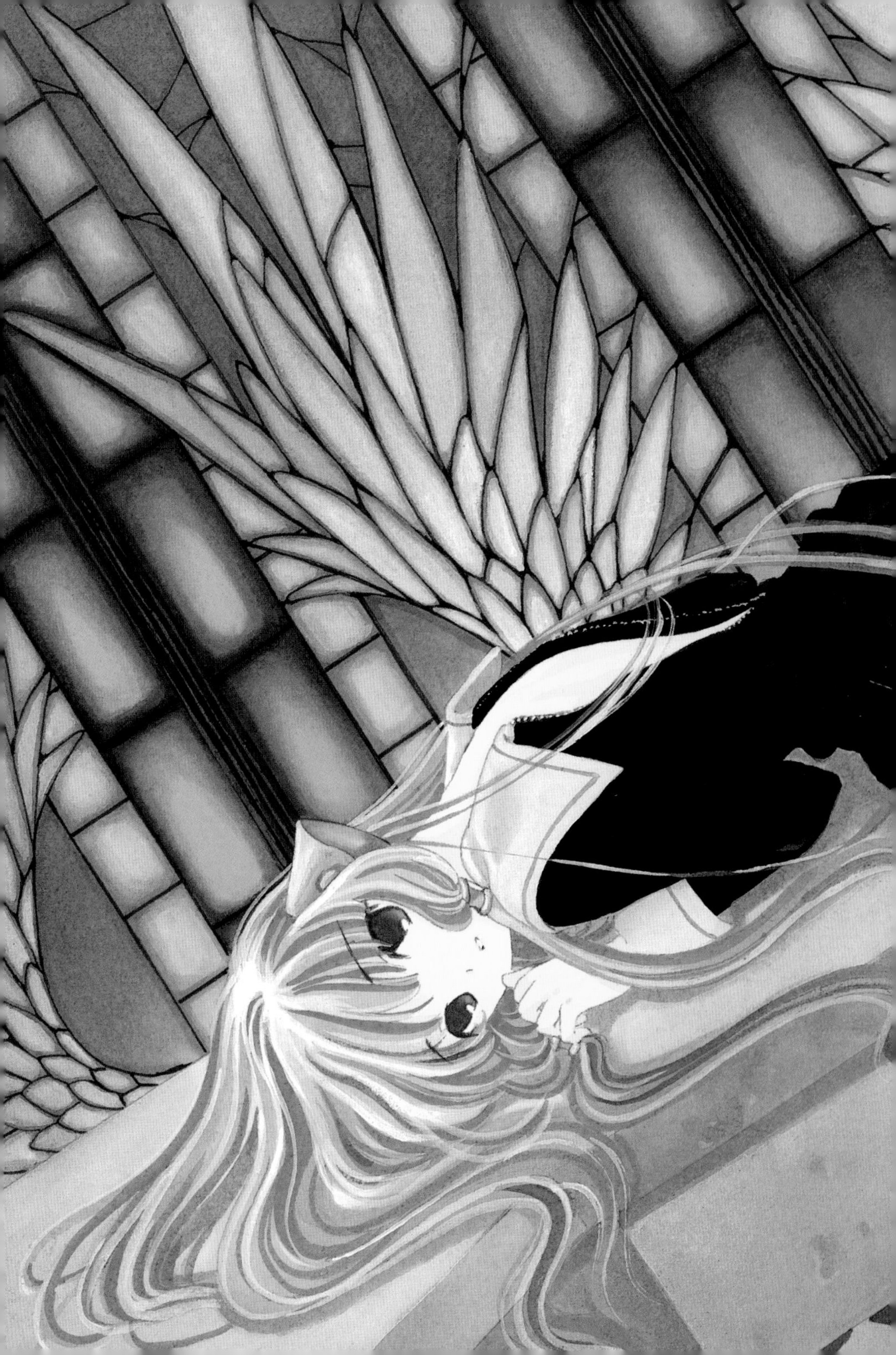

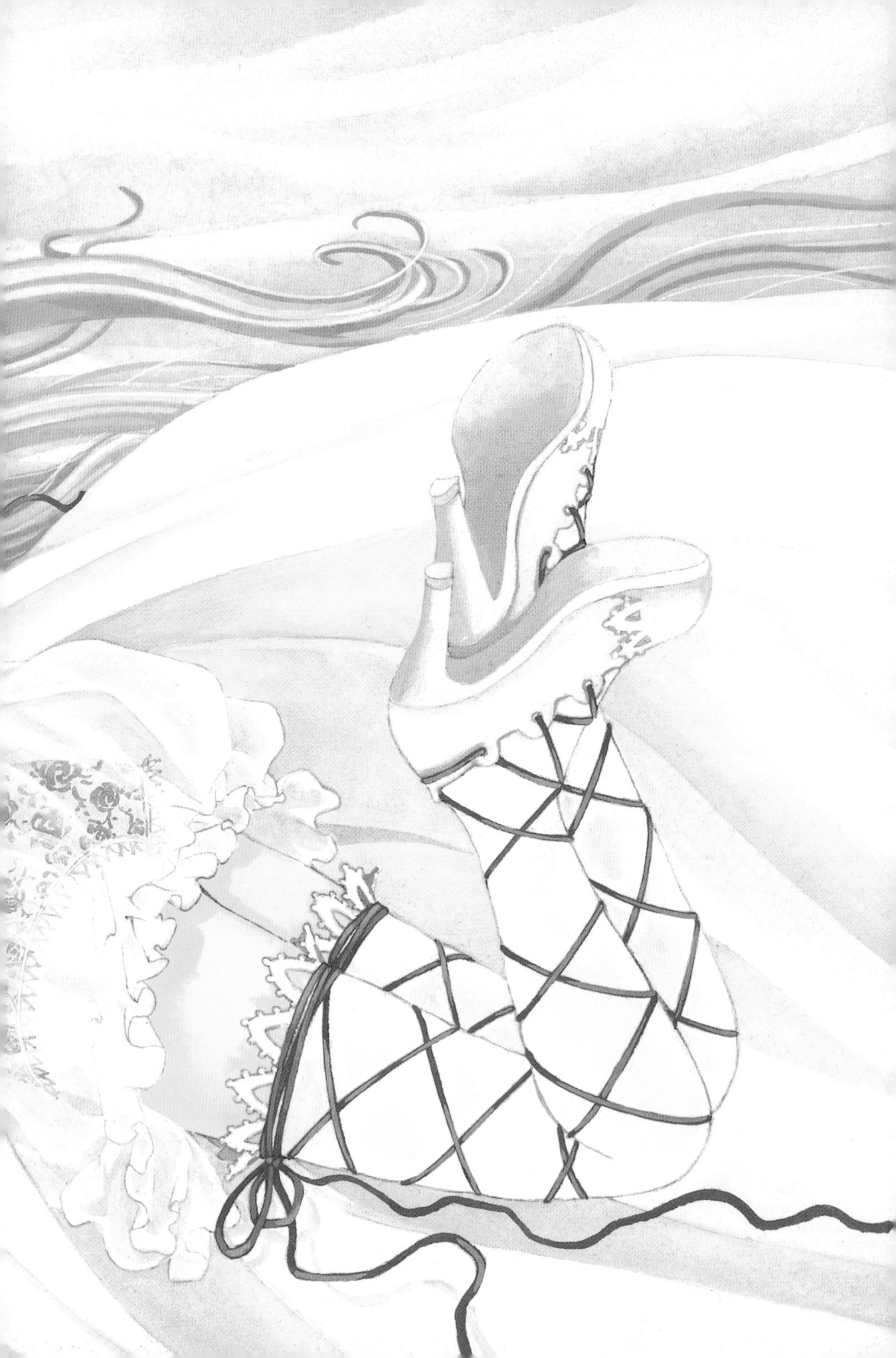

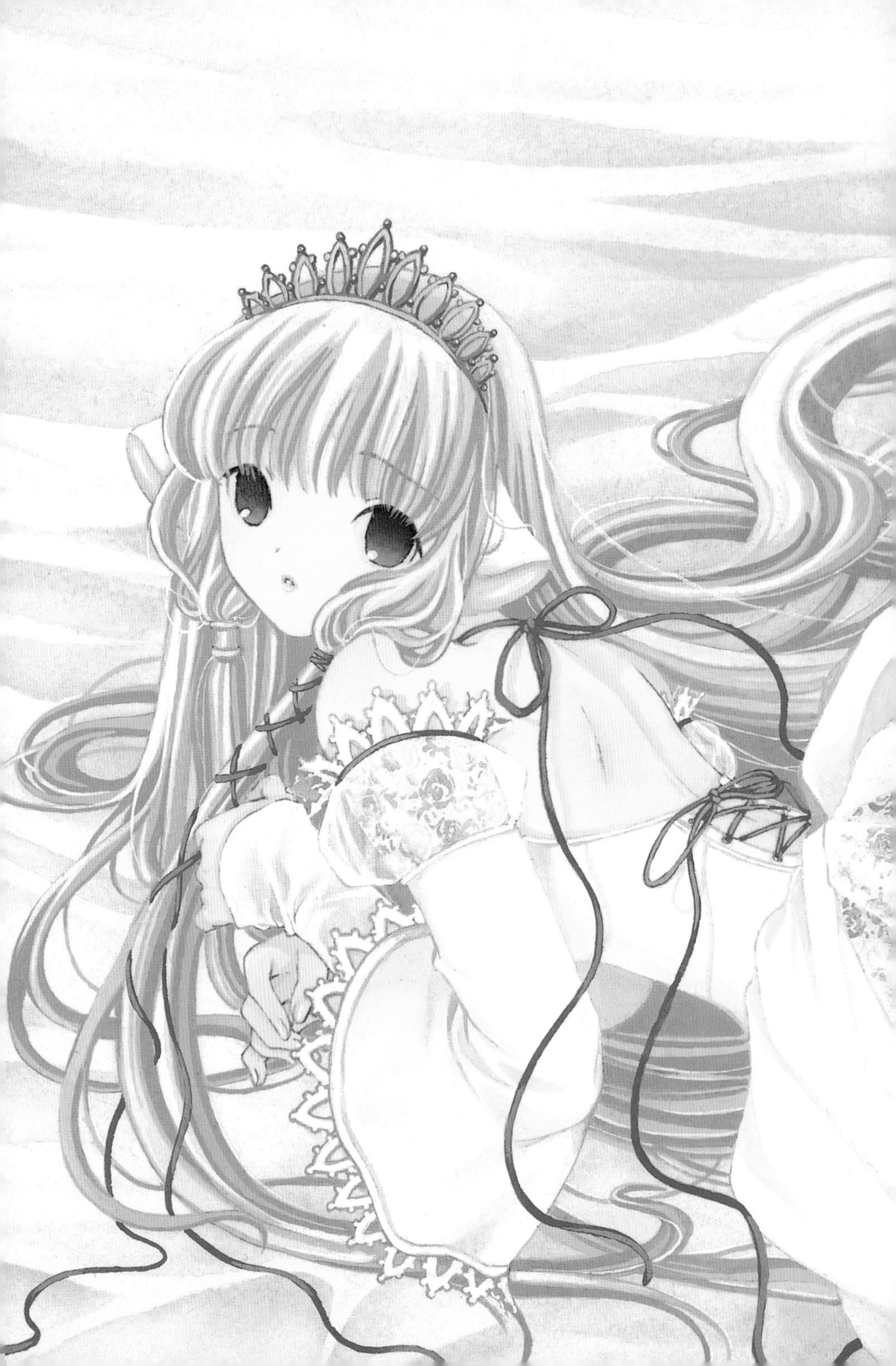

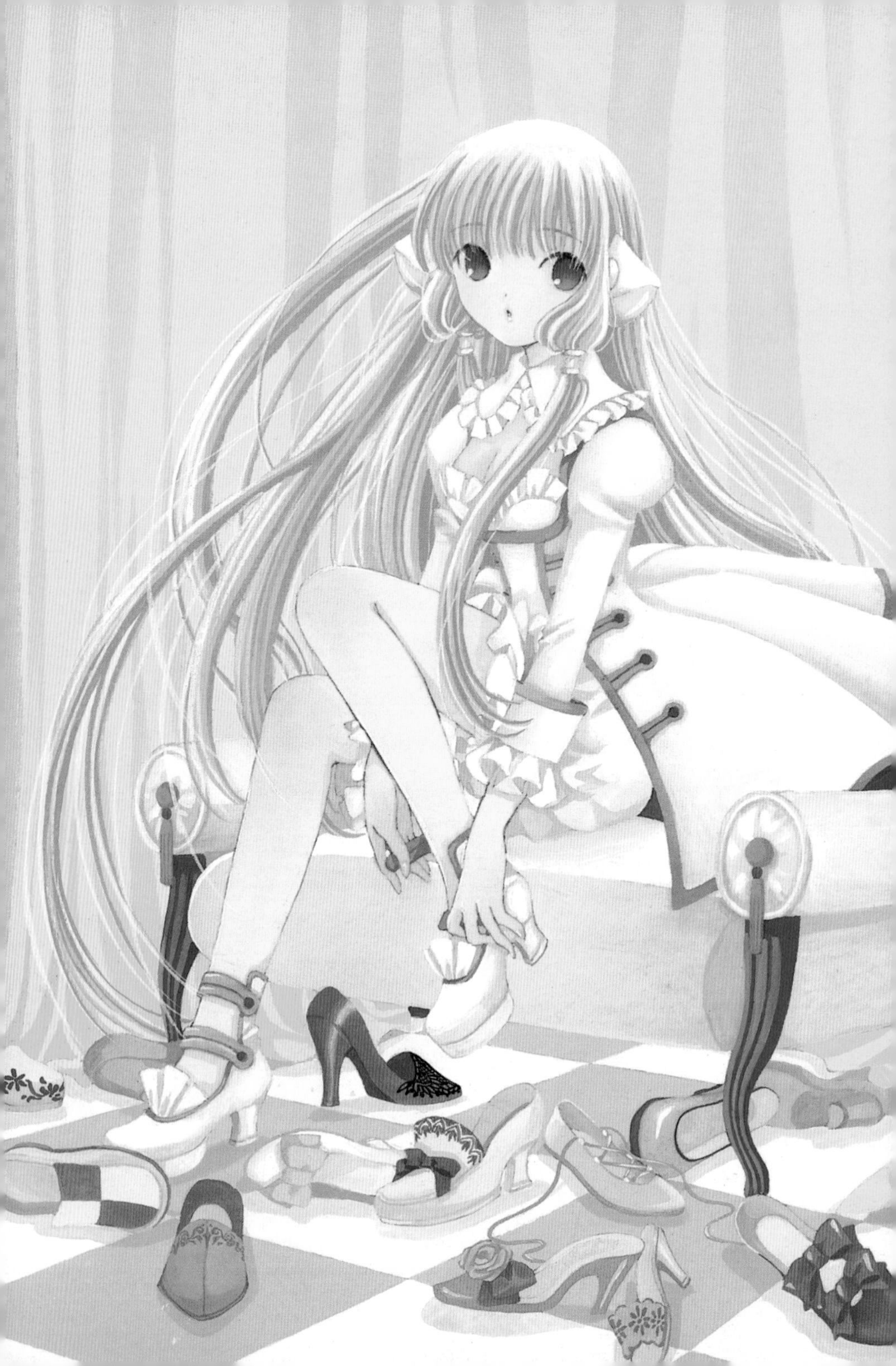

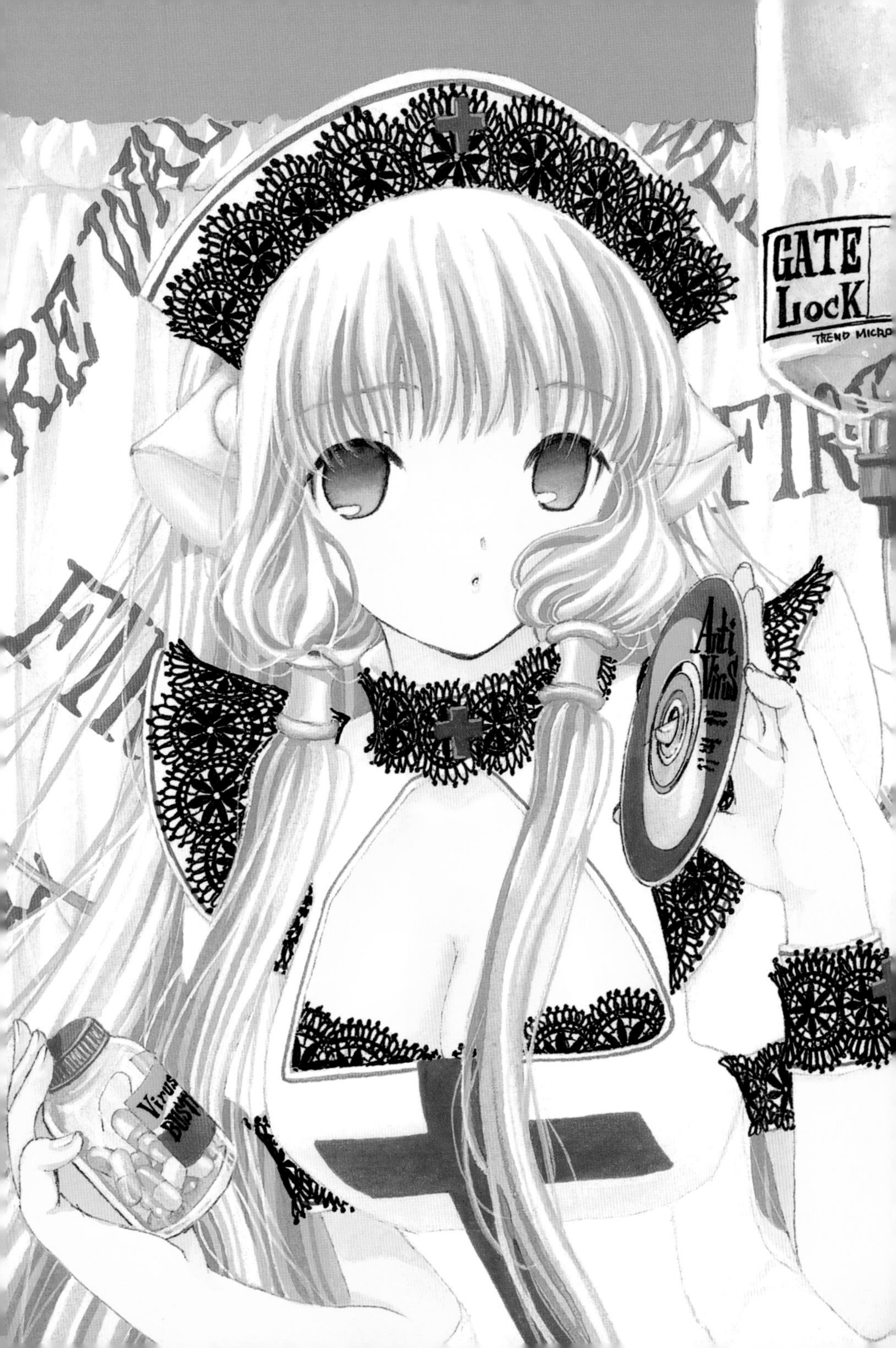

GATE LocK
TREND MICRO
Anti Virus
Virus BUST

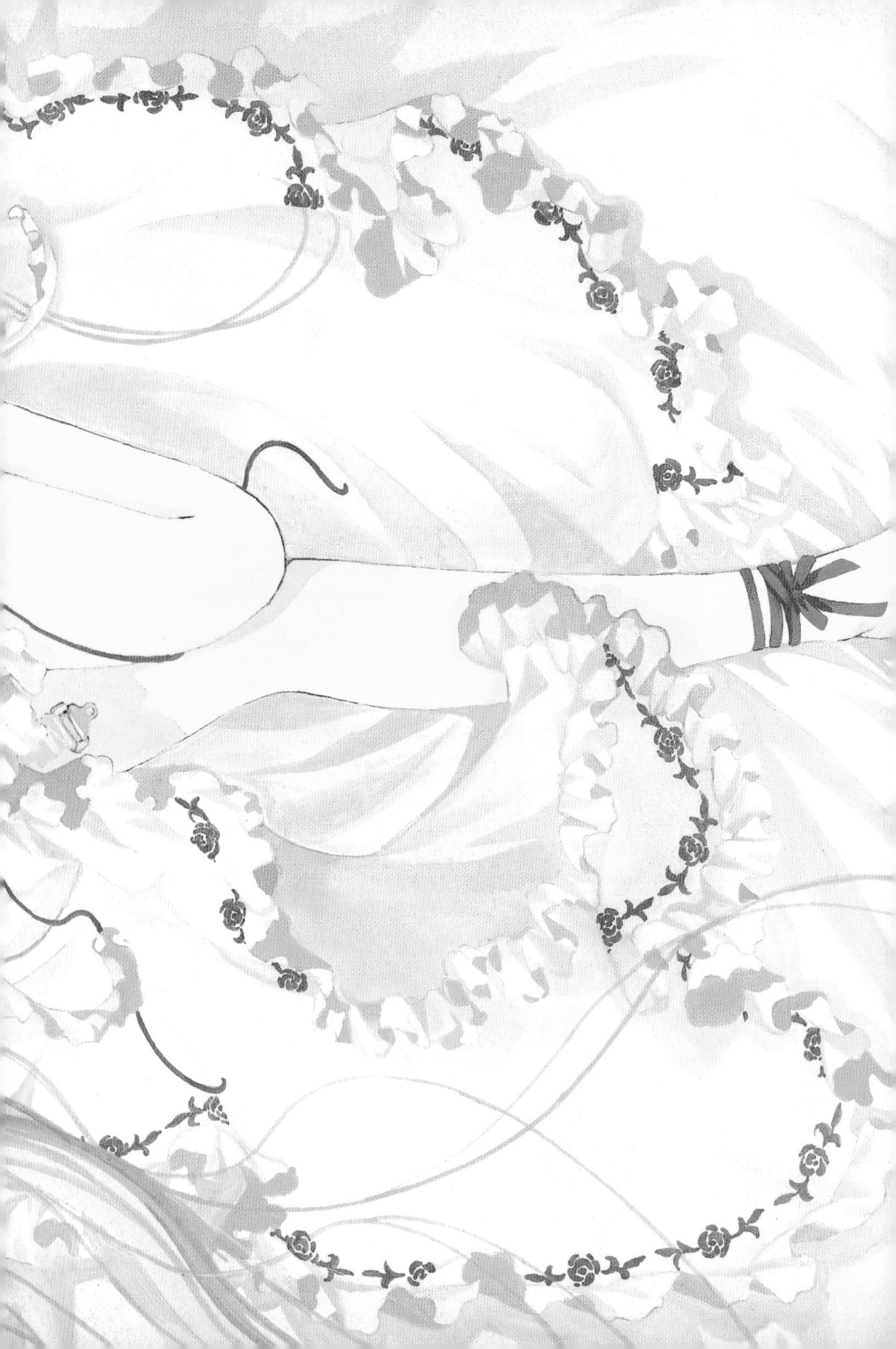

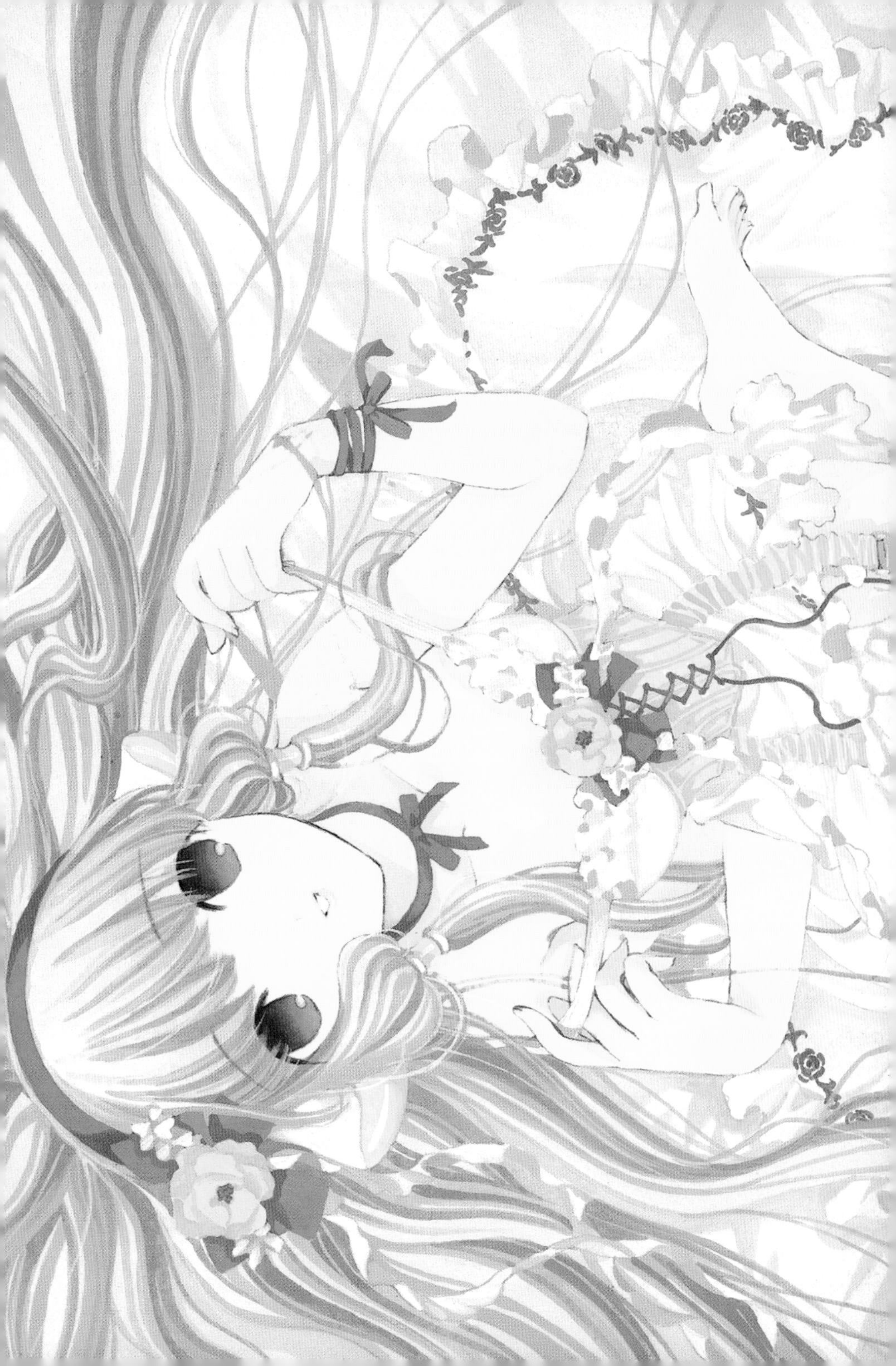

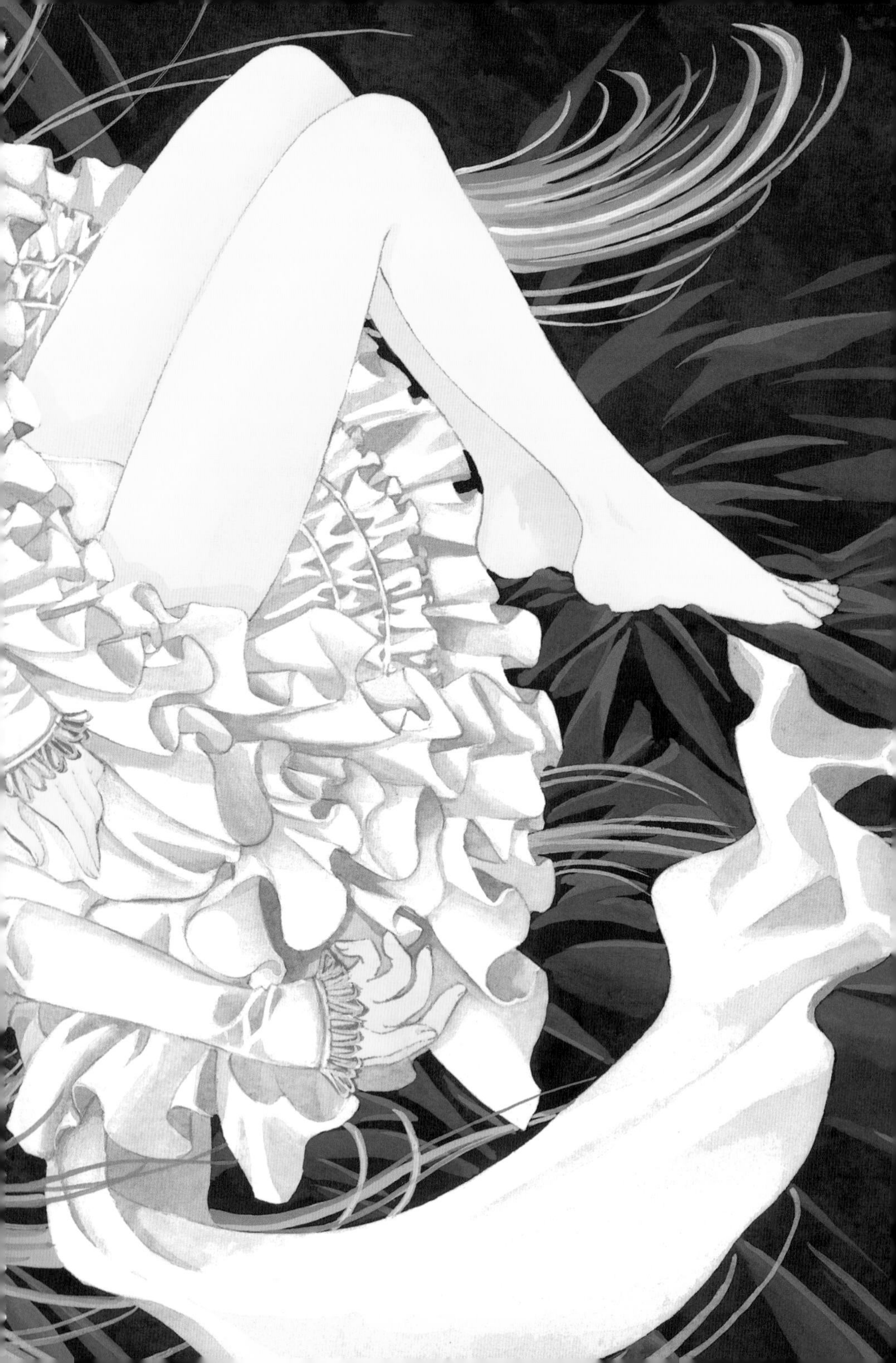

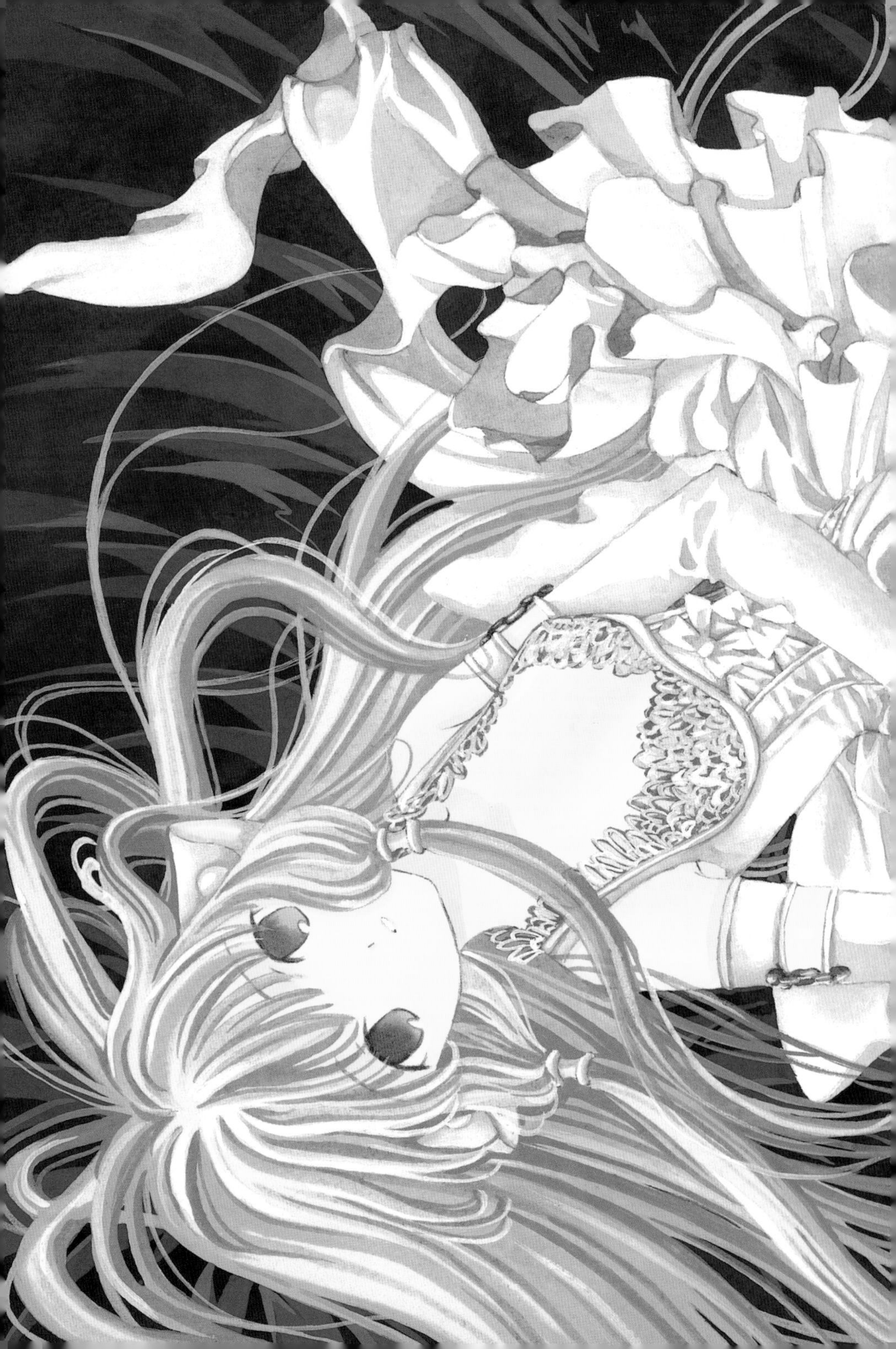

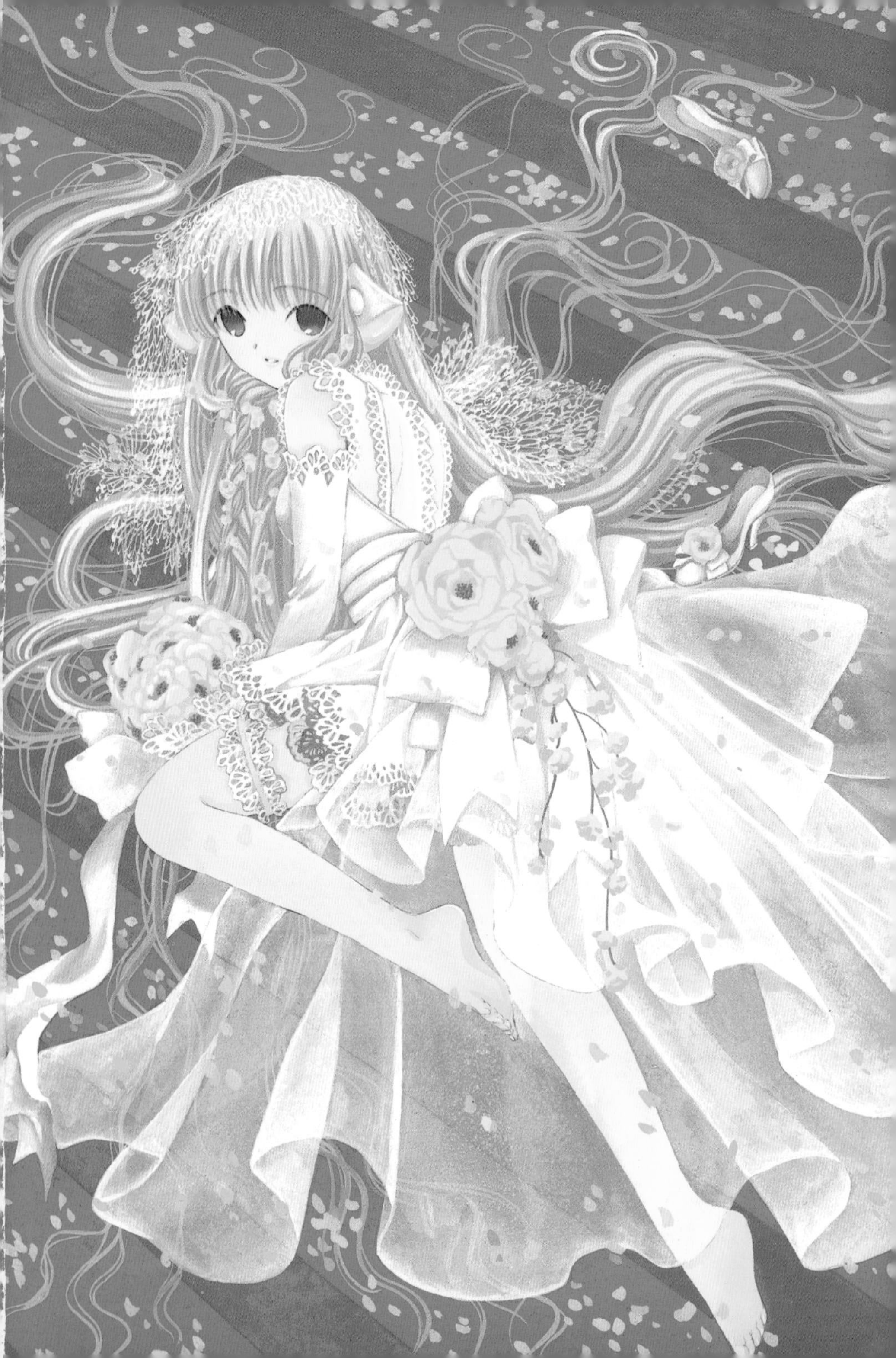

Date: 9/15/21

**GRA 741.5 CHO V.3
Chobits.**